NEW PERSPECTIVES ON

Microsoft® Windows® 7

COMPREHENSIVE

NEW PERSPECTIVES ON
Microsoft® Windows® 7

COMPREHENSIVE

June Jamrich Parsons
Dan Oja
Lisa Ruffolo

COURSE TECHNOLOGY
CENGAGE Learning™

Australia • Brazil • Japan • Korea • Mexico • Singapore • Spain • United Kingdom • United States

COURSE TECHNOLOGY
CENGAGE Learning

New Perspectives on Microsoft Windows 7, Comprehensive

Vice President, Publisher: Nicole Jones Pinard

Executive Editor: Marie L. Lee

Associate Acquisitions Editor: Brandi Shailer

Senior Product Manager: Kathy Finnegan

Product Manager: Leigh Hefferon

Associate Product Manager: Julia Leroux-Lindsey

Editorial Assistant: Zina Kresin

Director of Marketing: Cheryl Costantini

Senior Marketing Manager: Ryan DeGrote

Marketing Coordinator: Kristen Panciocco

Developmental Editor: Mary Pat Shaffer

Senior Content Project Manager:
   Jennifer Goguen McGrail

Composition: GEX Publishing Services

Art Director: Marissa Falco

Text Designer: Althea Chen

Cover Designer: Roycroft Design

Cover Art: © Veer

Copyeditor: Suzanne Huizenga

Proofreader: Andrea Schein

Indexer: Alexandra Nickerson

For product information and technology assistance, contact us at
Cengage Learning Customer & Sales Support, 1-800-354-9706
For permission to use material from this text or product, submit all requests online at **www.cengage.com/permissions**
Further permissions questions can be emailed to
permissionrequest@cengage.com

Some of the product names and company names used in this book have been used for identification purposes only and may be trademarks or registered trademarks of their respective manufacturers and sellers.

Microsoft and the Office logo are either registered trademarks or trademarks of Microsoft Corporation in the United States and/or other countries. Course Technology, Cengage Learning is an independent entity from the Microsoft Corporation, and not affiliated with Microsoft in any manner.

Disclaimer: Any fictional data related to persons or companies or URLs used throughout this book is intended for instructional purposes only. At the time this book was printed, any such data was fictional and not belonging to any real persons or companies.

Library of Congress Control Number: 2010926539

ISBN-13: 978-0-538-74600-7

ISBN-10: 0-538-74600-9

Course Technology
20 Channel Center Street
Boston, MA 02210
USA

Cengage Learning is a leading provider of customized learning solutions with office locations around the globe, including Singapore, the United Kingdom, Australia, Mexico, Brazil, and Japan. Locate your local office at:
international.cengage.com/global

Cengage Learning products are represented in Canada by Nelson Education, Ltd.

To learn more about Course Technology, visit **www.cengage.com/course technology**

To learn more about Cengage Learning, visit **www.cengage.com**

Purchase any of our products at your local college store or at our preferred online store **www.cengagebrain.com**

Printed in the United States of America
1 2 3 4 5 6 7 8 9 14 13 12 11 10

Preface

The New Perspectives Series' critical-thinking, problem-solving approach is the ideal way to prepare students to transcend point-and-click skills and take advantage of all that Microsoft Windows 7 has to offer.

In developing the New Perspectives Series, our goal was to create books that give students the software concepts and practical skills they need to succeed beyond the classroom. We've updated our proven case-based pedagogy with more practical content to make learning skills more meaningful to students.

With the New Perspectives Series, students understand *why* they are learning *what* they are learning, and are fully prepared to apply their skills to real-life situations.

About This Book

This book provides comprehensive coverage of the new Microsoft Windows 7 operating system, and includes the following:

- Hands-on instruction of fundamental skills such as personalizing the desktop, managing files, and securing computers, as well as new features such as the upgraded Windows Media Center, Homegroups, libraries, Windows Live Essentials, and Windows Touch
- Coverage of advanced skills including managing multimedia files, coordinating mobile computers and home networks, maintaining hardware and software, and improving system performance
- Exploration of Windows 7 innovations, including simplified networking features, streamlined troubleshooters, enhanced programs for working with graphics and video, and centralized maintenance tools

New for this edition!

- Each session begins with a Visual Overview, a new two-page spread that includes colorful, enlarged screenshots with numerous callouts and key term definitions, giving students a comprehensive preview of the topics covered in the session, as well as a handy study guide.
- New ProSkills boxes provide guidance for how to use the software in real-world, professional situations, and related ProSkills exercises integrate the technology skills students learn with one or more of the following soft skills: decision making, problem solving, teamwork, verbal communication, and written communication.
- Important steps are now highlighted in yellow with attached margin notes to help students pay close attention to completing the steps correctly and avoid time-consuming rework.

System Requirements

This book assumes a typical installation of Microsoft Windows 7 Ultimate using an Aero theme. (Note that most tasks in this text can also be completed using the Windows 7 Home Premium or Professional editions.) The browser used for any steps that require a browser is Internet Explorer 8.

www.cengage.com/ct/newperspectives

The New Perspectives Approach

Context

Each tutorial begins with a problem presented in a "real-world" case that is meaningful to students. The case sets the scene to help students understand what they will do in the tutorial.

Hands-on Approach

Each tutorial is divided into manageable sessions that combine reading and hands-on, step-by-step work. Colorful screenshots help guide students through the steps. **Trouble?** tips anticipate common mistakes or problems to help students stay on track and continue with the tutorial.

VISUAL OVERVIEW

Visual Overviews

New for this edition! Each session begins with a Visual Overview, a new two-page spread that includes colorful, enlarged screenshots with numerous callouts and key term definitions, giving students a comprehensive preview of the topics covered in the session, as well as a handy study guide.

PROSKILLS

ProSkills Boxes and Exercises

New for this edition! ProSkills boxes provide guidance for how to use the software in real-world, professional situations, and related ProSkills exercises integrate the technology skills students learn with one or more of the following soft skills: decision making, problem solving, teamwork, verbal communication, and written communication.

KEY STEP

Key Steps

New for this edition! Important steps are highlighted in yellow with attached margin notes to help students pay close attention to completing the steps correctly and avoid time-consuming rework.

INSIGHT

InSight Boxes

InSight boxes offer expert advice and best practices to help students achieve a deeper understanding of the concepts behind the software features and skills.

TIP

Margin Tips

Margin Tips provide helpful hints and shortcuts for more efficient use of the software. The Tips appear in the margin at key points throughout each tutorial, giving students extra information when and where they need it.

REVIEW
APPLY

Assessment

Retention is a key component to learning. At the end of each session, a series of Quick Check questions helps students test their understanding of the material before moving on. Engaging end-of-tutorial Review Assignments and Case Problems have always been a hallmark feature of the New Perspectives Series. Colorful bars and brief descriptions accompany the exercises, making it easy to understand both the goal and level of challenge a particular assignment holds.

REFERENCE
TASK REFERENCE
GLOSSARY/INDEX

Reference

Within each tutorial, Reference boxes appear before a set of steps to provide a succinct summary and preview of how to perform a task. In addition, a complete Task Reference at the back of the book provides quick access to information on how to carry out common tasks. Finally, each book includes a combination Glossary/Index to promote easy reference of material.

Our Complete System of Instruction

Coverage To Meet Your Needs

Whether you're looking for just a small amount of coverage or enough to fill a semester-long class, we can provide you with a textbook that meets your needs.

- Brief books typically cover the essential skills in just 2 to 4 tutorials.
- Introductory books build and expand on those skills and contain an average of 5 to 8 tutorials.
- Comprehensive books are great for a full-semester class, and contain 9 to 12+ tutorials.

So if the book you're holding does not provide the right amount of coverage for you, there's probably another offering available. Go to our Web site or contact your Course Technology sales representative to find out what else we offer.

CourseCasts – Learning on the Go. Always available…always relevant.

Want to keep up with the latest technology trends relevant to you? Visit our site to find a library of podcasts, CourseCasts, featuring a "CourseCast of the Week," and download them to your mp3 player at http://coursecasts.course.com.

Our fast-paced world is driven by technology. You know because you're an active participant—always on the go, always keeping up with technological trends, and always learning new ways to embrace technology to power your life.

Ken Baldauf, host of CourseCasts, is a faculty member of the Florida State University Computer Science Department where he is responsible for teaching technology classes to thousands of FSU students each year. Ken is an expert in the latest technology trends; he gathers and sorts through the most pertinent news and information for CourseCasts so your students can spend their time enjoying technology, rather than trying to figure it out. Open or close your lecture with a discussion based on the latest CourseCast.

Visit us at http://coursecasts.course.com to learn on the go!

Instructor Resources

We offer more than just a book. We have all the tools you need to enhance your lectures, check students' work, and generate exams in a new, easier-to-use and completely revised package. This book's Instructor's Manual, ExamView testbank, PowerPoint presentations, data files, solution files, figure files, and a sample syllabus are all available on a single CD-ROM or for downloading at http://www.cengage.com/coursetechnology.

SAM: Skills Assessment Manager

SAM is designed to help bring students from the classroom to the real world. It allows students to train and test on important computer skills in an active, hands-on environment.

SAM's easy-to-use system includes powerful interactive exams, training, and projects on the most commonly used Microsoft Office applications. SAM simulates the Office application environment, allowing students to demonstrate their knowledge and think through the skills by performing real-world tasks, such as bolding text or setting up slide transitions. Add in live-in-the-application projects, and students are on their way to truly learning and applying skills to business-centric documents.

Designed to be used with the New Perspectives Series, SAM includes handy page references, so students can print helpful study guides that match the New Perspectives textbooks used in class. For instructors, SAM also includes robust scheduling and reporting features.

Content for Online Learning

Course Technology has partnered with the leading distance learning solution providers and class-management platforms today. To access this material, visit www.cengage.com/webtutor and search for your title. Instructor resources include the following: additional case projects, sample syllabi, PowerPoint presentations, and more. For students to access this material, they must have purchased a WebTutor PIN-code specific to this title and your campus platform. The resources for students might include (based on instructor preferences): topic reviews, review questions, practice tests, and more. For additional information, please contact your sales representative.

Acknowledgments

I would like to thank the following reviewers for their contributions in the development of this text: Sylvia Amito'elau, Coastline Community College; Paulette Comet, The Community College of Baltimore County; Annette Kerwin, College of DuPage; Deborah Meyer, St. Louis Community College; and Fidelis Ngang, Houston Community College. Their valuable insights and excellent feedback helped to shape this text, ensuring it will meet the needs of instructors and students both in the classroom and beyond.

Many thanks to everyone on the New Perspectives team for their guidance, insight, and encouragement, including Marie Lee and Jennifer Goguen McGrail. Special thanks go to Kathy Finnegan, whose high standards and sensitivity to how people learn make this book more engaging, appealing, and useful; and to Mary Pat Shaffer, whose attention to detail make this a superior instructional text. I also appreciate the careful work of John Freitas, Serge Palladino, Susan Pedicini, and Danielle Shaw, Manuscript Quality Assurance testers. Additional thanks go to June Parsons and Dan Oja, on whose previous work this book is based.
– Lisa Ruffolo

BRIEF CONTENTS

WINDOWS

Level I Tutorials

Tutorial 1 Exploring the Basics of Microsoft Windows 7 . . . . WIN 1
Investigating the Windows 7 Operating System

Tutorial 2 Organizing Your Files . . . . WIN 49
Managing Files and Folders in Windows 7

Level II Tutorials

Tutorial 3 Personalizing Your Windows Environment . . . . WIN 105
Changing Desktop Settings

Tutorial 4 Working with the Internet and E-Mail . . . . WIN 173
Communicating with Others

Tutorial 5 Protecting Your Computer . . . . WIN 227
Managing Computer Security

Tutorial 6 Searching for Information and Collaborating with Others . . . . WIN 285
Finding and Sharing Information

Level III Tutorials

Tutorial 7 Managing Multimedia Files . . . . WIN 337
Working with Graphics, Photos, Music, and Movies

Tutorial 8 Connecting to Networks with Mobile Computing . . . . WIN 411
Accessing Network Resources

Tutorial 9 Maintaining Hardware and Software . . . . WIN 467
Managing Software, Disks, and Devices

Tutorial 10 Improving Your Computer's Performance . . . . WIN 541
Enhancing Your System and Troubleshooting Computer Problems

Appendix A Connecting Computers to the Internet . . . . WIN A1
Setting Up an Internet Connection

Appendix B Exploring Additional Windows 7 Tools . . . . WIN B1
Using Control Panel Tools and Windows Live Essentials

Glossary/Index   **REF 1**

Task Reference   **REF 16**

TABLE OF CONTENTS

Preface v

WINDOWS LEVEL I TUTORIALS

Tutorial 1 Exploring the Basics of Microsoft Windows 7
Investigating the Windows 7 Operating System . . . . **WIN 1**

SESSION 1.1 . . . . **WIN 2**

Starting Windows 7 . . . . .WIN 4

Touring the Windows 7 Desktop . . . . .WIN 6

   Interacting with the Desktop . . . . .WIN 6

Exploring the Start Menu .WIN 10

Running Multiple Programs . . . . .WIN 14

   Switching Between Programs . . . . .WIN 15

   Closing Programs from the Taskbar . . . . .WIN 17

Using Windows and Dialog Boxes . . . . .WIN 18

   Manipulating Windows . . . . .WIN 19

   Using the Ribbon . . . . .WIN 23

   Using List Boxes and Scroll Bars . . . . .WIN 26

   Working with Dialog Boxes . . . . .WIN 27

Session 1.1 Quick Check . . . . .WIN 29

SESSION 1.2 . . . . **WIN 30**

Exploring Your Computer .WIN 32

   Navigating with the Computer Window . . . . .WIN 32

   Changing the View . . . . .WIN 34

   Navigating with Windows Explorer . . . . .WIN 36

Getting Help . . . . .WIN 39

   Viewing Windows Basics Topics . . . . .WIN 40

   Selecting a Topic from the Contents List . . . . .WIN 41

   Searching the Help Pages . . . . .WIN 41

Turning Off Windows 7 . . . . .WIN 43

Session 1.2 Quick Check . . . . .WIN 44

Review Assignments . . . . .WIN 45

Case Problems . . . . .WIN 46

Tutorial 2 Organizing Your Files
Managing Files and Folders in Windows 7 . . . . **WIN 49**

SESSION 2.1 . . . . **WIN 50**

Getting Prepared to Manage Your Files . . . . .WIN 52

   Understanding the Need for Organizing
   Files and Folders . . . . .WIN 53

   Developing Strategies for Organizing Files
   and Folders . . . . .WIN 54

   Planning Your Organization . . . . .WIN 55

Exploring Files and Folders . . . . .WIN 55

   Using Libraries and Folders . . . . .WIN 58

   Navigating to Your Data Files . . . . .WIN 60

   Navigating with the Address Bar . . . . .WIN 63

Using the Search Box to Find Files . . . . .WIN 65

Managing Files and Folders . . . . .WIN 66

   Creating Folders . . . . .WIN 67

   Moving and Copying Files and Folders . . . . .WIN 69

   Selecting Files and Folders . . . . .WIN 71

   Copying Files and Folders . . . . .WIN 71

Session 2.1 Quick Check . . . . .WIN 73

SESSION 2.2 . . . . **WIN 74**

Naming and Renaming Files . . . . .WIN 76

Deleting Files and Folders .WIN 77

Working with New Files . . . . .WIN 78

   Creating a File . . . . .WIN 78

   Saving a File . . . . .WIN 79

   Opening a File . . . . .WIN 81

Refining the Organization of Files . . . . .WIN 82

   Sorting and Filtering Files . . . . .WIN 83

   Grouping Files . . . . .WIN 85

Customizing a Folder Window. . . . . .WIN 86

    Changing the Layout of a Folder Window . . . . .WIN 87

    Customizing the File List . . . . .WIN 89

    Customizing the Navigation Pane . . . . .WIN 91

Working with Compressed Files . . . . .WIN 92

Restoring Your Settings. . . . . .WIN 95

Session 2.2 Quick Check . . . . .WIN 95

Review Assignments . . . . .WIN 96

Case Problems. . . . . .WIN 97

ProSkills Exercise: Decision-Making . . . . .WIN 102

WINDOWS LEVEL II TUTORIALS

Tutorial 3 Personalizing Your Windows Environment
Changing Desktop Settings. . . . . **WIN 105**

SESSION 3.1 . . . . WIN 106

Accessing Common Tools on the Desktop. . . . . .WIN 108

    Adding Icons to the Desktop . . . . .WIN 109

    Changing the Appearance of Desktop Icons . . . . .WIN 111

Using Windows Gadgets . . . . .WIN 114

    Customizing a Gadget . . . . .WIN 115

Using Shortcuts. . . . . .WIN 117

    Creating a Shortcut to a Drive . . . . .WIN 117

    Creating Shortcuts to Folders and Documents . . .WIN 119

    Creating a Shortcut to a Program . . . . .WIN 121

    Organizing Icons on the Desktop . . . . .WIN 122

    Deleting Shortcut Icons .WIN 124

Personalizing with the Control Panel . . . . .WIN 124

    Selecting Themes. . . . . .WIN 127

    Changing Your Desktop's Background. . . . . .WIN 129

    Changing Desktop Colors and Fonts . . . . .WIN 131

    Activating a Screen Saver . . . . .WIN 134

    Saving Themes. . . . . .WIN 136

Changing Display Settings .WIN 137

    Changing the Size of the Desktop Area. . . . . .WIN 137

    Changing the Size of Text and Objects . . . . .WIN 138

Session 3.1 Quick Check . . . . .WIN 139

SESSION 3.2. . . . . .WIN 140

Managing the Desktop with Aero Tools . . . . .WIN 142

Modifying the Taskbar . . . . .WIN 147

    Pinning Programs to the Taskbar. . . . . .WIN 148

    Moving and Resizing the Taskbar. . . . . .WIN 151

    Setting Taskbar Appearance Properties . . . . .WIN 152

Working with Taskbar Toolbars. . . . . .WIN 153

    Adding Toolbars to the Taskbar . . . . .WIN 154

Customizing the Start Menu . . . . .WIN 155

    Controlling the Appearance of the Start Menu . . .WIN 155

    Pinning Programs to the Start Menu . . . . .WIN 157

    Adding Commands to the Right Pane of
the Start Menu . . . . .WIN 160

    Selecting Start Menu Settings . . . . .WIN 161

Restoring Your Settings. . . . . .WIN 164

Session 3.2 Quick Check . . . . .WIN 165

Review Assignments . . . . .WIN 166

Case Problems. . . . . .WIN 167

Tutorial 4 Working with the Internet and E-Mail
*Communicating with Others . . . .*WIN 173

SESSION 4.1 . . . . .WIN 174

Exploring the Internet and the Web . . . . .WIN 176

    Using Web Browsers. . . . . .WIN 178

Getting Started with Microsoft Internet Explorer . . .WIN 178

Opening a Page on the Web .WIN 179

    Opening a Web Page Using a URL. . . . . .WIN 180

    Navigating with Links . . . . .WIN 182

    Navigating with Internet Explorer Tools . . . . .WIN 184

Using the History List . . . . WIN 184

Managing Multiple Web Pages . . . . WIN 185

Using Favorites . . . . WIN 188

Adding an Item to the Favorites List . . . . WIN 189

Organizing the Favorites List . . . . WIN 190

Adding Links and Web Slices to the
Favorites Bar . . . . WIN 191

Finding and Using Accelerators . . . . WIN 194

Printing and Saving Web Pages . . . . WIN 196

Session 4.1 Quick Check . . . . WIN 197

SESSION 4.2 . . . . **WIN 198**

Getting Started with Windows Live Mail . . . . WIN 200

Examining How E-Mail Works . . . . WIN 200

Addressing E-Mail . . . . WIN 201

Setting Up Windows Live Mail . . . . WIN 203

Sending and Receiving E-Mail Using Windows
Live Mail . . . . WIN 206

Creating and Sending E-Mail Messages . . . . WIN 207

Receiving and Reading E-Mail Messages . . . . WIN 209

Replying to E-Mail Messages . . . . WIN 211

Deleting E-Mail Messages . . . . WIN 212

Attaching a File to a Message . . . . WIN 213

Adding Information to Windows Live Contacts . . . . . WIN 214

Managing Your Schedule with Windows Live
Calendar . . . . WIN 216

Starting Windows Live Calendar . . . . WIN 216

Scheduling Appointments . . . . WIN 217

Restoring Your Settings . . . . WIN 219

Session 4.2 Quick Check . . . . WIN 220

Review Assignments . . . . WIN 221

Case Problems . . . . WIN 222

Tutorial 5 Protecting Your Computer
Managing Computer Security . . . . **WIN 227**

SESSION 5.1 . . . . **WIN 228**

Using the Action Center . . . . WIN 230

Managing Windows Firewall . . . . WIN 232

Setting Up Windows Update . . . . WIN 235

Protecting Your Computer from Malware . . . . WIN 238

Defending Against Spyware . . . . WIN 240

Scanning Your Computer with Windows
Defender . . . . WIN 241

Setting Windows Defender Options . . . . WIN 244

Defending Against E-Mail Viruses . . . . WIN 247

Selecting Windows Live Mail Security Settings . . . WIN 247

Blocking Spam and Other Junk Mail . . . . WIN 249

Defending Against Phishing Messages . . . . WIN 250

Session 5.1 Quick Check . . . . WIN 251

SESSION 5.2 . . . . **WIN 252**

Managing Microsoft Internet Explorer Security . . . . WIN 254

Using the SmartScreen Filter . . . . WIN 254

Blocking Malware with Protected Mode and
Security Zones . . . . WIN 257

Blocking Pop-Up Windows . . . . WIN 259

Managing Add-On Programs . . . . WIN 261

Selecting Privacy Settings . . . . WIN 262

Protecting Your Privacy with InPrivate Browsing . . WIN 265

Using InPrivate Filtering . . . . WIN 267

Setting Up User Accounts . . . . WIN 269

Creating a Password-Protected Standard
User Account . . . . WIN 270

Controlling Access to Your Computer . . . . WIN 274

Locking Your Computer . . . . WIN 274

Securing and Sharing Folders . . . . .WIN 275

    Assigning Permissions to Folders . . . . .WIN 276

Restoring Your Settings . . . . .WIN 277

Session 5.2 Quick Check . . . . .WIN 278

Review Assignments . . . . .WIN 279

Case Problems . . . . .WIN 280

Tutorial 6 Searching for Information and Collaborating with Others
Finding and Sharing Information . . . . **WIN 285**

SESSION 6.1 . . . . **WIN 286**

Developing Search Strategies . . . . .WIN 288

Searching in a Folder Window . . . . .WIN 289

    Filtering the Search Results by Size . . . . .WIN 291

    Examining the Search Results . . . . .WIN 293

    Filtering Search Results by Date Modified . . . . . . .WIN 295

    Saving a Search . . . . .WIN 297

Using Tags and Other Properties . . . . .WIN 299

    Adding Tags to Files . . . . .WIN 300

    Adding Other Details to Files . . . . .WIN 302

Using Advanced Criteria in the Search Box . . . . . . .WIN 303

    Combining Criteria When Searching File
    Contents . . . . .WIN 304

    Combining Boolean Filters and File Properties . . .WIN 307

Session 6.1 Quick Check . . . . .WIN 307

SESSION 6.2 . . . . **WIN 308**

Searching for Programs from the Start Menu . . . . . .WIN 310

Searching the Internet . . . . .WIN 312

    Narrowing Your Search . . . . .WIN 314

    Choosing Search Providers . . . . .WIN 318

Collaborating with Other People . . . . .WIN 322

    Creating a Group . . . . .WIN 323

    Inviting Other People to Join the Group . . . . . . .WIN 325

Restoring Your Settings . . . . .WIN 328

Session 6.2 Quick Check . . . . .WIN 328

Review Assignments . . . . .WIN 329

Case Problems . . . . .WIN 330

ProSkills Exercise: Problem Solving . . . . .WIN 335

WINDOWS LEVEL III TUTORIALS

Tutorial 7 Managing Multimedia Files
Working with Graphics, Photos, Music, and Movies . . . . **WIN 337**

SESSION 7.1 . . . .**WIN 338**

Exploring Computer Graphics . . . . .WIN 340

Creating Graphics in Paint .WIN 342

    Opening a Graphic in Paint . . . . .WIN 345

    Saving a Graphic File . . . . .WIN 346

    Copying and Pasting to Create a Graphic . . . . . . .WIN 348

Modifying Graphics in Paint . . . . .WIN 350

    Resizing the Canvas and Moving an Image . . . . . .WIN 350

    Adding Text to a Graphic .WIN 353

    Moving Part of a Graphic . . . . .WIN 356

    Drawing Shapes . . . . .WIN 359

    Changing Colors . . . . .WIN 361

    Copying an Image . . . . .WIN 362

    Cropping a Graphic . . . . .WIN 366

Session 7.1 Quick Check . . . . .WIN 369

SESSION 7.2 . . . . **WIN 370**

Working with Photos . . . . .WIN 372

    Acquiring and Importing Photos . . . . .WIN 372

    Viewing and Organizing Photos . . . . .WIN 373

    Playing a Simple Slide Show . . . . .WIN 378

    Editing Photos . . . . .WIN 379

Sharing Photos . . . . .WIN 382

    Distributing Photos via E-Mail . . . . .WIN 382

    Printing Photos . . . . .WIN 384

Playing and Organizing Music Files . . . . .WIN 385

    Playing Music . . . . .WIN 387

    Creating a Playlist . . . . .WIN 389

    Syncing Files to a Portable Device . . . . .WIN 390

Creating a Multimedia Slide Show with Windows Media

Center . . . . .WIN 391

    Working with Videos. . . . . .WIN 396

    Burning a Video onto a DVD . . . . .WIN 398

Restoring Your Computer . . . . .WIN 399

Session 7.2 Quick Check . . . . .WIN 399

Review Assignments . . . . .WIN 400

Case Problems. . . . . .WIN 402

**Tutorial 8 Connecting to Networks with Mobile
Computing**
Accessing Network Resources . . . . **WIN 411**

SESSION 8.1. . . . . .WIN 412

Managing Mobile Computing Devices . . . . WIN 414

Using Mobility Center . . . . WIN 415

    Setting Speaker Volume. . . . . WIN 416

    Selecting a Power Plan. . . . . WIN 416

Customizing Power Options . . . . WIN 419

    Modifying a Power Plan . . . . .WIN 420

    Selecting Other Power Options . . . . .WIN 424

Presenting Information to an Audience . . . . .WIN 426

    Preparing a Computer for a Presentation . . . . . . .WIN 427

    Displaying Information on an External

    Display Device . . . . .WIN 429

    Connecting to a Network Projector . . . . .WIN 430

Exploring Network Concepts . . . . .WIN 432

    Setting Up a Small Office or Home Network. . . . .WIN 434

Managing Network Connections. . . . . .WIN 435

    Connecting to a Wireless Network. . . . . .WIN 436

Session 8.1 Quick Check . . . . .WIN 439

SESSION 8.2. . . . . **WIN 440**

Using a Windows Homegroup. . . . . .WIN 442

    Creating a Homegroup. . . . . .WIN 442

    Adding Other Computers to a Homegroup . . . . .WIN 443

    Sharing Files with a Homegroup . . . . .WIN 445

    Sharing a Printer with a Homegroup . . . . .WIN 447

Accessing Offline Files. . . . . .WIN 448

    Setting Up a Computer to Use Offline Files. . . . . .WIN 449

    Making a File or Folder Available Offline . . . . . . .WIN 451

Synchronizing Folders . . . . .WIN 452

    Using Sync Center . . . . .WIN 453

    Resolving Synchronization Conflicts . . . . .WIN 455

Using Remote Desktop Connection. . . . . .WIN 456

Restoring Your Settings. . . . . .WIN 459

Session 8.2 Quick Check . . . . .WIN 460

Review Assignments . . . . .WIN 461

Case Problems. . . . . .WIN 462

Tutorial 9 Maintaining Hardware and Software
Managing Software, Disks, and Devices . . . . **WIN 467**

SESSION 9.1. . . . . **WIN 468**

Backing Up and Restoring Files. . . . . .WIN 470

    Specifying Where to Save Your Backup File . . . . . .WIN 472

    Selecting the Folders and Files to Back Up . . . . . .WIN 473

    Indicating How Often to Back Up. . . . . .WIN 473

    Backing Up Files . . . . .WIN 474

    Changing Your Backup Settings. . . . . .WIN 478

    Restoring Files and Folders . . . . .WIN 480

Managing Software. . . . . .WIN 482

    Creating a System Restore Point . . . . .WIN 483

    Restoring a Shadow Copy of a File. . . . . .WIN 486

    Installing Software . . . . .WIN 487

    Uninstalling a Software Program. . . . . .WIN 491

    Installing and Uninstalling a Software Update . . .WIN 492

Setting Default Programs. . . . . .WIN 493

Setting Up a Program for Compatibility . . . . .WIN 495

Session 9.1 Quick Check. .WIN 497

SESSION 9.2. . . . .**WIN 498**

Maintaining Hard Disks. .WIN 500

Viewing Hard Disk Properties . . . . .WIN 500

Checking for Partitions. .WIN 502

Deleting Unnecessary Files with Disk Cleanup . . .WIN 504

Checking a Hard Disk for Errors. . . . . .WIN 505

Defragmenting a Disk . . . . .WIN 508

Working with Devices and Drivers . . . . .WIN 512

Understanding Device Resources. . . . . .WIN 514

Understanding Device Drivers. . . . . .WIN 515

Installing a USB Device .WIN 515

Enabling and Disabling Devices. . . . . .WIN 516

Installing and Updating Device Drivers. . . . . .WIN 518

Rolling Back a Driver to a Previous Version . . . . . .WIN 520

Safely Removing USB Devices . . . . .WIN 520

Maintaining Your Monitor . . . . .WIN 521

Adjusting the Display Refresh Rate . . . . .WIN 522

Selecting Color Settings. . . . . .WIN 524

Changing the Size of Icons and Text . . . . .WIN 525

Setting Up Multiple Monitors . . . . .WIN 526

Setting the Resolution of a Secondary Monitor . . .WIN 528

Installing and Setting Up a Printer. . . . . .WIN 529

Installing a Local Printer . . . . .WIN 529

Changing the Default Printer. . . . . .WIN 531

Restoring Your Settings. .WIN 532

Session 9.2 Quick Check .WIN 533

Review Assignments . . . . .WIN 534

Case Problems. . . . . .WIN 535

Tutorial 10 Improving Your Computer's Performance
Enhancing Your System and Troubleshooting
Computer Problems . . . . **WIN 541**

SESSION 10.1 . . . . **WIN 542**

Improving System Performance . . . . .WIN 544

Rating Your Computer's Performance . . . . .WIN 544

Using the Performance Troubleshooter . . . . .WIN 547

Optimizing Visual Effects and Other Options . . . .WIN 550

Using Advanced Performance Tools . . . . .WIN 552

Viewing Details About System Events . . . . .WIN 554

Monitoring System Performance . . . . .WIN 556

Using Resource Monitor . . . . WIN 561

Using Task Manager to Examine System
Information. . . . . .WIN 562

Examining System Information . . . . .WIN 566

Increasing Memory Capacity. . . . . .WIN 568

Generating a System Health Report. . . . . .WIN 569

Using ReadyBoost to Increase Memory Capacity . . . .WIN 571

Session 10.1 Quick Check. .WIN 573

SESSION 10.2. . . . .**WIN 574**

Finding Troubleshooting Information . . . . .WIN 576

Searching the Microsoft Solution Centers . . . . . . .WIN 579

Troubleshooting Printing Errors. . . . . .WIN 582

Recovering from Software Errors . . . . .WIN 585

Reporting and Solving Software Errors . . . . .WIN 585

Viewing Reliability History . . . . .WIN 588

Recovering the Operating System . . . . .WIN 590

Using the Problem Steps Recorder . . . . .WIN 592

Requesting and Managing Remote Assistance. . . . . .WIN 594

Requesting Remote Assistance . . . . .WIN 596

Restoring Your Settings. .WIN 598

Session 10.2 Quick Check .WIN 599

Review Assignments . . . . .WIN 600

Case Problems. . . . . .WIN 601

ProSkills Exercise: Teamwork . . . . .WIN 607

Appendix A Connecting Computers to the Internet
Setting Up an Internet Connection . . . . **WIN A1**

Preparing to Connect to the Internet . . . . WIN A4

    Using a Broadband Connection . . . . WIN A4

    Using a Wireless Connection . . . . WIN A6

    Using a Dial-Up Connection. . . . . WIN A7

Setting Up a Broadband Connection . . . . WIN A8

    Troubleshooting a Broadband Connection. . . . . . .WIN A10

Setting Up a Wireless Connection . . . . .WIN A11

Setting Up a Dial-Up Connection . . . . .WIN A12

    Troubleshooting a Dial-Up Connection . . . . .WIN A14

Appendix B Exploring Additional Windows 7 Tools
Using Control Panel Tools and Windows Live
Essentials . . . .**WIN B1**

Using BitLocker Drive Encryption . . . . .WIN B4

    Turning BitLocker On and Off. . . . . .WIN B4

Changing Hardware and Sound Settings . . . . .WIN B7

    Selecting AutoPlay Defaults. . . . . .WIN B8

    Changing the Sound Scheme. . . . . .WIN B9

    Using a Multitouch Monitor . . . . WIN B10

Adjust Tablet PC Settings . . . . WIN B14

Changing User Accounts and Family Safety Settings WIN B16

    Creating a Password Reset Disk. . . . . WIN B16

    Setting Parental Controls. . . . . WIN B17

    Managing Credentials . . . . WIN B19

Setting Ease of Access Options. . . . . .WIN B20

    Making the Computer Easier to See. . . . . .WIN B24

Using Windows Live Essentials . . . . .WIN B25

    Using Windows Live Photo Gallery. . . . . .WIN B27

    Using Windows Live Movie Maker . . . . .WIN B30

Restoring Your Settings. . . . . .WIN B36

GLOSSARY/INDEX . . . . **REF 1**

TASK REFERENCE . . . . **REF 16**

TUTORIAL **1**

OBJECTIVES

Session 1.1
- Start Windows 7 and tour the desktop
- Explore the Start menu
- Run software programs, switch between them, and close them
- Identify and use the controls in windows and dialog boxes

Session 1.2
- Navigate your computer using Windows Explorer and the Computer window
- Change the view of the items in your computer
- Get help when you need it
- Turn off Windows 7

Exploring the Basics of Microsoft Windows 7

Investigating the Windows 7 Operating System

Case | *Metro Learning Center*

Metro Learning Center is a small but growing training company in Des Moines, Iowa. It offers academic tutoring and supplemental classes to help high school students and others prepare for college and other postsecondary education. Laura Halverson is the director of computer education at Metro, and she coordinates demonstrations and classes on developing a wide range of computer skills.

Laura recently hired you as a computer trainer. She has asked you to prepare a demonstration on the fundamentals of the Microsoft Windows 7 operating system. She has scheduled demos with a few nonprofit agencies in Des Moines and surrounding communities, and offers to help you identify the topics you should cover and the skills you should demonstrate. In this tutorial, you will start Windows 7 and practice some fundamental computer skills. Then, you'll learn how to navigate using the Computer window and Windows Explorer. Finally, you'll use the Windows 7 Help system and turn off Windows 7.

STARTING DATA FILES

There are no starting Data Files needed for this tutorial.

SESSION 1.1 VISUAL OVERVIEW

The **Recycle Bin** holds deleted items until you remove them permanently.

Recycle Bin

The **pointer** is a small object, such as an arrow, that moves on the screen when you move your mouse.

This graphic is part of an Aero **theme**, a set of desktop backgrounds, window colors, sounds, and screen savers.

The **Start button** provides access to Windows 7 programs, documents, and information on the Internet.

The **taskbar** is a strip that contains buttons to give you quick access to common tools and running programs.

Windows 7 provides three default **taskbar buttons** you can click to open popular programs, such as Internet Explorer.

An **icon** is a small picture that represents an object available on your computer.

THE WINDOWS 7 DESKTOP

The Windows 7 **desktop** is your workspace on the screen.

The **notification area** displays icons corresponding to services running in the background, such as an Internet connection.

The **Date/Time control** is an element that shows the current date and time and lets you set the clock.

10:07 AM
9/3/2013

Starting Windows 7

The **operating system** is software that manages and coordinates activities on the computer and helps the computer perform essential tasks, such as displaying information on the computer screen and saving data on disks. (The term *software* refers to the **programs**, or **applications**, that a computer uses to complete tasks.) Your computer uses the **Microsoft Windows 7** operating system—**Windows 7** for short. *Windows* is the name of the operating system, and *7* indicates the version you are using.

Much of the software created for the Windows 7 operating system shares the same look and works the same way. This similarity in design means that after you learn how to use one Windows 7 program, you are well on your way to understanding how to use others. Windows 7 allows you to use more than one program at a time, so you can easily switch between them. It also makes it easy to access the **Internet**, a worldwide collection of computers connected to one another to enable communication.

Windows 7 starts automatically when you turn on your computer. After completing some necessary start-up tasks, Windows 7 displays a Welcome screen. Depending on how your computer is set up, the Welcome screen might list only your user name or it might list all the users for the computer. Before you start working with Windows 7, you might need to click your user name and type a password. A **user name** is a unique name that identifies you to Windows 7, and a **password** is a confidential series of characters that you must enter before you can work with Windows 7. After selecting your user name, the Windows 7 desktop appears.

To begin your demo of Windows 7, Laura asks you to start Windows 7.

To start Windows 7:

1. Turn on your computer. After a moment, Windows 7 starts and the Welcome screen appears.

   Trouble? If you are asked to select an operating system, do not take action. Windows 7 should start automatically after a designated number of seconds. If it does not, ask your instructor or technical support person for help.

2. On the Welcome screen, click your user name and enter your password, if necessary. The Windows 7 desktop appears, as shown in the Session 1.1 Visual Overview. Your desktop might look different.

   Trouble? If your user name does not appear on the Welcome screen, try pressing the Ctrl+Alt+Del keys to enter your name. If necessary, ask your instructor or technical support person for further assistance.

   Trouble? If you need to enter a user name and a password, type your assigned user name, press the Tab key, type your password, and then click the Continue button or press the Enter key to continue.

   Trouble? If a blank screen or an animated design replaces the Windows 7 desktop, your computer might be set to use a **screen saver**, a program that causes a monitor to go blank or to display an animated design after a specified amount of idle time. Press any key or move your mouse to restore the Windows 7 desktop.

The Windows 7 screen uses a **graphical user interface** (**GUI**, pronounced *gooey*), which displays icons that represent items stored on your computer, such as programs and files. A computer **file** is a collection of related information; typical types of files include text documents, spreadsheets, digital pictures, and songs. Your computer represents files with icons, which are pictures of familiar objects, such as file folders and documents. Windows 7 gets its name from the rectangular work areas called **windows** that appear on your screen as you work, such as those shown in Figure 1-1.

Figure 1-1   **Two windows open on the desktop**

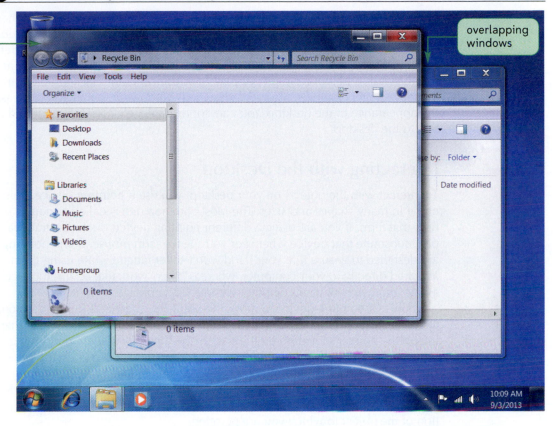

translucent color is characteristic of the Aero experience

overlapping windows

The user interface in Windows 7 is called **Aero**, and it provides a semitransparent glass design that lets you see many objects at the same time, such as two or more overlapping windows. Aero also offers other features for viewing windows and managing them on the desktop that are demonstrated later in this tutorial. Together, the translucent appearance and management features are called the Aero desktop experience.

INSIGHT

Windows 7 and the Aero Desktop Experience

Windows 7 provides themes, which are sets of desktop backgrounds, window colors, sounds, and screen savers that allow you to personalize the Aero desktop experience. The themes that take advantage of Aero's rich three-dimensional appearance are called Aero themes. You can use an Aero theme only if your computer hardware and version of Windows 7 support it. (The Microsoft Web site at *www.microsoft.com* provides detailed information about the requirements for using Aero themes.) Otherwise, your computer is set by default to use a desktop theme called Windows 7 Basic, which provides most of the same elements as the enhanced experience, including windows and icons, but not the same graphic effects. In this book, the figures show the Windows 7 Aero theme. If you are using Windows 7 Basic or another basic theme, the images on your screen will vary slightly from the figures, and some features will not be available. (These are noted throughout the book.)

Touring the Windows 7 Desktop

In Windows terminology, the background area displayed on your screen when Windows 7 starts represents a desktop—a workspace for projects and the tools that you need to manipulate your projects. When you first start a computer, it uses **default settings**, those preset by the operating system. The default desktop you see after you first install Windows 7, for example, displays a translucent blue background with a four-color Windows logo. However, Microsoft designed Windows 7 so that you can easily change the appearance of the desktop. You can, for example, change images or add patterns and text to the desktop.

Interacting with the Desktop

To interact with the objects on your desktop, you use a **pointing device**. Pointing devices come in many shapes and sizes. The most common one is called a **mouse**, so this book uses that term. If you are using a different pointing device, such as a trackball or touch-pad, substitute that device whenever you see the term *mouse*. Some pointing devices are designed to ensure that your hand won't suffer fatigue while using them. Some are attached directly to your computer, whereas others work like a TV remote control and allow you to access your computer without being plugged into it.

You use a pointing device to move the pointer over objects on the desktop, or to **point** to them. The pointer is usually shaped like an arrow, although it changes shape depending on the pointer's location on the screen and the tasks you are performing. As you move the mouse on a surface, such as a mouse pad, the pointer on the screen moves in a corresponding direction.

When you point to certain objects, such as the objects on the taskbar, a ScreenTip appears near the object. A **ScreenTip** is on-screen text that tells you the purpose or function of the object to which you are pointing.

Laura suggests that during your demo, you acquaint Metro Learning Center clients with the desktop by viewing ScreenTips for a couple of desktop objects.

To view ScreenTips:

▶ 1. Use the mouse to point to the **Start** button 🪟 on the taskbar. After a few seconds, you see a ScreenTip identifying the button, as shown in Figure 1-2.

   Trouble? If you don't see the ScreenTip, make sure you are holding the mouse still for a few seconds.

| Figure 1-2 | Viewing a ScreenTip |

ScreenTip
pointer
10:10 AM
9/3/2013

▶ 2. Point to the time and date displayed at the right side of the taskbar. A ScreenTip showing today's date (or the date to which your computer's calendar is set) appears in a longer format, such as Tuesday, September 03, 2013.

Clicking refers to pressing a mouse button and immediately releasing it. Clicking sends a signal to your computer that you want to perform an action with the object you click. In Windows 7, you perform most actions with the left mouse button. If you are told to click an object, position the pointer on that object and click the left mouse button, unless instructed otherwise.

When you click the Start button, the Start menu opens. A **menu** is a group or list of commands, and a **menu command** is text that you can click to complete tasks. If a right-pointing arrow follows a menu command, then you can point to the command to open a **submenu**, which is a list of additional choices related to the command.

The **Start menu** provides access to programs, documents, and much more. Laura suggests you click the Start button to open and explore the Start menu.

To open the Start menu:

1. Point to the **Start** button ⊞ on the taskbar.

2. Click the left mouse button. The Start menu opens. An arrow ▶ points to the All Programs command on the Start menu, indicating that you can view additional choices by navigating to a submenu. See Figure 1-3; your Start menu might show different commands.

Figure 1-3   Start menu

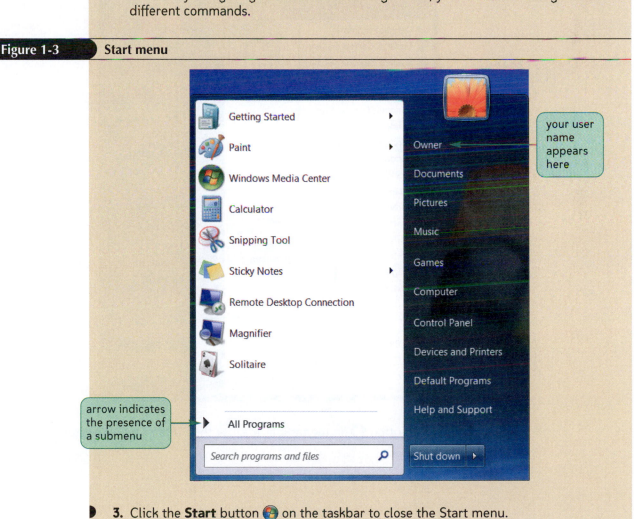

Getting Started
Paint
Windows Media Center
Calculator
Snipping Tool
Sticky Notes
Remote Desktop Connection
Magnifier
Solitaire
All Programs

Search programs and files

Owner — your user name appears here
Documents
Pictures
Music
Games
Computer
Control Panel
Devices and Printers
Default Programs
Help and Support
Shut down ▶

arrow indicates the presence of a submenu

3. Click the **Start** button ⊞ on the taskbar to close the Start menu.

You need to select an item, or object, before you can work with it. To **select** an object in Windows 7, you usually need to point to and then click that object. Windows 7 often shows you that an object is selected by highlighting it, typically by changing the object's color, putting a box around it, or making the object appear to be pushed in.

You can select certain objects simply by pointing to them. To demonstrate selecting a menu command by pointing, Laura suggests that you point to the All Programs command on the Start menu to open the All Programs submenu.

To select a menu command:

1. Click the **Start** button ⊞ on the taskbar.

2. Point to **All Programs** on the Start menu. The All Programs command is high-lighted to indicate it is selected. After a short pause, the All Programs list opens. See Figure 1-4.

Figure 1-4   All Programs list

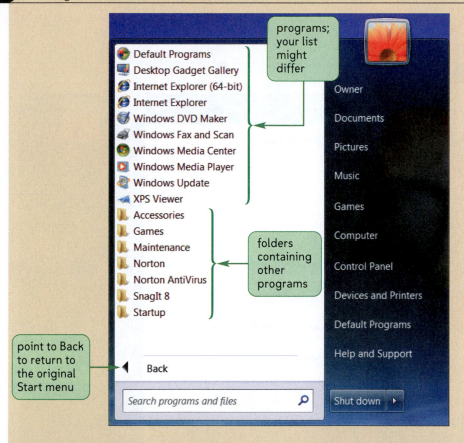

3. Click the **Start** button ⊞ on the taskbar to close the Start menu. You return to the desktop.

Clicking an object usually selects it; in contrast, you double-click an object to open or start the item associated with it. For example, you can double-click a folder icon to open the folder and see its contents. (A **folder** in Windows 7 is a container that helps to organize the contents of your computer, such as files and other folders.) Or you can double-click a program icon to start the program. **Double-clicking** means clicking the left mouse button twice in quick succession.

Laura suggests that you have students practice double-clicking by opening the Recycle Bin. The Recycle Bin holds deleted items until you remove them permanently.

To view the contents of the Recycle Bin:

1. Click the **Recycle Bin** icon on the desktop to select it, and then point to the selected icon. After a few moments, a ScreenTip appears that describes the Recycle Bin.

2. Click the left mouse button twice quickly to double-click the **Recycle Bin** icon. The Recycle Bin window opens, as shown in Figure 1-5.

Figure 1-5	Contents of the Recycle Bin

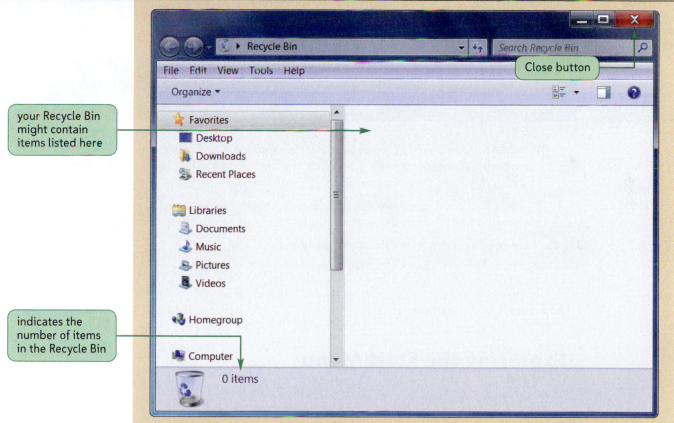

Trouble? If the Recycle Bin window does not open and you see only the Recycle Bin name highlighted below the icon, you double-clicked too slowly. Double-click the icon again more quickly.

Now you can close the Recycle Bin window.

3. Click the **Close** button ▣ in the upper-right corner of the Recycle Bin window.

You'll learn more about opening and closing windows later in this session.

Your mouse has more than one button. In addition to the left button, the mouse has a right button that you can use to perform certain actions in Windows 7. However, the term *clicking* refers to the left button; clicking an object with the right button is called **right-clicking**.

In Windows 7, right-clicking selects an object and opens its **shortcut menu**, which lists actions you can take with that object. You can right-click practically any object—the Start button, a desktop icon, the taskbar, and even the desktop itself—to view commands associated with that object. Laura suggests that when you're not sure what to do with an object in Windows 7, you should right-click it and examine its shortcut menu. She also reminds you that you clicked the Start button with the left mouse button to open the Start menu. Now you can right-click the Start button to open the shortcut menu for the Start button.

To right-click an object:

1. Position the pointer over the **Start** button 🟦 on the taskbar.

2. Right-click the **Start** button 🟦 to open its shortcut menu. This menu offers a list of actions you can take with the Start button. See Figure 1-6.

Figure 1-6	Start button shortcut menu

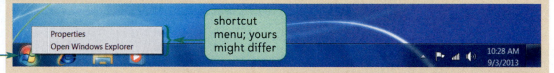

right-click the Start button

shortcut menu; yours might differ

Trouble? If the shortcut menu does not open and you are using a trackball or a mouse with a wheel, make sure you click the button on the far right, not the one in the middle.

Trouble? If your menu looks slightly different from the one in Figure 1-6, it is still the correct Start button shortcut menu. Its commands often vary by computer.

3. Press the **Esc** key to close the shortcut menu.

Now that you've opened the Start menu and its shortcut menu, you're ready to explore the contents of the Start menu.

Exploring the Start Menu

The Start menu is the central point for accessing programs, documents, and other resources on your computer. The Start menu is organized into two **panes**, which are separate areas of a menu or window. Each pane lists items you can point to or click. See Figure 1-7.

Figure 1-7   **Start menu**

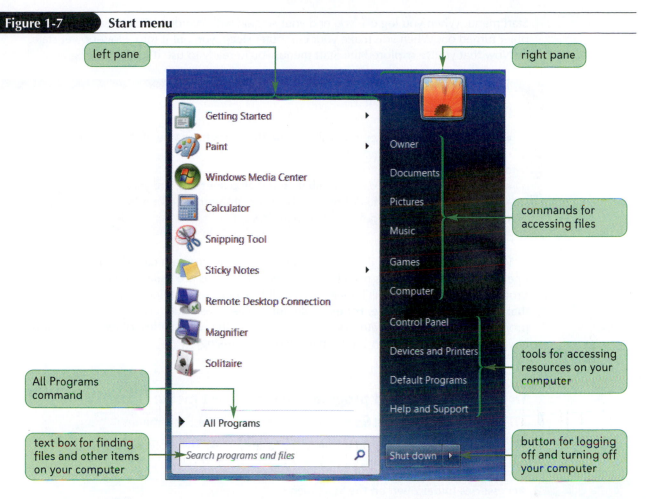

left pane

right pane

Getting Started
Paint
Windows Media Center
Calculator
Snipping Tool
Sticky Notes
Remote Desktop Connection
Magnifier
Solitaire

Owner
Documents
Pictures
Music
Games
Computer
Control Panel
Devices and Printers
Default Programs
Help and Support

commands for accessing files

tools for accessing resources on your computer

All Programs command

All Programs

text box for finding files and other items on your computer

Search programs and files

Shut down

button for logging off and turning off your computer

The left pane organizes programs for easy access. When you first install Windows 7, the left pane contains a short list of programs on your computer. After you use a program, Windows 7 adds it to this list so you can find it quickly the next time you want to use it. The Start menu can list only a certain number of programs—after that, the programs you have not opened recently are replaced by the programs you used last.

Near the bottom of the left pane is the All Programs command, which you have already used to display the All Programs list. The All Programs list provides access to the programs currently installed on your computer. You'll use the All Programs list shortly to start a program.

The **Search programs and files box** helps you quickly find anything stored on your computer, including programs, documents, pictures, music, videos, and e-mail messages. When you want to use the Search programs and files box, you open the Start menu and type one or more words related to what you want to find. For example, if you want to find and play the Happy Birthday song, which you have saved on your computer, you could type *birthday* in the Search programs and files box. Windows 7 searches your computer for that song and displays the search results in the Start menu, where you can click the song to play it.

From the right pane of the Start menu, you can access common locations and tools on your computer. For example, the **Computer window** is a tool that you use to view, organize, and access the programs, files, and drives on your computer.

From the bottom section of the right pane, you can open windows that help you work effectively with Windows 7, including the **Control Panel**, which contains specialized tools that help you change the way Windows 7 looks and behaves, and **Help and Support**, which provides articles, video demonstrations, and steps for performing tasks in Windows 7. You also log off your computer, shut it down, and put it to sleep from the

TIP

Point to an item in the right pane of the Start menu to display a ScreenTip describing the item.

Start menu. When you **log off**, you end your session with Windows 7 but leave the computer turned on. When you make your computer **sleep**, you put it into a low-power state. Now that you've explored the Start menu, you're ready to use it to start a program.

Starting a Program

- Click the Start button on the taskbar, and then click the name of the program you want to start.

or

- Click the Start button on the taskbar, and then point to All Programs.
- If necessary, click the folder that contains the program you want to start.
- Click the name of the program you want to start.

Windows 7 includes an easy-to-use word-processing program called WordPad. You open Windows 7 programs from the Start menu. Programs are usually located on the All Programs list or in one of its folders. In the All Programs list, a folder contains programs that share a similar purpose. For example, the Accessories folder contains standard useful programs, such as a calculator. WordPad is stored in the Accessories folder because it is a typical accessory you can use for basic word processing.

To start the WordPad program from the Start menu:

1. Click the **Start** button 🌐 on the taskbar to open the Start menu.

2. Point to **All Programs**, and then click **Accessories**. The Accessories folder opens, as shown in Figure 1-8.

Figure 1-8 Accessories folder open on the Start menu

contents of the Accessories folder (yours might show additional commands)

click WordPad to start the WordPad program

> **Trouble?** If a different menu or folder opens, point to Back to return to the initial Start menu, point to All Programs, and then click Accessories.

3. Click **WordPad**. The WordPad program window opens, as shown in Figure 1-9.

Figure 1-9   WordPad program window

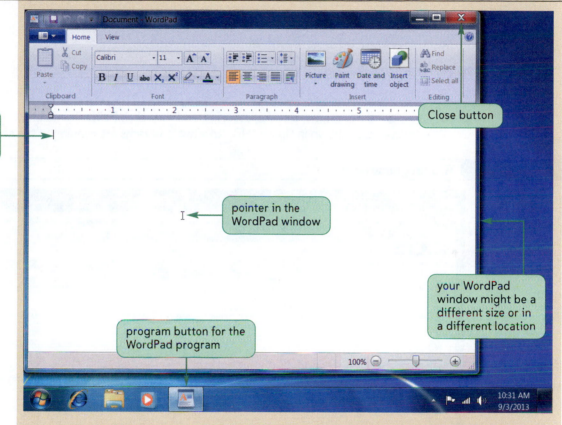

> **Trouble?** If the WordPad program window fills the entire screen, continue with the next step. You will learn how to manipulate windows shortly.

When a program is started, it is said to be open or running. A **program button** appears on the taskbar for each open program. You can click a program button on the taskbar to switch between open programs. When you are finished using a program, you can click the Close button located in the upper-right corner of the program window to **exit**, or close, that program.

To exit the WordPad program:

1. Click the **Close** button [X] in the upper-right corner of the WordPad window. The WordPad program closes and you return to the Windows 7 desktop.

Now that you have started one program, you can start another program and run two at the same time.

Running Multiple Programs

One of the most useful features of Windows 7 is its ability to run multiple programs at the same time. This feature, known as **multitasking**, allows you to work on more than one task at a time and to switch quickly between projects. To demonstrate multitasking, Laura suggests that you start WordPad and leave it running while you start Paint, which is a program used to draw, color, and edit digital pictures.

TIP

Because you have started WordPad before, it might now appear in the left pane of the Start menu.

To run WordPad and Paint at the same time:

1. Start WordPad again.

2. Click the **Start** button 🌐 on the taskbar.

3. Point to **All Programs**, click **Accessories**, and then click **Paint**. The Paint program window opens, as shown in Figure 1-10. Now two programs are running at the same time.

Figure 1-10 Two programs open

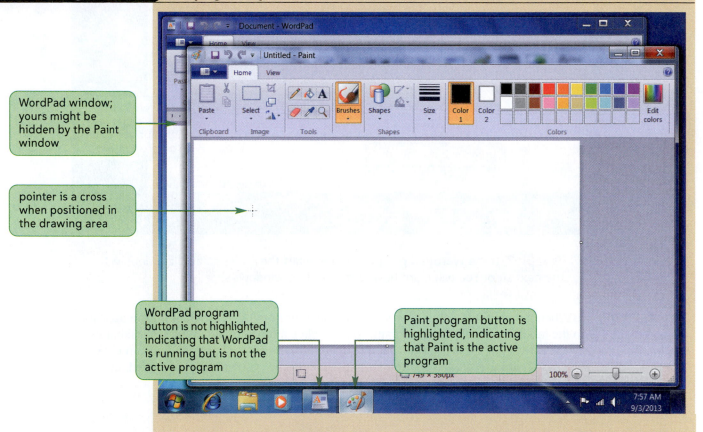

WordPad window; yours might be hidden by the Paint window

pointer is a cross when positioned in the drawing area

WordPad program button is not highlighted, indicating that WordPad is running but is not the active program

Paint program button is highlighted, indicating that Paint is the active program

Trouble? If the Paint program window fills the entire screen, continue with the next set of steps. You will learn how to manipulate windows shortly.

The **active program** is the one you are currently working with—Windows 7 applies your next keystroke or command to the active program. Paint is the active program because it is the one you are currently using. If two or more program windows overlap, the active window appears in front of the other windows. The program button for the active program is highlighted on the taskbar. The WordPad program button is still on the taskbar, indicating that WordPad is running even if you can't see its program window. The taskbar organizes all the open windows so you can quickly make a program active by clicking its taskbar button.

Switching Between Programs

Because only one program is active at a time, you need to switch between programs if you want to work in one or the other. The easiest way to switch between programs is to use the program buttons on the taskbar.

To switch between WordPad and Paint:

1. Click the **WordPad** program button 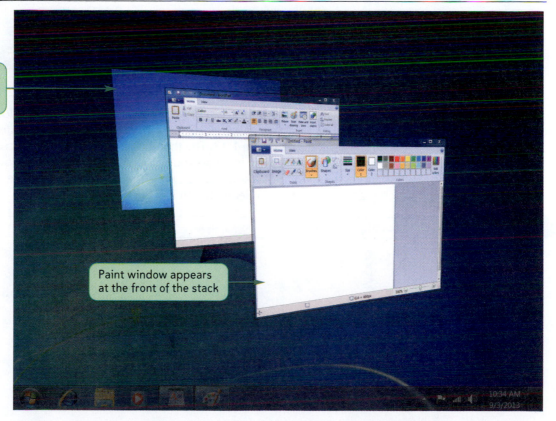 on the taskbar. The WordPad program window moves to the front, and the WordPad program button appears highlighted, indicating that WordPad is the active program.

2. Click the **Paint** program button on the taskbar to switch to the Paint program. The Paint program is again the active program.

You can also bypass the taskbar and use keyboard shortcuts to switch from one open window to another. A **keyboard shortcut** is a key or combination of keys that perform a command. When you press and hold the Windows key and then press the Tab key, Windows activates **Aero Flip 3D** (often shortened to *Flip 3D*), which displays all your open windows in a three-dimensional stack so you can see the windows from the side, the way you view the spine of a book. See Figure 1-11. To flip through the stack, you press the Tab key or scroll the wheel on your mouse while continuing to hold down the Windows button. When you release the Windows and Tab keys, you close Flip 3D and the window at the top of the stack becomes the active window.

Figure 1-11 **Aero Flip 3D**

two windows and the desktop image are flipped and stacked

Paint window appears at the front of the stack

Note that Aero Flip 3D is only available if you are using an Aero theme. If you are not using an Aero theme, you press the Alt+Tab keys to open a task switcher window that displays a generic icon for each program that is running. See Figure 1-12. You can point to an icon to display information about the program it represents. Clicking an icon makes that program the active program and closes the task switcher window; clicking outside the task switcher window closes it without changing the current active window.

Figure 1-12 **Using the task switcher window**

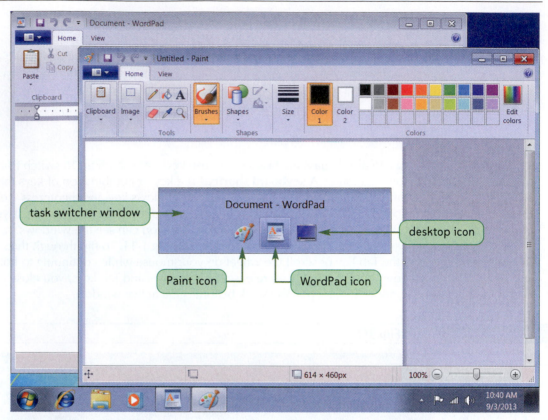

If you like to use keyboard shortcuts and are using an Aero theme, you can also switch from one window to another using Windows Flip. When you hold down the Alt key and press the Tab key once, Windows Flip displays thumbnails (miniature versions) of your open windows. See Figure 1-13. The thumbnails display the exact contents of the open windows instead of generic icons so you can easily identify the windows. While continuing to hold down the Alt key, you can press the Tab key to select the thumbnail for the program you want; you release the Alt key to close Windows Flip.

Figure 1-13 **Windows Flip**

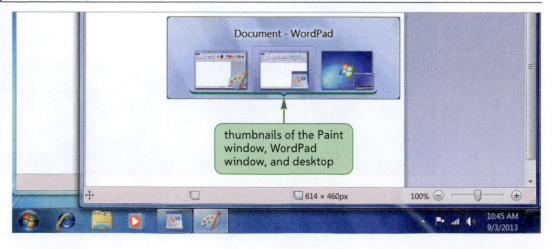

To switch between program windows using Aero Flip 3D:

1. Press and hold the **Windows** key and then press the **Tab** key. Windows arranges the Paint and WordPad windows and the desktop in a stack, with the Paint window at the top of the stack.

   Trouble? If a task switcher window similar to the one shown in Figure 1-12 opens when you press the Windows+Tab keys, you are not using an Aero theme. Click outside the task switcher window and then read, but do not perform, the remaining steps.

2. Press the **Tab** key to flip the WordPad window to the front of the stack. The Paint window moves to the back of the stack.

3. Press the **Tab** key to flip the desktop to the front of the stack, and then press the **Tab** key again to flip the Paint window to the front of the stack.

4. Release the **Windows** key to turn off Flip 3D and make Paint the active program.

Aero Flip 3D is especially useful when many windows are open on the desktop, and the one you want to use is hidden by other windows. Flip 3D provides a handy alternative to switching windows from the taskbar, which can get crowded with program buttons. In addition to using the taskbar and Aero Flip 3D to switch between open programs, you can also close programs from the taskbar.

Closing Programs from the Taskbar

You should always close a program when you are finished using it. Each program uses computer resources, such as memory, so Windows 7 works more efficiently when only the programs you need are open. Laura reminds you that you've already closed an open program using the Close button in the upper-right corner of the program window. You can also close a program, whether active or inactive, by using the shortcut menu associated with the program button on the taskbar.

To close WordPad and Paint using the program button shortcut menus:

1. Right-click the **Paint** program button ✏️ on the taskbar. The shortcut menu for the Paint program button opens. See Figure 1-14.

Figure 1-14	Program button shortcut menu

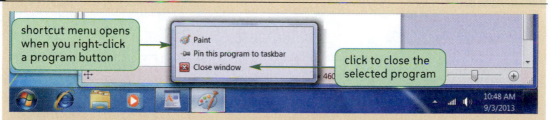

shortcut menu opens when you right-click a program button

Paint
Pin this program to taskbar
Close window

click to close the selected program

TIP

If you are using an Aero theme, you can also close a window by pointing to its button on the taskbar, pointing to the thumbnail until a Close button appears, and then clicking the Close button.

2. Click **Close window** on the shortcut menu. The Paint program closes and its program button no longer appears on the taskbar.

   Trouble? If a message appears asking if you want to save changes, click the Don't Save button.

3. Right-click the **WordPad** program button 📄 on the taskbar, and then click **Close window** on the shortcut menu. The WordPad program closes, and its program button no longer appears on the taskbar.

PROSKILLS

Problem Solving: Working Efficiently on the Desktop

When you work with Windows and its programs, especially on a complicated project, you often start and run more than one program and open many windows. This can lead to two common problems that affect your productivity: too many open windows can make it difficult to find the information you need, and running too many programs can slow the performance of your computer.

Deciding how many windows to open and how to arrange them on the desktop depends on your personal preference. Some people like to maximize all their open windows and use the taskbar to switch from one window to another. Other people like to size and arrange each window so it is visible on the desktop, even if that means having some small and overlapping windows. Keep in mind that a clean and organized desktop increases your productivity. Find an arrangement that works for you without cluttering your desktop.

If you find that your computer responds to your keystrokes and mouse actions more slowly than usual, you might have too many programs running at the same time. Closing the programs you are not using frees up system resources, which makes your computer faster and more responsive and can solve performance problems.

Now that you've learned the basics of using the Windows 7 desktop, you're ready to explore other Windows 7 features, including windows and dialog boxes.

Using Windows and Dialog Boxes

When you run a program in Windows 7, the program appears in a window. Recall that a window is a rectangular area of the screen that contains a program, text, graphics, or data. A window also contains **controls**, which are graphical or textual objects used for manipulating the window and for using the program. Figure 1-15 describes the controls you are likely to see in most windows.

Figure 1-15   Window controls

Control	Description
Program menu button	Lists commands for common program tasks, such as creating, opening, and saving documents
Quick Access Toolbar	Contains buttons for performing tasks, such as saving a document
Ribbon	Provides access to the main set of commands organized by task into tabs and groups
Sizing button	Lets you enlarge, shrink, or close a window
Status bar	Displays information or messages about the task you are performing
Tab	Organizes commands on the Ribbon related to similar tasks
Title bar	Contains the window title and basic window control buttons
Window title	Identifies the program and document contained in the window
Workspace	Includes the part of the window where you manipulate your work—enter text, draw pictures, and set up calculations, for example
Zoom controls	Magnifies or shrinks the content displayed in the workspace

Laura mentions that the WordPad program displays the controls you are likely to see in most windows. She suggests that you start WordPad and identify its window controls.

To look at the window controls in WordPad:

1. Start WordPad. On your screen, identify the controls that are labeled in Figure 1-16.

Figure 1-16 **WordPad window controls**

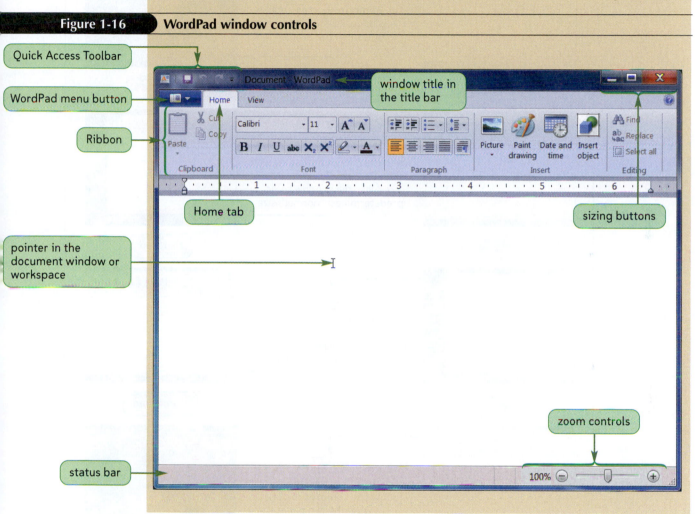

Quick Access Toolbar

WordPad menu button

Ribbon

window title in the title bar

Home tab

sizing buttons

pointer in the document window or workspace

zoom controls

status bar

After you open a window, you can manipulate it by changing its size and position.

Manipulating Windows

In most windows, three buttons appear on the right side of the title bar. The first button is the Minimize button, which hides a window so that only its program button is visible on the taskbar. Depending on the status of the window, the middle button either maximizes the window or restores it to a predefined size. You are already familiar with the last button—the Close button. Figure 1-17 illustrates how these buttons work.

Figure 1-17   Window buttons

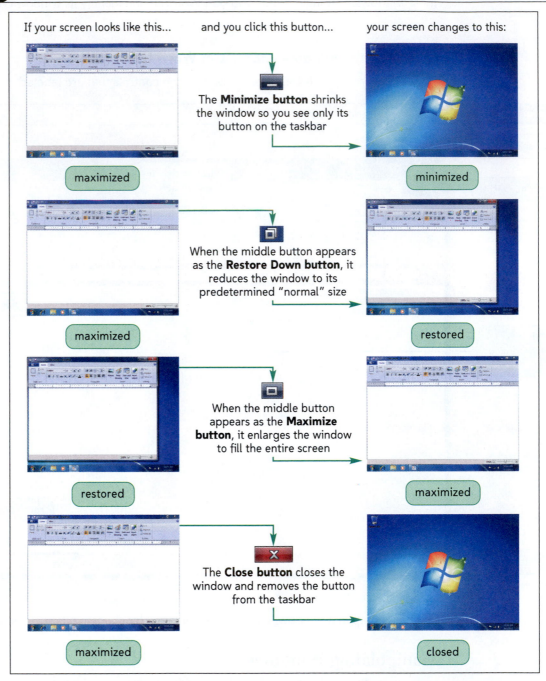

Now that WordPad is open, Laura encourages you to show students how to use its window controls to manipulate the program window. You can use the Minimize button when you want to temporarily hide a window but keep the program running.

To minimize the WordPad window:

1. Click the **Minimize** button ▬ on the WordPad title bar. The WordPad window shrinks so that only the WordPad program button on the taskbar is visible.

Trouble? If the WordPad program window closed, you accidentally clicked the Close button ☒. Use the Start button 🟢 to start WordPad again, and then repeat Step 1. If you accidentally clicked the Maximize button ▭ or the Restore Down button ⬚ , repeat Step 1.

You can redisplay a minimized window by clicking the program's button on the task-bar. When you redisplay a window, it becomes the active window.

To redisplay the WordPad window:

1. Click the **WordPad** program button 🖼 on the taskbar to redisplay the WordPad window.

   The taskbar button provides another way to switch between a window's minimized and active states.

2. Click the **WordPad** program button 🖼 on the taskbar again to minimize the window.

3. Click the **WordPad** program button 🖼 once more to redisplay the window.

The Maximize button enlarges a window so that it fills the entire screen. Laura recommends that you work with maximized windows when you want to concentrate on the work you are performing in a single program.

TIP

You can also double-click a window's title bar to maximize the window. Double-click the title bar again to restore the window to its previous size.

To maximize the WordPad window:

1. Click the **Maximize** button ▭ on the WordPad title bar.

   Trouble? If the window is already maximized, it fills the entire screen, and the Maximize button ▭ doesn't appear. Instead, you see the Restore Down button ⬚. Skip this step.

The Restore Down button reduces the window so that it is smaller than the entire screen. This feature is useful if you want to see more than one window at a time. Also, because the window is smaller, you can move the window to another location on the screen or change the dimensions of the window.

To restore a window:

1. Click the **Restore Down** button ⬚ on the WordPad title bar. After a window is restored, the Restore Down button ⬚ changes to the Maximize button ▭.

You can use the mouse to move a window to a new position on the screen. When you click an object and then press and hold down the mouse button while moving the mouse, you are **dragging** the object. You can move objects on the screen by dragging them to a new location. If you want to move a window, you drag the window by its title bar. You cannot move a maximized window.

To drag the restored WordPad window to a new location:

▶ **1.** Position the mouse pointer on the WordPad title bar.

▶ **2.** Press and hold down the left mouse button, and then move the mouse up or down a little to drag the window. The window moves as you move the mouse.

▶ **3.** Position the window anywhere on the desktop, and then release the left mouse button. The WordPad window stays in the new location.

▶ **4.** Drag the WordPad window near the upper-left corner of the desktop.

   Trouble? If the WordPad window becomes maximized when you drag it near the upper part of the desktop, click the Restore Down button ▣ before performing the next set of steps.

You can also use the mouse to change the size of a window. When you point to an edge or corner of a window, the pointer changes to the resize pointer, which is a double-headed arrow, similar to ⬊. You can use the resize pointer to drag an edge or corner of the window and change the size of the window.

To change the size of the WordPad window:

▶ **1.** Position the pointer over the lower-right corner of the WordPad window. The pointer changes to ⬊. See Figure 1-18.

Figure 1-18   Preparing to resize a window

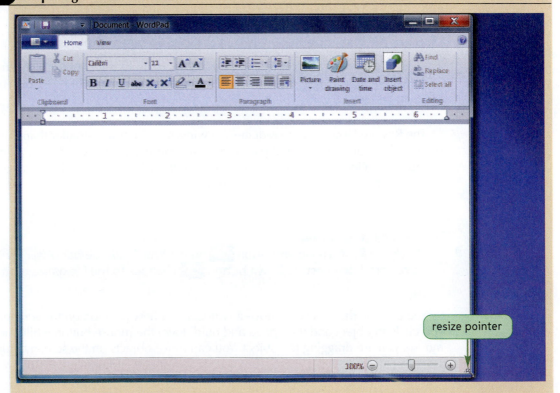

resize pointer

▶ **2.** Press and hold down the mouse button, and then drag the corner down and to the right.

> **3.** Release the mouse button. Now the window is larger.
>
> **4.** Practice using the resize pointer to make the WordPad window larger or smaller.

You can also use the resize pointer to drag any of the other three corners of the window to change its size. To change a window's size in any one direction only, drag the left, right, top, or bottom window borders left, right, up, or down.

Using the Ribbon

Many Windows 7 programs use a Ribbon to organize the program's features and commands. The **Ribbon** is located at the top of the program window, immediately below the title bar, and is organized into tabs. Each **tab** contains commands that perform a variety of related tasks. For example, the Home tab has commands for tasks you perform frequently, such as changing the appearance of a document. You use the commands on the View tab to change your view of the WordPad window.

To select a command and perform an action, you use a button or other type of control on the Ribbon. Controls for related actions are organized on a tab in **groups**. For example, to enter bold text in a WordPad document, you click the Bold button in the Font group on the Home tab. Figure 1-19 shows examples of the types of controls on the Ribbon.

Figure 1-19   **Examples of Ribbon controls**

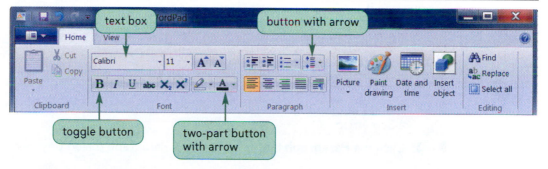

Figure 1-20 describes the Ribbon controls.

Figure 1-20 **Types of controls on the Ribbon**

Control	How to Use	Example
Button with arrow	Click the button to display a menu of related commands.	
Check box	Click to insert a check mark and select the option, or click to remove the check mark and deselect the option.	✓ Ruler
Text box	Click the text box and type an entry, or click the arrow button to select an item from the list.	Calibri
Toggle button	Click the button to turn on or apply a setting, and then click the button again to turn off the setting. When a toggle button is turned on, it is highlighted.	B B
Two-part button with arrow	If an arrow is displayed on a separate part of the button, click the arrow to display a menu of commands. Click the button itself to apply the current selection.	A

When you click some buttons on the Ribbon, you open a dialog box, such as the one shown in Figure 1-21. A **dialog box** is a special kind of window in which you enter or choose settings for how you want to perform a task. For example, you use the Paragraph dialog box to set the indentation, spacing, and alignment of the current paragraph.

Because the Paragraph dialog box contains many typical controls, Laura suggests that you open it.

To open the Paragraph dialog box:

 1. If necessary, click the **Home** tab on the WordPad Ribbon.

 2. In the Paragraph group, point to the **Paragraph** button 📑 to display its name in a ScreenTip.

 3. Click the **Paragraph** button to open the Paragraph dialog box. See Figure 1-21.

| Figure 1-21 | Paragraph dialog box |

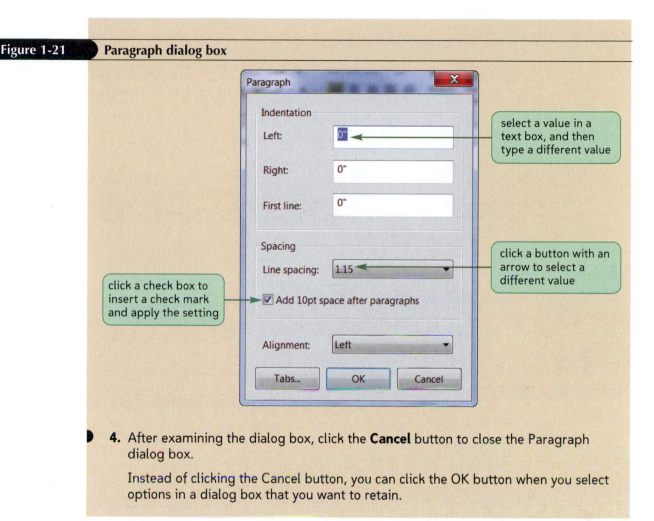

4. After examining the dialog box, click the **Cancel** button to close the Paragraph dialog box.

   Instead of clicking the Cancel button, you can click the OK button when you select options in a dialog box that you want to retain.

Laura reminds you that Windows 7 programs often display ScreenTips to indicate the name or function of a window component, such as a button. She suggests exploring the buttons on the WordPad Ribbon by looking at their ScreenTips.

To determine the names and descriptions of the buttons on the WordPad Ribbon:

1. On the Home tab of the WordPad Ribbon, position the pointer over the **Bold** button B in the Font group to display its ScreenTip.

2. Move the pointer over each remaining button on the Home tab to display its name.

Most Windows 7 programs, including WordPad and Paint, include a **Quick Access Toolbar**, which is a row of buttons on the title bar that give you one-click access to frequently used commands, such as saving a file and undoing an action. You can display the name of each button on the Quick Access Toolbar in a ScreenTip by pointing to the button, just as you do for buttons on the Ribbon. You also select a button on the Quick Access Toolbar or the Ribbon by clicking the button, which performs the associated command. One of the buttons you pointed to on the WordPad Ribbon is the Bold button, which you click to bold selected text. One of the buttons included on the Quick Access Toolbar is the Undo button, which you click to reverse the effects of your last action.

Laura says you can see how both buttons work by typing some bold text, and then clicking the Undo button to remove that text.

To use buttons on the WordPad Ribbon and Quick Access Toolbar:

▶ 1. Click the **Bold** button B in the Font group on the Home tab of the WordPad Ribbon. Now any text you type will appear as bold text.

▶ 2. Type your full name in the WordPad window.

▶ 3. Click the **Undo** button on the Quick Access Toolbar. WordPad reverses your last action by removing your name from the WordPad window.

Besides buttons, windows can contain list boxes and scroll bars, which you'll learn about next.

Using List Boxes and Scroll Bars

As you might guess from the name, a **list box** displays a list of available choices from which you can select one item. For example, to select a font size in WordPad, you use the Font size list box. A list box is helpful because it only includes options that are appropriate for your current task, such as selecting a font size. Sometimes a list might not include every possible option, so you can type the option you want to select. In most cases, the right side of the list box includes an arrow. You can click the list box arrow to view all the options and then select one or type appropriate text.

Buttons can also have arrows. The arrow indicates that the button has more than one option. Rather than crowding the window with a lot of buttons, one for each possible option, including an arrow on a button organizes its options logically and compactly into a list. Ribbon tabs often include list boxes and buttons with arrows. For example, the Font size button list box on the Home tab includes an arrow. Laura suggests you select a different font size using the arrow on the Font size button list box.

To select a new font size in the Font size button list box:

▶ 1. Click the **Font size button arrow** 11 in the Font group on the Home tab.

▶ 2. Click **18**. The Font size list closes, and the font size you selected appears in the list box.

▶ 3. Type your full name to test the new font size, and then press the **Enter** key.

▶ 4. Click the **Font size button arrow** 11 on the Home tab again, and then click **12**.

▶ 5. Type your full name again to test this type size. Your name appears in 12-point font.

List boxes sometimes include a scroll bar, which appears when the list of available options is too long or wide to fit in the list box. The vertical scroll bar includes an up and down arrow and a scroll box that you use to scroll the list. Horizontal and vertical scroll bars are more common in windows and dialog boxes. To practice scrolling, Laura advises you to open the Fonts window in WordPad and scroll the list of fonts.

To scroll the list of fonts in the Fonts window:

1. Click the **Font family button arrow** [Calibri ▾] in the Font group on the Home tab, and then click **Show more fonts** at the bottom of the list to open the Fonts window, which lists fonts installed on your computer. See Figure 1-22.

Figure 1-22	Fonts window

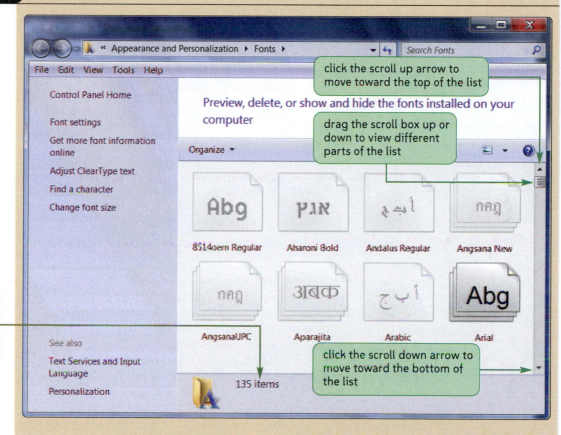

2. To scroll down the list, click the **scroll down arrow** button [▾] on the scroll bar.

3. Drag the **scroll box** to the top of the scroll bar by pointing to the scroll box, pressing and holding down the left mouse button, dragging the scroll box up, and then releasing the left mouse button. The list scrolls back to the beginning.

4. Close the Fonts window.

You'll examine a typical dialog box next.

Working with Dialog Boxes

Recall that a dialog box allows you to provide more information about how a program should carry out a task. Dialog boxes can include tabs, option buttons, check boxes, and other controls to collect information about how you want to perform a task. Figure 1-23 displays examples of common dialog box controls.

Figure 1-23   **Examples of dialog box controls**

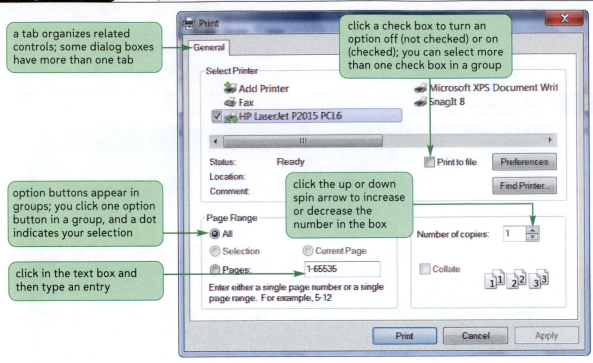

a tab organizes related controls; some dialog boxes have more than one tab

click a check box to turn an option off (not checked) or on (checked); you can select more than one check box in a group

option buttons appear in groups; you click one option button in a group, and a dot indicates your selection

click the up or down spin arrow to increase or decrease the number in the box

click in the text box and then type an entry

Besides using buttons on Ribbon tabs, you can also open dialog boxes by selecting a command on the WordPad button menu. The WordPad menu button ▇▼ appears in the upper-left corner of the WordPad window. You click the WordPad menu button to display a list of commands such as Open, Save, and Print. To open a dialog box, such as the Print dialog box, you click the appropriate command, such as Print. If you point to certain commands on the WordPad button menu, a submenu appears listing related commands. A right-pointing arrow indicates that a command has a submenu. For example, when you point to the Print command, a submenu appears listing the Print, Quick print, and Print preview commands.

Laura says a good way to learn how dialog box controls work is to open a typical Windows 7 dialog box in WordPad, such as the Page Setup dialog box. You use this dialog box to determine how text appears on a page by specifying margins, page numbers, orientation, and other settings. Before selecting options in the Page Setup dialog box, you can switch to Print Preview using the WordPad menu button to see exactly how your selections affect the WordPad document containing two copies of your name.

To work with a typical Windows 7 dialog box:

1. Click the **WordPad** menu button ▇▼ in the upper-left corner of the WordPad window, point to **Print**, and then click **Print preview**. The current document appears as it will when printed. Note that the page appears in portrait orientation, which is longer than it is wide, with a page number at the bottom of the page. The Ribbon now contains only one tab—the Print preview tab.

2. Click the **Page setup** button in the Print group on the Print preview tab. The Page Setup dialog box opens.

3. Click the **Landscape** option button to change the orientation of the page.

4. Click the **Print Page Numbers** check box to remove the check mark. This means no page numbers will appear in the document.

5. Click the **OK** button. WordPad accepts your changes and closes the Page Setup dialog box. Now the page appears in landscape orientation, so it is wider than it is long, and no page number appears at the bottom of the page.

Now that you're finished exploring dialog boxes, you can close Print Preview and exit WordPad. Besides using the Close button in the upper-right corner of the title bar, you can exit a program by clicking the program menu button and then clicking Exit.

To close Print Preview and exit WordPad:

1. Click the **Close print preview** button in the Close group on the Print preview tab. The WordPad window appears in its original view, including the Home and View tabs.

2. Click the **WordPad** menu button, and then click **Exit**. A WordPad dialog box opens asking if you want to save the document.

3. Click the **Don't Save** button to close WordPad without saving the document.

In this session, you started Windows 7 and toured the desktop, learning how to interact with the items on the desktop and on the Start menu. You also started two Windows programs, manipulated windows, and learned how to select options from a Ribbon, toolbar, menu, and dialog box.

Session 1.1 Quick Check

REVIEW

1. What does the operating system do for your computer?
2. In Windows 7, right-clicking selects an object and opens its _____.
3. The _____ is the central point for accessing programs, documents, and other resources on your computer.
4. Name two ways to change the size of a window.
5. How can you access the programs on the All Programs list?
6. True or False. When you're not sure what to do with an object in Windows 7, it's a good idea to right-click the object and examine its shortcut menu.
7. Even if you can't see an open program on your desktop, the program might be running. How can you tell if a program is running?
8. Name two ways to open a dialog box in WordPad.

SESSION 1.2 VISUAL OVERVIEW

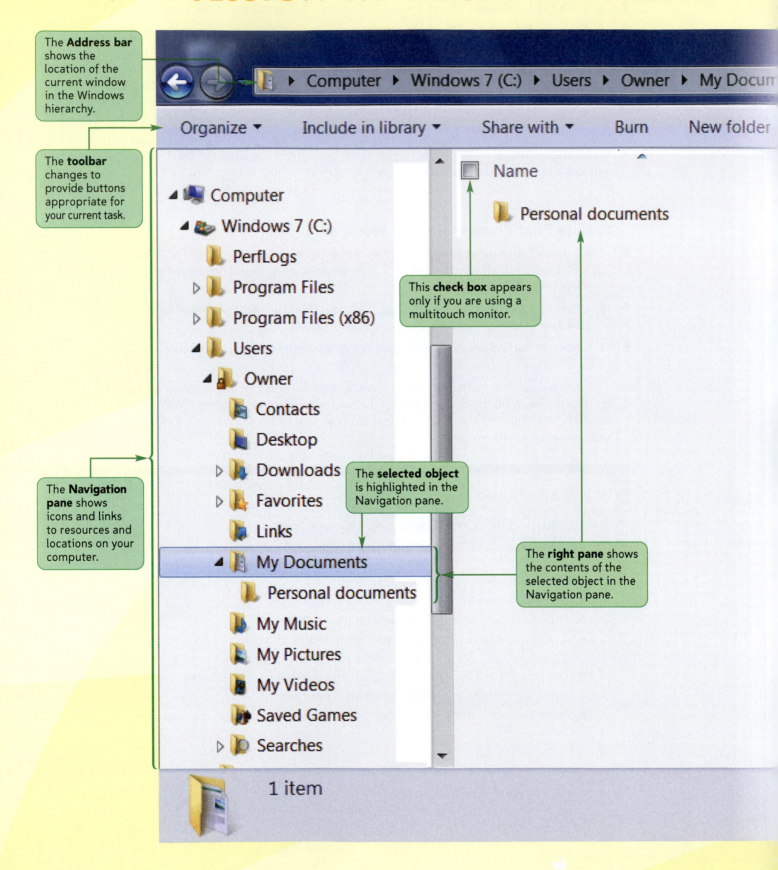

The **Address bar** shows the location of the current window in the Windows hierarchy.

The **toolbar** changes to provide buttons appropriate for your current task.

This **check box** appears only if you are using a multitouch monitor.

The **Navigation pane** shows icons and links to resources and locations on your computer.

The **selected object** is highlighted in the Navigation pane.

The **right pane** shows the contents of the selected object in the Navigation pane.

Computer ▸ Windows 7 (C:) ▸ Users ▸ Owner ▸ My Docum

Organize ▾   Include in library ▾   Share with ▾   Burn   New folder

☐ Name

📁 Personal documents

- 🖥 Computer
  - 💾 Windows 7 (C:)
    - 📁 PerfLogs
    - ▷ 📁 Program Files
    - ▷ 📁 Program Files (x86)
    - 📁 Users
      - 📁 Owner
        - 📇 Contacts
        - 🖿 Desktop
        - ▷ 📁 Downloads
        - ▷ ⭐ Favorites
        - 📁 Links
        - 📁 My Documents
          - 📁 Personal documents
        - 📁 My Music
        - 📁 My Pictures
        - 📁 My Videos
        - 🎮 Saved Games
        - ▷ 🔍 Searches

1 item

THE COMPUTER WINDOW

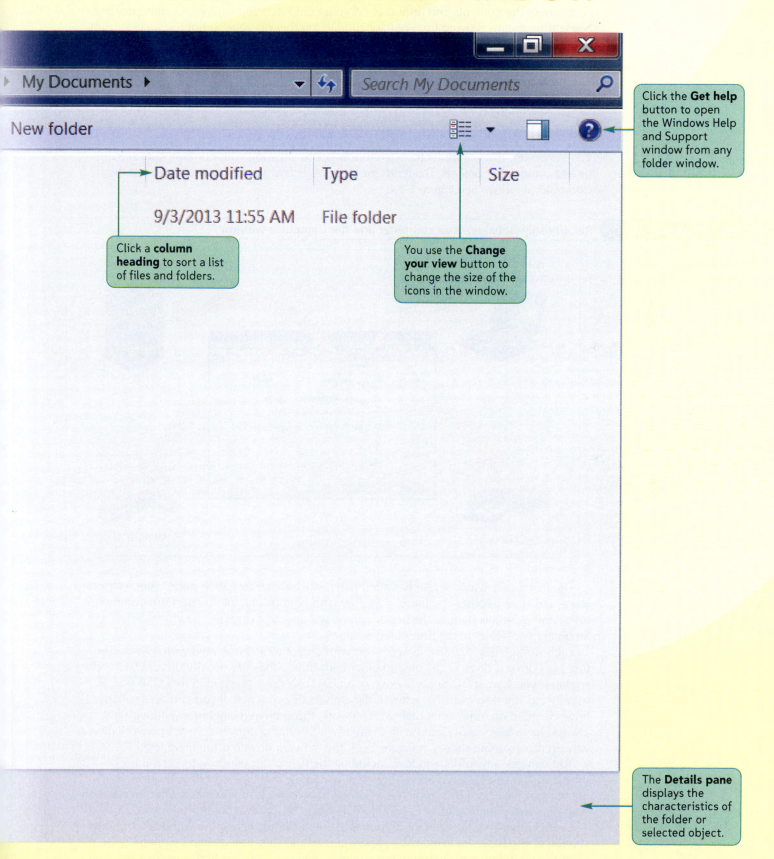

My Documents ▶

Search My Documents

New folder

Date modified   Type   Size

9/3/2013 11:55 AM   File folder

Click the **Get help** button to open the Windows Help and Support window from any folder window.

Click a **column heading** to sort a list of files and folders.

You use the **Change your view** button to change the size of the icons in the window.

The **Details pane** displays the characteristics of the folder or selected object.

Exploring Your Computer

To discover the contents and resources on your computer, you explore, or navigate, it. **Navigating** means moving from one location to another on your computer, such as from one file or folder to another. Windows 7 provides two ways to navigate, view, and work with the contents and resources on your computer—the Computer window (shown in the Session 1.2 Visual Overview) and Windows Explorer. Both are examples of **folder windows**, which display the contents of your computer.

Navigating with the Computer Window

When you use the Computer tool, a window opens showing your computer, its storage devices, and other objects. The icons for these objects appear in the right pane of the Computer window. See Figure 1-24.

Figure 1-24   Relationship between your computer and the Computer window

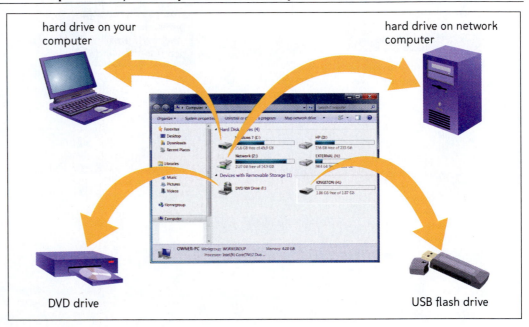

The Computer window also has a left pane, called the Navigation pane, which shows icons and links to other resources; a toolbar with buttons that let you perform common tasks; and a Details pane at the bottom of the window that displays the characteristics of an object you select in the Computer window.

Each storage device you can access on your computer is associated with a letter. The first hard drive is drive C. (If you add other hard drives, they are usually drives D, E, and so on.) If you have a CD or DVD drive or a USB flash drive plugged in to a USB port, it usually has the next available letter in the alphabetic sequence. If you can access hard drives located on other computers in a network, those drives sometimes (although not always) have letters associated with them as well. Naming conventions for network drives vary. In the example shown in Figure 1-24, the network drive has the drive letter Z.

You can use any folder window, including the Computer window, to keep track of where your files are stored and to organize your files. In this session, you explore the contents of your hard disk, which is assumed to be drive C. If you use a different drive on your computer, such as drive E, substitute its letter for C throughout this session.

Laura Halverson, the director of Metro Learning Center, is helping you plan a demonstration of the basics of Windows 7. She wants you to start this session by opening the Computer window and exploring the contents of your computer. She suggests exploring the Music library, which is a convenient location for storing your music files. (A **library** is a central place to view and organize files and folders stored anywhere that your computer can access, such as those on your hard disk, removable drives, and network. You explore libraries in more detail in Tutorial 2.) Even if you store some music files on your hard disk and others on an external drive such as a digital music player attached to your computer, they are all displayed in the Music library. Many digital music players use this location by default when you rip, download, play, and burn music.

The computer Laura provides for you has a multitouch monitor, which lets you interact with objects on the screen using your finger instead of a mouse. If you have a multitouch monitor, a feature in Windows 7 called Windows Touch lets you perform tasks such as selecting icons, opening folders, and starting programs using your finger as a pointing device. To make it easier to select objects and identify which ones are selected, Windows Touch displays a check box next to objects such as files and icons on the desktop and in folder windows. For example, you could touch the check box shown in Figure 1-25 to select all the folders in the Music library. If you are not using a multitouch monitor, these check boxes do not appear in your folder windows or on the desktop.

To explore the contents of your computer using the Computer window:

1. If you took a break after the previous session, make sure that your computer is on and Windows 7 is running.

2. Click the **Start** button on the taskbar, and then click **Computer** in the right pane of the Start menu. The Computer window opens.

3. In the Navigation pane, click the **Music** link. A window opens showing the contents of the Music library. See Figure 1-25.

Figure 1-25   **Contents of the Music library**

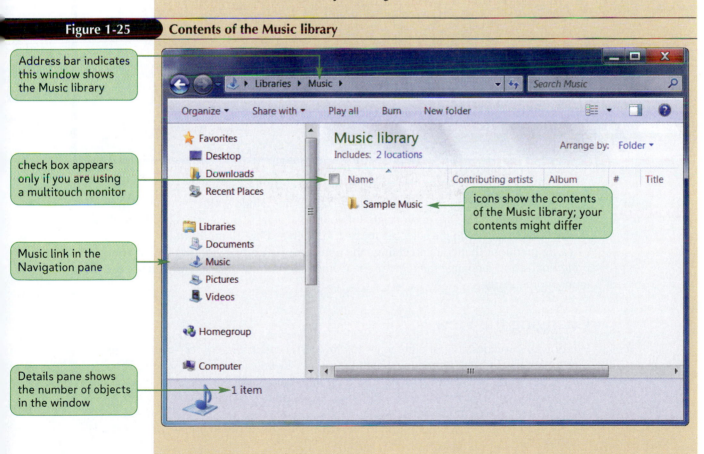

Address bar indicates this window shows the Music library

check box appears only if you are using a multitouch monitor

Music link in the Navigation pane

Details pane shows the number of objects in the window

Trouble? If your window looks different from Figure 1-25, you can still perform the rest of the steps. For example, your window might contain a different number of folders and files.

4. In the right pane, double-click the **Sample Music** icon to open the Sample Music folder. The right pane of the window shows the contents of the folder you double-clicked. You can learn more about the contents of a folder by selecting one or more of its files.

5. Click the first file listed in the Sample Music folder to select it. See Figure 1-26.

Figure 1-26 Viewing files in a folder window

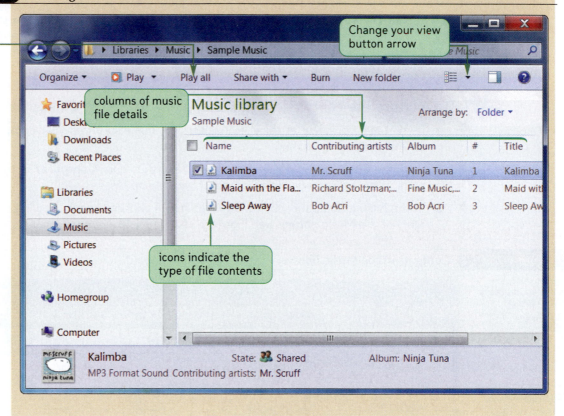

As you open folders and navigate with the Computer window, the contents of the toolbar change so that they are appropriate for your current task. In Figure 1-26, the toolbar lists actions to take with the selected music file, such as Play all and Burn.

Laura mentions that you can change the appearance of most windows to suit your preferences. You'll change the view of the Computer window next so you can see the file icons more clearly.

Changing the View

Windows 7 provides at least eight ways to view the contents of a folder—Extra Large Icons, Large Icons, Medium Icons, Small Icons, List, Details, Tiles, and Content. The default view is Details view, which displays a small icon and lists details about each file. The icon provides a visual cue about the file type. Although only Details view lists all file details, such as the contributing artists and album title for music files, you can see these details in any other view by pointing to an icon to display a ScreenTip.

Changing the Icon View

- In a folder window, click the Change your view button arrow on the toolbar, and then click a view.

or

- To cycle through the predefined views, click the Change your view button more than once.

or

- Click the Change your view button arrow on the toolbar, and then drag the slider.

To practice switching from one view to another, Laura says you can display the contents of the Sample Music folder in Tiles view. To do so, you'll use the Change your view button on the toolbar.

To view files in Tiles view:

1. In the Sample Music folder window, click the **Change your view button arrow** on the toolbar. See Figure 1-27.

   Trouble? If you click the Change your view button instead of the arrow, you cycle through the views. Click the Change your view button arrow, and then continue with Step 2.

Figure 1-27 **Preparing to change views**

TIP

To change the appearance of the icons using the Change your view button, you can also drag the slider to select an icon size or set a size somewhere between the predefined views.

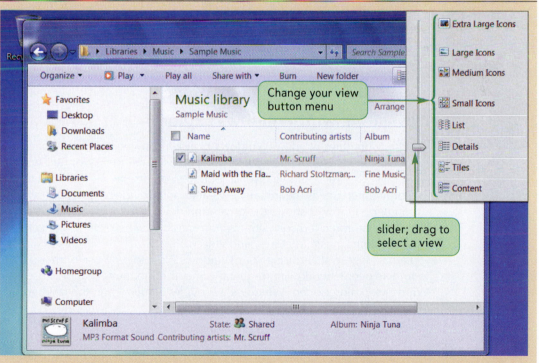

2. Click **Tiles**. The window shows the same files, but with larger icons than in Details view. The Change your view button changes to display tiles also.

3. Click the **Change your view button arrow** on the toolbar, and then click **Details** to return to Details view.

Selecting a View

When you display files in one of the large icon views, the icon displays a preview of the file's content. The preview images are big and easy to see; however, the window shows fewer files with large icons. When you display files using smaller icons, the window can show more files but the preview images are not as easy to see. The view you select depends on your preferences and needs.

No matter which view you use, you can sort the file list by filename or another detail, such as size, type, or date. If you're viewing music files, you can sort by details such as artist or album title; and if you're viewing picture files, you can sort by details such as date taken or size. Sorting helps you find a particular file in a long file listing. For example, suppose you want to listen to a song on a certain album, but you can't remember the song title. You can sort the music file list in alphabetic order by album to find the song you want.

To sort the music file list by album:

▶ **1.** Click the **Album** button at the top of the list of files. The up-pointing arrow in the upper-middle part of the Album button indicates that the files are sorted in ascending (A–Z) alphabetic order by album name.

▶ **2.** Click the **Album** button again. The down-pointing arrow on the Album button indicates that the sort order is reversed, with the albums listed in descending (Z–A) alphabetic order.

▶ **3.** Click the **Close** button **X** to close the Sample Music window.

Now Laura says you can compare the Computer window to Windows Explorer, another navigation tool.

Navigating with Windows Explorer

Like the Computer window, Windows Explorer also lets you easily navigate the resources on your computer. All of the techniques you use with the Computer window apply to Windows Explorer—and vice versa. Both let you display and work with files and folders. The only difference is the initial view each tool provides. By default, when you open the Computer window, it shows the drives and devices on your computer. When you start Windows Explorer, it displays the Libraries folder, which lets you access resources such as documents, music, pictures, and videos.

Laura suggests that during your Windows 7 demo, you use both tools to navigate to folders people work with frequently. She also mentions that because people use Windows Explorer often, Windows 7 provides its button on the taskbar for easy access.

To start Windows Explorer:

1. Click the **Windows Explorer** button 📁 on the taskbar. The Windows Explorer window opens, displaying the contents of the Libraries folder, as shown in Figure 1-28.

Figure 1-28   **Windows Explorer window**

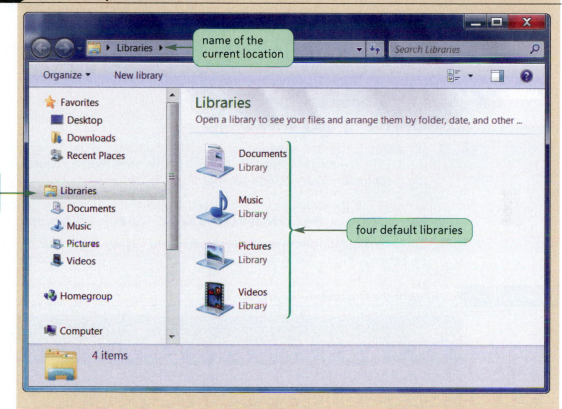

name of the current location

current location is highlighted in the Navigation pane

four default libraries

Trouble? If your Windows Explorer window looks slightly different from the one displayed in Figure 1-28, the configuration of your computer probably differs from the computer used in this figure.

Windows Explorer has the same tools and features you used in the Computer window: the Navigation pane, toolbar, Details pane, and file list in the right pane. The Navigation pane organizes resources into five categories: Favorites (for locations you access frequently), Libraries (for the Windows default libraries), Homegroup (for your shared home network, if any), Computer (for the drives and devices on your computer), and Network (for network locations your computer can access).

When you move the pointer into the Navigation pane, triangles appear next to some icons. An open triangle, or expand icon, ▷ indicates that a folder contains other folders that are not currently displayed in the Navigation pane. Click the triangle to expand the folder and display its subfolders. A filled triangle, or collapse icon, ◢ indicates the folder is expanded, and its subfolders are listed below the folder name. As you saw when working with the Computer window, you can click a folder in the Navigation pane to navigate directly to that folder and display its contents in the right pane.

INSIGHT

Exploring with the Navigation Pane

Using the Navigation pane to explore your computer usually involves clicking expand icons to expand objects and find the folder you want, and then clicking that folder to display its contents in the right pane. To display a list of all the folders on a drive, expand the Computer icon in the Navigation pane, and then expand the icon for the drive, such as Local Disk (C:). The folders list shows the hierarchy of folders on the drive, so you can use it to find and manage your files and folders.

Now you're ready to use the Navigation pane to find and open a folder people use often—the My Documents folder, which is a convenient place to store your documents and other work. The My Documents folder is stored in the Documents library by default.

To open the My Documents folder:

1. If necessary, click the **expand** icon ▷ next to Libraries in the Navigation pane to display the four built-in library folders for Documents, Music, Pictures, and Videos. (Your computer might include additional library folders.)

   Trouble? If the expand icon ▷ does not appear next to Libraries in the Navigation pane, the Libraries folder is already expanded. Skip step 1.

2. Click the **expand** icon ▷ next to Documents to display the folders in the Documents library. See Figure 1-29.

Figure 1-29   Folders in the Documents library

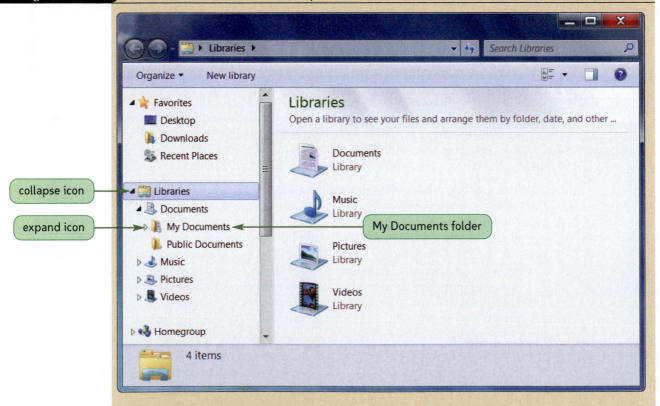

3. Click the **My Documents** folder to display its contents in the right pane. (Your My Documents folder might not contain any files or folders.)

4. Close the window.

Getting Help

Windows 7 Help and Support provides on-screen information about the program you are using. Help for the Windows 7 operating system is available by clicking the Start button and then clicking Help and Support on the Start menu.

When you start Help for Windows 7, the Windows Help and Support window opens, which gives you access to Help files stored on your computer as well as Help information stored on the Microsoft Web site. If you are not connected to the Web, you have access to only the Help files stored on your computer.

Laura suggests that you start Windows 7 Help, and then explore the information provided in the Windows Help and Support window.

TIP

You can also start Windows 7 Help and Support from any folder window by clicking the Get help button on the toolbar.

To start Windows 7 Help:

1. Click the **Start** button on the taskbar.

2. Click **Help and Support** in the right pane of the Start menu. The home page of Windows Help and Support opens. See Figure 1-30. The contents of the home page differ depending on whether you are connected to the Internet.

Figure 1-30   Windows Help and Support window

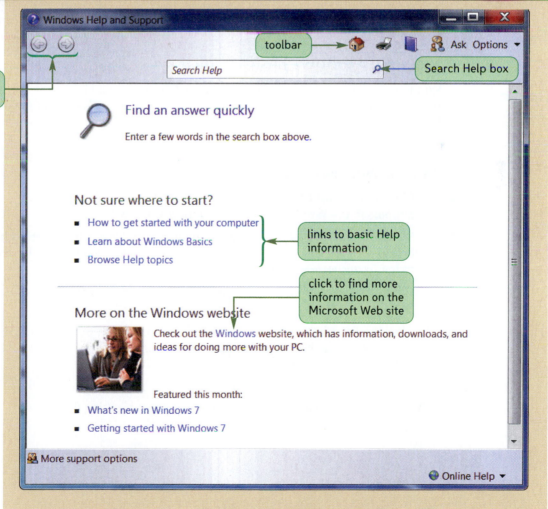

Trouble? If the Help and Support window does not display the page in Figure 1-30, click the Help and Support home button on the toolbar to view Help contents.

The home page in Windows Help and Support provides tools for finding answers and other information about Windows 7. For information about setting up your computer after installing Windows 7, click the *How to get started with your computer* link. If you are new to Windows or computers in general, click the *Learn about Windows Basics* link. To select a Help topic from a list of typical topics, click the *Browse Help topics* link. If you have an Internet connection, you can click the *Windows* link in the *More on the Windows website* section to find complete Windows 7 Help resources on the Microsoft Web site.

When you click a link on the Windows Help and Support home page, you display a list of Help topics. Click a topic to open an article providing detailed information about that topic or instructions for performing a task. You can also use the toolbar in the Windows Help and Support window to navigate Help topics. For example, click the Browse Help button ▊ to display the Contents list for Help pages. Click the Help and Support home button 🏠 to return to the Windows Help and Support home page. In addition to buttons providing quick access to pages in Windows Help and Support, the toolbar contains two other navigation buttons—the Back button ⬅ and the Forward button ➡. You use these buttons to navigate the pages you've already opened. Use the Back button to return to the previous page you viewed. By doing so, you activate the Forward button, which you can click to go to the next page of those you've opened.

For quick access to Help topics, you can use the Search Help box. Type any word or phrase in the Search Help box and press Enter, and Windows 7 lists all the Help pages that contain that word or phrase.

Viewing Windows Basics Topics

Windows 7 Help and Support includes instructions on using Help itself. You can learn how to find a Help topic by using the *Learn about Windows Basics* link on the Windows Help and Support home page.

To view Windows Basics topics:

▶ 1. Click **Learn about Windows Basics**. A list of topics related to using Windows 7 appears in the Windows Help and Support window.

▶ 2. Scroll down to the *Help and support* heading, and then click **Getting help**. An article explaining how to get help appears, with the headings in the article listed in the *In this article* section on the right.

▶ 3. Click **Getting help with dialog boxes and windows**. The Windows Help and Support window scrolls to that heading in the article.

▶ 4. Click the **Back** button ⬅ on the toolbar. You return to the previous page you visited, which is the Windows Basics: all topics page. The Forward button is now active.

You can access the full complement of Help pages by using the Contents list.

Selecting a Topic from the Contents List

The Contents list logically organizes all of the topics in Windows Help and Support into topics and categories. In the Contents list, you can click a category to display the titles of related topics. Click a topic to get help about a particular task or feature. For example, you can use the Contents list to learn more about files and folders.

To find a Help topic using the Contents list:

1. Click the **Help and Support home** button 🔴 on the toolbar to return to the home page for Windows Help and Support.

2. Click the **Browse Help** button 📘 on the toolbar. A list of categories appears in the Windows Help and Support window.

3. Click **Files, folders, and libraries** to display the list of topics and other categories related to files, folders, and libraries.

4. Click the topic **Working with files and folders**. The Windows Help and Support window displays information about that topic.

5. In the first paragraph below the *Working with files and folders* heading, click the word **icons**, which is green by default. A ScreenTip shows the definition of *icons*.

6. Click a blank area of the Windows Help and Support window to close the ScreenTip.

Another Help tool is the Search Help box, a popular way to find answers to your Windows 7 questions.

Searching the Help Pages

If you can't find the topic you need by clicking a link or using the toolbar, or if you want to quickly find Help pages related to a particular topic, you can use the Search Help box. Laura provides a typical example. Suppose you want to know how to exit Windows 7, but you don't know if Windows refers to this as exiting, quitting, closing, or shutting down. You can search the Help pages to find just the right topic.

To search the Help pages for information on exiting Windows 7:

1. Click in the Search Help box. A blinking insertion point appears.

2. Type **shut down** and then press the **Enter** key. A list of Help pages containing the words *shut down* appears in the Windows Help and Support window. See Figure 1-31. (Your results might differ.)

Figure 1-31   Search Help results

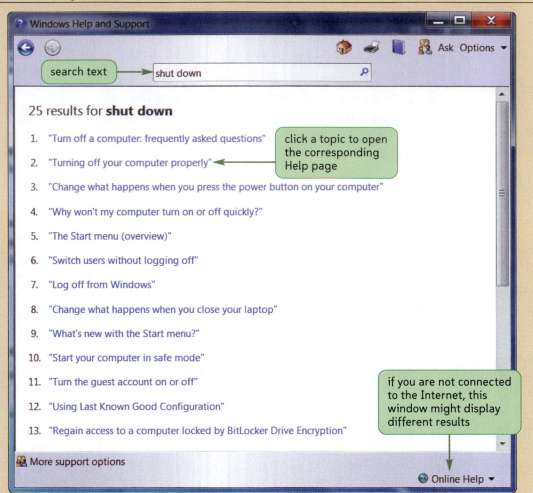

3. Click the **Turning off your computer properly** topic. The article appears in the Windows Help and Support window.

   Trouble? If a *Topic not found* message appears in the window instead of a Help topic, click the Back button ⬅ on the toolbar, and then click a different link in the Windows Help and Support window, such as *Turn off a computer: frequently asked questions*.

   If this article did not answer your question, you could click the Ask button on the toolbar. Doing so opens a page listing other ways to get Help information.

4. Click the **Close** button ❌ on the title bar to close the Windows Help and Support window.

Now that you know how Windows 7 Help works, Laura reminds you to use it when you need to perform a new task or want a reminder about how to complete a procedure.

Turning Off Windows 7

When you're finished working in Windows 7, you should always turn it off properly. Doing so saves energy, preserves your data and settings, and makes sure your computer starts quickly the next time you use it.

You can turn off Windows 7 using the Shut down button at the bottom of the Start menu. When you click the Shut down button, your computer closes all open programs, including Windows itself, and then completely turns off your computer. Shutting down doesn't save your work, so you must save your files first. For greater flexibility, you can click the arrow on the Shut down button to display a menu of shut down options, including Switch user, Log off, Lock, Restart, and Sleep. If you choose the Sleep option, Windows saves your work and then turns down the power to your monitor and computer. A light on the outside of your computer case blinks or turns yellow to indicate that the computer is sleeping. Because Windows saves your work, you do not need to close your programs or files before putting your computer to sleep. To wake a desktop computer, you press any key or move the mouse. To wake a notebook computer, you might need to press the hardware power button on your computer case instead. After you wake a computer, the screen looks exactly as it did when you turned off your computer.

When you select the Restart option, your computer shuts down and then immediately restarts, which you might need to do after installing new programs or hardware.

Instead of using the Shut down, Sleep, or Restart command, your school might prefer that you select the Log off command on the Shut down button menu. This command closes all programs and logs you off of Windows 7 but leaves the computer turned on, allowing another user to log on without restarting the computer. Check with your instructor or technical support person for the preferred method at your lab.

PROSKILLS

Decision Making: Log Off, Sleep, or Shut Down?

If you are using a computer on the job, your organization probably has a policy about what to do when you're finished working on the computer. If it does not, deciding on the best approach depends on who uses the computer and how long it will be idle. Keep the following guidelines in mind as you make your decision:

- **Log off:** If another person might use your computer shortly, log off Windows to protect your data and prepare the computer for someone else to use.
- **Sleep:** By default, Windows 7 is set to sleep after 15–30 minutes of idle time, depending on whether you are using a notebook or desktop computer. If you will be away from the computer for more than 15 minutes but less than a day, you can generally let the computer go to sleep on its own.
- **Shut down:** If your computer is plugged in to a power outlet and you don't plan to use the computer for more than a day, such as over the weekend, you save wear and tear on your electronic components and conserve energy by turning the computer off. You should also turn off the computer when it is susceptible to electrical damage, such as during a lightning storm, and when you need to install new hardware or disconnect the computer from a power source. If your notebook computer is running on battery power only and you don't plan to use it for more than a few hours, you should also turn it off to save your battery charge.

Laura suggests that you compare putting your computer to sleep and shutting down Windows 7.

To turn off Windows 7:

▶ 1. Click the **Start** button 🪟 on the taskbar, click the **Shut down button arrow**, and then click **Sleep**. Windows 7 saves your work and then puts the computer to sleep.

▶ 2. After a few moments, press any key or move the mouse. (If you are using a notebook computer, you might need to press the hardware power button, usually located on your computer case.) If necessary, enter your password.

Trouble? If your Shut down button menu does not include a Sleep option, skip to Step 3.

▶ 3. Click the **Start** button 🪟 on the taskbar and then click the **Shut down** button. Windows 7 turns off the computer.

Trouble? If you are supposed to log off rather than shut down, skip Step 3, click the Shut down button arrow, click Log off, and then follow your school's logoff procedures.

In this session, you learned how to start and close programs and how to use multiple programs at the same time. You learned how to work with windows and the controls they provide. Finally, you learned how to get help when you need it and how to turn off Windows 7. With Laura's help, you should feel comfortable with the basics of Windows 7 and well prepared to demonstrate the fundamentals of using this operating system.

REVIEW

Session 1.2 Quick Check

1. The Computer window and Windows Explorer are both examples of _____, which display the contents of your computer.
2. True or False. All of the techniques you use with the Computer window apply to Windows Explorer—and vice versa.
3. Explain how to expand a folder or other object in the Navigation pane.
4. When you navigate from the Computer window displaying the drives on your computer to the Sample Music folder, what happens to the toolbar in the Computer window?
5. In the Computer or Windows Explorer window, what appears in the right pane when you click a folder icon in the Navigation pane?
6. To display a Contents list or Help pages, you click the _____ button on the toolbar in the Windows Help and Support window.
7. How can you decide which view to use to display file and folder icons in the Computer window or Windows Explorer?
8. True or False. Instead of clicking the Shut down button at the bottom of the Start menu, you can turn off your computer by right-clicking the Start button and then clicking Turn Off on the shortcut menu.

Practice the skills you learned in the tutorial using the same case scenario.

PRACTICE

Review Assignments

There are no Data Files needed for the Review Assignments.

The day before your first Windows 7 demonstration for Metro Learning Center clients, Laura Halverson offers to observe your tour of the operating system and help you fine-tune your demo. You'll start working on the Windows 7 desktop, with no windows opened or minimized. Complete the following steps, recording your answers to any questions according to your instructor's preferences:

1. Start Windows 7 and log on, if necessary.
2. Use the mouse to point to each object on your desktop. Record the names and descriptions of each object as they appear in the ScreenTips.
3. Click the Start button. How many menu items or commands are on the Start menu?
4. Start WordPad. How many program buttons are now on the taskbar? (Don't count items in the notification area or the three default taskbar buttons to the right of the Start button.)
5. Start Paint and maximize the Paint window. How many programs are running now?
6. Switch to WordPad. What are two visual cues that tell you that WordPad is the active program?
7. Beginning on the left with the Start button, point to each object displayed in the taskbar, and then record the name and description of each object as they appear in the ScreenTips. The last item you point to should be the date and time.
8. Close WordPad, and then restore the Paint window to its original size.
9. Open the Recycle Bin window. Record the number of items it contains, and then drag and resize the Recycle Bin window so that you can see both it and the Paint window.
10. Close the Paint window from the taskbar. What command did you use?
11. In the Recycle Bin window, click the Organize button on the toolbar. Write down the commands on the menu.
12. Use any command on the Organize button menu to open a dialog box. What dialog box did you open? What do you think this dialog box is used for? Click Cancel to close the dialog box, and then close the Recycle Bin window.
13. Using the Computer window or Windows Explorer, open the Pictures library from the Navigation pane. List the contents of the Pictures library. Open a folder in the Pictures library. Explain how you opened the folder and describe its contents.
14. Change the view of the icons in the right pane of the folder window. What view did you select? Describe the icons in the folder window. Close all open windows.
15. Open Windows Help and Support. Use the *Learn about Windows Basics* link to learn something new about the Windows 7 desktop. What did you learn? How did you find this topic?
16. Return to the Home page, and then browse Help topics to find information about customizing your computer. How many topics are listed? (*Hint*: Don't include Help categories.)
17. Use the Search Help box to find information about customizing your computer. How many topics are listed?
18. Close Help, and then close any other open windows.
19. Turn off Windows 7 by using the Sleep command, shutting down, or logging off.
20. Submit your answers to the preceding questions to your instructor, either in printed or electronic form, as requested.

Use your skills to explore the contents of a computer for a client of a small business.

APPLY

Case Problem 1

There are no Data Files needed for this Case Problem.

At Your Service   At Your Service is a small business with three locations in Boulder, Colorado. The company provides troubleshooting and repair services for desktop and notebook personal computers. Roy Farwell, the manager of the west side branch, has hired you to do on-site troubleshooting and repair. You are preparing for a visit to a client who is new to Windows 7 and wants to determine the contents of his computer, including sample media files and related programs already provided in folders or menus. Complete the following steps:

1. Start Windows 7 and log on, if necessary.
2. From the Start menu, open the Computer window.
3. List the names of the drives on the computer.
4. Expand the Favorites link in the Navigation pane, if necessary, and then click the Desktop link. Does the Desktop contain any objects or folders? If so, what are their names?
5. Use the right pane to display the contents of the folder with your user name. For example, if your user name is Roy Farwell, display the contents of the Roy Farwell folder. What does this folder contain?
6. Open the Pictures library, and then open a folder containing images, if necessary. View the files in Details view, and then sort them by Size. Which file is the largest?
7. Navigate to a folder that contains music, video, or recorded TV files. Point to a file to open the ScreenTip. What type of file did you select? What details are provided in the ScreenTip? Close all open windows.
8. Use the Start menu to display the contents of the Accessories folder in the All Programs list, and then click Getting Started. Describe the contents of the Getting Started window.
9. Use the Start menu to open a program that you could use with CDs or DVDs. What program did you start?
10. Use the Start menu to open any program you might use with music or sound files. What program did you start?
11. Open Windows Help and Support, and then find and read topics that explain how to use a program you started in a previous step. Explain the purpose of one of the programs.
12. Close all open windows.
13. Submit your answers to the preceding questions to your instructor, either in printed or electronic form, as requested.

Use your skills to work with Windows 7 installed on a computer for a garden center.

APPLY

Case Problem 2

There are no Data Files needed for this Case Problem.

Dover Landscapes   After earning a degree in horticulture and working as a master gardener and landscape designer in Dover, Delaware, Liz Borowski started a garden center called Dover Landscapes that specializes in native plants and environmental planning. So that she can concentrate on landscape designs and marketing, she hired you to help her perform office tasks as her business grows. She asks you to start by teaching her the basics of using her computer, which runs Windows 7. She especially wants to know which programs are installed on her computer and what they do. Complete the following steps:

1. Open the Start menu and write down the programs listed in the left pane.

2. Start one of the programs in the left pane and then describe what it does. Close the program.

3. Open the Start menu, display the All Programs list, and then open the Accessories folder. Examine the list of programs in the Accessories folder and its subfolders.

4. Use Windows Help and Support to research one of the programs you examined in the previous step, such as Calculator or Notepad. Describe the purpose of the program and how to perform a task using that program.

5. Use the Search Help box in Windows Help and Support to list all the Help topics related to the program you researched in the previous step. How many topics are displayed in the results?

✦ EXPLORE 6. Start the program you researched. Click Help on the program's menu bar (or click the Help button) and then click each command on the Help menu or in the Help window to explore the Help topics. Compare these topics to the ones included in the Windows Help and Support window.

✦ EXPLORE 7. Use Windows Help and Support to search for Help topics about Notepad. Next, if you are connected to the Internet, use the Windows Help and Support window to find Help information about Notepad on the Microsoft Web site. Compare the two search results.

8. Close all open windows.

9. Submit the results of the preceding steps to your instructor, either in printed or electronic form, as requested.

Extend what you've learned to customize the Windows Explorer window.

CHALLENGE

Case Problem 3

There are no Data Files needed for this Case Problem.

Vernon Taylor Moe Vernon and Brett Taylor recently started their own small firm called Vernon Taylor in Bloomington, Indiana, which analyzes the finances of local businesses and recommends ways to plan for growth and success. Most of these businesses want to provide employee benefits while increasing revenues and profits. Brett Taylor uses his Windows 7 computer to write reports, study and compare data, and communicate with clients. He typically uses the Windows Explorer window to work with his files, but suspects he is not taking full advantage of its features. As his new assistant, one of your responsibilities is to show him around the Windows Explorer window and demonstrate how to customize its appearance. Complete the following steps:

1. Start Windows Explorer. Click the Organize button on the Windows Explorer toolbar, and write down any commands that seem related to changing the appearance of the window.

✦ EXPLORE 2. Select a command that lays out the Windows Explorer window so that it displays a single pane for viewing files. What command did you select? Then restore the window to its original condition.

3. Navigate to the Pictures library and display its contents. Double-click the Sample Pictures folder to open it. (If your computer does not contain a Sample Pictures folder, open any folder that displays pictures.) Display the icons using Large Icons view.

4. Change the view to Content view. Describe the differences between Large Icons and Content view.

✦ EXPLORE 5. Click the Slide show button on the toolbar. Describe what happens, and then press the Esc key.

6. With the Details pane open, click a picture file. Describe the contents of the Details pane.

✦ EXPLORE 7. Click the Organize button on the toolbar, point to Layout, and then click Menu bar to display the menu bar. Use the menu bar to display the window in Details view. Describe the steps you performed to do so.

⊕ **EXPLORE** 8. On the Organize button menu, click Folder and search options to open the Folder Options dialog box. Select the option that shows all folders in the Navigation pane, and then click the OK button. Describe the changes in the Sample Pictures window.

⊕ **EXPLORE** 9. Open the Folder Options dialog box again, click the Restore Defaults button, and then click the OK button.

10. Open the Windows Help and Support window and search for information about folder options. Find a topic explaining how to show hidden files. Explain how to do so.

11. Close all open windows.

12. Submit the results of the preceding steps to your instructor, either in printed or electronic form, as requested.

Use the Internet to provide information to an academic tour company.

RESEARCH

Case Problem 4

There are no Data Files needed for this Case Problem.

Go and Learn Tours   Years after spending their college junior year abroad in Salzburg, Austria, Rebecca Springer and Betsy Modine decided to start a travel service called Go and Learn Tours for people who want to learn about the history, art, literature, and music of Austria. Betsy spends most of the year in Washington, D.C., marketing the business and enrolling travelers in tours. Rebecca works part-time in the Washington, D.C., office and often travels to Salzburg to organize the local lecturers. Both use laptop computers running Windows 7 to manage their business when they are on the move.

They have hired you as a consultant to help them use and maintain their computers. For your first task, Betsy asks you to help her research wireless networks. Small networks are often called home networks. Betsy and Rebecca also want to connect their Bluetooth mobile phones to the network. Betsy wants to set up a small wireless network in the Go and Learn Tours office so that she and Rebecca can easily connect to the Internet wherever they are working within the office. You suggest starting with Windows Help and Support, and then expanding to the Internet to search for the latest information. Complete the following steps:

1. In Windows Help and Support, find information about the hardware Betsy and Rebecca need to set up a wireless home network.

2. Use the Ask button to visit the Microsoft Web site to obtain more information about wireless networks.

3. Choose a topic that describes how to set up a wireless network for a home or small office, and then read the topic thoroughly.

4. On the Microsoft Web site, search for information about adding a Bluetooth device to the network.

5. Write one to two pages for Betsy and Rebecca explaining what they need to set up a wireless network and the steps they should perform. Also explain how they can add their Bluetooth mobile phones to the network.

6. Submit the results of the preceding steps to your instructor, either in printed or electronic form, as requested.

ENDING DATA FILES

There are no ending Data Files needed for this tutorial.

TUTORIAL 2

Organizing Your Files

Managing Files and Folders in Windows 7

OBJECTIVES

Session 2.1
- Develop file management strategies
- Plan the organization of your files and folders
- Explore libraries, folders, and files
- Find files and folders quickly
- Create folders
- Copy and move files and folders

Session 2.2
- Name and delete files and folders
- Work with new files
- Sort and group files
- Set the appearance of a folder window
- Compress and extract files

Case | *Azalea Inn*

The Azalea Inn is a hotel in a historic mansion in Mobile, Alabama, owned by Andrew and Marilynne Ambrose. The Azalea Inn hosts travelers visiting Mobile, and it is a popular site for wedding parties and receptions, especially when the azaleas are in bloom. The Azalea Inn holds a ball during Mobile's Azalea Festival, an annual spring event. Andrew, the marketing manager, has worked hard to position the Azalea Inn at the center of the Azalea Festival. Andrew and Marilynne hired you to assist with marketing, particularly using computer tools to track repeat customers and measure the success of marketing campaigns. Before you begin, Andrew asks you to organize the files on his new computer. Although he has only a few files, he wants to use a logical organization to help him find his work as he stores more files and folders on his new computer.

In this tutorial, you'll work with Andrew to devise a strategy for managing files. You'll learn how Windows 7 organizes files and folders, and you'll examine Windows 7 file management tools. You'll create folders and organize files within them. You'll also use techniques to display the information you need in folder windows, and explore options for working with compressed files.

STARTING DATA FILES

Tutorial.02 →

Tutorial

Azalea Inn.jpg
Brochure.rtf
Budget.txt
Flyer.rtf
Logo.bmp
Pink Azalea.jpg
Purple Azalea.jpg
Rates.htm

Review

Alabama.jpg
Business Plan.rtf
Event Form.xlsx
Letterhead.bmp
Mobile.jpg
Schedule.rtf

Case1

Buffet.jpg   Ingredients.txt
Cherry.jpg   Menu-Fall.rtf
Classes.rtf   Menu-Spring.rtf
Fruit Bowl.jpg   Menu-Summer.rtf
Fruit Photo.jpg   Menu-Winter.rtf

Case2

Ely-BreakEven.xlsx   Shaw-BreakEven.xlsx
Ely-GL.xlsx   Shaw-Expenses.xlsx
Ely-Sales.xlsx   Shaw-GL.xlsx
Ely-Tax Notes.txt   Shaw-Tax Notes.txt

Case4

Contacts.accdb
Diagram.mht
Milestones.pptx
Presentations.pptx
Training.pptx

SESSION 2.1 VISUAL OVERVIEW

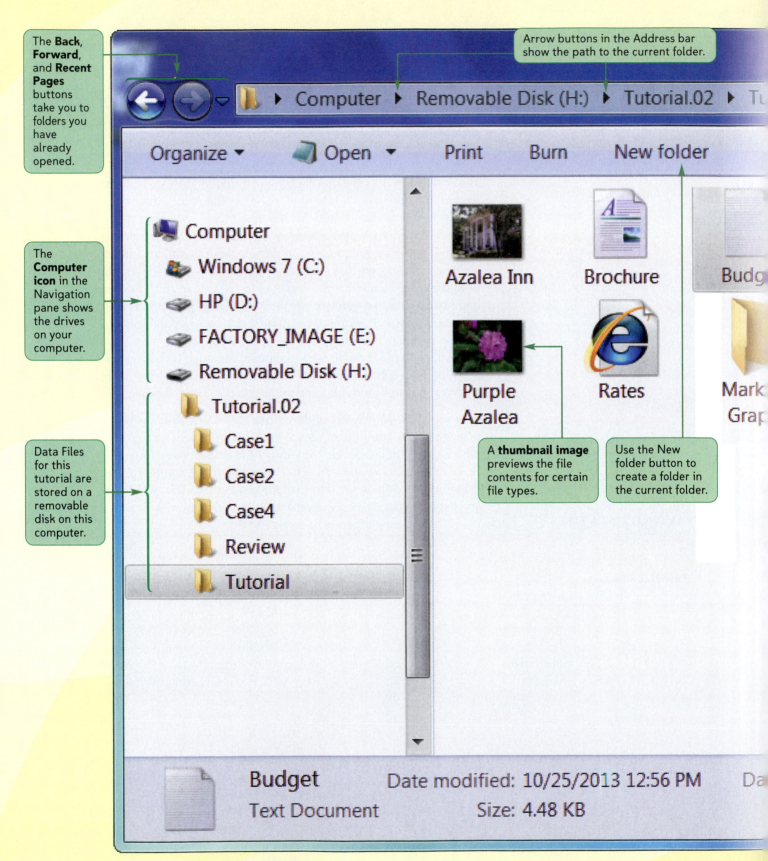

The **Back**, **Forward**, and **Recent Pages** buttons take you to folders you have already opened.

Arrow buttons in the Address bar show the path to the current folder.

The **Computer icon** in the Navigation pane shows the drives on your computer.

Data Files for this tutorial are stored on a removable disk on this computer.

A **thumbnail image** previews the file contents for certain file types.

Use the New folder button to create a folder in the current folder.

Computer ▸ Removable Disk (H:) ▸ Tutorial.02 ▸ Tu

Organize ▾   Open ▾   Print   Burn   New folder

Computer
Windows 7 (C:)
HP (D:)
FACTORY_IMAGE (E:)
Removable Disk (H:)
Tutorial.02
Case1
Case2
Case4
Review
Tutorial

Azalea Inn   Brochure   Budg

Purple Azalea   Rates   Mark Grap

Budget
Text Document   Date modified: 10/25/2013 12:56 PM   Da
Size: 4.48 KB

FILES IN A FOLDER WINDOW

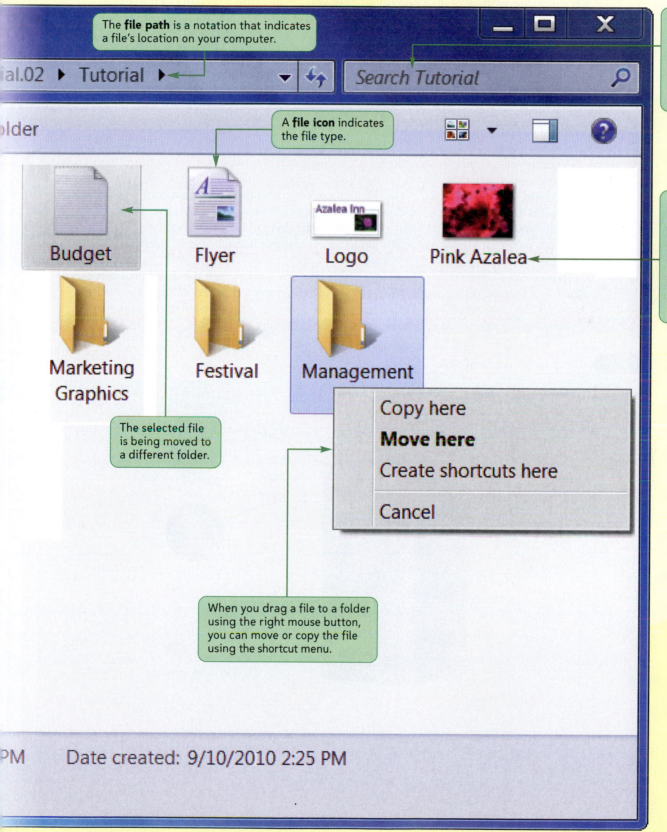

The **file path** is a notation that indicates a file's location on your computer.

Use the **Search box** to find a file in the current folder and its subfolders.

A **file icon** indicates the file type.

A **filename** is the name given to a file when it is saved and it identifies the file's contents.

The selected file is being moved to a different folder.

When you drag a file to a folder using the right mouse button, you can move or copy the file using the shortcut menu.

ial.02 ▶ Tutorial ▶

Search Tutorial

older

Budget   Flyer   Logo   Pink Azalea

Azalea Inn

Marketing Graphics   Festival   Management

Copy here

Move here

Create shortcuts here

Cancel

PM   Date created: 9/10/2010 2:25 PM

Getting Prepared to Manage Your Files

Knowing how to save, locate, and organize computer files makes you more productive when you are working with a computer. After you create a file, you can open it and in some cases edit the file's contents, print the file, and save it again—usually using the same program you used to create it. You organize files by storing them in folders. You need to organize files and folders so that you can find them easily and work efficiently.

A file cabinet is a common metaphor for computer file organization. A computer is like a file cabinet that has two or more drawers—each drawer is a storage device, or **disk**. Each disk contains folders that hold documents, or files. To make it easy to retrieve files, you arrange them logically into folders. For example, one folder might contain financial data, another might contain your creative work, and another could contain information you're gathering for an upcoming vacation.

A computer can store folders and files on different types of disks, ranging from removable media—such as USB drives (also called USB flash drives) and digital video discs (DVDs)—to **hard disks**, or fixed disks, which are permanently stored on a computer. Hard disks are the most popular type of computer storage because they provide an economical way to store many gigabytes of data. (A **gigabyte**, or **GB**, is about 1000 megabytes, and a **megabyte**, or **MB**, is 1 million bytes, with each byte roughly equivalent to a character of data.)

To have your computer access a removable disk, you must insert the disk into a **drive**, which is a computer device that can retrieve and sometimes record data on a disk. See Figure 2-1. A computer's hard disk is already contained in a drive inside the computer, so you don't need to insert it each time you use the computer.

Figure 2-1	Computer drives and disks

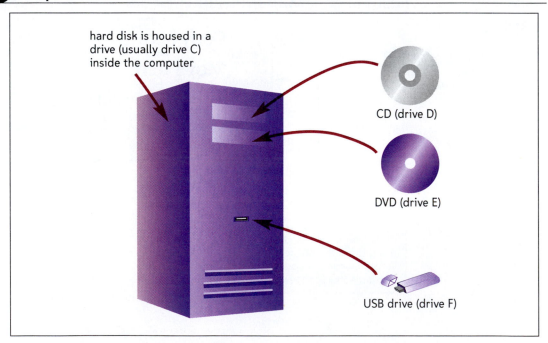

hard disk is housed in a drive (usually drive C) inside the computer

CD (drive D)

DVD (drive E)

USB drive (drive F)

A computer distinguishes one drive from another by assigning each a drive letter. Recall from Tutorial 1 that the hard disk is assigned to drive C. The remaining drives can have any other letters, but are usually assigned in the order that the drives were installed on the computer—so your USB drive might be drive D or drive F.

Understanding the Need for Organizing Files and Folders

Windows 7 stores thousands of files in many folders on the hard disk of your computer. These are system files that Windows 7 needs to display the desktop, use drives, and perform other operating system tasks. To ensure system stability and to find files quickly, Windows organizes the folders and files in a hierarchy, or **file system**. At the top of the hierarchy, Windows stores folders and important files that it needs when you turn on the computer. This location is called the **root directory** and is usually drive C (the hard disk). The term *root* refers to another popular metaphor for visualizing a file system—an upside-down tree, which reflects the file hierarchy that Windows uses. In Figure 2-2, the tree trunk corresponds to the root directory, the branches to the folders, and the leaves to the files.

Figure 2-2	Windows file hierarchy

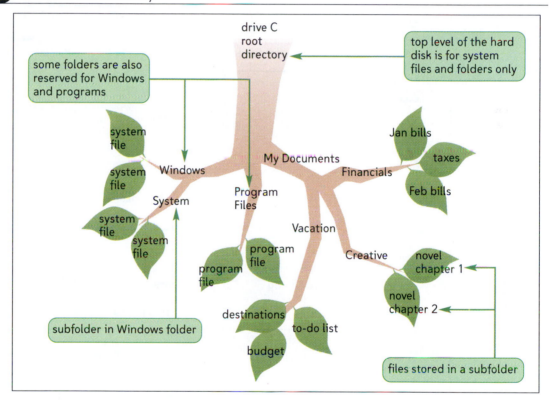

Note that some folders contain other folders. An effectively organized computer contains a few folders in the root directory, and those folders contain other folders, also called **subfolders**.

The root directory, or top level, of the hard disk is for system files and folders only—you should not store your own work here because it could interfere with Windows or a program. (If you are working in a computer lab, you might not be allowed to access the root directory.)

Do not delete or move any files or folders from the root directory of the hard disk; doing so could disrupt the system so that you can't run or start the computer. In fact, you should not reorganize or change any folder that contains installed software because Windows 7 expects to find the files for specific programs within certain folders. If you reorganize or change these folders, Windows 7 can't locate and start the programs stored in those folders. Likewise, you should not make changes to the folder (usually named Windows) that contains the Windows 7 operating system.

Developing Strategies for Organizing Files and Folders

The type of disk you use to store files determines how you organize those files. Figure 2-3 shows how you could organize your files on a hard disk if you were taking a full semester of business classes. To duplicate this organization, you would open the main folder for your documents, create four folders—one each for the Basic Accounting, Computer Concepts, Management Skills II, and Professional Writing courses—and then store the writing assignments you complete in the Professional Writing folder.

Figure 2-3   **Organizing folders and files on a hard disk**

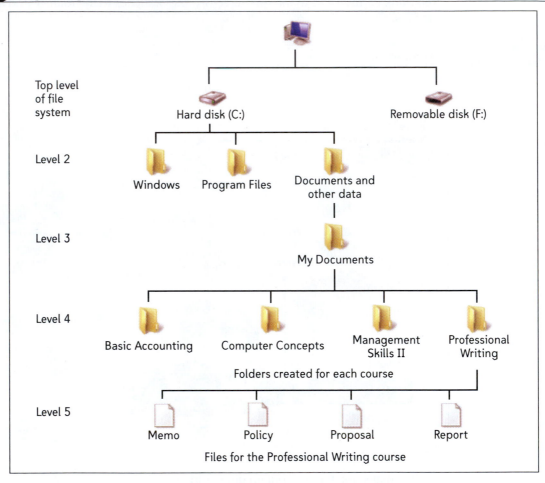

If you store your files on removable media, such as a USB drive, you can use a simpler organization because you do not have to account for system files. In general, the larger the medium, the more levels of folders you should use because large media can store more files and, therefore, need better organization. For example, if you were organizing your files on a 1-GB USB drive, you could create folders in the top level of the USB drive for each general category of documents you store—one each for Courses, Creative, Financials, and Vacation. The Courses folder could then include one folder for each course (Basic Accounting, Computer Concepts, Management Skills II, and Professional Writing), and each of those folders could contain the appropriate files.

If you have USB drives with a lower storage capacity, you might use one USB drive for your courses, another for creative work, and so on. If you needed to create large documents for your courses, you could use one USB drive for each course.

INSIGHT

Duplicating Your Folder Organization

If you work on two computers, such as one computer at an office or school and another computer at home, you can duplicate the folders you use on both computers to simplify transferring files from one computer to another. For example, if you have four folders in your My Documents folder on your work computer, you would create these same four folders on your removable medium as well as in the My Documents folder of your home computer. If you change a file on the hard disk of your home computer, you can copy the most recent version of the file to the corresponding folder on your removable disk so the file is available when you are at work. You also then have a **backup**, or duplicate copy, of important files.

Planning Your Organization

Now that you've explored the basics of organizing files on a computer, you can plan the organization of your files for this book by recording your answers to the following questions:

1. How do you obtain the files for this book (on a USB drive from your instructor, for example)? _____

    _____

2. On what drive do you store your files for this book (drive C or D, for example)?

    _____

3. Do you use a particular folder on this drive? If so, which folder do you use?

    _____

4. Is this folder contained within another folder? If so, what is the name of that main folder? _____

    _____

5. On what type of disk do you save your files for this book (hard disk, USB drive, or network drive, for example)?_____

If you cannot answer all of these questions, ask your instructor for help.

Exploring Files and Folders

Windows 7 provides two tools for exploring the files and folders on your computer—Windows Explorer and the Computer window. Both display the contents of your computer, using icons to represent drives, folders, and files. However, each initially presents a slightly different view of your computer. Windows Explorer opens to show the contents of the Windows default libraries, making it easy to find the files you work with often, such as documents and pictures. The Computer window shows the drives on your computer and makes it easy to perform system tasks, such as viewing system information. You can use either tool to open a folder window that displays the files and subfolders in a folder.

Using Folder Windows

The term *folder window* refers to any window that displays the contents of a folder, including the Computer, Windows Explorer, and Recycle Bin windows and the Save As and Open dialog boxes (which you'll examine later in this tutorial). In all of these windows, you can use the same techniques to display folders and their contents, navigate your computer, and filter, sort, and group files. Instead of distinguishing between the Computer window and Windows Explorer, think of managing your files in a folder window.

Folder windows are divided into two sections, called panes. The left pane is the Navigation pane, which contains icons and links to locations you use often. The right pane lists the contents of your folders and other locations. If you select a folder in the Navigation pane, the contents of that folder appear in the right pane. To display the hierarchy of the folders and other locations on your computer, you select the Computer icon in the Navigation pane, and then select the icon for a drive, such as Local Disk (C:) or Removable Disk (H:). You can then open and explore folders on that drive.

If the Navigation pane showed all the folders on your computer at once, it could be a very long list. Instead, you open drives and folders only when you want to see what they contain. If a folder contains undisplayed subfolders, an expand icon ▷ appears to the left of the folder icon. (The same is true for drives.) To view the folders contained in an object, you click the expand icon. A collapse icon ◢ then appears next to the folder icon; click the collapse icon to hide the folder's subfolders. To view the files contained in a folder, you click the folder icon, and the files appear in the right pane. See Figure 2-4.

Figure 2-4   **Viewing files in a folder window**

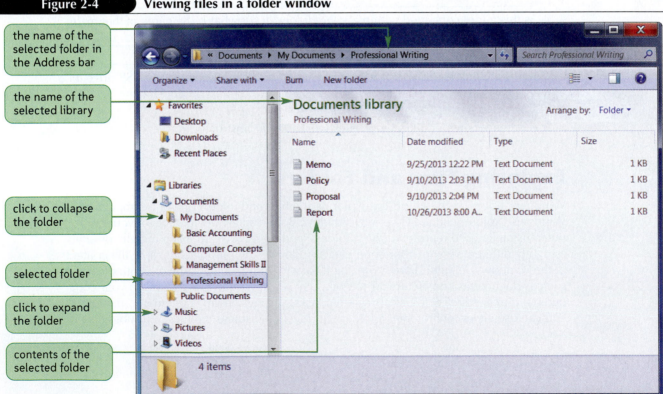

the name of the selected folder in the Address bar

the name of the selected library

click to collapse the folder

selected folder

click to expand the folder

contents of the selected folder

Using the Navigation pane helps you explore your computer and orients you to your current location. As you move, copy, delete, and perform other tasks with the files and folders in the right pane of a folder window, you can refer to the Navigation pane to see how your changes affect the overall organization.

In addition to using the Navigation pane, you can explore your computer from a folder window in other ways. Use the following navigation techniques in any folder window and many dialog boxes:

- **Opening drives and folders in the right pane:** To view the contents of a drive or folder, double-click the drive or folder icon in the right pane of the folder window. For example, to view the contents of the Professional Writing folder shown in Figure 2-5, you can double-click the Professional Writing icon in the right pane.

Figure 2-5	Viewing the contents of a folder

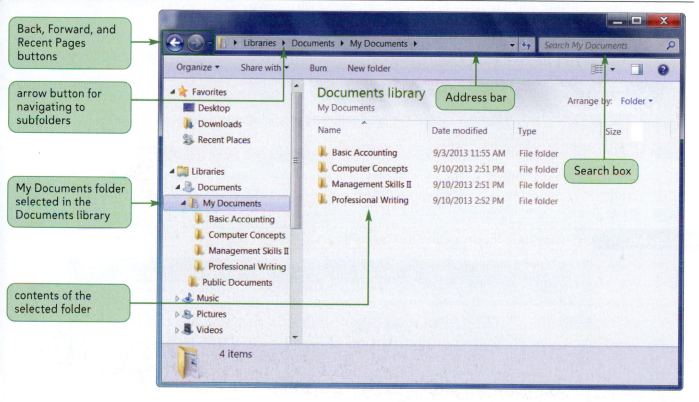

- **Using the Address bar:** You can use the Address bar to navigate to a different folder. The Address bar displays your current folder as a series of locations separated by arrows. Click a folder name, such as Documents in Figure 2-5, or an arrow button to navigate to a different location. You'll explore these controls later in the tutorial.
- **Clicking the Back, Forward, and Recent Pages buttons:** Use the Back, Forward, and Recent Pages buttons to navigate to other folders you have already opened. After you use the Address bar to change folders, for example, you can use the Back button to return to the original folder. As with the Address bar arrow button, you can click the Recent Pages button to navigate to a location you've visited recently.
- **Using the Search box:** To find a file or folder stored in the current folder or its subfolders, type a word or phrase in the Search box. The search begins as soon as you start typing. Windows finds files based on text in the filename, text within the file, and other characteristics of the file, such as tags (descriptive words or phrases you add to your files) or the author. For example, if you're looking for a document named September Income, you can type *Sept* in the Search box. Windows searches the current folder and its subfolders, and then displays any file whose filename contains a word starting with *Sept*, including the September Income document.

TIP

The name of the Search box reflects the location you are searching. If you select the My Documents folder in the left pane, for example, the Search box name is *Search My Documents.*

Using Libraries and Folders

When you open Windows Explorer, it shows the contents of the Windows built-in libraries by default. A library displays similar types of files together, no matter where they are stored. In contrast, a folder stores files in a specific location, such as in the Professional Writing subfolder of the My Documents folder on the Local Disk (C:) drive. When you want to open the Report file stored in the Professional Writing folder, you must navigate to the Local Disk (C:) drive, then the My Documents folder, and finally the Professional Writing folder. A library makes it easier to access similar types of files. For example, you might store some music files in the My Music folder and others in a folder named Albums on your hard disk. You might also store music files in a Tunes folder on a USB drive. If the USB drive is connected to your computer, the Music library can display all the music files in the My Music, Albums, and Tunes folders. You can then arrange the files to quickly find the ones you want to open and play.

Next, you'll navigate to the My Documents folder from the Documents library.

To open the My Documents folder from the Documents library:

1. Click the **Windows Explorer** button 📁 on the taskbar. The Windows Explorer window opens, displaying the contents of the default libraries.

2. In the Libraries section of the Navigation pane, click the **expand** icon ▷ next to the Documents icon. The folders in the Documents library appear in the Navigation pane; see Figure 2-6. The contents of your computer will differ.

   Trouble? If your window displays icons in a view different from the one shown in Figure 2-6, you can still explore files and folders. The same is true for all the figures in this session.

Figure 2-6 ▶ **Viewing the contents of the Documents library**

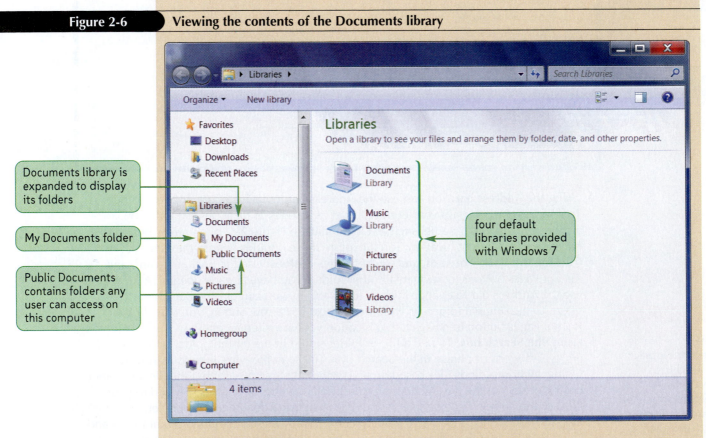

Documents library is expanded to display its folders

My Documents folder

Public Documents contains folders any user can access on this computer

four default libraries provided with Windows 7

3. Click the **My Documents** folder in the Navigation pane to display its contents in the right pane.

You can think of the Documents library as containing links to folders and files that are physically stored in other locations. The My Documents folder is not stored in the Documents library—it is actually located in your personal folder, which is labeled with the name you use to log on to the computer, such as *Andrew*. Your personal folder contains folders that most users open frequently, such as My Documents, My Music, and Favorites. The My Documents folder is designed to store your data files—the memos, reports, spreadsheets, presentations, and other files that you create, edit, and manipulate in a program. Although the My Pictures folder is designed to store graphics and the My Music folder is designed to store music files, you can store graphics, music, or any other type of file in the My Documents folder, especially if doing so makes it easier to find these files when you need them.

Now that you've shown Andrew how to display the contents of the My Documents folder from the Documents library, you can show him how to navigate to the actual location of the My Documents folder using the hierarchy of folders on your computer.

To open the My Documents folder using the hierarchy of folders on your computer:

1. In the Navigation pane of the open folder window, click the **Desktop** icon. This icon represents resources you can access from the desktop. See Figure 2-7.

Figure 2-7   **Resources accessed from the desktop**

Desktop is the selected location

Desktop icon in the Navigation pane

personal folder; yours is identified by your user name

locations to access from the desktop

2. In the right pane, double-click your personal folder, the one with your user name. In Figure 2-7, the personal folder is named Owner. A list of folders stored in your personal folder appears in the right pane. See Figure 2-8.

Figure 2-8   **Contents of your personal folder**

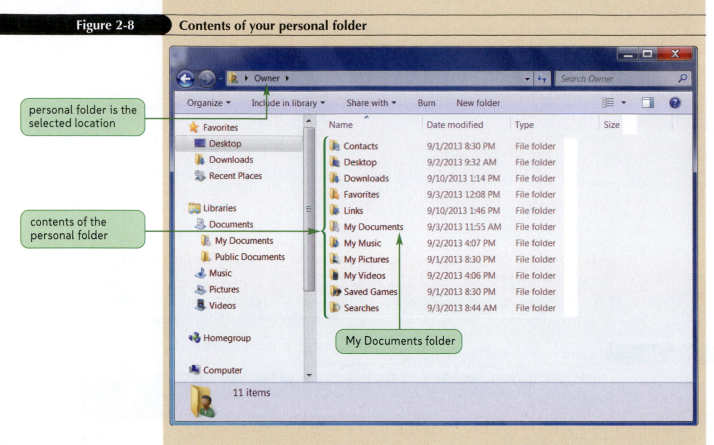

personal folder is the
selected location

contents of the
personal folder

My Documents folder

11 items

▶ **3.** In the right pane, double-click **My Documents**. The Address bar shows the actual location of the My Documents folder on your computer—in your personal folder.

You've already mastered the basics of using a folder window to navigate your computer. If necessary, you click expand icons in the Navigation pane until you find the folder that you want. Then, you click the folder icon in the Navigation pane to view the folders and files it contains, which are displayed in the right pane. You can also double-click folders in the right pane to display their contents.

Navigating to Your Data Files

TIP

To display the file path in a folder window, click to the right of the text in the Address bar.

To navigate to the files you want, it helps to know the file path. The file path leads you through the folder and file organization to your file. For example, the Logo file is stored in the Tutorial subfolder of the Tutorial.02 folder. If you are working on a USB drive, for example, the path to this file might be as follows:

H:\Tutorial.02\Tutorial\Logo.bmp

This path has four parts, with each part separated by a backslash (\ ):

- **H:** The drive name (For example, drive H might be the name for the USB drive. If this file were stored on the primary hard disk, the drive name would be C.)
- **Tutorial.02:** The top-level folder on drive H
- **Tutorial:** A subfolder in the Tutorial.02 folder
- **Logo.bmp:** The full filename

If someone tells you to find the file H:\Tutorial.02\Tutorial\Logo.bmp, you know you must navigate to your USB drive, open the Tutorial.02 folder, and then open the Tutorial folder to find the Logo file. Folder windows can display the full file path in their Address bars so you can keep track of your current location as you navigate. You can use the open folder window to navigate to the Data Files you need for the rest of this tutorial. Refer to the information you provided in the *Planning Your Organization* section and note the drive on your system that contains your Data Files. In the following steps, that drive is assumed to be Removable Disk (H:), a USB drive. If necessary, substitute the appropriate drive on your system when you perform the steps.

To navigate to your Data Files:

1. Make sure your computer can access your Data Files for this tutorial. For example, if you are using a USB drive, insert the drive into the USB port.

   Trouble? If you don't have the starting Data Files, you need to get them before you can proceed. Your instructor will either give you the Data Files or ask you to obtain them from a specified location (such as a network drive). In either case, make a backup copy of your Data Files before you start using them so you will have the original files available in case you need to start over. If you have any questions about the Data Files, see your instructor or technical support person for assistance.

2. In the open folder window, click the **expand** icon ▷ next to the Computer icon to display the drives on your computer, if necessary.

3. Click the **expand** icon ▷ next to the drive containing your Data Files, such as Removable Disk (H:). A list appears below the drive name showing the folders on that drive.

4. If the list of folders does not include the Tutorial.02 folder, continue clicking the **expand** icon ▷ to navigate to the folder that contains the Tutorial.02 folder.

5. Click the **expand** icon ▷ next to the Tutorial.02 folder to expand the folder, and then click the **Tutorial.02** folder. Its contents appear in the Navigation pane and in the right pane of the folder window. The Tutorial.02 folder contains the Case1, Case2, Case4, Review, and Tutorial folders, as shown in Figure 2-9. (Because Case Problem 3 does not require any files, the Tutorial.02 folder does not include a Case3 folder.) The other folders on your system might vary.

Figure 2-9   Navigating to the Tutorial.02 folder

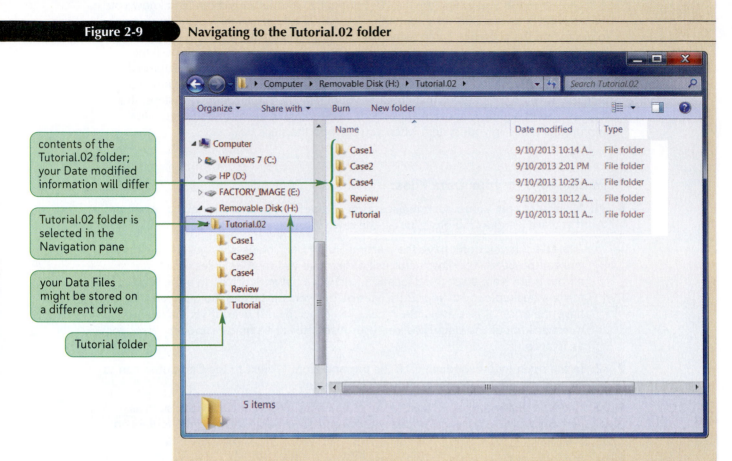

contents of the Tutorial.02 folder; your Date modified information will differ

Tutorial.02 folder is selected in the Navigation pane

your Data Files might be stored on a different drive

Tutorial folder

6. In the Navigation pane, click the **Tutorial** folder. The files it contains appear in the right pane. To preview the contents of the graphics, you can display the files as medium icons.

7. If necessary, click the **Change your view button arrow** ▤▾ on the toolbar, and then click **Medium Icons**. The files appear in Medium Icons view in the folder window. See Figure 2-10.

Figure 2-10	Files in the Tutorial folder in Medium Icons view

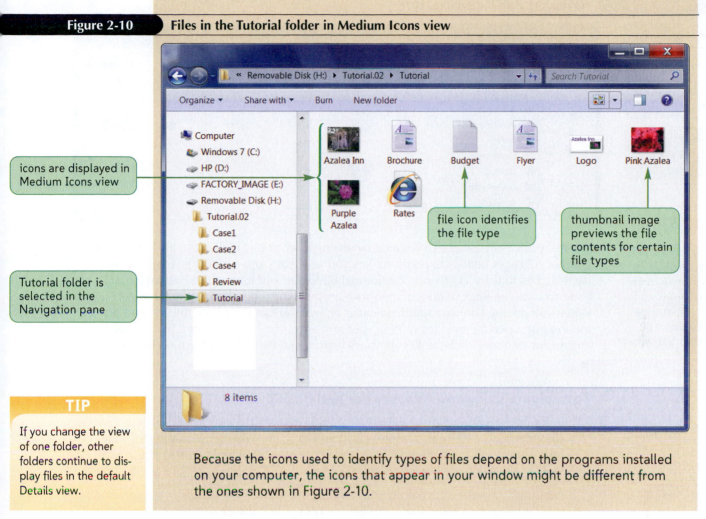

icons are displayed in Medium Icons view

file icon identifies the file type

thumbnail image previews the file contents for certain file types

Tutorial folder is selected in the Navigation pane

TIP

If you change the view of one folder, other folders continue to display files in the default Details view.

Because the icons used to identify types of files depend on the programs installed on your computer, the icons that appear in your window might be different from the ones shown in Figure 2-10.

Andrew wants to know how to use the Address bar effectively, so you offer to navigate with the Address bar to compare that technique to using the Navigation pane.

Navigating with the Address Bar

The Address bar, located at the top of every folder window, displays your current folder as a series of locations separated by arrows. For example, in Figure 2-11, the Address bar shows the Tutorial.02 and Tutorial folders separated by an arrow, indicating that Tutorial is the current folder and it's stored in the Tutorial.02 folder. If a chevron button « appears, you can click it to list the folders and drives containing the locations displayed in the Address bar. In Figure 2-11, the first item in this list is Computer, which contains Removable Disk (H:). This list also includes other locations your computer can access, such as Libraries and Recycle Bin.

To change your location, you can click or type a folder name in the Address bar. For example, you can click Tutorial.02 to navigate to that folder. You can also type the path to the folder you want, or type the name of a standard, built-in Windows folder or library, such as the My Documents or Favorites folders or the Music library.

Figure 2-11   **Navigating with the Address bar**

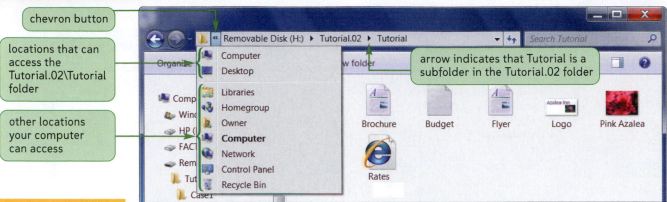

chevron button

locations that can
access the
Tutorial.02\Tutorial
folder

other locations
your computer
can access

arrow indicates that Tutorial is a
subfolder in the Tutorial.02 folder

After you've navigated to a location by any method, you can click the Back, Forward, and Recent Pages buttons to revisit folders you've already opened. For example, if you navigate first to drive H:, then to the Tutorial.02 folder, and then to the Tutorial folder, you can click the Back button to open your previous location, the Tutorial.02 folder. When you do, the Forward button becomes active. You can then click the Forward button to again open the next location in your sequence, the Tutorial folder. To navigate to any recent location, click the Recent Pages button, and then click a location in the list.

To navigate using the Address bar and Back button:

1. In the folder window displaying the contents of your Tutorial folder, click the **chevron** button « on the Address bar, and then click the drive containing your Data Files, such as Removable Disk (H:), in the list. The window displays the contents of the drive containing your Data Files.

   Trouble? If a chevron button does not appear in the Address bar, your window is wide enough to show the complete file path. Click the first arrow button in the Address bar.

   Trouble? If the drive containing your Data Files is not listed in the chevron button or arrow button menu, click Computer.

2. Click the **arrow** button ▸ to the right of Computer on the Address bar, and then click the name of a hard disk drive, such as **Local Disk** (C:).

3. Click the **Back** button ◉ on the Address bar one or more times to return to the Tutorial folder.

4. Click the **Recent Pages** button ▾ to display a list of locations you visited, and then click **Tutorial.02**. The subfolders in your Tutorial.02 folder appear in the right pane.

Leave the folder window open so that you can work with other file and folder tools.

Using the Search Box to Find Files

After you use a computer awhile, you're likely to have many hundreds of files stored in various folders. If you know where you stored a file, it's easy to find it—you can use any navigation technique you like to navigate to that location and then scan the file list to find the file. Often, however, finding a file is more time consuming than that. You know that you stored a file somewhere in a standard folder such as My Documents or My Music, but finding the file might mean opening dozens of folders and scanning many long file lists. To save time, you can use the Search box to quickly find your file.

The Search box appears next to the Address bar in any folder window. To find a file in the current folder or any of its subfolders, you start typing text associated with the file. This search text can be part of the filename, text within the file, tags (keywords you associate with a file), or other file properties. By default, Windows searches for files by examining the filenames and contents of the files displayed in the folder window, including files in any subfolders. If it finds a file whose filename contains a word starting with the search text you specify, it displays that file in the folder window. For example, you can use the search text *inn* to find files named Azalea Inn and Innsbruck Plans. If you are searching a hard drive, Windows also looks for files that contain a word starting with your search text. If it finds one, it displays that file in the folder window. For example, using *inn* as the search text also finds files containing words such as inning, inner, and innovate. If you are searching a removable drive, Windows searches filenames only, though you can specify that you want to search the file contents also. The following steps assume you are searching a removable drive.

Andrew asks you to find a digital photo of azaleas on his computer. He knows he has at least one photo of an azalea. You can find this file by starting to type *azalea* in the Search box.

To use the Search box to find a file:

1. In the folder window displaying the contents of your Tutorial.02 folder, click in the Search box.

2. Type **a** and then pause. Windows 7 examines the files in the Tutorial.02 folder and its subfolders, searching for a filename that includes a word starting with *a*. Several files in the Tutorial.02 folder meet this criterion. You can continue typing to narrow the selection.

3. Type **za** after the *a* so that the search text is now aza. Only three files have filenames that include a word beginning with *aza*.

   Trouble? If you are searching a hard drive, you will see additional files that contain words beginning with *aza*.

4. If you are searching files on a removable drive, click **File Contents** in the *Search again in* section of the folder window to search for files containing the text *aza*. Scroll down to view all the files. See Figure 2-12.

Figure 2-12   **Searching for a file**

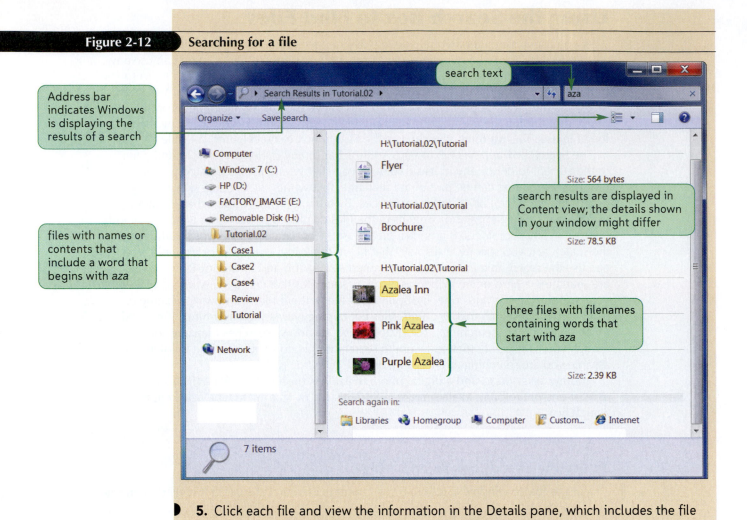

Address bar indicates Windows is displaying the results of a search

files with names or contents that include a word that begins with *aza*

search text

search results are displayed in Content view; the details shown in your window might differ

three files with filenames containing words that start with *aza*

7 items

5. Click each file and view the information in the Details pane, which includes the file properties, such as the filename, file type, and other details.

Three of the files you found using *aza* as the search text have filenames that contain words starting with *aza*: Azalea Inn, Pink Azalea, and Purple Azalea. Five of the files you found contain text that matches your criterion. By examining the file contents and properties in the Details pane, you found two photos of azaleas for Andrew—the Pink Azalea file and the Purple Azalea file.

Now that Andrew is comfortable navigating a computer to find files, you're ready to show him how to manage his files and folders.

Managing Files and Folders

After you devise a plan for storing your files, you are ready to get organized by creating folders that will hold your files. You can do so using any folder window. For this tutorial, you'll create folders in the Tutorial folder. When you are working on your own computer, you will usually create folders within the My Documents folder and other standard folders, such as My Music and My Pictures.

Examine the files shown in Figure 2-10 again and determine which files seem to belong together. Azalea Inn, Logo, Pink Azalea, and Purple Azalea are all graphics files that the inn uses for marketing and sales. The Brochure and Flyer files were created for a special promotion the inn ran during the spring Azalea Festival. The other files relate to general inn management.

One way to organize these files is to create three folders—one for graphics, one for the Azalea Festival, and another for the management files. When you create a folder, you give it a name, preferably one that describes its contents. A folder name can have up to 255 characters. Any character is allowed, except / \ : * ? " < > or |. Considering these conventions, you could create three folders as follows:

- **Marketing Graphics folder:** Azalea Inn, Logo, Pink Azalea, and Purple Azalea files
- **Festival folder:** Brochure and Flyer files
- **Management folder:** Rates and Budget files

Before creating the folders, you show your plan to Andrew. You point out that instead of creating a folder for the graphics files, he could store them in the My Pictures folder that Windows provides for photos, clip art, drawings, and other graphics. But Andrew wants to keep these marketing graphic files separate from any other files. He also thinks storing them in a folder along with the Festival and Management folders will make it easier to find his marketing files later.

Guidelines for Creating Folders

Keep the following guidelines in mind as you create folders:

- Keep folder names short and familiar: Long folder names can be more difficult to display in their entirety in folder windows, so use names that are short but clear. Choose names that will be meaningful later, such as project names or course numbers.
- Develop standards for naming folders: Use a consistent naming scheme that is clear to you, such as one that uses a project name as the name of the main folder, and includes step numbers in each subfolder name, such as 01Plan, 02Approvals, 03Prelim, and so on.
- Create subfolders to organize files: If a file listing in a folder window is so long that you must scroll the window, consider organizing those files into subfolders.

Andrew asks you to create the three new folders. After that, you'll move his files to the appropriate folders.

Creating Folders

You've already seen folder icons in the windows you've examined. Now, you'll create folders within the Tutorial folder using the toolbar that appears in all folder windows.

Creating a Folder in a Folder Window

- In the Navigation pane, click the drive or folder in which you want to create a folder.
- Click New folder on the toolbar.
- Type a name for the folder, and then press the Enter key.

or

- Right-click a folder in the Navigation pane or right-click a blank area in the folder window, point to New, and then click Folder.
- Type a name for the folder, and then press the Enter key.

Now you can create three folders in your Tutorial folder as you planned—the Marketing Graphics, Festival, and Management folders.

To create folders:

> 1. Navigate to the **Tutorial** folder included with your Data Files for Tutorial.02.

> 2. Click the **New folder** button on the toolbar. A folder icon with the label *New folder* appears in the right pane. See Figure 2-13.

Figure 2-13   Creating a folder in the Tutorial folder

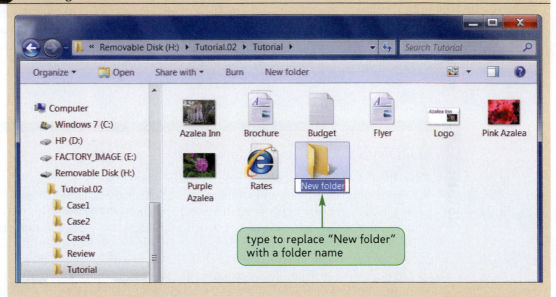

Trouble? If the *New folder* name is not selected, right-click the new folder, click Rename, and then continue with Step 3.

Windows uses *New folder* as a placeholder, and selects the text so that you can replace it with the name you want simply by typing the new name—you do not need to press the Backspace or Delete key to delete the *New folder* text.

> 3. Type **Marketing Graphics** as the folder name, and then press the **Enter** key. The new folder is named *Marketing Graphics* and is the selected item in the right pane.

You are ready to create a second folder. This time, you'll use a shortcut menu to create a folder.

> 4. Right-click a blank area in the right pane, point to **New** on the shortcut menu, and then click **Folder**. A folder icon with the label *New folder* appears in the right pane with the *New folder* text selected.

Trouble? If the *New folder* text is not selected, right-click the folder, and then click Rename on the shortcut menu.

> 5. Type **Festival** as the name of the new folder, and then press the **Enter** key.

> 6. Using the toolbar or the shortcut menu, create a folder named **Management**. The Tutorial folder now contains three new subfolders.

After creating three folders, you're ready to organize your files by moving them into the appropriate folders.

Moving and Copying Files and Folders

If you want to place a file into a folder from another location, you can either move the file or copy it. **Moving** a file removes it from its current location and places it in a new location that you specify. **Copying** also places the file in a new location that you specify, but does not remove it from its current location. Windows 7 provides several techniques for moving and copying files. The same principles apply to folders—you can move and copy folders using a variety of methods.

REFERENCE

Moving a File or Folder in a Folder Window

- Right-click and drag the file or folder you want to move to the destination folder.
- Click Move here on the shortcut menu.

or

- Right-click the file or folder you want to move, and then click Cut on the shortcut menu. (You can also click the file or folder and then press the Ctrl+X keys.)
- Navigate to and right-click the destination folder, and then click Paste on the shortcut menu. (You can also click the destination folder and then press the Ctrl+V keys.)

Andrew suggests that you move some files from the Tutorial folder to the appropriate subfolders. You'll start by moving the Budget file to the Management folder.

To move a file using the right mouse button:

1. Point to the **Budget** file in the right pane, and then press and hold the *right* mouse button.

2. With the right mouse button still pressed down, drag the **Budget** file to the **Management** folder. When the *Move to Management* ScreenTip appears, release the button. A shortcut menu opens.

3. With the left mouse button, click **Move here** on the shortcut menu. The Budget file is removed from the main Tutorial folder and stored in the Management subfolder.

   Trouble? If you release the mouse button before you've dragged the Budget file all the way to the Management folder and before seeing the *Move to Management* ScreenTip, press the Esc key to close the shortcut menu, and then repeat Steps 1–3.

4. In the right pane, double-click the **Management** folder. The Budget file is in the Management folder.

   Trouble? If the Budget file does not appear in the Management folder, you probably moved it to a different folder. Press the Ctrl+Z keys to undo the move, and then repeat Steps 1–4.

5. Click the **Back** button 🔙 on the Address bar to return to the Tutorial folder. The Tutorial folder no longer contains the Budget file.

The advantage of moving a file or folder by dragging with the right mouse button is that you can efficiently complete your work with one action. However, this technique requires polished mouse skills so that you can drag the file comfortably. Another way to move files and folders is to use the **Clipboard**, a temporary storage area for files and information that you have copied or moved from one place and plan to use somewhere else. You can select a file and use the Cut or Copy commands to temporarily store the file on the Clipboard, and then use the Paste command to insert the file elsewhere. Although using the Clipboard takes more steps, some users find it easier than dragging with the right mouse button.

You'll move the Brochure file to the Festival folder next by using the Clipboard.

To move files using the Clipboard:

1. Right-click the **Brochure** file, and then click **Cut** on the shortcut menu. Although the file icon is still displayed in the folder window, Windows 7 removes the Brochure file from the Tutorial folder and stores it on the Clipboard.

2. In the right pane, right-click the **Festival** folder, and then click **Paste** on the shortcut menu. Windows 7 pastes the Brochure file from the Clipboard to the Festival folder. The Brochure file icon no longer appears in the folder window.

3. In the Navigation pane, click the **expand** icon ▷ next to the Tutorial folder, if necessary, and then click the **Festival** folder to view its contents in the right pane. The Festival folder now contains the Brochure file. See Figure 2-14.

Figure 2-14	Moving a file

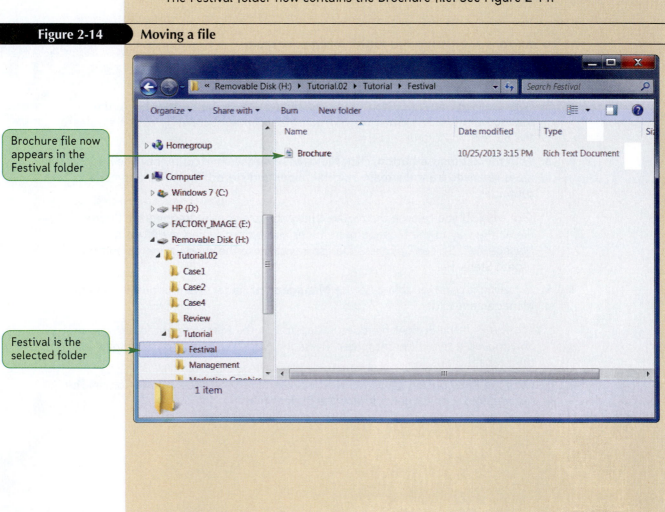

Brochure file now appears in the Festival folder

Festival is the selected folder

<table><tr><td>

TIP

To use keyboard shortcuts to move files, click the file you want to move, press Ctrl+X to cut the file, navigate to a new location, and then press Ctrl+V to paste the file.

</td><td>

Next, you'll move the Flyer file from the Tutorial folder to the Festival folder.

4. Click the **Back** button ⬅ on the Address bar to return to the Tutorial folder, right-click the **Flyer** file in the folder window, and then click **Cut** on the shortcut menu.

5. In the Navigation pane, right-click the **Festival** folder, and then click **Paste** on the shortcut menu.

6. Click the **Forward** button ➡ on the Address bar to return to the Festival folder. The Festival folder now contains the Brochure and Flyer files.

</td></tr></table>

One way to save steps when moving or copying multiple files or folders is to select all the files and folders you want to move or copy, and then work with them as a group. You'll show Andrew how to do that next.

Selecting Files and Folders

You can select multiple files or folders using several techniques, so you can choose the most convenient method for your current task. First, you open the folder that contains the files or folders you want to select. Then select the files or folders using any one of the following methods:

- To select files or folders that are listed together in a window, click the first item, hold down the Shift key, click the last item, and then release the Shift key.
- To select files or folders that are listed together in a window without using the keyboard, drag the pointer to create a selection box around all the items you want to include.
- To select files or folders that are not listed together, hold down the Ctrl key, click each item you want to select, and then release the Ctrl key.
- To select all of the files or folders, click Organize on the toolbar, and then click Select all.
- To clear the selection of an item in a selected group, hold down the Ctrl key, click each item you want to remove from the selection, and then release the Ctrl key.
- To clear the entire selection, click a blank area of the window.

Copying Files and Folders

When you copy a file or folder, you make a duplicate of the original item. You can copy files or folders using techniques similar to the ones you use when moving them.

REFERENCE

Copying a File or Folder in a Folder Window

- Right-click and drag the file or folder you want to move to the destination folder.
- Click Copy here on the shortcut menu.
or
- Right-click the file or folder you want to copy, and then click Copy on the shortcut menu. (You can also click the file or folder and then press the Ctrl+C keys.)
- Navigate to and right-click the destination folder, and then click Paste on the shortcut menu. (You can also click the destination folder and then press the Ctrl+V keys.)

You'll copy the four graphics files from the Tutorial folder to the Marketing Graphics folder now.

To copy files using the Clipboard:

1. Return to the Tutorial folder window, and then click the **Azalea Inn** file.

2. Hold down the **Ctrl** key, click the **Logo** file, click the **Pink Azalea** file, click the **Purple Azalea** file, and then release the **Ctrl** key. Four files are selected in the Tutorial folder window.

3. Right-click a selected file, and then click **Copy** on the shortcut menu. Windows copies the files to the Clipboard.

4. Right-click the **Marketing Graphics** folder, and then click **Paste** on the shortcut menu. Windows copies the four files to the Marketing Graphics folder.

Now that you have copied files using the Copy and Paste commands, you can use the right-drag technique to copy the Rates file to the Management folder. As with moving files, to copy a file using the right-drag technique, you point to the file, hold down the right mouse button, and then drag the file to a new location. When you release the mouse button, however, you click Copy here (instead of Move here) on the shortcut menu to copy the file.

To copy a file:

1. Right-drag the **Rates** file from the Tutorial folder to the Management folder.

2. Release the mouse button, and then click **Copy here** on the shortcut menu.

When you move or copy a folder, you move or copy all the files contained in the folder. You'll practice moving and copying folders in the Case Problems at the end of this tutorial.

You can use a third technique to copy or move a file or folder. You can drag the file or folder (using the left mouse button) to another location. Whether the file or folder is copied or moved depends on where you drag it. A ScreenTip appears when you drag a file to a new location—the ScreenTip indicates what happens when you release the mouse button. Figure 2-15 summarizes how to copy and move files and folders by dragging.

Figure 2-15   **Dragging to move and copy files**

Drag a File or Folder:	To:
Into a folder on the same drive	Move the file or folder to the destination folder
Into a folder on a different drive	Copy the file or folder to the destination folder

Although the copy and move techniques listed in Figure 2-15 are common ways to copy and move files and folders, be sure you can anticipate what happens when you drag a file or folder.

PROSKILLS

Decision Making: Determining Where to Store Files

When you create and save files on your computer's hard disk, you should store them in subfolders. The top level of the hard disk is off-limits for your files because they could interfere with system files. If you are working on your own computer, store your files within the My Documents folder, which is where many programs save your files by default. When you use a computer on the job, your employer might assign a main folder to you for storing your work. In either case, if you simply store all your files in one folder, you will soon have trouble finding the files you want. Instead, you should create subfolders within a main folder to separate files in a way that makes sense for you.

Even if you store most of your files on removable media, such as USB drives, you still need to organize those files into folders and subfolders. Before you start creating folders, whether on a hard disk or removable disk, you need to plan the organization you will use. Following your plan increases your efficiency because you don't have to pause and decide which folder to use when you save your files. A file organization plan also makes you more productive in your computer work—the next time you need a particular file, you'll know where to find it.

In this session, you examined why you need to organize files and folders, and you began to plan your organization. You also explored your computer using folder windows and learned how to navigate to your Data Files using the Navigation pane and the Address bar. You used the Search box to find files quickly based on their filenames and contents. Finally, you managed files and folders by creating folders and selecting, moving, and copying files.

REVIEW

Session 2.1 Quick Check

1. What is the term for a collection of data that has a name and is stored on a disk or other storage medium?
2. Explain how to use a folder window to navigate to a file in the following location: H:\Courses\Written Communications\Conference Report.txt
3. A(n) _____ displays similar types of files together, no matter where they are stored.
4. What can you follow through the folder and file organization on your computer to locate a file?
5. Describe two ways to find files using the Search box.
6. Describe three ways to navigate your computer in a folder window.
7. True or False. The advantage of moving a file or folder by dragging with the right mouse button is that you can efficiently complete your work with one action.
8. Describe two ways to select files that are listed in a folder window.

SESSION 2.2 VISUAL OVERVIEW

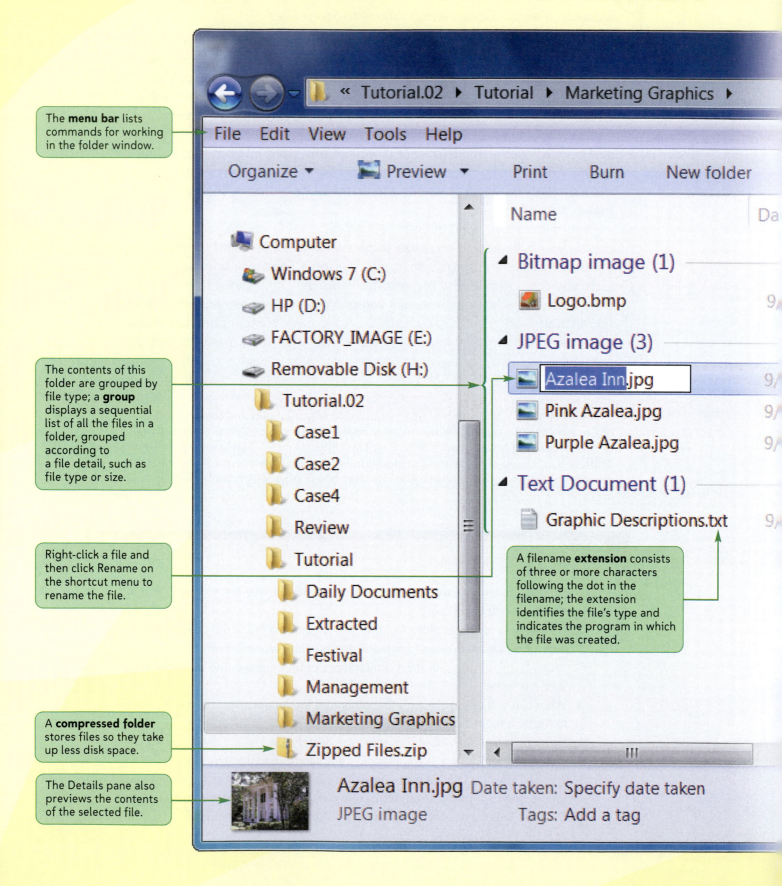

The **menu bar** lists commands for working in the folder window.

The contents of this folder are grouped by file type; a **group** displays a sequential list of all the files in a folder, grouped according to a file detail, such as file type or size.

Right-click a file and then click Rename on the shortcut menu to rename the file.

A **compressed folder** stores files so they take up less disk space.

The Details pane also previews the contents of the selected file.

A filename **extension** consists of three or more characters following the dot in the filename; the extension identifies the file's type and indicates the program in which the file was created.

Tutorial.02 ▶ Tutorial ▶ Marketing Graphics ▶

File   Edit   View   Tools   Help

Organize ▼   Preview ▼   Print   Burn   New folder

Name

- Computer
  - Windows 7 (C:)
  - HP (D:)
  - FACTORY_IMAGE (E:)
  - Removable Disk (H:)
    - Tutorial.02
      - Case1
      - Case2
      - Case4
      - Review
      - Tutorial
        - Daily Documents
        - Extracted
        - Festival
        - Management
        - Marketing Graphics
    - Zipped Files.zip

▲ Bitmap image (1)
   Logo.bmp   9

▲ JPEG image (3)
   Azalea Inn.jpg   9/
   Pink Azalea.jpg   9/
   Purple Azalea.jpg   9/

▲ Text Document (1)
   Graphic Descriptions.txt   9/

Azalea Inn.jpg   Date taken: Specify date taken
JPEG image   Tags: Add a tag

CUSTOMIZED FOLDER WINDOW

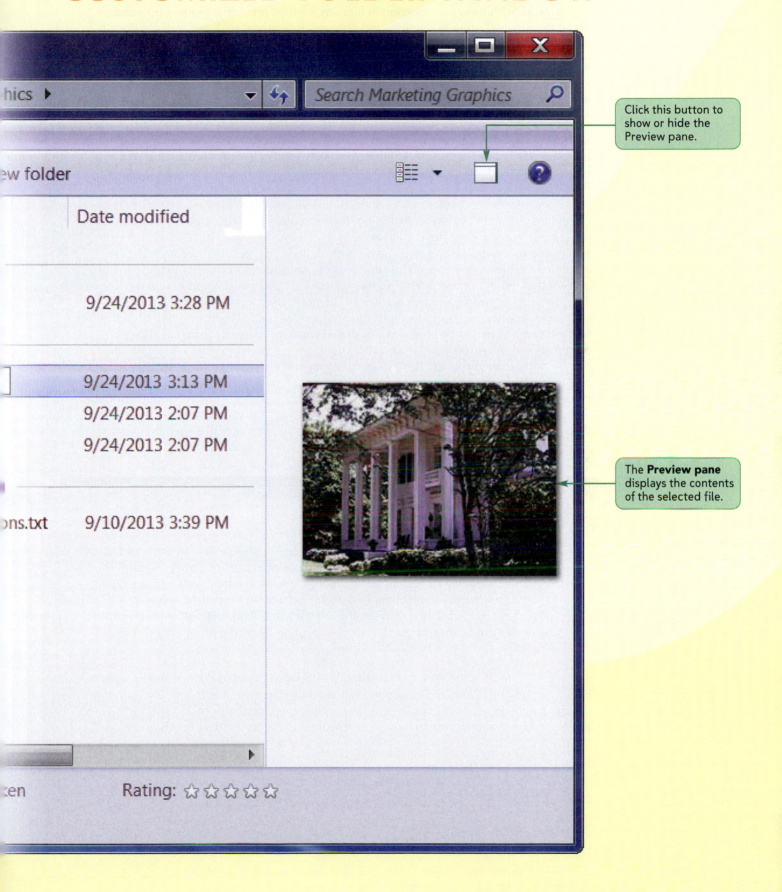

hics ▶

Search Marketing Graphics

Click this button to show or hide the Preview pane.

ew folder

Date modified

9/24/2013 3:28 PM

9/24/2013 3:13 PM
9/24/2013 2:07 PM
9/24/2013 2:07 PM

The **Preview pane** displays the contents of the selected file.

ons.txt   9/10/2013 3:39 PM

zen   Rating: ☆ ☆ ☆ ☆ ☆

Naming and Renaming Files

As you work with files, pay attention to filenames—they provide important information about the file, including its contents and purpose. A filename such as Car Sales.docx has three parts:

- **Main part of the filename:** The name you provide when you create a file, and the name you associate with a file
- **Dot:** The period (.) that separates the main part of the filename from the file extension
- **File extension:** Usually three or four characters that follow the dot in the filename

The main part of a filename can have up to 255 characters—this gives you plenty of room to name your file accurately enough so that you'll know the contents of the file just by looking at the filename. You can use spaces and certain punctuation symbols in your filenames. Like folder names, however, filenames cannot contain the symbols / \ : * ? " < > or | because these characters have special meaning in Windows 7.

A filename might display an extension. For example, in the filename Car Sales.docx, the extension *docx* identifies the file as one created by Microsoft Office Word, a word-processing program. You might also have a file called Car Sales.jpg—the *jpg* extension identifies the file as one created in a graphics program such as Paint. Though the main parts of these filenames are identical, their extensions distinguish them as different files. The filename extension also helps Windows identify what program should open the file. For example, the .txt extension in a file named Agenda.txt indicates that it is a text file and can be opened by programs associated with that extension, such as WordPad, Notepad, and Microsoft Word. You usually do not need to add extensions to your filenames because the program that you use to create the file adds the file extension automatically. Also, although Windows 7 keeps track of extensions, by default, Windows 7 is not set to display them. (You learn how to show filename extensions later in the tutorial.)

Be sure to give your files and folders meaningful names that will help you remember their purpose and contents. You can easily rename a file or folder by using the Rename command on the file's shortcut menu.

INSIGHT

Guidelines for Naming Files

The following are best practices for naming your files:

- Use common names: Avoid cryptic names that might make sense now but could cause confusion later, such as nonstandard abbreviations or imprecise names like Stuff08.
- Don't change the file extension: Do not change the file extension when renaming a file. If you do, Windows might not be able to find a program that can open it.
- Find a comfortable balance between too short and too long: Use filenames that are long enough to be meaningful, but short enough to be read easily on the screen.

Andrew notes that the Brochure file in the Festival folder could contain the information for any brochure. He recommends that you rename that file to give it a more descriptive filename. The Brochure file was originally created to store text specifically for the Azalea Festival brochure, so you'll rename the file Azalea Festival Brochure.

To rename the Brochure file:

1. If you took a break after the previous session, make sure that a folder window is open, and then navigate to the **Tutorial.02** folder included with your Data Files. Click the **Tutorial** folder in the left pane and change to **Medium Icons** view, if necessary.

2. Open the **Festival** folder to display its contents.

3. Right-click the **Brochure** file, and then click **Rename** on the shortcut menu. The filename is highlighted and a box appears around it.

4. Type **Azalea Festival Brochure**, and then press the **Enter** key. The file now appears with the new name.

   Trouble? If you make a mistake while typing and you haven't pressed the Enter key yet, press the Backspace key until you delete the mistake and then complete Step 4. If you've already pressed the Enter key, repeat Steps 2 and 3 to rename the file again.

   Trouble? If your computer is set to display file extensions, a message might appear asking if you are sure you want to change the file extension. Click the No button, right-click the Brochure file, click Rename on the shortcut menu, type *Azalea Festival Brochure.rtf*, and then press the Enter key.

All the files that originally appeared in the Tutorial folder are now stored in appropriate subfolders. You can streamline the organization of the Tutorial folder by deleting the duplicate files you no longer need.

Deleting Files and Folders

TIP

A file deleted from removable media, such as a USB drive, does not go into the Recycle Bin. Instead, it is deleted when Windows 7 removes its icon, and cannot be recovered.

You should periodically delete files and folders you no longer need so that your main folders and disks don't get cluttered. In a folder window, you delete a file or folder by deleting its icon. When you delete a file from a hard disk, Windows 7 removes the file from the folder but stores the file contents in the Recycle Bin. The Recycle Bin is an area on your hard disk that holds deleted files until you remove them permanently. When you delete a folder from the hard disk, the folder and all of its files are stored in the Recycle Bin. If you change your mind and want to retrieve a deleted file or folder you can double-click the Recycle Bin, right-click the file or folder you want to retrieve, and then click Restore. However, after you empty the Recycle Bin, you can no longer recover the files it contained.

REFERENCE

Deleting a File or Folder

- Click the file or folder you want to delete. (If you want to delete more than one file or folder, select them first.)
- Press the Delete key.
- Click Yes.
or
- Right-click the file or folder you want to delete. (If you want to delete more than one file or folder, select them first.)
- Click Delete on the shortcut menu.
- Click Yes.

Because you copied the Azalea Inn, Logo, Pink Azalea, Purple Azalea, and Rates files to the subfolders in the Tutorial folder, you can safely delete the original files. As is true for moving, copying, and renaming files and folders, you can delete a file or folder in many ways, including using a shortcut menu or selecting one or more files and then pressing the Delete key.

To delete files in the Tutorial folder:

1. Use any technique you've learned to navigate to and open the **Tutorial** folder.

2. Click the **first file** in the file list, hold down the **Shift** key, click the **last file** in the file list, and then release the **Shift** key. All the files in the Tutorial folder are now selected. None of the subfolders should be selected.

3. Right-click the selected files, and then click **Delete** on the shortcut menu. Windows 7 asks if you're sure you want to delete these files.

4. Click the **Yes** button.

So far, you've worked with files in folder windows, but you haven't viewed any file contents. To view a file's contents, you open the file. When you double-click a file in a folder window, Windows 7 starts the associated program and opens the file. You'll have a chance to try these techniques in the next section.

Working with New Files

The most common way to add files to a drive or folder is to create new files when you use a program. For example, you can create a text document in a word-processing program, a drawing in a graphics program, or a movie file in a video-editing program. When you are finished with a file, you must save it if you want to use the file again. To work with the file again, you open the file in an appropriate program; you can usually tell which programs can open a file by examining the filename extension or file icon.

Before you continue working with Andrew's files, you decide to create a to-do list to summarize your remaining tasks. You'll create the to-do list file, save it, close it, and then reopen it to add some items to the list.

Creating a File

You create a file by starting a program and then saving the file in a folder on your computer. Some programs create a file when you open the program. When you open WordPad, for example, it starts with a blank page. This represents an empty (and unsaved) file. You start typing and, when you are finished, you save your work using the Save As dialog box, where you can select a location for the file and enter a filename that identifies the contents. By default, most programs save files in a library such as Documents, Pictures, or Music, which makes it easy to find the files again later.

The to-do list you want to create is a simple text document, so you can create this file using Notepad, the basic text-editing program that Windows 7 provides.

To create a Notepad file:

1. Start Notepad by clicking the **Start** button 🪟 on the taskbar, pointing to **All Programs**, clicking **Accessories**, and then clicking **Notepad**. The Notepad program window opens. See Figure 2-16.

Figure 2-16   Creating a file

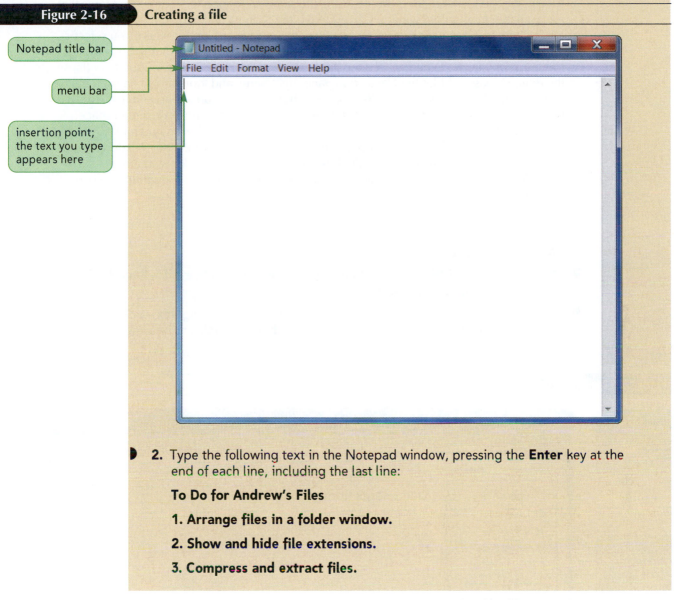

Notepad title bar

menu bar

insertion point; the text you type appears here

2. Type the following text in the Notepad window, pressing the **Enter** key at the end of each line, including the last line:

To Do for Andrew's Files

1. Arrange files in a folder window.

2. Show and hide file extensions.

3. Compress and extract files.

The Notepad title bar indicates that the name of this file is *Untitled*. To give it a more descriptive name, preserve the contents, and store the file where you can find it later, you must save the file.

Saving a File

As you are creating a file, you should save it frequently so you don't lose your work. When you save a new file, you use the Save As dialog box to specify a filename and a location for the file. When you open a file you've already created, you can usually click a toolbar button to save the file with the same name and location. If you want to save the file with a different name or in a different location, however, you use the Save As dialog box again to specify the new name or location. You can create a folder for the new file at the same time you save the file.

As a special type of folder window, the Save As dialog box can contain the same elements as all folder windows, such as an Address bar, Search box, Navigation pane, and right pane displaying folders and files. To display all of these navigation tools, you might need to click the Browse Folders button to expand the Save As dialog box. (When the dialog box is expanded, this button changes to the Hide Folders button.) Then you can specify the file location, for example, using the same navigation techniques and tools that are available in all folder windows. In addition, the Save As dialog box always includes a File name text box where you specify a filename, a Save as type list where you select a file type, and other controls for saving a file. If the expanded Save As dialog box covers too much of your document or desktop, you can click the Hide Folders button to collapse the dialog box so it hides the Navigation pane, right pane, and toolbar. You can still navigate with the Back, Forward, and Recent Pages buttons, the Address bar, and the Search box, and you can still use the controls for saving a file, but you conserve screen space.

Now that you've created a to-do list, you need to save it. The best name for this document is probably *To-Do List*. However, none of the folders you've already created for Andrew seems appropriate for this file. It belongs in a separate folder with a name such as *Daily Documents*. You can create the Daily Documents folder at the same time you save the to-do list file.

To save the Notepad file:

1. In the Notepad window, click **File** on the menu bar, and then click **Save As**. The Save As dialog box opens.

2. If the Navigation pane does not appear in the Save As dialog box, click the **Browse Folders** button. The Browse Folders button toggles to become the Hide Folders button, as shown in Figure 2-17.

Figure 2-17 Saving a new file

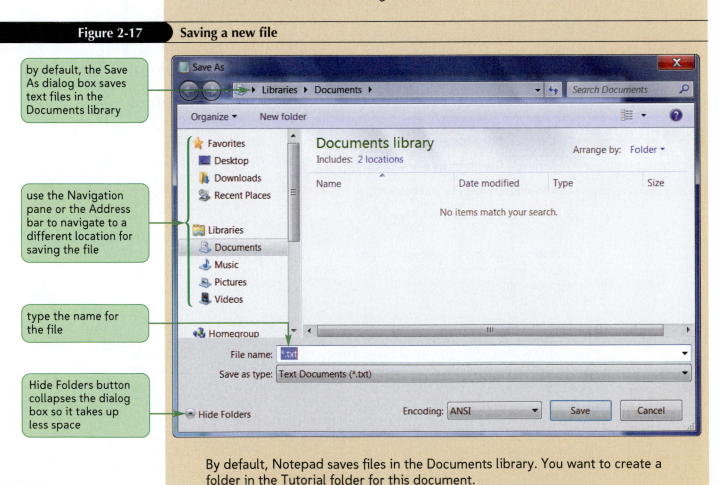

by default, the Save As dialog box saves text files in the Documents library

use the Navigation pane or the Address bar to navigate to a different location for saving the file

type the name for the file

Hide Folders button collapses the dialog box so it takes up less space

By default, Notepad saves files in the Documents library. You want to create a folder in the Tutorial folder for this document.

3. Use any technique you've learned to navigate to the **Tutorial.02\Tutorial** folder provided with your Data Files.

4. Click the **New folder** button on the toolbar. A new folder appears in the Tutorial folder, with the *New folder* name highlighted and ready for you to replace.

5. Type **Daily Documents** as the name of the new folder, and then press the **Enter** key.

6. Double-click the **Daily Documents** folder to open it. Now you are ready to specify a filename and save the to-do list file in the Daily Documents folder.

7. Click in the **File name** text box to select the *.txt text, and then type **To-Do List**. Notepad will automatically provide a .txt extension to this filename.

8. Click the **Save** button. Notepad saves the To-Do List file in the Daily Documents folder. The new filename now appears in the Notepad title bar.

9. Click the **Close** button [X] to close Notepad.

Next, you can open the file to add another item to the to-do list.

Opening a File

TIP

To select the default program for opening a file, right-click the file, point to Open with, and then click Choose default program. Click a program, and then click the OK button.

If you want to open a file in a running program, you use the Open dialog box, which is a folder window with additional controls for opening a file, similar to the Save As dialog box. You usually click an Open button on a toolbar or an Open command on a menu to access the Open dialog box. You use the Open dialog box to navigate to the file you want, select the file, and then click the Open button to open the file. If the program you want to use is not running, you can open a file by double-clicking it in a folder window. The file usually opens in the program that you used to create or edit it. If it's a text file with a .txt extension, for example, it opens in a text editor, such as Notepad. If it's a text file with a .docx extension, it opens in Microsoft Word.

Not all documents work this way. Double-clicking a digital picture file usually opens a picture viewer program, which displays the picture. To actually edit the picture, you need to use a graphics editor program. When you need to specify a program to open a file, you can right-click the file, point to Open with on the shortcut menu, and then click the name of the program that you want to use.

To open and edit the To-Do List file:

1. In the right pane of the Tutorial folder window, double-click the **Daily Documents** folder.

2. Double-click the **To-Do List** file. Notepad starts and opens the To-Do List file.

   Trouble? If a program other than Notepad starts, such as WordPad, click the Close button to close the program, right-click the To-Do List file, point to Open with, and then click Notepad.

3. Press the **Ctrl+End** keys to move the insertion point to the end of the document, and then type **4. Review how to customize folder windows.**

   Because you want to save this file using the same name and location, you can use the Save command on the File menu to save your work this time.

4. Click **File** on the menu bar, and then click **Save**. Notepad saves the To-Do List file without opening the Save As dialog box because you are using the same name and location as the last time you saved the file.

As long as Notepad is still open, you can create another simple text file that describes the graphics in the Marketing Graphics folder.

To create and save another file:

▶ **1.** Click **File** on the menu bar, and then click **New** to open a new, blank document.

▶ **2.** Type the following text in the Notepad window, pressing the **Enter** key at the end of each line:

Marketing Graphics files:

Azalea Inn: Photo of the inn

Logo: Copy of the inn's logo for stationery and ads

Pink Azalea: Photo of pink azaleas

Purple Azalea: Photo of a purple azalea

▶ **3.** Click **File** on the menu bar, and then click **Save**. The Save As dialog box opens.

▶ **4.** Navigate to the **Marketing Graphics** folder in the Tutorial folder.

▶ **5.** Click in the File name text box, and then type **Graphic Descriptions**.

▶ **6.** Click the **Save** button. Notepad saves the Graphic Descriptions file in the Marketing Graphics folder.

▶ **7.** Click the **Close** button [X] to close Notepad.

Now that you've organized Andrew's files and then created and saved new folders and files, you're ready to refine the organization of the files.

Refining the Organization of Files

To refine the organization of your files, you can fine-tune the view of your files and folders in a folder window. Changing the view can often help you find files and identify those that share common features, such as two versions of the same file. One way to change the view is to sort your files. **Sorting** files and folders means listing them in a particular order, such as alphabetically by name or type or chronologically by their modification date. You can also **filter** the contents of a folder to display only files and folders with certain characteristics, such as all those you modified yesterday. In short, sorting reorganizes all of the files and folders in a list, while filtering displays only those files and folders that share a characteristic you specify. Both actions change your view of the files and folders, not the items themselves.

Windows 7 provides another way to change the view of your files and folders—grouping. When you group your files by type, for example, Windows separates the files into several groups, such as Microsoft Word documents in one group and photo files (or JPEG files) in another group.

Problem Solving: Preventing Lost File Problems

Many computer users, even very experienced ones, fall into the trap of saving or moving a file to a folder and then forgetting where it's stored. You can prevent these types of "lost file" problems by managing your files systematically. To manage files so you know where to find them later, start by formulating a logical plan for organizing your files. Some people sketch a simple diagram of the file structure to help them visualize where to store files. Next, create the folders you need to store the files, and then move and copy your existing files into those folders. As you create files using programs, save them in an appropriate folder and use folder names and filenames that help you identify their contents. If possible, use a similar organization scheme in all of your folders. For example, if you organized the files for one project into subfolders such as Phase 1, Phase 2, Phase 3, and Follow Up, use the same organization for each project. To make it easier to find files, especially in a long file list, you can sort, filter, and group the files in a way that seems logical to you. Performing these basic management tasks helps you keep track of your files so you can easily find information when you need it.

You want to show Andrew how to change the view of his files by sorting, filtering, and grouping so he can choose one view that makes the most sense for him or his current task.

Sorting and Filtering Files

When you are working with a folder window in Details view, you can sort or filter the files using the column headings in the right pane of the window. To sort files by type, for example, click the Type column heading. You can sort files in ascending order (A to Z, zero to nine, or earliest to latest date) or descending order (Z to A, nine to zero, or latest to earliest date). To switch the order, click the column heading again. Sorting is often an effective way to find a file or folder in a relatively short file list. By default, Windows 7 sorts the contents of a folder in ascending alphabetic order by filename, so a file named April Budget appears at the top of the list, and a file named Winter Expenses appears at the end. You can change the sort criterion to list files according to any other file characteristic.

If you are working with a longer file list, filtering the list might help you find the file you want. To filter the contents of a folder, you click the arrow button to the right of a column heading, and then click one or more file properties such as a specific filename, date created or modified, author, or file type. Windows displays only files and folders with those properties. For example, if you want to list only music files by a particular artist, you can filter by that artist's name.

Details view always includes column headings corresponding to file details. To sort files in other views that do not display column headings, you can right-click a blank area of the folder window, point to Sort by on the shortcut menu, and then click a file detail such as Type. (You cannot filter files in views without column headings.)

To sort and filter the files in the Marketing Graphics folder:

1. Navigate to the **Marketing Graphics** folder in the Tutorial folder.

2. Click the **Change your view button arrow** 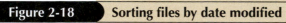 on the toolbar, and then click **Details**.

3. If necessary, click the **Size** column heading to sort the files in descending order according to file size. An indented sort arrow appears at the top of the Size column heading. The sort arrow points down to indicate the column is sorted in descending order.

   Trouble? If the Size column does not appear in your folder window, right-click any column heading and then click Size. Then complete Step 3.

4. Click the **Size** column heading again to reverse the sort order. The sort arrow now points up, indicating the column is sorted in ascending order.

5. Right-click any **column heading** to display a list of file details. Details with a check mark are displayed in the folder window. If the Date modified column heading does not appear in your folder window, click **Date modified** to display this column. Otherwise, click a blank area of the window. Your folder window should now display only the Name, Date modified, Type, and Size columns.

   Trouble? If your folder window contains columns other than Name, Date modified, Type, and Size, right-click any column heading, and then click the name of the column you want to remove from the folder window.

6. Click the **Date modified** column heading to sort the files chronologically by the date they were modified. See Figure 2-18.

Figure 2-18 **Sorting files by date modified**

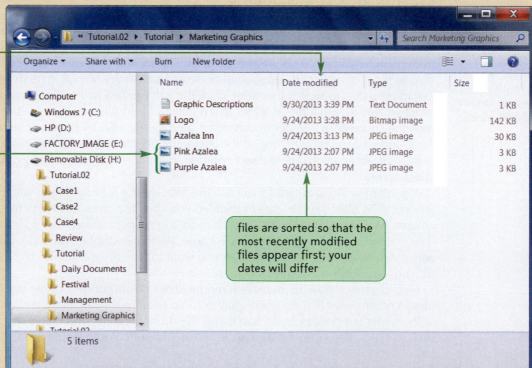

sort arrow points down, indicating the column is sorted in descending order

because these two files were modified at the same time, they are further sorted alphabetically by name

files are sorted so that the most recently modified files appear first; your dates will differ

To compare sorting and filtering, you can filter the files by their modified date to display only the files you modified today.

7. Point to the **Date modified** column heading, and then click its arrow button to display a list of filtering options.

8. Click the **Today** check box to select today's date. The folder window displays only the Graphic Descriptions file. See Figure 2-19.

Trouble? If you modified the Graphic Descriptions file on a different date, click that date on the calendar.

Trouble? If you clicked Today rather than the check box, repeat Steps 7 and 8 to select today's date.

Figure 2-19   **Filtering to display files modified today**

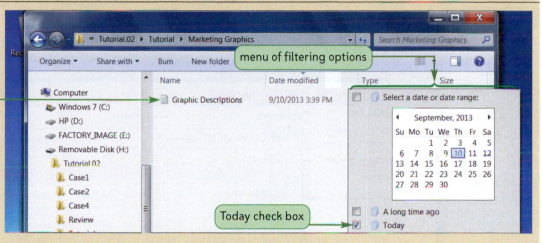

only files modified today appear in the filtered list

menu of filtering options

Today check box

Note that you can filter by two or more properties by selecting the corresponding check boxes.

9. Click a blank area of the window to close the list. A check mark appears next to the Date modified column heading to indicate the file list is filtered by a Date modified detail.

Next, you can group the files in the Marketing Graphics folder and compare this view to the views displayed when you sorted and filtered the files.

Grouping Files

To change your view of files and folders, you can group them—a technique that is especially effective when you are working with long file lists. You can group files according to any file detail such as Type or Authors. To group files by author, for example, right-click a blank area of the window, point to Group by, click More, and then click Authors. Windows divides the folder window into sections, with one section listing files you wrote, for example, and another section for files your colleague wrote.

Before grouping files, you must remove any filters you are using in the folder window. If you don't, you'll rearrange only the files that appear in the filtered list. After removing the filter, you'll group the files in the Marketing Graphics folder by type.

To remove the filter and group the files in the Marketing Graphics folder:

1. In the Marketing Graphics folder window, click the **check mark** on the Date modified column heading, and then click the **Today** check box (or the **Select a date** or **date range** check box if you selected a date on the calendar earlier) to clear the check box. Click a blank area of the folder window. The complete list of Marketing Graphics files appears in the window.

2. Right-click a blank area of the folder window, point to **Group by**, and then click **Type**. Windows arranges all five files in the Marketing Graphics folder into three groups, one for each file type. See Figure 2-20.

| Figure 2-20 | Grouping files |

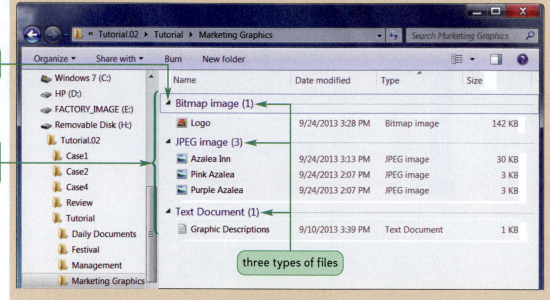

3. Right-click a blank area of the folder window, point to **Group by**, and then click **(None)** to ungroup the files.

After showing Andrew how to sort, filter, and group files in a folder window, he mentions that he might want to hide or show elements of the folder window itself, such as the Navigation pane or the Details pane. You'll show him how to customize the folder window elements next.

Customizing a Folder Window

You can change the way your folder windows look and work to suit your needs. For example, you can hide the Details pane or the Navigation pane to devote more space to file lists. To do so, you use the Layout command and the Folder and search options command on a folder window's Organize button. The Layout command lists the panes you can display in a folder window. When you select the Folder and search options command, the Folder Options dialog box opens, where you can select settings that change the behavior and appearance of the folder window. Figure 2-21 summarizes the ways you can customize the appearance of a folder window. Note that the Folder and search options command is not available for the Save As and Open dialog boxes.

Figure 2-21   Layout and folder options

Layout Options	
Option	**Description**
Menu bar	Hide or show the menu bar in this window only.
Details pane	Hide or show the Details pane.
Preview pane	Hide or show the Preview pane.
Navigation pane	Hide or show the Navigation pane.

Folder Options Dialog Box Settings	
Settings on the General Tab	**Description**
Navigation pane	Show all the folders on your computer in the Navigation pane, including your personal folder, and automatically expand the Navigation pane to display the folder selected in the folder window.
Restore Defaults	Restore the original settings for your folders.
Settings on the View Tab	**Description**
Always show icons, never thumbnails	Always show static icons of files and never show thumbnail previews of files. Use this setting if the thumbnail previews are slowing down your computer.
Show hidden files, folders, and drives	Display files, folders, and drives marked as hidden. Use this setting if you need to work with files that are usually hidden from view, such as user files that have been marked as hidden.
Hide extensions for known file types	Show or hide extensions as a part of filenames.
Restore Defaults	Restore the original settings on the View tab.

You'll show Andrew how to change the layouts in a folder window, and then how to customize the appearance of the folder contents. Finally, you'll demonstrate how to add items and make other changes to the Navigation pane.

Changing the Layout of a Folder Window

You can change the layout of a folder window by showing or hiding one or more of the following elements: the Navigation pane, Preview pane, Details pane, and menu bar. If you often use the Navigation pane to open a particular folder, you can drag that folder to the Favorites list to make it one of your favorite locations. Both the Details pane and the Preview pane display the contents of pictures and some other types of files. The Details pane also provides information such as the filename and file type. Figure 2-22 shows a folder window with all the panes open.

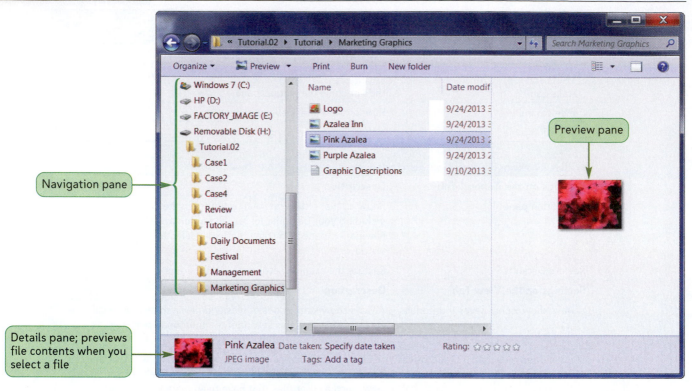

You have also used the toolbar to perform many tasks, particularly to change the appearance of your files and folders. If you used earlier versions of Windows, such as Windows XP, you probably performed many of these same tasks using a menu bar. As in programs, Windows 7 folder windows can display a menu bar that shows the names of the menus, such as File, Edit, and Help. The folder window menu bar in Windows 7 is hidden by default because you can use the toolbar or the shortcut menu that opens when you right-click a file or folder to perform the tasks associated with the menu bar commands.

Andrew likes using a menu bar in folder windows, so he asks you to display the menu bar and hide the Details pane. He is also curious about the Preview pane, so you'll open that for him. To show or hide the Preview pane, you can use the Layout command or the Preview pane button on the toolbar of any folder window. The Marketing Graphics folder window should currently be open in Details view, with files sorted according to type.

To change the layout of a folder window:

1. Click the **Organize** button on the toolbar, point to **Layout**, and then click **Details pane** to close the Details pane.

2. Click the **Show the preview pane** button ▢ on the toolbar to display the Preview pane.

3. Click the **Azalea Inn** file to display its contents in the Preview pane.

4. Click the **Organize** button on the toolbar, point to **Layout**, and then click **Menu bar** to display the menu bar in folder windows. See Figure 2-23.

Figure 2-23 **Folder window displaying the Navigation pane, Preview pane, and menu bar**

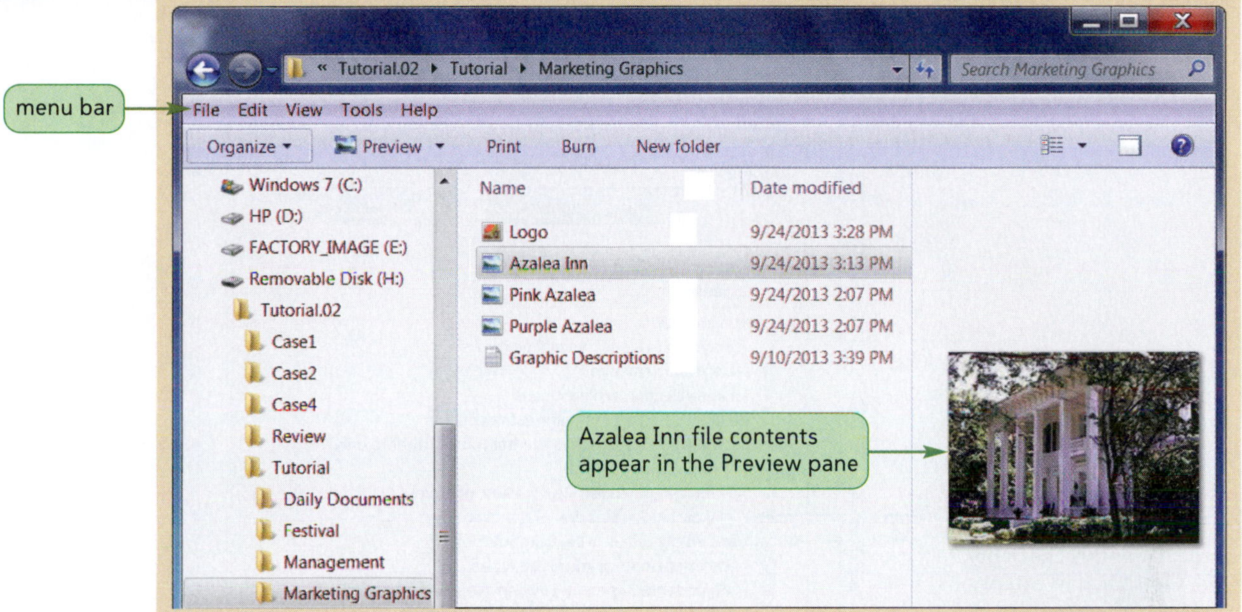

menu bar

Azalea Inn file contents appear in the Preview pane

Another way to customize a folder is to change its type. If you store mostly pictures in a folder, for example, right-click the folder, and then click Properties on the shortcut menu. In the folder's Properties dialog box, click the Customize tab, click the *Optimize this folder for* arrow button, and then click a folder type, such as Pictures. That folder window then includes features, such as toolbar buttons, designed for working with pictures.

Customizing the File List

Although Windows 7 refers to a file extension to identify a file's type, file extensions are not displayed by default in a folder window. Windows hides the extensions to make filenames easier to read, especially for long filenames. If you prefer to display file extensions, you can show them in all the folder windows (as you do in the following steps).

Another type of file not displayed by default in a folder window is a hidden file. A **hidden file** is not listed in a folder window, though it is actually stored in that folder. Windows hides many types of files, including temporary files it creates before you save a document. It hides these files so that you do not become confused by temporary filenames, which are similar to the names of the files you store on your computer. You can also use a file's Properties dialog box to hide files. Keep in mind that hidden files still take up space on your disk. By default, Windows 7 also hides system files, which are files the operating system needs to work properly. You should keep these files hidden unless a reliable expert, such as a technical support professional, instructs you to display them. You use the Folder Options dialog box to show and hide filename extensions, hidden files, and system files.

You can change folder settings in the Marketing Graphics window to show the filename extensions in all windows.

To show filename extensions:

1. Click the **Organize** button on the toolbar, and then click **Folder and search options** to open the Folder Options dialog box.

2. Click the **View** tab. See Figure 2-24. The settings on the View tab of your Folder Options dialog box might differ.

Figure 2-24 Folder Options dialog box

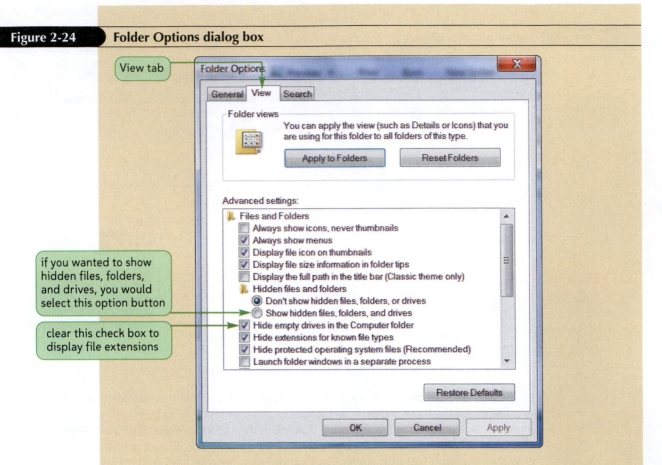

3. In the Advanced settings section, click the **Hide extensions for known file types** check box to clear the box and display file extensions.

   Trouble? If the Hide extensions for known file types check box is already cleared, skip Step 3.

4. Click the **OK** button. The Marketing Graphics folder window should look similar to Figure 2-25.

Figure 2-25   **Folder window showing file extensions**

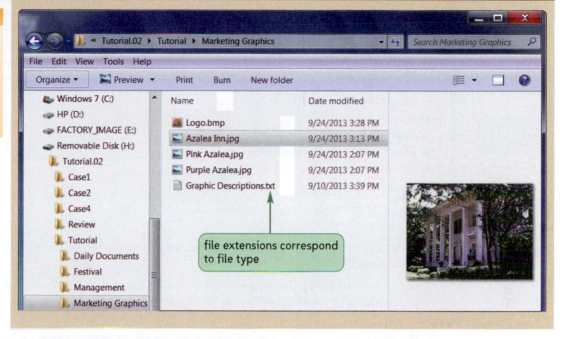

file extensions correspond to file type

Now the file list in the Marketing Graphics folder window includes file extensions. Next, you can customize the Navigation pane by changing its appearance and adding a folder to the Favorites list.

Customizing the Navigation Pane

You can customize the Navigation pane by adding, renaming, and removing items in the Favorites list. First, you'll add the Daily Documents folder to the Favorites list so you can access it quickly. Then you'll move and rename this link to distinguish it from the Documents library. When you rename an item in the Favorites list, you rename the link only—not the actual file or folder. Later, when you restore the settings on your computer, you'll delete this link.

To customize the Navigation pane:

1. Use any navigation method you've learned to display the folders in the Tutorial folder. Scroll to the top of the Navigation pane, if necessary.

2. Drag the **Daily Documents** folder from the Tutorial folder to the end of the Favorites list in the Navigation pane. When a *Create link in Favorites* ScreenTip appears, release the mouse button to insert a new link named Daily Documents. See Figure 2-26.

Figure 2-26   **Daily Documents folder as a link in the Favorites list**

Favorites list in the Navigation pane

Daily Documents link and folder

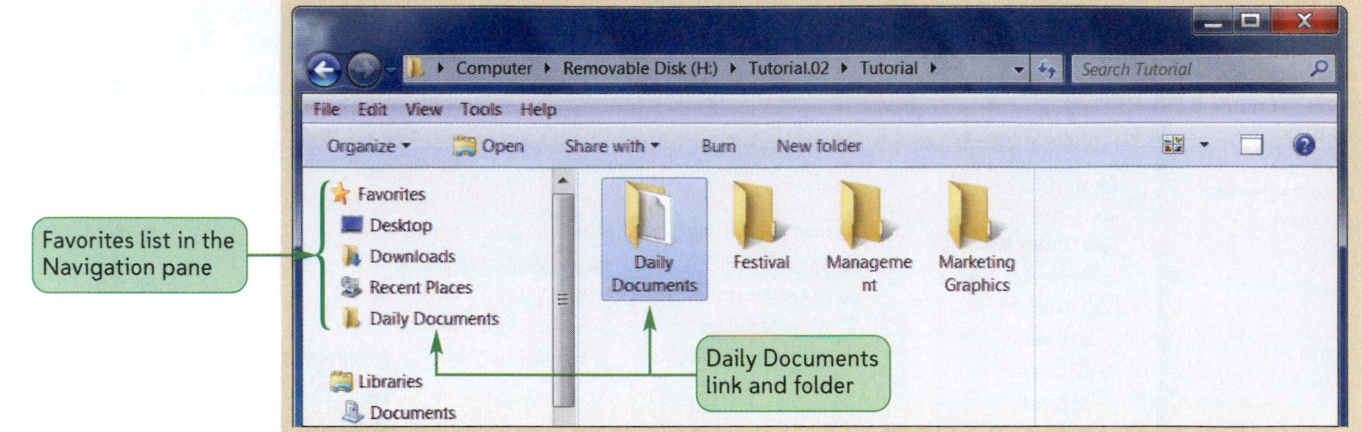

3. In the Favorites list, drag the **Daily Documents** folder to the top of the list, before the Desktop link.

4. Right-click the **Daily Documents** link in the Favorites list, and then click **Rename** on the shortcut menu. The current filename is selected.

5. Type **Daily Projects** as the new name of this link, and then press the **Enter** key. The link is renamed, but the Daily Documents folder in the Tutorial folder still has its original name. See Figure 2-27.

Figure 2-27   **Daily Documents link moved and renamed to Daily Projects**

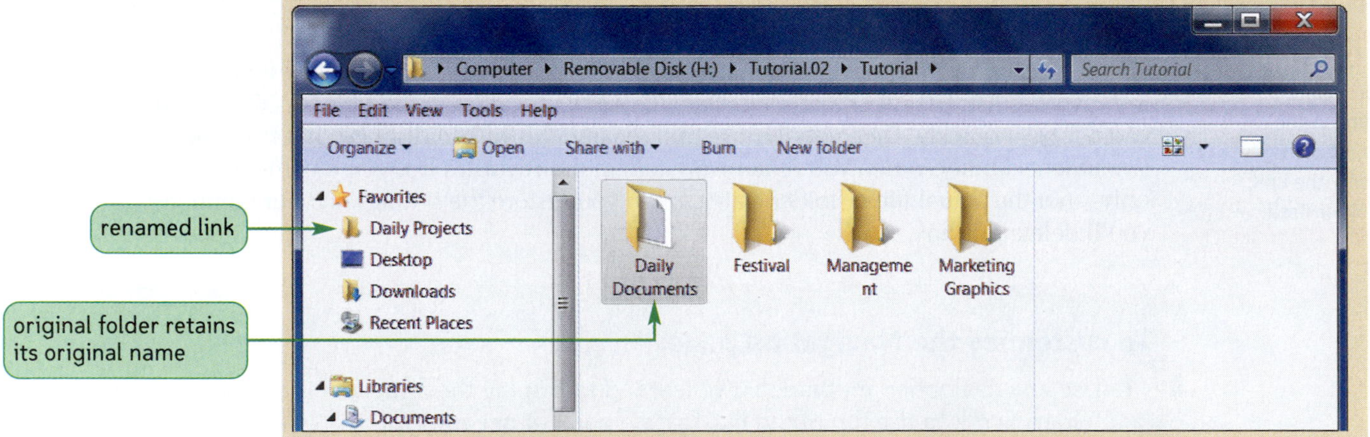

renamed link

original folder retains its original name

Now that you've refined your file organization and customized the folder window, you are ready to show Andrew two final tasks—compressing and extracting files.

Working with Compressed Files

If you transfer files from one location to another, such as from your hard disk to a removable disk or vice versa, or from one computer to another via e-mail, you can store the files in a compressed (zipped) folder so that they take up less disk space. You can then transfer the files more quickly. When you create a compressed folder using Windows 7's compression tool, a zipper appears on the folder icon.

You compress a folder so that the files it contains use less space on the disk. Compare two folders—a folder named Photos that contains about 8.6 MB of files and a compressed folder containing the same files, but requiring only 6.5 MB of disk space. In this case, the compressed files use about 25 percent less disk space than the uncompressed files.

You can create a compressed folder using the Send to Compressed (zipped) folder command on the shortcut menu of one or more selected files or folders. Then you can compress additional files or folders by dragging them into the compressed folder. You can open a file directly from a compressed folder, although you cannot modify the file. To edit and save a compressed file, you must extract it first. When you **extract** a file, you create an uncompressed copy of the file in a folder you specify. The original file remains in the compressed folder.

If a different compression program has been installed on your computer, such as WinZip, the Send to Compressed (zipped) folder command might not appear on the shortcut menu. Instead, it might be replaced by the name of your compression program. In this case, refer to your compression program's Help system for instructions on working with compressed files.

Andrew suggests that you compress the files and folders in the Tutorial folder so that you can more quickly transfer them to another location.

To compress the folders and files in the Tutorial folder:

1. Select all the folders in the Tutorial folder, right-click the selected folders, point to **Send to**, and then click **Compressed (zipped) folder**. After a few moments, a new compressed folder with a zipper icon appears in the Tutorial window.

   Trouble? If the Send to Compressed (zipped) folder command does not appear on the shortcut menu, this means that a different compression program is probably installed on your computer. Click a blank area of the Tutorial window to close the shortcut menu, and then read but do not perform the remaining steps.

2. Type **Zipped Files** and then press the **Enter** key to rename the compressed folder. See Figure 2-28.

Figure 2-28	Creating a compressed folder

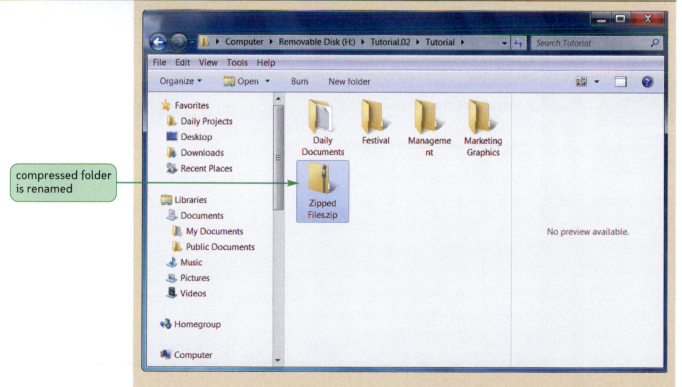

compressed folder is renamed

You open a compressed folder by double-clicking it. You can then move and copy files and folders in a compressed folder, although you cannot rename them. When you extract files, Windows 7 uncompresses and copies them to a location that you specify, preserving the files in their folders as appropriate.

Understanding Compressed File Types

Some types of files, such as JPEG picture files (those with a .jpg or .jpeg file extension), are already highly compressed. If you compress JPEG pictures into a folder, the total size of the compressed folder is about the same as the collection of uncompressed pictures. However, if you are transferring the files from one computer to another, such as by e-mail, it's still a good idea to store the compressed files in a zipped folder to keep them together.

To extract the compressed files:

1. Right-click the **Zipped Files.zip** compressed folder, and then click **Extract All** on the shortcut menu. The Extract Compressed (Zipped) Folders Wizard starts and opens the Select a Destination and Extract Files dialog box.

   Trouble? If you are using a different compression program, the Extract All command might not appear on the shortcut menu. Read but do not perform the remaining steps.

2. Press the **End** key to deselect the path in the text box, press the **Backspace** key as many times as necessary to delete the *Zipped Files* text, and then type **Extracted**. The final three parts of the path in the text box should be *Tutorial.02\\Tutorial\\ Extracted*. See Figure 2-29.

Figure 2-29	Extracting files from a compressed file

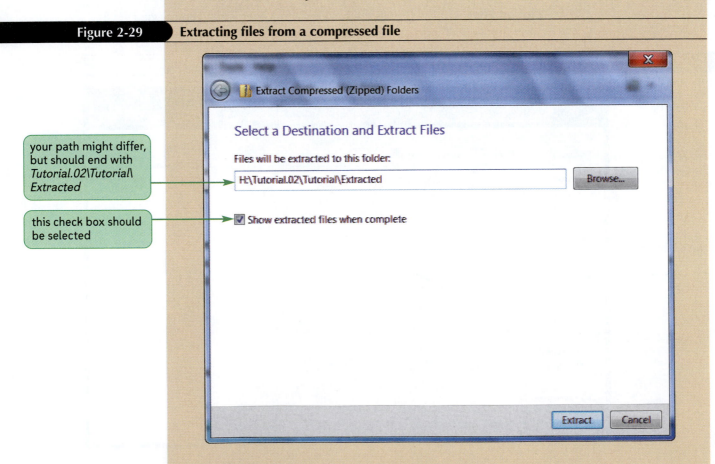

your path might differ, but should end with *Tutorial.02\\Tutorial\\ Extracted*

this check box should be selected

3. Make sure the Show extracted files when complete check box is checked, and then click the **Extract** button. Windows extracts the files, and then opens the Extracted folder, showing the Daily Documents, Festival, Management, and Marketing Graphics folders.

4. Open each folder to make sure it contains the files you worked with in this tutorial.

5. Close the Extracted folder window.

In this session, you renamed and deleted files according to your organization plan, and then created a file, saved it in a new folder, and opened and edited the file. Then you refined the organization of the files and folders, customized a folder window, and worked with compressed files. You tell Andrew that you have finished organizing the files on his Windows 7 computer. Before you end your Windows 7 session, however, you should restore your computer to its original settings.

Restoring Your Settings

If you are working in a computer lab or on a computer other than your own, complete the steps in this section to restore the original settings on the computer.

To restore your settings:

1. In the Tutorial folder window, click the **Organize** button on the toolbar, point to **Layout**, and then click the **Details pane** to display the Details pane in the folder window.

2. Click the **Hide the preview pane** button ▢ on the toolbar to hide the Preview pane.

3. Click the **Organize** button on the toolbar, point to **Layout**, and then click **Menu bar** to hide the menu bar.

4. Click the **Organize** button on the toolbar, and then click **Folder and search options** to open the Folder Options dialog box.

5. Click the **View** tab.

6. In the Advanced settings section, click the **Hide extensions for known file types** check box to check the box and hide file extensions. Click the **OK** button.

7. Right-click the **Daily Projects** link in the Navigation pane, and then click **Remove**.

8. Close all open windows.

REVIEW

Session 2.2 Quick Check

1. What does a filename extension indicate about a file?

2. The _____ is an area on your hard disk that holds deleted files until you remove them permanently.

3. Explain the difference between sorting and filtering files.

4. True or False. Renaming or deleting a link in the Favorites list renames or deletes the corresponding folder in the file list.

5. Name two ways that you can change the layout of a folder window.

6. By default, Windows hides _____ in a folder window to make the filenames easier to read.

7. Under what circumstances would you store files in a compressed folder?

8. True or False. When you extract a file, you create an uncompressed copy of the file in a folder you specify.

Practice the skills you learned in the tutorial using the same case scenario.

PRACTICE

Review Assignments

For a list of Data Files in the Review folder, see page WIN 49.

Andrew has saved a few files from his old computer on a removable disk. He gives you these files in a single, unorganized folder, and asks you to organize them logically into subfolders. Before you do, devise a plan for managing the files, and then create the subfolders you need. Also rename, copy, move, and delete files, and perform other management tasks to make it easy for Andrew to work with these files and folders. Complete the following steps, recording your answers to any questions in the spaces provided:

1. Use a folder window to navigate to and open the Tutorial.02\Review folder provided with your Data Files.

2. Examine the six files in the Review folder included with your Data Files, and then answer the following questions:
   - How will you organize these files? _____
   - What folders will you create? _____
   - Which files will you store in these folders? _____

3. In the Review folder, create three folders: Financial, Events, and Travel.

4. Move the **Business Plan** file from the Review folder to the Financial folder. Move the **Alabama**, **Letterhead**, and **Mobile** files to the Travel folder. Move the **Schedule** and **Event Form** files to the Events folder.

5. Copy the **Letterhead** file in the Travel folder to the Events folder.

6. Rename the **Event Form** file in the Events folder as **Promotional Events**. Rename the **Mobile** file in the Travel folder as **Historic Mobile**.

7. Return to the Review folder and use the Search box to find a file containing the text *Executive Summary*. Rename this file **Plan Form**.

8. Create a Notepad file that includes the following text:
   Agenda for Board Meeting
   7 p.m. Welcome and introductions

9. Save the Notepad file as **Agenda** in the Events folder. Close the Notepad window.

10. Navigate to the Events folder, open the **Agenda** file, and then add the following agenda item to the end of the document:
    7:15 Review business plan

11. Save the **Agenda** file with the same name and in the same location. Open a new document, and then type the following text:
    Financial Contact List
    Corgan, Richard (Banker) 555-4187

12. Save the file as **Contact List** in the Financial folder. Close Notepad.

13. Navigate to the Financial folder and make sure the Date modified column is displayed in the folder window. (*Hint*: Switch to Details view, if necessary, right-click a column heading, and then click Date modified if you need to display this column.) Sort the files by Date modified. How many files appear in the folder window? Filter the files by today's date (or the date you created the two text files). How many files appear in the folder window?

14. Remove the filter, and then group the files by type.

15. Navigate to the Travel folder, and then display file extensions in the folder window. Group the files by size.

16. Change the layout of the folder window by hiding the Details pane.

17. Display the Review folder, and then add the Travel folder to the top of the Favorites list in the Navigation pane. Rename the link **Travel Info**.

18. Click the Travel Info link, and then press the Alt+Print Screen keys to capture an image of the folder window. Start Paint, and then press the Ctrl+V keys to paste this image in a file. Save this file as **Review** in the Tutorial.02\Review folder provided with your Data Files. Close Paint.

19. Restore your computer's settings by displaying the Details pane, hiding file extensions in the folder window, and removing the Travel Info link from the Favorites list in the Navigation pane.

20. Create a compressed (zipped) folder in the Review folder named **Zipped Review Files** that contains all the files and folders in the Review folder.

21. Extract the contents of the Zipped Review Files folder to a new folder named **Extracted** in the Review folder. (*Hint*: The file path will end with *Tutorial.02*\ *Review**Extracted*.)

22. Close all open windows.

23. Submit the results of the preceding steps to your instructor, either in printed or electronic form, as requested.

Use your skills to manage files and folders for a catering service.

APPLY

Case Problem 1

For a list of Data Files in the Case1 folder, see page WIN 49.

Rossini Catering   Sharon Rossini owns Rossini Catering in Providence, Rhode Island, and provides catering services to businesses and others for conferences, weddings, and other events. Specializing in authentic regional Italian dishes, Sharon's business has expanded as word of her innovative menus has spread throughout Providence. She recently started offering cooking classes and was surprised to discover that her class on fruit plates was among the most popular. Knowing you are multitalented, Sharon hired you to help her design new classes and manage other parts of her growing business, including maintaining electronic business files and communications. Your first task is to organize the files on her new Windows 7 computer. Complete the following steps:

1. In the Tutorial.02\Case1 folder provided with your Data Files, create three folders: **Classes**, **Menus**, and **Photos**.

2. Move the **Menu-Fall**, **Menu-Spring**, **Menu-Summer**, and **Menu-Winter** files from the Case1 folder to the Menus folder.

3. Rename the four files in the Menus folder to remove *Menu-* from each name.

4. Move the four JPEG files from the Case1 folder to the Photos folder.

5. Copy the remaining two files to the Classes folder. Also copy the **Ingredients** and **Classes** files to the Menus folder.

6. Delete the **Classes** and **Ingredients** files from the Case1 folder.

7. Open the Recycle Bin folder by double-clicking the Recycle Bin icon on the desktop, and then complete the following steps:
   - Sort the contents of the Recycle Bin by filename in descending order.

- Filter the files by their deletion date to display only the files you deleted today. (*Hint*: If you deleted files from the Case1 folder on a different date, click that date on the calendar.)
- Do the Classes and Ingredients files appear in the Recycle Bin folder? Explain why or why not.
- Remove the filter, and then close the Recycle Bin window.

8. Make a copy of the Photos folder in the Case1 folder. The name of the duplicate folder appears as *Photos - Copy*. Rename the Photos - Copy folder as **Web Ads**.

9. Locate and copy the **Fruit Photo** file to the Classes folder. Rename this file **Green Grapes**.

10. Find a file in the Case1 subfolders that contains the text **Fruit plate**. Copy this file to the Classes folder and rename it **Sample Menu**.

11. Send one copy of each graphic file from the Web Ads folder to a new compressed folder named **Illustrations**, and then move the zipped Illustrations folder to the Case1 folder.

12. Close all open windows.

13. Submit the results of the preceding steps to your instructor, either in printed or electronic form, as requested.

Use your skills to manage files and folders for an accounting firm.

APPLY

Case Problem 2

For a list of Data Files in the Case2 folder, see page WIN 49.

Lincoln Small Business Accountants   Jack Takamoto is the vice president of Lincoln Small Business Accountants, a firm in Lincoln, Nebraska, that provides accounting services to local small businesses. You work as Jack's assistant and devote part of your time to organizing client files. Jack recently upgraded to Windows 7 and asks you to examine the folder structure and file system on his computer, and then begin organizing the files for two clients. Complete the following steps:

⊕ EXPLORE

1. Open a folder window, and then open each folder that appears in the Desktop list. Describe the contents of each folder in the Desktop list.

2. Open a folder in the Pictures library to display two or more picture files. Change the view to Large Icons. Group the files by Date. (If a Group command is not available, choose the Arrange command to arrange the files by Month.) Press the Alt+Print Screen keys to capture an image of the folder window. Start Paint, and then press the Ctrl+V keys to paste this image in a file. Save the file as **Group** in the Tutorial.02\Case2 folder provided with your Data Files. Close Paint, and then close the folder window displaying grouped picture files.

3. Examine the files in the Tutorial.02\Case2 folder provided with your Data Files. Based on the filenames and the descriptions displayed in the Details pane, devise an organization plan for the files.

4. In the Tutorial.02\Case2 folder, create the folders you need according to your plan.

5. Move the files from the Case2 folder to the subfolders you created. When you finish, the Case2 folder should contain at least two subfolders and the Group file.

6. Rename the files in each subfolder so that they are shorter but still clearly reflect their contents.

7. Search for a file in the Case2 folder that contains *refund* in the contents.

8. Open the text document you found, and then add the following note at the end of the file: **Client expects a tax refund this year**. Save and close the file.

9. Open the window for one of the subfolders you created. Display the menu bar in the folder window.

10. Click View on the menu bar and then click Tiles to change the view of the folder window. Press the Alt+Print Screen keys to capture an image of the folder window. Start Paint, and then press the Ctrl+V keys to paste this image in a file. Save the image as **Tiles** in the Tutorial.02\Case2 folder provided with your Data Files. Close Paint.

⊕ EXPLORE 11. Send all the spreadsheet files (that is, all the XLSX files) in one Case2 subfolder to a new compressed folder named **Spreadsheets** in the Case2 folder. (*Hint:* After you create the compressed folder in a Case2 subfolder, move it to the Case2 folder.)

12. Restore your computer by hiding the menu bar in the folder window.

13. Close all open windows.

14. Submit the results of the preceding steps to your instructor, either in printed or electronic form, as requested.

Explore other methods of managing files for a home healthcare organization.

CHALLENGE

Case Problem 3

There are no Data Files needed for this Case Problem.

MedFirst Hospital Home Health Services   Anders Guillickson is the director of MedFirst Hospital Home Health (MHHH) Services in Nashville, Tennessee. The company's mission is to connect licensed practical nurses with people who need health care at home, usually as part of their recovery from surgery. Anders has a dedicated staff of nurses who are just starting to use Windows 7 notebook computers to record the details of their home visits. Anders hires you as a part-time trainer to teach the nurses how to use their computers efficiently. They report that their major problem is finding files they have saved on their hard disks. Anders asks you to prepare a lesson on how to find files in Windows 7. Complete the following:

⊕ EXPLORE 1. Windows Help and Support includes topics that explain how to search for files on a disk without looking through all the folders. Click the Start button and then click Help and Support to open Windows Help and Support. Use one of the following methods to locate topics on searching for files:
   - On the Home page, click the Browse Help button on the toolbar. On the Contents page, click Files, folders, and libraries; then click Working with files and folders; and then click Finding files.
   - In the Search Help box, type **find file or folder**, and then click the Search Help button. Click Find a file or folder.

⊕ EXPLORE 2. Click the Show all link to show the complete contents of the Find a file or folder topic. Read the topic and click any See also links that provide information about finding files and folders to provide the following information:
   - Identify three ways to search for files.
   - If you do not know the entire name of a file, how can you find the file?

⊕ EXPLORE 3. Use Windows Help and Support to find topics about saving searches. Then explain how you can save a search so you can use it again.

EXPLORE

4. Use Windows Help and Support to locate topics about organizing and finding files using properties and tags.

5. Write a short description of one procedure for finding files and folders that was not covered in the tutorial.

6. Submit the results of the preceding steps to your instructor, either in printed or electronic form, as requested.

Use your skills and the Internet to organize files for an architectural design firm.

RESEARCH

Case Problem 4

For a list of Data Files in the Case4 folder, see page WIN 49.

Green Design   Green Design is an architectural design firm in St. Paul, Minnesota, known for its environmentally responsible buildings. The firm has been at the forefront of creating healthier and more resource-efficient models of construction, renovation, and maintenance. Maggie O'Donnell is the operations manager for Green Design, and you assist her in setting up systems so that the architects can work effectively. Maggie has recently installed Windows 7 on the firm's desktop and notebook computers. She has a collection of files she can't open with any program installed on her Windows 7 computer. You offer to help her identify the file types and organize the files. Complete the following:

1. Examine the files in the Tutorial.02\Case4 folder provided with your Data Files. Use the Folder Options dialog box to display the file extensions for all of these files. List the file extensions not already discussed in this tutorial.

EXPLORE

2. Use your favorite search engine to find information about each file type you listed in Step 1. For example, search for ACCDB files to learn what type of program can open files with an .accdb extension.

3. Based on what you learned about the file types, sketch an organization for these files. Then create the subfolders you need in the Case4 folder.

4. Move the files from the Case4 folder to the subfolders you created.

5. Open the **Presentations** file in Notepad, read the contents, and then close Notepad. Based on the contents of the Presentations file, move it to a different folder, if necessary.

EXPLORE

6. Right-click the **Presentations** file, and then point to Open with on the shortcut menu. Select a program other than Notepad to use to open the file. Type your name at the beginning of the file, click the program menu button or click File on the menu bar, and then click Save as. Use the Save As dialog box to save the file as a different type, such as .rtf or .doc, but using the same location. (*Hint*: Click the Save as type arrow and then click a file type.) Close the program window.

7. Double-click any other file in a Case4 subfolder and describe what happens.

EXPLORE

8. If a program did not start when you double-clicked the file in Step 7, right-click the file, and then click Open. If you are connected to the Internet, use a Web service to find the correct program. Describe what happens.

9. Double-click another file in a Case4 subfolder and describe what happens. Be sure to choose a file other than the one you chose for Step 7.

10. Close all open windows.
11. Submit the results of the preceding steps to your instructor, either in printed or electronic form, as requested.

ENDING DATA FILES

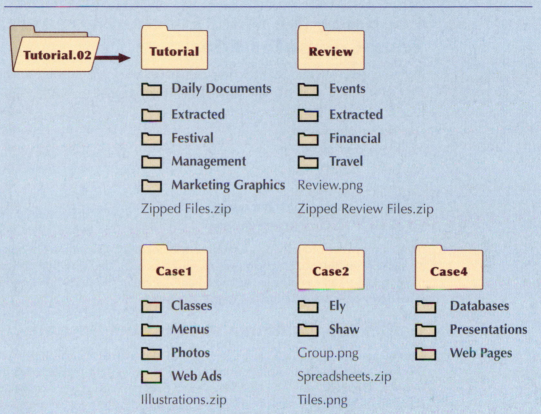

Tutorial.02 → **Tutorial**
- 📁 Daily Documents
- 📁 Extracted
- 📁 Festival
- 📁 Management
- 📁 Marketing Graphics

Zipped Files.zip

Review
- 📁 Events
- 📁 Extracted
- 📁 Financial
- 📁 Travel

Review.png

Zipped Review Files.zip

Case1
- 📁 Classes
- 📁 Menus
- 📁 Photos
- 📁 Web Ads

Illustrations.zip

Case2
- 📁 Ely
- 📁 Shaw

Group.png

Spreadsheets.zip

Tiles.png

Case4
- 📁 Databases
- 📁 Presentations
- 📁 Web Pages

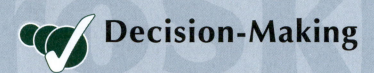

Decision-Making

Choosing the Most Efficient Organization for Your Computer Files

Decision making is choosing the best alternative from many possible alternatives. The alternative you select is your decision. When making a decision, you typically complete the following steps:

1. Gather information
2. Make predictions
3. Select the best alternative
4. Prepare an action plan
5. Perform tasks and monitor results
6. Verify the accuracy of the decision

If you are involved in making a complex decision that affects many people, you perform all six steps in the process. If you are making a simpler decision that does not affect many people, such as how to organize your computer files, you can condense the steps or perform only those that relate to your decision.

Gather Information and Select the Best Alternative

Start by gathering information to identify your alternatives. For example, when organizing your files, you could store most of your work on your computer hard disk or on removable media, such as a USB drive or an external hard drive. Also ask questions that quantify information, or use numbers to compare the alternatives, such as the following:

- How much space do you need for your files?
- In how many locations do you need to access the files?
- How often do you work with your files?

Also ask questions that compare the qualities of the alternatives, such as the following:

- Is one alternative easier to perform or maintain than another?
- Does each alternative make sense for the long term?
- Can you perform each alternative on your own?
- What is your final goal in selecting an alternative?

After testing each alternative by asking both types of questions, one alternative should emerge as the best choice for you. If one option does not seem like the best alternative, continue comparing alternatives by listing the pros and cons of each.

Prepare an Action Plan

After you make a decision, prepare an action plan by identifying the steps you need to perform to put the decision into practice. One way to do this is to work backwards from your final goal. If you are determining how best to manage your computer files, your final goal might be a set of folders and files organized so that you can find any file quickly. Start by listing the tasks you need to perform to meet your goal. Be as specific as possible to avoid confusion later. For example, instead of listing "Create folders" as a task, identify each folder and subfolder by name and indicate which files or types of files each should contain.

Next, estimate how long each task will take, and assign the task to someone. For simple decisions, you assign most tasks to yourself. If you need to use outside resources, include those in the action plan. For example, if you decide to store your files on USB drives, include a step to purchase the drives you need. If you are sharing a computer with someone else, include a step to discuss where you plan to store your files and how that might affect the other person. If someone else needs to approve your plan or any of its tasks, be sure to include that step in the action plan.

If appropriate, the action plan can also track your budget. For example, you could track expenses for a new hard disk or backup media.

Complete the Tasks and Monitor the Results

After you prepare an action plan and receive any necessary approvals, perform the tasks outlined in the plan. For example, create or rename the folders you identified in your action plan, and then move existing files into each folder. As you perform each step, mark its status as complete or pending, for example.

When you complete all the tasks in the action plan, monitor the results. For example, after reorganizing your files, did you meet your goal of being able to quickly find any file when you need it? If so, continue to follow your plan as you add files and folders to your computer. If not, return to your plan and determine where you could improve it.

PROSKILLS

Organize Your Files

Even if you are familiar with some features of Windows 7 or regularly use your computer for certain tasks, such as accessing Web sites or exchanging e-mail, take some time to explore the basics of Windows 7 on your computer. Then decide how you want to organize the files and folders you use for course work or for job-related projects on your own computer. Be sure to follow the guidelines you learned for developing an organization strategy, creating folders, naming files, and moving, copying, deleting, and compressing files. As you work through this ProSkills exercise, you will first record settings on your computer. To do so, you can capture and save images of the desktop and windows you open by pressing Alt+Print Screen to capture an image of the screen, and then saving the image in a WordPad or Paint file. You can print these images to use as references if you experience problems with your computer later or want to restore these settings. Complete the following tasks:

1. Start Windows 7 and log on, if necessary.
2. To solve system problems that might appear later, you should now capture and save images of your current desktop, the Start menu, the Computer window showing the drives on your computer, and your My Documents folder.
3. Determine which folder you plan to use as the main folder for your documents. Create this folder, if necessary. Navigate to that folder and make sure the Address bar shows the location of this folder on your computer. Capture and save an image of this window.

ProSkills

4. To determine which programs you will use that are included with Windows 7, start at least two accessory programs that are new to you. Open a menu in each program, and then capture and save the image of each program window.

5. Using the Ribbon, toolbar, or menu bar in the new programs, find a dialog box in each program that you are likely to use. Capture and save images of the dialog boxes.

6. Use Windows Help and Support to find information about a feature or technique covered in this tutorial. Choose a topic that you want to know more about. Capture and save an image of the Windows Help and Support window displaying information about this topic.

7. Use a program such as Word, WordPad, or Notepad to create a plan for organizing your files. List the types of files you work with, and then determine whether you want to store them on your hard disk or on removable media. Describe the folders and subfolders you will use to manage these files. If you choose a hard disk as your storage medium, make sure you plan to store your work files and folders in a subfolder of the My Documents folder.

8. Use a folder window to navigate to your files. Note which tools you prefer to use for navigating your computer.

9. Create any additional folders and subfolders you want to use for your files.

10. Move and copy files to the appropriate folders according to your plan, and rename and delete files as necessary.

11. Create a backup copy of your work files by creating a compressed file and then copying the compressed file to a removable medium, such as a USB flash drive.

12. Submit your finished plan to your instructor, either in printed or electronic form, as requested.

TUTORIAL 3

Personalizing Your Windows Environment

Changing Desktop Settings

Case | *Magellan Cartography*

OBJECTIVES

Session 3.1
- Access desktop icons and gadgets on the desktop
- Create and use shortcuts on the desktop
- Use the Control Panel
- Customize the desktop
- Activate a screen saver
- Change display settings

Session 3.2
- Manage the desktop with Aero tools
- Pin items to and modify the taskbar
- Customize taskbar toolbars
- Change Start menu settings
- Pin items on the Start menu

Magellan Cartography is a small business in Charlottesville, Virginia, that specializes in creating historical maps of American locations. Holly Devore started the company with Sarah Linder about two years ago. Sarah now travels to meet with clients, and Holly runs operations in Charlottesville.

You have been working as the office manager for Magellan Cartography for a few months, providing general assistance to Holly, Sarah, and the staff. Holly recently upgraded the office computers to Windows 7, and now she has asked you to customize the company's computers so that everyone can access important files and computer resources. She also wants the desktop to reflect the Magellan Cartography company image. You will start by personalizing Holly's computer, and then apply the changes to the other office computers.

STARTING DATA FILES

Tutorial.03 →

Tutorial
District 1.png
District 2.png
Facts.txt
Haleakala.jpg
Islands.png
Maui.jpg
Navigation.jpg
Volcano.jpg

Review
Charleston.jpg
Explorers.jpg
James River.jpg
N America.png
N America.png
NF Map.png
NF Outline.png
US 1800.jpg

Case1
Last Supper.jpg
Mona Lisa.jpg
Polyhedra.png
Tank.jpg
V Man.jpg
Vasari.txt

Case2
Beaux Arts.jpg
Colonial.jpg
For Sale.jpg
School.jpg
Syracuse.txt
Victorian.jpg

Case3
Bald Island.jpg
Bar Island.jpg
Birch Grass.jpg
Bridge.jpg
Directions.txt
Peregrine.jpg
Summit.jpg

Case4
(none)

SESSION 3.1 VISUAL OVERVIEW

The size of the desktop icons has been set to Small.

You can change the appearance of the desktop icons

Desktop icons, such as the Recycle Bin, are the easiest way to access Windows tools, drives, programs, and documents.

Besides the Recycle Bin, you can display additional desktop icons.

A **shortcut icon** provides a quick way to open a file, folder, device, or program without having to find its permanent location.

The icon font has been changed to Palatino.

Owner

Removable Disk (H) ...

Computer

Recycle Bin

Control Panel

Hawaii Maps - Shortcut

Paint

PERSONALIZED WINDOWS DESKTOP

The Clock is a Windows **gadget**, or miniprogram, that you can customize and display on the desktop.

The **desktop background** has been personalized with a custom picture, which is also part of a custom theme.

The color of the window borders, Start menu, and taskbar has been changed to pumpkin.

3:51 PM
10/3/2013

Accessing Common Tools on the Desktop

As you know, the large area you see on your screen when you start Windows 7 is called the desktop. The desktop displays a background image, the Recycle Bin icon, and the taskbar by default. Your desktop might also include other icons or windows.

Because the desktop provides your first view of the computer and its contents, it should contain the items you want to access when you start your computer. You can place icons on the desktop that represent objects you want to access quickly and frequently, such as Windows tools, drives, programs, and documents. Windows provides desktop icons for system tools, such as the Recycle Bin, the Computer window, and your My Documents folder. You can add or remove these icons according to your work preferences. Figure 3-1 shows the types of icons you can include on the desktop and the objects they represent.

Figure 3-1	Types of desktop icons

Icon	Description
	Computer desktop icon
	Control Panel desktop icon
	Document shortcut icon
	Drive shortcut icon
	Folder shortcut icon
	Network desktop icon
	Program shortcut icon (such as Paint)
	Recycle Bin desktop icon (full and empty)
	User's folder desktop icon

Besides these built-in desktop icons, you can use shortcuts to start a program or access an object. Shortcut icons include a small arrow in the lower-left corner, a reminder that the icon points to an item stored elsewhere on the computer. If you double-click a shortcut, its associated file, folder, device, or program opens. When you delete a shortcut or desktop icon, you delete only the icon—the file or resource it represents remains in its original location. You typically create shortcuts on the desktop (or elsewhere, such as in a folder or on the taskbar) to locations, files, and devices that you use often.

PROSKILLS

Problem Solving: Simplifying Tasks with Shortcuts

If you work with many devices, programs, or folders, it might be difficult to access all of these resources efficiently. One way to solve this problem is to add shortcuts to the desktop. Shortcut icons can simplify tasks you perform regularly. For example, you can create a shortcut icon for a USB flash drive, and then drag files to the shortcut icon to copy them to the flash drive. You also can create a shortcut icon for a program you use often, such as Calculator, and then double-click the icon to start the program. Many programs add a shortcut icon to the desktop when you install the program. If you work with a particular folder often, you can add a desktop shortcut to the folder. That way, you can double-click the folder shortcut to open the folder without navigating many folder windows.

Sarah is in Hawaii this week meeting with the tourism board and gathering data to create historic maps of the islands. This gives Holly time to work with you to customize her computer, starting with adding icons to the desktop for system tools she uses often. You'll also explore Windows gadgets and show her how to add one to the desktop. Then you'll show her how to create shortcut icons on the desktop, including those for a USB flash drive, folder, and program.

Adding Icons to the Desktop

Windows provides five standard icons that can be displayed on the desktop. Besides the Recycle Bin, you can include the Computer icon on the desktop to provide easy access to the Computer window. If you display the desktop icon for your personal folder (that is, the folder containing the current user's files), you can quickly find and open the folders containing your documents. Display the Network icon to access a window that lists the shared computers and other devices on your network. You can also add the Control Panel icon to the desktop. The Control Panel contains specialized tools you use to change the way Windows looks and behaves.

REFERENCE

Displaying Standard Desktop Icons

- Right-click an empty area of the desktop, and then click Personalize on the shortcut menu.
- In the left pane of the Personalization window, click Change desktop icons.
- In the Desktop Icon Settings dialog box, click to select a check box for each icon you want to add to the desktop.
- Click the OK button.

Holly mentions that the Windows tools she uses most frequently are her personal folder, the Computer window, and the Control Panel. You'll add these icons to Holly's desktop. First, you will make sure the desktop view options are set to the Windows 7 defaults so the icons appear in a column on the left side of the desktop. Make sure your computer is displaying only the Windows desktop before you perform the following steps.

To change the desktop view options to their default settings:

1. Right-click the **desktop**, and then point to **View** on the shortcut menu to display the desktop view options.

2. If Medium icons is not selected, click **Medium icons**. Then right-click the **desktop** and point to **View** again.

3. If the Auto arrange icons command does not appear with a check mark, click **Auto arrange icons** to select it. This sets the view to Auto arrange icons and closes the shortcut menu. Right-click the **desktop** and point to **View** again.

4. If the Align icons to grid command does not appear with a check mark, click **Align icons to grid** to select it. Then right-click the **desktop** and point to **View** again.

5. If the Show desktop icons command does not appear with a check mark, click **Show desktop icons** to select it. Then right-click the **desktop** and point to **View** again.

6. If the Show desktop gadgets command does not appear with a check mark, click **Show desktop gadgets** to select it. Then right-click the **desktop** and point to **View** again.

7. If the Medium icons, Auto arrange icons, Align icons to grid, Show desktop icons, and Show desktop gadgets are all selected, as shown in Figure 3-2, click the **desktop** to close the shortcut menu.

Figure 3-2	View settings on the desktop shortcut menu

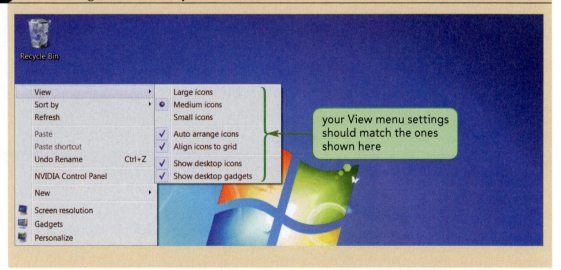

You're ready to add standard desktop icons to the desktop on Holly's computer.

To display standard desktop icons:

1. Right-click the **desktop**, and then click **Personalize** on the shortcut menu. The Personalization window opens.

2. In the left pane, click **Change desktop icons**. The Desktop Icon Settings dialog box opens. See Figure 3-3.

| Figure 3-3 | Desktop Icon Settings dialog box |

standard Windows icons you can display on the desktop

preview of the icons (except for Control Panel)

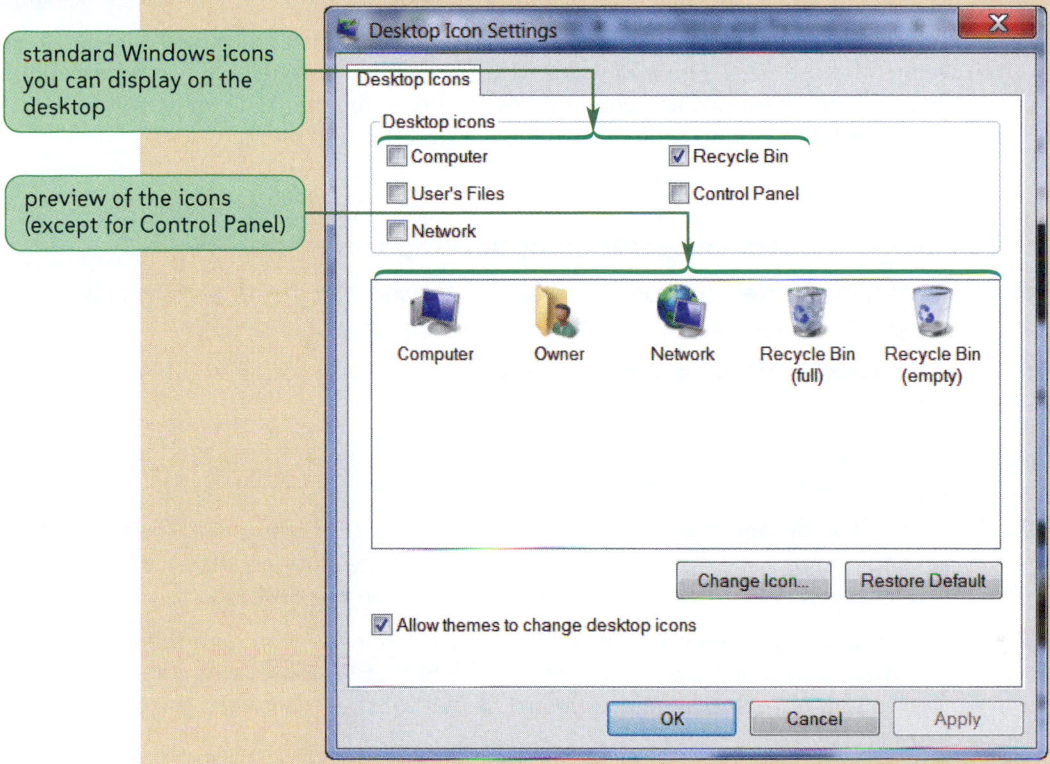

Trouble? If the settings in your Desktop Icon Settings dialog box differ from those in Figure 3-3, note the current options and change them so they match those in Figure 3-3.

TIP

Note that the Recycle Bin icon has two appearances: one when it is empty, and another when it contains deleted items.

3. Click the **Computer**, **User's Files**, and **Control Panel** check boxes.

   The Recycle Bin check box is already selected, indicating that Windows is displaying the Recycle Bin icon on the desktop.

4. Click the **OK** button.

5. Click the **Close** button [X] to close the Personalization window. The icons for your personal folder, the Computer window, and the Control Panel appear on the desktop.

Now that you've added desktop icons for Holly, you can customize their appearance to suit her preferences.

Changing the Appearance of Desktop Icons

You can change the size and appearance of desktop icons depending on how you like to work. Windows displays desktop icons at a medium size by default. If you have only a few icons on your desktop or you prefer to work with large icons, you can resize the desktop icons so they are larger. On the other hand, if you use many icons on your desktop, you might prefer small icons.

If you like a clean, uncluttered desktop, you can hide all of your desktop icons and show them only when you need to use one. By default, Windows lists icons in columns along the left side of your desktop and aligns the icons to an invisible grid so that they are evenly spaced on the desktop. You can change this arrangement to match your preferences, such as arranging the icons on the right or along the top of the desktop.

Besides personalizing the size and arrangement of the desktop icons, you can change the icon images. For example, the Computer icon shows an image of a desktop computer. If you work on a notebook or tablet computer, you might want to change this image to match your computer type.

Holly asks you to show her the desktop with large and small icons to see if she wants to use one of those sizes. She also wants to know how to move the icons on the desktop and then hide them for privacy when interns use her computer. You can perform all of these tasks using the View command on the desktop shortcut menu.

To change the size and location of desktop icons:

1. Right-click the **desktop**, point to **View** on the shortcut menu, and then click **Large icons**. The icons on the desktop now appear in a larger size.

2. Right-click the **desktop**, point to **View** on the shortcut menu, and then click **Small icons**. The icons appear in their smallest size.

   Next, you'll move the desktop icons so they no longer are displayed in a column along the left side of the desktop.

3. Right-click the **desktop**, point to **View** on the shortcut menu, and then click **Auto arrange icons** to remove the check mark. When the Auto arrange icons command is unchecked, you can move the icons anywhere on the desktop.

4. Drag the **Computer** icon to the right of the Recycle Bin icon, and then click the **desktop** to deselect the Computer icon. Note that Windows aligns the Computer icon to a grid, maintaining a standard amount of space between the two icons. See Figure 3-4.

Figure 3-4 | Arranging icons on the desktop

the name of your personal folder might differ

moving the Computer icon next to the Recycle Bin

5. Right-click the **desktop**, point to **View** on the shortcut menu, and then click **Align icons to grid** to remove the check mark. When the Align icons to grid command is unchecked, you can change the icons so they are no longer aligned with each other.

6. Drag the **Computer** icon closer to the Recycle Bin icon.

7. Right-click the **desktop**, point to **View** on the shortcut menu, and then click **Show desktop icons** to remove the check mark. When Show desktop icons is unchecked, Windows hides the icons so only the desktop appears on your screen.

8. Right-click the **desktop**, point to **View** on the shortcut menu, and then click **Show desktop icons**. A check mark appears next to the command, indicating that Windows is displaying the icons on the desktop.

Because she works on an all-in-one computer, with the computer and monitor built into the same case, Holly wants to change the image for the Computer icon on the desktop. To do so, you use the Personalization window.

To change the image of the Computer icon:

1. Right-click the **desktop**, and then click **Personalize** on the shortcut menu. The Personalization window opens.

2. In the left pane, click **Change desktop icons**. The Desktop Icon Settings dialog box opens.

3. In the box displaying desktop icons, click the **Computer** icon, and then click the **Change Icon** button. The Change Icon dialog box opens and highlights the current image. See Figure 3-5. Note the image currently used for the Computer icon so you can restore it later.

Figure 3-5	Change Icon dialog box

4. Click the image that is two icons to the left of the current image. This icon shows a monitor displaying a moon image.

   Trouble? If the computer image shown in Figure 3-5 does not appear in your Change Icon dialog box, click any other suitable image.

5. Click the **OK** button to close the Change Icon dialog box, and then click the **OK** button to close the Desktop Icon Settings dialog box.

6. Close the Personalization window. The Computer icon on the desktop now appears as a monitor displaying a moon image.

The standard Windows desktop icons provide quick access to common Windows tools. You can also personalize another desktop feature to save time when you're performing common tasks—Windows gadgets.

Using Windows Gadgets

Gadgets offer information at a glance and are similar to tools you might keep on your physical desk, such as a calendar or clock. Windows provides a collection of built-in gadgets, which are described in Figure 3-6.

| Figure 3-6 | Windows gadgets |

Gadget	Use to:
Calendar	Display the current date and browse a monthly calendar.
Clock	Display the time in your time zone or any other around the world.
CPU Meter	Gauge system performance.
Currency	Convert from one currency to another.
Feed Headlines	Track news headlines, sports scores, and entertainment information.
Picture Puzzle	Move the pieces of the puzzle to create an image.
Slide Show	Show a continuous slide show of pictures on your computer.
Weather	Check the weather in cities around the world.
Windows Media Center	Access home entertainment media, including recorded TV, videos, and music.

A few of the most popular gadgets are the Calendar, Clock, Feed Headlines, and Weather. The Calendar shows the current date by default and a monthly view when you double-click it. Besides using the Clock gadget to show the current time for your time zone, you can show one or more additional clocks to display the current time for other time zones around the world. The Feed Headlines gadget lists frequently updated headlines so you can keep up with the news from your desktop. The headlines are supplied by a Web site that publishes a **feed**, which is online content that is updated often. The Weather gadget also accesses online information to display the weather in various locations you specify around the world.

INSIGHT

Understanding Feeds

A feed, or a Really Simple Syndication (RSS) feed, is Web site content that is frequently updated, such as news or Web logs (more commonly called *blogs*). A feed often has the same content as the information provided on a Web site, but it can be delivered directly to your desktop if you are connected to the Internet. Then you can use the Feed Headlines gadget to display the changing content. If you want to keep up with news, sports scores, or other frequently updated information, use Internet Explorer to subscribe to a feed on a Web site. Then keep the Feed Headlines gadget open on your desktop so you can view the changing information at a glance.

Holly wants to display a Clock gadget on the desktop set to Hawaii time so she can call Sarah at appropriate times while she's visiting the islands. When Sarah returns from Hawaii, Holly can change the clock to a different time zone or remove it.

To display the Clock gadget on the desktop:

1. Right-click the **desktop**, and then click **Gadgets** on the shortcut menu. The gadget gallery opens, showing the gadgets that are currently installed on your computer. You can add any of these gadgets to the desktop. See Figure 3-7.

Figure 3-7   Gadget gallery

gadgets installed on your computer; yours might differ

click to find more gadgets on the Microsoft Web site

2. Double-click the **Clock** gadget. A clock appears on the desktop.

3. Close the gadget gallery.

Next, you'll show Holly how to customize the Clock gadget to display Hawaiian time.

Customizing a Gadget

You can customize many gadgets to suit your preferences, including the Clock, Currency, Feed Headlines, Slide Show, Picture Puzzle, and Weather. For example, you can select the pictures you want to display in the Slide Show and Picture Puzzle. First you will customize the Clock gadget to display the current time in Hawaii. You will also display a name for the clock so you can tell at a glance that it displays Hawaiian time.

To customize the Clock gadget:

1. Point to the new **Clock** gadget on the desktop, and then click the **Options** button 🔧. The Clock dialog box opens. See Figure 3-8.

Figure 3-8   Clock dialog box

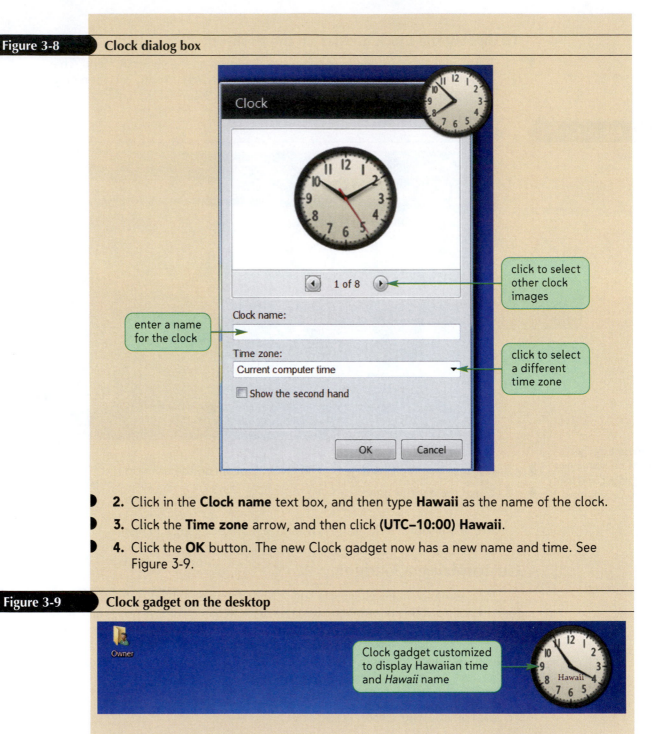

Clock

1 of 8

click to select
other clock
images

enter a name
for the clock

Clock name:

Time zone:

Current computer time

click to select
a different
time zone

☐ Show the second hand

OK   Cancel

▶ **2.** Click in the **Clock name** text box, and then type **Hawaii** as the name of the clock.

▶ **3.** Click the **Time zone** arrow, and then click **(UTC–10:00) Hawaii**.

▶ **4.** Click the **OK** button. The new Clock gadget now has a new name and time. See Figure 3-9.

Figure 3-9   Clock gadget on the desktop

Owner

Clock gadget customized
to display Hawaiian time
and *Hawaii* name

Hawaii

If you are connected to the Internet and want to add other gadgets to the gadget gallery, you can open the gadget gallery window, and then click Get more gadgets online. When the Personalization Gallery window opens, scroll down, if necessary, and then click the Desktop gadgets tab. Review the featured gadgets, or click the Get more desktop gadgets link to view all the available gadgets. When you find one that interests you, click the Download button to open a page describing the gadget. If you want to install it in your gadget gallery, click the Download button on the description page.

So far, you've explored how to personalize your desktop by displaying Windows desktop icons and gadgets. These are standard tools that Windows provides to simplify or enhance your computer work. However, other items you access often (such as documents, folders, and drives) might be different from the items other users access often.

In addition, the folders you use frequently one week might differ from those you'll use frequently next week. To personalize your desktop to provide quick access to these items, you can create and use shortcuts.

Using Shortcuts

You can create shortcuts to access drives, documents, files, Web pages, programs, or other computer resources such as a printer. For example, you can easily open a document from the desktop by creating a shortcut icon for the document. A shortcut icon for a document works much the same way as a document icon does in a folder window—you can double-click the shortcut icon to open the document in the appropriate program. However, a shortcut icon is only a link to the actual document. If you move the icon, for example, you move only the shortcut, not the document itself. One advantage of using shortcut icons is that if your desktop becomes cluttered, you can delete the shortcut icons without affecting the original documents.

You can also create shortcut icons for the folders, drives, and devices on your computer. This way, you can access your local hard disk, for example, directly from the desktop, instead of having to open a folder window and then navigate to the hard disk.

Windows 7 provides several ways of creating shortcuts. Figure 3-10 summarizes the techniques you can use to create shortcuts. The one you choose is a matter of personal preference.

Figure 3-10   **Methods for creating shortcuts**

Method	Description
Drag (for drives and devices only)	To create a drive shortcut on the desktop, use a folder window to locate the drive icon, and then drag the icon to the desktop.
Right-drag	Use a folder window to locate and select an icon, hold down the right mouse button, and drag the icon to a new location. Release the mouse button and click Create shortcuts here on the shortcut menu.
Right-click, Create shortcut	Use a folder window to locate an icon, right-click the icon, click Create shortcut on the shortcut menu, and then drag the shortcut icon to a new location.
Right-click, Send to	To create a shortcut on the desktop, use a folder window to locate an icon, right-click the icon, point to Send to, and then click Desktop (create shortcut).

Next, you'll create a shortcut to a USB flash drive. You could use any technique listed in Figure 3-10, but you'll use the drag method because it involves the fewest steps.

Creating a Shortcut to a Drive

To create a shortcut to a drive, you can open the Computer window and then drag the drive icon from the window to the desktop. Windows 7 creates a shortcut icon that looks like a drive icon with a shortcut arrow and includes an appropriate label, such as *Removable Disk (G) – Shortcut*. If you drag a *document* icon from a folder window to the desktop, you move the actual document from its original location to the desktop. However, you cannot move a drive, program, or other computer resource—its location is fixed during installation—so when you drag a drive icon to the desktop, you automatically create a shortcut.

When you create a shortcut to a USB flash drive, you can insert the drive in a USB port and then double-click the shortcut to view your Data Files, and you can move or copy documents to the drive without having to open a separate folder window.

Holly regularly copies image files from her computer to a USB flash drive, and wants to use a shortcut to simplify the task. You'll show her how to create a shortcut to a USB flash drive on her desktop.

The steps in this tutorial assume that your Data Files are stored on Removable Disk (G:), a USB drive. If necessary, substitute the appropriate name and drive on your system when you perform the steps.

To create a shortcut to a USB flash drive:

1. If necessary, insert the USB flash drive containing your Data Files into a USB port on your computer.

   Trouble? If you don't have the starting Data Files, you need to get them before you can proceed. Your instructor will either give you the Data Files or ask you to obtain them from a specified location (such as a network drive). In either case, make a backup copy of your Data Files before you start using them so you will have the original files available in case you need to start over. If you have any questions about the Data Files, see your instructor or technical support person for assistance.

   Trouble? If you do not have a USB flash drive, insert a different type of removable disk containing your Data Files, such as a memory card, but not a CD, into the appropriate drive.

2. Double-click the **Computer** icon on the desktop. Resize the Computer window so you can see the icons along the left side of the desktop. You need to see both the desktop icons and the Computer window to drag effectively.

3. Point to the **Removable Disk (G:)** icon in the Computer window, press and hold the left mouse button, and then drag the **Removable Disk (G:)** icon from the Computer window into an empty area of the desktop.

4. Release the mouse button. A shortcut labeled *Removable Disk (G) – Shortcut* now appears on the desktop. See Figure 3-11.

Figure 3-11	Shortcut to a removable disk

shortcut to removable disk

your shortcut might appear in a different location on the desktop

removable disk icon

Trouble? If you dragged with the right mouse button instead of the left, a shortcut menu appears when you release the mouse button. Click Create shortcuts here to add the Removable Disk (G) – Shortcut to the desktop.

5. Point to the **Removable Disk (G) – Shortcut** icon to view its ScreenTip, which indicates the permanent location of the drive on your computer.

Holly received a few files from Sarah containing map images. Use the shortcut on the desktop to copy the files from the USB flash drive to a new folder for Hawaiian maps.

To use the removable disk shortcut:

1. In the Navigation pane of the Computer window, click **Pictures** to open the Pictures library.

2. Click the **New folder** button on the toolbar to create a new folder in the Pictures library.

3. Type **Hawaii Maps** as the name of the new folder, and then press the **Enter** key.

4. Double-click the **Hawaii Maps** folder to open it.

5. Double-click the **Removable Disk (G) – Shortcut** icon on the desktop. A new window opens showing the contents of the USB flash drive.

6. Open the **Tutorial.03** folder and then the **Tutorial** folder.

7. Select all of the files in the Tutorial folder, and then drag them to the right pane of the **Hawaii Maps** folder window. All eight files are copied to the Hawaii Maps folder.

8. Close the Tutorial folder window.

Using a shortcut to a drive saves a few steps when you transfer files from one computer to another. If you regularly use certain folders and documents, you can save even more time by creating shortcuts to those items.

Holly expects to receive many documents from Sarah while she's working in Hawaii, and Holly plans to store those in the Hawaii Maps folder. In addition, Holly needs to use the Facts document when she is creating basic maps of the islands. You'll show her how to create a shortcut to the Hawaii Maps folder and the Facts document to save time.

Creating Shortcuts to Folders and Documents

Creating shortcuts to folders and documents is similar to creating shortcuts to drives—with one crucial difference. Instead of dragging a drive icon from a window to the desktop, you right-drag the folder or document icon to the desktop. (That is, you press and hold the right mouse button as you drag.) If you drag a folder or document icon from a folder window to the desktop, you move or copy the folder or document from its original location to the desktop rather than creating a shortcut.

INSIGHT

Keeping a Clean Desktop

Storing actual files and folders on the desktop instead of shortcuts can slow your computer's performance and make it difficult to find documents when you need them. Instead, follow good file management principles and store your documents and other files in your personal folder and its subfolders. Create desktop shortcuts only to the documents and folders you use most often.

You'll show Holly how to create a shortcut to the Hawaii Maps folder using the right-drag method. Then you'll create a shortcut to the Facts document using a different method—the Send to menu. When you right-click a file or folder and point to Send to on the shortcut menu, Windows displays a list of the drives and other locations on your computer, including the desktop. If you send an item to the desktop, you create a shortcut to that file or folder.

To create a shortcut to a folder by right-dragging:

1. In the Hawaii Maps folder window, click the **Back** button ⬅ to display the contents of the Pictures library, including the Hawaii Maps folder. Resize and move the window as necessary to see both the Hawaii Maps folder icon in the window and the icons on the left side of the desktop.

   Trouble? If the Hawaii Maps folder window is not open on your computer, open any folder window, and then click Pictures in the Navigation pane to open the Pictures library. Resize and move the window as necessary to see both the Hawaii Maps folder icon in the window and the icons on the left side of the desktop.

2. Point to the **Hawaii Maps** folder, press and hold the right mouse button, drag the **Hawaii Maps** folder icon from the Pictures window onto the desktop, and then release the mouse button. A shortcut menu appears listing the tasks you can perform with this document. Recall that you can use the shortcut menu to copy or move a document as well as create a shortcut to it.

3. Click **Create shortcuts here**. An icon labeled *Hawaii Maps – Shortcut* appears on the desktop.

4. Point to the **Hawaii Maps – Shortcut** icon to display the ScreenTip, which indicates the location of the original folder. See Figure 3-12.

| Figure 3-12 | Creating a shortcut to the Hawaii Maps folder |

5. Close the Pictures window.

Now you can test the folder shortcut and create another shortcut on the desktop, this time to the Facts document.

To test the folder shortcut and create a shortcut to a document using the Send to menu:

1. Double-click the **Hawaii Maps – Shortcut** icon on the desktop. A window opens displaying the contents of the Hawaii Maps folder. Move or resize the window as necessary to see the contents of the Hawaii Maps folder and a blank area on the left side of the desktop.

2. Right-click the **Facts** document in the Hawaii Maps window, and then point to **Send to**. The Send to menu opens. See Figure 3-13.

Figure 3-13	Creating a shortcut using the Send to menu

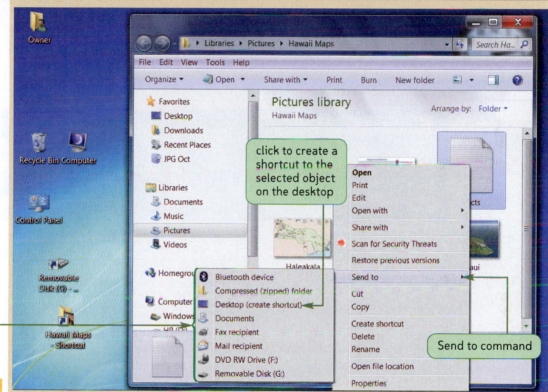

TIP

You can rename a shortcut icon by right-clicking the shortcut icon, clicking Rename, and then entering the new name.

3. Click **Desktop (create shortcut)**. An icon labeled *Facts – Shortcut* appears on the desktop.

4. Double-click the **Facts – Shortcut** icon on the desktop to open this document in Notepad.

5. Close all open windows.

You now have three shortcuts on the desktop that provide efficient ways to open the Hawaii Maps folder, the Facts document, and a USB flash drive. Next, you want to add a program shortcut to the desktop so that Holly can easily view and edit image files.

Creating a Shortcut to a Program

The easiest and safest way to create a program shortcut is to use the right mouse button to drag a program icon from the Start menu to the desktop. When you right-drag a program icon, Windows creates a program shortcut icon on the desktop. (If you drag the program icon using the left mouse button, you might move the program file.) You can then open an appropriate file by dragging its icon to the program shortcut icon on the desktop. For example, if you create a Paint shortcut icon on the desktop, you can drag a picture file from a folder window to the Paint shortcut icon to view and edit the picture.

Holly often edits image files when she's working on a map. Instead of starting Paint and then using the Open dialog box to navigate to and select an image file, she can drag a file to the Paint shortcut icon to open and edit the image. You'll show her how to create a program shortcut on the desktop.

To create a program shortcut:

1. Click the **Start** button 🟦 on the taskbar, point to **All Programs**, and then click **Accessories**.

> Make sure you create a Paint shortcut icon; if you drag the Paint program icon, you move it to the desktop.

2. Right-drag the Paint program icon to a blank area of the desktop, and then release the mouse button. When a shortcut menu opens, click **Create shortcuts** here. Windows creates a Paint shortcut icon.

3. Click a blank area of the desktop to deselect the new shortcut icon. See Figure 3-14.

Figure 3-14 **Creating a shortcut to a program**

Paint shortcut icon

You'll show Holly how to open an image file using the Paint and Hawaii Maps – Shortcut icons.

To open an image file using the Paint shortcut icon:

1. Double-click the **Hawaii Maps – Shortcut** icon on the desktop to open the Hawaii Maps folder.

2. If necessary, resize and move the Hawaii Maps folder window so you can see the window and the Paint shortcut icon.

3. Using the left mouse button, drag the **District 1** image file from the folder window to the **Paint** shortcut icon.

4. When an *Open with Paint* ScreenTip appears, release the mouse button. Paint starts and displays the District 1 image.

5. Close all open windows.

Now that your desktop contains a variety of icons, including standard desktop icons and shortcuts, you can arrange the icons so they are easy to access.

Organizing Icons on the Desktop

When you turn off the Auto arrange icons setting and then add icons to the desktop, Windows 7 lists the shortcut icons where you add them or where it finds room. You can change this order by selecting a sort option to list the shortcut icons by name, size, item type, or date modified. These sort options are similar to the ones you use when sorting files and folders in a folder window. Sorting by name organizes the shortcut icons in alphabetical order by the icon name. Sorting by size organizes them according to the size of their source files (unless the icon is a shortcut to a program—then Windows uses the size of the shortcut itself). Sort by item type when you want to keep shortcuts to files of the same type, such as text documents, next to each other on the desktop. Sort by date modified to arrange the icons according to the date you modified the shortcuts.

Before you organize the icons on the desktop, restore the original Auto arrange icons and Align icons to grid settings to arrange the icons in a neat column. Then you can sort the shortcut icons by name to make them easy to find.

To restore the desktop settings and sort the icons:

1. Right-click the **desktop**, point to **View** on the shortcut menu, and then click **Auto arrange icons** to select that option.

2. Right-click the **desktop**, point to **View** on the shortcut menu, and then click **Align icons to grid** to select that option.

3. Right-click the **desktop**, point to **Sort by** on the shortcut menu, and then click **Name** to select that option, if necessary. The shortcut icons are organized on the desktop in alphabetical order. See Figure 3-15.

Figure 3-15 Desktop icons sorted by name

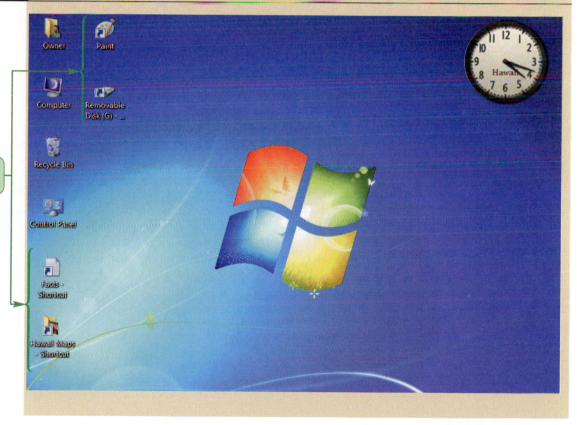

shortcut icons listed alphabetically

Finally, you can delete a shortcut icon to verify that doing so does not affect its associated device, drive, program, folder, or document.

Deleting Shortcut Icons

If you delete a document icon in a folder window, you also delete the document. If you delete a shortcut icon, however, you don't delete the document itself because it is stored elsewhere; you delete only the shortcut that links to the document. The same is true for other types of shortcuts, including those to folders, drives, and devices. You can verify this by deleting the Facts – Shortcut icon on the desktop when the Hawaii Maps folder is open.

To delete a shortcut:

▶ **1.** Double-click the **Hawaii Maps – Shortcut** icon on your desktop. The Hawaii Maps window opens, displaying the contents of the Hawaii Maps folder, including the Facts document.

▶ **2.** If necessary, arrange the Hawaii Maps window so that it doesn't overlap the Facts – Shortcut icon on the desktop.

▶ **3.** Click the **Facts – Shortcut** icon on the desktop, and then press the **Delete** key.

▶ **4.** Click the **Yes** button when you are asked if you are sure you want to move this shortcut to the Recycle Bin.

▶ **5.** Verify that the Facts document is still stored in the Hawaii Maps folder, and then close the folder window.

Because you selected Auto arrange icons and Align icons to grid using the View command on the desktop shortcut menu, Windows rearranges the icons when you delete the Facts shortcut icon so they remain in columns and are aligned to one another on the desktop.

Personalizing with the Control Panel

You've worked with Windows gadgets and with standard desktop and shortcut icons to personalize your desktop. You can also personalize Windows 7 using the Control Panel, a window that contains specialized tools you use to change the way Windows 7 looks and behaves. Some tools help you adjust settings that make your computer more fun to use. For example, use the Personalize tool to change the theme, which is a background plus a set of colors, sounds, and other elements. Other Control Panel tools help you set up Windows so that your computer is easier to use. For example, you can change display settings so that the desktop, icons, and windows are sharp and clear. All of the Control Panel tools provide access to dialog boxes that let you select or change the **properties**, or characteristics, of an object.

If you added the Control Panel icon to the desktop, you can open the Control Panel by double-clicking that icon. Otherwise, you can open the Control Panel from the Start menu.

To open the Control Panel:

1. Double-click the **Control Panel** icon on your desktop. The Control Panel window opens. See Figure 3-16. Your Control Panel window might differ.

Figure 3-16   **Control Panel**

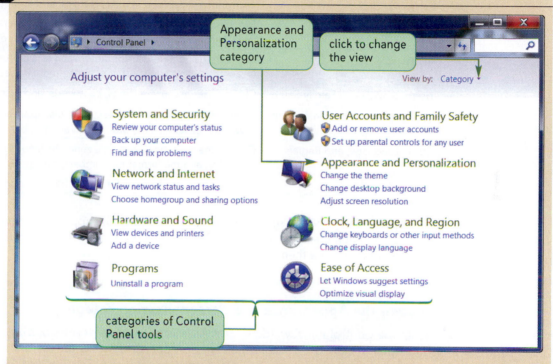

Trouble? If your desktop does not display a Control Panel icon, click the Start button 🪟 on the taskbar, and then click Control Panel.

Trouble? If a message appears indicating that the Control Panel is not available, you might be in a computer lab with limited customization access. Ask your instructor or technical support person for options.

TIP

You can click the View by button arrow and then click Large icons or Small icons to list each tool in alphabetic order.

The main window of the Control Panel shown in Figure 3-16 is called the Control Panel Home page. By default, this page displays tools in Category View, which groups similar tools into categories. See Figure 3-17.

Figure 3-17   Control Panel categories

Control Panel Category	Typical Tasks
System and Security	Schedule maintenance checks, increase the space on your hard disk, maintain Windows security settings, and keep Windows up to date.
Network and Internet	Set Internet options, view network status, and set up a homegroup to share files and perform other network tasks.
Hardware and Sound	Change the sounds on your computer, and change the settings for your printer, keyboard, mouse, camera, and other hardware.
Programs	Install and uninstall programs and Windows features, set options for default settings and programs, and work with desktop gadgets.
Mobile PC	If you are using a mobile computer such as a laptop, change battery settings and adjust other common mobility settings.
User Accounts and Family Safety	Change user account settings, passwords, and associated pictures.
Appearance and Personalization	Change the appearance of desktop items, apply a theme or screen saver, and customize the Start menu and taskbar.
Clock, Language, and Region	Change the date, time, and time zone, the language you use on your computer, and the format for numbers, currencies, dates, and times.
Ease of Access	Change computer settings for vision, hearing, and mobility.

To open a category and see its related tools, you click the appropriate link. For example, you can open the Appearance and Personalization window to change the desktop background or to set a theme.

To open the Appearance and Personalization category:

1. In the Control Panel window, click **Appearance and Personalization**. The Appearance and Personalization window opens, showing the tasks and tools related to personalizing your computer's appearance. See Figure 3-18.

Figure 3-18   **Appearance and personalization options in the Control Panel**

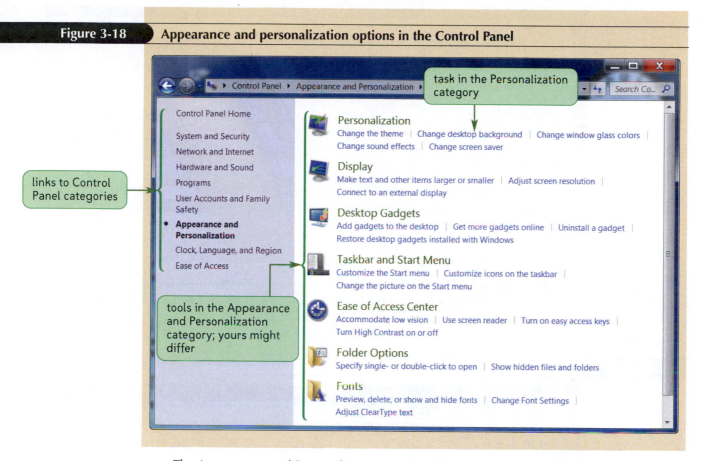

links to Control Panel categories

task in the Personalization category

tools in the Appearance and Personalization category; yours might differ

The Appearance and Personalization window, like the other Control Panel category windows, lists tasks and tools in the right pane and links to the Control Panel Home page and other categories in the left pane. To change the desktop background, for example, you click the Change desktop background task in the right pane. The Desktop Background window opens so you can select a new desktop background and set other background options.

Holly wants her office computers to reflect the company image of Magellan Cartography, and she'd like the desktop itself to be more appealing to her and her employees. You will work with the Control Panel to personalize Holly's desktop.

Selecting Themes

The easiest way to personalize your desktop in Windows 7 is to select a theme. When you select a theme, you select one or more desktop background images; a color for window borders, the Start menu, and the taskbar; a collection of sounds to play to signal system tasks, such as shutting down Windows; and a screen saver. If your computer and edition of Windows are designed to run with Aero, you can choose an Aero theme to personalize your computer. Otherwise, you can use the Windows 7 Basic theme, which is also a good choice if your computer is performing slowly. In addition, Windows provides a few high-contrast themes, which make the items on your screen easier to see. When you use a Windows 7 Aero or Basic theme, you can set up a slide show (a rotating series of pictures) to use as your desktop background. You can use your own pictures or pictures that Windows provides as part of a theme.

Selecting a Theme

- Open the Control Panel window and switch to Category view, if necessary.
- Click Appearance and Personalization.
- Click Personalization.
- Click a theme.

Holly's computer and edition of Windows support Aero themes, so you offer to show her some Aero themes to see if one would be suitable for Magellan Cartography.

To change the theme:

1. In the Appearance and Personalization window, click **Personalization** to open the Personalization window, which lists many types of themes. See Figure 3-19. Your Personalization window might differ. Note your current theme so you can restore it later.

Figure 3-19 Personalization window

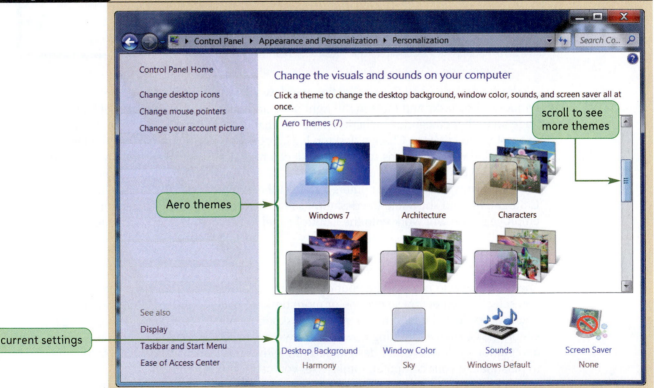

2. If necessary, scroll the themes, and then click **Landscapes**. The desktop background changes to a landscape image, the taskbar and window borders change color, and a sound plays (if your speakers are turned on).

Trouble? If the Landscapes theme does not appear in your Personalization window, your computer might not be able to use Aero themes. Read but do not perform Step 2.

3. Minimize the Personalization window.

Holly thinks the Landscapes theme might work for her, but she wants to display a different landscape image. You'll show her how to do so by changing the desktop background.

Changing Your Desktop's Background

You can change the desktop background, or its **wallpaper**, to display one of the images that Windows 7 provides, or you can select your own graphic to use as wallpaper. When you change the background, you are not placing a new object on the desktop; you are only changing its appearance. You can also determine how you want to position the picture—resized to fill the screen, resized to fit the screen, stretched across the screen (which might distort the image), tiled (repeated across the screen), or centered. If you center the wallpaper on the screen, you can select a color to frame the background image.

You and Holly decide to examine the desktop backgrounds that Windows 7 provides to find a suitable landscape image.

To change the desktop background:

1. Click the **Control Panel** button 🖼 on the taskbar to restore the Personalization window, and then click **Desktop Background** to open the Desktop Background window. See Figure 3-20. All six Landscapes images are selected because Windows uses all the images for the desktop slide show. Your Desktop Background window might differ. Note your current desktop background so you can restore it later.

Figure 3-20 ▶ Desktop Background window

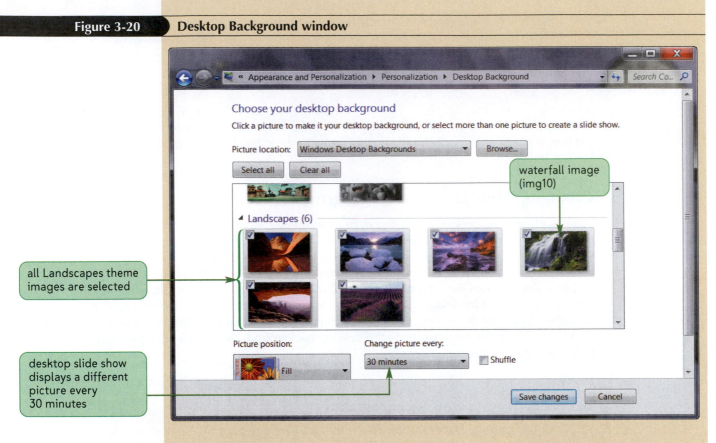

all Landscapes theme images are selected

desktop slide show displays a different picture every 30 minutes

2. Scroll the wallpapers as necessary, and then click the **waterfall** image in the Landscapes category. (The ScreenTip indicates this image is named img10.) Windows displays the image you selected on the desktop. Now only the waterfall image is selected in the Landscapes category of themes.

3. Minimize the Desktop Background window to see the new background image.

TIP

You can display any picture saved on your computer as your desktop background by right-clicking the picture, and then clicking Set as desktop background.

After examining the desktop, Holly doesn't think the waterfall image is right for her company after all. She mentions that she has an image file of historical maps that she has used in marketing materials. That image might be right for the desktop background.

You'll show Holly how to display her graphic as the desktop background.

To use a graphic image as a desktop background:

1. Click the **Control Panel** button 🖼 on the taskbar to restore the Desktop Background window.

2. Click the **Browse** button near the top of the window to open the Browse For Folder dialog box.

3. Expand the **Libraries** folder, expand the **Pictures** library, expand the **My Pictures** folder, and then click the **Hawaii Maps** folder.

4. Click the **OK** button to add the images in the Hawaii Maps folder to the Desktop Background window.

5. All the image files are selected when you first add them to the Desktop Background window, so click the **Clear all** button to clear the selection.

6. Double-click the **Navigation** image file, the one displaying a spyglass. The Navigation image appears on the desktop.

7. Minimize the Personalization window. See Figure 3-21.

| Figure 3-21 | Navigation image as the desktop background |

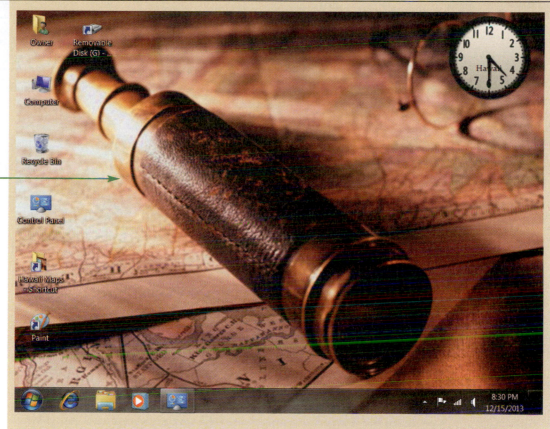

Holly's image used as a desktop background

Holly likes the Navigation wallpaper but comments that the color of the taskbar is not coordinated with that wallpaper. She also wants to change the font of the desktop icon labels to match the font Magellan Cartography uses in its marketing materials, which is Palatino. You'll show her how to change the window colors and the font of the desktop elements.

Changing Desktop Colors and Fonts

Besides changing the desktop background, you can use the Window Color tool in the Personalization window to set the color of windows, the Start menu, and the taskbar. Each theme uses a particular color for window borders, the Start menu, and the taskbar. You can change this color using the Window Color and Appearance window. For example, the Windows 7 Aero theme uses Sky by default for the window borders, Start menu, and taskbar, though you can change this to another color, such as Slate.

You can also use the Window Color and Appearance window to change the properties of the text for Windows elements, including icons, window title bars, and buttons. For example, you can increase the size or change the font of the text for desktop icons.

To change the window colors and icon font:

1. Click the **Control Panel** button 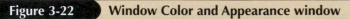 on the taskbar to restore the Personalization window.

2. Near the bottom of the window, click **Window Color**. The Window Color and Appearance window opens. See Figure 3-22. Note the current window color so you can restore it later.

Figure 3-22   **Window Color and Appearance window**

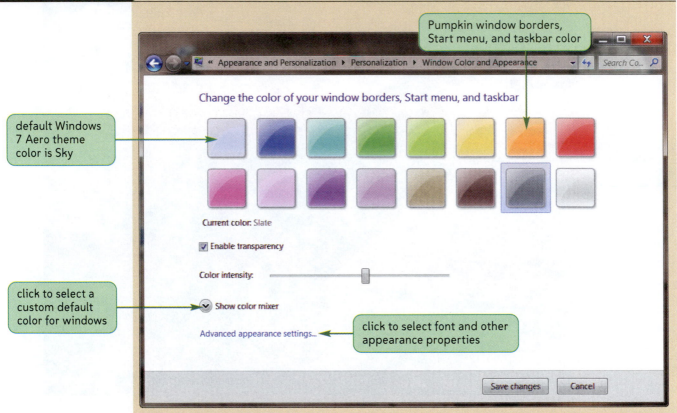

3. Click **Pumpkin**, which is the second color square from the right in the first row. The title bar and border change to pumpkin, which coordinates with Holly's Navigation wallpaper.

   Now you want to change the font for the desktop icon labels.

4. Click **Advanced appearance settings**. The Window Color and Appearance dialog box opens. See Figure 3-23.

Figure 3-23   **Window Color and Appearance dialog box**

click to select a desktop item to change

click to change the font of the selected item

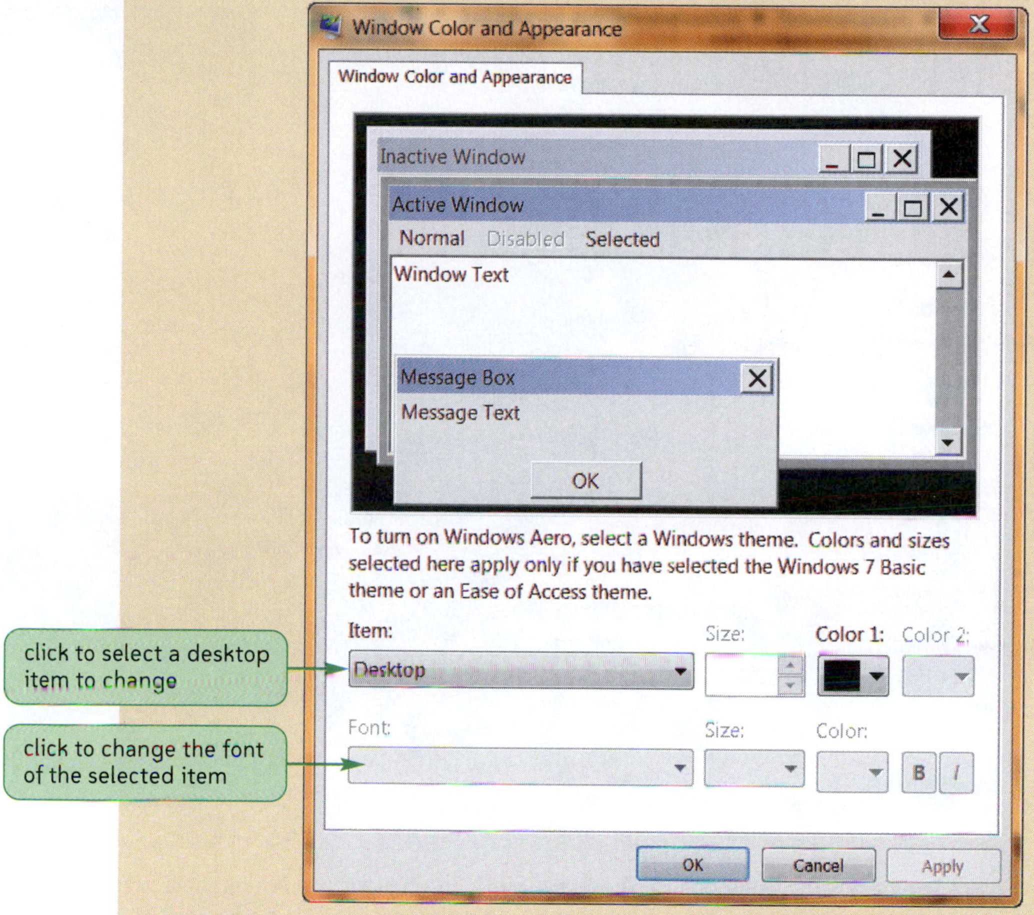

5. Click the **Item** button (which currently displays *Desktop*), and then click **Icon**. The controls for selecting font properties become active.

6. Click the **Font** button (which currently displays *Segoe UI*), scroll up, and then click **Palatino Linotype**.

7. Click the **OK** button to close the Window Color and Appearance dialog box.

8. Click the **Save changes** button to close the Window Color and Appearance window and apply your changes to the desktop, and then minimize the Personalization window. See Figure 3-24.

Figure 3-24 Personalized desktop

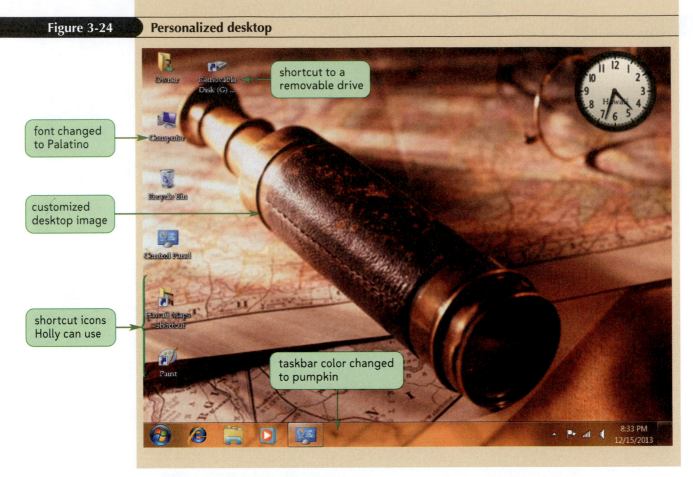

font changed to Palatino

customized desktop image

shortcut icons Holly can use

shortcut to a removable drive

taskbar color changed to pumpkin

The desktop is now personalized for Holly. It displays the Navigation wallpaper, pumpkin window elements, and Palatino icon labels. Holly's desktop does not include a screen saver, so you'll add one next.

Activating a Screen Saver

A screen saver blanks the screen or displays a moving design whenever you haven't worked with the computer for a specified period of time. Screen savers are entertaining and handy for hiding your data from the eyes of others if you step away from your computer. When a screen saver is on, you restore your desktop by moving your mouse or pressing a key. Windows 7 comes with several screen savers. Some show an animated design and others play a slide show of the pictures stored on your computer.

You can select how long you want the computer to sit idle before the screen saver starts. Most users find settings between 3 and 10 minutes to be the most convenient. You can change this using the options on the Screen Saver Settings dialog box.

INSIGHT

Using a Screen Saver for Security

To enhance the security of your computer and prevent unauthorized people from accessing your files, take advantage of a security setting available in the Screen Saver Settings dialog box. If you select the On resume, display logon screen check box in this dialog box, the screen saver will request your user name and password before displaying your desktop. This means that only you and other people who know your user name and password can work with your desktop and files.

Holly wants to examine the screen savers that Windows provides and then choose the most appropriate one for her company.

To activate a screen saver:

1. Click the **Control Panel** button 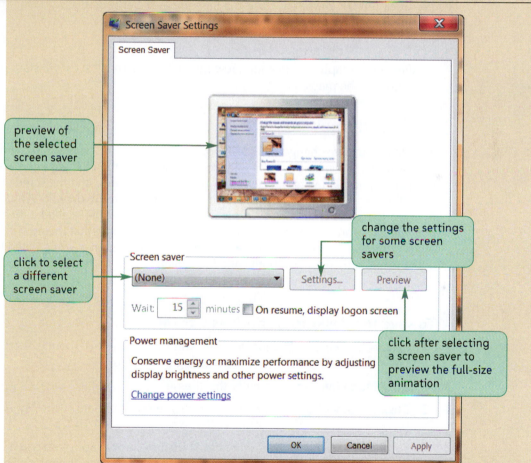 on the taskbar to restore the Personalization window. In the Personalization window, click **Screen Saver**. The Screen Saver Settings dialog box opens. See Figure 3-25. Note the name of the current screen saver so you can restore it later.

Figure 3-25   Screen Saver Settings dialog box

preview of the selected screen saver

change the settings for some screen savers

click to select a different screen saver

click after selecting a screen saver to preview the full-size animation

2. Click the **Screen saver** button, which currently displays *(None)*, to display the screen savers installed on your computer.

3. Click **Ribbons**. The animated screen saver plays in the Preview window. Holly likes that screen saver, but it's not appropriate for her desktop theme. You suggest the Photos screen saver, which plays a slide show of the pictures and videos stored in the Pictures library, by default. You can change this to any location on the computer, including the Hawaii Maps folder.

4. Click the **Screen saver** arrow, and then click **Photos**. The preview window plays a slide show of the graphic files stored in the Pictures library, including those in the Hawaii Maps folder.

5. To restrict the screen saver to display photos in the Hawaii Maps folder only, click the **Settings** button to open the Photos Screen Saver Settings dialog box. You use this dialog box to specify which files to include in the slide show and other settings, such as the slide show speed.

6. Click the **Browse** button. The Browse For Folder dialog box opens.

7. Expand the **Pictures** library and the **My Pictures** folder, if necessary, click the **Hawaii Maps** folder, and then click the **OK** button.

8. Click the **Save** button to close the Photos Screen Saver Settings dialog box. Now only the pictures in the Hawaii Maps folder appear in the Preview window.

9. Click the **OK** button to close the Screen Saver Settings dialog box.

10. Minimize the Personalization window.

After your computer is idle for a few minutes, the screen saver will start, playing a slide show of the maps.

Saving Themes

Now that you have changed the desktop, you can save the settings as a theme. If you save your current settings as a theme, you can apply all the changes—the Navigation wallpaper, pumpkin window elements, Palatino icon labels, and the screen saver—at the same time, without selecting the individual settings again. By default, Windows stores the theme in a system folder. You can also create a theme file—called a theme pack—that you can store in a folder of your choice, and then share that theme with people on other Windows 7 computers. You will save the desktop settings you created for Holly as a theme and a theme pack, both called Magellan.

To save the desktop settings as a theme:

1. Restore the Personalization window, and then in the My Themes section, click **Save theme**. The Save Theme As dialog box opens.

2. Type **Magellan** as the name of this theme.

3. Click the **Save** button. The Magellan theme now appears in the My Themes section.

4. To save the theme so that others at Magellan Cartography can use it, right-click the **Magellan** theme in the Personalization window, and then click **Save theme for sharing** on the shortcut menu.

5. In the Save Theme Pack As dialog box, navigate to the **Hawaii Maps** folder in the Pictures library. In the File name text box, type **Magellan**.

6. Click the **Save** button. The Magellan theme pack is stored in the Hawaii Maps folder.

7. Close the Personalization window.

Next, you can explore the display properties that affect the sharpness of the images on your desktop.

Changing Display Settings

After working with the properties for the desktop background, theme, and screen saver, you're ready to explore the display properties that affect the computer monitor itself. The Screen Resolution window lets you control the display settings for your monitor, such as the size of the desktop and whether to use more than one monitor. Windows chooses the best display settings, including screen resolution and orientation, based on your monitor. **Screen resolution** refers to the clarity of the text and images on your screen. At higher resolutions, items appear sharper and smaller, so more items fit on the screen. At lower resolutions, fewer items fit on the screen, but they are larger and easier to see. At very low resolutions, however, images might have jagged edges. Selecting the best display settings for your monitor enhances your Windows experience.

INSIGHT

Selecting the Best Display Settings for Your Monitor

Display settings vary depending on whether you have a liquid crystal display (LCD) or cathode-ray tube (CRT) monitor. (Notebooks and other devices with flat screens often use LCD monitors, while desktop computers sometimes have CRT monitors.) Screen resolution is measured horizontally and vertically in **pixels**, short for *picture elements*, which are the tiny dots that make up a computer image. The recommended resolution for a CRT monitor depends on its size. For a 15-inch monitor, use 1024 x 768 (that is, 1024 pixels horizontally and 768 pixels vertically); for a 17-inch to 19-inch monitor, use 1280 x 1024; and for a 20-inch or larger monitor, use 1600 x 1200.

LCD monitors generally come in two shapes: a standard aspect ratio of 4:3 or a widescreen ratio of 16:9 or 16:10. (An **aspect ratio** is the ratio of the width to the height.) A widescreen monitor has a wider aspect ratio than a standard monitor. The resolutions available on your computer vary depending on your monitor. Standard LCD monitors have different options from widescreen monitors. All LCD monitors display the sharpest images and clearest text at a particular resolution, which is called their native resolution. For example, most 19-inch standard LCD monitors have a native resolution of 1280 x 1024. A 22-inch widescreen LCD monitor usually has a native resolution of 1680 x 1050. You can change the resolution to a lower setting, such as 1024 x 768, though the text might not be as clear as text displayed at the native resolution.

Changing the Size of the Desktop Area

You use the Screen Resolution window to change the display settings. This window has a Resolution button that you click to display a slider bar. You can drag the slider bar to increase or decrease the resolution, or sharpness, of the image.

To change the screen resolution:

1. Right-click the **desktop**, and then click **Screen resolution** on the shortcut menu to open the Screen Resolution window. Note the original setting on the Resolution button so you can restore it later.

2. To select the 1280 x 800 resolution, if it is not already selected, click the **Resolution** button, and then drag the slider to 1280 x 800. The settings appear as you drag. The preview area shows the relative size of the new resolution. See Figure 3-26.

Figure 3-26 **Changing the screen resolution**

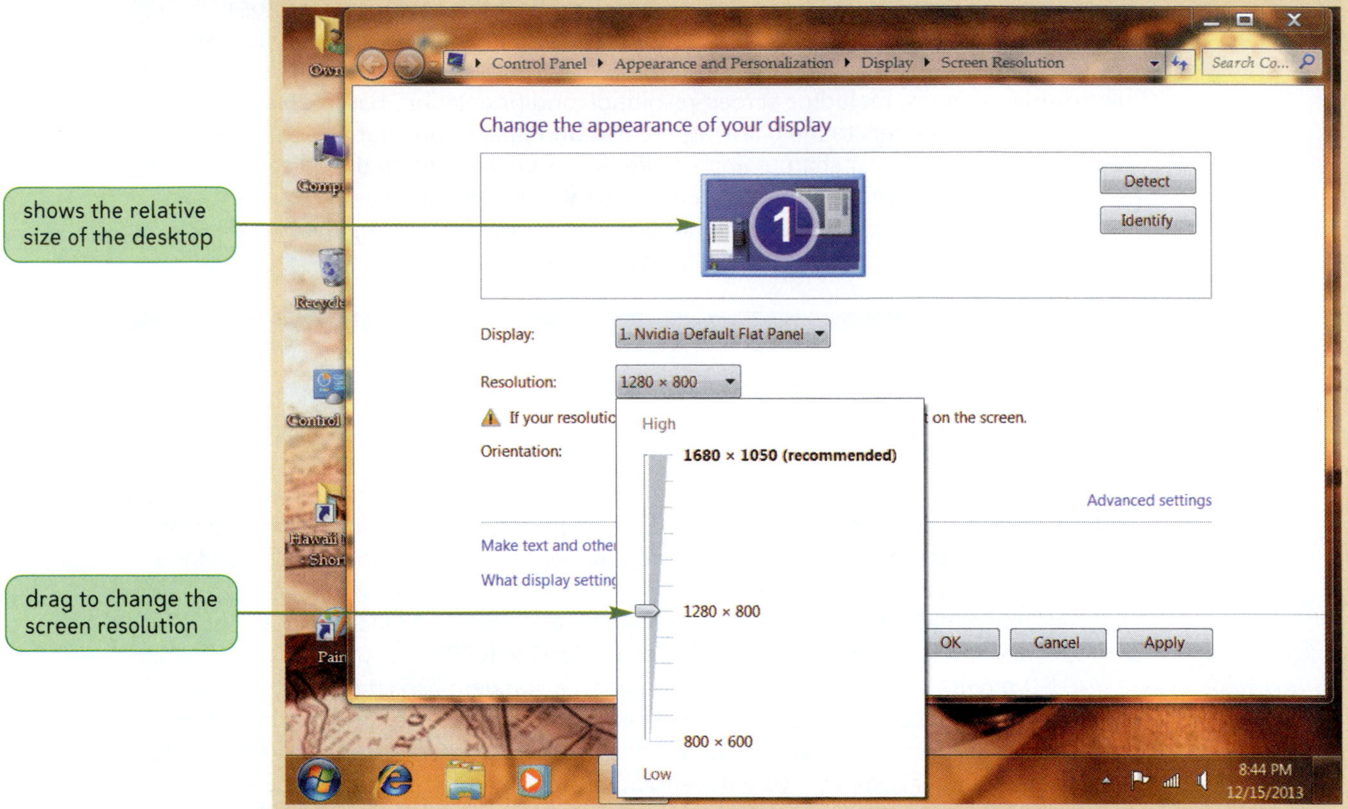

shows the relative size of the desktop

drag to change the screen resolution

Trouble? If your monitor does not display a 1280 × 800 resolution, choose a different resolution, such as 1280 × 720 or 1280 × 1024.

3. To select the 1024 × 768 resolution, if possible, drag the **Resolution** slider to that setting.

4. Return the **Resolution** slider to its original setting, and then click a blank area of the Screen Resolution window to close the list of resolution settings.

If you select a screen resolution recommended for your monitor, but find the text and objects are now too large or small, you can adjust the size of the text and objects.

Changing the Size of Text and Objects

Without adjusting your screen resolution, you can change the size of the text and objects such as icons on your screen. This means you can increase or decrease the size of text and objects while maintaining the native resolution of your monitor. For example, if you use a low screen resolution, such as 1024 × 768, you can make text and objects smaller to display more information on the screen. Conversely, if you use a high resolution, you can make text and objects easier to see by making them larger while retaining the sharpness of the high resolution.

Holly's computer uses the Medium – 125% setting, which is the default for her monitor. You'll view the other settings to see if they would improve her desktop.

To view the display settings:

1. In the Screen Resolution window, click **Make text and other items larger or smaller**. The Display window opens, showing the display settings: Smaller – 100%, Medium – 125%, and Larger – 150%.

2. Click **Smaller – 100%**, and then note the image in the Preview area. This setting would not noticeably improve Holly's desktop.

   Trouble? If Smaller – 100% is already selected, click Medium – 125%.

3. Click **Larger – 150%**, and then note the image in the Preview area. The desktop objects are much larger and easy to see, but they take up too much space.

4. Click the original setting, such as **Medium – 125%**, and then close the Display window without applying any changes.

So far, you have learned how to access the tools you need from the desktop by displaying system icons and customizing Windows gadgets. You have also learned how to create desktop shortcuts to a drive, folder, document, and program, and then organize all the icons on your desktop. In addition, you have learned how to work with the Control Panel to customize the desktop and personalize your Windows experience.

REVIEW

Session 3.1 Quick Check

1. _____ are icons that provide quick ways to start a program or open a file, folder, or other object without having to find its permanent location on your computer.

2. True or False. By default, you cannot change the image of the icons that appear on the Windows 7 desktop.

3. When you delete a shortcut icon, what happens to the file or resource it represents?

4. Name three gadgets you can display on the desktop.

5. Name three ways you can create a shortcut to the USB flash drive on your desktop.

6. What are the properties of an object?

7. What is a theme?

8. True or False. At low screen resolutions, items appear sharper and smaller, so more items fit on the screen.

SESSION 3.2 VISUAL OVERVIEW

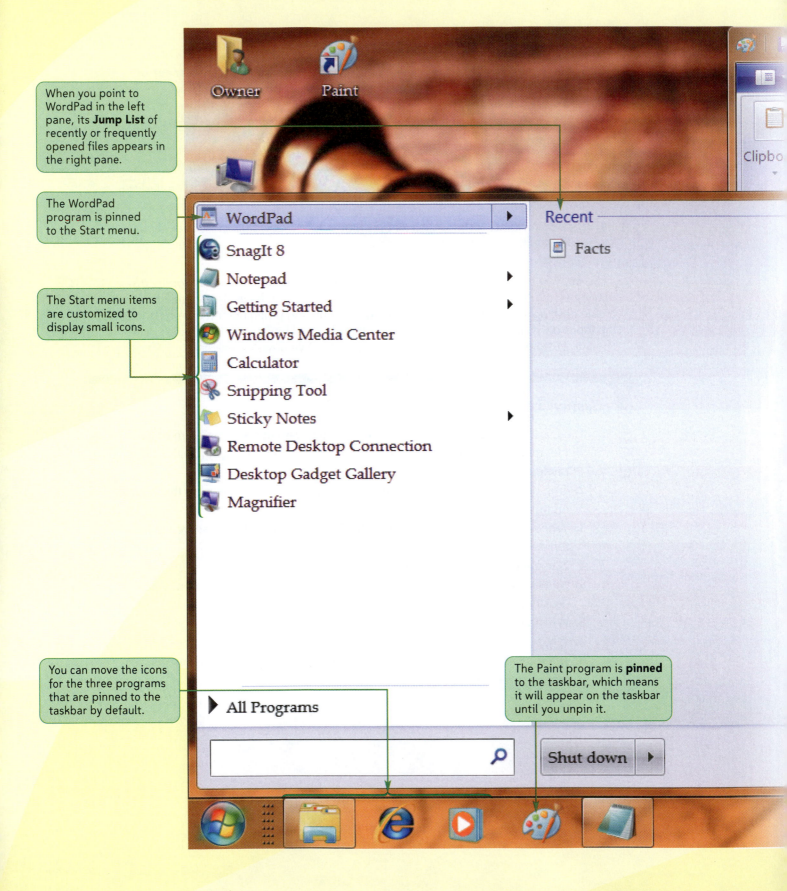

When you point to WordPad in the left pane, its **Jump List** of recently or frequently opened files appears in the right pane.

The WordPad program is pinned to the Start menu.

The Start menu items are customized to display small icons.

You can move the icons for the three programs that are pinned to the taskbar by default.

The Paint program is **pinned** to the taskbar, which means it will appear on the taskbar until you unpin it.

Owner

Paint

Clipbo

WordPad

SnagIt 8

Notepad

Getting Started

Windows Media Center

Calculator

Snipping Tool

Sticky Notes

Remote Desktop Connection

Desktop Gadget Gallery

Magnifier

Recent

Facts

All Programs

Shut down

MANAGING THE DESKTOP

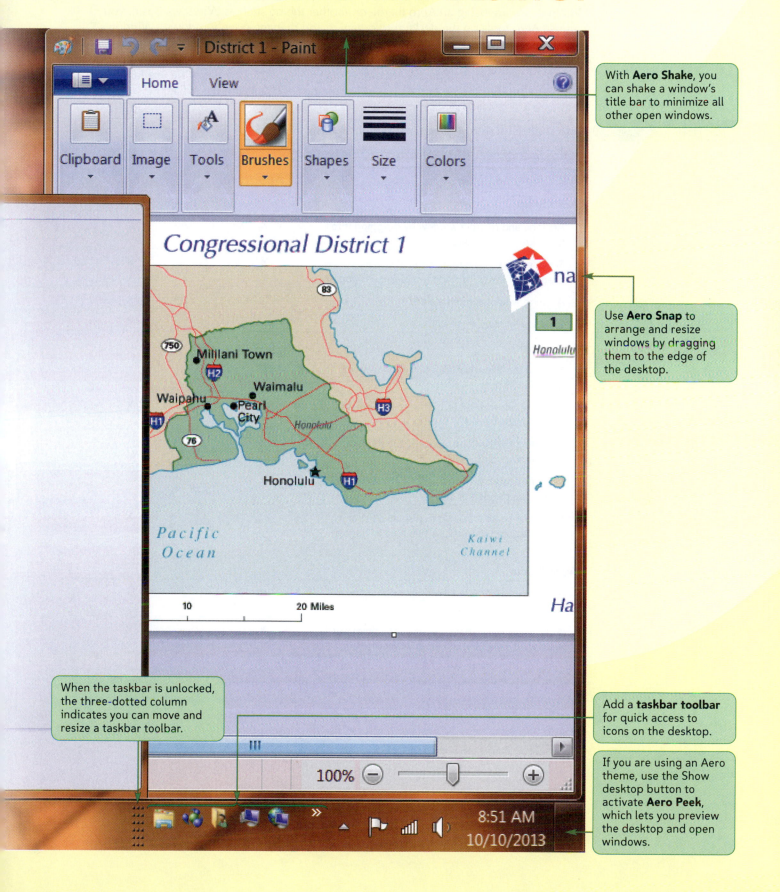

With **Aero Shake**, you can shake a window's title bar to minimize all other open windows.

Use **Aero Snap** to arrange and resize windows by dragging them to the edge of the desktop.

When the taskbar is unlocked, the three-dotted column indicates you can move and resize a taskbar toolbar.

Add a **taskbar toolbar** for quick access to icons on the desktop.

If you are using an Aero theme, use the Show desktop button to activate **Aero Peek**, which lets you preview the desktop and open windows.

District 1 - Paint

Home   View

Clipboard   Image   Tools   Brushes   Shapes   Size   Colors

Congressional District 1

Mililani Town

Waimalu

Waipahu   Pearl City

Honolulu

Pacific Ocean

Kaiwi Channel

10   20 Miles

100%

8:51 AM
10/10/2013

Managing the Desktop with Aero Tools

Whether you are using an Aero theme or another theme such as Windows Basic, you can use Aero tools on the desktop to organize and manage open windows. (Windows 7 Home Premium, Professional, and Ultimate editions include Aero themes, but you need certain graphics hardware to display them correctly. See the Microsoft Web site at *www.microsoft.com* for specific requirements.) Figure 3-27 compares the available Aero tools with an Aero theme and with another theme such as Windows Basic.

Figure 3-27   Aero tools with Aero themes and Windows Basic

Aero Tool and Behavior	With Aero Theme	Without Aero Theme
Aero Snap		
Arrange and resize a window by dragging it to the edge of the desktop.	X	X
Restore the window to its original size by dragging it away from the top of the desktop.	X	X
Arrange windows side by side.	X	X
Expand windows vertically.	X	X
Aero Peek		
Point to the Show desktop button to fade all open windows.	X	
Click the Show desktop button to minimize all open windows.	X	X
Point to a taskbar button to display thumbnails of open files.	X	
Point to a taskbar button, and then click a thumbnail to open or close a window.	X	
Point to a taskbar button to display a list of filenames, and then click a filename to open a window.		X
Aero Shake		
Shake a window to minimize all other open windows.	X	X
After using Aero Shake, restore the minimized windows by shaking the open window again.	X	X

With Aero Snap you can drag the title bar of an open window to the top of the desktop to maximize the window. To restore the window to its original size, drag the title bar away from the top of the desktop. You can also use Aero Snap to arrange windows side by side and expand windows vertically on the desktop.

Aero Peek also helps you manage open windows. To use Aero Peek to preview the desktop without minimizing windows, you use the Show desktop button on the far right side of the taskbar. When you point to the Show desktop button, any open windows fade from view to reveal the desktop. Move the mouse away from the Show desktop button when you want the windows to reappear. To minimize all open windows, click the Show desktop button.

To use Aero Peek to preview open windows without leaving your current window, you point to a taskbar button to display thumbnails of open files, and then point to a thumbnail. Any open windows fade to reveal the selected window, and then reappear when you move the pointer away from the thumbnail. To open the window you're previewing, you click the thumbnail.

Another handy tool for managing windows is Aero Shake. Use Aero Shake to quickly minimize all open windows on the desktop except the one you want to focus on—you don't have to minimize the windows one by one. Click and hold the title bar of the window you want to keep open, and then shake it by quickly dragging the window to the right and left. When you do, you minimize all the other open windows. To restore the minimized windows, shake the open window again.

Holly sometimes needs to work with two windows open so she can compare current and historical map information. You offer to show her how to quickly arrange windows side by side using Aero Snap.

To arrange windows side by side with Aero Snap:

1. Double-click the **Paint** shortcut icon on the desktop, and then double-click the **Hawaii Maps – Shortcut** icon.

   Trouble? If a window opens as maximized, click the Restore down button ▣ to resize the window.

2. Arrange the windows so that you can see parts of both windows, and then drag the **Volcano** image file from the Hawaii Maps folder window to the **Paint** window to open the Volcano image in Paint.

3. In the Hawaii Maps window, double-click **Facts** to open the Facts text document in Notepad.

4. If the Notepad window is maximized, click the **Restore down** button ▣ in the Notepad window.

5. Click the title bar of the Paint window to make it the active window, and then drag the **title bar** to the left of the desktop until an outline of the expanded window appears. See Figure 3-28.

Figure 3-28   Arranging windows with Aero Snap

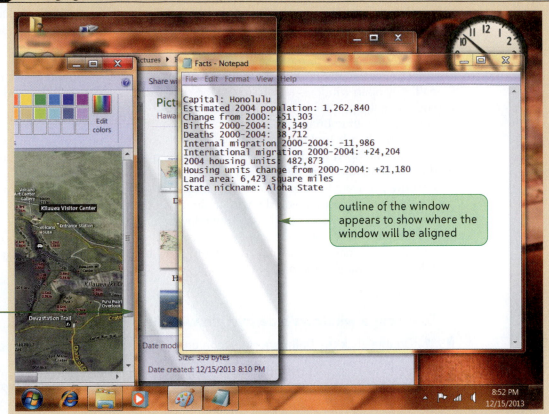

Paint window being dragged to the left side of the desktop

outline of the window appears to show where the window will be aligned

6. Release the mouse button to expand the Paint window to cover the left side of the desktop.

7. Drag the **title bar** of the Notepad window to the right of the desktop until an outline of the expanded window appears.

8. Release the mouse button to expand the Notepad window to cover the right side of the desktop. Now each window covers half of the desktop, with the Volcano - Paint window on the left and the Facts - Notepad window on the right.

Holly can use Aero Snap when she needs to work with two windows side by side. However, she typically has many windows open, and often has to stop working on a map to manage those windows. For example, she might open a few more Hawaiian map files and then call Sarah in Hawaii to verify a fact. She'd like to quickly view the desktop to check the time in Hawaii on her Clock gadget. She also wants to know how to briefly display a particular window to view its contents. You'll show her how to use Aero Peek to perform both tasks.

To use Aero Peek:

1. Point to the **Show desktop** button ▌ on the taskbar until the three open windows fade from view and reveal the desktop. See Figure 3-29.

Figure 3-29   Previewing the desktop with Aero Peek

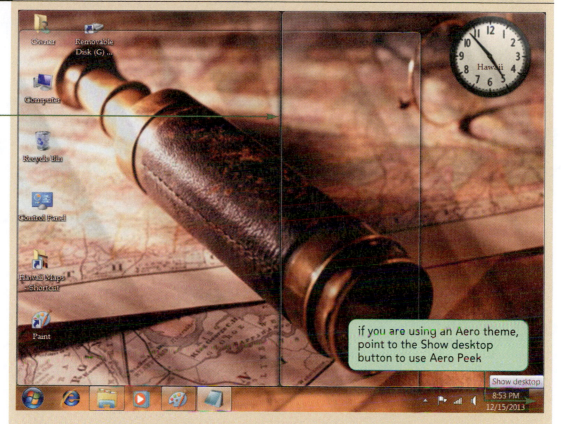

open windows fade and display only their outlines so you can preview the desktop

if you are using an Aero theme, point to the Show desktop button to use Aero Peek

2. Move the pointer away from the **Show desktop** button ▮ so the windows reappear.

3. Click the **Show desktop** button ▮ to minimize all the open windows, and then click the **Windows Explorer** button 🖼 on the taskbar to display the Hawaii Maps folder.

4. Drag the **District 1** file from the Hawaii Maps window to the **Paint** shortcut icon, and when the *Open with Paint* ScreenTip appears, release the mouse button to open the District 1 map in Paint.

    Trouble? If the District 1 file appears on the desktop, you moved the file. Press the Ctrl+Z keys to undo the move, and then repeat Step 4.

5. Minimize the Paint window.

6. Drag the **District 2** file from the Hawaii Maps window to the **Paint** shortcut icon, and when the *Open with Paint* ScreenTip appears, release the mouse button to open the District 2 map in Paint.

    Trouble? If the District 2 file appears on the desktop, you moved the file. Press the Ctrl+Z keys to undo the move, and then repeat Step 6.

7. Minimize the Paint window.

8. Point to the **Paint** taskbar button to display thumbnail previews of the three pictures open in Paint. See Figure 3-30.

Figure 3-30   ▶ **Previewing windows with Aero Peek**

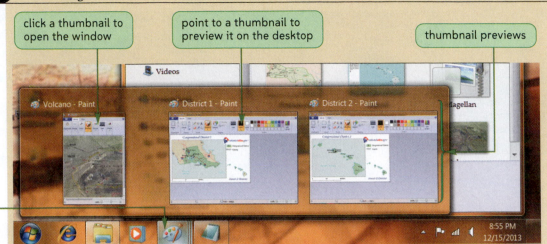

click a thumbnail to open the window

point to a thumbnail to preview it on the desktop

thumbnail previews

if you are using an Aero theme, point to the Paint taskbar button to preview the minimized windows

Trouble? If a list of filenames appears instead of thumbnails when you point to the Paint taskbar button, you are not using an Aero theme. Read but do not perform Steps 8 and 9.

▶ **9.** To preview the District 1 map, point to the **District 1** thumbnail. The other open windows fade so that the District 1 window is the only one open on the desktop.

▶ **10.** Click the **District 1** thumbnail to display District 1 and make it the active window.

Holly mentions that when she needs to focus on the contents of a window, she likes to minimize all the other open windows. You suggest she use Aero Shake to do so.

To use Aero Shake:

▶ **1.** Point to the **title bar** of the District 1 window, hold down the mouse button, and then quickly drag to the right and left to shake the window. The District 1 window remains open while all the other open windows are minimized.

▶ **2.** To restore the minimized windows, shake the **District 1** window again.

▶ **3.** Click the **Show desktop** button ▮ to minimize all open windows.

You have used the taskbar to manage open windows. Next, you'll learn how to modify the taskbar to work effectively on the desktop.

Modifying the Taskbar

As you know, the bar that contains the Start button and appears by default at the bottom of the desktop is the taskbar. The taskbar is divided into the following three sections:

- Start button: You are already familiar with the Start button, which you click to open the Start menu.
- Middle section: This section of the taskbar displays program buttons, which you click to manipulate windows.
- Notification area: The far-right section of the taskbar is the notification area, which shows the current time, program icons, and system status information. You have already used the Show desktop button on the right side of the notification area.

Figure 3-31 shows the taskbar with these default sections.

| Figure 3-31 | Default taskbar sections |

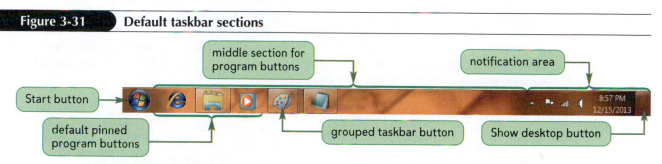

The middle section contains taskbar buttons for three programs by default: Internet Explorer, Windows Explorer, and Windows Media Player. (You will learn how to add programs to this section shortly.) In addition, Windows displays taskbar buttons for each open program. By default, each button is identified by an icon, not a text label, to conserve space. If you open another file in one of these programs, Windows groups the buttons for that program into a single button. In Figure 3-31, for example, a few windows are grouped on the Paint program button. The Paint icon appears on top, and the outlines of the open windows are stacked behind it.

As you saw when working with Aero Peek, when you point to a taskbar button and are using an Aero theme, Windows displays a thumbnail preview of the corresponding window. The preview is designed to help you identify a window by more than the title alone. If a window is playing a video or an animation, it also plays in the preview. When you point to a grouped taskbar button, Windows arranges the thumbnail previews in a row above the taskbar. You can click a thumbnail to open a window. To close a window, you point to a thumbnail until a Close button appears, and then you click the Close button.

You can personalize the taskbar to suit your preferences. For example, you can reorder the taskbar buttons by dragging them to a new location. You can also change the appearance of taskbar buttons by displaying button labels and specifying when buttons should be grouped together. To further customize the taskbar, you can change the size and position of the taskbar or hide it altogether. In addition, you can display toolbars on the taskbar. These toolbars can contain buttons for the icons on your desktop or for Web pages to which you want quick access.

PROSKILLS

Decision Making: Monitoring the Notification Area

The icons in the notification area of the taskbar let you access some computer settings, such as the system time. The icons also communicate the status of programs running in the background. Background programs are those programs that Windows runs to provide a service, such as an Internet connection. By default, the notification area displays only a few icons, which are usually determined by your computer manufacturer and the programs installed on your computer. One of these icons (the flag) is for the Action Center, a window that displays notification messages about security and maintenance settings. Briefly read these messages when they appear so you can make decisions about your computer. You can also point to the Action Center icon to display a summary of Action Center issues, and then click the flag icon to open the Action Center, which categorizes messages by color. Items highlighted by a red bar are important and need your immediate attention. For example, a message reminding you to update an antivirus program is flagged as important. Items highlighted by a yellow bar are suggestions you can address later, such as recommended maintenance tasks. To respond to Action Center messages, click the Action Center icon.

In addition, you might receive notifications from other programs running in the background about a change in status, such as the addition of a new hardware device. Read the notification to find out whether you need to respond to or correct a problem. You can also point to any icon in the notification area to display its status or name. (You might need to click the Show hidden icons button on the taskbar to display all the icons in the notification area.) For example, if you're having trouble hearing sounds on your computer, point to the Speakers icon to determine whether you need to turn up the volume.

Now you can personalize the taskbar on Holly's computer. You'll start by showing her how to pin items to the taskbar.

Pinning Programs to the Taskbar

Internet Explorer, Windows Explorer, and Windows Media Player are pinned to the middle section of the taskbar by default. If you use another program often, you can also pin that to the taskbar as an alternative to creating a program shortcut on the desktop. In fact, pinning a program to the taskbar increases your efficiency because the pinned program is always visible, and you can start it with a single click. You can rearrange the buttons for pinned and running programs on the taskbar to suit your preferences.

Pinning Programs to the Taskbar

- If the program is already running, right-click the program button, and then click Pin this program to taskbar.

or

- If the program is not running, click the Start button, locate the program in the Start menu, right-click the program icon, and then click Pin to Taskbar.

Because Holly frequently uses Paint, you suggest she pin Paint to the taskbar. This task is particularly easy because Paint is already running and its button appears on the taskbar.

To pin Paint to the taskbar:

1. Right-click the **Paint** program button 🖌 on the taskbar, and then click **Pin this program to taskbar**.

2. To confirm that Paint is pinned to the taskbar, right-click the **Paint** program button 🖌 on the taskbar again, and then click **Close all windows**. All the Paint windows close, but the Paint program button remains on the taskbar.

In addition to starting a program from the taskbar, you can use a pinned item to open favorite and recent files from that program. To do so, you use a Jump List, a list of recently or frequently opened files, folders, or Web sites. When you right-clicked the Paint program button in the previous steps, you displayed its Jump List, which included the image files you opened for Holly, such as District 1, District 2, and Volcano. If you want to make sure you can always access one of those files, you can pin it to the Jump List. To open a pinned file, you right-click the Paint program button on the taskbar to display its Jump List, and then click a recent or favorite file you want to open in Paint.

Holly plans to use the Volcano image file often, so you'll show her how to pin the file to the Paint program button's Jump List and then open the file from the taskbar.

To pin a file to the Paint program button's Jump List:

1. Right-click the **Paint** program button 🖌 on the taskbar to display its Jump List. See Figure 3-32.

Figure 3-32 Paint program button's Jump List

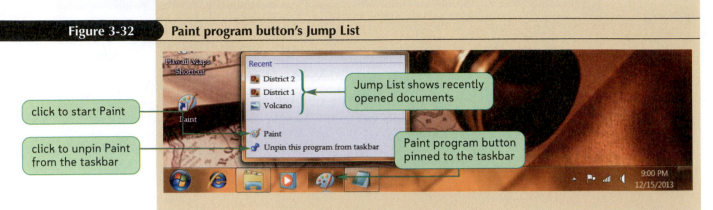

click to start Paint

click to unpin Paint from the taskbar

Jump List shows recently opened documents

Paint program button pinned to the taskbar

Trouble? If your Jump List contains different files, continue to Step 2.

2. Point to **Volcano**, and then click the **Pin to this list** icon 📌 to pin Volcano to the Jump List. See Figure 3-33.

Figure 3-33 File pinned to the Paint Jump List

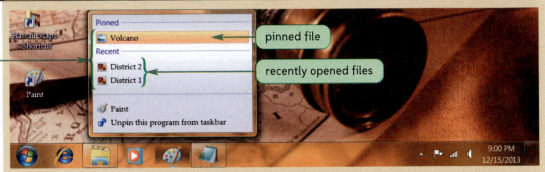

click a file to open it in Paint

pinned file

recently opened files

TIP

To unpin a file, open the Jump List, point to the filename, click the Unpin from this list icon, and then click Unpin from this list.

Trouble? If your Jump List does not include the Volcano file, click the Windows Explorer button 📁 on the taskbar, drag the Volcano file to the Paint shortcut icon to open the image in Paint, save the file, close Paint, minimize the folder window, and then repeat Step 2.

3. To open the Volcano file in Paint, click **Volcano** on the Jump List. Paint starts and opens the Volcano image file.

4. Minimize the Paint window.

Holly says that the changes you made to the taskbar will help her work more efficiently. She'd also like to adjust the position of the taskbar buttons. She frequently uses the Windows Explorer button, and she asks you to move it just to the right of the Start button for easy access.

To move a taskbar button:

1. Point to the **Windows Explorer** button 📁 on the taskbar, and then drag it to the left.

2. When it appears just to the right of the Start button, release the mouse button. See Figure 3-34.

Figure 3-34   **Moving a taskbar button**

Windows Explorer
button moved to
the left

Trouble? If the Hawaii Maps folder window opens, minimize the window.

You can move any taskbar button, even those for programs that are not pinned to the taskbar. When you do, you move the entire button group so the open files remain grouped on a program button.

Moving and Resizing the Taskbar

When you first install Windows 7, the taskbar is locked in its position at the bottom of the desktop. That way, as you learn your way around Windows, you always have access to the Start menu so you can start programs and shut down Windows. Before you can move or resize the taskbar, however, you must unlock it. You can do so by right-clicking the taskbar to open its shortcut menu, and then clicking the Lock the taskbar command, which is listed with a check mark by default to indicate that it is selected. Clicking it removes the check mark, indicating the taskbar is no longer locked. Then you can move the taskbar to the sides or top of the desktop.

REFERENCE

Moving and Resizing the Taskbar

- Make sure the taskbar is unlocked. To unlock it, right-click any blank spot on the task-bar, and then click Lock the taskbar on the shortcut menu to remove the check mark.
- To move the taskbar, click a blank spot on the taskbar, hold down the left mouse button, and drag the taskbar to a new location (the top, bottom, left, or right edge of the desktop).
- To resize the taskbar, point to a taskbar border until a resize pointer appears, and then drag the border to a different height or width.

When Holly is working with graphics programs, she occasionally drags objects onto the taskbar by accident. You'll show her how to move the taskbar to the top of the desktop, where it's out of her way. Dragging the taskbar is slightly different from dragging a folder or window because a dim image of the taskbar does not appear as you drag it—it appears only after you release the mouse button when you're finished dragging. Before you can move the taskbar, however, you need to unlock it.

TIP

You can also select commands on the taskbar shortcut menu that let you cascade windows, stack them, or show them side by side.

To move the taskbar:

1. Right-click a blank spot on the taskbar, and then, if necessary, click **Lock the taskbar** on the shortcut menu to uncheck this command.

   Trouble? If the Lock the taskbar command is already unchecked, skip Step 1.

2. Drag the taskbar to the top of the desktop. See Figure 3-35. Notice that the icons on the desktop moved down slightly to make room for the newly positioned taskbar.

Figure 3-35 **Moving the taskbar to the top of the desktop**

taskbar at the top of the desktop

3. Drag the taskbar back down to the bottom of the desktop.

Holly thinks that if she pins programs to the taskbar and has many other programs running at the same time, the buttons for all those programs could fill up the middle section of the taskbar. You'll show her how to increase the size of the taskbar to make more room for taskbar buttons.

To increase the size of the taskbar:

1. Point to the upper edge of the taskbar until the pointer changes to ↕.

2. Drag up to double the height of the taskbar. See Figure 3-36.

Figure 3-36 **Resizing the taskbar**

taskbar is twice as high

3. Drag the upper border of the taskbar down to return it to its original height.

Besides changing the appearance of the taskbar, you can change taskbar properties, such as one that determines when the taskbar is displayed.

Setting Taskbar Appearance Properties

In addition to resizing and relocating the taskbar, you can set taskbar appearance properties using the Taskbar and Start Menu Properties dialog box. Using this dialog box, you can increase the amount of screen space available for your program windows by hiding the taskbar. In this case, the taskbar is not closed, removed, or minimized, but hidden either under the border of the desktop or under the program windows open on the desktop. It still remains active and accessible—you can point to the area of your screen where the taskbar would be located to redisplay the taskbar.

You can also use the Taskbar and Start Menu Properties dialog box to determine whether to display small icons on the taskbar, group similar taskbar buttons, and use Aero Peek to preview the desktop.

You'll show Holly how to increase the amount of screen space by hiding the taskbar and using small icons.

To set taskbar appearance properties:

1. Right-click a blank area on the taskbar, and then click **Properties** on the shortcut menu. The Taskbar and Start Menu Properties dialog box opens. See Figure 3-37.

Figure 3-37   **Taskbar and Start Menu Properties dialog box**

taskbar settings

this setting is available only if you are using an Aero theme

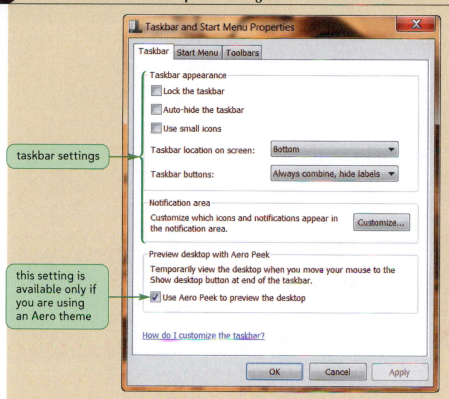

Note the options currently selected in this dialog box so you can restore them later.

2. Click to select the **Auto-hide the taskbar** check box, and then click the **Apply** button. Windows hides the taskbar.

3. Point to the bottom of the desktop to redisplay the taskbar.

4. In the Taskbar and Start Menu Properties dialog box, click the **Auto-hide the taskbar** check box to remove the check mark, and then click the **Apply** button. The taskbar appears in its default position at the bottom of the desktop.

5. Click to select the **Use small icons** check box, and then click the **Apply** button. The taskbar icons shrink and the height of the taskbar decreases accordingly.

6. Click the **Use small icons** check box to remove the check mark, and then click the **Apply** button to display the taskbar icons at their default size.

7. Make sure the options in the Taskbar and Start Menu Properties dialog box are in their original state, and then click the **OK** button to close the dialog box.

Knowing how to resize the taskbar itself and its icons will be helpful when you perform the next task—adding toolbars to the taskbar.

Working with Taskbar Toolbars

As you probably know, a toolbar displays buttons representing tasks you can perform in a program. Besides pinning programs and files to the taskbar, you can use taskbar toolbars to access tools such as the Address bar, which you can use to visit Web sites or open a folder on your computer. Figure 3-38 describes the toolbars you can include on the taskbar. Your taskbar might be able to display additional toolbars.

Figure 3-38 Taskbar toolbars

Taskbar Toolbar	Description
Address	Use to open any Web page or computer location you specify.
Desktop	Use to access items on your desktop, such as the Recycle Bin and Computer, from the taskbar.
Links	Use to access links to Web pages and add Web links by dragging them to the toolbar.
New	Create a custom taskbar toolbar to store shortcuts to folders, documents, or other objects you use often.
Tablet PC Input Panel	Use to open the Tablet PC Input Panel, a Windows tool that lets you write directly on your computer.

The New taskbar toolbar is a custom toolbar you can create to store shortcuts to folders, documents, or other objects you use often. In fact, you can move all the shortcut icons you created from the desktop to a custom taskbar toolbar.

Adding Toolbars to the Taskbar

You can add several toolbars to the taskbar by using the Toolbars tab on the Taskbar and Start Menu Properties dialog box, or by using the taskbar's shortcut menu.

Holly often has several programs running at once, filling up the screen and hiding the desktop. Although she can now use Aero Shake and Aero Peek to quickly access or clear the desktop, she also wants to use the desktop icons when her program windows are open. You suggest that she place a Desktop toolbar on her taskbar, which contains all the icons on the desktop plus those for common locations such as the Libraries folder. Although it displays only its name, Desktop, by default, the Desktop toolbar includes an expand button that you can click to display all of the icons that appear on the desktop. You can also resize the Desktop toolbar, though it typically takes up a lot of room on the taskbar because it shows the toolbar title and both icon names and images by default. You'll show Holly how to add the Desktop toolbar to the taskbar, display only the toolbar icons, and then use it to open her personal folder, which is one of the icons on her desktop.

To display and modify the Desktop toolbar:

1. Right-click a blank area of the taskbar, point to **Toolbars** on the shortcut menu, and then click **Desktop**. The Desktop toolbar appears on the taskbar. See Figure 3-39.

Figure 3-39 Displaying the Desktop toolbar

Desktop toolbar

click to display all the icons on the Desktop toolbar

2. Click the **expand** button ⁞ on the Desktop toolbar to display a menu of its icons.

3. Click a blank area on the desktop to close the menu, point to the left border of the Desktop toolbar until the pointer changes to ⟷, and then drag left until you see the first item on the toolbar, such as Libraries. As you can see, the icon name and image take up a lot of taskbar space.

4. To display only icon images, not names, right-click a blank area of the Desktop toolbar (such as above the *Desktop* title), and then click **Show Text** to remove the check mark. Now the toolbar shows only icon images, not names.

   Trouble? If the Show Text command does not appear on the shortcut menu, you probably right-clicked one of the buttons on the Desktop toolbar. Be sure to click a blank area on the Desktop toolbar.

   Trouble? If the Show Text command does not appear with a check mark on the shortcut menu, skip Step 4.

5. Right-click a blank area on the Desktop toolbar again, and then click **Show title** on the shortcut menu to uncheck this command.

   Trouble? If the Show title command does not appear with a check mark on the shortcut menu, skip Step 5.

6. Click **your user folder** icon 🖳 on the Desktop toolbar menu to open this folder, and then close the folder window.

   Figure 3-40 displays the final appearance of the toolbar. Note that each item on the desktop is matched by an item in the toolbar, and that the icons are smaller than those pinned to the taskbar.

Figure 3-40   **Modified Desktop toolbar**

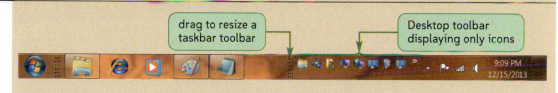

drag to resize a taskbar toolbar

Desktop toolbar displaying only icons

Now Holly can access all the items on her desktop while leaving windows open. Next, you can turn to the other major element you can open from the taskbar—the Start menu.

Customizing the Start Menu

Most of the items on the Start menu are created for you by Windows 7 or by the various programs you install. Windows 7 personalizes the left pane of the Start menu as you work to show the programs you use most frequently. However, you also can determine the content and appearance of your Start menu, removing items you don't use and adding those you do. You can pin icons to the Start menu for programs you use most often, as you can on the taskbar, and use Jump Lists to access recent or favorite files, folders, and Web sites. Finally, you can organize the Start menu and control its appearance to use it most effectively.

Controlling the Appearance of the Start Menu

The picture associated with the current user appears at the top of the Start menu. When you point to commands in the right pane of the Start menu, this picture changes. For example, when you point to the Documents command, the picture shows an image of a document. Although you can't change the images associated with commands, you can change the user picture to personalize the Start menu.

You'll select a user picture for Holly that fits the appearance of her desktop.

To change the user picture on the Start menu:

1. Click the **Start** button  on the taskbar, and then click the **user picture** at the top of the right pane. The User Accounts window opens. See Figure 3-41.

Figure 3-41   **User Accounts window**

Control Panel ▸ User Accounts and Family Safety ▸ User Accounts

Control Panel Home

Manage your credentials

Create a password reset disk

Link online IDs

Manage your file encryption certificates

Configure advanced user profile properties

Change my environment variables

Make changes to your user account

Create a password for your account

Change your picture

Change your account name

Change your account type

Manage another account

Change User Account Control settings

Owner
Administrator

click to change the user picture

current user picture

2. Click **Change your picture**. The Change Your Picture window opens, displaying a collection of pictures you can use on the Welcome screen and Start menu.

3. Click the image of the **starfish**, which is the second picture in the collection.

4. Scroll down, if necessary, and then click the **Change Picture** button.

5. Click the **Start** button  again to verify the new user picture, and then point to the commands in the right pane to see the picture change to reflect the current command.

6. Click the **Start** button  to close the Start menu.

7. Close the User Accounts window.

Another feature of the Start menu you can control is whether the menu displays small or large icons. The default is to use large icons, but you can fit more commands on the Start menu by changing to the smaller icon style. Because the Start button is considered part of the taskbar, you change settings for the Start menu using the same dialog box you used earlier to control the appearance of the taskbar.

To change the size of the icons on the Start menu:

1. Right-click the **Start** button  on the taskbar, and then click **Properties** on the shortcut menu. The Taskbar and Start Menu Properties dialog box opens to the Start Menu tab.

2. Click the **Customize** button. The Customize Start Menu dialog box opens. See Figure 3-42.

Figure 3-42	Customize Start Menu dialog box

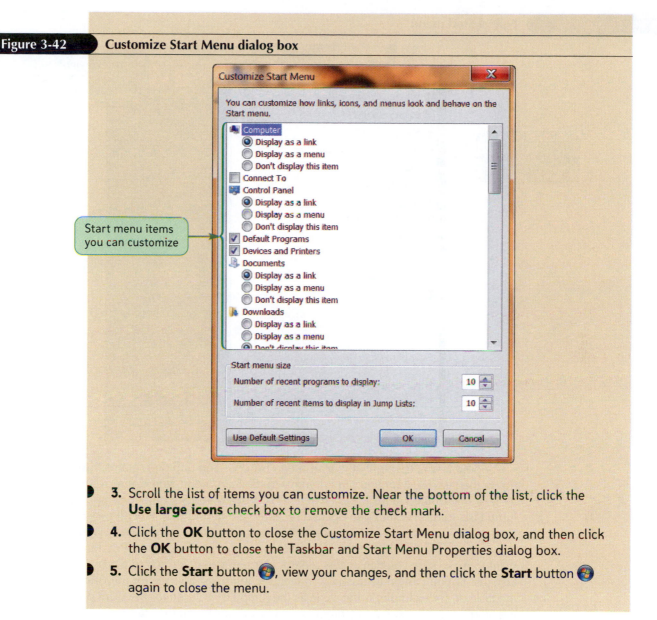

3. Scroll the list of items you can customize. Near the bottom of the list, click the **Use large icons** check box to remove the check mark.

4. Click the **OK** button to close the Customize Start Menu dialog box, and then click the **OK** button to close the Taskbar and Start Menu Properties dialog box.

5. Click the **Start** button, view your changes, and then click the **Start** button again to close the menu.

Now that you have plenty of room on the Start menu, you can learn how to add items to it.

Pinning Programs to the Start Menu

As you open programs, Windows 7 adds their shortcuts to the left pane of the Start menu. For example, if you use WordPad often, Windows 7 adds a WordPad shortcut to the left pane of the Start menu. The items on the right of the Start menu allow you to easily access locations and tools on your computer through dialog boxes or submenus. See Figure 3-43.

Figure 3-43 Typical Start menu

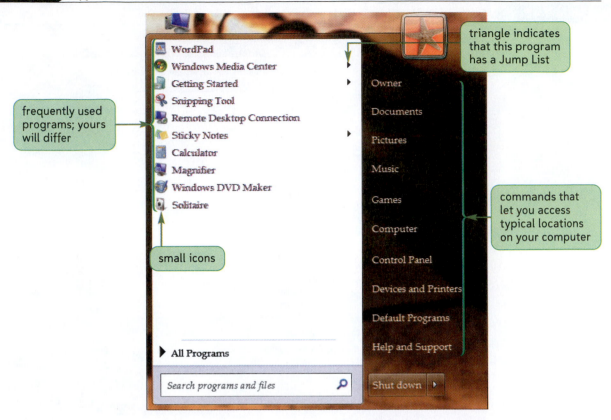

triangle indicates that this program has a Jump List

frequently used programs; yours will differ

commands that let you access typical locations on your computer

small icons

A popular way to modify the Start menu is to pin and unpin programs, just as you do on the taskbar. After you pin programs to the Start menu, you can move the program icons in the pinned items list to change their order. Some Start menu programs also have Jump Lists to display files you opened recently in that program. Not all programs on the Start menu can have Jump Lists—only those with a triangle, as shown in Figure 3-43, or those you pin to the Start menu. (Jump Lists do not appear in the All Programs list.) If you want to make sure you can access a particular file, you can pin it to a program's Jump List, just as you can on the taskbar. In fact, the Jump List you see for the Paint program on the taskbar, for example, is the same as the Jump List you see for the Paint program on the Start menu. You point to a program or click its arrow on the Start menu to display the program's Jump List in the right pane.

Besides personalizing the left pane of the Start menu, you can add and remove commands from the right pane of the Start menu. For example, you can add the Recent Items command to access all your recent files.

Holly uses WordPad for her word-processing tasks. Instead of clicking the Start button on the taskbar, pointing to All Programs, clicking the Accessories folder, and then clicking WordPad, you can pin WordPad to the Start menu for easy access.

To pin WordPad to the Start menu:

1. Click the **Start** button on the taskbar, point to **All Programs**, and then click the **Accessories** folder.

2. Right-click **WordPad**, and then click **Pin to Start Menu** on the shortcut menu.

3. Point to **Back** on the Start menu to verify that WordPad is now pinned to the top of the Start menu. See Figure 3-44.

TIP

To pin a folder to the Start menu, drag the folder from a window to the Start button.

Figure 3-44   **WordPad pinned to the Start menu**

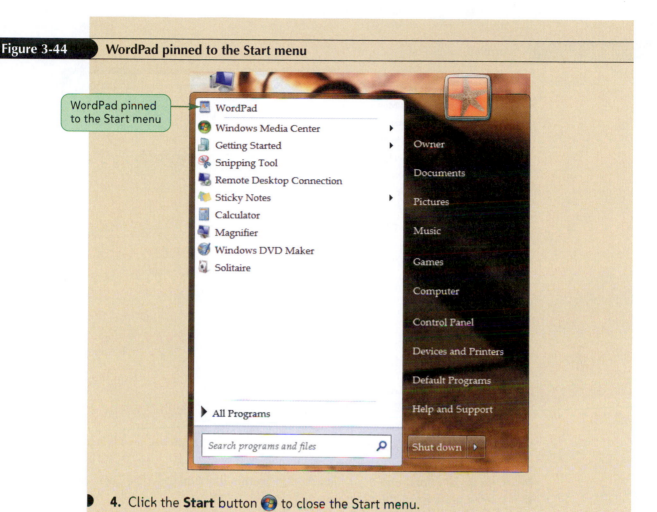

WordPad pinned to the Start menu

- WordPad
- Windows Media Center ▶
- Getting Started ▶
- Snipping Tool
- Remote Desktop Connection
- Sticky Notes ▶
- Calculator
- Magnifier
- Windows DVD Maker
- Solitaire

▶ All Programs

Search programs and files 🔍

Owner

Documents

Pictures

Music

Games

Computer

Control Panel

Devices and Printers

Default Programs

Help and Support

Shut down ▶

▶ **4.** Click the **Start** button 🟦 to close the Start menu.

Holly mentions that she would rather use WordPad than Notepad to open the Facts document because she prefers working with the WordPad editing tools. Next, you'll show her how to pin the Facts document to the WordPad Jump List.

To pin a document to the WordPad Jump List:

▶ **1.** Click the **Start** button 🟦 on the taskbar, and then click **WordPad** to start WordPad.

▶ **2.** Click the **WordPad menu** button ▣▾ , click **Open**, navigate to the Hawaii Maps folder in the Pictures library, and then double-click **Facts** to open the Facts document.

▶ **3.** Click the **Close** button ❌ to close WordPad.

▶ **4.** Click the **Start** button 🟦 on the taskbar, and then point to **WordPad** to display its Jump List. See Figure 3-45. The Facts document appears in the Jump List because you just opened it in WordPad.

| Figure 3-45 | WordPad Jump List |

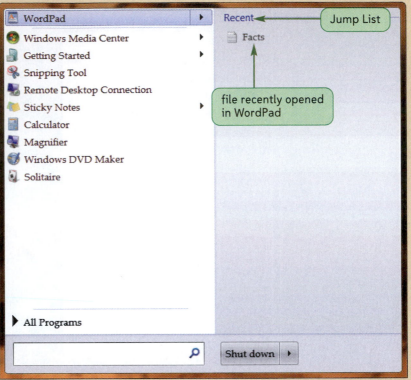

5. Point to **Facts**, and then click the **Pin to this list** icon ![pin]. The Facts document now appears in the Pinned section of the Jump List.

Besides pinning programs to the left pane of the Start menu, you can add commands to the right pane.

Adding Commands to the Right Pane of the Start Menu

You can add or remove items—such as the Computer, Control Panel, and Pictures commands—that appear on the right side of the Start menu. You can also change some items so that they appear as links or menus.

Holly wants to see how she could use the Start menu to access the Recent Items list, which displays a list of your recently used files, no matter what program you used to open them. She asks you to add the Recent Items command to the Start menu.

To add the Recent Items command to the Start menu:

1. Right-click the **Start** button 🪟 on the taskbar, and then click **Properties** to open the Taskbar and Start Menu Properties dialog box.

2. Click the **Customize** button to open the Customize Start Menu dialog box.

3. Scroll the Start menu items, and then click the **Recent Items** check box.

4. Click the **OK** button, and then click the **Apply** button. The Taskbar and Start Menu Properties dialog box stays open. Before you open the Start menu to view the new command, you can drag this dialog box out of the way.

5. Drag the Taskbar and Start Menu Properties dialog box to the right side of the desktop.

6. Click the **Start** button 🪟 on the taskbar to verify that the Recent Items command is now displayed in the right pane.

Holly can now open a recent file by pointing to Recent Items on the Start menu, and then clicking a file.

Selecting Start Menu Settings

The Customize Start Menu dialog box lists options and settings for your Start menu. For example, you can display a command on the Start menu as a link or as a submenu. If you display a command as a link, you click it to open the appropriate dialog box or window. For example, the Computer command appears on the Start menu as a link by default—you click Computer to open its window. If you display a command as a submenu, you point to the command until a submenu appears, and then you click a command on the submenu. Instead of a link, you can display the Computer command as a submenu. When you point to Computer, a submenu appears listing the contents of the Computer window, including your local hard disk. Figure 3-46 describes the settings you can select for your Start menu.

| Figure 3-46 | Common Start menu settings |

Start Menu	Description
Computer	Display this item as a link you click to open the Computer window or as a submenu that lists the contents of the Computer window, or don't display this item.
Connect To	Display an item that lets you select a network to which you can connect.
Control Panel	Display this item as a link you click to open the Control Panel or as a submenu that lists individual tools or categories in the Control Panel, or don't display this item.
Default Programs	Display an item that lets you choose the default programs you use for Web browsing, e-mail, playing music, and other activities.
Devices and Printers	Display this item to open the Devices and Printers window.
Documents	Display this item as a link you click to open the Documents library or as a submenu that lists the contents of Documents, or don't display this item.
Downloads	Display this item as a link you click to open the Downloads folder or as a submenu that lists the contents of the Downloads folder, or don't display this item.
Favorites menu	Display this item to list your favorite Web sites, files, and folders.
Games	Display this item as a link you click to open the Games folder or as a submenu that lists the contents of the Games folder, or don't display this item.
Help	Display this item to open the Help and Support window.
Highlight newly installed programs	Before you start a newly installed program for the first time, highlight the program name.
Homegroup	Display this item to open the Homegroup window, which displays information about your personal home network.
Music	Display this item as a link you click to open the Music library or as a submenu that lists the contents of the Music library, or don't display this item.
Network	Display this item to open the Network window.
Personal folder	Display this item as a link you click to open your personal folder or as a submenu that lists the contents of your personal folder, or don't display this item.
Pictures	Display this item as a link you click to open the Pictures library or as a submenu that lists the contents of the Pictures library, or don't display this item.
Recent Items	Display a list of recently opened files.
Use large icons	Display large program icons on the Start menu.
Videos	Display this item as a link you click to open the Videos library or as a submenu that lists the contents of the Videos library, or don't display this item.

Holly wants to display the Computer item as a submenu so she has another easy way to access her USB flash drive. The Computer submenu will then contain a shortcut icon that she can click to quickly open her USB flash drive.

To change the Computer command on the Start menu to display a submenu:

1. With the Taskbar and Start Menu Properties dialog box open on the desktop, click the **Customize** button. The Customize Start Menu dialog box opens.

2. Click the **Display as a menu** option button under the Computer icon.

3. Click the **OK** button, click the **Apply** button, and then close the Taskbar and Start Menu Properties dialog box. Now you can test the Computer submenu on the Start menu.

4. Click the **Start** button 🔵 on the taskbar, and then point to **Computer**. The icons in the Computer window appear in the submenu. See Figure 3-47.

Figure 3-47   New Computer submenu on the Start menu

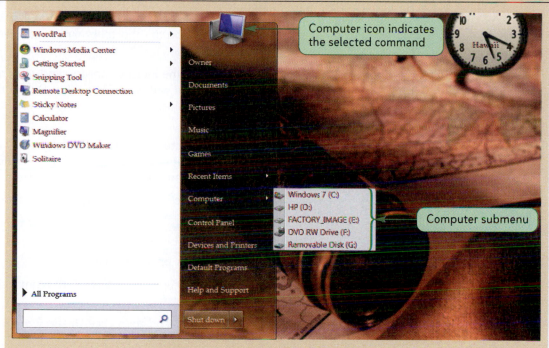

5. Click **Removable Disk (G:)** or another item on the Computer submenu. The contents of this drive appear in the Computer window.

6. Close all open windows and dialog boxes.

Now that you've finished personalizing the Windows 7 environment on Holly's computer, you should restore your computer to its original settings.

Restoring Your Settings

Complete the steps in this section to restore the original settings on your computer.

To restore your settings:

1. Right-click the **desktop**, and then click **Personalize** on the shortcut menu.

2. Click your original theme, such as **Windows 7** or **Windows Basic**, to restore your original desktop background, window color, and screen saver.

3. Click **Change desktop icons**. Click check boxes to restore the original settings. By default, only the Recycle Bin appears on the desktop.

4. If the Computer desktop icon is not restored to its default image, click **Computer** in the box displaying desktop icons, and then click the **Restore Default** button. Click the **OK** button to close the Desktop Icon Settings dialog box. Close the Personalization window.

5. Right-click the **desktop**, point to **View** on the shortcut menu, and then click **Medium icons**.

6. Navigate to the **Hawaii Maps** folder in the Pictures library, and then move it to the **Tutorial.03\Tutorial** folder provided with your Data Files. Delete the original files in the Tutorial.03\Tutorial folder, which should now contain only the Hawaii Maps folder. Close all folder windows.

7. Click a desktop **shortcut icon** that you created in this tutorial, hold down the **Ctrl** key, and then click all the other **shortcut icons** you created in this tutorial. Press the **Delete** key to delete the shortcuts, and then click the **Yes** button.

8. Right-click the **Clock** gadget, and then click **Close gadget** on the shortcut menu.

9. Right-click the **Paint** program button [icon] on the taskbar, point to **Volcano**, and then click the **Unpin from this list** icon [icon].

10. On the Paint Jump List, click **Unpin this program from taskbar**.

11. Click the **Start** button [icon] on the taskbar, point to **WordPad**, point to **Facts**, and then click the **Unpin from this list** icon [icon].

12. Right-click **WordPad** on the Start menu, and then click **Unpin from Start Menu**. Close the Start menu.

13. Drag the **Windows Explorer** icon [icon] on the taskbar to its original location: to the right of the Internet Explorer icon.

14. Right-click a blank area of the taskbar, point to **Toolbars**, and then click **Desktop** to remove this toolbar from the taskbar.

15. Right-click the taskbar, and then click **Lock the taskbar** on the shortcut menu.

16. Click the **Start** button [icon] on the taskbar, click the **user picture**, click **Change your picture**, click the original user picture, and then click the **Change Picture** button. Close the User Accounts window.

▶ **17.** Right-click the **Start** button 🟦, click **Properties**, click the **Customize** button, click the **Use large icons** check box to select it, click the **Recent Items** check box to remove the check mark, click the **Display as a link** option button under the Computer icon, click the **OK** button to close the Customize Start Menu dialog box, and then click the **OK** button to close the Taskbar and Start Menu Properties dialog box.

▶ **18.** Close Paint, Notepad, and any other open windows.

Session 3.2 Quick Check

REVIEW

1. True or False. To use any Aero tools on the desktop to organize and manage open windows, you must be using an Aero theme.

2. The _____ on the taskbar shows the current time, program icons, and system status information.

3. What does a program's Jump List contain?

4. Why would you pin a program such as Paint to the Start menu?

5. You can place a(n) _____ toolbar on the taskbar to provide access to all the icons on the desktop plus those for common locations such as the Libraries folder.

6. True or False. Only Windows 7 can set the user picture that appears on the Start menu—you cannot change it.

7. You can display a Start menu command as a link. Identify the other way you can display a command on the Start menu.

8. True or False. The Jump List for the Paint program on the taskbar is the same as the Jump List for the Paint program on the Start menu.

PRACTICE

Practice the skills you learned in the tutorial using the same case scenario.

Review Assignments

For a list of Data Files in the Review folder, see page WIN 105.

Magellan Cartography keeps a computer in its conference area for any employee or intern to use when needed. Holly asks you to customize that computer so it is appropriate for the company. Holly is also preparing a map of Newfoundland, and she wants to store current Newfoundland maps and historical map images on that computer for her employees to use as models. As you perform the following steps, note the original settings of the desktop and other items so you can restore them later. Complete the following steps:

1. Change the desktop icon settings on your computer to display the Computer and Control Panel icons in addition to the default Recycle Bin icon. Change the image for the Computer icon so that it displays any other appropriate image. Close all open windows.
2. Change the size of the desktop icons to display the icons in their smallest size.
3. Display a Clock gadget that displays the time in the Atlantic time zone. Name the clock Atlantic.
4. Insert the USB flash drive or other removable media containing your Data Files in the appropriate drive, and then create a shortcut to this drive on the desktop. Name the shortcut Removable Disk Shortcut.
5. Use the Removable Disk Shortcut to move the files from the Tutorial.03\Review folder to a new folder named **Historical Maps** in your Pictures library.
6. On the desktop, create a shortcut to the Historical Maps folder. Then create a shortcut to the **NF Facts** text document. Test the shortcut by double-clicking the NF Facts shortcut to start Notepad and open the document.
7. Sort the desktop icons by size so that the Computer icon is the last icon in the list.
8. Change the desktop background to display any image in the Historical Maps folder.
9. Change the icon font to MS UI Gothic.
10. Change the screen saver to play a slide show of the images in the Historical Maps folder.
11. Save the current desktop settings as a theme for sharing. Name the theme Historical, and store it in the Historical Maps folder. Close all open windows.
12. Pin the Paint program to the taskbar. Use it to open the Charleston image in the Historical Maps folder. Pin the Charleston image file to the Paint program's Jump List.
13. Use Aero Snap to align the Paint window on the left side of the desktop.
14. Unlock the taskbar, and then increase its height so it is about twice as high as its current setting.
15. Change the appearance of the Start menu so that it displays small icons.
16. Change the user picture on the Start menu so it displays a guitar.
17. Pin WordPad to the Start menu, pin the NF Facts document to WordPad's Jump List, and then change the Documents command on the Start menu from a link to a menu. Close all open dialog boxes.
18. Open the Start menu, point to WordPad, and then press the Print Screen key to capture an image of your desktop with the Start menu open. Open a new file in Paint, and then press Ctrl+V to paste the image in the Paint file. Save the file as **Review***XY*, where *XY* are your initials, in the Tutorial.03\Review folder provided with your Data Files.
19. Use the shortcuts on your desktop to move the Historical Maps folder from the Pictures library to the Tutorial.03\Review folder provided with your Data Files. Close all open windows.

20. Restore the settings on your computer. Restore the image of the Computer icon, and then display the original set of icons on the desktop. Change the size of the desktop icons to Medium, and change the icon font back to Segoe UI. Remove the Clock gadget from the desktop. Delete the shortcut icons on the desktop. Restore the desktop background and the screen saver to their original images. Resize the taskbar to its original size, unpin the Charleston image file from the Paint program's Jump List, and unpin the Paint program from the taskbar. Lock the taskbar. Change the user picture to display the original image. Unpin NF Facts from WordPad's Jump List, unpin WordPad from the Start menu, change the Documents command from a submenu to a link, and use large icons on the Start menu.

21. Close any open windows.

22. Submit the results of the preceding steps to your instructor, either in printed or electronic form, as requested.

Use the skills you learned in the tutorial to set up Windows 7 for an engineering firm.

APPLY

Case Problem 1

For a list of Data Files in the Case1 folder, see page WIN 105.

Da Vinci Engineering   When Hank Van Hise started his own engineering firm in Columbus, Ohio, he named it after Leonardo da Vinci, one of his engineering heroes. Da Vinci Engineering is an environmental engineering firm that participates in public works projects such as building dams and bridges while working to minimize their effect on the environment. When he is not on site, Hank manages 15 employees in an office in downtown Columbus. He has hired you to help him run the office. Because he just installed Windows 7, he asks you to personalize the desktop on his computer. As you perform the following steps, note the original settings of the desktop and other items so you can restore them later. Complete the following steps:

1. Change the desktop icon settings on your computer to display the Computer, User's Files, and Control Panel icons. Change the image for the User's Files icon so that it displays any other appropriate image.

2. Change the size of the desktop icons to display the icons in their largest size.

3. Open the gadget gallery, and then display the Calendar gadget on the desktop. Double-click the Calendar gadget to display it as a monthly calendar.

4. Insert the USB flash drive or other removable media containing your Data Files in the appropriate drive, and then create a shortcut to this drive on the desktop. Name the shortcut Removable Disk Shortcut.

5. Use the Removable Disk Shortcut to move the files in the Tutorial.03\Case1 folder to a new folder named **Leonardo** in your Documents library.

6. On the desktop, create a shortcut to the Leonardo folder. Then create a shortcut to the **Vasari** text document, an account of the life of Leonardo da Vinci by one of his contemporaries. Test the shortcut by double-clicking the Vasari shortcut to start Notepad and open the document.

7. Create shortcuts to two other files in the Leonardo folder.

8. Sort the desktop icons by item type.

9. If possible, change the theme to a Windows Aero theme other than Windows 7 Aero such as Architecture. Also change the color of the window borders, Start menu, and taskbar to Slate.

10. Increase the height of the taskbar so it is about twice as high as its current setting.

11. Pin the WordPad program to the taskbar.

12. Change the user picture on the Start menu so it displays a top (the image in the first row, sixth from the left).

13. Open the Screen Saver Settings dialog box and select the Ribbons screen saver. Move the dialog box so that some or all of the desktop items are clearly visible. Use an Aero tool to minimize any other open windows.

14. Open the Start menu, and then press the Print Screen key to capture an image of your desktop with the Start menu open. Open Paint, and then press Ctrl+V to paste the image in a Paint file. Save the file as **Case1XY**, where XY are your initials, in the Tutorial.03\Case1 folder provided with your Data Files.

15. Move the Leonardo folder to the Tutorial.03\Case1 folder.

16. Restore the settings on your computer. Restore the image of the User's Files icon, and then display the original set of icons on the desktop. Change the size of the desktop icons to Medium. Sort the icons by name. Delete the shortcut icons on the desktop. Remove the Calendar gadget from the desktop. Restore the original theme and screen saver. Return the taskbar to its default state, including its original size. Lock the taskbar. Unpin the WordPad program from the taskbar. Change the user picture to display the original image.

17. Close any open windows.

18. Submit the results of the preceding steps to your instructor, either in printed or electronic form, as requested.

Use the skills you learned in the tutorial to personalize Windows.

APPLY

Case Problem 2

For a list of Data Files in the Case2 folder, see page WIN 105.

B&B Realty   Ed Bolton and Kevin Bestmuller own B&B Realty in Syracuse, New York, and concentrate on home sales and appraisals. One way they distinguish their business from other realty agencies is by providing computers in their downtown office and inviting people to browse real estate listings, learn about architectural styles, and find local businesses that can help them prepare a house for sale or restore a fixer-upper. Some of this information is stored on the office computers, and some, such as the Multiple Listing Service, is on the Web. You are the office manager and work with the agents and clients to help them use B&B Realty resources. After installing Windows 7 on all the office computers, Ed asks you to personalize the desktop so it reflects the B&B Realty company image. As you perform the following steps, note the original settings of the desktop and other items so you can restore them later. Complete the following steps:

1. Change the desktop icon settings on your computer to display the Network and Control Panel icons in addition to the default Recycle Bin icon. Change the image for the Network icon so that it displays any other appropriate image.

2. Change the size of the desktop icons to display the icons in their smallest size.

3. Display the Clock, Calendar, and CPU Meter gadgets on the desktop.

4. Insert the USB flash drive or other removable media containing your Data Files in the appropriate drive, and then create a shortcut to this drive on the desktop. Name the shortcut Removable Disk Shortcut.

5. Use the Removable Disk Shortcut to move the files in the Tutorial.03\Case2 folder to a new folder named **Houses** in the Documents library.

6. On the desktop, create a shortcut to the Houses folder. Then create a shortcut to the **Syracuse** text document. Test the shortcut by double-clicking the Syracuse shortcut to start Notepad and open the document.

7. Create a shortcut to WordPad on the desktop.

⊕ **EXPLORE**   8. Create a shortcut to your printer on the desktop. (*Hint:* Click the Start button, click Devices and Printers, and then drag the printer icon to the desktop.)

9. Arrange all of the desktop icons in a row along the top of the desktop. (*Hint*: Turn off the Auto arrange icons option on the desktop shortcut menu before moving the icons.)

10. Change the desktop background to display any image in the Houses folder. Center the image on the desktop.

11. If possible, change the theme to a Windows Aero theme other than Windows 7 Aero.

12. Change the color of the window borders, Start menu, and taskbar to Sun.

13. Save the current desktop settings as a theme for sharing. Name the theme B&B, and store it in the Houses folder.

14. Change the screen saver to Mystify.

15. Auto-hide the taskbar.

16. Display the Desktop toolbar on the taskbar. Pin the Paint program to the taskbar.

17. Remove the Default Programs item from the Start menu.

18. Use Paint to open all the picture files in the Houses folder. Open the Syracuse file in WordPad. If you are using an Aero theme, point to the Show desktop button on the taskbar to activate Aero Peek.

19. Press the Print Screen key to capture an image of your desktop. Open WordPad, and then press Ctrl+V to paste the image in a WordPad document. Save the document as **Case2XY**, where *XY* are your initials, in the Tutorial.03\Case2 folder provided with your Data Files. Open a folder window displaying the files in the Tutorial.03\Case2 folder.

⊕ EXPLORE 20. Right-click the printer shortcut icon on the desktop, click See what's printing, and then drag the Case2*XY* document from the Case2 folder window to the open printer window to print the document. Close all open windows.

21. Use the shortcuts on your desktop to move the Houses folder from the Documents folder on your hard disk to the Tutorial.03\Case2 folder provided with your Data Files.

22. Restore the settings on your computer. Restore the image of the Network icon, and then display the original set of icons on the desktop. Change the size of the desktop icons to Medium, delete the shortcut icons, and then move the Recycle Bin icon to the upper-left corner of the desktop. Auto-arrange the icons. Remove the gadgets from the desktop. Restore the desktop background and screen saver to their original images. Restore the original theme. Unpin the Paint program from the taskbar. Restore the taskbar to its default state. Restore the Start menu to its original condition.

23. Close any open windows.

24. Submit the results of the preceding steps to your instructor, either in printed or electronic form, as requested.

Extend what you've learned to discover other ways to customize Windows for a nature conservancy.

CHALLENGE

Case Problem 3

For a list of Data Files in the Case3 folder, see page WIN 105.

Acadia Nature Conservancy   Ellie Larsen is the director of the Acadia Nature Conservancy in Augusta, Maine. The mission of the organization is to protect the most ecologically important lands and waters in Maine. Ellie organizes projects to study and preserve the natural history and diversity of Maine's plants, animals, and natural habitats. Because of your earlier work for the Acadia Nature Conservancy as a dedicated volunteer, Ellie hired you as a project assistant. Ellie recently upgraded to Windows 7, and she asks you to customize her computer. As you perform the following steps, note the original settings of the desktop and other items so you can restore them later. Complete the following steps:

1. Change the desktop icon settings on your computer to display all of the built-in desktop icons. Change the image for the Computer icon so that it displays any other appropriate image.

2. Insert the USB flash drive or other removable media containing your Data Files in the appropriate drive, and then create a shortcut to this drive on the desktop. Name the shortcut Removable Disk Shortcut.

3. Use the Removable Disk Shortcut to move the files in the Tutorial.03\Case3 folder to a new folder named **Nature** in the Pictures library.

4. On the desktop, create a shortcut to the Nature folder. Then create a shortcut to the **Directions** text document. Test the shortcut by double-clicking the Directions shortcut to start Notepad and open the document. Close all open windows.

5. On the desktop, create a shortcut to the Calculator program. Pin the Calculator to the Start menu, and pin Paint to the taskbar.

✦ EXPLORE   6. Display the Slide Show and Clock gadgets on the desktop. Right-click the Slide Show gadget, and then click Options to open the Slide Show dialog box. If necessary, click the Folder arrow, and then click Pictures Library to play a slide show of the images in the Pictures library, including the Nature folder. (Make sure the Include subfolders check box is selected.) Click the Shuffle pictures check box, and then click the OK button.

✦ EXPLORE   7. Right-click the Clock gadget, and then click Options to open the Clock dialog box. Display image 6 of 8 for the Clock, show the second hand, and then close the Clock dialog box.

8. If possible, change the theme to the Aero Nature theme. If you cannot use a Windows Aero theme, change the theme to Windows Classic.

9. Use Paint to open and view each picture stored in the Nature folder. Then close Paint.

✦ EXPLORE   10. Open the Customize Start Menu dialog box, and then change the Number of recent items to display in Jump Lists to 4. Click the OK button in the dialog boxes to accept your changes.

11. Right-click the Paint program button on the taskbar to display its Jump List, and then press the Print Screen key to capture an image of your desktop with the Jump List open. Open Paint, and then press Ctrl+V to paste the image in a Paint file. Save the file as **Case3XY**, where *XY* are your initials, in the Tutorial.03\Case3 folder provided with your Data Files.

12. Use the shortcuts on your desktop to move the Nature folder from the Pictures library to the Tutorial.03\Case3 folder provided with your Data Files.

13. Restore the settings on your computer, and then close all open windows.

14. Submit the results of the preceding steps to your instructor, either in printed or electronic form, as requested.

Using Figure 3-48 as a guide, personalize the desktop for an animation design firm.

CREATE

Case Problem 4

There are no Data Files needed for this Case Problem.

Animated Ventures After working for a video game developer, Adam Wolff decided to start his own company in San Diego, California, that provides animation to the computer industry. Adam recently upgraded all the computers at Animated Ventures to Windows 7, and then hired you to manage the office. After working with a client in Los Angeles, Adam shows you a screen shot of that client's desktop. See Figure 3-48. He thinks this desktop would be appropriate for the computers at Animated Ventures, and he asks you to re-create it on your computer.

Figure 3-48 | **Model desktop for Animated Ventures**

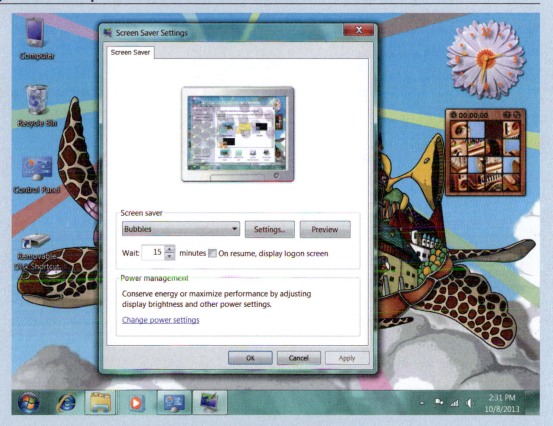

To create this Windows environment, complete the following:

1. Select the following Windows 7 settings:
   - Img19.jpg desktop background
   - Sea window borders, Start menu, and taskbar color
   - Bubbles screen saver
   - Clock gadget on the desktop showing image 5 of 8 and the second hand displayed, and with the Picture Puzzle gadget displaying image 6 of 11
   - Computer, Control Panel, and Recycle Bin desktop icons, with the Computer icon image showing a handheld computer
2. Insert the USB flash drive or other removable media containing your Data Files in the appropriate drive, and then create a shortcut to this drive on the desktop. Name the shortcut Removable Disk Shortcut.

3. Open the Screen Saver Settings dialog box, and then minimize the Personalization window.

4. Capture an image of the desktop, and then save the image in a Paint file named **Case4XY**, where *XY* are your initials, in the Tutorial.03\Case4 folder provided with your Data Files.

5. Restore the original settings, and then close all open windows.

6. Submit the results of the preceding steps to your instructor, either in printed or electronic form, as requested.

ENDING DATA FILES

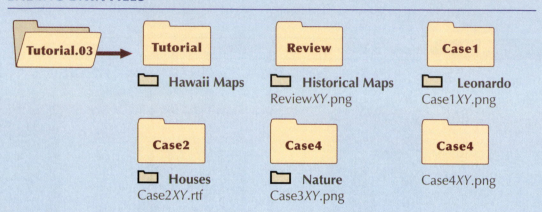

OBJECTIVES

Session 4.1
- Define the relationship between the Internet and the World Wide Web
- Open, view, and navigate Web pages in Internet Explorer
- Revisit recently opened Web pages
- Organize links to your favorite Web pages
- Use Web Slices and Accelerators

Session 4.2
- Explain how e-mail works
- Send, receive, reply to, and delete e-mail with Microsoft Windows Live Mail
- Attach a file to an e-mail message
- Add and delete a contact in Windows Live Contacts
- Create appointments with Windows Live Calendar

Working with the Internet and E-Mail

Communicating with Others

Case | *Entrée Tours*

David Sanchez started Entrée Tours in Fort Collins, Colorado, to run bus and van tours in states west of the Mississippi River for limited-mobility travelers. David's clients include people who ride in wheelchairs or otherwise need assistance to visit scenic destinations in Colorado and other western states. Recently, David hired you as a travel planner to help him expand his business. In addition to Entrée Tours' popular ski and snowboard vacations, David wants to offer sightseeing and wilderness trips. One of your main tasks is to research western destinations that are suitable for Entrée Tours and find information that states and businesses provide for adaptive travelers. You regularly use Microsoft Internet Explorer to gather this information on the Web. You also use Windows Live Mail to exchange e-mail with Entrée Tours' contacts and clients. David has asked you to get him up to speed in using these programs.

In this tutorial, you'll explore how the Internet and the Web work, and use Internet Explorer to visit and organize Web pages. You'll examine e-mail technology and use Windows Live Mail to send, receive, and reply to e-mail messages. You'll also use two programs that work with Windows Live Mail to help you manage your contacts and your schedule.

STARTING DATA FILES

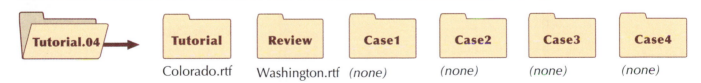

Tutorial.04 →	Tutorial	Review	Case1	Case2	Case3	Case4
	Colorado.rtf	Washington.rtf	*(none)*	*(none)*	*(none)*	*(none)*

SESSION 4.1 VISUAL OVERVIEW

Internet Explorer is a **browser**, a program that locates, retrieves, and displays Web pages.

The **Favorites bar** contains buttons for Web Slices and links to Web pages you view often.

Bing is a **search engine**, a program that conducts searches to retrieve Web pages.

The **Favorites Center** displays links to your favorites, feeds, and recently visited Web pages.

The **uniform resource locator (URL)** of the Web page indicates the location of a Web page.

Each hyperlinked text document—or hypertext document—on the Web is called a **Web page**.

Internet Explorer provides a few Accelerators by default.

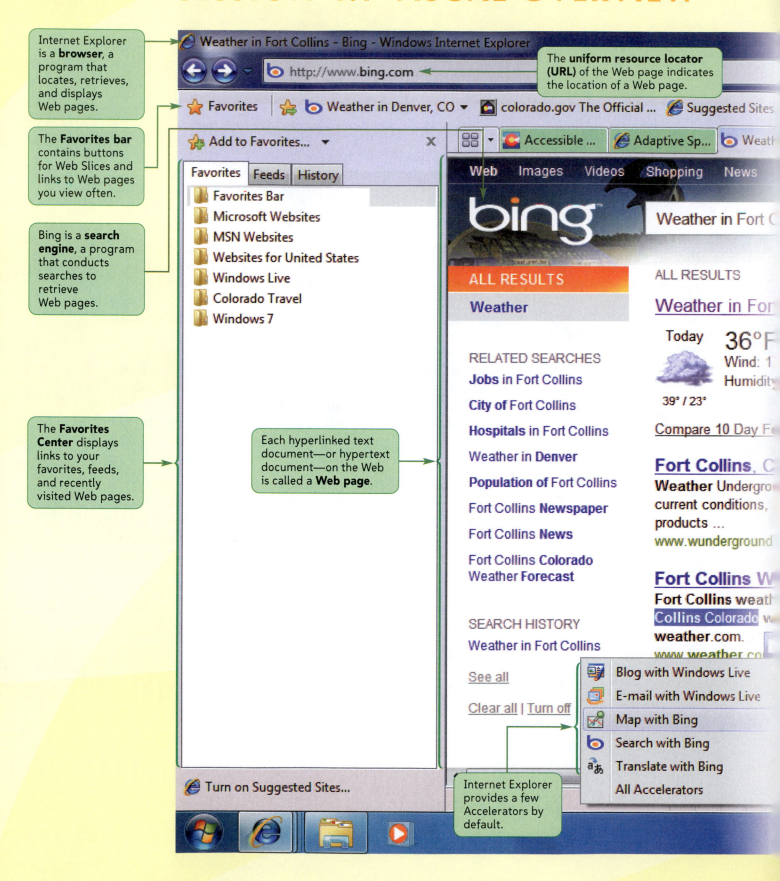

Weather in Fort Collins - Bing - Windows Internet Explorer

http://www.bing.com

⭐ Favorites | 🔖 b Weather in Denver, CO ▾ 🏠 colorado.gov The Official ... 🌐 Suggested Sites

🔖 Add to Favorites... ▾   ✕ | ⊞ ▾ | 🏳 Accessible ... 🌐 Adaptive Sp... b Weath

Favorites | **Feeds** | **History**

- 📁 Favorites Bar
- 📁 Microsoft Websites
- 📁 MSN Websites
- 📁 Websites for United States
- 📁 Windows Live
- 📁 Colorado Travel
- 📁 Windows 7

Web   Images   Videos   Shopping   News

bing™   Weather in Fort C

ALL RESULTS   ALL RESULTS

Weather   Weather in For

Today   **36°** F
☁️   Wind: 1
39° / 23°   Humidit

Compare 10 Day F

RELATED SEARCHES

Jobs in Fort Collins
City of Fort Collins
Hospitals in Fort Collins
Weather in **Denver**
Population of Fort Collins
Fort Collins **Newspaper**
Fort Collins **News**
Fort Collins **Colorado** Weather **Forecast**

Fort Collins, C
Weather Undergro
current conditions,
products ...
www.wunderground

Fort Collins W
Fort Collins weath
Collins Colorado w
weather.com.
www.weather.co

SEARCH HISTORY

Weather in Fort Collins

See all

Clear all | Turn off

🖥️ Blog with Windows Live
📧 E-mail with Windows Live
🗺️ Map with Bing
b Search with Bing
a̲ả Translate with Bing
   All Accelerators

🌐 Turn on Suggested Sites...

MICROSOFT INTERNET EXPLORER

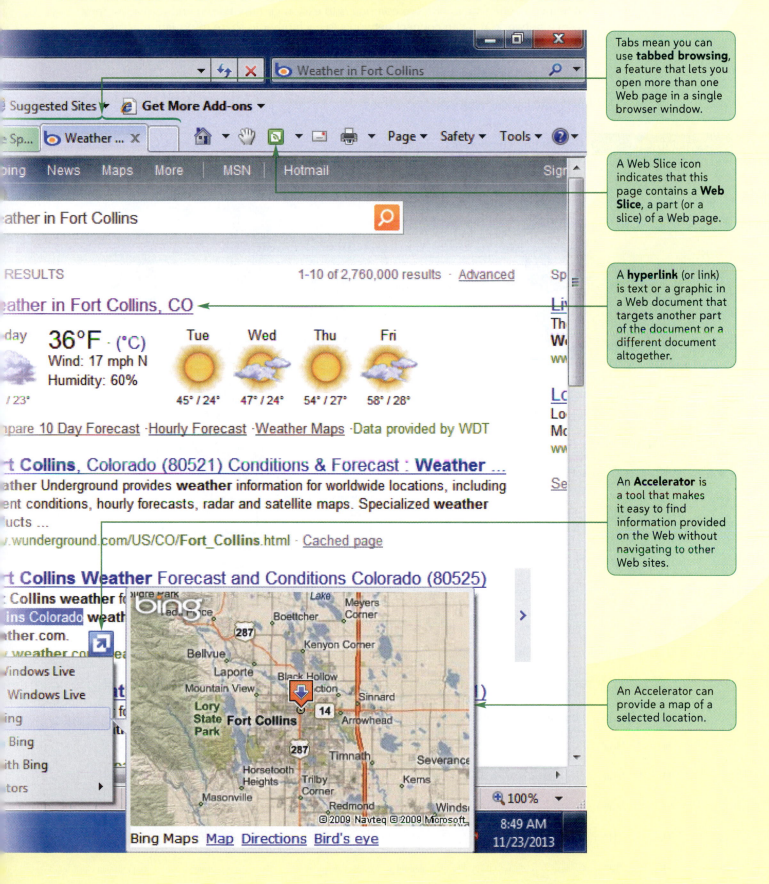

Tabs mean you can use **tabbed browsing**, a feature that lets you open more than one Web page in a single browser window.

A Web Slice icon indicates that this page contains a **Web Slice**, a part (or a slice) of a Web page.

A **hyperlink** (or link) is text or a graphic in a Web document that targets another part of the document or a different document altogether.

An **Accelerator** is a tool that makes it easy to find information provided on the Web without navigating to other Web sites.

An Accelerator can provide a map of a selected location.

Exploring the Internet and the Web

When you connect two or more computers to exchange information and resources, they form a **network**. You can connect networks to each other to share information across a wide area. The worldwide, publicly accessible collection of networks is called the Internet, and it consists of millions of computers linked to networks all over the world. The Internet lets you access and exchange information via electronic mail (e-mail), online newsgroups, file transfer, and the linked documents of the **World Wide Web**, better known as the **Web**. See Figure 4-1.

Figure 4-1 | Connecting computers to the Internet

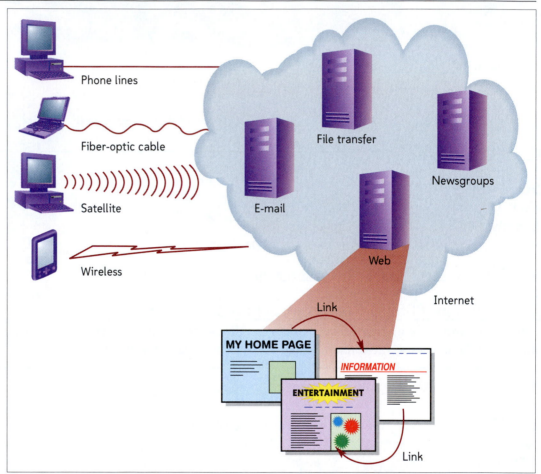

The Web is a service that you can access via the Internet. Whereas the Internet is a collection of networks connected by communication media such as fiber-optic cables and wireless connections, the Web is a collection of documents connected by hyperlinks. You click the link to display the targeted information. For example, in Figure 4-2, you can click links on the first Library of Congress Web document to display related documents.

Figure 4-2 Library of Congress Web page with links to other Web pages

Web pages are stored on Internet computers called **Web servers**. A **Web site** is a collection of Web pages that have a common theme or focus, such as all the pages containing information about the Library of Congress. The Web is appealing because it generally displays up-to-date information in a colorful, lively format that can use sound and animation.

When you want to find information on the Web, you typically use a search engine. To work with a search engine, you enter a word or expression as the search criteria. The search engine lists links to Web pages that fit your criteria. Popular general search engines include Google and Bing.

A recent innovation in Web technology is called **cloud computing**, which refers to providing and using computer tools, such as software, via the Internet (or the cloud). With cloud computing you can use your Web browser to access and work with software. You do not need to purchase and install a complete application. Instead, you use the software services you need for free or for a usage fee. For example, when you use a Web mapping service such as MapQuest or Google Maps to find directions from one location to another, you are using cloud computing. The software and data for the maps are not stored on your computer—they're on the cloud at the mapping service's Web site. You'll see an example of cloud computing when you use Windows Live Essentials later in this tutorial.

Using Web Browsers

You use a browser to visit Web sites around the world; interact with Web pages by clicking links; view multimedia documents; transfer files, images, and sounds to and from your computer; conduct searches for specific topics; and run programs on other computers. The browser included with Windows 7 is called Internet Explorer.

When you attempt to view a Web page, your browser locates and retrieves the document from the Web server and displays its contents on your computer. The server stores the Web page in one location, and browsers anywhere in the world can display it.

For your browser to access the Web, you must have an Internet connection. In a university setting, your connection might come from your campus network. If you are working on a home computer, you have a few options for connecting to the Internet. You might use your phone line and computer modem to establish a **dial-up connection**. More likely, you are using a **broadband connection**, a high-capacity, high-speed medium for connecting to the Internet. Popular broadband technologies include a **digital subscriber line (DSL)**, which is a high-speed connection through your telephone line, and **digital cable**, which uses a cable modem attached to cable television lines. A **wireless connection** uses infrared light or radio-frequency signals to communicate with devices that are physically connected to a network or the Internet. Home connections also require an account with an **Internet service provider (ISP)**, a company that sells Internet access. The ISP provides instructions for connecting your computer to one of its servers, which is connected to the Internet. You can then use your browser to visit Web sites and access other Internet services.

Getting Started with Microsoft Internet Explorer

Microsoft Internet Explorer, the Web browser that comes with Windows 7, lets you communicate, access, and share information on the Web. When you start Internet Explorer, it opens to your **home page**, which is the Web page a browser is set to open by default. The default home page for Internet Explorer is the MSN Web page, a Microsoft Web site with links to information and services. Your computer manufacturer or school might have set up a different home page.

Your first step in showing David how to research travel destinations is to start Internet Explorer. You must be connected to the Internet to perform all the steps in this session. Mute your speakers, if necessary, so the sounds that certain Web pages play do not disturb others.

To start Internet Explorer:

▶ 1. Click the **Internet Explorer** button 🌐 on the taskbar.

   Trouble? If a Dial-up Connection dialog box opens, enter your user name and password, and then click the Connect button. If you do not know your user name or password, ask your instructor or technical support person for help; you must have an Internet connection to complete the steps in this tutorial.

▶ 2. If necessary, click the **Maximize** button 🗖 to maximize the Internet Explorer window. Figure 4-3 shows the MSN main page in the Internet Explorer window. You might have a different home page.

Figure 4-3   Internet Explorer window

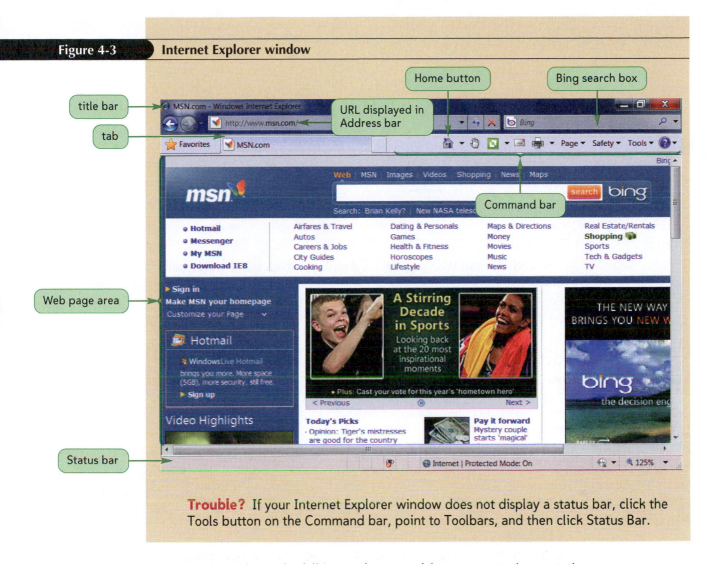

Trouble? If your Internet Explorer window does not display a status bar, click the Tools button on the Command bar, point to Toolbars, and then click Status Bar.

Figure 4-3 shows the following elements of the Internet Explorer window:

- Title bar: Shows the name of the open Web page and includes the resizing and Close buttons
- Command bar: Contains buttons you can click to perform common tasks, such as displaying the home page and printing a Web page
- Address bar: Shows the address of the Web page; you can also type an address here
- Web page area: Shows the current Web page
- Status bar: Shows information about the browser's actions; for example, indicates that a page is loading or is done loading
- Bing search box: Provides a way to search for Web pages
- Home button: Lets you open the Web page specified as the home page for your browser
- Tab: Displays each Web page you open, letting you switch from one Web page to another
- URL: Uniform resource locator; the address of the Web page you want to visit

Now you're ready to use Internet Explorer to open and view a Web page.

Opening a Page on the Web

To find a particular Web page among the billions stored on Web servers, your browser needs to know the uniform resource locator (URL) of the Web page. URLs are like addresses—they indicate the location of a Web page. A URL can consist of the following four parts, which are also shown in Figure 4-4:

- Protocol to use when transferring the Web page
- Address of the Web server storing the page
- Pathname of the folder containing the page
- Filename of the Web page

Figure 4-4   **Parts of a URL**

The URL for most Web pages starts with *http*, which stands for **Hypertext Transfer Protocol**, the most common way to transfer information around the Web. (A **protocol** is a standardized procedure used by computers to exchange information.) When the URL for a Web page starts with *http://*, the Web browser uses Hypertext Transfer Protocol to retrieve the page.

The server address indicates the location of the Web server storing the Web page. In *www.loc.gov*, the *www* indicates that the server is a Web server, *loc* is the name the Library of Congress chose for this Web site, and *.gov* means that a government entity runs the Web server. Other common types of Web servers in the United States are .com (commercial), .net (network server providers or resources), .org (not-for-profit organizations), and .edu (educational institutions). The server address in a URL corresponds to an Internet Protocol (IP) address, which identifies every computer on the Internet. An **IP address** is a unique number that consists of four sets of numbers from 0 to 255 separated by periods, or dots, as in 216.35.148.4. Although computers can easily use IP addresses, they are difficult for people to remember, so domain names were created. A **domain name** identifies one or more IP addresses, such as loc.gov in Figure 4-4. URLs use the domain name in the server address part of an address to identify a particular Web site.

In addition, each file stored on Web servers has a unique pathname, just like files stored on a disk. The pathname in a URL includes the names of the folders containing the file, the filename, and its extension. The filename extension for Web pages is usually .html, or just .htm. In Figure 4-4, the pathname is library/index.html, which specifies a file named index.html stored in a folder named library.

Not all URLs include a pathname. If you don't specify a pathname or filename in a URL, most Web browsers open a file named index.htm or index.html, which is the default name for a Web site's main page.

Opening a Web Page Using a URL

One way to open a Web page in Internet Explorer is to enter a URL, which you can often find in advertisements, informational materials, and on the Web. You enter the URL in the Address bar of Internet Explorer.

In most cases, URLs are not case sensitive, so you can enter a URL using all lower-case or all uppercase text. However, if the Web server storing a Web page uses the UNIX operating system, the URL might be case sensitive. For mixed-case URLs, it's safer to enter them using the mixed case exactly as printed.

The first Web page you want to open for David is for the Colorado Tourism Office.

To open a page on the Web using a URL:

1. Click the **Address** box on the Address bar. The contents of the Address box, which should be the URL for your home page, are selected. Anything you now type replaces the selected URL.

   Trouble? If the contents of the Address box are not selected, drag to select the entire address.

2. Type **www.colorado.com** in the Address box, and then press the **Enter** key. Internet Explorer adds the *http://* protocol for you, and then opens the main page for the Colorado Tourism Office Web site. Maximize the window, if necessary, and then scroll to view the entire page. See Figure 4-5. This page might display images and videos promoting Colorado.

   Trouble? If you receive a Not Found error message, you might have typed the URL incorrectly. Repeat Steps 1 and 2, making sure that the URL in the Address box matches the URL in Step 2. If you still receive an error message, ask your instructor or technical support person for help.

   Trouble? If the Web site plays music, mute your speakers.

Figure 4-5   **Opening the Colorado Tourism Office Web page**

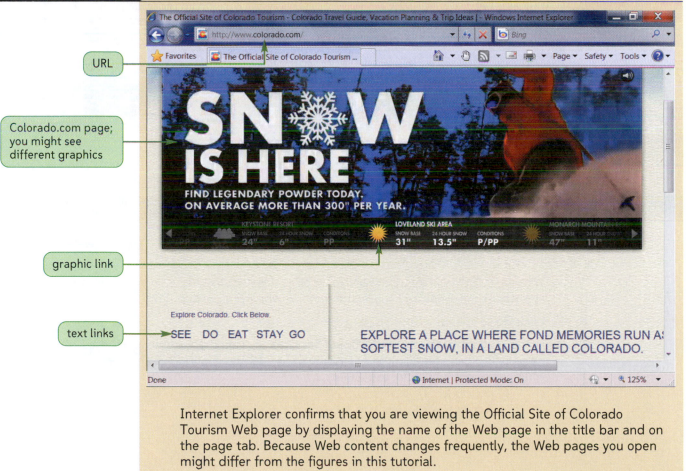

Internet Explorer confirms that you are viewing the Official Site of Colorado Tourism Web page by displaying the name of the Web page in the title bar and on the page tab. Because Web content changes frequently, the Web pages you open might differ from the figures in this tutorial.

The term *home page* has at least two definitions. The definition already introduced in this tutorial is the Web page a browser is set to open by default. The main page for a Web site is also called a home page, though this tutorial uses *main page* to avoid confusion. On a Web site, pages link to and are organized in relation to the main page.

Navigating with Links

The main page for a typical Web site includes plenty of links to help you navigate to its Web pages, and those pages also include links you can click to navigate from one page to another. Recall that links can be text, images, or a combination of both. Text links are usually colored and underlined, though the exact style can vary from one Web site to another. To determine whether something on a Web page is a link, point to it. If the pointer changes to 🖑, the text or image is a link you can click to open a Web page. A URL often appears in the status bar of your Web browser as well. For some graphic links, a ScreenTip appears next to your pointer.

To navigate a Web site using links:

1. Point to **Go** on the Colorado main page. The pointer changes to 🖑 and the URL for that link appears in the status bar. See Figure 4-6.

Figure 4-6   **Pointing to a link**

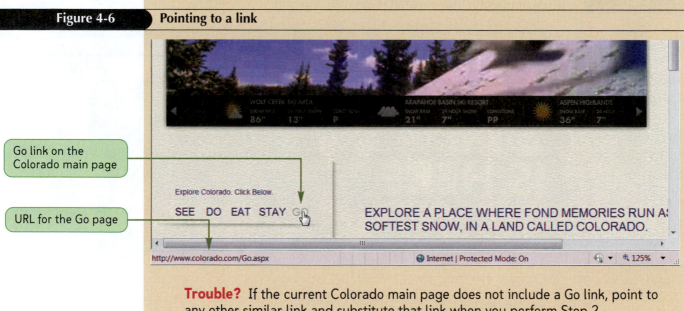

Go link on the Colorado main page

URL for the Go page

Trouble? If the current Colorado main page does not include a Go link, point to any other similar link and substitute that link when you perform Step 2.

2. Click **Go** to open the Go Web page.

3. In the list on the left, click **Additional Services** to open the Additional Services page, which includes a link to Accessible Colorado. See Figure 4-7. The Web page you open might look different.

Figure 4-7   **Additional Services Web page**

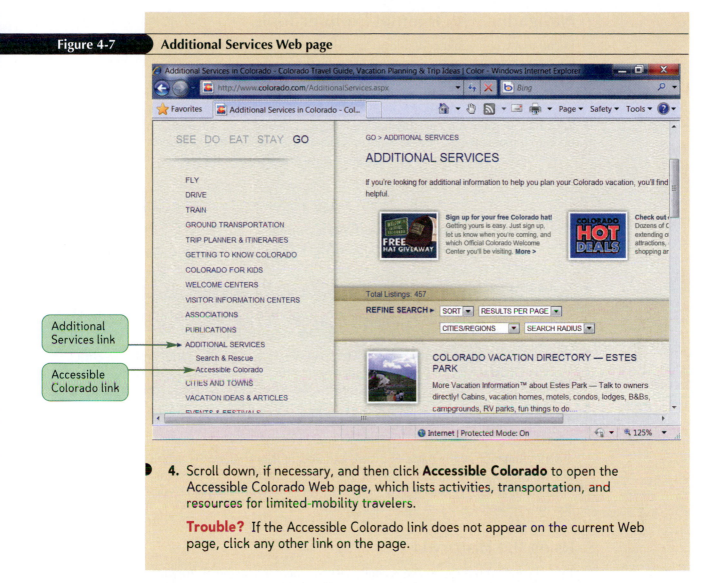

4. Scroll down, if necessary, and then click **Accessible Colorado** to open the Accessible Colorado Web page, which lists activities, transportation, and resources for limited-mobility travelers.

   Trouble? If the Accessible Colorado link does not appear on the current Web page, click any other link on the page.

INSIGHT

Displaying Web Pages Designed for Earlier Versions of Internet Explorer

Windows 7 includes Internet Explorer version 8. If you visit a Web site designed for earlier versions of Internet Explorer, the Web pages might not be formatted for Internet Explorer 8. For example, the menus, images, or text might appear out of place or the Web page might not scroll its full length. To improve the appearance of a Web site in your browser, you can turn on Compatibility View. When you do, the Web pages are displayed as if you were using an earlier version of Internet Explorer. If Internet Explorer detects a Web page that might not appear correctly, the Compatibility View button appears on the Address bar. You can click the Compatibility View button to display the page in Compatibility View. The Web page will be displayed in Compatibility View until you turn it off or the Web page is updated so it displays correctly in the current version of Internet Explorer.

Besides clicking links to navigate from one Web page to another, you can use tools that Internet Explorer provides.

Navigating with Internet Explorer Tools

Recall that when you use Windows Explorer and the Computer window, you can click the Back and Forward buttons to navigate the devices and folders on your computer. Internet Explorer includes similar buttons. As you navigate from one Web page to another, Internet Explorer keeps track of the pages you visited. To return to the previous page, you can click the Back button. To retrace even earlier pages, continue clicking the Back button. After you click the Back button, you can click the Forward button to continue to the next page in the sequence. You can also use the Recent Pages menu to revisit a Web page in the sequence. Click the arrow next to the Forward button, and then select a page in the list.

To return to previously viewed Web pages:

1. Click the **Back** button ⬅ to return to the Additional Services in Colorado Web page.

2. Click the **Forward** button ➡ to return to the Accessible Colorado page.

   Trouble? If you opened different Web pages in the previous set of steps, substitute the names of the pages as appropriate in Steps 1 and 2.

3. Click the **Recent Pages** button ⬇ to open the Recent Pages menu, and then click **The Official Site of Colorado Tourism** to return to the Colorado Tourism main page.

4. Click the **Close** button ✖ to close Internet Explorer.

One limitation of the Back, Forward, and Recent Pages buttons is that they apply only to your current session in the browser. If you close and then restart Internet Explorer, it starts keeping track of a fresh sequence of pages. To revisit Web pages you opened in previous sessions, you can use the History list.

Using the History List

To open any Web page you've recently visited, you can use the History list, which is available in the Internet Explorer Favorites Center. The Favorites Center organizes Web page links and other information, including the History list. (You'll explore the Favorites Center shortly.) The History list includes the Web sites you visited today, last week, and up to three weeks ago by default. You can also click the View By Date button in the History list to change the default setup and view pages by date, by site, by the number of times visited, and in the order visited today. You can also search the pages in the History list to locate a specific Web site you've recently visited.

David wants to open the Web page on the Colorado Web site that provides accessibility information. Because you already closed Internet Explorer, you can't use the Back button to return to that page. You'll use the History list to revisit the Accessible Colorado Web page.

To use the History list:

1. Start Internet Explorer.

2. Click the **Favorites** button on the Command bar to open the Favorites Center.

3. Click the **Pin the Favorites Center** 🔖 button on the Favorites Center toolbar to keep the Favorites Center open.

Trouble? If the Pin the Favorites Center button 🔘 does not appear on your Favorites Center toolbar, the Favorites Center is already pinned to the Internet Explorer window. Skip Step 3.

4. If the History tab in the Favorites Center is not currently selected, click the **History** tab to display the History list. See Figure 4-8.

Figure 4-8 Displaying the History list

Trouble? If your History list is not organized by date as shown in Figure 4-8, click the History button arrow and then click View By Date.

5. Click **Today** in the History list. The list expands to show the Web sites you visited today.

6. Click **colorado (www.colorado.com)** to expand the list to show the pages you visited on that Web site.

7. Click **Accessible Colorado**. The corresponding Web page opens in Internet Explorer. See Figure 4-9.

Figure 4-9 Revisiting a Web page

Next, you want to show David how to open other Web pages without closing the Accessible Colorado Web page.

Managing Multiple Web Pages

If you want to open a new Web page without closing the one you're currently viewing, you can use tabbed browsing to open more than one Web page in a single browser window. To use tabbed browsing, you open a tab for each new page you want to view.

On the new tab, you open a Web page as you usually do. You can also open a new tab by pressing the Ctrl key as you click a link on a Web page or by right-clicking the link and then clicking Open in New Tab on the shortcut menu. You can then switch from one Web page to another by clicking their tabs. If you have two or more tabs open, you can use the Quick Tabs button to display a thumbnail of each Web page so you can see all of your open pages at once. You click a thumbnail to switch to the corresponding page. To close a tab, you click its Close button.

Now that you've explored a few pages on the Colorado Tourism Office site, you can compare that information to information on the State of Colorado Web site, which provides instructions for applying for hunting and fishing licenses, buying state park passes, reserving campsites in state parks, and other information David's clients often need. You'll show David how to open a new tab in Internet Explorer, and then use it to open the State of Colorado Web main page.

To open other Web pages on new tabs:

1. Click the **New Tab** button ⬜ on the Command bar. (This button changes to 🖺 when you point to it.) An information page opens on the new tab.

2. Click in the Address bar, if necessary, type **www.colorado.gov**, and then press the **Enter** key. The Colorado.gov: The Official State Web portal page opens on the new tab. See Figure 4-10. The Web page you open might look different.

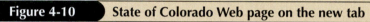

Figure 4-10	State of Colorado Web page on the new tab

URL for the Colorado.gov page

new tab for the Colorado.gov page

Tourism link

TIP

You can also switch to a different Web page by clicking the Tab List button next to the Quick Tabs button and then clicking the name of a Web page.

3. Right-click the **Tourism** link on the Web page, and then click **Open in New Tab** on the shortcut menu. The Tourism Overview Web page opens in a new tab.

   Trouble? If the Tourism link does not appear on the current Web page, right-click a different link on the page.

4. Click the **Quick Tabs** button 🞖 on the Command bar. Thumbnails appear showing a miniature version of each open Web page. See Figure 4-11.

Figure 4-11   **Thumbnails of the open Web pages**

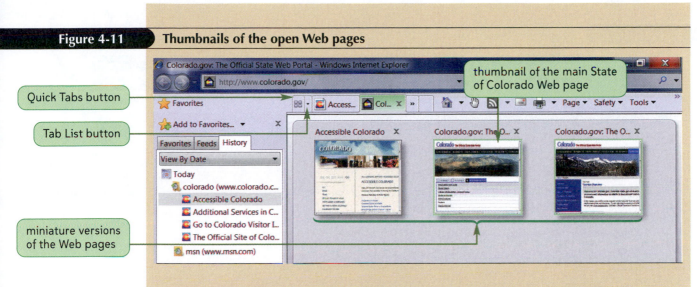

Quick Tabs button

Tab List button

thumbnail of the main State of Colorado Web page

miniature versions of the Web pages

> **5.** Click the **Colorado.gov: The Official State Web Portal** thumbnail to display the main State of Colorado Web page.

If you close tabs during a browsing session, you can quickly reopen all the tabs. This is especially helpful when you are viewing related information on two or more tabs—instead of opening a tab for each Web page and then retyping its Web address, you can use the Open All command on a new tab.

To close and then reopen the Web page tabs:

> **1.** Click the **Close Tab** button **X** on the Colorado.gov: The Official State Web Portal tab.

> **2.** Close the other Colorado.gov tab.

> **3.** Click the **New Tab** button ☐ to open a new tab. At least one tab must be open in the Internet Explorer window. Now that a new tab is open, you can close the Accessible Colorado tab.

> **4.** Click the **Accessible Colorado** tab, and then close it. The new tab displays links to Web pages you opened in the current browsing session. See Figure 4-12.

Figure 4-12   **Reopening closed tabs**

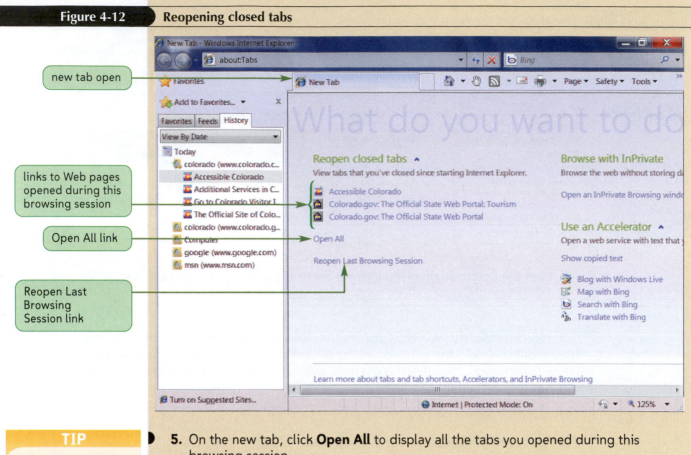

new tab open

links to Web pages opened during this browsing session

Open All link

Reopen Last Browsing Session link

TIP

If you close and then reopen Internet Explorer and want to reopen the tabs from your last browsing session, click Reopen Last Browsing Session.

▶ **5.** On the new tab, click **Open All** to display all the tabs you opened during this browsing session.

Although tabbed browsing helps you manage open Web pages, the Favorites Center helps you organize Web pages you open often. You'll show David how to use the Favorites Center next.

Using Favorites

As you explore the Web, you'll find pages that are your favorites, those you visit frequently. You can save the location of your favorite Web pages in the Favorites list, a collection of links to the Web pages that you visit often. To display the Favorites list, you open the Favorites Center, where you can manage the Favorites list, Feeds, and the History list. The Favorites list initially includes a few folders of links, such as those to Microsoft Web sites. Your computer manufacturer might also include a few links in the Favorites list. If you find a Web page you want to visit often, you can add it to your Favorites list. When you want to retrieve one of your favorite Web pages, you can click its link in the Favorites list and display the page in your browser. As your list of favorite pages grows, you can organize the links into folders. For example, you could create a Favorites folder for travel Web sites and another for news Web sites.

To display the Favorites list:

▶ **1.** Click the **Favorites** tab in the Favorites Center. Internet Explorer displays the Favorites list. See Figure 4-13. Your Favorites list might be different.

Figure 4-13   Displaying the Favorites list

Add to Favorites arrow

Add to Favorites button

Favorites tab

initial set of Favorites installed on this computer; yours might be different

The Accessible Colorado Web page provides the kind of information you often need when organizing trips for Entrée Tours. You'll also add that page to the Favorites list.

Adding an Item to the Favorites List

To add a Web page to the Favorites list, you access the page in Internet Explorer, and then you use the Add to Favorites command. By default, Windows 7 adds the new page to the end of the Favorites list. If you organize the Web pages into folders, you can add a Web page to one of the folders. You can store the page using the title of the Web page as its name, or you can change the name.

REFERENCE

Adding a Web Page to the Favorites List

- Open the Web page in Internet Explorer.
- Click the Add to Favorites button on the toolbar.
- Enter a new name for the Web page and select a folder, if necessary.
- Click the Add button.

If you are working on a network, you might not be able to change the content of the Favorites list. In that case, read through the following steps and examine the figures, but do not perform the steps.

To add Web pages to your Favorites list:

1. Click the **Accessible Colorado** tab to open that Web page.

2. Click the **Add to Favorites** button. The Add a Favorite dialog box opens, displaying the name of the Web page in the Name text box.

3. With Accessible Colorado displayed in the Name text box, click the **Add** button to add the Web page to the Favorites list.

Next, you can organize your favorite Web pages into folders.

Organizing the Favorites List

As you add more items to the Favorites list, you can organize its links by deleting some and moving others to new folders. Using folders is an excellent way to organize your favorite files and pages.

REFERENCE

Organizing the Favorites List

- Click the Add to Favorites arrow on the Favorites Center toolbar, and then click Organize Favorites to open the Organize Favorites dialog box.
- To create a new folder, click the New Folder button, enter a folder name, and then press the Enter key.
- To move a link into a Favorites folder, drag the link to the folder or select the item, click the Move button, select the new folder for the item, and then click the OK button.
- To remove an item from the Favorites list, select the item, and then click the Delete button.
- Click the Close button to close the Organize Favorites dialog box.

To organize your Favorites list:

TIP

If you have many links and folders in the Favorites list, use the Move button in the Organize Favorites dialog box instead of dragging.

1. Click the **Add to Favorites** arrow on the Favorites Center toolbar, and then click **Organize Favorites**. The Organize Favorites dialog box opens.

   Trouble? If the Add a Favorite dialog box opens, you clicked the Add to Favorites button instead of the arrow. Close the Add a Favorite dialog box, and then repeat Step 1.

2. Click the **New Folder** button, type **Colorado Travel** as the new folder name, and then press the **Enter** key.

3. In the Organize Favorites dialog box, drag the **Accessible Colorado** link to the Colorado Travel folder.

4. Click the **Close** button to close the Organize Favorites dialog box. The new link you added is now stored in the Colorado Travel folder in the Favorites list. See Figure 4-14.

Figure 4-14 | **New folders in the Favorites list**

your Favorites list might contain different links

Favorites list now includes a new folder

Next, you want to show David another way to work with favorites—the Favorites bar.

Adding Links and Web Slices to the Favorites Bar

The Favorites bar provides another way to quickly access your favorite Web pages. The Favorites bar contains links to Web pages you view often, buttons for RSS feeds you subscribe to, and buttons for Web Slices you subscribe to. Recall that an RSS feed is frequently updated Web site content, such as news or blogs, delivered directly to your desktop when you are connected to the Internet. A Web Slice is a part (or a slice) of a Web page. For example, on a weather Web page, the current temperature might be a Web Slice. Any type of frequently changing information such as temperatures, auction details, sports scores, and stock quotes can be a Web Slice. As with an RSS feed, Web Slice information is delivered to your browser to provide up-to-date information.

When a Web page contains a Web Slice, an Add Web Slices button 🟢 appears on the Command bar. For example, an Add Web Slices button might appear on a page containing sports scores. Point to parts of the Web page to display a Web Slice icon next to the content you can add to your Favorites bar, such as the score for a particular game. Click the Add Web Slices button on the Command bar or the Web Slices icon on the Web page to subscribe to the information, indicating that you want to receive updates, such as whenever the score changes. After you subscribe to a Web Slice, it appears on the Favorites bar. The button name becomes bold when the related information, such as the score, changes. Click the bold Web Slice button to see up-to-date information from the full Web page. You can also click a link to open the full Web page itself.

First, you want to show David how to add the main Colorado.gov Web page to the Favorites bar because you know he will use that page often. The Favorites bar is not open by default, so you need to open it before you can add links to it.

To display the Favorites bar and add a link to it:

1. Click the **Tools** button on the Command bar, point to **Toolbars**, and then click **Favorites Bar**. The Favorites bar appears above the Command bar in the Internet Explorer window.

2. Click the **Colorado.gov: The Official State Web Portal** tab to display the main Colorado.gov Web page.

3. Click the **Add to Favorites Bar** button ⭐ on the Favorites bar to add the main Colorado.gov Web page to the Favorites bar. See Figure 4-15.

Figure 4-15 | Adding a link to the Favorites bar

David wants up-to-date reports on Denver weather because most tours are based in Denver. You'll show him how to add a Web Slice to the Favorites bar that provides current Denver weather information.

To add a Web Slice for Denver weather:

▶ 1. Click the **Home** button ⌂ on the Command bar to display the main MSN.com page.

   Trouble? If MSN.com is not the home page in your browser, click the Address bar, type *www.msn.com*, and then press the Enter key.

▶ 2. If necessary, click in the Search text box at the top of the page, type **Denver weather**, and then press the **Enter** key. A list of links to Web pages about Denver weather appears on a new Web page.

▶ 3. Point to the first result in the list to display a Web Slice icon. See Figure 4-16. Your links will likely be different. Note that the Add Web Slices button appears on the Command bar because this Web page contains a Web Slice.

Figure 4-16	Add Web Slices button on the Command bar

▶ 4. Click the **Web Slice** icon 🟢 next to the first result in the list. The Internet Explorer dialog box for adding a Web Slice opens.

▶ 5. Click the **Add to Favorites Bar** button. A new button appears on the Favorites bar for Weather in Denver, CO. The name appears in bold, indicating an update is available.

▶ 6. Click the **Weather in Denver, CO** button on the Favorites bar to display a preview of the Web Slice. See Figure 4-17.

TIP

You can also click the Add Web Slices button arrow on the Command bar, and then click a Web Slice name to subscribe to the Web Slice.

| Figure 4-17 | Add Web Slices button on the Command bar |

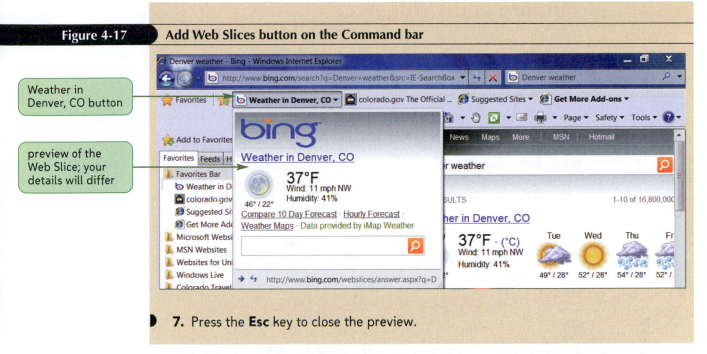

Weather in Denver, CO button

preview of the Web Slice; your details will differ

▶ **7.** Press the **Esc** key to close the preview.

Now that David can easily access the Web pages he needs in the Favorites list and on the Favorites bar, you can close the Favorites Center and Internet Explorer. If you have only one tab open, you close Internet Explorer the way you do any other program: click the Close button on the title bar. If more than one tab is open, however, you can choose to close a tab for a single Web page instead of closing the entire program. To close the tab for the current Web page, you click the Close Tab button. If you have more than one tab open and exit Internet Explorer, it asks if you want to close all tabs before exiting the program.

To close the Favorites Center, close tabs, and exit Internet Explorer:

▶ **1.** Click the **Close** button ⊠ to close the Favorites Center.

▶ **2.** Click the **Close** button ▇✕▇ on the Internet Explorer title bar. A dialog box opens and asks if you want to close all tabs.

▶ **3.** Click the **Close all tabs** button to close all the tabs and exit Internet Explorer.

INSIGHT

Letting Internet Explorer Suggest Sites

To help you discover Web sites that might interest you, you can use the Suggested Sites feature. When you turn on Suggested Sites, Internet Explorer reviews the Web pages open in your browser and those stored in your browsing history. Based on that information, it suggests other Web sites related to the content of the sites you visit most often. To view these suggestions, you click the Suggested Sites button on the Favorites bar. Suggested Sites is turned off by default. To turn it on, you can click the Tools button on the Command bar and then click Suggested Sites.

Now that you've added the Favorites bar and Web Slices to Internet Explorer, you are ready to explore another time-saving feature: Accelerators.

Finding and Using Accelerators

Like Web Slices, Accelerators are tools that make it easier to find information on the Web without navigating to other Web sites. For example, if you are viewing a Web page about a hotel in a city you plan to visit, you can select the hotel's address, and then use an Accelerator to quickly display a map showing the location of the hotel. Instead of copying the address, navigating to the Web page for a mapping service, pasting the address, and then viewing a map, you point to the Accelerator icon to display a preview of the map. In this case, you perform one step instead of four.

Accelerators are services provided by Web sites, so some sites have them and others do not. Internet Explorer comes with a selection of default Accelerators, including Bing Maps and Translate with Bing. (Bing is a search engine designed by Microsoft and replaces Live Search, the search engine in previous versions of Internet Explorer.) You can add or remove Accelerators as necessary using the Manage Add-ons dialog box.

David wants to review the list of outdoor activities for limited-mobility travelers provided on one of the Colorado Web pages, and then find a map to the location of one activity. You already closed the Favorites Center and Internet Explorer, so you need to start a new browsing session. You'll show David how to use the Address bar to revisit a Web page you have already opened.

To reopen a Web page using the Address bar:

▶ **1.** Start Internet Explorer.

▶ **2.** Click in the Address bar and then type **www.color**. As you type, a list of Web pages you visited that have an address starting with *www.color* appears below the Address bar. See Figure 4-18.

Figure 4-18	Reopening a Web page using the Address bar

text entered in the Address bar

list of Web pages visited that start with *www.color*

▶ **3.** Click **Accessible Colorado** to open the Accessible Colorado Web page.

Trouble? If the Accessible Colorado link does not appear below the Address bar when you type *www.color*, click in the Address bar, type *www.colorado.com/ AccessibleColorado.aspx*, and then press the Enter key.

▶ **4.** In the Outdoor Activities and Winter Sports list, hold down the **Ctrl** key and then click **Adaptive Sports Center at Crested Butte**. The Web page opens in a new tab.

Trouble? If the Adaptive Sports Center at Crested Butte does not appear in the Outdoor Activities and Winter Sports list, hold down the Ctrl key and click a different activity in the list.

▶ **5.** Click the **Adaptive Sports Center of Crested Butte Colorado** tab to display its Web page. This page provides exactly the type of information David needs.

David wants a map and directions to Crested Butte from Denver, Colorado. You'll show him how to use the Bing Maps Accelerator to find directions to any location in the United States. First, you'll verify that the Bing Maps Accelerator is installed on David's computer.

To use the Bing Maps Accelerator:

1. Click the **Page** button on the Command bar, point to **All Accelerators**, and then click **Manage Accelerators**. The Manage Add-ons dialog box opens, displaying a list of installed Accelerators. Scroll the list as necessary to display the Map section. See Figure 4-19.

Figure 4-19   Manage Add-ons dialog box listing installed Accelerators

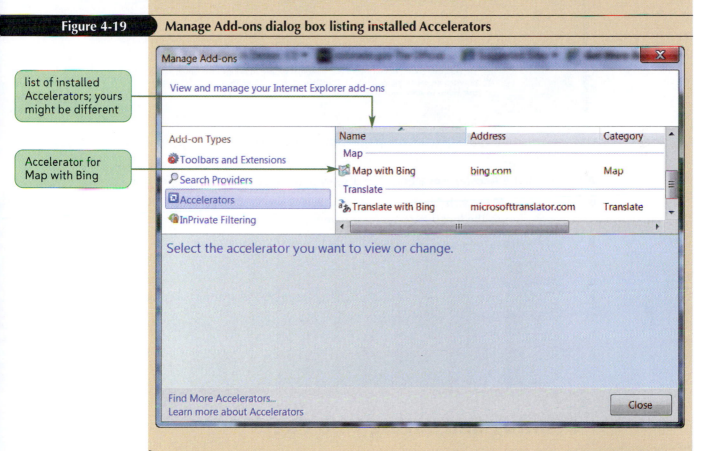

list of installed Accelerators; yours might be different

Accelerator for Map with Bing

2. Check to see whether Map with Bing is listed in the Map section, and then click the **Close** button.

3. If Map with Bing was not listed as one of the installed Accelerators, click the **Page** button on the Command bar, point to **All Accelerators**, click **Find More Accelerators**, find and click **Bing Maps** on the Accelerators Web page, click the **Add to Internet Explorer** button, click the **Add** button, and then click the **Back** button ⬅ on the Address bar to return to the Adaptive Sports Center Web page.

4. In the first descriptive paragraph on the Adaptive Sports Center Web page, drag to select the text **Crested Butte, Colorado**. A blue Accelerator icon ⬛ appears next to the selected text. See Figure 4-20.

Figure 4-20 Displaying an Accelerator

Trouble? If a different Web page is displayed, select an address or city name on the page.

5. Click the **Accelerator** icon ⬈ to display a menu of available Accelerators.

6. Point to **Map with Bing**. A preview map of Crested Butte appears with an arrow pointing to the location of the Adaptive Sports Center.

7. In the preview, click **Directions**. A Bing Maps Web page opens in a new tab. Crested Butte, Colorado, is already entered as the destination in the second text box.

8. Click in the first Directions text box, type **Denver, Colorado**, and then press the **Enter** key. The Bing Maps Web page shows driving directions from Denver to Crested Butte.

9. Close the Bing Maps tab. David can quickly find these directions again using the Bing Maps Accelerator.

Printing and Saving Web Pages

TIP

To preview a Web page before printing, click the Print button arrow on the Command bar, and then click Print Preview.

If you find a page on the Web and want to refer to it when you don't have computer access, you can print the Web page. Sometimes, Web pages include a Printer-Friendly Format link for printing a Web page, indicating that the Web site formats the page for a standard size sheet of paper before printing. However, not all Web pages provide such an option. Therefore, you should preview the page before you print it to see how it will look when printed. To print a Web page, you click the Print button on the Internet Explorer Command bar.

You can also save Web pages and the content they contain. To save a Web page as a file on your computer, click the Page button on the Command bar, and then click Save As. Enter a name for the file in the File name text box, and then select one of four file types by clicking the Save as type button. To save all the files associated with the page, including graphics, frames, and style sheets in their original format, select Webpage, complete. To save all the information as a single file, select Web Archive, single file. To save only the current page without graphics or other media files, select Webpage, HTML only. To save only the text from the current Web page, select Text File. Finally, click the Save button.

PROSKILLS

Decision Making: Determining Whether to Save Web Page Content

Using a browser, you can easily save Web page content on your computer, including the graphic images displayed on the page, files the Web page provides, such as text or music files, and the Web page itself. However, doing so is not always legal or ethical. Before you save any Web page content on your computer, you need to determine whether you have the legal right to do so. This is especially important when you want to save and use images, video, and other media for work projects because commercial use of such content is often prohibited.

Web content such as software, video, music, and images is easy to copy in its digital form. However, if this material is protected by copyright, you usually are not allowed to copy or share it unless you receive permission from the owner. The term **copyright** refers to the originator's exclusive legal right to reproduce, publish, or sell works they create. If you copy someone else's work without giving that person credit, you are committing plagiarism, and you may also be violating copyright laws.

Before you copy or save content from Web sites that you visit, you need to find out if and how you can use the materials. If you want to use material you find on a Web site, first get permission from the owner of the site. Often, Web sites include their copyright and permission-request information on their main pages. Even if you think that information or material you found is not copyrighted, you should always request permission to use it and give credit to any Web site that you use in your work or school projects.

David does not want to print or save any information you found for Entrée Tours because he can access it quickly using Internet Explorer tools. You can close all the open tabs and exit Internet Explorer.

To close tabs and exit Internet Explorer:

▸ **1.** Click the **Close** button [X] on the Internet Explorer title bar. A dialog box opens and asks if you want to close all tabs.

▸ **2.** Click the **Close all tabs** button to close the tabs and exit Internet Explorer.

So far, you have learned about the structure of the Internet and the Web, and how to use Internet Explorer to open, navigate, and organize Web pages. In the next session, you'll use another service the Internet provides—e-mail.

REVIEW

Session 4.1 Quick Check

1. Explain the relationship between the Internet and the Web.
2. True or False. A Web site is a collection of Web pages that have a common theme or focus.
3. A(n) _____ is a program that locates, retrieves, and displays Web pages.
4. When you start Internet Explorer, what does it display by default?
5. The address of a Web page is called a(n) _____.
6. Explain why you would use an Accelerator in Internet Explorer.
7. Describe three ways you can open a Web page you visited recently.
8. A(n) _____ lets you see when updated information is available on a Web page.

SESSION 4.2 VISUAL OVERVIEW

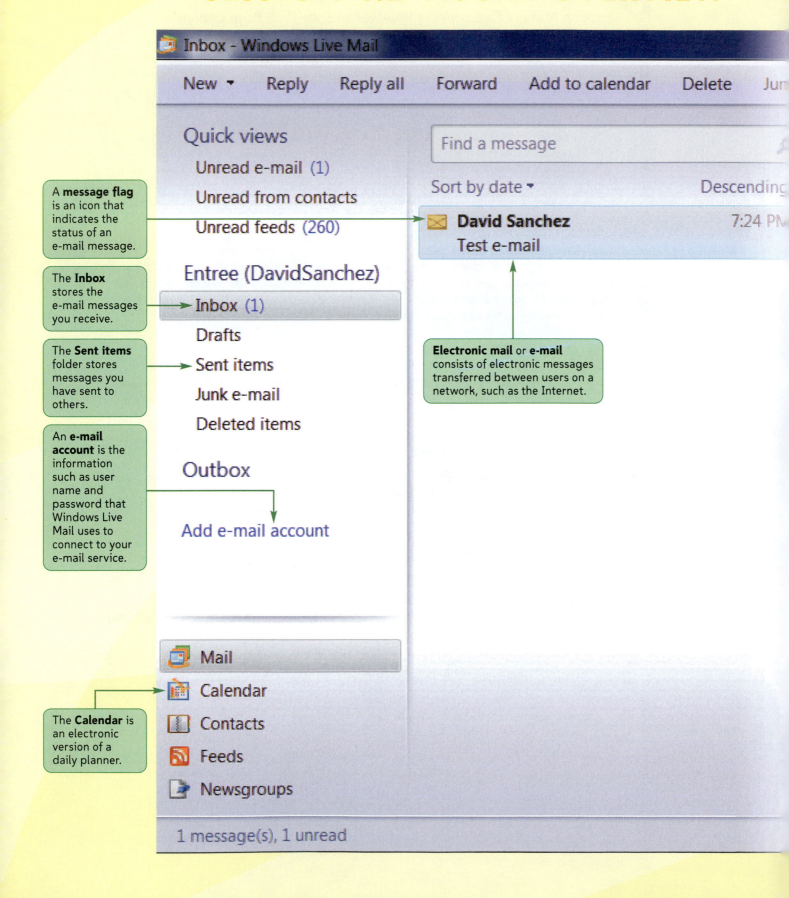

Inbox - Windows Live Mail

New ▾   Reply   Reply all   Forward   Add to calendar   Delete   Jun

Quick views

A **message flag** is an icon that indicates the status of an e-mail message.

Unread e-mail (1)
Unread from contacts
Unread feeds (260)

Find a message

Sort by date ▾   Descending

✉ **David Sanchez**   7:24 PM
Test e-mail

Entree (DavidSanchez)

The **Inbox** stores the e-mail messages you receive.

Inbox (1)

Electronic mail or **e-mail** consists of electronic messages transferred between users on a network, such as the Internet.

Drafts

The **Sent items** folder stores messages you have sent to others.

Sent items
Junk e-mail
Deleted items

Outbox

An **e-mail account** is the information such as user name and password that Windows Live Mail uses to connect to your e-mail service.

Add e-mail account

📧 Mail
📅 Calendar
📖 Contacts
📶 Feeds
📲 Newsgroups

The **Calendar** is an electronic version of a daily planner.

1 message(s), 1 unread

WINDOWS LIVE MAIL

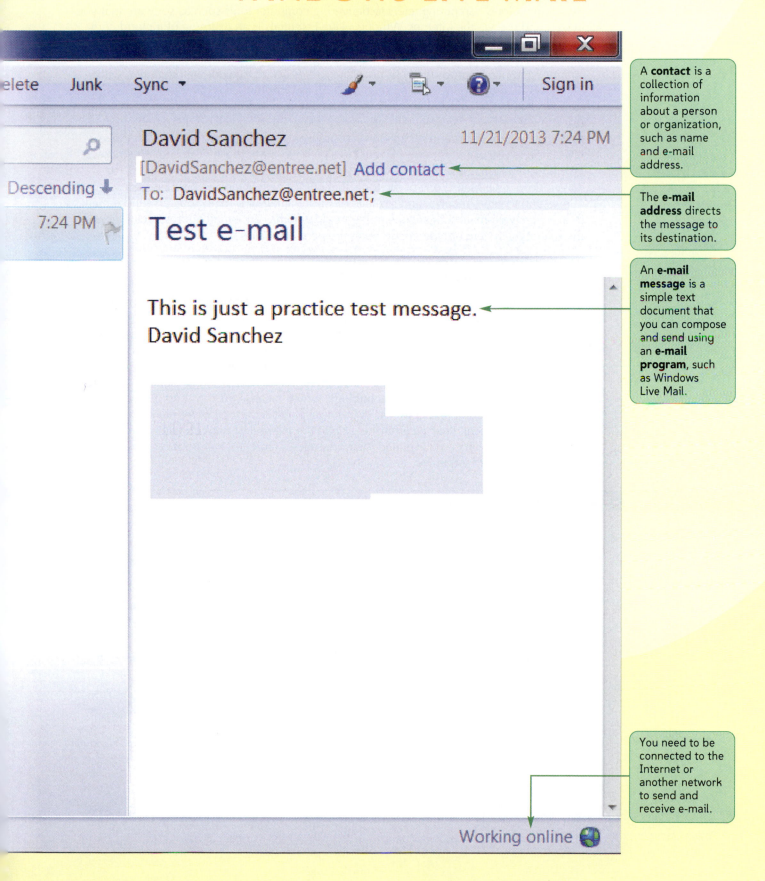

A **contact** is a collection of information about a person or organization, such as name and e-mail address.

The **e-mail address** directs the message to its destination.

An **e-mail message** is a simple text document that you can compose and send using an **e-mail program**, such as Windows Live Mail.

You need to be connected to the Internet or another network to send and receive e-mail.

Getting Started with Windows Live Mail

Recall that cloud computing refers to delivering computer tools such as software that you access and use via the Internet. Windows Live Essentials is an example of a cloud computing tool because you access it on the Web and can use some of its programs in your browser. Windows Live Essentials includes programs for e-mail, instant messaging, photo sharing, and other purposes. These programs are designed to work well together, with Windows 7, and with Web-based services such as Windows Live Photos (which lets you send photos to the computing cloud and share them with other people). Before you can use some Windows Live Essentials programs, you need to download them free of charge onto your computer from a Microsoft Web site. For other programs, such as Windows Live Photos, you use a Windows Live ID to sign on to a Microsoft Web site. A Windows Live ID is a user name and password that lets you access Microsoft services.

Windows Live Mail is one of the tools that comes with Windows Live Essentials. It allows you to send, receive, and manage electronic mail or e-mail. You can send e-mail to and receive e-mail from anyone in the world who has an e-mail address, regardless of the operating system or type of computer the person is using.

Examining How E-Mail Works

An e-mail message is a simple text document that you can compose and send using an e-mail program, such as Windows Live Mail. When you send a message, it travels from your computer, through a network, and arrives at a computer called an **e-mail server**. The e-mail server stores the e-mail messages until the recipients request them. Then the server forwards the messages to the appropriate computers. Typically, the system administrator of your network or ISP manages the e-mail server.

E-mail uses **store-and-forward technology**, which means you can send messages to anyone on the Internet or a network, even if they don't have their computers turned on. When it's convenient, your recipients log on to the Internet or network and use their e-mail programs to receive and read their messages. Figure 4-21 illustrates sending and receiving e-mail messages.

Figure 4-21 **Sending and receiving e-mail**

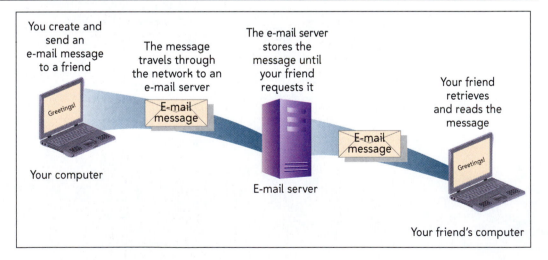

You create and send an e-mail message to a friend

The message travels through the network to an e-mail server

The e-mail server stores the message until your friend requests it

Your friend retrieves and reads the message

E-mail message

Greetings!

Your computer

E-mail server

E-mail message

Greetings!

Your friend's computer

To send and receive e-mail, you must be able to access an e-mail server on the network. If your computer is part of a network at a college or university, for example, you log on to the network to access its services. An e-mail server provides mail services to faculty, staff, and students who have access to the network. When someone sends you a message, it is stored on your e-mail server until you log on to the network and use an e-mail program to check your mail. The e-mail server then transfers new messages to your electronic mailbox. You use an e-mail program to open, read, print, delete, reply to, forward, and save the mail.

If your computer is not part of a network, you can access an e-mail server on the Internet. To do so, you open an e-mail account with a service that provides Internet access. For example, e-mail accounts are included as part of the subscription fee for most ISPs. E-mail accounts are also provided free of charge by advertiser-supported Web sites, such as Yahoo! and Google. After you establish an e-mail account, you can connect to the Internet to send and receive your e-mail messages.

Addressing E-Mail

Just as you must address a piece of ordinary mail, you need to supply an address for an e-mail message. The e-mail address you enter directs the message to its destination. Your e-mail address is included in the message as the return address, so your recipients can easily respond to your message. Anyone who has an e-mail address can send and receive electronic mail. If you work for a company or attend a school that provides e-mail, a system administrator probably assigns an e-mail address for you. Other times, you create your own e-mail address, though it must follow a particular format. See Figure 4-22.

Figure 4-22	Typical format of an e-mail address

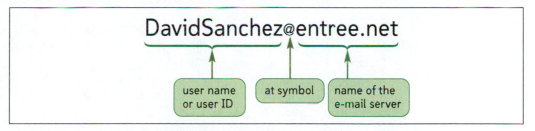

The **user name**, or **user ID**, is the name entered when your e-mail account is set up. The @ symbol signifies that the e-mail server name is provided next. In Figure 4-22, *DavidSanchez* is the user name and *entree.net* is the e-mail server.

The easiest way to learn a person's e-mail address is to ask the person what it is. You can also look up an e-mail address in a network or Internet directory. Most businesses and schools publish a directory listing e-mail addresses of those who have e-mail accounts on their network. Many Web sites also provide e-mail directories for people with e-mail accounts on the Internet, such as *www.people.yahoo.com*.

When you sign up for an e-mail account, you can send your new e-mail address to friends, colleagues, and clients. If your e-mail address changes, such as when you change e-mail services, you can subscribe to an e-mail forwarding service so you don't miss any mail sent to your old address.

Written Communication: Observing E-Mail Etiquette

Because e-mail is a widespread form of communication, you should follow standard guidelines when using it. Most of these guidelines are common sense practices, such as using appropriate language. Others might be new to you. For example, you should understand that e-mail is not private. When you correspond with others using e-mail, the information you send can be read by other users, especially if you work for a corporation or private institution. Your correspondents can easily forward your message to others, deliberately or inadvertently revealing information you consider confidential. It's a good idea to be professional and careful about what you say to and about others.

Keep the following guidelines in mind when you are composing messages so that you use e-mail to communicate effectively, without offending or annoying your correspondents:

- *Include meaningful subjects.* Most e-mail programs show the subject line, date, and sender address for incoming mail. Let your correspondents know the purpose of your message by including information in the subject line that concisely and accurately describes the message contents. For example, a subject such as *Staff meeting rescheduled* is more informative than *Meeting.*
- *Reply only as necessary.* When you want to respond to an e-mail message, you can click the Reply button to reply to the original sender or you can click the Reply all button to respond to everyone who received the original message. When you use the Reply all button, make sure that everyone listed as recipients really needs to receive the message so that you are not flooding electronic inboxes with unnecessary e-mails.
- *Include your response first.* When you reply to an e-mail, you can include text from the original message. If you do, make sure that your response is at the top of the message so your recipients can find it easily.
- *Don't e-mail sensitive or confidential information.* Keep in mind that e-mail is not private, and your recipients can forward your message to others, either intentionally or accidentally.
- *Be concise and direct.* People often read e-mail messages while they are doing something else. As a courtesy to your correspondents and to make sure your message is read, get right to the point and keep your messages short.
- *Avoid abbreviations.* Although you should strive to be brief, don't overcompensate by using nonstandard abbreviations. Stick to the abbreviations that are common in business writing, such as FYI and ASAP.
- *Don't use all capital letters.* Using all capital letters, as in *SEND ME THE REPORT TODAY,* makes it look like you're shouting and can be difficult to read.
- *Pause and reread before sending.* Be sure to read the e-mails you write before you send them, and consider how they could be received. A message that you intend to be funny could be misinterpreted as rude. If you wrote an e-mail in anger, calm down and revise your message before sending it. After you send an e-mail message, you can't retrieve or stop it.

Setting Up Windows Live Mail

To use e-mail, you need an Internet connection, an e-mail program such as Windows Live Mail, and an e-mail address. Make sure you have an Internet connection and e-mail address before performing the steps in this section. Windows Live Mail is not installed with Windows 7. Your first task is to download and install Windows Live Mail from the Windows Live Essentials Web site.

After you install Windows Live Mail, it can be the standard e-mail software you use on your computer, similar to Outlook Express or Windows Mail in previous editions of Windows. In this case, you do not need to have a Windows Live ID to use Windows Live Mail. If you use a Web-based e-mail service such as Hotmail or Gmail, you also can use Windows Live Mail to access, read, and send e-mail using those accounts. However, you must have a Windows Live ID account to use Web-based e-mail services with Windows Live Mail.

This tutorial assumes that you are not using a Windows Live ID e-mail account. If you are, some of the steps will be different. These are noted throughout the tutorial. You must be connected to the Internet to perform all the steps in this session.

To download and install Windows Live Mail:

1. Click the **Start** button 🟦 on the taskbar. The insertion point appears in the Search programs and files text box.

2. Type **Windows Live Essentials** in the text box to search for links on your computer to the Windows Live Essentials Web site.

3. Click **Go online to get Windows Live Essentials** on the Start menu. The main Windows Live Essentials Web page opens in your browser. See Figure 4-23.

Figure 4-23	Windows Live Essentials Web page

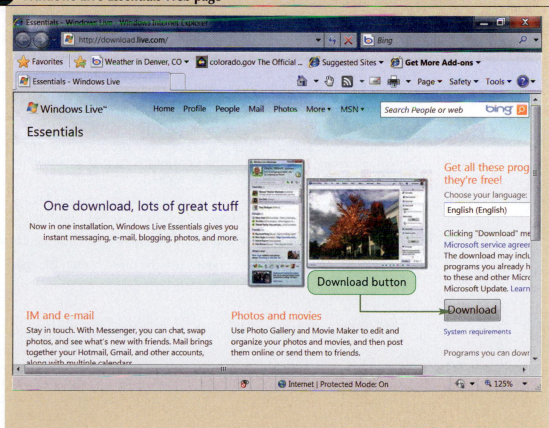

4. Click the **Download** button. A File Download – Security Warning dialog box opens.

5. Click the **Run** button. The Windows Live Essentials program files begin to download from the Web site. If a User Account Control dialog box opens asking if you want to allow the program to make changes to the computer, click the **Yes** button. After a few moments, the Welcome to Windows Live window opens.

Make sure you select the Mail check box before completing this step.

6. When a window opens listing programs you can install, make sure the Mail check box is selected. Then click all the other check boxes to deselect them. See Figure 4-24.

Figure 4-24   Selecting Windows Live Essentials programs to install

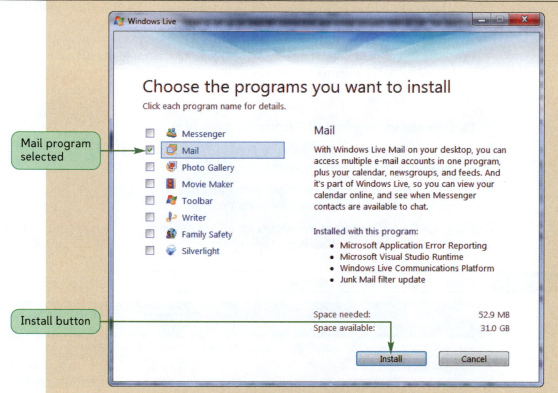

Mail program selected

Install button

7. Click the **Install** button. If a window opens asking you to close an open program such as Internet Explorer, click the **Close these programs for me** option button, if necessary, and then click the **Continue** button. Wait a few minutes while Windows Live Mail is installed on your computer.

8. When installation is complete, a Windows Live window opens asking you to select settings. Click the **Continue** button to accept the default settings.

9. When a window opens welcoming you to Windows Live, click the **Close** button.

Trouble? If Internet Explorer opens, click the Close button ![X] to close Internet Explorer.

After you install Windows Live Mail and set up an account with an e-mail service provider (usually this is your ISP), you add your account to Windows Live Mail so you can use it to exchange e-mail. If you are at a university or other institution, this might have been done for you; but if you are using your own computer, you probably have to add it yourself. At a minimum, Windows Live Mail needs to know your e-mail address, password, and the names of your incoming and outgoing e-mail servers. The type of server you choose corresponds to the type of account you have with your service provider. Windows Live Mail supports the following types of e-mail accounts:

- Post Office Protocol 3 (POP3): These servers hold incoming e-mail messages until you check your e-mail; then they deliver it to your computer. After delivering messages, e-mail servers usually delete them. POP3 is the most common account type for personal e-mail.
- Internet Message Access Protocol (IMAP): With this type of account, your e-mail is stored on an e-mail server, not on your computer. You can access your e-mail directly on the server, and then preview, delete, and organize messages. IMAP is usually used for business e-mail accounts.
- Simple Mail Transfer Protocol (SMTP): These accounts are for outgoing e-mail. You use them with a POP3 or IMAP account for incoming e-mail.

The first time you start Windows Live Mail, a series of dialog boxes guides you through the process of setting up an account. The following steps show you how to set up a Windows Live Mail account. If you already have an e-mail account, read but do not perform the following steps.

David Sanchez has an e-mail account with Entrée Tours, but he hasn't set up Windows Live Mail to use that account. Because this is the first time you're starting Windows Live Mail on his Windows 7 computer, you'll show him how to set up Windows Live Mail to use his Entrée Tours account.

To set up Windows Live Mail:

1. Click the **Start** button 🪟 on the taskbar, point to **All Programs**, if necessary, click the **Windows Live** folder, and then click **Windows Live Mail**. The Windows Live Mail program starts. If this is the first time you started Windows Live Mail, the Add an E-mail Account dialog box opens, requesting your e-mail account information.

   Trouble? If you have already set up Windows Live Mail, the main Windows Live Mail window opens instead of the Add an E-mail Account dialog box. Read but do not perform the rest of the steps.

   Trouble? If the main Windows Live Mail window opens instead of the Add an E-mail Account dialog box and you have not set up an e-mail account yet, click the Add e-mail account link in the Folder pane to open the Add an E-mail Account dialog box.

   Trouble? If a dialog box opens asking if you want Windows Live Mail to be your default mail program, click the Yes button only if you are using your own computer and want to use Windows Live Mail as your mail program. If you are using a school or institutional computer, click the No button or ask your technical support person for assistance.

2. Enter your e-mail address, such as **DavidSanchez@entree.net**.

3. Click the **Password** text box, and then enter the password for your e-mail account. (Your ISP might provide this information initially, though you can often change it.)

4. Click the **Display Name** text box, and then enter the name you want to appear as the sender of the e-mails you send, such as **David Sanchez**. Click the **Next** button. The next dialog box opens, requesting information about your e-mail server.

   Trouble? If you already have an e-mail account on Windows Live (*www.windowslive.com*) and have signed in to your Windows Live account, a summary window might open instead of a dialog box requesting information about your e-mail server. Skip Steps 5–9.

TIP

Check the Remember password check box, if necessary, if you don't want to enter the password each time you send and receive e-mail.

5. Click the **POP3** button, if necessary, to select a different type of incoming e-mail server. (Your ISP typically provides this information.)

6. Click the **Incoming server** text box, and then enter the name of your incoming e-mail server, such as **pop.entree.net**. (Your ISP usually provides this information.)

7. If necessary, click the **Login ID (if different from your e-mail address)** text box, and then enter the user name you use to access your e-mail account.

8. Click the **Outgoing server** text box, and then enter the name of your outgoing e-mail server, such as **smtp.entree.net**. (Your ISP usually provides this information.) If your server requires a user name and password when sending mail in addition to when receiving it, click the **My outgoing server requires authentication** check box.

9. Click the **Next** button. A dialog box opens indicating you have entered all the information required to set up your account.

10. Click the **Finish** button.

   Trouble? If a dialog box opens asking if you want to import mail from another e-mail program, do not import the e-mail unless your instructor indicates that you should do so.

Now you can show David how to send and receive e-mail.

Sending and Receiving E-Mail Using Windows Live Mail

You can use the Windows Live Mail program to compose, send, and receive e-mail messages. After you set up an e-mail account, you're ready to start using Windows Live Mail to manage your e-mail.

To start Windows Live Mail:

1. Start Windows Live Mail, if necessary. (Click the **Start** button 🔵 on the taskbar, point to **All Programs**, if necessary, click the **Windows Live** folder, and then click **Windows Live Mail**.) The main Windows Live Mail program window opens. See Figure 4-25. The e-mail account shown in the figures in this tutorial belongs to David Sanchez. Your screens will look different from the figures.

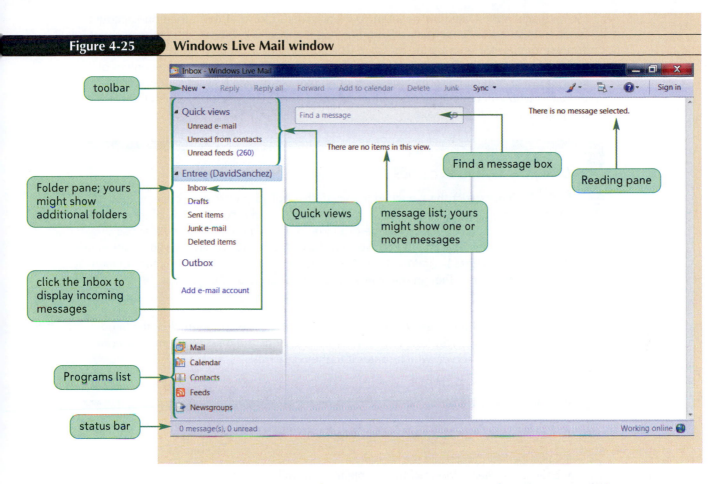

Figure 4-25   Windows Live Mail window

In addition to the standard Windows components, such as the title bar, Close button, and scroll bars, the Windows Live Mail window includes the following elements:

- Toolbar: The toolbar provides buttons for frequently performed commands, such as creating, replying to, and forwarding e-mail.
- Find a message box: This box lets you find e-mail messages by searching for text contained in any part of the message.
- Folder pane: This pane displays the default Windows Live Mail folders, including the Inbox, Drafts, Sent items, Junk e-mail, Deleted items, and Outbox folders. Windows Live Mail organizes your e-mail into these folders automatically. You can create additional folders for the messages you create and receive.
- Programs list: This list provides shortcuts to programs related to Windows Live Mail, including Calendar, Contacts, Feeds, and Newsgroups.
- Quick views: This section shows you the categories of e-mail and other accounts you use most often, such as unread e-mail.
- Message list: When you start Windows Live Mail, it displays a list of the messages in your Inbox by default. These are the messages you've received. If you select a different folder, Windows Live Mail displays those messages in the list.
- Reading pane: This pane displays the contents of the selected message.

Creating and Sending E-Mail Messages

An e-mail message uses a format similar to a standard memo: It typically includes Date, To, and Subject lines, followed by the content of the message. The To line indicates who will receive the message. Windows Live Mail automatically supplies the date you send the message in the Date line (as set in your computer's clock). If more than one account is set up in Windows Live Mail, a From line might appear so you can select the account you want to use for sending the message. The Subject line, although optional, alerts the recipient to the topic of the message. Finally, the message area contains the content of your message. You can also include additional information, such as a Cc line, which indicates who will receive a copy of the message, or a Priority setting, which indicates the new importance of the message.

INSIGHT

Using the Cc and Bcc Lines

In the To line, restrict the e-mail addresses to those of your primary recipients. Use the Cc (carbon copy) line for secondary recipients who should receive a copy of the message. If you are sending an e-mail message to a large group of people, you can also use the Bcc (blind carbon copy) line. (Click the Show Cc & Bcc link to specify that you want to use these additional lines.) Windows Live Mail sends an individual message to each person listed in the Bcc line, though the only other e-mail address that appears is the sender's.

To send an e-mail message, you first compose the message and then click the Send button on the message window. Windows Live Mail sends the message from your computer to your e-mail server, which routes it to the recipient.

REFERENCE

Creating and Sending an E-Mail Message

- Click the New button on the toolbar.
- Enter the e-mail address of the recipient in the To box.
- Click the Subject box and then type the subject of the message.
- Click the message area and then type the content of the message.
- Click the Send button.

To create and send an e-mail message:

1. Click the **New** button on the Windows Live Mail toolbar. The New Message window opens. See Figure 4-26.

Figure 4-26 | **New Message window**

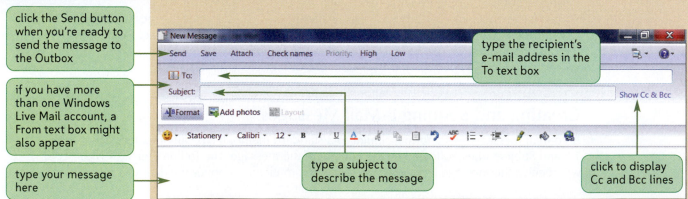

click the Send button when you're ready to send the message to the Outbox

if you have more than one Windows Live Mail account, a From text box might also appear

type your message here

type the recipient's e-mail address in the To text box

type a subject to describe the message

click to display Cc and Bcc lines

2. Type your e-mail address in the To text box.

   Trouble? If you're not sure what e-mail address you should enter, check with your instructor or technical support person.

3. Click the **Subject** text box, and then type **Test e-mail**.

4. Click in the message area, type **This is just a practice test message.**, press the **Enter** key, and then type your name.

5. Click the **Send** button on the toolbar. Windows Live Mail places the message in the Outbox. After a second or two, Windows Live Mail removes the message from the Outbox, sends the message to your e-mail server, and then places a copy of the sent message in the Sent items folder.

   To make sure your message has been sent, you can open the Sent items folder to see all the messages you have sent.

   Trouble? If, after several seconds have passed, Windows Live Mail still displays *(1)* to the right of the Outbox folder in the Folder pane, indicating that there is one unsent message, then Windows Live Mail is not configured to send messages immediately. In that case, click the Sync button on the toolbar to send your message.

6. Click the **Sent items** folder in the Folder pane. Your message appears in the Message list and the content of the message appears in the Reading pane. See Figure 4-27.

Figure 4-27 | **Sent items folder**

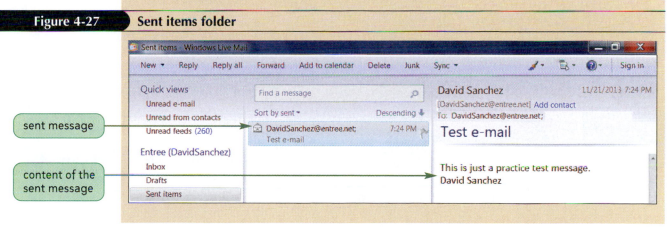

If you had wanted to send this message to many people, you could have typed more than one e-mail address in the To or Cc text boxes. Separate each address with a comma or semicolon. You can also add the e-mail addresses of people (your contacts) to Windows Live Contacts, which you'll do shortly.

Receiving and Reading E-Mail Messages

Windows Live Mail automatically checks to see if you've received e-mail whenever you start the program and periodically after that. (Every 30 minutes is the default.) Windows Live Mail also checks for received e-mail when you click the Sync button. E-mail you receive appears in your Inbox. By default, the Inbox shows only the name of the sender, the subject, and the date you received the message. Mail you have received but have not read yet appears in bold. To preview a message, you click the message in the list to display its contents in the Reading pane, or you can double-click the message to open it in a separate window. In either case, you can print the messages you receive.

To receive, read, and print the Test e-mail message:

1. Click **Inbox** in the Folder pane to display the contents of the Inbox folder in the right pane. (Your Inbox might not contain any messages yet.)

2. Click the **Sync** button on the toolbar. Windows Live Mail retrieves your messages from your e-mail server, routes them to your Inbox, and displays the number of unread messages to the right of the Inbox folder. See Figure 4-28. Your Inbox folder might contain additional e-mail messages from other people.

Figure 4-28   **Inbox folder**

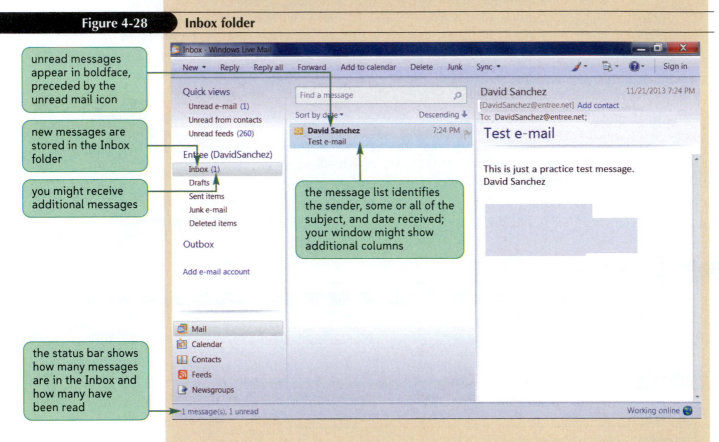

unread messages appear in boldface, preceded by the unread mail icon

new messages are stored in the Inbox folder

you might receive additional messages

the message list identifies the sender, some or all of the subject, and date received; your window might show additional columns

the status bar shows how many messages are in the Inbox and how many have been read

Trouble? If a dialog box opens requesting your user name and password, enter the information and continue with Step 3. See your instructor or technical support person if you need help entering the correct user name or password.

Trouble? If the message you sent doesn't appear in the Inbox, wait a few minutes, and then click the Sync button again.

3. If necessary, click the **Test e-mail** message to display its contents in the Reading pane.

4. Double-click the **Test e-mail** message in the Message list. The Test e-mail message window opens. See Figure 4-29.

TIP

To sort messages, click the Sort by button, and then select a category such as From, Date, or Subject.

Figure 4-29   **Reading a message**

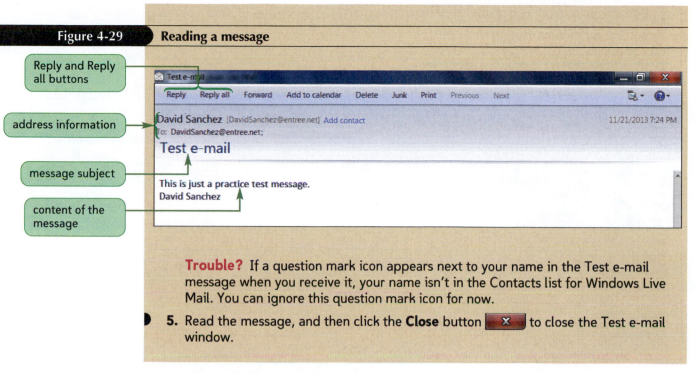

Reply and Reply all buttons

address information

message subject

content of the message

Trouble? If a question mark icon appears next to your name in the Test e-mail message when you receive it, your name isn't in the Contacts list for Windows Live Mail. You can ignore this question mark icon for now.

5. Read the message, and then click the **Close** button 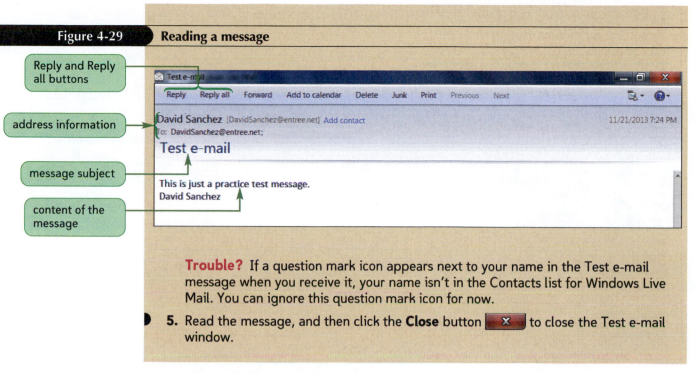 to close the Test e-mail window.

Next, you'll show David how to perform another common e-mail task—replying to the messages you receive.

Replying to E-Mail Messages

Some of the e-mail you receive may ask you to provide information, answer questions, or confirm decisions. Instead of creating a new e-mail message, you can reply directly to a message that you receive. When you reply to a message, Windows Live Mail inserts the e-mail address of the sender and the subject into the proper lines in the message window, and includes the text of the original message.

You can reply to messages by clicking the Reply or Reply all button. If the original message was sent to more than one person, click the Reply button to respond to only the original sender. Use the Reply all button to respond to all the other recipients as well. Keep in mind the e-mail etiquette guideline about using the Reply all button carefully so that the only messages people receive from you are those they need to read.

You can reply to an open message or to one selected in your Message list.

To reply to the Test e-mail message:

1. With the Test e-mail message selected in the Message list, click the **Reply** button on the toolbar. The Re: Test e-mail window opens. See Figure 4-30.

| Figure 4-30 | Replying to a message |

recipient's user name automatically appears

subject automatically appears, preceded by Re:

space for the new message

original message is included for reference

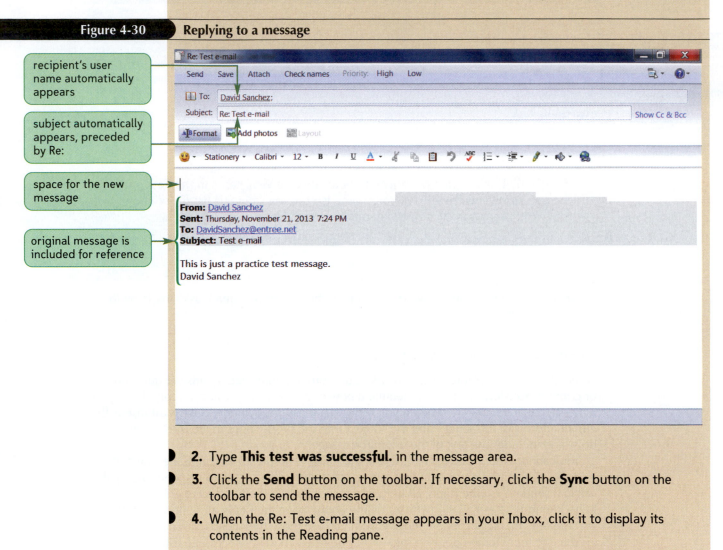

2. Type **This test was successful.** in the message area.

3. Click the **Send** button on the toolbar. If necessary, click the **Sync** button on the toolbar to send the message.

4. When the Re: Test e-mail message appears in your Inbox, click it to display its contents in the Reading pane.

David might want to delete the e-mail messages he's read. You'll show him how to delete e-mail messages next.

Deleting E-Mail Messages

After you read and respond to your messages, you can delete any message you no longer need. When you delete a message, it moves to the Deleted items folder. Messages remain in the Deleted items folder until you empty, or permanently delete, the folder contents. This folder might be set up to permanently delete its contents when you close Windows Live Mail. If not, you should do so periodically by right-clicking the Deleted items folder in the Folder pane, clicking Empty 'Deleted items' folder on the shortcut menu, and then clicking the Yes button to confirm the deletion.

To delete the Test e-mail messages:

► **1.** Click the **Test e-mail** message in the Message list, hold down the **Shift** key, click the **Re: Test e-mail** message, and then click the **Delete** button on the toolbar. The Inbox Message list no longer displays the Test messages.

INSIGHT

Dealing with Junk E-Mail

Junk e-mail, or spam, is unsolicited e-mail, often containing advertisements, fraudulent schemes, or legitimate offers. Windows Live Mail includes a junk e-mail filter that analyzes the content of the e-mail messages you receive and moves suspicious messages to the Junk e-mail folder, where you can examine and manage them as necessary. To reduce the amount of junk e-mail you receive, avoid posting your e-mail address on Web sites or other public areas of the Internet. If a Web site requests your e-mail address, read its privacy statement to make sure it doesn't disclose your e-mail address to others. Finally, never respond to junk e-mail—you're likely to receive even more spam.

David mentions that clients often request itineraries of upcoming trips, which he stores in separate documents. You'll show him how to attach a file to an e-mail message so he can reply to clients and provide the documents they request.

Attaching a File to a Message

Besides sending e-mail to others, you can also transfer files to them by attaching the files to messages. You can send any kind of file, including documents, pictures, music, or videos.

You'll show David how to send and open an e-mail message that includes an attachment. As before, you'll create a test message and send it to yourself.

To create and send a message with an attachment:

► **1.** Click the **New** button on the toolbar.

► **2.** Type your e-mail address in the To box.

► **3.** Type **Itinerary you requested** in the Subject text box.

► **4.** Click the **Attach** button on the toolbar. The Open dialog box opens.

► **5.** Navigate to the **Tutorial.04\Tutorial** folder provided with your Data Files, and then double-click **Colorado**. Windows Live Mail attaches the file to the message and displays the filename and size below the Subject text box.

► **6.** Type **This is a test e-mail message with a file attachment.** in the message area.

► **7.** Click the **Send** button on the toolbar.

Trouble? If a Spelling dialog box opens indicating that a word you typed is not in the dictionary, click the Ignore button.

► **8.** If necessary, click the **Sync** button on the toolbar to send and receive the message.

When you receive a message that contains an attachment, you can choose to save or open the attached file. You should open files only after scanning them with antivirus software. Some people spread harmful software, called viruses, in e-mail attachments. (You will learn more about viruses in Tutorial 5.) To open the file, you need to make sure the program used to create the attachment is installed on your computer. If it's not, you can sometimes use a text editor, such as WordPad or Notepad, to open and read the attached file.

To receive and open a message with an attachment:

▶ **1.** When the Itinerary you requested message appears in your Inbox, click the message in the Message list so the contents appear in the Reading pane.

▶ **2.** Right-click the **Colorado.rtf** filename in the Reading pane to display a shortcut menu, which lets you open, print, or save the attachment.

▶ **3.** Click **Open** on the shortcut menu. A Mail Attachment dialog box might open, asking you to confirm that you want to open the file.

▶ **4.** If necessary, click the **Open** button. The file opens in a word-processing program, such as Word or WordPad. You could save the document now if necessary.

▶ **5.** Close the word-processing program.

Avoiding E-Mail Viruses

Windows Live Mail blocks certain types of file attachments that are commonly used to spread e-mail viruses, including files with the following filename extensions: .exe, .pif, and .scr. If Windows Live Mail blocks an attachment in an e-mail message, an Information bar appears below the toolbar and displays a message letting you know that it has blocked an attachment.

Another bit of e-mail etiquette applies to attachments. If you attach a large file to an e-mail message, it might take a long time for your recipient to download your message. Most e-mail servers limit the size of the files you can attach; some allow files no larger than 1 MB. Check with your correspondents before sending large file attachments to find out about size restrictions and set up a convenient time to send the attachment.

A new feature in Windows Live Mail lets you avoid using attachments when you send photographs. Instead of attaching photos, which usually are large files, you can click the Add photos button in a New Message window to send thumbnails, which are smaller versions of your photos. Recipients can click the thumbnail to display larger versions, and everyone avoids the problems of attaching large files.

Adding Information to Windows Live Contacts

You can use Windows Live Contacts to keep track of all your e-mail correspondents—it works like an address book for Windows Live Mail. You can also use Windows Live Contacts on its own to save information about people and organizations. In addition to storing e-mail addresses, you can store related information such as street addresses, home phone numbers, and personal information such as anniversaries and birthdays. When you create an e-mail message, you can click the To button to open a dialog box listing your contacts. Click the name you want, and then click the To button to indicate that you want to send a message to this contact.

You can add contact information to Windows Live Contacts by creating a new contact, and then entering as much information as you want about that contact in the Add a Contact dialog box. When you send an e-mail message to someone, you can add his or her information to Windows Live Contacts by clicking Add Contact in the Reading pane.

Adding a Contact in Windows Live Mail

- Click Contacts in the Programs area of the Folder pane.
- Click the New button on the toolbar.
- Enter contact information in the Add a Contact dialog box.
- Click Add Contact.

You'll show David how to use Windows Live Contacts to add a new contact.

To add a contact:

1. Click **Contacts** in the Programs area of the Folder pane. The Windows Live Contacts window opens, listing your contacts. Your Windows Live Contacts window might not contain any contacts.

2. Click the **New** button on the toolbar. The Add a Contact dialog box opens with the Quick add category selected.

3. Type **David** in the First name text box, press the **Tab** key, and then type **Sanchez** in the Last name text box.

4. Press the **Tab** key, and then type **DavidSanchez@entree.net** in the Personal e-mail text box.

5. Press the **Tab** key twice, and then type **Entree Tours** in the Company text box. See Figure 4-31.

| Figure 4-31 | Adding a new contact |

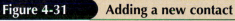

click to add fields for other contact information, such as home address

contact information

6. Click the **Add contact** button. If necessary, click **David Sanchez** in the Windows Live Contacts window to display his detailed contact information in the Reading pane. See Figure 4-32.

Figure 4-32   **New contact in Windows Live Contacts**

> **7.** Click the **Close** button [X] to close the Windows Live Contacts window.

You're finished showing David how to use Windows Live Mail to exchange e-mail. Next, you want to help him manage his schedule with the Windows Live Calendar.

Managing Your Schedule with Windows Live Calendar

Windows Live Calendar is another tool available in Windows Live Mail. You use it to schedule appointments, track tasks, and stay on top of deadlines. Windows Live Calendar also lets you schedule recurring events, such as weekly staff meetings, and set reminders so you don't miss an important appointment. When you schedule an event, Windows Live Calendar blocks out the time in your schedule, helping you avoid scheduling conflicts.

Because David works so often at his computer, he is ready to use an electronic calendar. You'll show him how to start Windows Live Calendar and schedule an appointment.

Starting Windows Live Calendar

As with Windows Live Contacts, you can open Windows Live Calendar from the Programs area of the Folder pane.

To start Windows Live Calendar:

1. Click **Calendar** in the Programs area of the Folder pane. The Calendar - Windows Live Mail window opens, showing a calendar for the current day, week, or month.

2. If necessary, click **Day** on the toolbar to display your schedule for the day. See Figure 4-33.

Figure 4-33   **Calendar in Day view**

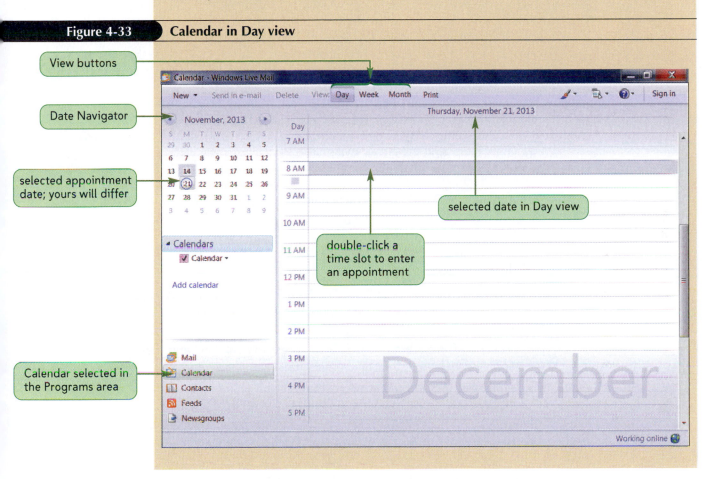

Now that you've opened Windows Live Calendar, you can use it to schedule appointments.

Scheduling Appointments

In Windows Live Calendar, you can schedule appointments such as meetings that occur for part of a day. You can also schedule events that last 24 hours or longer. An appointment appears as a colored block in your calendar, while a day-long event appears in a banner at the beginning of a day. When you schedule appointments, you can specify that they are recurring, such as training that takes place once a week, sales meetings scheduled once a month, or birthdays and other annual events.

Scheduling an Appointment in Windows Live Calendar

- Click Calendar in the Programs area of the Folder pane.
- Click the New button on the Windows Live Calendar toolbar.
- Type a description of the appointment, and then press the Tab key.
- In the Location box, enter the location of the appointment.
- If you have more than one calendar, click the Calendar arrow, and then select the calendar you want to use to schedule the appointment.
- If you are scheduling an all-day appointment, click the All day appointment check box.
- In the Start and End date boxes, click the arrow, and then click a date on the calendar.
- In the Start and End time boxes, click the arrows to change the times, or click to select the times and then enter the times you want.
- To specify a recurring appointment, click the Recurrence arrow, and then click how often the appointment recurs.
- To invite someone to the event, click the Send in e-mail button on the menu bar, and then compose and send the e-mail invitation.

The first appointment David wants to schedule is the weekly Tuesday morning staff meeting, which is usually 30 minutes long.

To schedule an appointment:

1. Click the **New** button on the toolbar. The New Event dialog box opens, displaying the details you can enter for the new appointment, such as subject, location, and start and end times.

2. Type **Weekly staff meeting** as the Subject, press the **Tab** key, and then enter **West conference room** in the Location text box.

3. Click the **Start** arrow, and then click the date for this coming Tuesday on the calendar.

4. Click the **arrow** in the Start time text box, and then click **9:00 AM**. The Start time now appears as next Tuesday at 9:00 AM, and the End time is the same day at 9:30 AM.

5. Click the **No recurrence** button, and then click **Weekly** to specify that this appointment occurs once a week. See Figure 4-34.

Figure 4-34 Scheduling an appointment

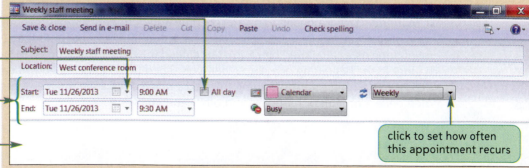

6. Click the **Save & close** button on the toolbar.

TIP

To edit an appointment already scheduled in a calendar, double-click the appointment.

You've created an appointment for David's weekly staff meeting. Next, you'll show David how to print his calendar. He can print the calendar using one of many formats: Day, Week, or Month. David wants to print the calendar using the Work Week format.

To print a calendar:

1. Click the **Print** button on the toolbar. The Print dialog box opens. See Figure 4-35.

Figure 4-35 ▶ **Printing a calendar**

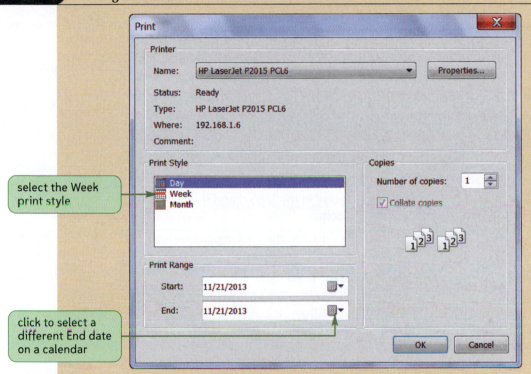

select the Week print style

click to select a different End date on a calendar

2. In the Print Style box, click **Week**.

3. In the Print Range section, click the **End** arrow, and then use the calendar to select the date one week from today.

4. Click the **OK** button to print the calendar.

Trouble? If you are not connected to a printer or your instructor does not want you to print the calendar, click the Cancel button instead.

5. Close all open windows.

Now that you've finished exploring the Internet and e-mail on David's computer, you should restore the computer to its original settings.

Restoring Your Settings

If you are working in a computer lab or using a computer other than your own, complete the steps in this section to restore the original settings on the computer.

To restore your settings:

1. Start Internet Explorer, click the **Safety** button on the Command bar, click **Delete Browsing History**, click the **History** check box, if necessary, deselect the other check boxes, and then click the **Delete** button.

2. Open the Favorites Center, click the **Add to Favorites** arrow on the Favorites Center toolbar, and then click **Organize Favorites**.

3. Click the **Colorado Travel** folder, click the **Delete** button, and then click the **Yes** button. Click the **Close** button to close the Organize Favorites dialog box.

4. Right-click the **Weather in Denver, CO** Web Slice on the Favorites bar, click **Delete** on the shortcut menu, and then click the **Yes** button to delete the Web Slice.

5. Right-click the **Colorado.gov** button on the Favorites bar, click **Delete** on the shortcut menu, and then click the **Yes** button to delete the Web Slice.

6. Click the **Tools** button on the Command bar, point to **Toolbars**, and then click **Favorites Bar** to remove the Favorites bar from the Internet Explorer window.

7. Close the Favorites Center, and then close Internet Explorer.

8. Start Windows Live Mail, click the **No** button if a dialog box asks if you want to set Windows Live Mail as your default e-mail program, click the **Itinerary you requested** message in the Inbox, and then click the **Delete** button on the Windows Live Mail toolbar.

9. Click the **Sent items** folder in the Folder pane, select the **Test e-mail**, **Re: Test e-mail**, and **Itinerary you requested** messages, and then click the **Delete** button.

10. Right-click the **Deleted items** folder in the Folder pane, click **Empty 'Deleted items' folder**, and then click the **Yes** button.

11. Click **Contacts** in the Programs area of the Folder pane. Right-click **David Sanchez** in the list of contacts, click **Delete Contact** on the shortcut menu, and then click the **OK** button. Close the Windows Live Contacts window.

12. Click **Calendar** in the Programs area of the Folder pane. Right-click the appointment you added to the calendar, click **Delete** on the shortcut menu, click the **Delete all occurrences** option button, and then click the **Delete** button.

13. Close all open windows.

REVIEW

Session 4.2 Quick Check

1. True or False. You can send e-mail messages to anyone on the Internet or network, even if they don't have their computers turned on.

2. A(n) _____ is a simple text document that you can compose and send using Windows Live Mail or another e-mail program.

3. Identify the user name and the e-mail server name in the following e-mail address: EdParks@forest.net.

4. Explain the purpose of the Inbox in Windows Live Mail.

5. If an e-mail message has a large file _____, it might take a long time to download your message.

6. True or False. You can open Windows Live Contacts when you are working in Windows Live Mail or you can open it from the Start menu.

7. In Windows Live Calendar, how can you tell the difference between an hour-long appointment, for example, and an all-day event?

Practice the skills you learned in the tutorial using the same case scenario.

PRACTICE

Review Assignments

For a list of Data Files in the Review folder, see page WIN 173.

You already showed David how to conduct research on tours in Colorado for limited-mobility travelers. He also needs information about accessible travel in the state of Washington. Some of his clients want to use wheelchairs or scooters on hiking trails, and then fish on a lake or stream. You'll use Internet Explorer to research this information. Complete the following steps:

1. Start Internet Explorer, click in the Address bar, type **www.parks.wa.gov**, and then press the Enter key to open the Washington State Parks Web page.

2. Click the ADA Recreation link on this page to open the Washington State Accessible Outdoor Recreation Guide Web page.

3. Click a link on this page to display information about accessible hiking trails in coastal Washington. Find at least one location that provides accessible fishing for low-mobility people. (*Hint*: Scroll down and look for the blue fishing icon.)

4. Scroll to the top of the Web page, click the Find a Park arrow, click the name of the park you found, and then click the Go button to open the Web page.

5. Click the New Tab button to open a new tab in the browser, type **www.fs.fed.us/gpnf** in the Address bar, and then press the Enter key to open the Web page for the Gifford Pinchot National Forest.

6. Click the Recreation link, and then click the Accessibility link to open a page on accessible recreation. Click a few links to learn about accessible recreation in the Gifford Pinchot National Forest. Find at least two pages that provide information that people in wheelchairs and scooters can use to access recreational sites.

7. Open the Favorites Center. Use the History list or other Internet Explorer tools to navigate to a Web page you think will be especially useful to Entrée Tours, and then add it your Favorites list.

8. Open the Favorites bar, go to *www.msn.com*, and then search for a Web site that displays weather information for Tacoma, Washington.

9. Add a Web slice to the Favorites bar for weather in Tacoma, Washington. Close the tab displaying search results.

10. On any open Web page displaying information about a Washington state recreation area, select the name of a location, and then use the Bing Maps Accelerator to preview a map of the location.

11. Press the Alt+Print Screen keys to capture an image of the Internet Explorer window. Start Paint or WordPad, paste the screen image in a new file, and then save the file as **WA Web Pages** in the Tutorial.04\Review folder provided with your Data Files.

12. Start Windows Live Mail and create an e-mail message. Enter your e-mail address and your instructor's e-mail address in the To box and the following text in the Subject box: **Best spots for Entrée Tours in Washington State**.

13. In the message area, write a message describing the best places in Washington state for disabled and low-mobility travelers, based on your research.

14. Attach the **Washington** file to the message. (This file is stored in the Tutorial.04\Review folder provided with your Data Files.)

15. Send the message, and then add your e-mail address and your instructor's e-mail address to the Contacts list.

16. Add an appointment to Windows Live Calendar to meet with David at Entrée Tours today for 30 minutes. Then print the calendar using the Day view.

17. Restore your computer by clearing the History list in Internet Explorer, deleting the Web page you added to the Favorites list, deleting the Web slice on the Favorites bar, closing the Favorites bar, deleting the e-mails you sent and received, emptying the Deleted items folder, deleting yourself and your instructor from the Windows Live Contacts window, and deleting the appointment you created on the Windows Live Calendar.

18. Close Internet Explorer and Windows Live Mail.

19. Submit the results of the preceding steps to your instructor, either in printed or electronic form, as requested.

Use the skills you learned in the tutorial to conduct research for an organization.

APPLY

Case Problem 1

There are no Data Files needed for this Case Problem.

Supernova Center   Gordon Bernhardt is the director of the Supernova Center, a non-profit organization in Santa Fe, New Mexico, that promotes astronomy and planetary science for kids from kindergarten through eighth grade. Gordon wants to take advantage of the astronomy information posted on the Web by national science organizations and compile it for science teachers. Recently, Gordon hired you to help provide outreach to educators. To prepare for an upcoming presentation at an educators conference, you want to pull together some innovative ideas for teaching astronomy in the classroom. Complete the following steps:

1. Start Internet Explorer, and go to the NASA for Kids' Club Web page at *kids.msfc.nasa.gov*.

2. On new tabs, open three other astronomy Web pages:
   - Astronomy for Kids: *www.kidsastronomy.com*
   - Starchild: *starchild.gsfc.nasa.gov*
   - Windows to the Universe: *www.windows.ucar.edu*

3. Click links on these Web pages and use the Internet Explorer tools to find three other Web pages that provide ideas for teaching astronomy in the classroom.

4. Save the three Web pages you found in Step 3 in your Favorites list in a folder named **Astronomy**.

5. Pin the Favorites Center to the Internet Explorer window, if necessary, so that the Favorites list stays open. Open the Astronomy folder in the Favorites list to display the Web pages you found.

6. With the Internet Explorer window displaying the contents of the Astronomy folder and at least four tabs containing Astronomy Web pages suitable for school-age children, press the Alt+Print Screen keys to capture an image of the Internet Explorer window. Start Paint or WordPad, paste the screen image in a new file, and then save the file as **Astronomy Web Pages** in the Tutorial.04\Case1 folder provided with your Data Files.

7. Start Windows Live Mail and create an e-mail message addressed to you and your instructor. Enter the following text in the Subject box: **Ideas for astronomy lessons**.

8. In the message area, write a message describing one of the ideas you found for teaching astronomy to students in grades kindergarten through eighth grade.

9. Attach the **Astronomy Web Pages** file to the message, and then send it.

10. Add an appointment to Windows Live Calendar to make a presentation to the educator's conference one month from today. Print the calendar showing the presentation appointment using the Week view.

11. Restore your computer by clearing the History list in Internet Explorer, deleting the folder you added to the Favorites list, closing the Favorites Center, deleting the e-mails you sent and received, emptying the Deleted items folder, and deleting the appointment you created on the Windows Live Calendar.

12. Close Internet Explorer and Windows Live Mail.

13. Submit the results of the preceding steps to your instructor, either in printed or electronic form, as requested.

Use the skills you learned in the tutorial to do online research for an art restoration company.

APPLY

Case Problem 2

There are no Data Files needed for this Case Problem.

Leroux Fine Art Restoration   Evelyn Leroux is the owner of Leroux Fine Art Restoration, a company in Philadelphia, Pennsylvania, that provides expert restoration services to authenticate, conserve, and scientifically study paintings. Her specialty is early American portrait painting. Evelyn often works with the conservation departments of Philadelphia museums to restore paintings and is interested in expanding her company to work with museums around the United States. As her marketing and sales assistant, you offer to research the restoration services provided by museums outside of Philadelphia. Complete the following steps:

1. Start Internet Explorer, and go to the Metropolitan Museum of Art Web page at *www.metmuseum.org*.

2. On additional tabs, open the Web pages for the Minneapolis Institute of Arts at *www.artsmia.org*, and the Smithsonian Institution at *www.si.edu*.

3. Click links and use the Internet Explorer tools to find at least one Web page for each museum that describes its restoration or conservation services. For the Metropolitan Museum of Art, start by clicking Science and Conservation. You can access the Objects Conservation page from the Features page in the Works of Art category. For the Minneapolis Institute of Arts, restoration information is considered an online education resource. (*Hint*: Look for a "Restoring a Masterwork" link.) For the Smithsonian, look for links to the Museum Conservation Institute, which is part of Smithsonian Research.

4. Save the Web pages you found in Step 4 in your Favorites list in a folder named **Restoration**.

⊕ **EXPLORE**

5. Display the Favorites bar, click the Suggested Sites button, click the Turn on Suggested Sites button, and then click the Yes button to let Internet Explorer discover Web sites you might like based on the Web sites you've visited. Click the Suggested Sites button on the Favorites bar again, and then click See Suggested Sites. Open two suggested art museum sites on separate tabs, and then add them to your Restoration folder in your Favorites list.

6. On the Metropolitan Museum of Art – Works of Art: Objects Conservation Web page, scroll to the bottom of the page, select the street address for the Metropolitan Museum of Art, and then use the Bing Maps Accelerator to find directions from Times Square to the museum.

7. Display all the open Web pages as thumbnails. Press the Alt+Print Screen keys to capture an image of the Internet Explorer window. Start Paint or WordPad, paste the screen image in a new file, and then save the file as **Museums** in the Tutorial.04\Case2 folder provided with your Data Files.

8. Start Windows Live Mail and create an e-mail message addressed to you and your instructor. Enter the following text in the Subject box: **Restoration programs**.

9. In the message area, write a message listing examples of the types of art objects the Metropolitan Museum of Art, the Minneapolis Institute of Arts, or the Smithsonian restores.

10. Add a one-hour appointment to Windows Live Calendar to research restoration services at museums next week.

EXPLORE 11. With the New Event window open, click the Send in e-mail button on the toolbar. Enter your instructor's e-mail address, and then enter your name in the Subject text box. Send the e-mail to your instructor.

12. Restore your computer by clearing the History list in Internet Explorer and deleting the folder you added to the Favorites list. Click Tools on the Command bar and then click Suggested Sites to remove the check mark. Delete the e-mails you sent and received, empty the Deleted items folder, and delete the appointment you created in Windows Live Calendar.

13. Close Internet Explorer and Windows Live Mail.

14. Submit the results of the preceding steps to your instructor, either in printed or electronic form, as requested.

Extend what you've learned to find information for a start-up magazine.

CHALLENGE

Case Problem 3

There are no Data Files needed for this Case Problem.

Northern Gardening Magazine The *Northern Gardening Magazine* is a new monthly periodical published in St. Paul, Minnesota, for gardeners in the upper midwestern states of Michigan, Wisconsin, and Minnesota. Michael Nilsson is the publisher and a master gardener. He hired you as his director of communications, and asked you to find Web sites providing basic information for the readers of *Northern Gardening Magazine*. Complete the following steps:

1. Start Internet Explorer, and go to the Minnesota Department of Natural Resources Web page at *www.dnr.state.mn.us*.

2. On additional tabs, open the gardening Web pages for the UM Extension at *www.extension.umn.edu* and the UW Extension at *www.uwex.edu/topics/agriculture*.

3. Click links and use the Internet Explorer tools to find at least one Web page from each site that recommends gardening techniques or plants for home gardeners in the upper Midwest.

EXPLORE 4. Save the group of open tabs in your Favorites list in a folder named **Gardening**. (*Hint*: Click the Add to Favorites arrow, click Add Current Tabs to Favorites, name the folder **Gardening**, and then click the Add button.)

EXPLORE 5. Return to the main page for the UM Extension Web site. Scroll down and click the Extensión en Español link. If necessary, click the En Español link on the left to display the Web page text in Spanish. Select the first paragraph on the page, click the blue Accelerator icon, and then point to Translate with Bing. Press the Alt+Print Screen keys to capture an image of the Internet Explorer window. Start Paint or WordPad, paste the screen image in a new file, and then save the file as **Spanish** in the Tutorial.04\Case3 folder provided with your Data Files.

EXPLORE 6. On the main Web page for the UW Extension agriculture topics, click the Urban Horticulture link, and then click a link for Wisconsin Garden Facts. On the Wisconsin Garden Facts page, look for files you can download. For example, look for a WORD or PDF link next to the name of an article. (PDFs, or Portable Document Format files, contain text and images that you can often download from a Web site and read with a program called Adobe Reader. DOC files are Microsoft Word documents, which you can also open in WordPad.) Right-click the link to a horticulture file, click Save Target As, and then save the file as **Wisconsin Horticulture** in the Tutorial.04\Case3 folder provided with your Data Files.

7. Start Windows Live Mail and create an e-mail message addressed to you and your instructor. Enter the following text in the Subject box: **Midwestern gardening**.

8. In the message area, write a message listing a few types of plants that can be grown in the upper Midwest.

9. Attach the **Wisconsin Horticulture** file to the message, and then send the message.

10. Add an appointment in Windows Live Calendar to meet with Michael to discuss next month's issue of *Northern Gardening Magazine* two days from today at 1:00 in the afternoon. Print the calendar showing the appointment using the Day view.

11. Restore your computer by clearing the History list in Internet Explorer, deleting the folder you added to the Favorites list, deleting the e-mail you sent, emptying the Deleted items folder, and deleting the appointment you created in Windows Live Calendar.

12. Close Internet Explorer and Windows Live Mail.

13. Submit the results of the preceding steps to your instructor, either in printed or electronic form, as requested.

Extend what you've learned to help a booster club promote women's college volleyball.

CHALLENGE

Case Problem 4

There are no Data Files needed for this Case Problem.

Volleyball Boosters   Volleyball Boosters is a club in Kalamazoo, Michigan, that supports and promotes women's college volleyball teams at small U.S. colleges. Felicia Andrade, the club president, recently hired you as a part-time assistant. You help Felicia write the club newsletter and organize promotional events. Felicia wants you to visit college Web sites periodically to make sure they are promoting their women's volleyball teams. Complete the following steps:

1. Start Internet Explorer, and go to the Web page for Hiram College at *www.hiram.edu*.

2. On additional tabs, open the college Web pages for Kalamazoo College at *www.kzoo.edu*, Mount Holyoke College at *www.mtholyoke.edu*, and Northland College at *www.northland.edu*.

3. Click links and use the Internet Explorer tools to find at least one Web page for each college that describes or reports on the women's volleyball team.

⊕ **EXPLORE**   4. Save all the open tabs in your Favorites list in a folder named **Volleyball**. (*Hint*: Click the Add to Favorites arrow, click Add Current Tabs to Favorites, name the folder **Volleyball**, and then click the Add button.)

⊕ **EXPLORE**   5. On the Web site for any of the four colleges, find a schedule for the current or upcoming volleyball season. Click the Page button arrow, click Save As, navigate to the Tutorial.04\Case4 folder provided with your Data Files, click the Save as type button, click Text File (*.txt), and then type **Schedule** as the filename. Click the Save button.

⊕ **EXPLORE**   6. Display the Web pages as thumbnails. Press the Alt+Print Screen keys to capture an image of the Internet Explorer window. Start Paint or WordPad, paste the screen image in a new file, and then save the file as **Volleyball** in the Tutorial.04\Case4 folder provided with your Data Files.

7. Restore your computer by clearing the History list in Internet Explorer and deleting the folder you added to the Favorites list.

8. Close Internet Explorer.

9. Submit the results of the preceding steps to your instructor, either in printed or electronic form, as requested.

ENDING DATA FILES

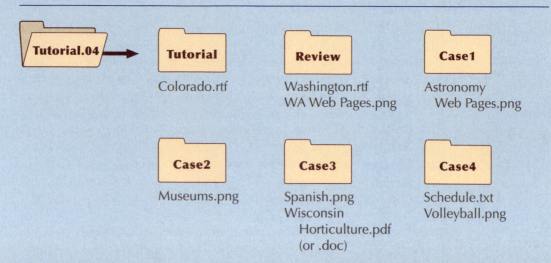

Tutorial.04 → **Tutorial**
Colorado.rtf

Review
Washington.rtf
WA Web Pages.png

Case1
Astronomy
   Web Pages.png

Case2
Museums.png

Case3
Spanish.png
Wisconsin
   Horticulture.pdf
   (or .doc)

Case4
Schedule.txt
Volleyball.png

WINDOWS

Protecting Your Computer

Managing Computer Security

Case | *Presto Global Translators*

A few years ago, Curt Mickelson founded Presto Global Translators in Ithaca, New York. Presto translates written material to and from English and dozens of other languages for corporate clients around the world. Recently, Curt has become concerned with the security of Presto's computers. Many of Curt's translators work at their client's offices, using notebook computers running Windows 7. Although these translators can access the Internet with their computers, they can't usually connect to the Presto network, where an administrator oversees security. Instead, they must take advantage of the security tools in Windows 7 to prevent problems stemming from viruses, spyware, and other types of harmful software. Curt recently hired you to support the translation staff. One of your first duties is to investigate the security features in Windows 7 and show Curt how to use them to address security threats.

In this tutorial, you'll explore the tools in the Action Center, including Windows Firewall and Windows Update. You'll learn how to set up Windows 7 to work with antivirus software and how to take other security measures, including setting up user accounts, and securing and sharing folders. You will also examine Microsoft Internet Explorer security settings so that you can use the Internet safely.

OBJECTIVES

Session 5.1
- Use the Action Center
- Set up Windows Firewall and Windows Update
- Protect your computer from viruses and other malicious software
- Use Windows Defender to protect against spyware
- Manage Windows Live Mail security

Session 5.2
- Manage Microsoft Internet Explorer security
- Protect privacy with InPrivate Browsing and InPrivate Filtering
- Set up user accounts
- Control access to your computer
- Secure and share folders

STARTING DATA FILES

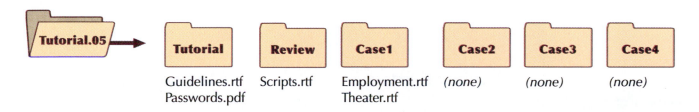

Tutorial.05	Tutorial	Review	Case1	Case2	Case3	Case4
	Guidelines.rtf Passwords.pdf	Scripts.rtf	Employment.rtf Theater.rtf	*(none)*	*(none)*	*(none)*

SESSION 5.1 VISUAL OVERVIEW

The **Action Center** is a Control Panel tool that helps you manage security from a single window.

Spyware is software that secretly gathers information about you and your computer actions and passes it to advertisers and others.

Important Action Center messages are highlighted by a red bar in the Action Center.

A **virus** is a program attached to a file that runs when you open the file and copies itself to infect a computer.

Suggestions for improving your computer experience are highlighted by a yellow bar.

▶ Control Panel ▶ System and Security ▶ Action Center

File   Edit   View   Tools   Help

Control Panel Home

Change Action Center settings

Change User Account Control settings

View archived messages

View performance information

See also

Backup and Restore

Windows Update

Windows Program Compatibility Troubleshooter

Review recent messages and re

Action Center has detected one or more

Security

Spyware and unwanted softwar

Windows Defender and Trend Mic report that they are out of date. Note: Running two or more antisp same time can cause your compu

Turn off messages about spyware

Virus protection (Important)

Trend Micro Internet Security repo

Turn off messages about virus pro

Maintenance

Set up backup

Your files are not being backed u

Turn off messages about Window

THE ACTION CENTER

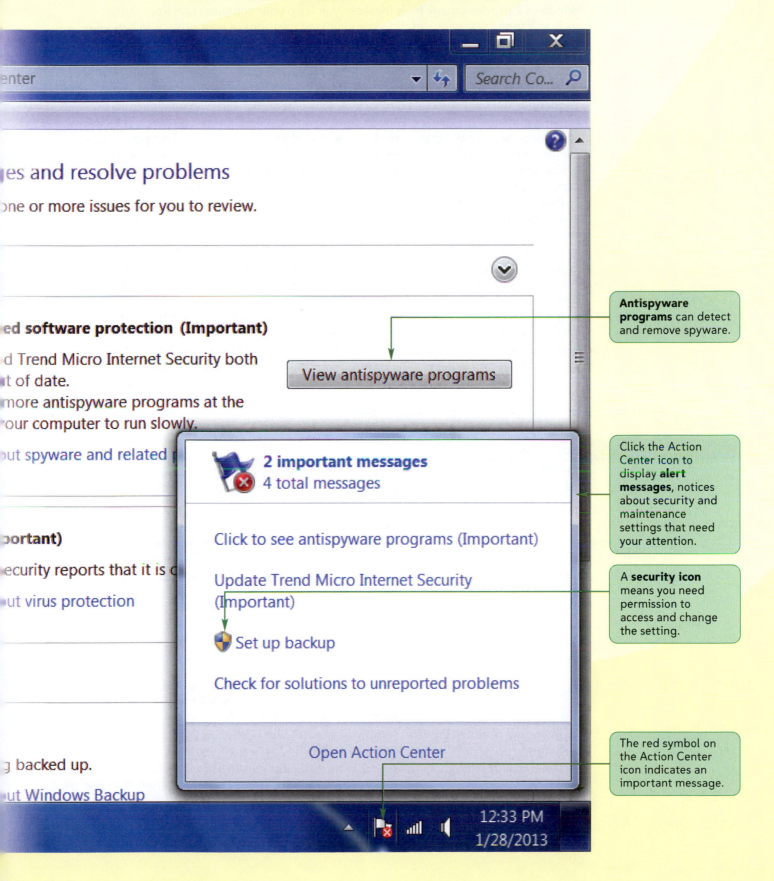

es and resolve problems

one or more issues for you to review.

ed **software protection (Important)**

d Trend Micro Internet Security both
t of date.
more antispyware programs at the
our computer to run slowly.

ut spyware and related

View antispyware programs

2 important messages
4 total messages

Click to see antispyware programs (Important)

Update Trend Micro Internet Security
(Important)

Set up backup

Check for solutions to unreported problems

Open Action Center

ortant)

ecurity reports that it is c

ut virus protection

g backed up.

ut Windows Backup

12:33 PM
1/28/2013

Antispyware
programs can detect
and remove spyware.

Click the Action
Center icon to
display **alert
messages,** notices
about security and
maintenance
settings that need
your attention.

A **security icon**
means you need
permission to
access and change
the setting.

The red symbol on
the Action Center
icon indicates an
important message.

Using the Action Center

Windows 7 provides many tools that help you keep your computer safe from threats such as harmful software, unsolicited e-mail, and invasions of your privacy. When you connect to the Internet, send and receive e-mail, or share your computer or files with others, your computer is vulnerable to harm from people who might attempt to steal your personal information, damage your files, or interrupt your work. You should use the Windows 7 security tools and other techniques to defend against these threats.

Harmful software (also called malicious software, or malware) includes viruses. By copying itself and triggering computer code, a virus can infect your computer. The damage a virus causes can range from changing your desktop settings to deleting or corrupting files on your hard disk. Viruses are often spread by e-mail and run when you open an e-mail attachment or the e-mail message itself. Files you download from Web sites can also contain viruses that run when you save the files on your computer.

People who create and send malware are called **hackers**, a generic term that refers to anyone who intends to access a computer system without permission. (Hackers with criminal intent are sometimes called **crackers** or black hat hackers.) Hackers can also invade your privacy by accessing your computer via the Internet to find information such as passwords and financial account numbers. Hackers sometimes access your computer using spyware, software that secretly gathers information about you and your computer actions, including sensitive information.

If you are working on a computer that is connected to a network, a network administrator probably defends the network against security threats such as viruses, worms, spyware, and hackers. Otherwise, if you are working on a home computer, for example, you should take advantage of the security features that Windows 7 provides.

The first place to go to secure your computer is the Action Center, a Control Panel tool that helps you manage security from a single window. Some of the security settings you can manage in the Action Center are listed in Figure 5-1.

Figure 5-1   **Action Center features**

Security Feature	Description
Network Firewall	This feature uses Windows Firewall by default to monitor and restrict communication with the Internet, which helps protect your computer from hackers. Before a program can send or receive information via the Internet, Windows Firewall must allow it to do so.
Windows Update	This feature checks for the latest Windows updates on the Microsoft Web site, and then downloads and installs the updates for you. Because Windows updates often include security enhancements, using this feature helps to make sure that your computer is secure against most current threats.
Virus protection	Antivirus software is your best protection against viruses, worms, and other types of harmful software. If you have antivirus software, Windows reminds you to use it regularly to scan your computer for virus infections and to monitor e-mail. If you do not have antivirus software, Windows lists vendors that provide it.
Spyware and unwanted software protection	Antispyware software such as Windows Defender prevents some types of malware from infecting your system.
Internet security settings	Action Center checks that your Web browser is using appropriate security settings to block malware from being installed on your system when you visit Web sites.
User Account Control	This service displays a dialog box requesting your permission to install software or open programs that could harm your computer.

Most of the features listed in Figure 5-1 are considered essential—you should turn on all of these features to keep your computer secure. If Windows detects a problem with one of these essential security features, such as when your firewall is turned off, an alert message appears near the Action Center icon ⬚ in the notification area of your taskbar. For example, the alert message might be *Solve PC issues: 1 message*. You can click the alert message or click the Action Center icon and then click Open Action Center to open the Action Center and find out how to address the problem. You can also see if the Action Center lists any new messages by pointing to the Action Center icon.

You'll start showing Curt how to use the security features in Windows 7 by opening the Action Center.

To open the Action Center:

▶ **1.** Click the **Action Center** icon ⬚ in the notification area of the taskbar. A message window opens.

▶ **2.** In the message window, click **Open Action Center** to open the Action Center window.

▶ **3.** If necessary, click the **Security** heading to expand the Security section. See Figure 5-2.

Figure 5-2   Action Center window

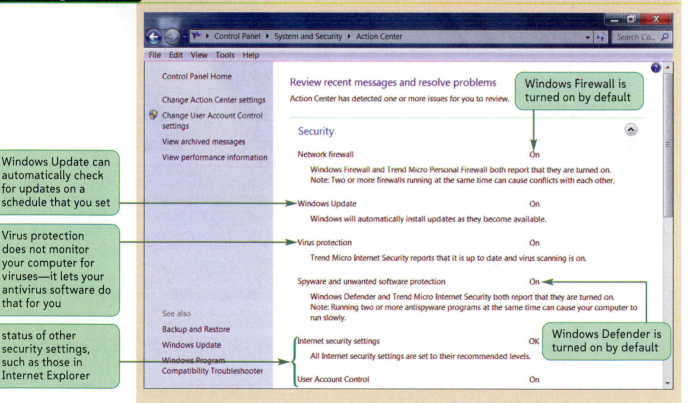

When you click the Action Center icon in the taskbar, the message window might list links to alert messages. If a security icon ⬚ appears next to a link, you need permission to access and change the setting. You usually indicate that you have permission by entering an administrator password. Requiring a user to enter a password to change system settings is another way to protect your computer.

Leave the Action Center window open to perform the tasks described in the following sections.

Managing Windows Firewall

Windows Firewall is software that serves as a barrier between your computer and a network or the Internet. As shown in Figure 5-3, Windows Firewall checks information coming from the network or the Internet and either blocks it from your computer or allows it to pass, depending on your settings. In this way, Windows Firewall prevents unauthorized users from accessing your computer and is the first line of defense against malware. Many antivirus programs include a firewall that works in a similar way.

Figure 5-3   How Windows Firewall protects your computer

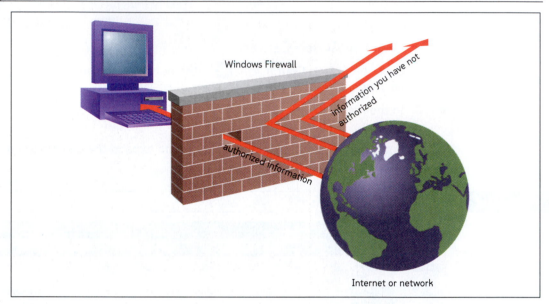

A firewall defends against malware trying to gain access to your computer by monitoring your network and Internet connections. However, a firewall does not scan e-mail, so it cannot detect viruses sent in e-mail messages (a common way to spread viruses). Neither can a firewall detect viruses in files you download from the Web. Furthermore, a firewall can't protect you from e-mail scams, called phishing, that try to deceive you into revealing private information, such as passwords. To protect against viruses in e-mail and downloaded files, use antivirus software. To minimize phishing attempts, use the Internet Explorer phishing filter. (Both topics are covered later in this tutorial.)

Windows Firewall is turned on by default, so it doesn't allow communications with most programs via the Internet or a network. However, your computer manufacturer or someone else might turn off Windows Firewall, so you should verify that it is running. Typically, Windows Firewall is turned off only if another firewall is protecting your computer.

To turn on Windows Firewall:

▶ **1.** In the Action Center window, click **System and Security** in the Address bar to display the System and Security window.

▶ **2.** Click **Windows Firewall** to open the Windows Firewall window. See Figure 5-4.

Figure 5-4   **Windows Firewall window**

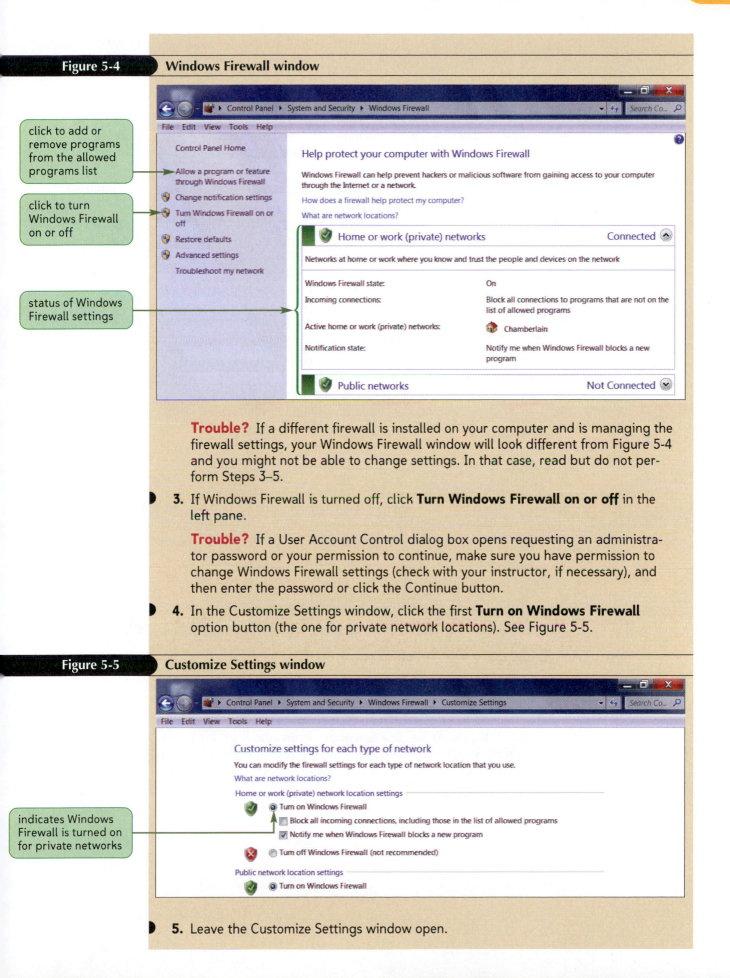

click to add or remove programs from the allowed programs list

click to turn Windows Firewall on or off

status of Windows Firewall settings

Trouble? If a different firewall is installed on your computer and is managing the firewall settings, your Windows Firewall window will look different from Figure 5-4 and you might not be able to change settings. In that case, read but do not perform Steps 3–5.

3. If Windows Firewall is turned off, click **Turn Windows Firewall on or off** in the left pane.

   Trouble? If a User Account Control dialog box opens requesting an administrator password or your permission to continue, make sure you have permission to change Windows Firewall settings (check with your instructor, if necessary), and then enter the password or click the Continue button.

4. In the Customize Settings window, click the first **Turn on Windows Firewall** option button (the one for private network locations). See Figure 5-5.

Figure 5-5   **Customize Settings window**

indicates Windows Firewall is turned on for private networks

5. Leave the Customize Settings window open.

When Windows Firewall is turned on and someone tries to connect to your computer from the Internet, Windows Firewall blocks the connection. Instead of turning off Windows Firewall every time you want to use a blocked program, you can customize it by adding programs to its allowed list so that it maintains a level of security that's right for you.

In the Customize Settings window, you can specify firewall settings for each type of network location that you use. For example, you might use a private network at home or work and a public network in other locations. For each network location, you can select one of the following settings:

- Turn on Windows Firewall: This setting is selected by default, meaning that most programs are blocked from communicating through the firewall.
- Block all incoming connections, including those in the list of allowed programs: When you connect to a public network, such as in a hotel or airport, you might want to select this setting. Windows blocks all programs, even those in the allowed list.
- Notify me when Windows Firewall blocks a new program: When you select this check box, Windows Firewall informs you when it blocks a new program, giving you the option of adding the program to the allowed programs list.
- Turn off Windows Firewall (not recommended): The only time you should select this setting is when another firewall is running on your computer.

Curt often uses network projectors to give presentations to potential clients in other locations. (A network projector is a video projector connected to a wireless or wired network, and it lets you give presentations using a network connection.) Before a network projector can communicate with a computer to indicate it is turned on and ready for the presentation, Windows Firewall must allow incoming connections from the network projector. You'll show Curt how to add the Connect to a Network Projector program to the allowed programs list so he can give network presentations without any problems.

If you are performing the following steps in a computer lab, you might not be allowed to change allowed programs. Check with your instructor or technical support person to determine whether you can specify Connect to a Network Projector as an allowed program in Windows Firewall. If you cannot, read but do not perform the following steps.

To add a program to the allowed programs list:

1. Click the **Back** button ⬅ to return to the Windows Firewall window.

2. In the left pane, click **Allow a program or feature through Windows Firewall** to open the Allowed Programs window. See Figure 5-6.

   Trouble? If the Allow a program or feature through Windows Firewall link is inactive in the Windows Firewall window, click the Back button ⬅ to return to the System and Security window, and then click Allow a program through Windows Firewall.

   Trouble? If a dialog box opens requesting an administrator password or your permission to continue, make sure you have permission to change Windows Firewall settings (check with your instructor, if necessary), and then enter the password or click the Continue button.

Figure 5-6 | Allowed Programs window

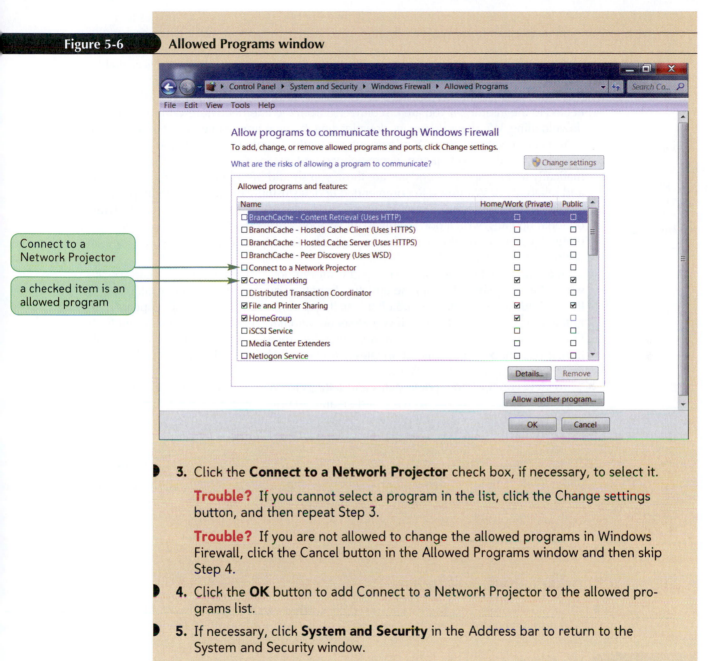

3. Click the **Connect to a Network Projector** check box, if necessary, to select it.

Trouble? If you cannot select a program in the list, click the Change settings button, and then repeat Step 3.

Trouble? If you are not allowed to change the allowed programs in Windows Firewall, click the Cancel button in the Allowed Programs window and then skip Step 4.

4. Click the **OK** button to add Connect to a Network Projector to the allowed programs list.

5. If necessary, click **System and Security** in the Address bar to return to the System and Security window.

Keep in mind that when you add a program to the Windows Firewall allowed programs list, you are making your computer easier for programs to access, and therefore more vulnerable to malware infection. You should therefore allow a program only when you really need it, and never allow a program that you don't recognize—it could be a virus or a worm. Finally, be sure to remove a program from the allowed programs list when you no longer need it.

Setting Up Windows Update

An **update** is a change to software that can prevent or repair problems, enhance the security of a computer, or improve a computer's performance. Microsoft occasionally releases updates to Windows 7 and provides them for download from its Web site. You can look for, download, and install these updates any time you visit the Microsoft Web site. However, because updates often include critical security repairs and enhancements, Microsoft also makes them available to you through the Windows Update feature.

When you use the Update feature, Windows periodically checks for updates to the operating system from Microsoft, including security updates, critical updates, and service packs. (When Microsoft combines many updates in one package, the collection of updates is called a service pack and is often abbreviated as *SP*.) If an update is available, Windows Update can download the software and install it for you. Windows downloads the updates in the background according to a schedule you set, as long as you're connected to the Internet. If you are disconnected from the Internet before Windows finishes downloading, Windows continues downloading the next time you connect to the Internet.

You can specify whether Windows automatically downloads only important updates, downloads both important and recommended updates, or does not download automatically at all. Important updates are those you should install to maintain the security and reliability of Windows. Recommended updates usually enhance your computing experience and repair problems that are not considered critical. Microsoft also provides optional updates, which don't apply to all Windows users. For example, if you use a particular piece of hardware, such as a digital music player, Windows might provide an optional update for the player's driver.

In addition to the types of updates you want Windows to download, you can specify when Windows should install the updates. To notify you that updates are available or that Windows is ready to download or install updates, an Update icon 🖼 appears in the notification area of the taskbar. If you've set up automatic updating, you can point to the Update icon to display a ScreenTip indicating the progress of the download and installation. If you choose to download updates automatically but install them yourself, click the Update icon to install the updates.

To view your current update status and settings for Windows Update, you open the Windows Update window from the System and Security category of the Control Panel. You can also use this window to review your update history.

You recommend that Curt turn on automatic updating for important and recommended updates so he doesn't miss any for Windows 7. He wants to check for updates every morning at 8:00 while he is typically meeting with his staff. That way, Windows will not interrupt his work if it needs to install updates. Although he is not using his computer then, it is turned on and connected to the Internet.

As you perform the following steps, note your original settings so you can restore them later.

TIP

To visit the Windows Update Web site and download an update, click the Start button, point to All Programs, and then click Windows Update.

To set up Windows Update:

1. In the System and Security window, click **Windows Update**. The Windows Update window opens. See Figure 5-7. Your settings might differ.

Figure 5-7 Windows Update window

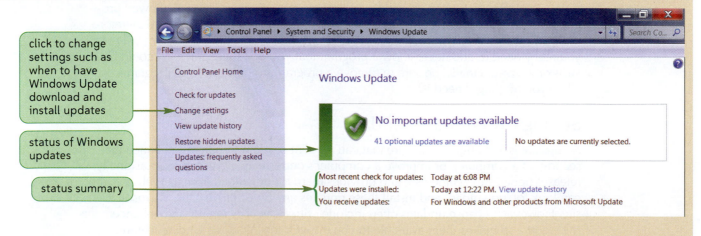

click to change settings such as when to have Windows Update download and install updates

status of Windows updates

status summary

2. In the left pane, click **Change settings**. The Change settings window opens. See Figure 5-8.

Figure 5-8 **Changing Windows Update settings**

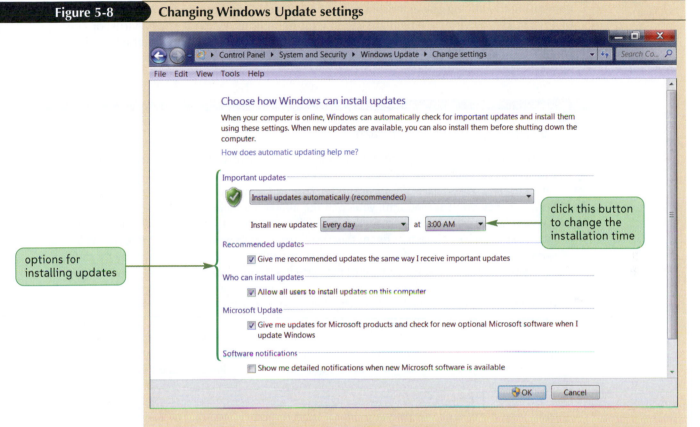

3. If *Install updates automatically (recommended)* does not appear on the first button in the Important updates section as shown in Figure 5-8, click the button and then click **Install updates automatically (recommended)**. Selecting this option means that Windows checks for updates according to a schedule, and then downloads and installs them for you when they are available.

4. In the Install new updates section, click the time (which appears as 3:00 AM by default), and then click **8:00 AM**.

5. If necessary, click the **Give me recommended updates the same way I receive important updates** check box to select it.

6. Click the **OK** button.

Trouble? If a dialog box opens requesting an administrator password or your permission to continue, enter the password or click the Continue button.

7. Click **System and Security** in the Address bar to return to the System and Security window.

Now that you know Curt's copy of Windows 7 is up to date, you can turn to protecting his computer from viruses and other types of malware.

Protecting Your Computer from Malware

Your best protection against malware is to use the current version of your antivirus software, which scans e-mail messages, attachments, and other files on your computer for viruses, worms, and other types of malware. Antivirus software locates a virus by comparing identifying characteristics of the files on your computer to the characteristics of a list of known viruses, which are called virus definitions. When it finds a virus, or any type of malware, antivirus software notifies you about the virus and then quarantines it by moving it to an isolated place on your computer or deletes the harmful file before it can damage your computer.

INSIGHT

Recognizing Types of Malware

Recall that a virus is a program that replicates itself and attaches to files or programs, usually affects your computer's performance and stability, and sometimes damages or removes files. Viruses are often transmitted through e-mail attachments or downloaded files, but they don't spread until you open the infected attachment or file. In contrast, a **worm** is harmful computer code that spreads without your interaction. A worm slips from one network connection to another, replicating itself on network computers. As it does, a worm consumes network resources, overwhelming computers until they become slow or unresponsive. Another type of malware is a **Trojan horse**, which is malware that hides inside another program, such as a photo viewing program you download from the Web. When you install the program, the Trojan horse infects the operating system, allowing a hacker to access your computer. Trojan horses can't spread on their own; they depend on programs, including viruses and worms, to proliferate. Common symptoms of malware are when your computer runs much slower than normal, messages appear unexpectedly, programs start or close on their own, or Windows shuts down suddenly.

Most vendors of antivirus software offer a subscription service that provides regular updates for current virus definitions. Like Windows, antivirus programs often use an automatic update feature that downloads and installs updates to the software and adds new viruses to your virus definition list. Keeping the virus definition list current helps to protect your computer from new attacks. If your list of viruses is out of date, your computer is vulnerable to new threats.

Windows 7 does not provide antivirus software, so you should make sure that you have an antivirus program installed and running on your computer. (Your computer manufacturer probably installed antivirus software for you—look on the All Programs submenu of the Start menu and then point to the icons in the notification area of the taskbar to make sure antivirus software is installed and running on your computer.) Be sure to select the options in the antivirus software to scan incoming e-mail automatically and to scan your entire system for malware periodically (usually once a week). Windows recognizes most types of antivirus software and displays their status in the Action Center window.

Refer to the antivirus software's help system to learn how to run the software and receive regular updates. In most cases, you can also use the Action Center to determine whether your antivirus software needs to be updated.

Curt is certain that antivirus software is installed on his computer, but asks you to check to make sure it is up to date and that virus scanning is turned on.

TIP

If antivirus software is not installed on your computer, visit the Microsoft Web site (*www.microsoft. com*) and search for *Windows 7 antivirus partners* to find antivirus software for Windows 7.

To check for virus protection on your computer:

1. In the System and Security window, click **Action Center** to return to the Action Center window. If necessary, click **Security** to expand the Security section.

2. Examine the settings in the Virus protection section, which should report that an antivirus program is up to date and virus scanning is on.

   Trouble? If the Action Center window reports that your virus protection is up to date and virus scanning is on, read but do not perform the remaining steps. If virus protection is turned on but not up to date, skip Steps 3–4.

   Trouble? If the Action Center window reports that antivirus software is not installed on your computer, read but do not perform the remaining steps.

3. If necessary, click the **Turn on now** button.

4. When a dialog box opens requesting your permission to run the antivirus program, click the **Yes** button. The Action Center window reports that virus scanning is on, but the antivirus program is not up to date. See Figure 5-9.

Figure 5-9	Antivirus software needs to be updated

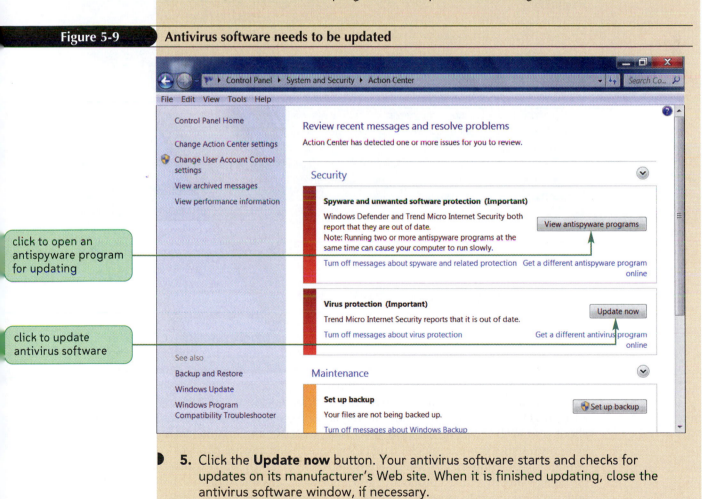

click to open an antispyware program for updating

click to update antivirus software

5. Click the **Update now** button. Your antivirus software starts and checks for updates on its manufacturer's Web site. When it is finished updating, close the antivirus software window, if necessary.

PROSKILLS

Problem Solving: Avoiding and Removing Viruses

One of the most difficult computer problems to solve is removing a virus from your system. To avoid this problem, you can defend against viruses in the following ways so that they do not infect your computer:

- *Do not open unexpected e-mail attachments.* If the message containing the attachment is from a trusted source, send an e-mail to that person asking about the file and what it contains.
- *Regularly scan your hard drive with an antivirus program.* Most antivirus software includes an option to schedule a complete system scan. You only need to make sure your computer is turned on to perform the scan.
- *Set your antivirus program to scan all incoming e-mail.*
- *Keep your antivirus software up to date.* New viruses are introduced frequently, and your antivirus software needs to use the latest virus definitions to protect your computer.
- *Back up your work files periodically.* Viruses can corrupt or destroy data files, which are the most valuable files on your computer.

When you notice symptoms such as your computer running slowly or turning off on its own, suspect a virus. You can try to remove a virus in the following ways:

- *Update your antivirus software.* Look for an update feature that connects with the Web site of your antivirus software developer to download the latest virus definitions.
- *Use the antivirus software to scan your entire computer.* The software might be able to remove the virus for you or identify the virus by name.
- *Use an online scanner.* If your antivirus software does not find or report a virus, visit the Microsoft Web site (*www.microsoft.com*) and search for *Windows security software providers*. Look for vendors in the search results that provide free online virus scanners to help you find and remove the virus.
- *Search for instructions on removing the virus.* If your antivirus software or online scanner identifies but does not remove the virus, search an antivirus vendor's Web site to find information about removing the virus.

Another security concern is spyware, which can also affect your computing experience.

Defending Against Spyware

Spyware can install itself or run on your computer without your consent or control. It's called *spyware* because it monitors your computing actions, usually while you are online, to collect information about you. Spyware can change system settings, interrupt programs, and slow your computer's performance. Spyware may infect your computer when you visit a certain Web site or download a free program, such as a screen saver or search toolbar. Less frequently, spyware is distributed along with other programs on a CD, DVD, or other type of removable media. Sometimes, spyware passes information about your Web browsing habits to advertisers, who use it to improve their products or Web sites. Other times, a special type of spyware called **adware** changes your browser settings to open **pop-up ads**, which are windows that appear while you are viewing a Web page and advertise a product or service. Pop-up ads interrupt your online activities and can be difficult to close; they can also be vehicles for additional spyware or other types of malware.

Because spyware can download, install, and run on your computer without your knowledge or consent, it's often difficult to know if spyware is infecting your computer. If you are experiencing any of the following symptoms, they are most likely due to spyware; you should scan your computer with a program that detects and removes spyware:

- New toolbars, links, or favorites appear in your Web browser unexpectedly.
- Your home page, mouse pointer, or search program changes without your consent.
- When you enter a URL for a Web site, such as a search engine, you go to a different Web site without notice.
- Pop-up ads interrupt you, even when you're not on the Internet.
- Your computer suddenly starts or runs slowly.

Scanning Your Computer with Windows Defender

To protect your computer against spyware, you can run up-to-date antispyware software. Some antivirus programs include antispyware components. Windows 7 also provides Windows Defender, which helps prevent spyware from installing itself and running on your computer. Windows Defender periodically scans your computer to detect and remove spyware. Besides monitoring and scanning your computer, Windows Defender also provides access to the Microsoft SpyNet community, where you can learn how others respond to software that hasn't been classified as spyware. When you are considering whether to download a free screen saver, for example, you can check the SpyNet Web site first to see if that program includes spyware or other types of malware.

REFERENCE

Performing a Quick Scan with Windows Defender
- Click the Start button, and then type Windows Defender.
- Click Windows Defender in the search results.
- Click the Scan button arrow on the toolbar.
- Click Quick scan.

As with antivirus software, you need to keep the spyware definitions in Windows Defender up to date. Windows Defender refers to the definitions to determine if software it detects is spyware or another type of malware. When you update your computer, Windows Update installs any new spyware definitions. You can also set Windows Defender to check for updated definitions before scanning your computer.

Next, you'll show Curt how to start Windows Defender and scan for spyware. You can run a quick scan or a full system scan. A quick scan checks the locations on your computer that spyware is most likely to infect. A full scan checks all your files and programs, but takes longer and can make your computer run slowly.

To start Windows Defender and perform a quick scan:

1. Close the Action Center window.
2. Click the **Start** button 🔵 on the taskbar, type **Windows Defender**, and then click **Windows Defender** in the search results. The Windows Defender window opens. Maximize the window. See Figure 5-10, which shows that Windows Defender needs to check for new definitions. Your settings might differ.

Figure 5-10	Windows Defender

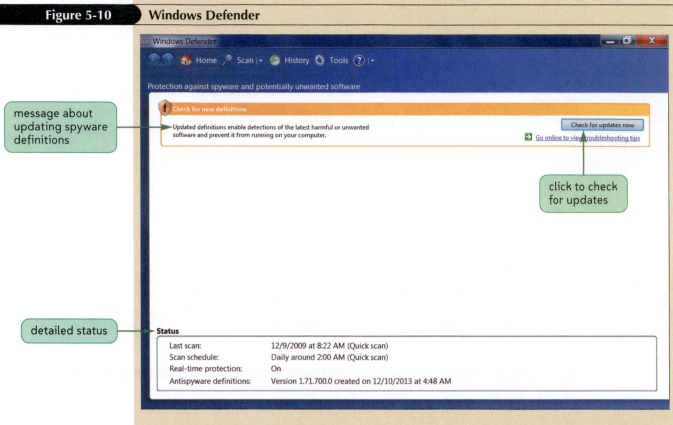

message about updating spyware definitions

click to check for updates

detailed status

Trouble? If a dialog box opens indicating that Windows Defender is turned off, click the *click here to turn it on* link.

▶ **3.** If necessary, click the **Check for updates now** button. Windows Defender checks for program updates, downloads and installs any updates, and then reports the update status.

▶ **4.** Click the **Scan button arrow** on the toolbar, and then click **Quick scan**. Windows Defender scans your computer, displaying first its progress and then the results of the scan. Depending on the number of programs on your computer, your scan might take a few minutes. Wait for the scan to finish and for the results window to open before continuing.

If Windows Defender finds files that might be spyware, it **quarantines** the files, which means it moves them to another location on your computer and prevents them from running until you remove or restore the files. Windows Defender alerts you if it quarantines any files. You can then open the Quarantined items page to review those files. Windows Defender lists the quarantined files by their name, alert level, and date of quarantine. Remove any files with a Severe or High alert level. If you do not recognize and trust the publisher of files with Medium or Low alert levels, remove those also.

The Quarantined items page also provides alert details to help you determine your best course of action. For example, it might indicate that a file is an adware program that has potentially unwanted behavior. The alert details sometimes include a link to a Web page on the Microsoft Web site that provides an up-to-date description of the program and identifies whether it is a known threat.

If Windows Defender quarantined any items, you should review the quarantined files and then remove or restore them.

To remove a quarantined file:

1. In the Windows Defender window, click the **Tools** button on the toolbar to open the Tools and Settings page, and then click **Quarantined items**. The Quarantined items page opens.

2. If necessary, click the **View** button to display quarantined items. See Figure 5-11.

Figure 5-11   **Quarantined items in Windows Defender**

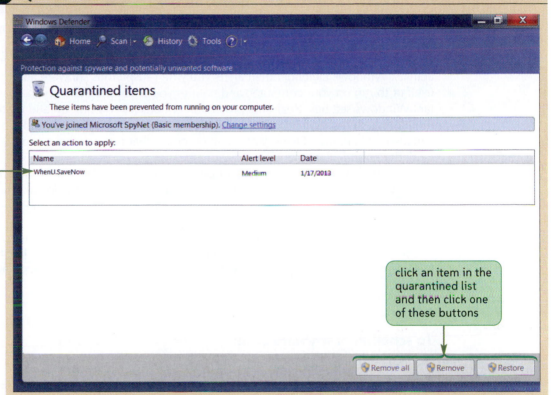

quarantined item to remove

click an item in the quarantined list and then click one of these buttons

Trouble? If Windows Defender did not quarantine any items after its quick scan, or if you do not have permission to work with quarantined items, read but do not perform Step 3.

The item shown in Figure 5-11, WhenU.SaveNow, has a Medium alert level, and its details indicate this is adware that can behave in an unwanted manner. Curt does not recognize the publisher of this program, so you should remove it.

TIP

Do not restore software with a Severe or High alert level.

3. In the Quarantined items list, click **WhenU.SaveNow** (or other item with a Severe, High, or Medium alert level and a publisher you do not recognize), and then click the **Remove** button.

Trouble? If a dialog box opens requesting an administrator password or your permission to continue, enter the password or click the Continue button.

Now that you've scanned Curt's computer and handled the items Windows Defender found, you can set options to make sure Windows Defender runs effectively.

Setting Windows Defender Options

The Options page in Windows Defender lets you set seven categories of options: Automatic scanning, Default actions, Real-time protection, Excluded files and folders, Excluded file types, Advanced, and Administrator options. You are most likely to use the first three options. When you select Automatic scanning options, you choose whether you want Windows Defender to scan your computer according to a schedule, and then set the frequency, approximate time, and type of scan (quick scan or full system scan). You can also indicate whether Windows Defender should check for updated definitions before scanning, which is the recommended setting for keeping the spyware definitions up to date.

Default actions are those you want Windows Defender to perform when it detects potentially unsafe software installed or trying to install itself on your computer. You can specify default actions according to alert level. For example, if Windows Defender detects a program with a Low alert level, you can set it to automatically allow the program to continue running.

By default, Windows Defender is set to constantly monitor your computer for spyware activity. Windows Defender then alerts you when suspicious software attempts to install itself or to run on your computer, and notifies you when programs try to change important Windows settings. Real-time protection options let you turn on and off this constant monitoring, and specify which Windows programs and settings it should monitor. You can also set Windows Defender to scan programs that run on your computer and downloaded files and attachments.

You can also use an Administrator option to specify whether you want to turn Windows Defender on or off. Windows Defender is turned on by default, though you can turn it off if it interferes with another antispyware program running on your computer.

Curt wants to follow your recommendation of performing a quick scan every day. You'll show him how to schedule the daily spyware scan for 5:00 p.m., just before he leaves the office. As you perform the following steps, note your settings so you can restore them later.

To schedule a spyware scan:

1. In the Windows Defender window, click the **Tools** button on the toolbar to open the Tools and Settings page, and then click **Options**. The Options page opens.

2. Click **Automatic Scanning** in the left pane, if necessary, to display the Automatic Scanning options. See Figure 5-12.

Figure 5-12   **Automatic scanning options**

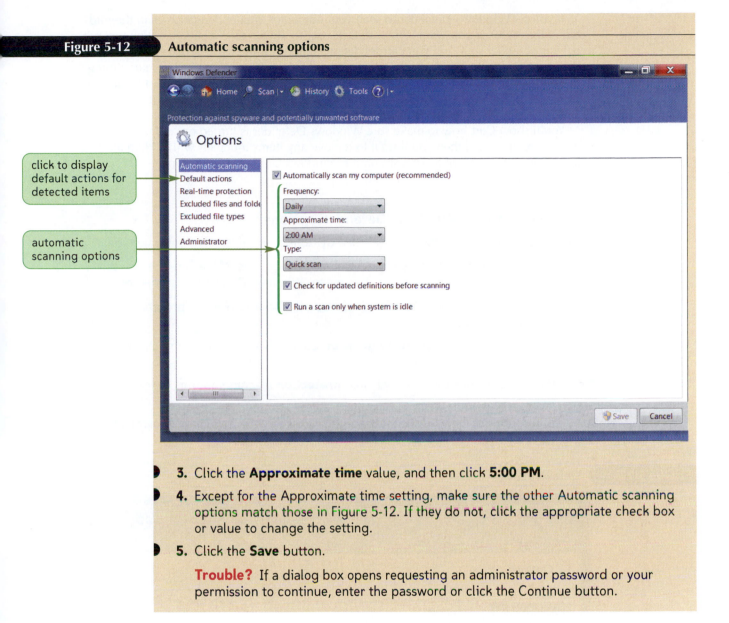

click to display
default actions for
detected items

automatic
scanning options

3. Click the **Approximate time** value, and then click **5:00 PM**.

4. Except for the Approximate time setting, make sure the other Automatic scanning options match those in Figure 5-12. If they do not, click the appropriate check box or value to change the setting.

5. Click the **Save** button.

Trouble? If a dialog box opens requesting an administrator password or your permission to continue, enter the password or click the Continue button.

You should keep Windows Defender turned on whenever you are using your computer. Windows Defender alerts all users if it detects spyware or other unwanted software trying to run or install itself on your computer. You can use the real-time protection feature to monitor certain Windows programs that spyware often attempts to change, such as Internet Explorer options that prevent programs from switching your home page or installing a toolbar without your consent. As with quarantined items, when Windows Defender detects suspicious software, it assigns an alert level to the software. Then it displays a dialog box where you can choose one of the following actions:

- Quarantine: Quarantine the program. Windows Defender prevents the software from running and allows you to restore it or remove it from your computer.
- Remove: Permanently delete the software from your computer.
- Allow: Add the software to the Windows Defender Allowed items list and run it on your computer. Windows Defender does not alert you to risks that the software might pose to your privacy or your computer unless you remove the program from the Allowed items list.

If you set Windows Defender to scan your computer unattended (such as in the middle of the night) or you want Windows Defender to always take a certain action when it detects potential spyware, you can set default actions for the items it detects. By default, Windows Defender checks its definition list and then acts accordingly, by quarantining items with a High alert level, for example. You can specify whether you want Windows Defender to allow or remove items with Medium and Low alert levels. For items with Severe or High alert levels, you can remove or quarantine the items.

You'll show Curt how to make sure Windows Defender is turned on and using real-time protection, and then you'll set it to remove any items it detects with a High alert level. You perform all of these tasks on the Windows Defender Options page.

To verify and set Windows Defender options:

1. On the Tools and Settings page, click **Options** to open the Options page again.

2. Click **Administrator** to view the Administrator options. Make sure the Use this program check box is selected. This means Windows Defender is turned on.

   Trouble? If Windows Defender is turned off, click the Use this program check box to turn it on.

3. In the Options list, click **Real-time protection** to view the Real-time protection options.

4. If necessary, click the **Use real-time protection (recommended)** check box to select it.

5. In the Options list, click **Default actions** to display the actions Windows Defender takes by default. See Figure 5-13.

Figure 5-13	Default actions

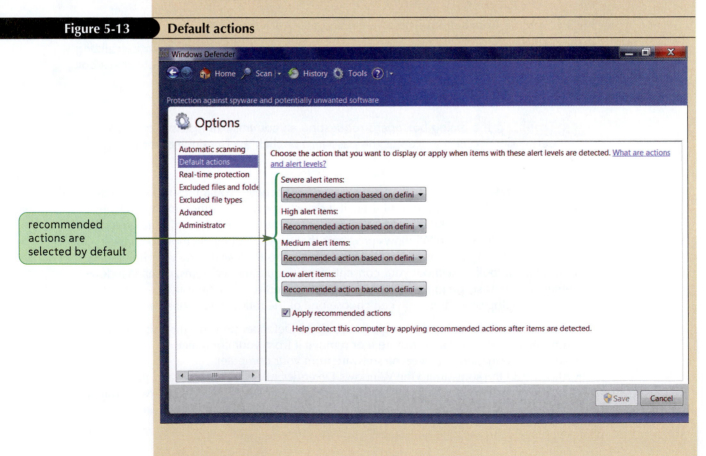

recommended actions are selected by default

6. Click the **High alert items** value and then click **Remove**.

7. If necessary, click the **Apply recommended actions** check box to select it, and then click the **Save** button.

   Trouble? If a dialog box opens requesting an administrator password or your permission to continue, enter the password or click the Continue button.

8. Close Windows Defender.

Defending Against E-Mail Viruses

An annoying and potentially dangerous type of privacy invasion is **spam**, or junk e-mail, offering products and services that are sometimes fake or misleading. Some users receive thousands of spam messages a day; the volume alone makes spam a nuisance. In addition, spam can be a vehicle for malware. Sending and reading e-mail messages is one of the most popular activities on the Internet, and e-mail is the most common way for computer viruses to spread. Because viruses and other security threats are often contained in e-mail attachments, the security settings in Windows Live Mail block e-mail attachments that might be harmful. Files with filename extensions such as *.exe*, *.bat*, and *.js*, for example, can contain malware, and are blocked by default. When Windows Live Mail blocks an attachment, it displays an Information bar below the toolbar that includes a message explaining that it blocked an attachment

To help prevent spam and potentially offensive material, Windows Live Mail does not download graphics with messages sent in HTML format. People sending spam (called spammers) often use graphics to access your e-mail address; that's why using plain text for e-mail messages is more secure than using the HTML format. Windows Live Mail displays an Information bar when it blocks graphics. If you trust the sender, you can click an option on the Information bar to download and display the pictures.

Spammers can also take advantage of vulnerabilities in your computer to use it to send spam to other computers without your permission, a practice known as an **e-mail relay**. This lets spammers work without being detected and can seriously downgrade the performance of your computer. By default, Windows Live Mail helps prevent spammers from using your computer for e-mail relays.

TIP

Viewing a picture in a junk e-mail message might validate your e-mail address and result in more junk e-mail.

Selecting Windows Live Mail Security Settings

You select your e-mail security settings using the Security tab of the Windows Live Mail Safety Options dialog box.

INSIGHT

Encrypting E-Mail Messages

When you exchange unencrypted e-mail messages, they are sent across the Internet in a plain text format. On their way to their recipients, hackers or automated programs can intercept, read, and even change the messages. Encrypted messages have a digital ID and are sent in a scrambled format that only your recipient can read. The encryption hides the e-mail contents, and the digital ID indicates whether a message has been altered in transit. However, to send and read encrypted messages, both the sender and receiver must have copies of one another's digital ID. If you need a digital ID for your recipient, ask your recipient to send you a digitally signed message. Whenever you receive a digitally signed e-mail message, Windows Live Mail automatically adds the sender's digital ID to the appropriate record in Windows Live Contacts.

You'll show Curt how to examine the security settings in Windows Live Mail. If he is using the default settings, you don't need to change them. Windows Live Mail must be installed before you can complete the following steps. (See "Setting Up Windows Live Mail" in Tutorial 4 for instructions.) If you are not allowed to install Windows Live Mail on your computer, read but do not perform the steps in this section.

To examine security settings in Windows Live Mail:

1. Click the **Start** button 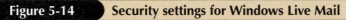 on the taskbar, point to **All Programs**, and click **Windows Live**, if necessary, and then click **Windows Live Mail** to start Windows Live Mail.

2. Click the **Menus** button on the toolbar, and then click **Safety options**. The Safety Options dialog box opens.

3. Click the **Security** tab to examine the enhanced security settings. See Figure 5-14.

Figure 5-14   **Security settings for Windows Live Mail**

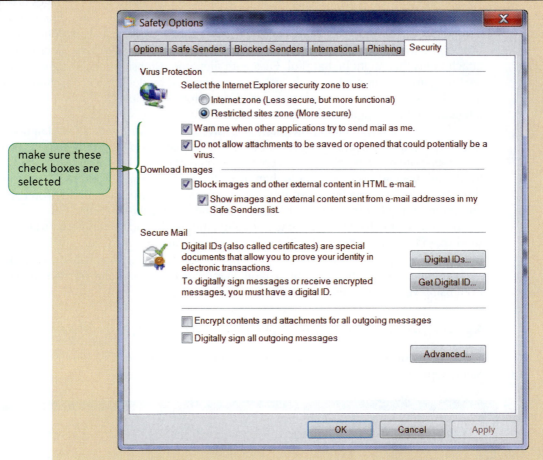

4. The check boxes in the Virus Protection and Download Images sections are for enhanced security features in Windows Live Mail. If one of these boxes is unchecked, click the check box to select it, and then click the **Apply** button.

5. Leave the Safety Options dialog box open.

In addition to selecting security settings in Windows Live Mail, some of the security settings you select for Internet Explorer apply to Windows Live Mail. You'll work with Internet Explorer security settings in the next session.

Blocking Spam and Other Junk Mail

Windows Live Mail includes a junk e-mail filter that catches obvious spam messages and moves them to a built-in Junk e-mail folder. You can then examine the messages in the Junk e-mail folder and delete them, open them, or move them back to your Inbox, if necessary. Windows Live Mail also maintains two lists of senders. The Safe Senders list contains addresses of messages you never want to treat as junk mail. The Blocked Senders list contains addresses of messages you always want to treat as junk mail. You can add e-mail addresses to these lists to customize the kind of security Windows Live Mail provides.

Usually, you add an address to the Safe Senders or Blocked Senders list when you review the messages in your Junk e-mail folder. You can block further messages from a sender by adding the sender or the domain to the Blocked Senders list. For example, if you receive spam from *JSmith@domain.net*, you can block all future e-mail from either that specific address or from any address in domain.net. Any further e-mail from that sender or domain will then be stored in the Junk e-mail folder automatically. Adding people to the Safe Senders list works the same way—you can add either an address or a domain to the Safe Senders list.

If you haven't received any e-mail from someone you want to add to your Safe or Blocked Senders list, you can do so manually by using the Safety Options dialog box. If you somehow include the same person on both lists, you'll receive e-mail from that person in your Inbox because the Safe Senders list has priority over the Blocked Senders list.

REFERENCE

Adding a Sender to the Blocked Senders or Safe Senders List

- To block a sender in Windows Live Mail, right-click a message whose sender you want to add to the Blocked Senders list, point to Junk e-mail, and then click Add sender to blocked senders list on the shortcut menu.
- To always allow a sender, right-click a message whose sender you want to add to the Safe Senders list, point to Junk e-mail, and then click Add sender to safe senders list on the shortcut menu.
- Click the OK button.

In addition, you can set the level of junk e-mail protection you want in Windows Live Mail. By default, Windows Live Mail uses a low level of junk e-mail protection; you can change this based on how much junk e-mail you receive. You can use any of the following protection levels:

- No Automatic Filtering: This setting does not block any junk e-mail messages except for those from senders on your Blocked Senders list.
- Low: This setting blocks only the most obvious spam. Choose this level if you don't receive many junk e-mail messages.
- High: This setting blocks most potential spam. Choose this level if you receive a large volume of junk e-mail messages. However, be sure to review the messages in your Junk e-mail folder frequently to make sure it doesn't contain legitimate e-mail messages.
- Safe List Only: This setting blocks all e-mail messages except for those from senders on your Safe Senders list. If you choose this setting, review the messages in your Junk e-mail folder frequently for legitimate e-mail.

To set junk e-mail options:

1. In the Safety Options dialog box, click the **Options** tab to display the junk e-mail options. See Figure 5-15.

Figure 5-15   **Safety Options dialog box displays options for junk e-mail**

Low setting is selected by default; your setting might differ

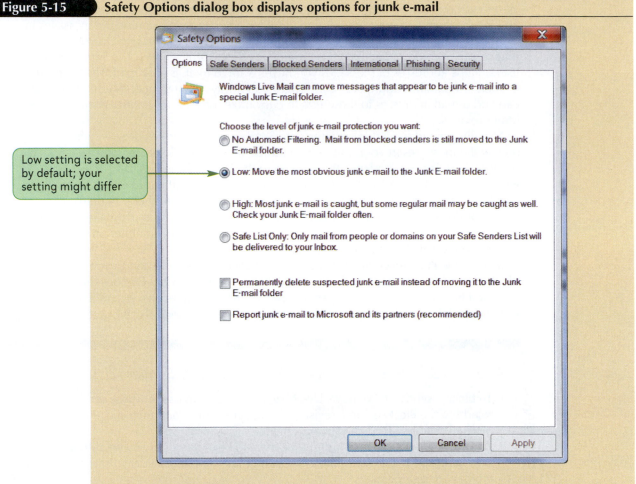

Curt doesn't receive much junk e-mail, so the Low setting selected in Figure 5-15 is appropriate for him.

> **2.** Click the **Safe Senders** tab to view the Safe Senders list. You can add your e-mail address to this list.

> **3.** Click the **Add** button to open the Add address or domain dialog box.

> **4.** Type your e-mail address, and then click the **OK** button.

> **5.** Click the **Blocked Senders** tab to view the Blocked Senders list. Adding a sender to this list works the same way as the Safe Senders list—you click the Add button and enter an e-mail address.

Before closing the Safety Options dialog box, you want to show Curt one more way to protect his computer from harmful e-mail.

Defending Against Phishing Messages

Phishing (pronounced *fishing*) is an attempt to deceive you into revealing personal or financial information when you respond to an e-mail message or visit a Web site. A typical phishing scam starts with an e-mail message that looks like an official notice from a trusted person or business, such as a bank, credit card company, or reputable online merchant. The e-mail message asks you to reply with sensitive information, such as an account number or password, or directs you to a fraudulent Web site that requests this information. Phishers usually use the information for identity theft.

By default, if Windows Live Mail detects links to Web sites in the e-mail messages you receive, and the links seem fraudulent, Windows Live Mail blocks access to the links in that message and displays a message on the Information bar explaining its actions. If you are certain the message contains legitimate links, you can click an option on the Information bar to turn on the links in the message. You can also specify that when Windows Live Mail suspects a message is a phishing e-mail, it moves the message to the Junk e-mail folder. You'll show Curt how to select this setting.

To set phishing e-mail options:

1. In the Safety Options dialog box, click the **Phishing** tab.

2. If necessary, click the **Protect my Inbox from messages with potential Phishing links** check box to select it.

3. Click the **Move phishing E-mail to the Junk e-mail folder** check box, if necessary, to select that option.

4. Click the **OK** button to close the Safety Options dialog box.

5. Close Windows Live Mail.

In the next session, you'll also work with Internet Explorer settings to protect against phishing attempts.

REVIEW

Session 5.1 Quick Check

1. _____ is malicious or harmful software.
2. What is the Action Center?
3. What does Windows Firewall do?
4. True or False. You add a program to the Windows Firewall allowed programs list to allow that program to communicate with your computer now and in the future.
5. A(n) _____ is a change to software that can prevent or repair problems, enhance the security of the computer, or improve the computer's performance.
6. True or False. Windows 7 does not provide any type of malware protection.
7. _____ monitors your computing actions to collect information about you, change settings on your computer, or interrupt programs and slow your computer's performance.
8. What is spam, and why can it be dangerous?

SESSION 5.2 VISUAL OVERVIEW

The **Information bar** is the place where Internet Explorer displays information about security, downloads, and blocked pop-up windows.

InPrivate Browsing helps prevent Internet Explorer from storing data about your browsing session.

Protected Mode guards against Web sites that try to save files or install malware on your computer.

Use the **Pop-up Blocker** to limit or block most pop-up windows.

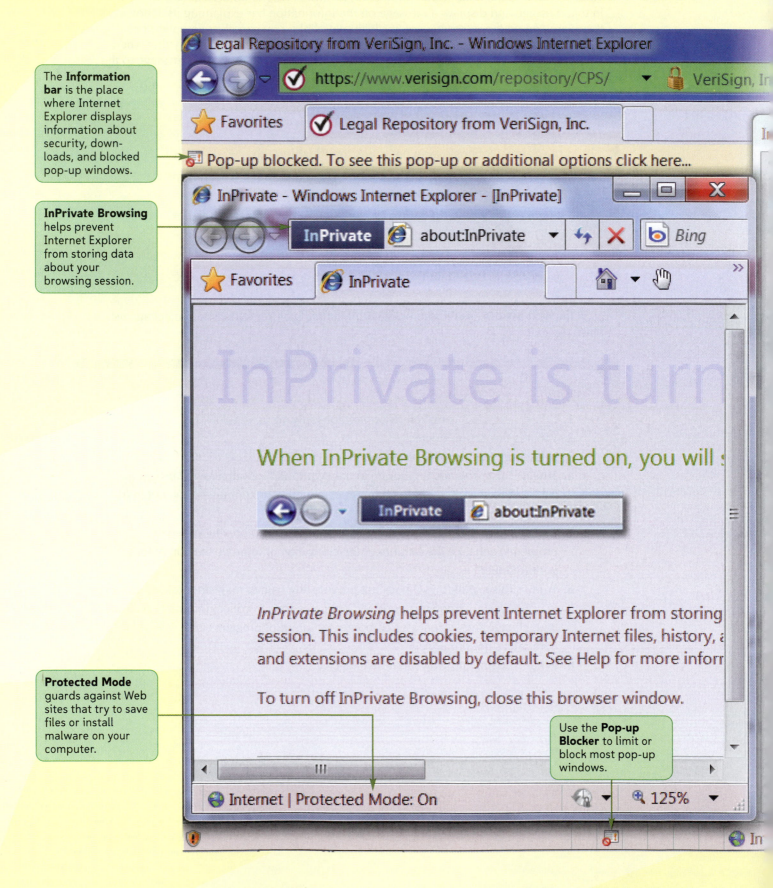

Legal Repository from VeriSign, Inc. - Windows Internet Explorer

https://www.verisign.com/repository/CPS/   VeriSign, In

Favorites   Legal Repository from VeriSign, Inc.

Pop-up blocked. To see this pop-up or additional options click here...

InPrivate - Windows Internet Explorer - [InPrivate]

InPrivate   about:InPrivate   Bing

Favorites   InPrivate

InPrivate is turn

When InPrivate Browsing is turned on, you will s

InPrivate   about:InPrivate

InPrivate Browsing helps prevent Internet Explorer from storing session. This includes cookies, temporary Internet files, history, a and extensions are disabled by default. See Help for more inforr

To turn off InPrivate Browsing, close this browser window.

Internet | Protected Mode: On   125%

INTERNET EXPLORER SECURITY FEATURES

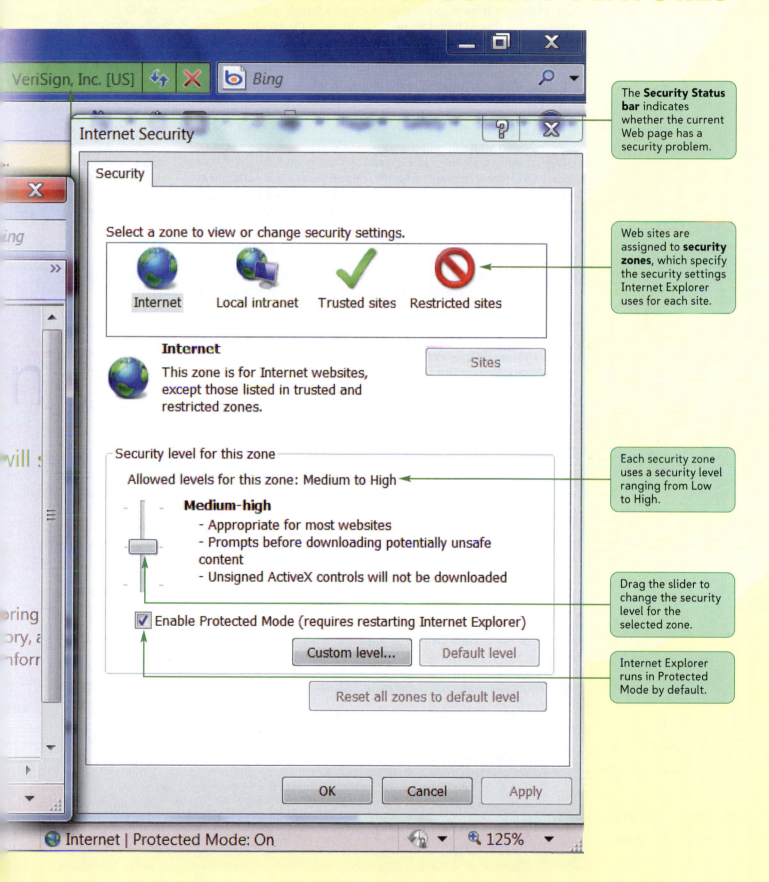

The **Security Status bar** indicates whether the current Web page has a security problem.

Web sites are assigned to **security zones**, which specify the security settings Internet Explorer uses for each site.

Each security zone uses a security level ranging from Low to High.

Drag the slider to change the security level for the selected zone.

Internet Explorer runs in Protected Mode by default.

Managing Microsoft Internet Explorer Security

Your computer is most vulnerable to security threats when you are connected to the Internet. You should therefore take advantage of the security settings in Internet Explorer to help protect your computer by identifying viruses and other security threats that are circulated over the Internet and to guard your privacy, making your computer and personal information more secure. Internet Explorer offers the following security features:

- SmartScreen filter: This feature helps detect online scams, such as Web sites that try to trick you into revealing financial account information.
- Protected Mode: This feature guards against Web sites that try to save files or install malware on your computer.
- Digital signatures: Internet Explorer can detect and display digital signatures, which are electronic security marks added to files to verify their authenticity.
- Pop-up Blocker: This tool allows you to limit or block most pop-up windows.
- Add-on Manager: This tool lets you disable or allow programs or controls that extend your browser's features.

Internet Explorer also protects your privacy with the following tools and features:

- Privacy settings and alerts: These settings specify how to handle identifying information when you're online and alert you when a Web site you're visiting doesn't meet your criteria.
- InPrivate Browsing: This feature helps prevent Internet Explorer from storing data about your browsing session by opening a separate InPrivate Browsing Internet Explorer window to keep your browsing actions private.
- InPrivate Filtering: This feature helps prevent Web site content providers from collecting information about sites you visit.
- Secure connections: Internet Explorer informs you when it is using a secure connection to communicate with Web sites that handle sensitive personal information.

Using the SmartScreen Filter

Recall that phishing is an attempt to deceive you into revealing personal or financial information when you respond to an e-mail message or visit a Web site. Internet Explorer can help protect you from phishing scams by detecting possible phishing Web sites. The SmartScreen Filter helps to protect you from phishing attacks, online fraud, and spoofed Web sites. (A **spoofed Web site** is a fraudulent site posing as a legitimate one.) The SmartScreen Filter operates in the background to analyze a Web site you visit by comparing its address to a list of reported phishing and malicious software Web sites. If SmartScreen Filter finds that the Web site you're visiting is on the list of known malware or phishing sites, Internet Explorer shows a blocking Web page and displays the Address bar in red. On the blocking page, you can choose to bypass the blocked Web site and go to your home page instead. If you are certain the blocked Web site is safe, you can continue to the site, though Microsoft does not recommend this.

INSIGHT

Protecting Yourself from Phishing Attempts

In addition to using the Internet Explorer SmartScreen Filter, use the following guidelines to protect yourself from online phishing:

- Never provide personal information in an e-mail, instant message, or pop-up window.
- Do not click links in e-mail and instant messages from senders you do not know or trust. Even messages that seem to be from friends and family can be faked, so check with the sender to make sure he or she actually sent the message.
- Only use Web sites that provide privacy statements or indicate how they use your personal information.

You can turn on SmartScreen Filter to check Web sites automatically, or you can check Web sites manually by clicking the Safety button on the Internet Explorer Command bar, pointing to SmartScreen Filter, and then clicking Check This Website.

To turn on the SmartScreen Filter and check a Web site:

1. Start Internet Explorer.

2. Click the **Safety** button on the Command bar, point to **SmartScreen Filter**, and then click **Check This Website**. Internet Explorer sends the URL of your home page to Microsoft for verification.

   Trouble? If a dialog box opens explaining how the SmartScreen Filter works, click the OK button.

   Trouble? If you are not connected to the Internet, skip Steps 2 and 3.

3. When the SmartScreen Filter dialog box opens to indicate this is not a phishing Web site, click the **OK** button.

4. Click the **Safety** button on the Command bar, point to **SmartScreen Filter**, and then click **Turn On SmartScreen Filter**. The Microsoft SmartScreen Filter dialog box opens. See Figure 5-16. Internet Explorer selects the Turn on automatic SmartScreen Filter (recommended) option button for you.

Figure 5-16   **Microsoft SmartScreen Filter dialog box**

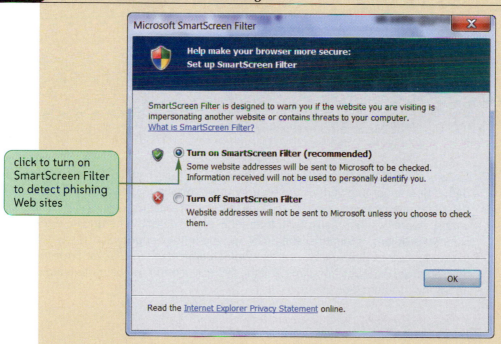

click to turn on SmartScreen Filter to detect phishing Web sites

Trouble? If Turn Off SmartScreen Filter appears when you point to SmartScreen Filter, the SmartScreen Filter is already turned on. Skip Steps 4 and 5.

▶ 5. Click the **OK** button.

▶ 6. To see how to report a possible phishing site, click the **Safety** button on the Command bar, point to **SmartScreen Filter**, and then click **Report Unsafe Website**. The Microsoft SmartScreen Filter Web page opens where you can report information about the Web site. See Figure 5-17.

Figure 5-17	Microsoft SmartScreen Filter Web page

select this check box if you think you encountered a phishing Web site

▶ 7. Close the Microsoft SmartScreen Filter Web page.

As you visit Web sites, Internet Explorer checks their certificates. A **certificate** is a digital document that verifies the security of a Web site you visit. Internet Explorer can detect certificate errors, which are signs that you are visiting a phishing site or one that uses spyware or other malware. If Internet Explorer detects a certificate error or other security problem, it identifies the problem type in the Security Status bar, which appears to the right of the Address bar. For example, the message *Certificate Error* might appear in the Security Status bar. You can click the security icon in the Security Status bar to learn about the problem. See Figure 5-18.

| Figure 5-18 | Security Status bar |

red Address bar indicates a problem with this site's certificate

security notice displayed in the Security Status bar

detailed message about the potentially unsafe Web site

The color of the Address bar also indicates the type of error or problem. Red means the certificate is out of date, is invalid, or has an error. Yellow signals that the certificate cannot be verified, which sometimes happens with a suspected phishing site. White means the certificate is normal, and green indicates sites that have high security, such as those for financial transactions.

Blocking Malware with Protected Mode and Security Zones

To install or run programs on your computer, hackers often take advantage of Web programming tools, such as scripts and ActiveX controls, that are designed to enhance your online experience. A **script** is programming code that performs a series of commands and can be embedded in a Web page. For example, a Web site designer might use a script to verify that you've completed all the necessary fields in an online form. In contrast, hackers use scripts on a Web page to automatically download programs that can collect and transmit information about you without your knowledge or authorization. A common way for hackers to distribute adware and spyware is to download **ActiveX controls**, which are small, self-contained programs, from a Web page to your computer. Some ActiveX controls make it easier to perform tasks, such as submitting information to a Web site. Other ActiveX controls can harm your computer and files, especially those controls that lack digital signatures, meaning they are unverified. Similar to a Web site certificate, a **digital signature** is an electronic security mark that can be added to files. It identifies the publisher of a file and verifies that the file has not changed since it was signed. Internet Explorer offers a few ways to protect against malicious scripts and ActiveX controls, including Protected Mode and security zones.

INSIGHT

Digital Signatures

Internet Explorer (and other programs, including Windows 7) detects whether a file has a digital signature. A file without a valid digital signature might not be from the stated source or might have been tampered with (possibly by a virus) since it was published. Avoid opening an unsigned file unless you know for certain who created it and whether the contents are safe to open. However, even a valid digital signature does not guarantee that the contents of the file are harmless. When you download a file, determine whether to trust its contents based on the identity of the publisher and the site providing the file.

Internet Explorer runs in Protected Mode by default, making it difficult for hackers to install malware on your computer. When Protected Mode is turned on, a notification appears in the Internet Explorer status bar. If a Web page tries to install any type of software or run a script, Internet Explorer displays a dialog box warning you about the attempt. If you trust the program, you can allow it to run once or always. If you are not familiar with the program or don't want to run it, you can deny it once or always.

In addition to Protected Mode, Internet Explorer uses security zones so you can tailor your security settings to the kind of online computing you do. Internet Explorer classifies all Web sites in one of four security zones: Internet, Local intranet, Trusted sites, and Restricted sites. Each zone uses a certain level of security setting ranging from Low to High. When you visit a Web site that has been assigned to a security zone, the appropriate icon appears in the Internet Explorer status bar. Figure 5-19 summarizes the four security zones. Note that the security zone settings in Internet Explorer also apply to Windows Live Mail.

Figure 5-19	Internet Explorer security zones

Security Zone	Description
Internet	Internet Explorer assigns all Internet Web sites to this zone by default and applies a Medium-high security level, which is appropriate for most sites. You can change the security level to Medium or High.
Local intranet	Internet Explorer assigns Web sites on your intranet (a corporate or business network) to this zone and applies a Medium-low security level. You can change this to any other level.
Trusted sites	You can assign Web sites to this zone that you trust not to damage your computer or files. This zone has a Medium level of security by default, but you can change it to any other level.
Restricted sites	You assign Web sites to this zone that might damage your computer or files. Adding sites to this zone does not block them, but it does prevent them from using scripts or active content. This zone has a High level of security by default and cannot be changed.

You'll show Curt how to check the security level of his home page.

To check the security level of your home page:

1. With Internet Explorer open to your home page, double-click the **Protected Mode** notification in the status bar. The Internet Security dialog box opens. See Figure 5-20.

| Figure 5-20 | Internet Security dialog box |

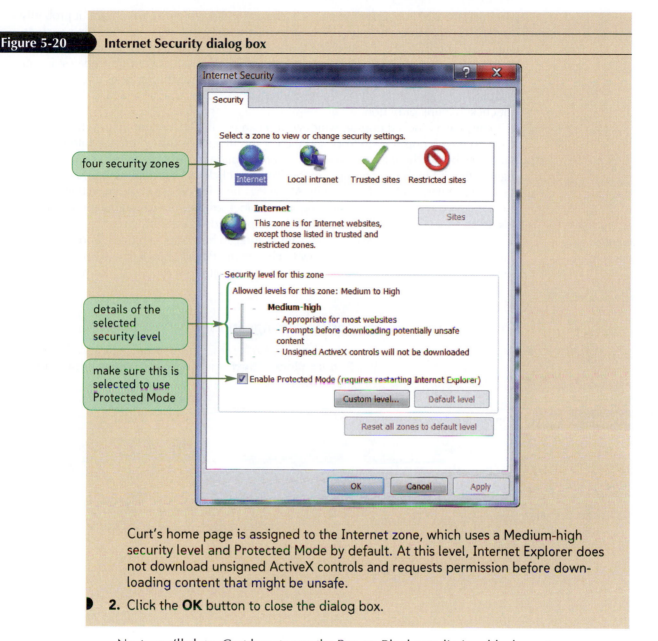

four security zones

details of the selected security level

make sure this is selected to use Protected Mode

Curt's home page is assigned to the Internet zone, which uses a Medium-high security level and Protected Mode by default. At this level, Internet Explorer does not download unsigned ActiveX controls and requests permission before downloading content that might be unsafe.

2. Click the **OK** button to close the dialog box.

Next, you'll show Curt how to use the Pop-up Blocker to limit or block most pop-up windows when he visits Web sites.

Blocking Pop-Up Windows

A pop-up ad is a small Web browser window that appears when you visit a Web site and that advertises a product or service. Many legitimate advertisers use pop-up ads because they effectively get your attention and provide information or services that might interest you. However, some pop-up ads are annoying because they repeatedly interrupt your online activities, are difficult to close, or display objectionable content. Other pop-up ads are dangerous; they can download spyware or **hijack** your browser, meaning they seize control of the browser, opening many more new windows each time you close one pop-up window until you have to close your browser or restart your computer.

To avoid the nuisance and danger of pop-up ads, Internet Explorer includes a Pop-up Blocker so it can warn you about or block pop-up ads. The Pop-up Blocker is turned on by default, meaning that Internet Explorer blocks most pop-up windows. Not all pop-up windows are ads. If a pop-up window opens as soon as you visit a Web site, it probably contains an ad. However, many Web sites use pop-up windows to display tools such as calendars. For example, if you visit a travel Web site to make flight or hotel reservations, you can use a calendar displayed in a pop-up window to select your travel dates. If you click a link or button to open the pop-up window, Internet Explorer does not block it by default. However, it does block pop-up windows that appear automatically if you have not clicked a link or button.

To display a blocked pop-up window, you can use the Information bar. When you visit a Web site with pop-up windows and the Pop-up Blocker is turned on, the Information bar opens below the Internet Explorer Command bar and displays a message informing you that it blocked a pop-up window. You can click the Information bar to display a menu of settings, such as Temporarily Allow Pop-ups. To select long-term settings, you use the Pop-up Blocker Settings dialog box to block all pop-up ads, allow more pop-up ads, or specify which Web sites can display pop-up ads in your browser.

Curt has had problems with pop-up ads before, so he wants to block all pop-ups in Internet Explorer. You'll show him how to change the Pop-up Blocker settings to do so. As you perform the following steps, note your original settings so you can restore them later.

TIP

To display a menu of pop-up settings, click the Pop-ups were blocked icon that appears in the status bar when a Web page contains pop-up ads.

To change the Pop-up Blocker settings in Internet Explorer:

1. Click the **Tools** button on the Internet Explorer Command bar, point to **Pop-up Blocker**, and then click **Pop-up Blocker Settings**. The Pop-up Blocker Settings dialog box opens. See Figure 5-21.

Figure 5-21 | **Pop-up Blocker Settings dialog box**

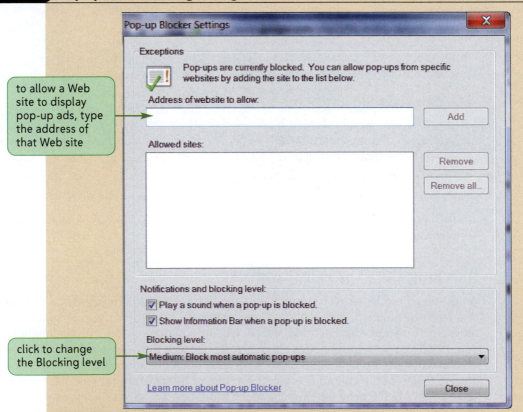

to allow a Web site to display pop-up ads, type the address of that Web site

click to change the Blocking level

> **2.** Click the Blocking level setting, and then click **High: Block all pop-ups (Ctrl+Alt to override)**.
>
>   **Trouble?** If you are working in a computer lab, you might not have permission to change the Pop-up Blocker settings. In that case, skip Step 2.
>
> **3.** Click the **Close** button.

Next, you'll learn how to find out which add-on programs are installed to work with Internet Explorer.

Managing Add-On Programs

A browser **add-on** is a program offered by any software vendor that provides enhancements such as a toolbar or an improved search feature. For example, Silverlight is a popular add-on that enhances the multimedia, animation, and other effects displayed in Internet Explorer. Some add-ons are safe and make your browser more effective; other add-ons, especially those that are installed without your permission, can affect the performance of Internet Explorer and even make it stop working. Internet Explorer provides an add-on manager so you can review, disable, update, or report add-ons to Microsoft. Other security features, such as Protected Mode, security levels, and the Information bar, warn you when a Web site is trying to download add-on software to your computer.

You can usually install and use browser add-ons without any problems, but some cause Internet Explorer to shut down unexpectedly. If this happens, you can disable the add-on.

Internet Explorer usually asks for permission before running an add-on for the first time. If you don't recognize the program or its publisher, you can deny permission. Internet Explorer also maintains a list of preapproved add-ons that have been checked and digitally signed. It runs add-ons in this list without requesting your permission. You can view the list of preapproved add-ons in the Manage Add-ons dialog box.

Curt isn't aware of any add-ons his browser uses, so he wants to view the preapproved add-ons and any others that Internet Explorer is running.

> **To examine and manage add-ons:**
>
> **1.** Click the **Tools** button on the Command bar, and then click **Manage Add-ons**. The Manage Add-ons dialog box opens. By default, this dialog box displays the toolbar and extension add-ons that are currently loaded in Internet Explorer.
>
> **2.** Click the **Currently loaded add-ons** button, and then click **Run without permission**. The preapproved add-ons appear in the list.
>
> **3.** Click the first add-on in the list to display details about it. See Figure 5-22.

Figure 5-22   **Manage Add-ons window**

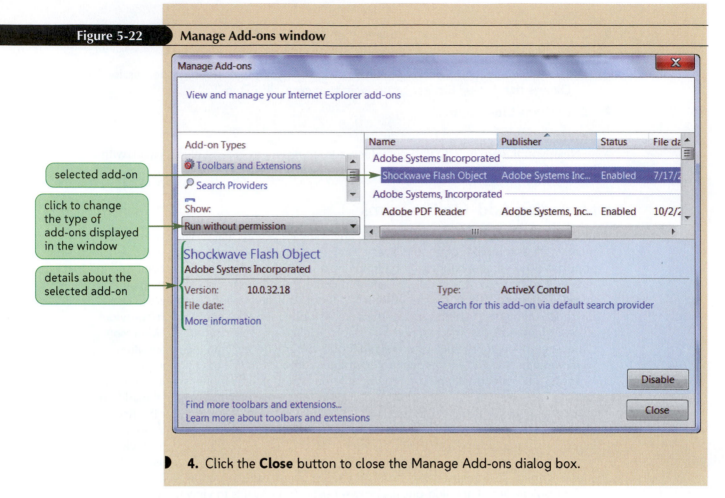

selected add-on

click to change the type of add-ons displayed in the window

details about the selected add-on

▶ **4.** Click the **Close** button to close the Manage Add-ons dialog box.

Now that you have explored the security settings in Internet Explorer, you can turn your attention to the privacy settings.

Selecting Privacy Settings

In addition to security protection, Internet Explorer also includes tools to protect your privacy. One privacy concern is cookies, which many Web sites store on your computer when you visit them. A **cookie** is a small file that records information about you, such as the type of browser you are using, your e-mail address, and your preferences for using a Web site. Like other Web tools, cookies can enhance your online experience by helping trusted Web sites customize their service to you; but they can also pose a security risk—hackers can retrieve cookies to search for private information such as passwords or use cookies to track the Web sites you visit. In Internet Explorer, you can specify privacy settings to either allow or prevent Web sites from saving cookies on your computer.

One way to protect your privacy with Internet Explorer is to block cookies on some or all of the Web sites you visit. You should be selective about which Web sites you allow to store cookies on your computer. Blocking all cookies keeps your Web site visits private, but might also limit your experience or prove annoying. Allowing all cookies might compromise your privacy. Most users find that the default medium-high privacy setting provides a good balance because it allows most **first-party cookies**, which are generated from the Web sites you visit and contain information the Web site reuses when you return. For example, to keep track of products you add to an electronic shopping cart or wish list, a Web site saves a first-party cookie on your computer. In contrast, the medium-high privacy setting blocks most **third-party cookies**, which are generated from Web site advertisers, who might use them to track your Web use for marketing purposes.

Selecting Privacy Settings

- Click Tools on the Internet Explorer Command bar, and then click Internet Options.
- Click the Privacy tab in the Internet Options dialog box.
- Drag the slider to select a privacy setting ranging from Block All Cookies to Accept All Cookies.
- Click the OK button.

Curt often visits his clients' Web sites for research as he prepares or performs translation projects. He wants to protect the privacy of Presto Global Translators and his clients by blocking all cookies and then allowing only those issued by sites he trusts.

As you perform the following steps, note your original settings so you can restore them later.

To change privacy settings for saving cookies:

1. Click the **Tools** button on the Internet Explorer Command bar, and then click **Internet Options**. The Internet Options dialog box opens.

2. Click the **Privacy** tab to view privacy settings. See Figure 5-23.

Figure 5-23   **Privacy tab in the Internet Options dialog box**

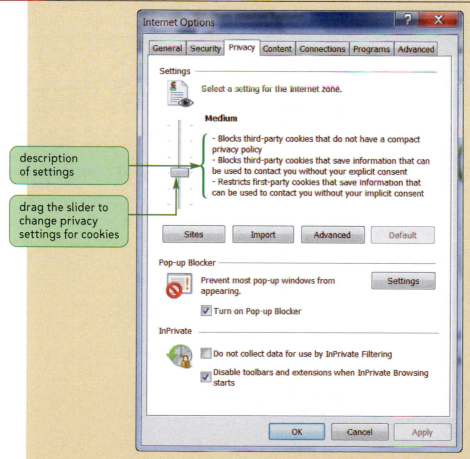

description of settings

drag the slider to change privacy settings for cookies

Trouble? If you are working in a computer lab, you might not have permission to change the privacy settings. In that case, read but do not perform Steps 3–6.

3. Drag the slider up to the **Block All Cookies** setting. When you select this setting, Internet Explorer will not let a Web site store any cookies on your computer unless you explicitly allow it to do so.

4. Drag the slider back to **Medium**. This setting blocks cookies except for those created by Web sites you identify.

5. Click the **Sites** button to open the Per Site Privacy Actions dialog box. You use this dialog box to specify the Web sites you want to allow to store cookies on your computer. (If you had selected a lower privacy setting, you could also use this dialog box to block certain Web sites from storing cookies.)

6. Click the **OK** button to close the Per Site Privacy Actions dialog box.

Internet Explorer will block most cookies on Curt's computer from now on. However, if Web sites stored cookies on his computer before you changed the privacy setting, they will remain there until you delete them. You can delete cookies by clearing your Web page history. In addition to cookies, Internet Explorer stores temporary Internet files, a history of the Web sites you've visited, information you've entered in the Address bar, and Web passwords you've saved. (A temporary Internet file is a copy of a Web page you viewed. Internet Explorer stores this file for a specified number of days, such as 20, so it can display the page quickly if you open it again.) Usually, maintaining this history information improves your Web browsing because it can fill in information that you would otherwise have to retype. If you have particular privacy concerns, however, such as when you are using a public computer, you can clear some or all of your browsing history to delete this information. Curt wants to delete all of the cookies and the list of Web sites he has visited.

> **TIP**
>
> To view temporary files before deleting them, click the Tools button, click Internet Options, click the General tab, click the Settings button in the Browsing history section, and then click View files.

To clear your browsing history:

1. Click the **General** tab in the Internet Options dialog box, and then click the **Delete** button in the Browsing history section. The Delete Browsing History dialog box opens. See Figure 5-24.

Figure 5-24   Delete Browsing History dialog box

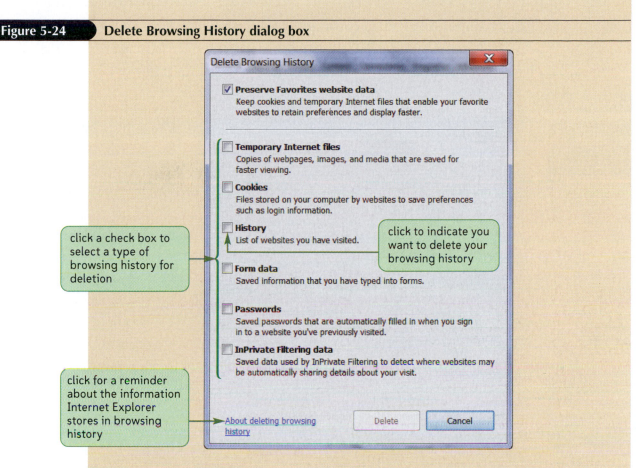

click a check box to select a type of browsing history for deletion

click to indicate you want to delete your browsing history

click for a reminder about the information Internet Explorer stores in browsing history

Trouble? If you are working in a computer lab, you might not have permission to clear your browsing history. In that case, read but do not perform Steps 2–5.

2. If necessary, click the **Cookies** check box to indicate you want to delete all the cookies stored on your computer.

3. If necessary, click the **History** check box to indicate you want to delete the list of Web sites you have visited.

4. Click the **Delete** button to delete cookies and your browsing history.

5. Click the **OK** button to close the Internet Options dialog box.

Another privacy feature of Internet Explorer is InPrivate Browsing, which you'll explore next.

Protecting Your Privacy with InPrivate Browsing

If you want to keep information about your Web browsing private, you can use InPrivate Browsing. This feature prevents Internet Explorer from storing data about your browsing session. If you are searching online for a gift, for example, or want to prevent another user from retracing your steps to a Web site containing your financial information, use InPrivate Browsing to hide the history of the Web pages you visited. When you do, Internet Explorer opens a new window and displays *InPrivate* in the Address bar. As you work in the InPrivate window, Internet Explorer protects your privacy. To end your InPrivate Browsing session, close the browser window.

Keep in mind that InPrivate Browsing does not make you anonymous on the Internet. Web sites might still be able to identify you through your Web address, and any forms you complete and selections you make can be recorded and saved by those Web sites.

To turn on InPrivate Browsing:

1. Click the **Safety** button on the Internet Explorer Command bar, and then click **InPrivate Browsing**. See Figure 5-25.

Figure 5-25	InPrivate Browsing window

InPrivate appears in the Address bar and title bar

click the link to review information about InPrivate Browsing

2. Click in the Address bar, type **www.whitehouse.gov**, and then press the **Enter** key. The home page for the White House Web site appears in the InPrivate browser window.

3. Point to the **Briefing Room** link near the top of the page, and then click **Your Weekly Address**.

    Trouble? If the Your Weekly Address link does not appear on the Web page you are viewing, click any other link.

4. Click the **Recent Pages** button 🔽 on the Address bar to display a list of pages you visited during your InPrivate Browsing session. These include the Your Weekly Address page and The White House home page.

5. Close all open Internet Explorer windows.

6. Start Internet Explorer again.

7. Click the **Favorites** button on the Command bar to open the Favorites Center, click the **History** tab, and then click the **Today** link. None of the Web pages you visited while using InPrivate Browsing appear in the History list.

Internet Explorer includes another privacy feature—InPrivate Filtering—which you'll learn about next.

Using InPrivate Filtering

Many Web pages use content such as ads, maps, or Web analysis tools that count the number of visitors to the Web site. This content is typically supplied by other Web sites called content providers or third-party Web sites. When you visit a Web site with third-party content, information that identifies your computer is sent to the content provider. For example, the content provider can learn your browser type, operating system, Web address, and screen resolution. If you visit many Web sites that the same content provider uses, the content provider can create a profile of your browsing preferences. The profile can be used to target ads that are likely to appeal to you, for example.

Web tracking tools such as visitor counters sometimes appear as visible content, but not always. For example, Web beacons are transparent images that invisibly track Web site usage. Web analysis tools often contain scripts that can track information such as the pages you visit and the selections you make. To control the information sent to content providers, you can use InPrivate Filtering.

InPrivate Filtering analyzes the content of Web pages you visit. If it finds content that is used on other Web sites, InPrivate Filtering lets you allow or block the content. You can also have InPrivate Filtering automatically block content from third-party Web sites.

By blocking content, InPrivate Filtering can protect your privacy on the Web. However, content providers often pay for Web site content that you can view or use for free. Blocking all third-party content can make Web pages load slowly and prevent Web sites you like from earning income they need. Instead of blocking all third-party content, you can use InPrivate Filtering to examine which content providers supply content to Web sites you've visited. The Web address of the content provider collecting information on a Web page is often displayed in the Internet Explorer status bar as the Web page opens. If you notice that you have trouble displaying Web pages when a content provider's address appears in the status bar, you can block that content provider to improve performance. Content providers who supply content to 30 or more Web pages might be collecting too much information about you, so you can block them as well.

Curt notices that when he has trouble opening Web pages, a Web address such as *ads.doubleclick.net* appears in the status bar. You suggest he block this content provider to see if that improves his browsing experience.

To turn on InPrivate Filtering and block a content provider:

1. Click the **Safety** button on the Internet Explorer Command bar, and then click **InPrivate Filtering**. The InPrivate Filtering dialog box opens.

   Trouble? If you already turned on InPrivate Filtering, click the Safety button, and then click InPrivate Filtering Settings. Skip Steps 1 and 2.

> **2.** Click **Let me choose which providers receive my information**. The InPrivate Filtering settings dialog box opens. See Figure 5-26.

Figure 5-26 InPrivate Filtering settings dialog box

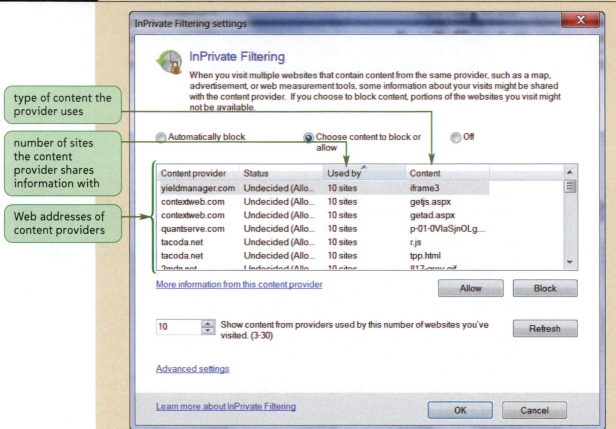

type of content the provider uses

number of sites the content provider shares information with

Web addresses of content providers

> **3.** Scroll to the bottom of the list, and then click **doubleclick.net** where *test_domain.js* appears in the Content column. The .js file in this column indicates that this Web site provides a script file to other Web sites. Because the content is used by many sites, you can block the content to improve performance.
>
> **Trouble?** If *doubleclick.net* does not appear in your InPrivate Filtering settings dialog box, select any other content provider with content used by 20 or more sites.
>
> **4.** Click the **Block** button to block this content.
>
> **5.** Click the **OK** button to close the InPrivate Filtering settings dialog box.

If Curt is having trouble displaying Web pages, he can return to the InPrivate Filtering settings dialog box and allow content from *doubleclick.net*.

PROSKILLS

Decision Making: Deciding Whether to Trust a Web Site

Your decision about whether to trust a Web site should be based on who publishes the Web site, what information the publisher wants from you, and what you want from the site. To make your Web browsing more efficient and productive, consider the following guidelines when deciding whether to trust a Web site with confidential information:

- *Ensure you have a secure connection to the Web site.* Look in the Address bar for a Web site address that begins with *https* rather than *http*. Also look for a security icon such as a padlock in the Address bar or status bar, which indicates that the Web site is secure.
- *Confirm that you are familiar with the organization that sponsors the Web site.* If you are a satisfied customer of a business that provides products in a physical location, you can probably trust its Web site. Read the Web site's privacy or terms of use statement to make sure you are comfortable with the terms. Avoid Web sites that require you to accept e-mail offers or advertising from the Web site.
- *Check to see if the Web site is certified by an Internet trust organization.* An Internet trust organization verifies that a Web site has a privacy statement and gives you a choice about how it uses your information. Approved Web sites display one or more privacy certification seals, usually on their home page or order forms. However, unscrupulous Web sites sometimes fraudulently display these trust logos. You can contact the trust organization to see if the Web site is registered with it. Reputable trust organizations include TRUSTe (*www.truste.com*), BBBOnLine (*www.bbb.org/online*), and WebTrust (*www.webtrust.org*). On the Web site of each trust organization, you can display a list of certified Web sites.
- *Stay away from sites that unnecessarily request confidential personal information.* Provide personal or confidential information such as credit card numbers only when necessary and only on a secure form. Make sure you are using a secure connection when completing the form. Also look for a message explaining that your information will be encrypted for security.
- *Avoid sites that use untrustworthy ways to contact you.* Untrustworthy Web sites are often referred to you through an e-mail message from someone you don't know. Stay away from Web sites making offers that seem too good to be true.

Now that you have thoroughly explored the privacy and security settings in Internet Explorer, you can review another way to protect your computer—by using user accounts.

Setting Up User Accounts

In Windows 7, a **user account** is a collection of information that indicates the files and folders you can access, the types of changes you can make to the computer, and your preferred appearance settings (such as your desktop background or color scheme). If you have a user account on a computer that you share with other people, you can maintain your own files and settings separate from other users. When you start Windows 7, the Welcome screen appears and displays the accounts that are available on the computer. To access your user account, you select your user name. For security purposes, you can also set Windows to request your password.

Windows 7 provides the following three types of user accounts, and each type gives the user a different level of control over the computer:

- Standard: This type of account is designed for everyday computing, and can protect your computer and data by preventing users from changing settings that affect all users. To make changes such as installing software or changing security settings, Windows requests permission or a password for an Administrator account. Microsoft recommends that every regular user on a computer have a Standard account.
- Administrator: This type of account is created when Windows 7 is installed, and provides full access to the computer. The Administrator can access the files of any user, install software, and change any settings. The intention is that when you install Windows 7, you first log on to the computer as the Administrator and then create a Standard user account for yourself and for each person who will use the computer.
- Guest: This type of account is primarily for people who need temporary access to the computer and is not used often.

To create an account, you provide a user name and select an account type. You are not required to protect every account with a password, but Microsoft strongly recommends that you do so. Using a password is one of the most effective ways you can keep your computer secure. When your computer is protected with a password, only someone who knows the password can log on to it.

REFERENCE

Creating a Password-Protected User Account

- Open the Control Panel in Category view, click User Accounts and Family Safety, and then click User Accounts.
- Click Manage another account.
- Click Create a new account.
- Type the new account name, click the Standard user option button or the Administrator option button, and then click the Create Account button.
- In the Manage Accounts window, click the icon of the new user account and then click Create a password.
- Click in the New password text box, and then type your password.
- Click in the Confirm new password text box, and then type your password again.
- Click in the Type a password hint text box, and then type a hint to help you remember your password.
- Click the Create password button.

Curt is concerned that he and his staff at Presto Global Translators are all using the Administrator accounts that Windows created when it was installed. He wants to make sure that everyone creates a Standard user account with a password. Some part-time employees share a single computer, and Curt wants those employees to create separate Standard accounts on the same computer.

Creating a Password-Protected Standard User Account

When you create a user account, you provide a name for the account, which is usually your name, and then select the account type. You can then change the picture for the account and create a password. In Windows 7, a password is a series of letters, numbers, spaces, and symbols that you provide to access your files, programs, and other resources on the computer. Windows passwords are case sensitive, so *CuBote18* is different from *cubote18*. Passwords strengthen computer security because they help to make sure that no one can access the computer unless he or she is authorized to do so. Therefore, you should not give your passwords to others or write them in a place where others can see them.

When creating a password, make sure you devise a **strong password**, one that is difficult to guess but easy for you to remember. Strong passwords have the following characteristics:

- Contain at least eight characters
- Do not include your user name, real name, or company name
- Are not words you can find in the dictionary
- Are significantly different from your previous passwords
- Contain characters from each of the following categories: uppercase letters, lowercase letters, numbers, and symbols (including spaces)

INSIGHT

Creating Strong Passwords

Microsoft provides the following guidelines for creating strong passwords:
- Create an acronym that's easy for you to remember. For example, select a phrase that is meaningful to you, such as *My birthday is February 12*. From that phrase, you could create *Mbdi02/12* as your password.
- Use numbers, symbols, and misspellings in place of letters or words in an easy-to-remember phrase. For example, you could change *My birthday is February 12* to *MiBD I$ Two12*.
- Relate your password to something that interests you, such as a hobby, sport, pet, or goal. For example, *Travel to Central America* could become *Trvl 2 Cntrl@mrca*.

Curt wants to start by creating a Standard user account on his computer with a strong password to protect it. If you can use an Administrator account to perform the following steps, log on to Windows using that Administrator account. If you do not have access to an Administrator account, read but do not perform the following steps.

To create a Standard user account:

1. Click the **Start** button 🔵 on the taskbar, and then click **Control Panel** to open the Control Panel.

2. In Category view, click **User Accounts and Family Safety**. The User Accounts and Family Safety window opens.

   Trouble? If the Control Panel opens displaying small or large icons instead of Category view, click the View by button, click Category, and then repeat Step 2.

3. Click **User Accounts** to open the User Accounts window. See Figure 5-27. Your window will differ.

Figure 5-27 User Accounts window

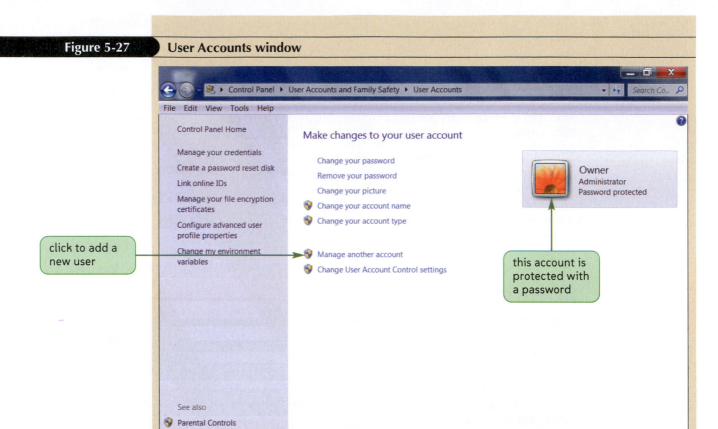

click to add a new user

this account is protected with a password

4. Click **Manage another account** to open the Manage Accounts window.

   Trouble? If a dialog box opens requesting an Administrator password or confirmation, enter the password or click the Continue button.

5. Click **Create a new account**. The Create New Account window opens. See Figure 5-28.

Figure 5-28 Create New Account window

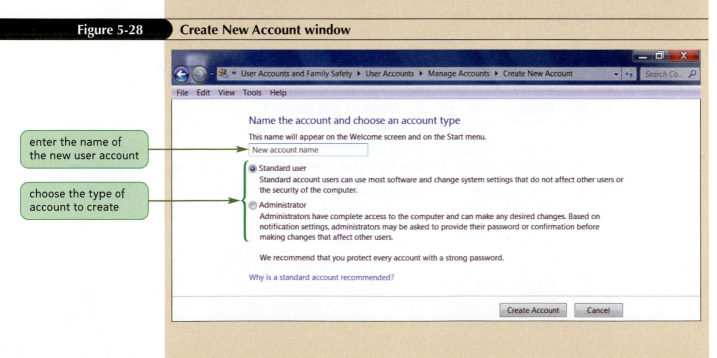

enter the name of the new user account

choose the type of account to create

6. Type **Curt** as the new account name, and then click the **Standard user** option button, if necessary.

7. Click the **Create Account** button. The Manage Accounts window opens, listing the new account.

After you create a user account, you can change its properties, such as the user picture, account type, or account name, and you can create a password for the account. When you create a password, you can also create a hint to help you remember it. Using a hint is a more secure way to remember a password than writing it where others might see it. You'll create a password for Curt's account. For security, he can log on to his account later and change the password. For now, you'll use *Prsto! 08* as the password, a combination of the name of Curt's company and the year it was founded.

To create a password:

1. In the Manage Accounts window, click the **icon** for Curt's account, and then click **Create a password**. The Create Password window opens. See Figure 5-29.

Figure 5-29 Create Password window

icon for the new user

enter and confirm a password for this user

2. In the New password text box, type **Prsto! 08** (including the space after the exclamation mark). You must type the password again to confirm it.

3. Click in the Confirm new password text box, and then type **Prsto! 08**.

4. Click in the Type a password hint text box, and then type **Company and first year**.

5. Click the **Create password** button. The Change an Account window opens, displaying the new account and indicating that it is password protected.

6. Click **User Accounts** in the Address bar to return to the User Accounts window.

Microsoft recommends that you create a password reset disk when you create a password. That way, if you forget the password for your account, you can reset it using the password reset disk. To create a password reset disk, insert a USB drive or other removable media in your computer, open the User Accounts window from the Control Panel, click Create a password reset disk in the left pane, and then follow the on-screen instructions. The next time you log on to Windows, enter an incorrect password. When Windows displays a message that the password is incorrect, click the OK button, click Reset password, insert your password reset disk, and then follow the steps in the Password Reset Wizard to create a new password.

Now you and Curt can show all of the Presto Global employees how to create accounts and passwords on their computers.

Controlling Access to Your Computer

One way to manage access to your computer is to take advantage of User Account Control (UAC), a feature that is turned on by default and can help prevent unauthorized changes to your computer. As you performed the previous steps, you might have seen UAC at work, asking for permission or an Administrator password before performing actions that could affect your computer's settings. A UAC dialog box usually opens when a program or action is about to start. The dialog box requests an Administrator password or your permission to start the program. By notifying you, UAC can help prevent malware from installing itself on or changing your computer without permission. Make sure the name of the action or program in the UAC dialog box is one that you intended to start. The dialog box indicates whether the program or action is part of Windows, is not part of Windows, is unidentified, or is blocked by the Administrator. The dialog box also indicates whether the program has an electronic certificate. If you are working on a computer on which you've set up an Administrator account and one or more Standard accounts, the UAC dialog box asks for an Administrator password so that software can't be installed without your knowledge or permission.

The UAC feature is turned on by default, and should not be turned off. You'll show Curt how to make sure UAC is turned on for all the Presto Global computers.

To verify User Account Control is turned on:

1. In the User Accounts window, click **Change User Account Control settings**. The User Account Control Settings window opens.

   Trouble? If a User Account Control dialog box opens requesting an Administrator password or confirmation, enter the password or click the Continue button.

2. If necessary, drag the slider to the **Default – Notify me only when programs try to make changes to my computer** setting, and then click the **OK** button.

3. Close the User Accounts window.

   Trouble? If a User Account Control dialog box opens asking if you want to allow the program to make changes to this computer, click the Yes button.

Another way to control access to your computer is to simply lock it, which you'll explore next.

Locking Your Computer

Another way to protect your privacy and reduce power consumption is to let your computer go to sleep after a specified amount of idle time, which it does by default. Before going to sleep, Windows saves your files, your settings, and the current state of your desktop in temporary memory so you can return to work easily, and then displays a screen saver or blanks the screen. To wake the computer, you might move the mouse, press a key, or press the Power button, depending on your settings. Windows then displays your user account icon, and indicates the account is locked. If you use a password to log on to Windows, you must enter your password when the Welcome screen appears. This extra precaution of locking your account helps to protect the confidential information you store on your computer. To manually lock your computer, click the Start button, point to the arrow next to the Shut down button, and then click Lock.

Besides controlling access to your computer with passwords and User Account Control, you can secure folders that contain files you share with other users.

Securing and Sharing Folders

If more than one person uses your computer, you can share files and folders with them in two ways: by explicitly allowing another user to share a folder, and by storing files in the Public folder. The Public folder is designed for files any user can access. To share files from the Public folder, you copy or move your files to your Public folder so that other users can access them. Be aware, however, that any user on your computer can view all the files in the Public folder. You cannot restrict users from viewing only some of the files in the Public folder, though you can restrict them from changing the files or creating new ones. Use the Public folder for sharing if you prefer sharing your files from a single location on your computer, you want to monitor your shared files by opening a single folder, you want to keep your shared files separate from your other personal files, or you don't need to set sharing permissions for individual users.

When you explicitly share files, you set sharing permissions that determine who can change your files and what kinds of changes they can make. In this way, you can allow only some users on your computer to view, change, or create files in your folders. Set permissions to share any folder if you prefer to share folders directly from their original location (such as when you store many large photos in your Pictures folder), or when you want to allow only some users to access the folder.

Curt has a document named Guidelines that contains some general guidelines for translating documents. He wants to create a Translation folder in the Public folder on his computer and add other documents to it so that any user can access the documents. You'll show him how to do so.

To share a document in the Public folder:

1. If necessary, insert the USB flash drive containing your Data Files into a USB port on your computer.

2. In a folder window, open the **Tutorial.05** folder and then the **Tutorial** folder in your Data Files.

3. Right-click the **Guidelines** document, and then click **Copy** on the shortcut menu.

4. In the Navigation pane, expand the **Documents** library, if necessary, right-click the **Public Documents** folder, point to **New**, and then click **Folder**.

   Trouble? If User Account Control dialog boxes open requesting your permission, an Administrator password, or confirmation, enter the password or click the Continue button.

5. Type **Translation** as the name of the new folder, and then press the **Enter** key.

   Trouble? If User Account Control dialog boxes open requesting your permission, an Administrator password, or confirmation, enter the password or click the Continue button.

6. Right-click the **Translation** folder, and then click **Paste** on the shortcut menu.

Now any user logged on to Curt's computer can access the Translation folder and its files.

Assigning Permissions to Folders

To specify which users can access a folder you want to share, you click the folder in a folder window, click Share with on the toolbar, and then select the users with whom you want to share files in that folder. If you select the Specific people option, you indicate whether that user can Read (can only read the files in the shared folder) or Read/Write (can read, change, add, or delete any file in the shared folder).

Curt has a sample password policy that he wants you to review before he revises it and distributes it to his employees. He wants you to store it in a shared folder that only you and he can access. First, you'll create a folder for the password policy document. Then you can assign permissions to the new folder so that Curt can open and revise the file.

To create and share a folder:

1. Click the **Documents** library in the Navigation pane of the open folder window.

2. Create a folder named **Policies** in the My Documents folder.

3. Copy the **Passwords** file from the Tutorial.05\Tutorial folder in your Data Files to the Policies folder.

4. Click the **Policies** folder, click the **Share with** button on the toolbar, and then click **Specific people**. The File Sharing dialog box opens.

5. Click the **arrow button** to the right of the first text box. See Figure 5-30.

Figure 5-30 | File Sharing dialog box

File Sharing

Choose people to share with

Type a name and then click Add, or click the arrow to find someone.

click to select a user for sharing →

| | Add |

Curt
Owner
Everyone
Homegroup

Level

I'm having trouble sharing

Share | Cancel

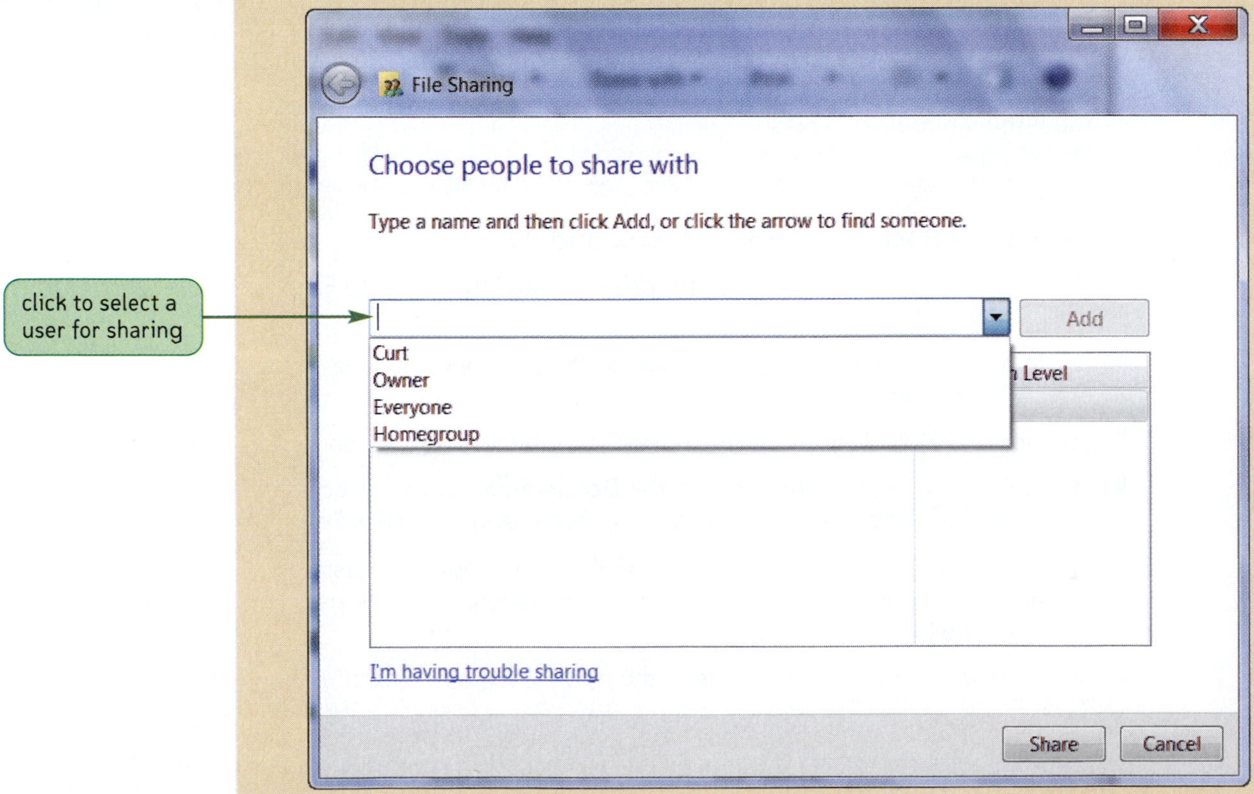

▶ **6.** Click **Curt** to insert his user name in the text box.

   Trouble? If you created an account with a different user name, click that user name instead of *Curt*. If you could not create a new account, read but do not perform Steps 7–11.

▶ **7.** Click the **Add** button to add Curt's user name to the list.

▶ **8.** Click the **permission level** (such as Read) for Curt.

▶ **9.** Click **Read/Write** so that Curt can view, add, and change files in the Policies folder.

▶ **10.** Click the **Share** button. Windows briefly displays the progress of the sharing process, and then confirms your folder is shared.

   Trouble? If a dialog box opens requesting an Administrator password or confirmation, enter the password or click the Continue button.

▶ **11.** Close all open windows.

After you receive confirmation that your folder is shared, you can send a link to your shared files to the people with whom you are sharing the files. That way, the other users will know the files are shared and how to access them. You can click the e-mail link in the File Sharing confirmation window to open an e-mail message in your default e-mail program with the link to your shared files.

Restoring Your Settings

If you are working in a computer lab or on a computer other than your own, complete the steps in this section to restore the original settings on the computer. If a User Account Control dialog box opens requesting an Administrator password or confirmation after you perform any of the following steps, enter the password or click the Continue button.

To restore your settings:

▶ **1.** Open the Control Panel in Category view, click **System and Security**, and then click **Windows Firewall**.

▶ **2.** In the left pane of the Windows Firewall window, click **Allow a program or feature through Windows Firewall**, and then click the **Change settings** button.

▶ **3.** Click the **Connect to a Network Projector** check box to remove the check mark, and then click the **OK** button.

▶ **4.** Click **System and Security** in the Address bar, click **Windows Update**, and then click **Change settings** in the left pane. In the Install new updates section, click the update time, click the original time set for installing updates, and then click the **OK** button. Close the Windows Update window.

▶ **5.** Click the **Start** button 🟦 on the taskbar, type **Windows Defender**, and then click **Windows Defender**. Click the **Tools** button on the toolbar, and then click **Options**. Click the **Approximate time** value, click the original time set for scanning, and then click the **Save** button. Close all open windows.

▶ **6.** Start Windows Live Mail, click the **Menus** button 🔲▾ on the toolbar, and then click **Safety options**. Click the **Safe Senders** tab, click **your e-mail address** in the list, and then click the **Remove** button.

▶ 7. Click the **Phishing** tab, click the **Move phishing E-mail to the Junk e-mail folder** check box to remove the check mark, click the **OK** button to close the Safety Options dialog box, and then close Windows Live Mail.

▶ 8. Start Internet Explorer, click the **Tools** button on the Command bar, point to **Pop-up Blocker**, and then click **Pop-up Blocker Settings**. Click the **Blocking level** setting, and then click your original setting. Click the **Close** button to close the Pop-up Blocker Settings dialog box.

▶ 9. Click the **Tools** button on the Command bar, click **Internet Options**, click the **Privacy** tab, and then drag the slider to its original setting. Click the **OK** button to close the Internet Options dialog box.

▶ 10. Click the **Safety** button on the Internet Explorer Command bar, click **InPrivate Filtering Settings**, scroll to the bottom of the content provider list, click **doubleclick.net** (or the name of another content provider), click the **Allow** button, and then click the **OK** button. Close Internet Explorer.

▶ 11. Open the Control Panel in Category view, click **User Accounts and Family Safety**, click **User Accounts**, and then click **Manage another account**. Click the **Curt** account icon, click **Delete the account**, click the **Delete Files** button, and then click the **Delete Account** button.

▶ 12. Navigate to the **Public Documents** folder on your hard disk, and then move the **Translation** folder to the Tutorial.05\Tutorial folder provided with your Data Files.

▶ 13. Navigate to the **My Documents** folder on your hard disk, and then move the **Policies** folder to the Tutorial.05\Tutorial folder provided with your Data Files. Delete the files in the Tutorial.05\Tutorial folder so that the folder contains only subfolders.

▶ 14. Close all open windows.

REVIEW

Session 5.2 Quick Check

1. True or False. The BlockScam feature in Internet Explorer helps protect you from phishing scams.
2. How do you know when Protected Mode is turned on in Internet Explorer?
3. When you visit a Web site with pop-up ads and the Pop-up Blocker is turned on, you can use the _____ to open the pop-up window.
4. A browser _____ program provides enhancements such as a toolbar or an improved search feature.
5. True or False. All cookies pose some type of security risk.
6. When would you use InPrivate Browsing?
7. Name three characteristics of a strong password.
8. If more than one person uses your computer, you can share files and folders with them in two ways: by explicitly allowing another user to share a folder, and by storing files in a(n) _____ folder.

Practice the skills you learned in the tutorial using the same case scenario.

PRACTICE

Review Assignments

For a list of Data Files in the Review folder, see page WIN 227.

Curt Mickelson, owner of Presto Global Translators, recently bought a new Windows 7 computer for you to share with Donna Cordoza, one of his project managers. Donna specializes in translating videos, which she plays using Windows Media Player, including those she plays when visiting Web sites. You'll show Donna how to keep the new computer secure and set up accounts for the two of you. Complete the following steps, noting your original settings so you can restore them later:

1. Open Windows Firewall, choose to allow a program through Windows Firewall, and then add Windows Media Player Network Sharing Service (Internet) to the allowed programs list.

2. Change the settings in Windows Update to automatically check for and install updates every day at 7:00 a.m.

3. Open and maximize the Action Center window, expand the Security section, and then press the Alt+Print Screen keys to capture an image of the window. Open Paint or WordPad, and then press the Ctrl+V keys to paste the image in a new file. Save the file as **ActionCenter** in the Tutorial.05\Review folder provided with your Data Files.

4. Open the Windows Defender window, and then change the Windows Defender settings to scan every day at 10:00 p.m.

5. Use Windows Defender to perform a quick scan on your computer.

6. With the Windows Defender home page window open on your desktop and displaying the scan statistics, press the Alt+Print Screen keys to capture an image of the window. Open Paint or WordPad, and then press the Ctrl+V keys to paste the image in a new file. Save the file as **Defender** in the Tutorial.05\Review folder provided with your Data Files. Close all open windows.

7. In Windows Live Mail, add the following e-mail address to your Safe Senders list: **DonnaCordoza@presto.net**.

8. In Internet Explorer, open a Web page in your Favorites list or go to the home page of a popular search engine, such as Google (*www.google.com*) or Yahoo! (*www.yahoo.com*). Use the SmartScreen Filter to verify this Web site is not a phishing Web site.

9. Make sure the Pop-up Blocker in Internet Explorer is turned on, and then visit a popular news Web site, such as *www.cnn.com*, until you find one that includes pop-up windows. Make sure the Information bar is displayed in the Internet Explorer window.

10. Turn on InPrivate Browsing in Internet Explorer. Visit the New York State Web site at *www.ny.gov*. Click the Cities & Towns link, click the I box to list city and town names that start with the letter *I*, and then click Ithaca, City of.

11. In the original Internet Explorer window with the news Web site and Information bar, pin the Favorites Center to the window, click the History tab, if necessary, and then click the Today link to visit Web sites you visited today.

12. Arrange the Ithaca InPrivate Browsing window so it appears on top of the news Web site window. Resize the windows as necessary so that the Favorites Center and the Information bar are visible. Click the Recent Pages button in the Ithaca InPrivate Browsing window, and then press the Print Screen key to capture an image of the desktop. Open Paint or WordPad, and then press the Ctrl+V keys to paste the image in a new file. Save the file as **InPrivate** in the Tutorial.05\Review folder provided with your Data Files. Close all open windows.

13. Create a Standard user account for Donna Cordoza. Type **Donna** as the name, **iLuv MVs98** as the password for Donna's account, and **Favorite things and birth year** as the password hint.

14. With the Create Password window open on the desktop, press the Alt+Print Screen keys to capture an image of the window. Open Paint or WordPad, and then press the Ctrl+V keys to paste the image in a new file. Save the file as **User** in the Tutorial.05\ Review folder provided with your Data Files. Finish creating the password and account for Donna, and then close the User Accounts window.

15. Move the **Scripts** document from the Tutorial.05\Review folder provided with your Data Files to a new folder named **Marketing** created in your My Documents folder.

16. Share the **Marketing** folder with Donna and give her a Read/Write permission level. With the final File Sharing dialog box open on your desktop, press the Alt+Print Screen keys to capture an image of the window. Open Paint or WordPad, and then press the Ctrl+V keys to paste the image in a new file. Save the file as **Sharing** in the Tutorial.05\Review folder provided with your Data Files.

17. Restore the settings on your computer. Remove Windows Media Player Network Sharing Service (Internet) from the Windows Firewall allowed programs list. Restore the settings in Windows Update and Windows Defender to install updates and scan at their original times. Remove Donna Cordoza's e-mail address from the Windows Live Mail Safe Senders list. Move the **Marketing** folder to the Tutorial.05\Review folder provided with your Data Files. Delete the user account you created for Donna Cordoza.

18. Close all open windows.

19. Submit the results of the preceding steps to your instructor, either in printed or electronic form, as requested.

Use the skills you learned in the tutorial to select security settings for a theater restoration company.

APPLY

Case Problem 1

For a list of Data Files in the Case1 folder, see page WIN 227.

Trang Renewals Alice and Lou Trang run a small business in Portland, Oregon, called Trang Renewals, which restores old theaters, many from the vaudeville era. Alice conducts most of her marketing work on a laptop computer running Windows 7, and she is concerned about maintaining security as she communicates with clients and researches restoration materials on the Internet. She has experienced problems with spam and wants to know how to block senders in Windows Live Mail. You'll help her use the Windows 7 security settings to protect her computer. Complete the following steps, noting your original settings so you can restore them later:

1. Add Wireless Portable Devices to the Windows Firewall allowed programs list.

2. Change the settings in Windows Update to automatically check for and install updates every day at 5:00 a.m.

3. Change the Windows Defender settings to scan every day at 11:00 p.m.

4. Arrange both windows so both schedules are visible, and then press the Print Screen key to capture an image of the desktop. Open Paint or WordPad, and then press the Ctrl+V keys to paste the image in a new file. Save the file as **Security** in the Tutorial.05\Case1 folder provided with your Data Files. Close all open windows.

5. In Windows Live Mail, add your e-mail address to the Blocked Senders list. Send an e-mail to yourself. When Windows Live Mail receives and blocks this message, press the Alt+Print Screen keys to capture an image of the dialog box. Open Paint or WordPad, and then press the Ctrl+V keys to paste the image in a new file. Save the file as **BlockedMail** in the Tutorial.05\Case1 folder provided with your Data Files. Close Windows Live Mail.

6. In Internet Explorer, change the security level for the Trusted sites zone to Low. Press the Alt+Print Screen keys to capture an image of the window. Open Paint or WordPad, and then press the Ctrl+V keys to paste the image in a new file. Save the file as **SecurityZone** in the Tutorial.05\Case1 folder provided with your Data Files.

7. In the Manage Add-ons dialog box, display a list of the currently loaded add-ons for toolbars and extensions. Press the Alt+Print Screen keys to capture an image of the window. Open Paint or WordPad, and then press the Ctrl+V keys to paste the image in a new file. Save the file as **AddOns** in the Tutorial.05\Case1 folder provided with your Data Files. Close all open windows.

8. Turn on InPrivate Filtering, and then open the InPrivate Filtering settings dialog box. Block a content provider that provides content with a .js extension. Press the Alt+Print Screen keys to capture an image of the dialog box. Open Paint or WordPad, and then press the Ctrl+V keys to paste the image in a new file. Save the file as **Filtering** in the Tutorial.05\Case1 folder provided with your Data Files.

9. Create Standard user accounts for Alice and Lou Trang. For Alice's account, use **Alice** as the name and **MiBd I$ 05/14** as her password. For Lou's account, use **Lou** as the name and **ILuv*The8tr** as his password.

10. With the Manage Accounts window open on the desktop, press the Alt+Print Screen keys to capture an image of the window. Open Paint or WordPad, and then press the Ctrl+V keys to paste the image in a new file. Save the file as **Accounts** in the Tutorial.05\Case1 folder provided with your Data Files. Close all open windows.

11. Move the **Theater** document from the Tutorial.05\Case1 folder provided with your Data Files to a new folder named **Projects** in the Public Documents folder on your computer.

12. Move the **Employment** document from the Tutorial.05\Case1 folder provided with your Data Files to a new folder named **Jobs** in your My Documents folder.

13. Restore the settings on your computer. Remove Wireless Portable Devices from the Windows Firewall allowed programs list. Restore the settings in Windows Update and Windows Defender to install updates and scan at their original times. Remove your e-mail address from the Windows Live Mail Blocked Senders list. Restore the security level for the Trusted sites zone to its original setting. Move the **Projects** and **Jobs** folders to the Tutorial.05\Case1 folder provided with your Data Files. Delete the user accounts you created for Alice and Lou Trang.

14. Close all open windows.

15. Submit the results of the preceding steps to your instructor, either in printed or electronic form, as requested.

Use the skills you learned in the tutorial to select security settings for a day spa.

APPLY

Case Problem 2

There are no Data Files needed for this Case Problem.

Revive Day Spa   Rita Patel owns the Revive Day Spa in Charleston, West Virginia, which is part of the Charleston Golf Resort. Revive offers spa services ranging from massage therapy to facial treatments for day or weeklong packages. Rita uses Remote Desktop to connect to other computers at the Charleston Golf Resort, and regularly uses Windows Live Mail and Internet Explorer to run her business. She has experienced problems with spyware and viruses, and wants to know when to trust e-mail she receives and Web sites she visits. You'll help her use the Windows 7 security settings to protect her computer. Complete the following steps, noting your original settings so you can restore them later:

1. Add Remote Desktop to the Windows Firewall allowed programs list. Capture an image of the Allowed Programs window, and save it in a Paint file named **Firewall** in the Tutorial.05\Case2 folder provided with your Data Files.

⊕ EXPLORE

2. In Windows Update, view your update history, and then check for updates. (*Hint*: In the Windows Update window, click View update history, click Windows Update in the Address bar, and then click Check for updates.) When Windows Update finishes checking for updates, capture an image of the View update history window, and save it as a Paint file named **Updates** in the Tutorial.05\Case2 folder provided with your Data Files. Close all open windows.

3. In Windows Live Mail, find out how to get a digital ID. (*Hint*: Click the Get Digital ID button on the Security tab of the Safety Options dialog box.) Find the Web page explaining how to find services that issue or use a digital ID, and then save the page as a Web Archive, single file named **Digital ID** in the Tutorial.05\Case2 folder provided with your Data Files. Close all open windows.

4. In Internet Explorer, open a Web page in your Favorites list or go to the home page of a popular search engine, such as Google (*www.google.com*) or Yahoo! (*www.yahoo.com*). Use the SmartScreen Filter to verify this Web site is not a phishing Web site. Capture an image of the Internet Explorer window and SmartScreen Filter dialog box, and save it in a Paint file named **Phishing** in the Tutorial.05\Case2 folder provided with your Data Files.

5. In Internet Explorer, change the security level for the Internet sites zone to High. Capture an image of the dialog box, and save it in a Paint file named **HighSecurity** in the Tutorial.05\Case2 folder provided with your Data Files. Close all open windows.

6. Create a Standard user account for Rita Patel. Use **Rita** as the name and **Re: VeyeV10** as her password.

⊕ EXPLORE   7. Create a guest account on the computer. (*Hint*: In the Manage Accounts window, click the Guest account, and then click the Turn On button.)

8. With the Manage Accounts window open on the desktop, capture an image of the window, and save it in a Paint file named **UserAccounts** in the Tutorial.05\Case2 folder provided with your Data Files.

9. Restore the settings on your computer. Remove Remote Desktop from the Windows Firewall allowed programs list. Restore the security level for the Internet sites zone to its original setting. Delete the user account you created for Rita Patel, and turn off the Guest account.

10. Close all open windows.

11. Submit the results of the preceding steps to your instructor, either in printed or electronic form, as requested.

Extend what you've learned to protect a computer at a sports center.

CHALLENGE

Case Problem 3

There are no Data Files needed for this Case Problem.

Urban Sports   Urban Sports is a sports center in Bloomington, Indiana, that organizes leagues in soccer, football, basketball, softball, and other sports for children and adults. Henry Lange manages the center and provides computers with Internet connections to members who want to use them. Henry is particularly concerned about the security of these computers. You'll help him use the Windows 7 security settings to protect a public computer. Complete the following steps, noting your original settings so you can restore them later:

⊕ EXPLORE   1. In Windows Firewall, block all incoming connections. (*Hint*: Select an option in the Customize Settings window.)

⊕ EXPLORE   2. Set Windows Defender to perform a full scan of your computer every day at 11:00 p.m. Also set default actions for High and Medium alert items so that Windows Defender removes these items.

3. Arrange the Windows Defender Options window and the Windows Firewall window to display the settings you changed, and then capture an image of the desktop. Save the image as a Paint file named **FullScan** in the Tutorial.05\Case3 folder provided with your Data Files. Close all open windows.

4. In Windows Live Mail, set the Junk e-mail protection level to High. Also specify that you want to move phishing e-mail to the Junk e-mail folder. Close Windows Live Mail.

5. In Internet Explorer, change the privacy level for the Internet zone to High. Capture an image of the dialog box, and save it in a Paint file named **HighPrivacy** in the Tutorial.05\Case3 folder provided with your Data Files.

6. Delete all temporary files and cookies in Internet Explorer.

⊕ EXPLORE

7. Set Internet Explorer so that it does not store a list of browsing history. (*Hint*: On the General tab of the Internet Options dialog box, click the Delete browsing history on exit check box.) Capture an image of the dialog box, and save it in a Paint file named **NoHistory** in the Tutorial.05\Case3 folder provided with your Data Files

⊕ EXPLORE

8. Create a password for your account on your computer, if necessary, and then create a guest account. (*Hint*: In the Manage Accounts window, click the Guest account, and then click the Turn On button.)

9. With the Manage Accounts window open on the desktop, capture an image of the window, and save it in a Paint file named **GuestAccount** in the Tutorial.05\Case3 folder provided with your Data Files.

10. Restore the settings on your computer. Restore the original general settings in Windows Firewall. Restore the settings for a Windows Defender scan to their original settings, including the default actions. Restore the safety options in Windows Live Mail to their original settings. In Internet Explorer, restore the privacy level for the Internet zone to its original setting, and restore the original setting of the Delete browsing history on exit check box. Turn off the Guest account.

11. Close all open windows.

12. Submit the results of the preceding steps to your instructor, either in printed or electronic form, as requested.

Use the Internet to research computer security for a group of soil scientists.

RESEARCH

Case Problem 4

There are no Data Files needed for this Case Problem.

Osborne & Associates   Tyler Osborne is the head scientist for Osborne & Associates, a firm providing soil science services in Columbia, Missouri. Osborne & Associates maps and classifies soils for land planners and managers, and conducts research on soil degradation and erosion. Tyler wants to protect the computers his scientists use against security threats. To do so, he first wants to understand who typically attacks computers and their data. He also wants to learn more about the types of attacks people use to access computers, and how much damage such attacks have caused. He asks you to research these topics and report your findings. Complete the following steps:

1. Use your favorite search engine to find information about the types of people behind attacks on desktop computers. (Attacks on networks are in a separate category.) Try searching for information about the following types of attackers:
   - Hackers
   - Crackers
   - Script kiddies
   - Social engineers

2. Use your favorite search engine to find information about the types of attacks that can affect a desktop computer. Try searching for information about the following types of attacks:
   - Malicious software, or malware
   - Viruses
   - Worms
   - Logic bombs
   - Password cracking

3. Use a word processor to summarize your findings in one or two pages. Be sure to define any new terms and cite the Web sites where you found your information. Save the document as an RTF file named **Attacks**.

4. Submit the results of the preceding steps to your instructor, either in printed or electronic form, as requested.

ENDING DATA FILES

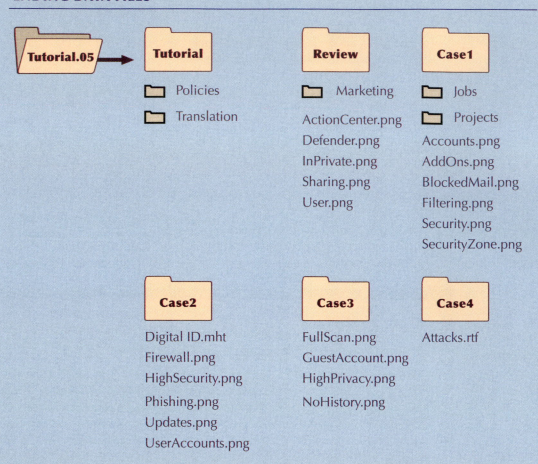

Tutorial.05 → **Tutorial**

📁 Policies
📁 Translation

Review

📁 Marketing
ActionCenter.png
Defender.png
InPrivate.png
Sharing.png
User.png

Case1

📁 Jobs
📁 Projects
Accounts.png
AddOns.png
BlockedMail.png
Filtering.png
Security.png
SecurityZone.png

Case2

Digital ID.mht
Firewall.png
HighSecurity.png
Phishing.png
Updates.png
UserAccounts.png

Case3

FullScan.png
GuestAccount.png
HighPrivacy.png
NoHistory.png

Case4

Attacks.rtf

TUTORIAL 6

OBJECTIVES

Session 6.1
- Develop search strategies
- Find files by name, type, and category
- Examine search results and save a search
- Add tags and other details to files
- Use Boolean filters in advanced searches

Session 6.2
- Search for programs from the Start menu
- Search the Internet
- Narrow searches using advanced search features
- Select search providers in Internet Explorer
- Collaborate with others using Windows Live

Searching for Information and Collaborating with Others

Finding and Sharing Information

Case | *TrendSpot Magazine*

TrendSpot is an online magazine for marketing professionals that features articles, profiles, and commentary about consumer trends. Kendra Cho, the founder of *TrendSpot*, works out of an office in Roswell, Georgia, and collaborates with *TrendSpot* editors around the country. As Kendra's editorial assistant, your duties include organizing article information and finding supporting material, such as photos and quotations.

In this tutorial, you'll learn how to develop strategies for finding information, and then use the Windows 7 search tools to find files. You'll refine your searches by using advanced techniques such as Boolean filters and multiple criteria. You'll also learn how to apply these search strategies when using Internet Explorer to find information on the Web. To share this information, you'll use Windows Live Groups to collaborate with others.

STARTING DATA FILES

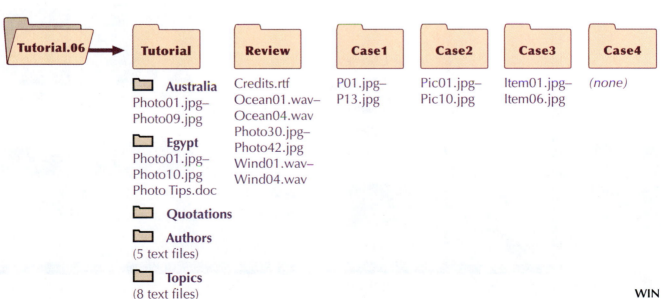

Tutorial.06 →

Tutorial
- **Australia**
  Photo01.jpg–
  Photo09.jpg
- **Egypt**
  Photo01.jpg–
  Photo10.jpg
  Photo Tips.doc
- **Quotations**
- **Authors**
  (5 text files)
- **Topics**
  (8 text files)

Review
Credits.rtf
Ocean01.wav–
Ocean04.wav
Photo30.jpg–
Photo42.jpg
Wind01.wav–
Wind04.wav

Case1
P01.jpg–
P13.jpg

Case2
Pic01.jpg–
Pic10.jpg

Case3
Item01.jpg–
Item06.jpg

Case4
(none)

SESSION 6.1 VISUAL OVERVIEW

Windows displays **search results**, the files that meet your search conditions, in a folder window.

If the search results do not include the file you need, click an option in the *Search again in* section to expand the search.

Click the Save search button to save the search criteria.

Saved searches are displayed in the Favorites list in the Navigation pane.

A **tag** is a word or phrase you add to photos and other types of files to describe them.

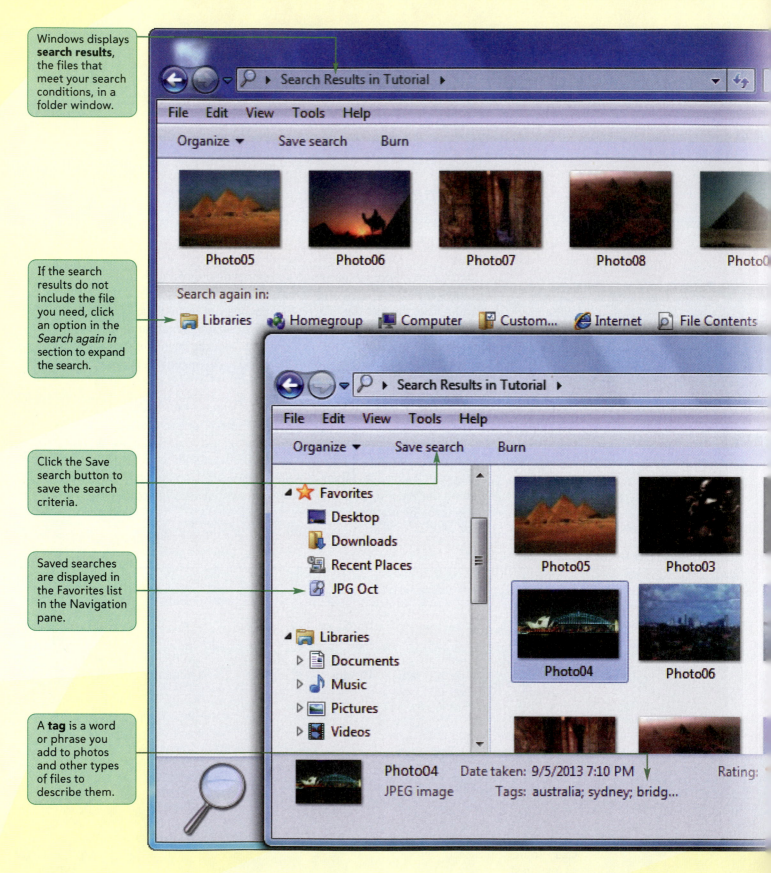

SEARCHING FOR FILES

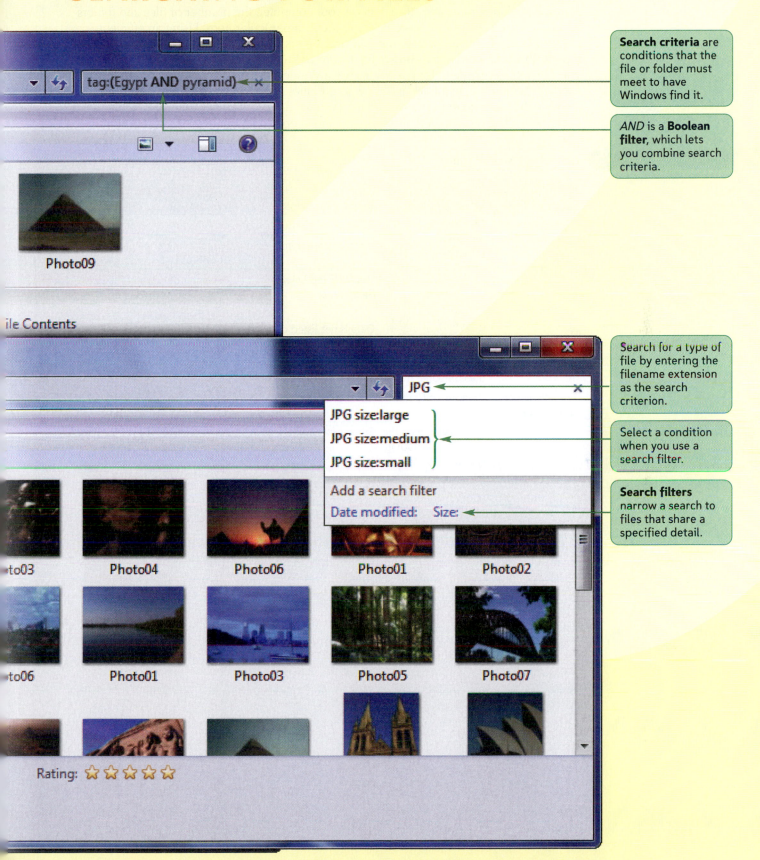

Search criteria are conditions that the file or folder must meet to have Windows find it.

AND is a **Boolean filter**, which lets you combine search criteria.

Search for a type of file by entering the filename extension as the search criterion.

Select a condition when you use a search filter.

Search filters narrow a search to files that share a specified detail.

Developing Search Strategies

As you install programs and store data on your computer, the number of files and folders you have grows, and it becomes harder to locate a particular item. Using an efficient organization scheme helps you find files and folders when you need them. However, if pinpointing an item means browsing dozens or hundreds of files and folders or if you don't know where to look, you can use a Windows 7 search tool. You have already used the Search box in a folder window to find files by name and file contents. You can also use the Start menu to search for files along with programs and Control Panel items. Figure 6-1 offers recommendations on when to choose one search tool over another.

| Figure 6-1 | Choosing a search tool |

Search Tool	What to Find	What You Know	Technique to Use
Search box in a folder window	File in the current folder or its subfolders	Some or all of the filename	Enter some or all of the filename
		Word or phrase in the file	Enter some or all of the word or phrase
		Details listed below the Search box	Select a detail, such as size, and then select a filter, such as Large
		Details not listed below the Search box	Enter a detail, colon, and filter
	File anywhere on the computer	Name, contents, or details	Expand the search, such as to libraries or the entire computer
Search box on the Start menu	Program or Control Panel item	Some or all of the name	Enter some or all of the name
	File anywhere on the computer, including system files	Some or all of the name	Enter some or all of the name

When you use any of the Windows 7 search tools, you provide search criteria, which are conditions that the file or folder must meet to have Windows find it. These conditions help you define and narrow your search so you can quickly find the item you want. For example, if you provide a filename, such as *Budget*, as the search condition, Windows locates and displays every file that matches that condition—in other words, all files whose filename contains a word starting with *Budget*.

If you use text from the filename or the file contents as search criteria, you are conducting a basic search. If you use other properties such as tags or authors as search criteria, you are conducting an advanced search. The other properties you can use as search criteria include any detail you can display as a column in a folder window. (Recall that you can display additional columns in a folder window by right-clicking any column heading, and then clicking a detail on the shortcut menu. If the detail you want to display does not appear on the shortcut menu, click More to open the Choose Details dialog box.) Figure 6-2 describes common criteria you can use when you conduct basic and advanced searches to find a file.

Figure 6-2	Typical search criteria

File Property	Description	What to Find	Search Criterion
Basic Searches			
Filename	All or part of the filename	File named *April sales.docx*	Apr or sales
File type	Filename extension	All of your photos	jpg
Contents	Text the file contains	File that uses *Trends for June* as a heading	Trends for June
Advanced Searches			
Date	Date the file was modified, created, or accessed	Document edited on May 2, 2013	5/2/2013
Size	Size of the file in kilobytes (KB)	Files larger than 1,000 KB, or 1 MB	1000
Tag	Word or phrase in the file properties	Photo with *winter*, *vacation*, *ski* as tags	winter vacation ski
Author	Name of the person who created the file	Document that Kendra created	Kendra

When you combine criteria, such as to find a file named *Agenda* that you created last Monday, you are also conducting an advanced search. You'll learn how to combine search criteria later in the tutorial.

Before you start looking for a file or folder on your computer, determine what you already know about the item; this helps you develop a search strategy. Choose the search tool that best fits your needs, and use search criteria that are most likely to find the item. For example, suppose you want to find a photo that you took last New Year's Eve and stored somewhere in the Pictures library. Because you know the location of the photo, you can use the Search box in the Pictures library window. You also know when you took the photo, so you can conduct an advanced search using 12/31/2012 as the search condition.

Kendra asks you to help her prepare a column on travel trends for the upcoming issue of *TrendSpot*. She has received photos and text files from various contributors and asks you to help find the right content for the travel column. You'll use the Windows 7 search tools to assist Kendra and complete this task.

Searching in a Folder Window

You have already used the Search box in a folder window to find files based on their filenames and contents. To conduct these kinds of basic searches, you type text in the Search box. Windows then displays only those files in the current folder or its subfolders that match the criterion: files whose contents or filename include a word starting with the text you typed.

You can also use a filename extension as the search criterion to find files by type. For example, you could enter *jpg* to find files with a JPG extension (also called JPEGs), which are usually photo files. When you search for files by type, you can enter the filename extension on its own (*JPG* or *jpg*) or use an asterisk and a dot before the filename extension (**JPG* or **.jpg*). In this case, the asterisk is a **wildcard**, a symbol that stands for one or more unspecified characters in the search criterion.

Using a wildcard is a good idea if you want to search for certain types of files, such as those with a DOC extension, but suppose some of your filenames include words that start with the extension text, such as *Doctor Visit*, *June Docket*, or *Kendra Docs*. In this case, using a wildcard and a dot makes it clear that you are searching by filename extension only, and produces more accurate search results.

Kendra is writing her travel column about Australia and Egypt. First, she wants to know how many photos her contributors have submitted featuring these two locations. Because all of these photos are stored in two subfolders, you can provide the information Kendra wants by conducting a basic search in a folder window using the filename extension .jpg as the search criterion.

To search for files by type:

TIP

To display the location of the files in the search results, switch to Details view, if necessary.

1. If necessary, insert the USB flash drive containing your Data Files into a USB port on your computer.

2. In a folder window, open the **Tutorial.06** folder and then the **Tutorial** folder in your Data Files. Maximize the window.

3. Click in the Search box, and then type **jpg**. Windows displays only the files with a .jpg extension in the folder window.

4. If necessary, click the **Change your view button arrow** [icon], and then click **Large Icons** to see the contents of the files clearly. See Figure 6-3.

Figure 6-3   **Searching for files with a JPG filename extension**

some files have the same name, but are stored in different folders

criterion entered in the Search box

search results

19 items

Details pane indicates the search results contain 19 items

Note that the Details pane at the bottom of the folder window indicates that the subfolders in the Tutorial folder contain 19 files that meet the search condition.

PROSKILLS

Decision Making: Searching vs. Sorting, Filtering, or Grouping

Recall that instead of using the Search box, you can often quickly find files by sorting, filtering, or grouping files using the column headings or View menu in a folder window. The method you choose depends on the number of files you want to search, the location of the files, and their names. For example, suppose you need to find JPEG files. If you want to search the current folder *and* its subfolders, use the Search box—the other options find files only in the current folder.

If you're searching a single folder, the Search box is also preferable if the folder contains similar filenames (because sorting would list many files that start with the same text) or many different types of files (because grouping would produce many groups). If you want to find a particular file in a very large folder, it is often easier to use the Search box rather than dealing with a long file list; however, if the folder doesn't contain too many files, then sorting, grouping, or filtering is usually a more efficient method.

The 19 JPEG files you found all have filenames starting with *Photo* followed by a number, such as Photo01 and Photo02. Kendra asked the contributors to name the files this way to streamline the layout and publication of the magazine. As Kendra prepares the column on Egypt, for example, she'll indicate where to insert photos in sequence. For the first photo, she'll include a note such as *Insert Egypt Photo01 here*; for the second photo, *Insert Egypt Photo02 here*; and so on. That way, when the page designers compose the column on travel in Egypt, they don't have to find files with long or cryptic names. They can also tell from the filenames the total number of files to include and the sequence in which they should appear. Although this file-naming scheme works well for editing and producing the magazine, it poses challenges for your research because the filenames do not reveal anything about the content except that they are photos.

Filtering the Search Results by Size

Besides simply typing a few letters in the Search box, you can also conduct more advanced searches from a folder window. To search for files modified on a certain date or files of a certain size, for example, you can add search filters to narrow a search to files that share a specified detail. For example, if you are searching the Pictures library for photos you took last week, you can click the Search box in the Pictures library, click the Date taken filter, and then select last week as the condition. Windows displays only the files in the Pictures library that meet your criteria.

When you add a search filter, Windows automatically adds a keyword to the Search box. The keyword is shorthand for the detail you want to use in the filter and includes the required colon (:). For example, when you select the Date modified filter, Windows inserts *datemodified:* as the keyword.

After you select a filter, you can click the Search box again to display a list of options appropriate for that filter. For example, if you select a date filter such as Date taken or Date modified, Windows displays a calendar and a list of date options, such as Yesterday and Earlier this week. The filter options vary depending on where you're searching. If you're searching the Documents library, you can use Authors, Type, Date modified, and Size as filters. If you're searching the Pictures library, you can use Date taken, Tag, and Type as filters. In folders on a removable USB drive, you can typically use Date modified and Size as filters.

REFERENCE

Filtering Search Results

- Open the folder, library, or drive you want to search.
- If necessary, enter a filename or file contents search criterion in the Search box.
- Click in the Search box, and then click a search filter.
- Click an available option for the selected filter.

Kendra wants to find a text file that Sam Moriarity, a novice contributor, submitted. The document describes the type of photograph that would best illustrate a travel tips sidebar he wrote. He does not recall where he saved the file or its filename, though it's likely the word *photo* appears in the filename or contents. Kendra also wants to find a photo of Sydney that Sam took. Sam can't remember the name, but he does know it is a large file, almost 3 MB in storage size.

You offer to help Kendra find Sam's files. First, you'll concentrate on finding the Sydney photo, which is a large file with a filename that starts with *photo*. If you conduct a basic search by using *photo* as the search text, you will find the 19 JPEG files as well as any other files containing the word *photo* in their filenames or contents. To narrow the search to large files only, you'll filter the results.

To narrow a search using a search filter:

1. In the Tutorial folder window, select the text in the Search box, and then type **pho** to begin entering *photo*. Windows displays all the files in the Tutorial subfolders with a filename that contains a word beginning with *pho* and highlights the search text in the filenames.

2. Click the **Search** box to display the Add a search filter list, and then click **Size:** to insert *size:* as a keyword and display a list of size options. See Figure 6-4.

Figure 6-4   **Selecting a search filter**

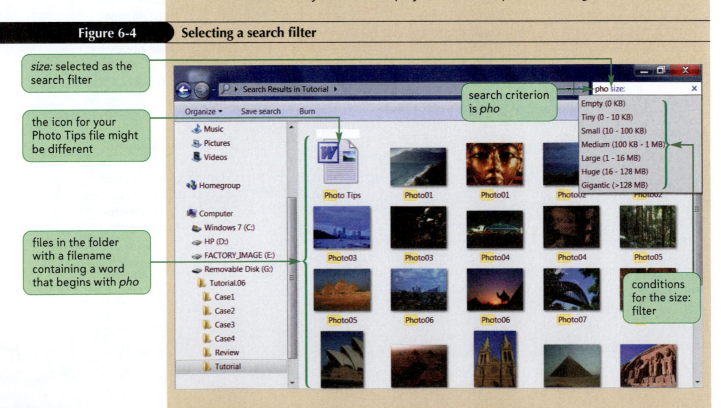

> **3.** Click **Large (1 – 16 MB)** in the options list. Windows reduces the search results to files that meet both criteria—only large files whose filenames contain a word beginning with *pho*.

Two files meet the search criteria. One is a digital photo named *Photo04*, which shows the Sydney Harbor at night. The other is a document named *Photo Tips*.

Examining the Search Results

After you enter search criteria using the Search box, Windows filters the view of the folder window to display files that meet your criteria. These are your search results. Figure 6-5 shows the results of the search performed in the preceding set of steps: large files (those from 1 to 16 MB) whose filenames contain a word beginning with *pho*. When a folder window displays search results, it provides extra tools to help you work with the files you found. For example, the toolbar contains a Save search button for saving the criteria you used to perform a search. If you often look for a certain group of files, you can save the search criteria so you don't have to reconstruct it.

| Figure 6-5 | Search results |

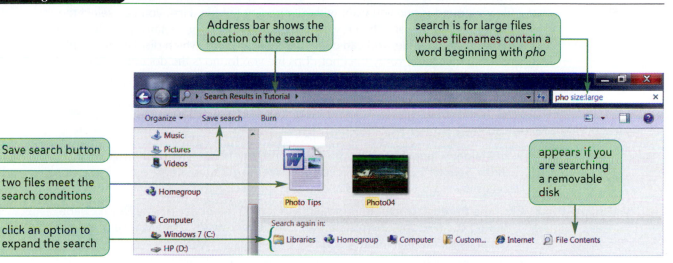

The right pane of a search results window also displays a section with the heading *Search again in*. When you search in a folder window, Windows searches the current folder and its subfolders. To expand the search to other locations, you can click an option in the *Search again in* section of a search results window. Select Libraries to search all the libraries on your computer. Select Homegroup to search the computers in your home network, if you have one. Click Computer to search your entire computer, though the search might be slow. Click Custom to search specific locations, or click Internet to search online using your default Web browser and search provider.

As you know, when you enter text in a folder window's Search box, Windows searches in the names of the folders and files in the folder window. If you are searching an indexed location, such as in the Documents library or Pictures library on your hard disk, Windows also looks in the file contents. An **indexed location** is one or more folders that Windows indexes so it can search them quickly. Libraries and other locations that contain your work files (not system files) are indexed locations.

By default, Windows searches *both* filenames and contents when you are searching an indexed location. However, searching filenames and contents can take a long time in large folders that are not indexed. Because removable disks are not included in the indexed locations, Windows searches only the names of the files on a removable disk by default. In the *Search again in* section of the search results window, you click File Contents to search the contents of a removable disk.

You want to show Kendra how to search in the Tutorial folder for medium-sized files whose filenames contain a word beginning with *pho*, and then use the same search conditions to find files that meet the same criteria in any library on her computer.

To search for files in other locations:

1. In the Tutorial folder window, select the text in the Search box, and then type **jpg** again.

2. Click the **Search** box to display the Add a search filter list, click **Size:**, and then click **Medium (100 KB – 1 MB)**. The search results show one medium JPEG file: Photo01.

3. Click **Libraries** in the *Search again in* section of the folder window. Windows expands the search to find medium JPEG files in the Documents, Pictures, Videos, and Music libraries. These include all the photos in the Sample Pictures folder.

In addition to the extra tools provided in a search window, you can use the standard folder window tools to open, move, copy, rename, or delete a file. You can also verify that a file you found is one you want without opening the file. First, you can select the file in the folder window and then review the information in the Details pane. If you're not sure this is the right file, you can open the Preview pane, which displays the contents of the selected file. You'll verify the Photo Tips file you found is the document Sam sent describing the type of photograph that would best illustrate his list of travel tips.

To verify you found the right file:

1. In the folder window, click the **Back** button ⬅ to return to the Tutorial window, click the **Search** box, and then click **pho size:large** to display the previous search results showing the Photo Tips and Photo04 files.

2. Click the **Photo Tips** file. Information about the file appears in the Details pane, including the file type, the file size, and the date it was modified. (Your window might show additional information.)

3. Click the **Show the preview pane** button 🔲 on the toolbar. The Preview pane opens in the folder window, displaying the contents of the Photo Tips file. See Figure 6-6.

   Trouble? If Microsoft Office Word is not installed on your computer, the contents do not appear in the Preview pane.

   Trouble? If the Preview pane doesn't seem to open, widen the folder window to display the Preview pane.

Figure 6-6   **Verifying a found file**

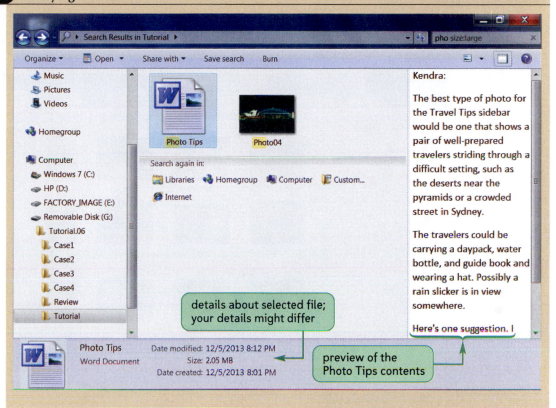

details about selected file; your details might differ

preview of the Photo Tips contents

The Photo Tips file appears to be the text file that Kendra needs. Now she needs to find the most recent photos she has of Australia and Egypt. To do that, you can conduct a new search that filters the results by the Date modified file detail.

Filtering Search Results by Date Modified

In her travel trends column, Kendra wants to use recent photos of Egypt and Australia, which are those taken after September 30, 2013. To find these files, you can start with the same criterion you used to find the 19 JPEG files, using a wildcard this time, and then filter the results to specify the date condition.

To find JPEG files taken after September 30, 2013:

1. In the folder window, click the **Tutorial** folder in the Folders list to return to the Tutorial window. Click the **Hide the preview pane** button 🗔 to close the Preview pane.

2. Click the **Search** box, and then type ***.jpg**. Windows displays the 19 JPEG files in the search results. Next, you'll enter additional criteria to narrow the results to JPEG files taken after September 30, 2013.

3. Click the **Search** box again to display the Add a search filter list.

4. Click **Date modified:**. The date options list opens. See Figure 6-7.

Figure 6-7   **Using file type and date modified as search criteria**

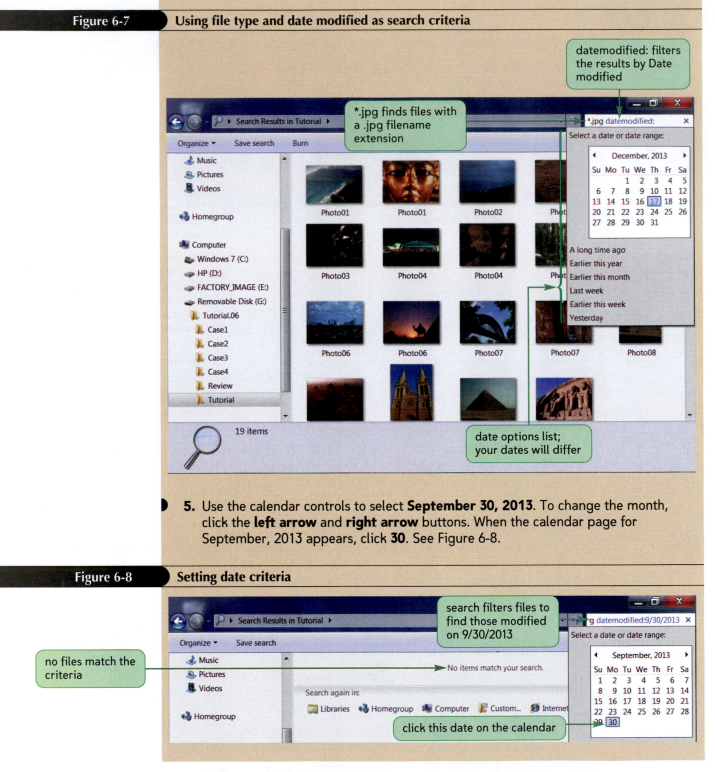

5. Use the calendar controls to select **September 30, 2013**. To change the month, click the **left arrow** and **right arrow** buttons. When the calendar page for September, 2013 appears, click **30**. See Figure 6-8.

Figure 6-8   **Setting date criteria**

No files appear in the search results because no files in the Tutorial folder were modified on September 30, 2013. You want to find files that were modified after September 30. To do that, you use the greater than (>) operator. You can use the greater than operator with any keyword you enter in the Search box. For example, to find files that are larger than 500 KB, enter *size:>500KB*. (You can include a space after the colon or omit it—the space does not affect the search results.) You can also use the less than (<) operator the same way. To find files less than 500 KB, enter *size:<500KB*. To find files modified before September 30, 2013, enter *datemodified:<9/30/2013*.

To modify the search criteria:

1. Click the **Search** box.

2. Move the insertion point after the colon (:) in datemodified, and then type **>**. Twelve files appear in the search results. See Figure 6-9.

Figure 6-9   Modifying search criteria

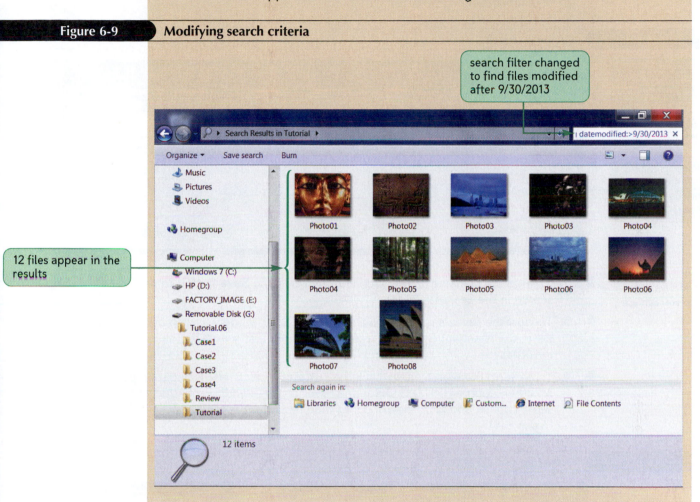

search filter changed to find files modified after 9/30/2013

12 files appear in the results

This search worked well, and Kendra anticipates that she'll want to conduct this search again as she prepares her travel trends column. You'll save the search so you can use it later.

Saving a Search

If you conduct a successful search, especially one that uses two or more criteria, you might want to save the search. Saving a search preserves your original criteria and folder location so you can perform the search again without reconstructing the criteria. By default, Windows saves the search in the Searches folder, which you can open from your personal folder (the one you can open by clicking the Start button and then clicking your user name). The Searches folder lists your searches by name so you can easily find the one you want. Windows also displays saved searches in the Favorites list of any folder window's Navigation pane. You can double-click a saved search to use the same criteria in a new search. The search results display the most current files that match the original conditions, so the results might differ from other times you conducted the same search.

To save a search and perform it again:

1. In the search results window, click the **Save search** button on the toolbar. The Save As dialog box opens, providing .jpg datemodified9-30-2013 as the filename. (Windows doesn't include the greater than symbol because > is not allowed in filenames.) See Figure 6-10.

Figure 6-10   **Saving a search**

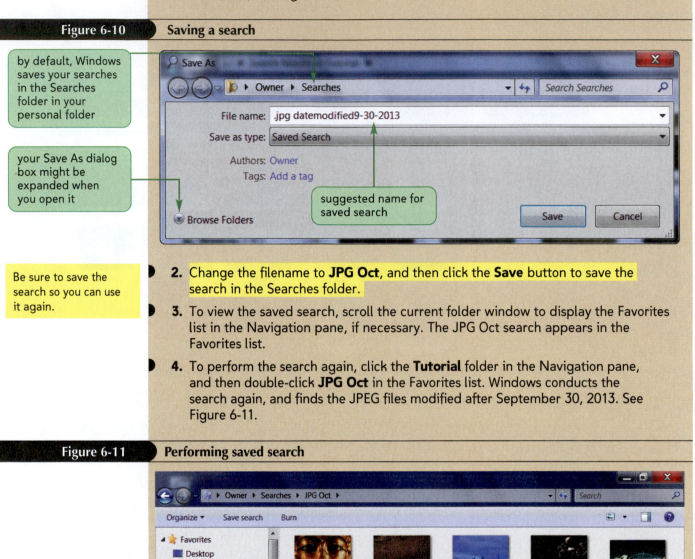

by default, Windows saves your searches in the Searches folder in your personal folder

your Save As dialog box might be expanded when you open it

suggested name for saved search

2. Change the filename to **JPG Oct**, and then click the **Save** button to save the search in the Searches folder.

Be sure to save the search so you can use it again.

3. To view the saved search, scroll the current folder window to display the Favorites list in the Navigation pane, if necessary. The JPG Oct search appears in the Favorites list.

4. To perform the search again, click the **Tutorial** folder in the Navigation pane, and then double-click **JPG Oct** in the Favorites list. Windows conducts the search again, and finds the JPEG files modified after September 30, 2013. See Figure 6-11.

Figure 6-11   **Performing saved search**

JPG Oct appears in the Searches folder

As you were performing searches, Kendra noticed the Tags property in the Details pane, and she asks you if using tags would help her find and identify files. In fact, one of the most useful properties you can use when searching for files is a file tag, which is one or more descriptive words you store with a file to help identify its purpose or contents. You are sure that adding tags to the photo files would save you and Kendra a lot of time when searching for photos. You'll show her how to do so next.

Using Tags and Other Properties

As you know, properties are characteristics of files, such as their name and size. When you create or modify a file, you set some file properties, including the filename, location, and date created or modified. You can add other properties later, including tags, ratings, titles, authors, and comments. Tags are often the most useful because they make files easier to find.

To add properties to a file, you can use the Details pane or the file's Properties dialog box. (You can use the Details pane to add or modify the properties of only some types of files, such as Microsoft Office documents, but not TXT or RTF files.) To use the Details pane, you select a file, click a property text box in the Details pane, and then enter the appropriate information, such as the author's name or comments about the file. Figure 6-12 shows the Details pane when the Photo04 file in the Australia folder is selected.

| Figure 6-12 | File properties in the Details pane |

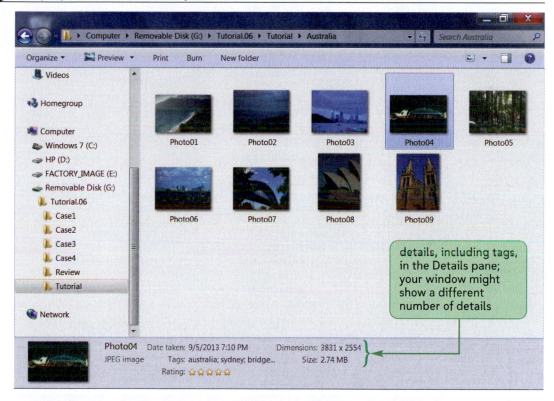

details, including tags, in the Details pane; your window might show a different number of details

Most of the other properties you can add using the Details pane work the same way, and vary by file type. For photos, you can specify date taken, tags, and other properties by using the appropriate text box in the Details pane. You can also rate photos by clicking a star in a series of five stars. If you click the first star, you apply a one-star rating. If click the fourth star, you apply a four-star rating.

If you want to specify file properties other than the ones that appear in the Details pane by default, you can open the Properties dialog box for a file. To do so, you right-click a file, and then click Properties on the shortcut menu. On the Details tab, you can add or modify dozens of properties. Figure 6-13 shows the Properties dialog box for the Photo04 file.

Figure 6-13 File details in the Properties dialog box

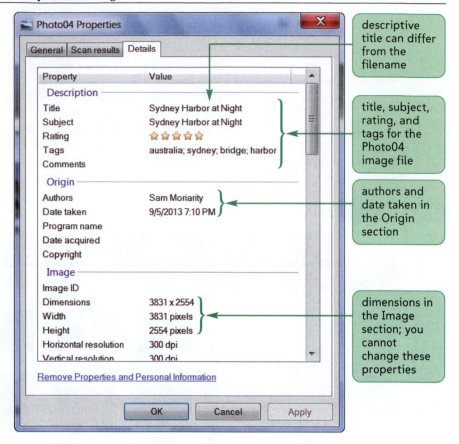

Adding Tags to Files

You can add a tag to a file by using the Save As dialog box when you save the file, or by using the Details pane or the file's Properties dialog box after you save the file. To use the Details pane, you select the file, click the Tags text box in the Details pane, and then type a word or phrase that will help you find the file later. To add more than one tag, separate each word or phrase with a semicolon. For example, if you have a photo of yourself on the peak of the Blackrock Mountain in Virginia, you could use *Blackrock; mountain; Virginia* as tags.

Much of the research you do for Kendra involves finding photos suitable for the columns and articles published in *TrendSpot*. Some photographers already add details to files, including tags and titles, to help identify their photos. (A file's title is a description, and usually differs from the filename.) To facilitate your research, you'll review the files photographers recently submitted for Kendra's column on budget travel in Australia and Egypt and add tags to the files that need them.

To add tags to files:

1. Open the **Australia** folder in the Tutorial.06\Tutorial folder, and then switch to Details view, if necessary. Maximize the window.

2. Display the Tags column, if necessary, by right-clicking any column heading and clicking **Tags** on the shortcut menu. Note that Photo02 and Photo08 do not have any tags.

3. Click **Photo02** and then point to the **Title** text box in the Details pane. The photographer has provided *Middleton Beach, Western Australia* as the title.

   Trouble? If the Details pane does not display a Title text box, drag the top border of the Details pane up to display additional details, including titles.

4. Click the **Tags** text box in the Details pane, and type **Australia** as the first tag. Windows inserts an ending semicolon for you. Type **;** to enter a second tag, and then type **Landscape**. As you type, Windows might suggest *Landscape* or other typical tags that start with the letter *L*. See Figure 6-14.

Figure 6-14	Adding tags to a file

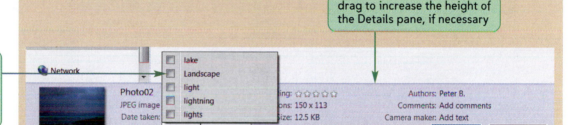

drag to increase the height of the Details pane, if necessary

if a list of suggested tags appears that includes *Landscape*, click Landscape to add it as a tag

TIP

Be sure to click the Save button or press the Enter key to save the changes you make to properties in the Details pane.

5. Click the **Save** button in the Details pane. Windows saves the tags you added.

6. Add the following tags to the Photo08 file: **architecture; Australia; buildings; Sydney**, and then click the **Save** button. Note that after you save a tag in one file, that tag appears in the list of suggested tags for other files.

7. If necessary, resize the **Tags** column in the folder window to display all of the tag text.

INSIGHT

Selecting Tags for Files

To create tags that will help you find files later, keep the following guidelines in mind:

- *Include the obvious.* Use words or phrases that describe the overall purpose or content of the file. For photo files, use tags that list the people in the picture, the location of the photo, and the occasion. For documents, describe the type of document, such as a proposal or report, and its subject.

- *Consider the sample tags.* If you are working with files on a hard drive, you can find typical tags by typing a letter in the Tags text box in the Details pane. For example, type *p* to find sample tags that start with *p*, such as people, pet owners, pets, and photography.

- *Use complete words and phrases.* Avoid abbreviations and codes because you might not remember them later. Assign complete words or use phrases to be as clear as possible. Feel free to use text that appears in the filename; doing so might help you find other related files with the same tag but a different filename.

Adding Other Details to Files

You can add dozens of details to files to help you identify or find the files later. The Details pane provides the most common ones, and a file's Properties dialog box includes those and many others. Kendra wants to add details to the Photo Tips document that Sam sent earlier. In particular, she wants to add a subject, tags, and the name of Sam's manager in California, who is Taylor Baldwin. To do so, you'll use the Properties dialog box.

To add details using a file's Properties dialog box:

1. Open the **Egypt** folder in the Tutorial.06\Tutorial folder.

2. Right-click **Photo Tips** and then click **Properties** on the shortcut menu. The Photo Tips Properties dialog box opens.

3. Click the **Details** tab to work with the details for this file. See Figure 6-15. Windows scanned the first line of this file, which is *Kendra:*, and provided that text as the title. The details in your file might differ.

Figure 6-15 Photo Tips.doc Properties dialog box

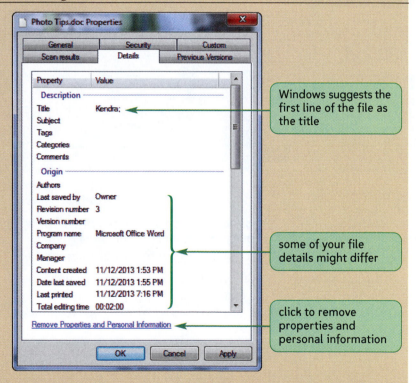

Windows suggests the first line of the file as the title

some of your file details might differ

click to remove properties and personal information

4. In the **Title** text box, delete **Kendra:**, type **Travel Tips**, and then press the **Enter** key.

5. Point to the right of Subject, and then click in the **Subject** text box. Type **General photo suggestions**, and then press the **Enter** key.

6. Click the **Tags** text box, type **Sam; sidebar; travel tips; photo suggestions**, and then press the **Enter** key.

7. Click the **Manager** text box, and then type **Taylor Baldwin**.

8. Click the **OK** button to save the details with the file and close the dialog box.

Now that you've entered tags and other properties for files, you're ready to use this information to build advanced criteria for smarter searching.

Using Advanced Criteria in the Search Box

If the filter options in the Search box don't help you find the files you need, you can use the Search box to search for other properties, including tags, title, and subject. To use any property as a criterion in the Search box, you specify the property using the following shorthand notation: *property name:criterion*. For example, if you want to search for files that include the word *landscape* as a tag, you could enter *tag:landscape*. (The properties are not case sensitive, so you could also enter *Tag:Landscape*.) The properties you can use as search criteria include any detail you can display as a column in a folder window. Figure 6-16 provides examples of the shorthand notation you can use to specify file properties as search criteria in the Search box.

Figure 6-16   **Examples of using file properties in the Search box**

Property	Example	Finds
Name	Name:city	Files and folders with names that contain a word beginning with *city*
Date modified	DateModified:10/28/2013	Files and folders modified on October 28, 2013
	DateModified:<10/28/2013	Files and folders modified before October 28, 2013
Date created	DateCreated:>10/28/2013	Files and folders created after October 28, 2013
	DateCreated:2013	Files and folders created during the year 2013
Size	Size:200KB	Files with a size of 200 KB
	Size:>1MB	Files larger than 1 MB
Type	Type:doc	Files with a .doc filename extension
Tags	Tag:Egypt	Files that include *Egypt* as a tag
Authors	Author:Peter	Files that specify *Peter* as the author
Artists	Artist:Elvis	Files that specify artists with *Elvis* in their names, such as Elvis Presley and Elvis Costello
Rating	Rating: 4 stars	Files with a rating of four stars

When you use the shorthand notation in the Search box, you can use any file detail as the filter. This is especially useful when you are working with photos, music, and videos, because they have special properties for their file types, such as Artists, Album, Rating, and Length, that are useful when searching.

As Kendra plans her travel trends column, she decides to include at least two close-up photos of Sydney, Australia's largest city. Besides showing the Sydney Opera House, she'd like to show a contrasting work of architecture. You recall that some photographers provided titles for their photos. You'll use the title property in the Search box to find photographs of Sydney.

To find files by specifying a property in the Search box:

▶ **1.** Open the **Australia** folder in the Tutorial.06\Tutorial folder.

▶ **2.** Click the **Search** box, and then type **title:Sydney**. As you type, Windows filters the view of the files in the folder window, and then displays three files that contain the word *Sydney* in their Title property: Photo04, Photo08, and Photo09.

3. Click **Photo04** and examine the information in the Details pane. Even though this is a photo of Sydney, it is not a close-up photo, so Kendra doesn't want to use it.

4. Click **Photo08** and look for the title in the Details pane. This is a fairly close-up photo of the Sydney Opera House.

5. Click **Photo09**. Point to the **Title** text box in the Details pane to display the full title in a ScreenTip. Kendra thinks this photo of St. Andrew's Cathedral in Sydney will work well with the close-up of the Sydney Opera House. See Figure 6-17.

| Figure 6-17 | Title property in the Details pane |

Photo09 — JPEG image — Date taken: 11/15/2013 9:41 AM — Tags: church; cathedral; Austr... — Rating: ☆☆☆☆☆ — Dimensions: 113 x 150 — Size: 18.5 KB — Title: St. Andrews Cathedral, Sydney — Authors: Peter B. — Comments: Add comments — Camera maker: Add text — Title property

Trouble? If the Title property does not appear in the Details pane, drag the right or left edge of the window to widen it.

By searching for text in the Title property, you found two photos for Kendra—one showing the Sydney Opera House and the other showing St. Andrew's Cathedral in Sydney.

Combining Criteria When Searching File Contents

To perform a precise search, you can combine criteria in the Search box. For example, suppose you store your financial documents on your computer and need to find a list of charitable donations you made in 2013. You don't recall where you've stored this information, and scanning the filenames in your Financial folder doesn't reveal the file. If you search the contents of the files using *donation* as the search criterion, you'll find lists of donations for many years as well as other documents, including e-mail messages with text such as *Thanks for your support! Every donation helps*. If you search the contents of files using *2013* as the search criterion, you'll find dozens of documents that mention that year. To pinpoint your search, you can combine the criteria to find files that contain the word *donations* and the year *2013*. When you search file contents, you can use Boolean filters, which let you search for specific information using the words AND, OR, and NOT to combine search criteria. You can use quotation marks and parentheses to refine the search conditions further. Figure 6-18 describes how to use AND, OR, and NOT along with quotation marks and parentheses when combining search criteria.

TIP

When you use two or more words as a search condition, Windows searches as if the condition uses the AND Boolean filter.

| Figure 6-18 | Combining search criteria |

Word or Punctuation	Examples	When to Use
AND	donations AND 2013 donations 2013	To narrow the search to files that contain *donations* and *2013* even if the words are not next to each other
OR	donations OR 2013	To broaden the search to files that contain *donations* or *2013*
NOT	donations NOT 2013	To restrict the search to files that contain *donations* but not *2013*
" " (quotation marks)	"donations 2013"	To pinpoint the search to files that contain the exact phrase *donations 2013*
( ) (parentheses)	(donations 2013)	To open the search to files that contain both items next to each other in any order

Note that when you use the words AND, OR, and NOT, you must enter them using all uppercase letters.

One of your ongoing projects for *TrendSpot* is maintaining an archive of quotations, which Kendra and the *TrendSpot* editors use in columns and articles; they often request a quotation from a particular author or on a particular topic just before publishing an issue of the magazine. You have therefore created a Quotations folder with two subfolders: an Authors folder that contains documents of quotations listed alphabetically by author, and a Topics folder that contains documents of quotations listed by general topic. Because authors and editors use a variety of word-processing programs, you've stored collections of quotations in TXT documents to make sure anyone at *TrendSpot* can use the documents. However, this means that you cannot add tags or other properties to the files—you can add these details only to Microsoft Office documents.

In one part of her column, Kendra plans to highlight a few contemporary Australian writers, and wants to start that section with a quotation about Australian writers. You can use Boolean logic to combine search criteria and search the contents of the Quotations folder to find suitable quotations.

INSIGHT

Preparing to Combine Search Criteria

Before you combine search criteria, select the search text, select the filter you plan to use, if any, and then select the condition. For example, choose **.txt* as the search text to find text files. If you want to find text files modified after a certain date, use the *datemodified:* filter, and then select the appropriate date, such as *>9/30/2013*. Next, determine whether you should use AND, OR, or NOT to combine the criteria, and whether you need quotation marks or parentheses to find the files you want. For example, if you want to find files that use *Egypt* as a tag and have *Sam* as the author, you use the AND filter, whether you insert AND or not. In other words, *tag:Egypt AND author:Sam* is the same as *tag:Egypt author:Sam*.

If you want to find text files or Word documents, you need to insert OR, as in **.txt OR *.doc**. (The condition **.doc** finds Word documents that have a .doc or a .docx filename extension.) To determine the best criteria, test each method in order starting with AND. Keep in mind that AND narrows the search results, while OR broadens the results. For example, if you search for files that are photos AND use *Egypt* as a tag, you find fewer files than searching for files that are photos OR use *Egypt* as a tag.

Although you want to find quotations about Australian writers, using *Australian* and *writers* as search criteria won't find quotations that include *Australia* or *writer* or even *write*, which might be appropriate quotations. A good rule of thumb when selecting search text is to use the root of the word, such as using *writ* to find documents containing *writer*, *writers*, *writes*, and *writing*. For your purposes, you should use *Australia* and *writ* as search criteria.

Next, determine the best way to combine the criteria, as shown in the following list:

- *Australia writ* (or *Australia AND writ*) finds documents that include both words.
- *Australia OR writ* finds documents that include at least one of the words.
- *Australia NOT writ* finds documents that include *Australia*, but not those that include *writ*.
- *"Australia writ"* finds documents that include the exact phrase *Australia writ*.
- *(Australia writ)* finds documents that include the exact words *Australia* and *writ* consecutively in either order.

Because *Australia writ* produces the results you want, you'll use that as your search criteria to find quotations about Australian writers.

To find files using AND criteria:

1. Open the **Quotations** folder in the Tutorial.06\Tutorial folder.

2. Click the **Search** box, and then type **Australia writ**. As you type, Windows searches filenames that meet your criteria.

3. If necessary, click **File Contents** in the *Search again in* section of the folder window to search the file contents instead of filenames. Windows finds one file that meets your criteria. See Figure 6-19.

Figure 6-19   **Finding files that contain *Australia* AND *writ***

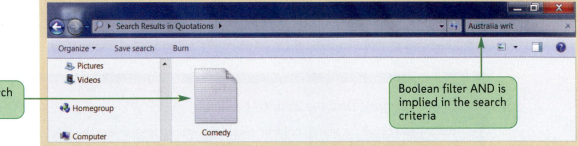

one file in the search results

Boolean filter AND is implied in the search criteria

4. To verify this file contains a quotation you can use, double-click **Comedy** to open it in a text-editing program such as Notepad.

5. Press the **Ctrl+F** keys to open the Find dialog box, type **Australia** in the Find what text box, click the **OK** button to find a quotation by Geoffrey Cottrell (*In America only the successful writer is important, in France all writers are important, in England no writer is important, and in Australia you have to explain what a writer is.*), and then close the text-editing program.

Kendra says that she could use quotations that mention Australia or mention writers—she can work either type into her column. You can try your search again, this time using the Boolean filter OR to find files that contain either *Australia* or *writ*.

To find files using OR criteria:

1. Display the contents of the **Quotations** folder again.

2. Click the **Search** box, and then type **Australia OR writ**.

3. If necessary, click **File Contents** in the folder window to search the file contents instead of filenames. Now Windows finds three files that contain the word *Australia* or the text *writ*. See Figure 6-20.

Figure 6-20   **Finding files that contain *Australia* OR *writ***

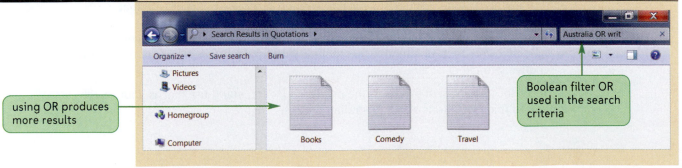

using OR produces more results

Boolean filter OR used in the search criteria

To really pinpoint what you want to find and to refine your search criteria, you can combine Boolean filters and file properties.

Combining Boolean Filters and File Properties

When you search files by file property, you can use Boolean filters to combine criteria. For example, Kendra is working on the Egypt section of her travel column, and requests a photo of an Egyptian pyramid. You can search the tags of the photo files to find those that contain this text. To search efficiently, you can use the Boolean filter AND to combine the criteria and search for photos that include the tags *Egypt* and *pyramid*. (If you used the Boolean filter OR, you would find photos of Egypt, but not necessarily of a pyramid, and photos of pyramids that are not necessarily in Egypt.) If you use *tag: Egypt pyramid*, Windows searches for files that include *Egypt* as a tag and *pyramid* in any property. To restrict the search to tags only, enclose the criteria in parentheses.

To find files by combining file property criteria:

1. Display the contents of the **Tutorial** folder.

2. Click the **Search** box, and then type **tag: (Egypt pyramid)**. Windows finds five files that meet your criteria. See Figure 6-21.

Figure 6-21   Combining Boolean filters with file properties

You've already explored many ways to search for files on your computer. Besides searching filenames and contents, you've learned how to use shorthand notation to specify tags and other file properties in search criteria, and how to combine criteria using Boolean filters. In the next session, you'll apply these techniques to search for programs and for files that could be stored anywhere on your computer. You'll also develop techniques for searching the Internet, and collaborate with other people.

REVIEW

Session 6.1 Quick Check

1. What are search criteria?
2. Explain how to search for JPEG files in a folder window.
3. True or False. When you develop a search strategy, you choose the search tool that best fits your needs and select search criteria that are most likely to find the item.
4. Name two ways you can verify that a file you found is the one you want without opening the file.
5. True or False. Saving a search saves the results in a folder you specify.
6. A(n) _____ is a word or phrase you add to a file's properties to help you find the file later.
7. Name three types of properties you can add to photo files.
8. If you use *tag: landscape OR beach*, what files would you find?

SESSION 6.2 VISUAL OVERVIEW

Use the **Find toolbar** to find specific information on the page.

Bing is a search engine, a program that searches Web pages.

The **search expression** is the word or phrase that best describes the information you want to find.

Bing highlights text on the page that matches the search text in the Find toolbar.

Each link in the search results is called a **hit**.

---

sydney australia - Bing - Windows Internet Explorer

http://www.bing.com/search?q=sydney+australia&src=IE-Searc

⭐ Favorites   b sydney australia - Bing

X   Find: Opera   Previous   Next   ✏️   Opti

Web   Images   Videos   Shopping   News   Maps   More | MSN   Hotmail

bing   sydney australia

SYDNEY AUSTRALIA   ALL RESULTS   1-20 of 6

Sydney Australia **Weather**   SYDNEY, AUSTRALIA

Sydney Australia **Airport**   **City of Sydney Homepage**
                                      www.cityof**sydney**.nsw.gov.au · Official si
Sydney Australia **Map**   The City of **Sydney** council is responsible
                                      and surrounds - the commercial,...
Sydney Australia **Tourism**

Sydney Australia **Attractions**   **Weather »**   **Attractions »**   Neigh

Reference   ☁️ **65°**F   Sydney Opera House   City C
                                         70° / 63°   Sydney Jewish Museum   The R
Images   Cloudy   Sydney Harbour Bridge   Darling
                                                          Powerhouse Museum   Circula

RELATED SEARCHES   **Sydney – Wikipedia, the free encyclopedia**
Sydney Australia   **Sydney** is the largest city in **Australia**, and the state capital
Employment   **Sydney** has a metropolitan area population of approximately
                                      History · Geography · Urban structure · Economy
Sydney Opera House   en.wikipedia.org/wiki/**Sydney** · Enhanced view

Sydney Australia **Stores**   **There's no place in the world like Sydney**
                                      Sydney Australia There's no place in the world like Sydney

Done   🌐 Int

SEARCHING THE INTERNET

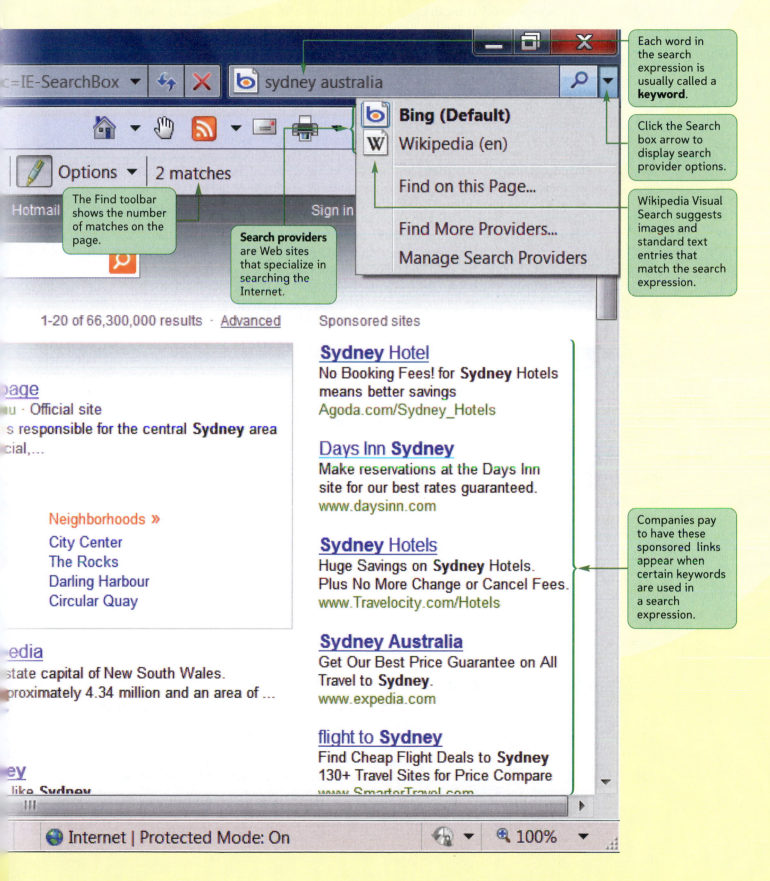

Each word in the search expression is usually called a **keyword**.

Click the Search box arrow to display search provider options.

Wikipedia Visual Search suggests images and standard text entries that match the search expression.

The Find toolbar shows the number of matches on the page.

Search providers are Web sites that specialize in searching the Internet.

Companies pay to have these sponsored links appear when certain keywords are used in a search expression.

Searching for Programs from the Start Menu

As you've learned, you can use the Search box in a folder window to find any file or folder on your computer. But if you're looking for a program, you can use the Search programs and files text box on the Start menu. As the name of the text box indicates, you can also use the Search programs and files box to find files. Using the Start menu is no better or worse than using the Search box in a folder window—the method you choose depends on what you're doing on your computer. If you are already working in a folder window, it's more convenient to use the Search box. If you are working on the desktop, it's easier to access the Search programs and files text box on the Start menu.

When you use the Search programs and files text box on the Start menu, you enter text just as you do when you use the Search box in a folder window. As you type, Windows displays in the left pane of the Start menu the programs and files that meet your criteria, filtering the list with every character you type. At the top of the list are programs that meet your criteria, followed by Control Panel items and then files. First are files with filenames that match your criteria, and then come the files with tags that match your criteria. Windows also displays a link at the bottom of the search results—See more results. You can click the See more results link to display the files in a search results window that identifies the path and other details about the file.

When you search from the Start menu, Windows finds only files that have been indexed and displays them in the Search results. Recall that most files on your computer are indexed automatically, such as any file stored in a library.

REFERENCE

Searching for Programs on the Start Menu

- Click the Start button.
- Click the Search programs and files text box.
- Type your search criteria.

Now that you have found a few photos and quotations for Kendra's travel column, she wants to find programs on her computer that will let her work with photos. In particular, she wants to play a slide show of the photos she is using in an upcoming issue of *TrendSpot* magazine. She can play the show on a computer when she gives presentations to business and community groups. She has heard that Windows 7 provides at least one program she can use to play media files. You'll show her how to search for programs from the Start menu.

To search for programs from the Start menu:

1. Click the **Start** button 🟦 on the taskbar, and then click in the **Search programs and files** text box, if necessary.

2. Type **med** to start entering *media* as the search text. The Start menu lists programs for working with media at the top of the menu. It also lists Control Panel items that contain a word starting with *med* and files with tags that start with *med*. See Figure 6-22. Your search results might differ.

Figure 6-22   Searching for programs

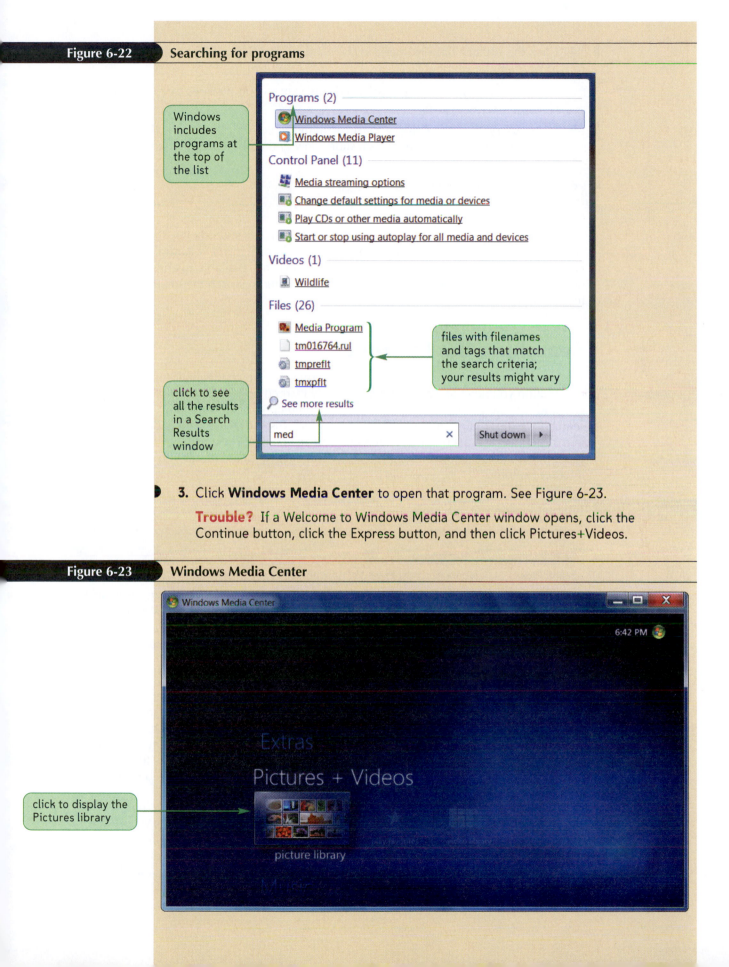

Windows includes programs at the top of the list

files with filenames and tags that match the search criteria; your results might vary

click to see all the results in a Search Results window

3. Click **Windows Media Center** to open that program. See Figure 6-23.

Trouble? If a Welcome to Windows Media Center window opens, click the Continue button, click the Express button, and then click Pictures+Videos.

Figure 6-23   Windows Media Center

click to display the Pictures library

> **4.** Click the **picture library** image in the window. The Sample Pictures folder appears in the window.
>
>   **Trouble?** If a window opens asking if you want to add pictures to your library, click the Cancel button.
>
> **5.** If necessary, click the **Sample Pictures** folder to select it, and then click **play slide show**. Windows plays a slide show of the photos in the Sample Pictures folder.
>
> **6.** Close Windows Media Center.

Now that you've found a program Kendra can use to play slide shows, she asks you to continue researching information for her column on budget travel in Australia and Egypt. However, the information she now wants you to find is not available in any of the files on your computer. Instead, you can use Internet Explorer to search the Internet for the information.

Searching the Internet

The Internet provides access to a wealth of information; the challenge is to find the information you need or want. You have already learned how to develop search strategies and specific criteria to find files on your computer. You can use many of the same search strategies to find information on the Internet. Instead of using tools provided in a folder window, such as the Search box and Search pane, you use the search tools provided in Internet Explorer. Figure 6-24 summarizes the search tools you can use in Internet Explorer.

Figure 6-24 **Internet Explorer search tools**

Search Tool	Description
Search box	Type a word or phrase to find Web pages associated with that topic.
Address bar	Type *Find*, *Go*, or *?* followed by a word or phrase to find Web pages associated with that topic. If the word or phrase you enter is the name of a Web site, its main page opens in Internet Explorer.
Search provider	Click the Search box arrow, and then select a search provider to use its tools to search the Internet.

The terminology that you use when searching the Internet is slightly different from the terminology you use to search for files on your computer. The word or phrase you use to search the Internet is typically called a search expression. Each word in the search expression is called a keyword. After you enter a search expression using one of Internet Explorer's search tools, Internet Explorer displays the results, which are links to Web pages that meet your criteria. You can click these links, or hits, to access Web pages that contain the keywords in your search expression.

When you provide a search expression to Internet Explorer, it uses a search provider, which is a search engine such as Bing or a reference Web site such as Wikipedia. Because searching all of the Web pages on the Internet to find those that contain your search expression would take a prohibitive amount of time, search providers typically search a database of indexed Web pages. These databases are updated periodically, though not often enough to keep all of the indexed Web pages up to date. This is why a page of search results might include inactive or broken links.

Web site designers and owners can make their Web pages easier for search providers to find by **optimizing** the site. In its Web page headings, an optimized site lists keywords and phrases that you and other Web users are likely to use to find the information on the Web page. Conversely, you are more likely to find the Web pages you want if you are aware of the types of keywords Web designers often use.

PROSKILLS

Problem Solving: Searching the Internet Effectively

Because the Internet provides access to a vast amount of information, finding the information you need can be a problem. Conducting a search that finds millions of results is inefficient, even if search providers list the Web pages most relevant to your search first. To work effectively, you need to use search techniques that provide a few high-quality results. Keep the following guidelines in mind to search the Internet efficiently:

- *Be specific.* If you search for general categories, you'll find an overwhelming number of pages. Searching for specific terms or details is more likely to provide results you can use. For example, instead of searching for *desserts*, search for *pear cake recipe*.
- *Form a question.* Think of your search expression as a question you want answered, such as *Are there restaurants in the Denver area that serve vegetarian food?* Eliminate the articles and common words to form a workable search expression, such as *restaurants Denver vegetarian*.
- *Search the results.* Most search providers let you reduce the number of pages to review by searching your results. For example, suppose you search for *pear cake recipe* and find many thousands of results. If you want a recipe similar to the one your Swedish grandmother made, you can search the results using *Swedish* as your search expression.

Kendra is now working on a section of her column that describes the popular restaurants in the capital cities of Australia and Egypt. So far, she has plenty of information on the restaurants in Sydney, but she wants to know more about the restaurants in Cairo. You offer to search the Internet to find the information. You'll start by using *Cairo Egypt restaurants* as the search expression to find Web pages describing restaurants in Cairo.

Because Web pages and search indexes change frequently, the search results you find when you perform the steps in this section will differ from those shown in the figures. The following steps use Bing as the search provider. If you are using a different search provider, your results will differ from those shown in Figure 6-25.

To search using a search expression:

1. Start Internet Explorer.

2. Click in the Search box, type **Cairo Egypt restaurants**, and press the **Enter** key. Bing looks for Web pages containing the search expression you entered, and then displays the results. Maximize the Internet Explorer window, if necessary. See Figure 6-25.

| Figure 6-25 | Search results for the search expression *Cairo Egypt restaurants* |

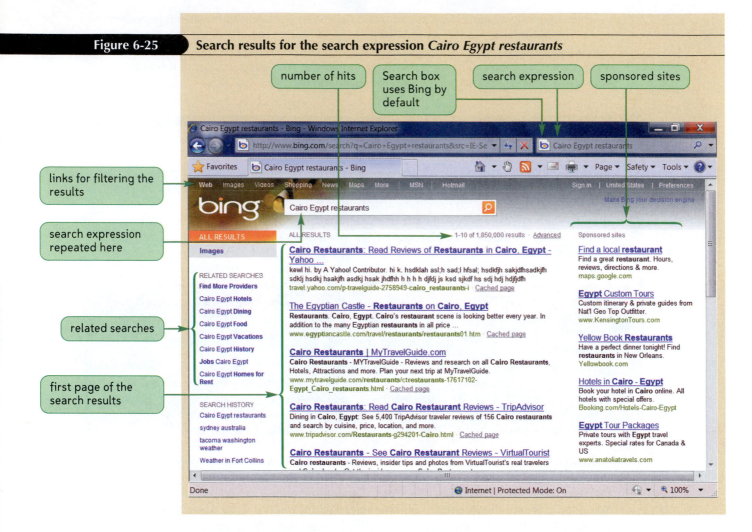

Using *Cairo Egypt restaurants* as the search expression produced nearly 2 million results, which is not unusual. Although the first few Web pages listed might provide the information you seek, to find more useful Web pages, you need to narrow your search.

Narrowing Your Search

You can narrow your Internet search by modifying your search expression or by limiting the kinds of Web pages you want in your results. One way to modify your search expression is to use quotation marks to search for specific phrases. If you enclose a phrase in quotation marks, you restrict the results to Web pages that contain that exact phrase. For example, using a search expression such as *Radcliffe College Library* finds Web pages that include those three words anywhere on the page. If you enclose the search expression in quotation marks, as in *"Radcliffe College Library"*, you find only Web pages that include the exact text in the specified order.

Another way to modify your search expression is to use the advanced search features that search providers typically offer. Figure 6-26 shows the Advanced Search page from Google, a popular search provider.

Figure 6-26   **Google Advanced Search page**

select one or more of these options to use a more precise search expression

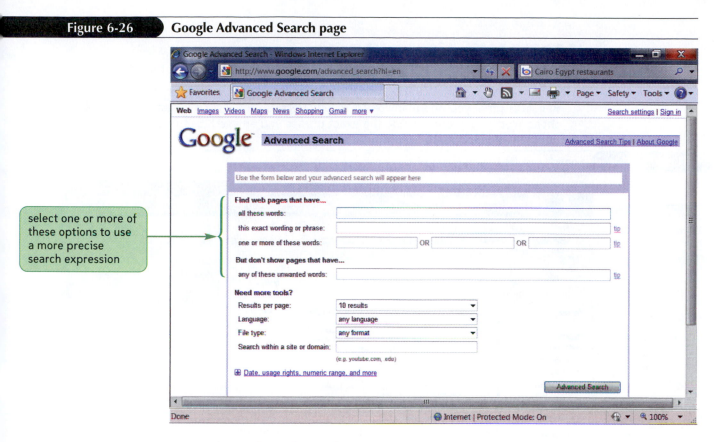

An advanced search page lets you specify and combine search conditions. Most advanced search pages provide the following types of options:

- Find pages that include all of the words. This is the default for most search providers.
- Limit the results to pages that match the exact phrase. This is the same as using quotation marks to enclose an expression.
- Find pages that include at least one of the words in the search expression.
- Specify keywords that you do not want included on the Web page.
- Search only pages written in a particular language.
- Find pages of a certain type, such as Microsoft Word or Adobe Acrobat PDF.
- Search pages that have been updated within a specified period of time.
- Limit results to pages in a specified Web site or domain.

Besides providing an advanced search page for narrowing your search expression, most search providers include tabs or links that specify the kind of results you want. For example, the Bing results page shown in Figure 6-25 includes seven links in the navigation bar at the top of the page: Web, Images, Videos, Shopping, News, Maps, and More. By default, Bing displays Web pages in the results. If you are searching for images, such as photos and drawings, you can click the Images link before or after you enter a search expression to restrict the results to pages including images that meet your criteria.

Some of the Web pages you found when you used *Cairo Egypt restaurants* as a search expression described Cairo, Egypt, but didn't necessarily focus on restaurants. You can try narrowing your search by enclosing the expression in quotation marks to see if the results are more useful.

To narrow a search to an exact match:

1. On the search results page, click in the **search** text box at the top of the page.

2. Edit the text so it appears as **"Cairo Egypt restaurants"** and press the **Enter** key. This time, you find many fewer results because the search is restricted to only those Web pages that include the exact phrase you entered. See Figure 6-27.

Figure 6-27   Search results for an exact phrase search expression

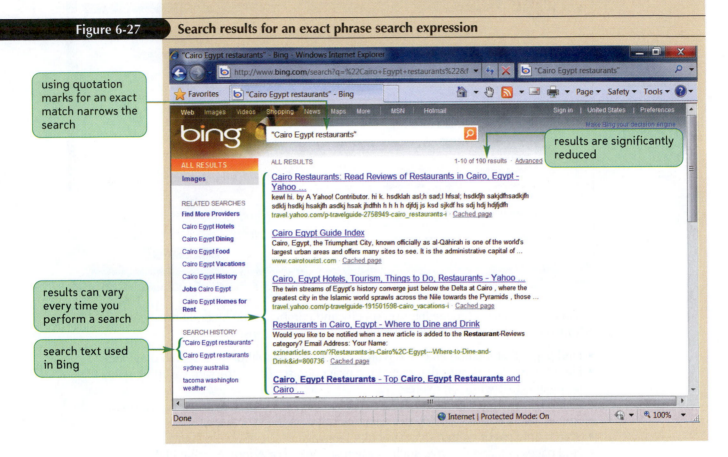

using quotation marks for an exact match narrows the search

results are significantly reduced

results can vary every time you perform a search

search text used in Bing

Using an exact phrase produced a list of restaurants in Cairo, Egypt, that is useful to you and Kendra. Now Kendra wants to briefly mention some restaurants in other parts of Egypt that budget travelers might want to visit. These are any budget restaurants that are not located in Cairo. To specify this kind of search condition, you can use a search provider's advanced search page. You have used Google in the past, so you can try this search using Google instead of Bing. You'll specify that you want to search for budget restaurants in Egypt, but not those in Cairo.

To narrow a search by excluding keywords:

1. Click the Address bar, type **www.google.com**, and then press the **Enter** key to open the main page on the Google Web site. See Figure 6-28.

Figure 6-28 | **Main page on the Google Web site**

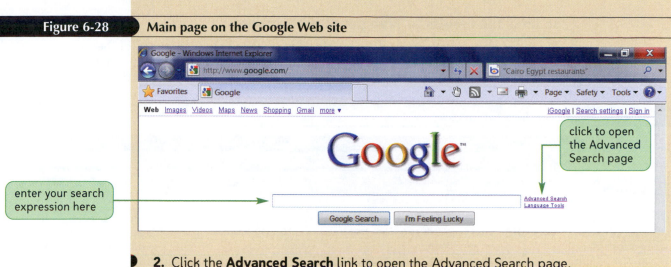

enter your search
expression here

click to open
the Advanced
Search page

2. Click the **Advanced Search** link to open the Advanced Search page.

3. In the Find web pages that have section, click the **all these words** text box, and then type **Egypt budget restaurants**.

4. Click the **any of these unwanted words** text box, type **Cairo**, and then press the **Enter** key. The search results list several million Web pages, including many for hotels. Next, you'll exclude the keyword *hotel* from the search.

5. Click the **Advanced Search** link near the top of the page, click the **any of these unwanted words** text box, press the **Spacebar**, and then type **hotel** so that *Cairo* and *hotel* both appear in the text box.

6. Click the **Advanced Search** button. The search results page includes fewer hits, with the best matches on the first page, which will help you find a few restaurants for Kendra's column.

Evaluating Web Pages in the Search Results

Although a Web page might be listed at the top of the search results, that doesn't guarantee the page provides reliable and up-to-date information that will meet your needs. On a search engine's Web page, the search results are usually organized into sections. At the top or in another prominent location on the page are sponsored links; companies pay to have these links appear when certain keywords are used in a search expression. The companies pay an additional fee when you click one of their sponsored links. Using sponsored links helps search engines offer their services free to the public. However, that doesn't mean a sponsored link will lead to the information you want. Before using a Web page or citing it as a source, review the content with a critical eye. At the bottom of the Web page, look for the author's name and evidence of the author's credentials. Look for links to the original source of quoted information, which tends to validate the information on a Web page. Also look for signs of bias, such as unsubstantiated claims or extreme points of view.

Kendra wonders if you can find any photos of Egyptian restaurants that she can include in her column. She'd prefer those that show restaurant interiors. To fulfill her request, you can use the Images tab in Google. Recall that Bing and other search providers include a similar tool.

To limit the results to Web pages with images:

1. In the Google search results page, click the **Images** link near the top of the page. Google looks for Web pages containing images that meet your search criteria—those of budget restaurants not in Cairo. See Figure 6-29.

Figure 6-29	Searching for images

These are not promising results. However, Kendra said the photos she needs could be of any Egyptian restaurant, so you can change the search expression.

2. Click the **text box** near the top of the Images page, and edit the search expression to be **Egypt restaurants interior**.

3. Click the **Search** button. Google displays images that meet your criteria, interiors of restaurants in Egypt.

TIP

The *-Cairo* in the search expression is a shorthand way of excluding *Cairo* from the search.

After Kendra selects images of Egyptian restaurants, she will contact the copyright owners and request permission to use the photos in *TrendSpot*.

Choosing Search Providers

In Internet Explorer, you can choose which provider you want to use when you search for information on the Internet. You can change the search provider for a specific search, and you can specify which search provider you prefer to use by default. When you first install Internet Explorer, only one provider might be available; however, you can add search providers to increase your searching options. Keep in mind that you can use a search provider's Web site, such as google.com, to perform a search even if it is not selected as your search provider.

REFERENCE

Selecting a Search Provider

- Click the Search box arrow next to the Address bar.
- Click Find More Providers.
- Click a provider in the list, and then click Add to Internet Explorer. In the Add Search Provider dialog box, click Add.

You and Kendra often use Wikipedia, an online encyclopedia, to search for information. Internet Explorer lets you use Wikipedia to conduct visual searches—that is, searches that include images and standard text entries in the results. You'll add Wikipedia Visual Search to the provider list, which you can access by clicking the Search box arrow. You can also choose to make a new search provider the default one to use when you search from the Address bar or Search box.

To add a search provider to the provider list:

1. Click the **Search** box arrow, and then click **Find More Providers**. A list of possible search providers appears in a Web page. See Figure 6-30.

Figure 6-30 | **Adding search providers**

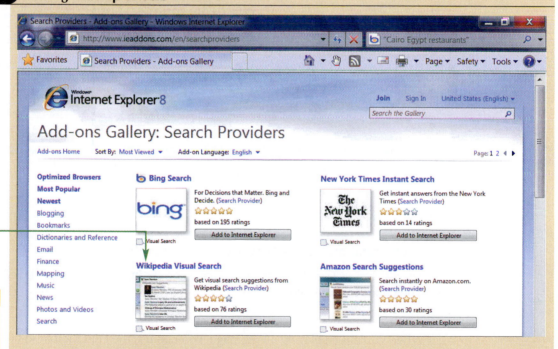

select Wikipedia Visual Search in the list of search providers

TIP

To set the default search provider, click the Search box arrow, click Manage Search Providers, click a search provider, and then click the Set as default button.

2. Next to Wikipedia Visual Search, click the **Add to Internet Explorer** button to open the Add Search Provider dialog box.

3. Click the **Add** button.

4. Click the **Search** box arrow to verify that Internet Explorer added Wikipedia to the list of search providers.

Kendra wants to verify some facts about the Giza pyramid in Egypt. She can use Wikipedia as the search provider to make sure the Giza complex includes the famous monument called the Sphinx.

To use Wikipedia as the search provider:

1. If necessary, click the **Search** box arrow to display the list of search providers, and then click **Wikipedia** to make Wikipedia the current search provider.

2. Click the **Search** box, and then type **Giza**. A window below the text box displays Wikipedia entries that contain the search text, including an entry that displays a photo of the Sphinx. See Figure 6-31.

Figure 6-31   **Using Wikipedia as a search provider**

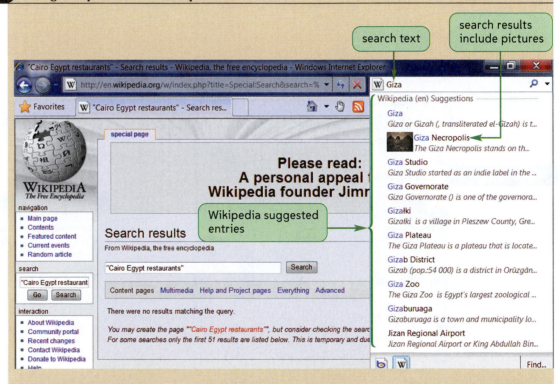

3. Point to the Giza Necropolis entry to read a summary of the Wikipedia entry, and then click **Giza Necropolis** to display the entry at the Wikipedia Web site. The entry confirms that the Giza complex includes the Sphinx.

   Trouble? If *Giza Necropolis* does not appear in the search results, click any other link about Giza, Egypt.

When you are displaying a Web page, you can use the Find toolbar in Internet Explorer to find specific information on the page. For example, you'll show Kendra how to search for a map on the Giza Necropolis Web page.

To find information on a Web page:

1. Click the **Search** box arrow, and then click **Find on this Page**. The Find toolbar opens below the Command bar. It inserts the search text from the Search box and highlights the matching text on the page. It also displays the number of matches on the page. See Figure 6-32.

Figure 6-32	Using the Find toolbar

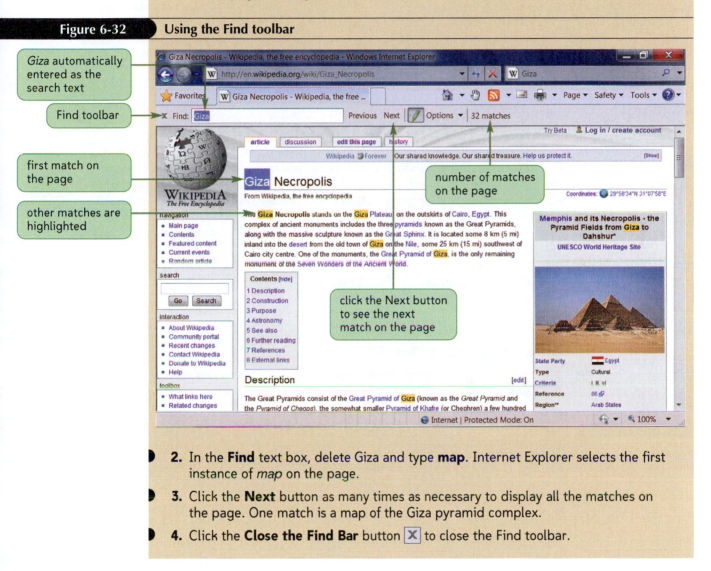

Giza automatically entered as the search text

Find toolbar

first match on the page

other matches are highlighted

number of matches on the page

click the Next button to see the next match on the page

2. In the **Find** text box, delete Giza and type **map**. Internet Explorer selects the first instance of *map* on the page.

3. Click the **Next** button as many times as necessary to display all the matches on the page. One match is a map of the Giza pyramid complex.

4. Click the **Close the Find Bar** button X to close the Find toolbar.

Now that you have explored some ways to search the Internet and completed your research for Kendra, you are ready to turn to another task—preparing for an online meeting.

Collaborating with Other People

Windows Live Groups is part of Windows Live, a free collection of programs and services provided on the Web. (Tutorial 4 introduced you to Windows Live Essentials, programs that perform essential tasks, such as Windows Live Mail.) Windows Live Groups is a place on the Web where you can organize a group of people who work together or share a common interest. Because people often work together from separate locations, they occasionally need a way to meet online to exchange information or collaborate on projects without physically traveling to convene in the same place. You can use Windows Live Groups to have discussions and share files with other meeting participants who are not in the same location. To do so, you create a group and invite other people to join it, or you join an existing group.

Tutorial 4 includes steps to download and install Windows Live Mail, the basic e-mail program provided as part of Windows Live Essentials. To use Windows Live Groups, however, you do not need to download and install the software. Instead, you can access and use Windows Live Groups via your Web browser, which makes Windows Live Groups one of many cloud computing programs (a concept introduced in Tutorial 4).

Before you start using Windows Live Groups, you must create a Windows Live account, and then sign in with your Windows Live ID, which is a user name and password. Signing in keeps your group collaboration private and ensures the communication and files you share are secure. After you set up a Windows Live ID, you can use it to access other Windows Live services, such as Windows Live Photos, which lets you post and share photo albums online, and Windows Live SkyDrive, which provides space where you can store and share files.

The following steps show you how to set up a Windows Live ID. You must be connected to the Internet to complete the steps in the rest of the tutorial.

To set up a Windows Live ID account:

1. In Internet Explorer, click in the Address bar, type **home.live.com**, and then press the **Enter** key. The Windows Live home page opens. See Figure 6-33.

| **Figure 6-33** | **Creating a Windows Live ID** |

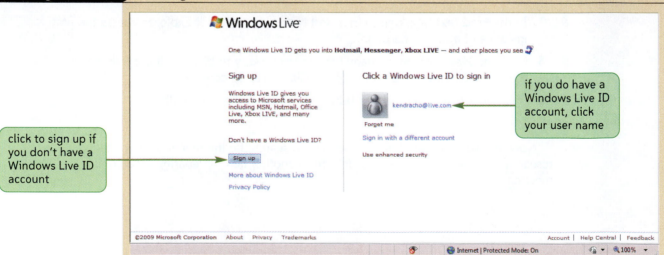

click to sign up if you don't have a Windows Live ID account

if you do have a Windows Live ID account, click your user name

2. If you already have a Windows Live ID, click your ID, enter your Windows Live password, and then click the **Sign in** button. Skip Steps 3–5.

Trouble? If a blank text box appears instead of your user name, enter your Windows Live ID, enter your password, and then click the Sign in button.

3. If you do not have a Windows Live ID, click the **Sign up** button. A Web page opens where you can create your Windows Live ID.

4. Follow the on-screen instructions to create a Windows Live ID.

   Trouble? If you are not sure whether you should use your e-mail address or another ID, check with your instructor.

5. Click the **I accept** button (or a similar button) to display your home page on Windows Live. See Figure 6-34.

Figure 6-34   Windows Live home page

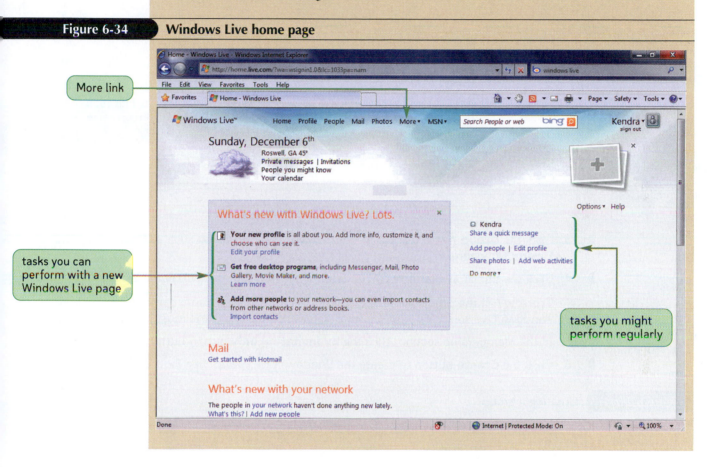

Creating a Group

Kendra is nearly finished with her column, and wants to meet online with Bev Parkinson, a *TrendSpot* page designer, to discuss the layout and illustrations for the column. You'll show Kendra how to use Windows Live Groups to meet with Bev. First, you need to create a group that includes Kendra and Bev.

To create a group in Windows Live Groups:

1. On your Windows Live home page, click **More** on the navigation bar, and then click **Groups**. The Windows Live Groups page opens.

2. Click the **Create a group** link to open a page where you can create a group. See Figure 6-35.

Figure 6-35 Creating a group

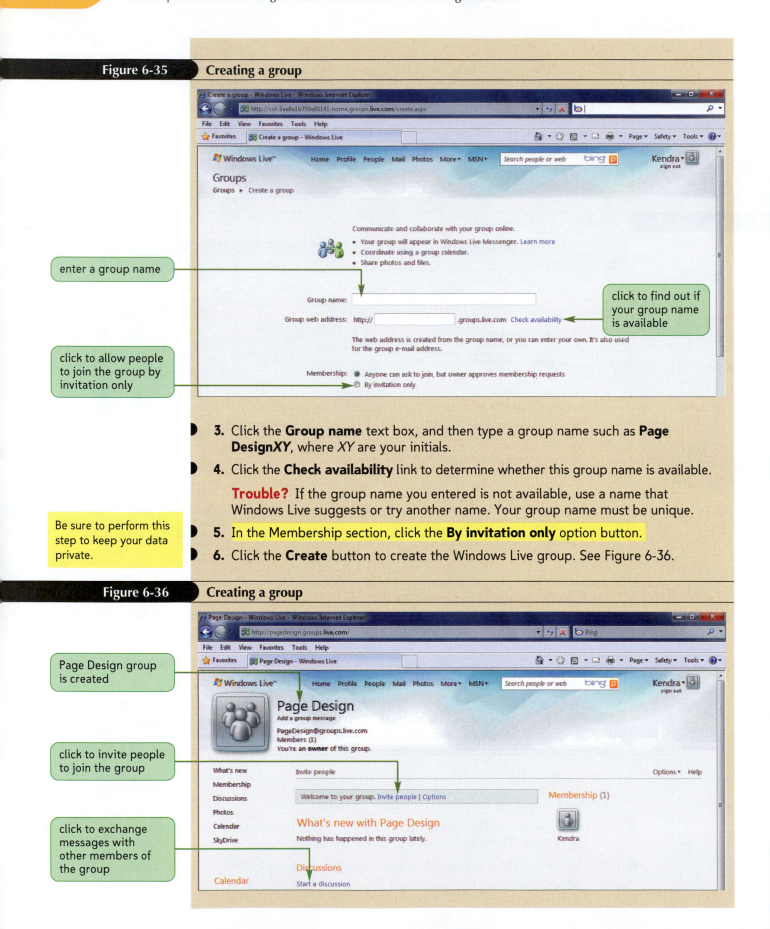

enter a group name

click to find out if your group name is available

click to allow people to join the group by invitation only

3. Click the **Group name** text box, and then type a group name such as **Page DesignXY**, where *XY* are your initials.

4. Click the **Check availability** link to determine whether this group name is available.

   Trouble? If the group name you entered is not available, use a name that Windows Live suggests or try another name. Your group name must be unique.

Be sure to perform this step to keep your data private.

5. In the Membership section, click the **By invitation only** option button.

6. Click the **Create** button to create the Windows Live group. See Figure 6-36.

Figure 6-36 Creating a group

Page Design group is created

click to invite people to join the group

click to exchange messages with other members of the group

Inviting Other People to Join the Group

When you create a group, you become the owner of that group. As the owner, you can invite others to become members of the group. Group members can view the group's page, participate in a discussion, add photos, share files, and add items to the group calendar. You can invite people to join the group at any time, including just before an online meeting.

Kendra is ready to meet with Bev, so you'll show Kendra how to invite Bev to join the group.

In the following steps, enter the e-mail address of a classmate or someone else you know, instead of Bev Parkinson's e-mail address. If you are sending the message to someone other than a classmate, first ask their permission to send the message described in the following steps. You can use any e-mail address, not just Windows Live e-mail addresses.

To invite someone to join a group:

1. On the home page of your group, click **Invite people**.

2. In the Invite people window, click the **To** text box, and then type the e-mail address of someone you know, such as **BevParkinson@live.com**.

3. In the **Include your own message** text box, type **Bev:** and press the **Enter** key, and then type the following text: **Let's meet to work out the page design and illustrations for the next issue of TrendSpot. —Kendra**.

4. Scroll down, if necessary, and then click the **Send** button. Windows Live sends the invitation to the e-mail address you provided.

When Bev (or another person you invited) receives the invitation, it looks similar to the e-mail message shown in Figure 6-37.

Figure 6-37   **Invitation to join a Windows Live group**

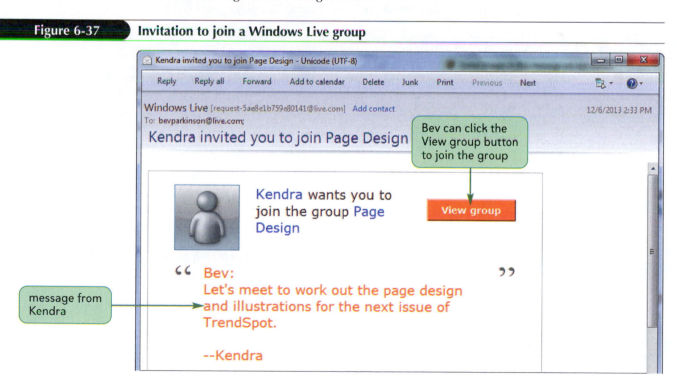

To join the group, Bev clicks the View group button, signs in to the Windows Live group, and then clicks the Join button. See Figure 6-38.

Figure 6-38 Group page is updated when Bev joins

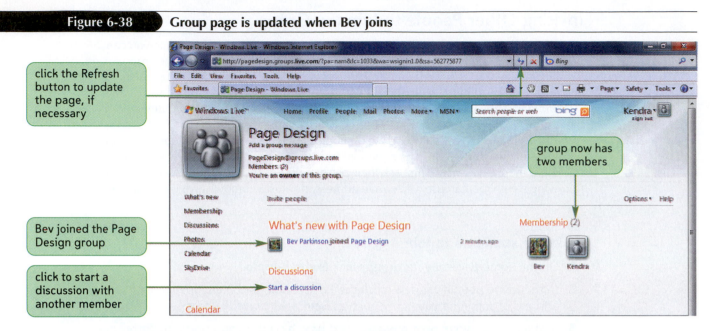

click the Refresh button to update the page, if necessary

group now has two members

Bev joined the Page Design group

click to start a discussion with another member

Now that Bev has joined the Page Design group, Kendra wants to share some of the photos for the travel trends column. First, you start a discussion so Bev knows which photos Kendra is sending.

To start a discussion:

1. On the group page, click **Start a discussion**. The Group discussion page opens and you can enter the text of your discussion. See Figure 6-39.

Figure 6-39 Preparing a message to Bev

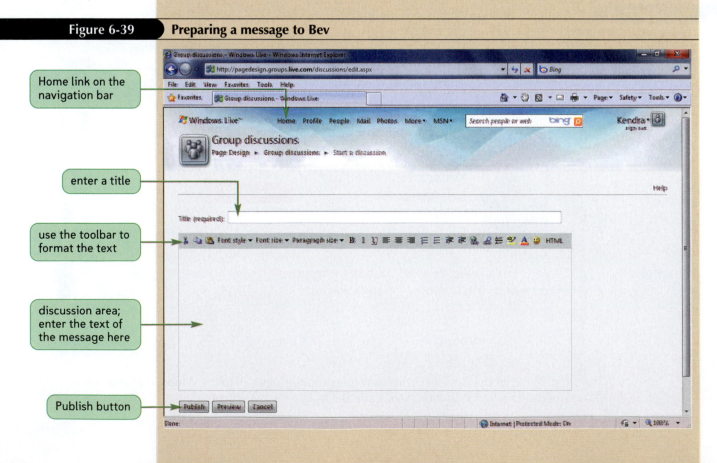

Home link on the navigation bar

enter a title

use the toolbar to format the text

discussion area; enter the text of the message here

Publish button

2. Click the **Title (required)** text box, and then type **Photos for travel trends column**.

3. Click in the discussion area, type **Bev:**, and then type the following text: **What do you think about two Australia photos for the column? I'll send them to you in a minute.**

4. Click the **Publish** button to send the message to Bev.

When Bev receives the message, she can click the Title of the discussion on her Groups home page, click Reply to open a Group discussions page similar to the one shown in Figure 6-39, and then respond. Next, Kendra wants Bev to review the two photos. First, you need to create an album for the photos, and then send Bev a link to the online album.

To create a photo album and send a link to another person in your group:

1. Click the **Home** link on the navigation bar to return to your Windows Live home page.

2. In the list on the right below your user name, click **Share photos**. The Select an album page opens where you can select or create an album to store your photos.

3. Click **New album**. Enter **Australia** as the name of the album, click the **Share with** arrow, and then click **My network**. Click the **Next** button.

4. Click the **Select photos from your computer** link, navigate to the **Tutorial** folder in the Tutorial.06 folder provided with your Data Files, and then open the **Australia** folder.

5. Click **Photo08**, hold down the **Ctrl** key, and then click **Photo09** to select the two photos.

6. Click the **Open** button to add the photos to the Australia album. See Figure 6-40.

| Figure 6-40 | Creating a new photo album |

two photos provided for the album

click the Upload button to add the two photos to the Australia album

7. Click the **Upload** button to store the photos in the Australia album.

Now you should let Bev know the photos are available.

To send links to the photos:

TIP

You can also click the To button and then select a contact.

1. On the Australia album page, click the **More** arrow in the middle of the page, and then click **Send a link**.

2. Click the **To** text box, and then type the e-mail address of someone you know, such as **BevParkinson@live.com**. Bev is expecting the photos, so you don't need to include a message.

3. Click the **Send** button. An e-mail message is sent to Bev (or the person whose e-mail address you entered) with a link to the Australia photo album.

Bev will receive an e-mail with a View album button that she can click to open the Windows Live Web page displaying the photos in the Australia album. She can respond to Kendra when she begins to work on the layout of the magazine.

To end the Windows Live session:

1. Click the **sign out** link below your user name.

2. Close Internet Explorer.

Restoring Your Settings

If you are working in a computer lab or on a computer other than your own, complete the steps in this section to restore the original settings on the computer.

To restore your settings:

1. Move the JPG Oct search file from the Navigation pane to the Tutorial.06\Tutorial folder provided with your Data Files.

2. Start Internet Explorer, click the **Search** box arrow, click **Manage Search Providers**, click **Wikipedia**, and then click the **Remove** button.

3. Close all open windows.

REVIEW

Session 6.2 Quick Check

1. What three types of searches can you perform using the Start menu?
2. True or False. In Internet Explorer, you can specify which search provider you prefer to use by default.
3. Name three guidelines for searching the Internet efficiently.
4. True or False. When you enter a search expression in a Web browser, a search provider searches all of the Web pages on the Internet to find those that match your criteria.
5. One way to modify an Internet search expression is to use _____ to search for specific phrases.
6. To sign in to Windows Live, you need a(n) _____.

Practice the skills you learned in the tutorial using the same case scenario.

PRACTICE

Review Assignments

For a list of Data Files in the Review folder, see page WIN 285.

You are now working with Kendra Cho on a *TrendSpot* article about a disturbing trend: the number of extreme or destructive weather incidents has been increasing in recent years. Kendra is editing an article on weather and needs your help to research the photos she'll use in the upcoming issue of the magazine. As an online publication, the magazine often includes multimedia files so that readers can play sound, music, and videos as they read articles. Kendra wants you to help her search for audio and video files, and find a program that can play them. She also wants to meet with Bev Parkinson and her assistant, Corinne Andrews, to select weather photos. Complete the following:

1. In a folder window, open the **Review** folder in the Tutorial.06 folder provided with your Data Files.

2. Use the Search box to search for WAV files. Move the WAV files to a new subfolder named **Sounds** in the Review folder.

3. Display the Review folder again, and then use the Search box to find files containing the text *pho* in their filenames or contents. Search the file contents, if necessary. Verify that a file you found lists credits for the photos in the Review folder. If it does, move the file you found to a new subfolder named **Documents** in the Review folder. Otherwise, do not move the file you found.

4. Add the following tags to Photo30: **storm; clouds**.

5. Add the following tags to Photo41: **lightning; night; sky; thunderstorm**.

6. In the folder window, verify that the new tags are now assigned to Photo30 and Photo41. If necessary, maximize the folder window, switch to Details view, right-click a column heading, and then click Tags to display the Tags column.

7. In the Review folder, search for photos that have *tornado* as a tag. Move the files you found to a new subfolder named **Tornado** in the Review folder.

8. In the Review folder window, find a photo that has *snow* and *winter* as tags. Change the name of this file to **Winter**.

9. Search for a program on your computer that lets you play media files. Start the program, and then explore its toolbars. (If you need to set up the program, choose the Recommended Settings option.) Press the Alt+Print Screen keys to capture an image of the program window, and then paste the image in a new Paint or WordPad file. Save the file as **Media Program** in the Tutorial.06\Review folder provided with your Data Files. Close the media program.

10. Find video files in the Tutorial.06\Review folder and in the libraries on your computer. (*Hint*: Use *video* in your search criteria.) Press the Alt+Print Screen keys to capture an image of the Search Results window, and then paste the image in a new Paint or WordPad file. Save the file as **Videos** in the Tutorial.06\Review folder provided with your Data Files.

11. Start Internet Explorer, and use Bing to find Web pages providing information about extreme weather in the current year. Narrow the search by finding only images of extreme weather in the current year. Press the Alt+Print Screen keys to capture an image of the first screen of search results, and then paste the image in a new Paint or WordPad file. Save the file as **Images** in the Tutorial.06\Review folder provided with your Data Files.

12. Switch to Wikipedia as your search provider, and use *weather* as the search text. With the search results displayed below the Search box, press the Alt+Print Screen keys to capture an image of the first screen of search results, and then paste the image in a new Paint or WordPad file. Save the file as **Weather** in the Tutorial.06\Review folder provided with your Data Files.

13. Go to Windows Live and sign in. Create a group named Weather*XY*, where *XY* are your initials. Membership should be by invitation only. Invite two people to join the group by sending the following message: **Let's meet to select weather photos.** With the Weather*XY* page showing that your invitations have been sent or that two people joined the group, press the Print Screen key to capture an image of the desktop, and then paste the image in a new Paint or WordPad file. Save the file as **Meeting** in the Tutorial.06\Review folder provided with your Data Files.

14. Sign out of Windows Live Groups, and then close all open windows.

15. Submit the results of the preceding steps to your instructor, either in printed or electronic form, as requested.

Use your skills to conduct research for a graphic arts firm.

APPLY

Case Problem 1

For a list of Data Files in the Case1 folder, see page WIN 285.

G & K Graphic Arts Marco Garcia and Joel Knightly own G & K Graphic Arts, a small firm in Nashville, Tennessee, that provides graphic design services to local businesses. They are currently working for a recording studio on a project to design a Web page and a CD insert for a CD featuring the work of studio musicians, tentatively called Bluegrass Studio. Marco and Joel ask you to help them find images they can use for the Web page and CD. They also want to back up their files on a DVD, and ask you to find information about programs they can use to do so. Complete the following steps:

1. Open the Case1 folder in the Tutorial.06 folder provided with your Data Files.

2. Review the tags and other properties already assigned to the files in the Case1 folder. Then add the tag **fiddle** or **bluegrass** to files as appropriate.

3. Using a file's Properties dialog box, add **Marco** as the author of the following photos: P01, P02, P05, P10, P12, and P13.

4. Use the Search box to find photos that include the tag *guitar* and have *Marco* as the author. Move the file(s) you found to a new subfolder named **Marco Guitar** in the Case1 folder.

5. In any of the indexed locations on your computer, search for MP3 music files. Save the search as **MP3**, and then move it to the Case1 folder.

6. Remove all the properties and personal information from the **P09** file in the Case1 folder. (*Hint*: Click the appropriate link in the P09 Properties dialog box, click the option button to Remove the following properties from this file, click the Select All button, and then click the OK button.)

7. Search for a program on your computer that lets you store files on a DVD. Start the program, and then press the Alt+Print Screen keys to capture an image of the program window. Paste the image in a new Paint or WordPad file. Save the file as **DVD Program** in the Tutorial.06\Case1 folder provided with your Data Files. Close the DVD program.

8. Search for a program on your computer that lets you back up and restore files. Start the program, and then press the Alt+Print Screen keys to capture an image of the program window. Paste the image in a new Paint or WordPad file. Save the file as **Backup Program** in the Tutorial.06\Case1 folder provided with your Data Files. Close the backup program.

9. Start Internet Explorer, and use Bing to find Web pages providing information on bluegrass music in Nashville. Narrow the search to find only images of bluegrass music in Nashville. Press the Alt+Print Screen keys to capture an image of the first screen of search results, and then paste the image in a new Paint or WordPad file. Save the file as **Nashville** in the Tutorial.06\Case1 folder provided with your Data Files.

10. Go to *www.google.com*, and then display the results of the original search for information about bluegrass music in Nashville. Modify the search to show information about bluegrass music not in Nashville. Press the Alt+Print Screen keys to capture an image of the first screen of search results, and then paste the image in a new Paint or WordPad file. Save the file as **Not Nashville** in the Tutorial.06\Case1 folder provided with your Data Files.

11. Close all open windows.

12. Submit the results of the preceding steps to your instructor, either in printed or electronic form, as requested.

Use your skills to conduct searches for a pet adoption agency.

APPLY

Case Problem 2

For a list of Data Files in the Case2 folder, see page WIN 285.

Amherst Pet Adoption   Michelle Rangely is the director of the Amherst Pet Adoption agency in Amherst, Massachusetts. She is developing a presentation to give to local groups such as parent-teacher organizations, neighborhood associations, and senior centers about the pets available at the agency and the value they provide to individuals and families. She asks you to help her organize the pictures she has of pets and to research information about the benefits of keeping a pet. She also wants to find photographs of wildlife for part of her presentation. Because she will eventually distribute the presentation via e-mail, she wants to be aware of file size so that she can select small image files. Complete the following steps:

1. Open the Case2 folder in the Tutorial.06 folder provided with your Data Files.

2. Add a tag to each file in the Case2 folder to identify the type of animal shown in the photo. Use **cat**, **dog**, **duck**, **rabbit**, or **parrot** as tags. (*Hint*: Use a Large Icons or Extra Large Icons view to see the images clearly.)

3. Using a file's Properties dialog box, add **Available for adoption** as the comment in the following photos: Pic01, Pic04, Pic05, Pic06, and Pic09.

⊕ **EXPLORE**   4. Search for photos of cats that are available for adoption. (*Hint*: Start your search using **comment** as the property name in the Search box.) Move the files you found to a new subfolder named **Cats to Adopt** in the Case2 folder.

⊕ **EXPLORE**   5. Using **dimensions** as the property name in the search box, find files that are 120 pixels wide. Press the Alt+Print Screen keys to capture an image of the search results window showing the files you found. Paste the image in a new Paint or WordPad file, and save the file as **Dim 120** in the Tutorial.06\Case2 folder provided with your Data Files.

6. In libraries, your personal folder, and the Tutorial.06\Case2 folder, search for files that are exactly 16 KB in size. (*Hint*: Add **KB** to the search text.) Press the Alt+Print Screen keys to capture an image of the search results window showing the files you found. Paste the image in a new Paint or WordPad file, and save the file as **16 KB** in the Tutorial.06\Case2 folder provided with your Data Files.

7. In the libraries on your computer, search for picture files that have *wildlife* as a tag. Press the Alt+Print Screen keys to capture an image of the search results window showing the files you found. Paste the image in a new Paint or WordPad file, and save the file as **Wildlife** in the Tutorial.06\Case2 folder provided with your Data Files.

8. In the libraries on your computer, search for photos that have *Corbis* as an author and a rating of 4 Stars. Press the Alt+Print Screen keys to capture an image of the search results window showing the files you found. Paste the image in a new Paint or WordPad file, and save the file as **Good Pix** in the Tutorial.06\Case2 folder provided with your Data Files.

9. Search for a program on your computer that lets you connect to a network projector to play presentations. Start the program, allowing Windows Firewall to unblock the program, if necessary, and then Press the Alt+Print Screen keys to capture an image of the opening window. Paste the image in a new Paint or WordPad file. Save the file as **Projector** in the Tutorial.06\Case2 folder provided with your Data Files. Close the projector program.

10. Start Internet Explorer, and use Bing to find Web pages providing information on the benefits of adopting pets. Narrow the search to Web pages that provide this information only about Amherst, Massachusetts. Press the Alt+Print Screen keys to capture an image of the first screen of search results, and then paste the image in a new Paint or WordPad file. Save the file as **Amherst Pets** in the Tutorial.06\Case2 folder provided with your Data Files.

11. Switch to any other search provider, and use it to conduct a search for information about pets. Open a page displaying information about this topic. Use the Find toolbar to find information on the page about adopting pets. Press the Alt+Print Screen keys to capture an image of the screen showing the Find toolbar, and then paste the image in a new Paint or WordPad file. Save the file as **Pets** in the Tutorial.06\Case2 folder provided with your Data Files. Close all open windows.

12. Submit the results of the preceding steps to your instructor, either in printed or electronic form, as requested.

Using the figure as a guide, find files and information for a small antiques shop.

CREATE

Case Problem 3

For a list of Data Files in the Case3 folder, see page WIN 285.

Vandemain Antiques Harold Dougal recently bought an antiques shop named Vandemain Antiques in Asheville, North Carolina. Harold wants to promote his most unusual objects in the local visitor's magazine. He asks you to help him find appropriate images and to research information about his competitors in Asheville. Complete the following steps:

1. Open the Case3 folder in the Tutorial.06 folder provided with your Data Files.

2. Conduct a search to find files with *time* as a tag or *Hal* as an author.

3. Press the Alt+Print Screen keys to capture an image of the search results, and then paste the image in a new Paint or WordPad file. Save the file as **Search1** in the Tutorial.06\Case3 folder provided with your Data Files.

4. Conduct another search to find files with *time* as a tag and *Hal* as an author.

5. Press the Alt+Print Screen keys to capture an image of the search results, and then paste the image in a new Paint or WordPad file. Save the file as **Search2** in the Tutorial.06\Case3 folder provided with your Data Files.

6. Conduct another search to find files with *boat* or *antique* as a tag.

7. Press the Alt+Print Screen keys to capture an image of the search results, and then paste the image in a new Paint or WordPad file. Save the file as **Search3** in the Tutorial.06\Case3 folder provided with your Data Files.

8. Start Internet Explorer, and conduct a search to produce the results shown in Figure 6-41.

Figure 6-41	Bing search results

9. Press the Alt+Print Screen keys to capture an image of the first screen of search results, and then paste the image in a new Paint or WordPad file. Save the file as **Search4** in the Tutorial.06\Case3 folder provided with your Data Files. Close all open windows.

10. Submit the results of the preceding steps to your instructor, either in printed or electronic form, as requested.

Use your skills and the Internet to learn about other ways to search for information.

RESEARCH

Case Problem 4

There are no Data Files needed for this Case Problem.

Ask Me Anything   Diana and Paul Seefert are former librarians who recently started a company called Ask Me Anything in San Antonio, Texas. They provide a wide range of research services, including finding marketing and demographic information for businesses, answering trivia questions, and uncovering local history stories. When they were trained as librarians, they learned to use mostly print documents as source materials. They hired you as an intern to help them learn how to take full advantage of the Internet. Complete the following steps:

1. Start Internet Explorer and use any search provider to research the difference between search engines, metasearch engines, and subject directories.

2. Find an example of each type of search tool and capture an image of its main page. Save the search engine image in a file named **Search Engine** in the Case4 folder. Save the metasearch engine image in a file named **Metasearch** in the Case4 folder. Save the subject directory image in a file named **Subject Directory** in the Case4 folder.

3. Use any search provider to find information about Boolean logic or Boolean operators. Narrow the results to find pages that explain how to use Boolean logic or operators to find information on the Web. Create a document using WordPad or another word-processing program with four column headings: **Operator**, **Alternate Operator**, **Description**, and **Examples**. Enter information in each column to describe at least four Boolean operators you can use to search the Web. Complete the columns according to the following descriptions:

Operator	Alternate Operator	Description	Examples
List text terms for Boolean operators.	List symbols used for Boolean operators, if any.	Provide a brief description of the operator or its purpose.	Give examples of how to use the operator: one using the text operator, and one using the symbol (if possible).

4. Save the document as **Boolean** in the Case4 folder provided with your Data Files.

5. Submit the results of the preceding steps to your instructor, either in printed or electronic form, as requested.

ENDING DATA FILES

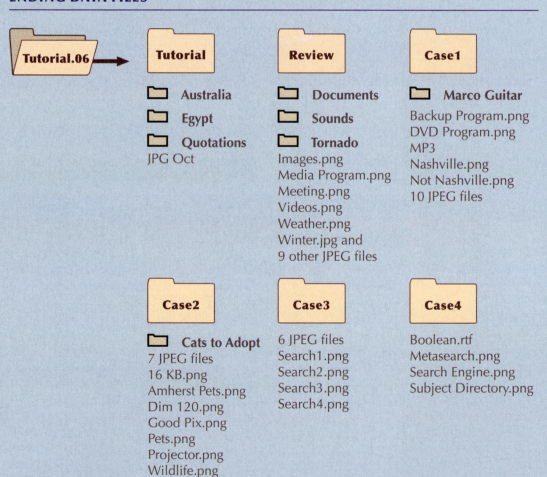

Tutorial.06 → **Tutorial**
- Australia
- Egypt
- Quotations
- JPG Oct

Review
- Documents
- Sounds
- Tornado
- Images.png
- Media Program.png
- Meeting.png
- Videos.png
- Weather.png
- Winter.jpg and 9 other JPEG files

Case1
- Marco Guitar
- Backup Program.png
- DVD Program.png
- MP3
- Nashville.png
- Not Nashville.png
- 10 JPEG files

Case2
- Cats to Adopt
- 7 JPEG files
- 16 KB.png
- Amherst Pets.png
- Dim 120.png
- Good Pix.png
- Pets.png
- Projector.png
- Wildlife.png

Case3
- 6 JPEG files
- Search1.png
- Search2.png
- Search3.png
- Search4.png

Case4
- Boolean.rtf
- Metasearch.png
- Search Engine.png
- Subject Directory.png

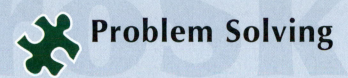

Problem Solving

Selecting the Best Settings for Efficient Computer Work

When you solve problems, you work through a series of stages to gather information about the problem and its possible solutions. Problem solving in general involves the following tasks:

1. Recognize and define the problem.
2. Determine possible courses of action.
3. Collect information needed to evaluate alternative courses of action.
4. Evaluate each alternative's merits and drawbacks.
5. Select an alternative.
6. Implement the decision.
7. Monitor and evaluate performance to provide feedback and take corrective action.

If you are involved in solving a complex problem with many possible causes, you perform all seven steps in the process. If you are solving a simpler problem or have limited time to explore solutions, you can condense the steps. For example, you might recognize the problem in one step, determine possible actions, evaluate and select an alternative in the next step, and then implement and evaluate your decision in another step.

Recognize and Define the Problem

A problem is an obstacle that prevents you from reaching a goal. This definition is especially fitting for work with a computer. For example, suppose your goal is to create a report containing text and graphics, but you don't know which program to use. In this case, your lack of familiarity with the programs on your computer is an obstacle preventing you from reaching your goal of efficiently creating a report with text and graphics.

After identifying a simple problem, such as which computer program to use, you can focus on solutions. Start by considering any possible solution. For example, start each program on your computer related to text and graphics and examine its features. Next, compare and evaluate those alternatives. Which programs help you meet your goal most effectively? Select the best solution and then try it, observing the results to make sure it actually solves the problem. Can you efficiently create the report with the program you selected? If not, try a different program until you find the best possible solution.

ProSkills

Set Up Your Computer to Work Efficiently

The way you set up your computer can help you avoid problems and work with efficiency. Two common problems for Windows users are not being familiar with the programs installed on their computers and not being able to quickly access folders, files, devices, and information they use often. You can avoid or solve these problems by personalizing your computer and using a few Windows programs that let you work efficiently and securely. As you select settings, capture and save images of your computer so you can document what you've done. Complete the following tasks:

1. Start Windows 7 and log on, if necessary.

2. Set up shortcuts on your desktop to the folders, devices, and documents you use often.

3. Change the desktop icons, taskbar, and Start menu to suit your preferences and provide access to programs you use often.

4. Use Internet Explorer to research themes you can use on your computer. If you find a theme you like, download and install it on your computer.

5. Pin programs you use often to the taskbar or the Start menu. Add files you use often to the Jump Lists for these programs. Open the Start menu, and then capture an image of the desktop.

6. In Internet Explorer, add the Web pages that you visit often to your Favorites list. Open the Favorites Center, and then capture an image of the Internet Explorer window.

7. Using Windows Live Contacts, create contacts for your correspondents. Capture an image of the main Windows Live Contacts window.

8. Using Windows Live Calendar, set up your appointments and tasks for the upcoming week. Capture an image of the appointment calendar.

9. Open the Windows 7 Action Center and make sure you are using all of the recommended security settings. In particular, make sure you are using an up-to-date antivirus program and that Windows Update is set to check for updates regularly. Both settings help you avoid the problems of security threats to your computer. Capture an image of the Action Center window. Do the same for Windows Live Mail and Internet Explorer.

10. Submit the images you captured to your instructor, either in printed or electronic form, as requested.

OBJECTIVES

Session 7.1
- Examine computer graphics
- Create and edit graphics in Paint
- Add text to a graphic
- Apply color and draw shapes in an image

Session 7.2
- Acquire, view, and edit photos
- Organize and play music
- Sync music files to a portable device
- Create a multimedia slide show
- Burn video files to a DVD

Managing Multimedia Files

Working with Graphics, Photos, Music, and Movies

Case | *Oak Park Landscaping*

Bernie Quinn and Hector Torres own Oak Park Landscaping in Oak Park, Illinois, which provides landscaping and design services for businesses and homeowners. You are a part-time designer helping Bernie and Hector prepare landscaping proposals and create graphics used to market and sell their services. Your first projects are to create a logo for the company's Web site and e-mail stationery, and to assemble a multimedia presentation to showcase its designs and services.

In this tutorial, you'll learn how to create, acquire, and modify multimedia files, including graphics, photos, and videos. You'll also explore how to organize and play music files. To share multimedia files with others, you'll learn how to e-mail, sync, and burn the files and how to create a multimedia slide show.

STARTING DATA FILES

Tutorial.07 → **Tutorial**

Frame.png
Garden01.jpg–
Garden13.jpg
Oak.png
Summer.wmv

Review

Border.jpg
Buttercup.jpg
Dahlia.jpg
Fuschia.jpg
Iris.jpg
Lily.jpg

Lupin.jpg
Phlox.jpg
Plan.jpg
Rose.jpg
Violet.jpg

Case1

Austen.jpg
Bronte.jpg
Browning.jpg
Cather.jpg
Flourish.png
Letters AZ.png

McCullers.jpg
Millay.jpg
Moore.jpg

Case2

LH01.jpg–LH08.jpg
Lighthouse.png
Ocean.wav

Case3

Bird01.jpg–
Bird10.jpg
BirdSong.wav
WaterFowl.wav
Window.tif
Wren.tif

Case4

Apples.jpg
Banner.jpg
Berries.jpg
Market.jpg
Onions.jpg
Peppers.jpg

Potatoes.jpg
Squash.jpg
Tomatoes.jpg
Wheat.jpg

SESSION 7.1 VISUAL OVERVIEW

Paint is a **graphics program**, which is software that includes drawing and graphics-editing tools.

To space and align shapes effectively, you can display **gridlines**, which are horizontal and vertical lines that do not appear in the graphic itself.

In Paint, you create, edit, and manipulate **bitmapped graphics**, which are made up of small dots that form an image.

The **sizing coordinates** display the size of the shape you are drawing.

The **pixel coordinates** in the status bar specify the exact location of the pointer on the canvas relative to the pixels on your screen.

The status bar shows the dimensions of the canvas.

Logo - Paint

Home   View

Paste   Select   Brushes   Shapes   Outline   Fill

Clipboard   Image   Tools   Shapes

Oak Park Landsca

⊹ 5, 185px   ☐ 20 × 26px   ☐ 310 × 250p

CREATING GRAPHICS IN PAINT

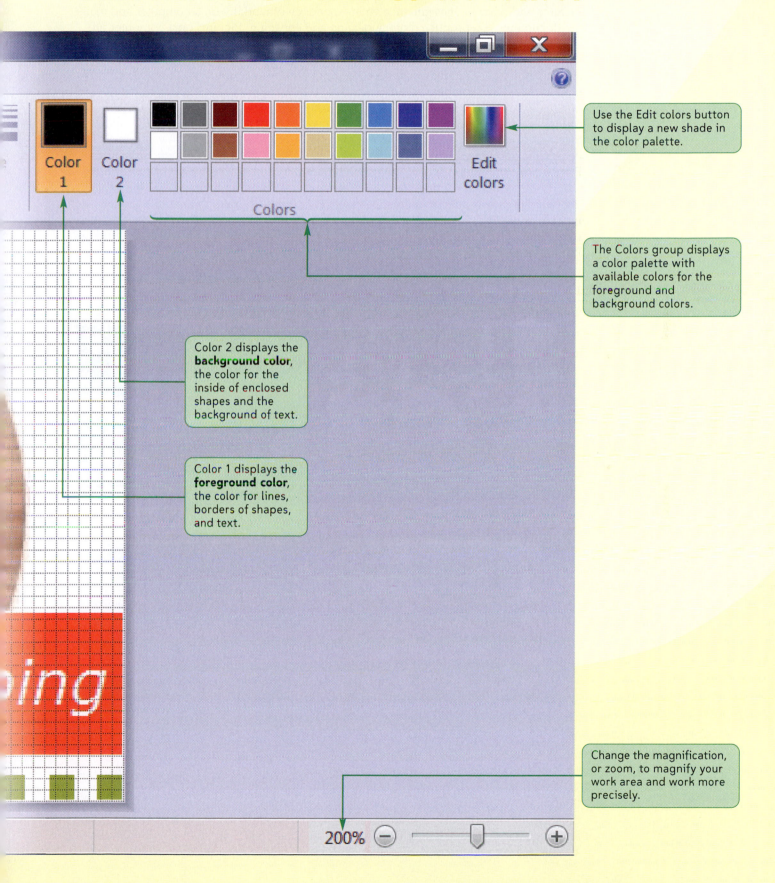

Use the Edit colors button to display a new shade in the color palette.

The Colors group displays a color palette with available colors for the foreground and background colors.

Color 2 displays the **background color**, the color for the inside of enclosed shapes and the background of text.

Color 1 displays the **foreground color**, the color for lines, borders of shapes, and text.

Change the magnification, or zoom, to magnify your work area and work more precisely.

Color 1

Color 2

Colors

Edit colors

200%

Exploring Computer Graphics

Pictures and other images enhance your experience of working on a computer and make the documents you produce more appealing and engaging. Pictures on a computer are called **graphic images**, or **graphics**. A computer graphic is different from a drawing on a piece of paper because a drawing is an actual image, whereas a computer graphic is a file that displays an image on a computer monitor. Computer graphics come in two fundamental types: bitmapped and vector.

When you manipulate a bitmap graphic, you work with a grid of dots, called pixels. A bitmapped graphic (or *bitmap* for short) is created from rows of colored pixels that together form an image. The simplest bitmaps have only two colors, with each pixel being black or white. Bitmaps become more complex as they include more colors. Photographs or pictures with shading can have millions of colors, which increases file size. Bitmaps are appropriate for detailed graphics, such as photographs and the images displayed on a computer monitor. See Figure 7-1. Typical types of bitmap file formats include PNG, JPG, GIF, and BMP. (You'll learn more about graphic file formats later.) You create and edit bitmaps using graphics programs such as Adobe Photoshop and Windows Paint. Bitmap-editing programs are also called painting programs.

| Figure 7-1 | Bitmapped graphics |

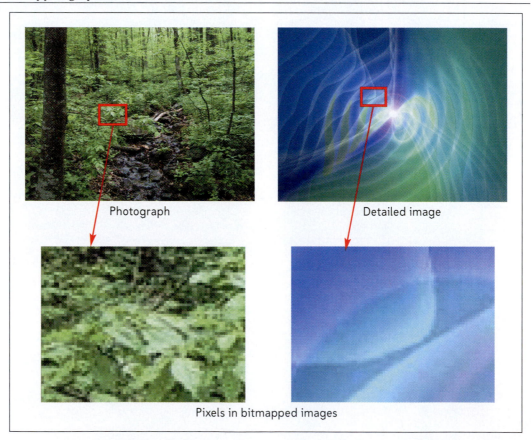

Photograph   Detailed image

Pixels in bitmapped images

In contrast, a **vector graphic** is created by mathematical formulas that define the shapes used in the image. When you work with a vector graphic, you interact with a collection of lines. Rather than a grid of pixels, a vector graphic consists of shapes, curves, lines, and text that together make a picture. While a bitmapped image contains information about the color of each pixel, a vector graphic contains instructions about where to place each component. Vector images are appropriate for simple drawings, such as line art and graphs, and for fonts. See Figure 7-2. Typical types of vector file formats include

WMF, SWF, and SVG, a standard for vector images on the Web. You use drawing programs such as Adobe Illustrator and CorelDRAW to create and edit vector images.

Figure 7-2   **Vector graphics**

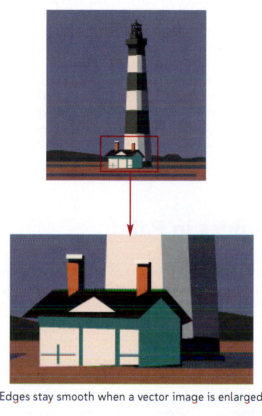

Aa Bb Cc

Aa Bb Cc

Fonts are a kind of vector image

Edges stay smooth when a vector image is enlarged

A vector shape is a collection of points, lines, and curves

Decision Making: Selecting Bitmapped or Vector Graphics

If you're designing materials that include graphics, such as a Web page or flyer, one of your first decisions is whether to use bitmapped or vector graphics. Keep the following guidelines in mind as you make this decision:

- In general, a bitmap file is much larger than a similar vector file, making vector files more suitable for displaying graphics on Web pages.
- Avoid resizing bitmapped graphics because resolution (the number of pixels in an image) affects their quality. If you enlarge a bitmapped graphic, it often looks jagged because you are redistributing the pixels in the image. If you reduce the size of a bitmapped graphic, its features might be indistinct and fuzzy. On the other hand, you can resize vector graphics without affecting quality because vectors redraw their shapes when you resize them.
- To edit vector graphics, you often need to use the same drawing program used to create the graphic. Before you acquire vector graphics from various sources, make sure you have the program that created them in case you need to edit them. In contrast, most painting programs can open many types of bitmapped graphic formats.
- Bitmaps are suitable for photographs and photorealistic images, while vector graphics are more practical for typesetting or graphic design.

By default, Windows 7 provides sample bitmapped graphics in its Pictures library. You can add your own graphic files to your computer in a few ways. One way is to use a **scanner**, which is a device that converts an existing paper image into an electronic file that you can open and work with on your computer. Another popular method is to use a digital camera to take photos and then transfer the images to your computer. Software and Web sites also provide graphics you can use. The clip art images they provide are usually line drawings and therefore vector images. Many Web sites maintain online catalogs of drawings, images, and photographs that are available for download. Some of these sites charge a membership fee, some charge per image, and others provide copyright-free images that are also free of charge.

To edit a graphic or create one from scratch, you use a graphics program. Windows 7 includes a basic graphics program called Paint, which lets you create, edit, and manipulate bitmap graphics, though not vector graphics. Many programs designed for Windows 7, including Microsoft Office, include tools for creating and editing vector graphics such as charts, flowcharts, and other drawings in a document or worksheet, for example. Bernie wants to combine two images to create the Oak Park logo; because they are both bit-mapped graphics, you can use Paint for this project.

Creating Graphics in Paint

As you already know, Paint is a Windows 7 accessory program that you can use to create and modify bitmapped graphics. Using Paint, you can draw shapes, add and change colors, insert text, remove parts of a picture, and copy and paste images, including those you capture on your computer screen. Bernie is ready to learn about Paint, so you can start the program and introduce him to its graphic tools.

To start Paint:

 1. Click the **Start** button 🪟 on the taskbar, point to **All Programs**, and then click **Accessories**. The Accessories folder opens in the Start menu.

 2. Click **Paint**. The Paint window opens. If necessary, maximize the window.

When you start Paint without opening a picture, the Paint window is mostly blank, providing a few tools for drawing and painting. The white area in the Paint window is the canvas, where you work with your graphic. Above the canvas is the Ribbon, which opens to the Home tab by default. See Figure 7-3. Your Home tab might display a Shapes gallery and additional button names depending on the resolution of your monitor and the size of text and other objects on the screen.

Figure 7-3   Paint window

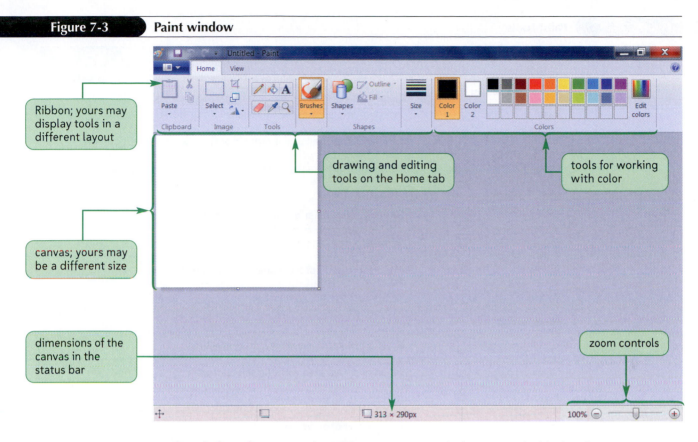

The Clipboard group on the Ribbon contains tools that are probably familiar to you—the Paste, Cut, and Copy buttons. You use these buttons the same way you would in a Microsoft Office program, such as Microsoft Word. In Paint, you can click the Paste button arrow to paste entire image files into the current image, which is often a helpful timesaver.

You use the buttons in the Image group to select and edit images. The buttons in the Tools group help you change an image. For example, you use the Eraser to remove pixels from an image. The Shapes group includes tools you use to draw lines and shapes in various styles on the canvas. Use the tools in the Colors group to select colors for the outline and background color or fill of shapes and text. The status bar at the bottom of the window provides information about the tools you select and about the location of the pointer when it's in the canvas.

Figure 7-4 describes the tools you can use on the Paint Home tab shown in Figure 7-3 to create and edit graphics.

Figure 7-4 Paint tools

Tool	Icon	Description
Clipboard Group		
Paste		Insert an image from the Clipboard or one stored on your computer
Cut		Remove some or all of the graphic and store it on the Clipboard
Copy		Copy some or all of the graphic and store it on the Clipboard
Image Group		
Select		Select a rectangular or free-form part of an image
Crop		Remove part of an image from the sides
Resize		Make some or all of an image larger or smaller
Rotate		Rotate some or all of an image
Tools Group		
Pencil		Draw a free-form line or one pixel at a time
Fill with color		Fill an enclosed area with the selected color
Text		Add text to an image
Eraser		Erase a part of an image
Color picker		Pick up a color in an image to set the current foreground or background color
Magnifier		Change the magnification and zoom in or out of an image
Brushes		Paint free-form lines and curves using a brush in a variety of styles
Shapes Group		
Shapes		Draw various shapes, including lines, rectangles, and ellipses (circles)
Outline		Select a style for the line or border as you draw
Fill		Select a style for the fill (inside area) as you draw
Size		Select a width for the line or border as you draw
Colors Group		
Color 1		Select the foreground color, the color for lines, borders of shapes, and text
Color 2		Select the background color, the color for the inside of enclosed shapes and the background of text
Color palette	[n/a]	Select a color to change the foreground or background color
Edit colors		Select a color that does not appear on the palette

Opening a Graphic in Paint

You open a graphic in Paint the same way you open a file in any Windows 7 program—use the Open dialog box to navigate to where you store the image file, select the file, and then open it. Paint can keep only one graphic open at a time, similar to the way Notepad handles files. If you are working with a graphic and then try to open another one, Paint closes the first graphic and gives you a chance to save your changes before opening the new graphic. If you want to work with a second image at the same time as the first image, you can start another session of Paint and open the second image.

Bernie asks you to show him how to open the two JPG files he found so you can discuss how to combine them to create a single image.

To open the Oak Park graphics:

1. Make sure you have created your copy of the Windows 7 Data Files, and that your computer can access them.

   Trouble? If you don't have the starting Data Files, you need to get them before you can proceed. Your instructor will either give you the Data Files or ask you to obtain them from a specified location (such as a network drive). In either case, make a backup copy of the Data Files before you start so that you will have the original files available in case you need to start over. If you have any questions about the Data Files, see your instructor or technical support person for assistance.

2. Click the **Paint menu** button ▣▾, and then click **Open**. The Open dialog box opens.

3. Navigate to the Tutorial folder in the Tutorial.07 folder provided with your Data Files.

4. Click **Oak** and then click the **Open** button. The Oak file opens in the Paint window. See Figure 7-5.

Figure 7-5   Oak picture open in Paint

image opens in the upper-left corner of the Paint window

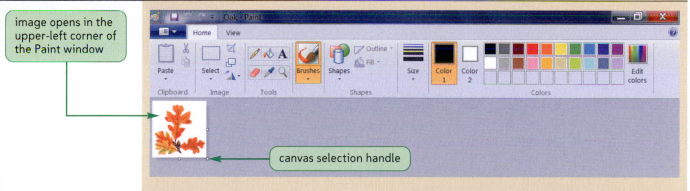

canvas selection handle

5. To examine the second picture, click the **Paint menu** button ▣▾, and then click **Open**.

6. In the file list, click **Frame** and then click the **Open** button. The oak picture closes and the frame picture opens in the Paint window.

Now that you've seen the two images Bernie wants to use, you can plan the logo graphic. Clearly, the best way to combine these images is to insert the oak picture inside the frame picture. You also need to add the name of Bernie's company—Oak Park Landscaping. After making a few sketches, you and Bernie agree on the design shown in Figure 7-6.

Figure 7-6 Design for Oak Park Landscaping logo

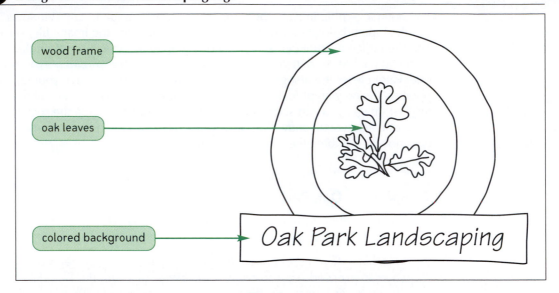

To start creating this design, you need to add the oak picture to the center of the round frame. You'll show Bernie how to do this shortly. Before you do, you should save the Frame graphic file with a new name in case you need the original again in its unchanged state.

Saving a Graphic File

When you save a graphic file with a new name, you use the Save As dialog box, as you do in other Windows 7 programs. In the Save As dialog box, you select a location for the file, provide a filename, and select a file type, or format, if necessary. Paint can save and open images in many bitmap formats, and each format has its pros and cons. To work effectively with graphics, you should understand the basics of the most popular Paint file bitmap formats: PNG, JPG, GIF, and BMP. A fifth file format—TIF—is useful if you are creating images for print. PNG is the default format in Windows 7, while JPG was the default format in Windows Vista.

When you create a graphics file, you choose its format based on what you intend to do with the image and where you want to display it. If you want to use the image on a Web site or send it via e-mail, for example, you need an image with a small file size. In this case, you should choose a file format that compresses color information. For example, if a picture has an area of solid color, it doesn't need to store the same color information for each pixel. Instead, the file can store an instruction to repeat the color until it changes. This space-saving technique is called **compression**. Some compression methods save space without sacrificing image quality, and others are designed to save as much space as possible, even if the image is degraded. Figure 7-7 summarizes the pros and cons of five bitmapped graphics formats.

Figure 7-7 **Graphic file formats**

File Format	Advantages	Disadvantages	Use for
Graphics Interchange Format (GIF)	Compresses images without losing quality and allows animation	Not suitable for photographs	Graphics such as logos, line drawings, and icons
Joint Photographic Experts Group (JPG or JPEG)	Efficiently compresses photographic images	Can reduce quality	Photographs and images with fine detail
Portable Network Graphics (PNG)	Compresses images without losing quality	Does not allow transparency	Nonphotographic images designed for the Web
Tagged Image File Format (TIF or TIFF)	Maintains image quality in print and on screen	Some Web browsers cannot display TIF images	Images used in desktop publishing, faxes, and medical imaging
Windows Bitmap (BMP)	Simplest way to store a bitmapped graphic	Can waste large amounts of storage space	Basic shapes and images with few colors

The Frame and Oak files are both PNG files, which is an appropriate file format for displaying graphics on a Web page or distributing graphics via e-mail. You'll save a copy of the Frame file as a PNG file. However, if you need to provide a graphic in a different file format, you can convert it in Paint by choosing that format when you save the file.

To save the Frame image with a new name:

1. Click the **Paint menu** button, and then click **Save as**. The Save As dialog box opens.

2. If necessary, click the **Browse Folders** button to open the Navigation pane, and then navigate to the **Tutorial** folder in the Tutorial.07 folder provided with your Data Files.

3. In the File name text box, type **Logo**. The file type is already displayed in the Save As dialog box. See Figure 7-8.

TIP

To save a file as a different type, point to Save as and then click a different file type, such as JPEG picture.

Make sure you save the file with a different name—you might need the original files later.

Figure 7-8	Saving the Frame image with a new name

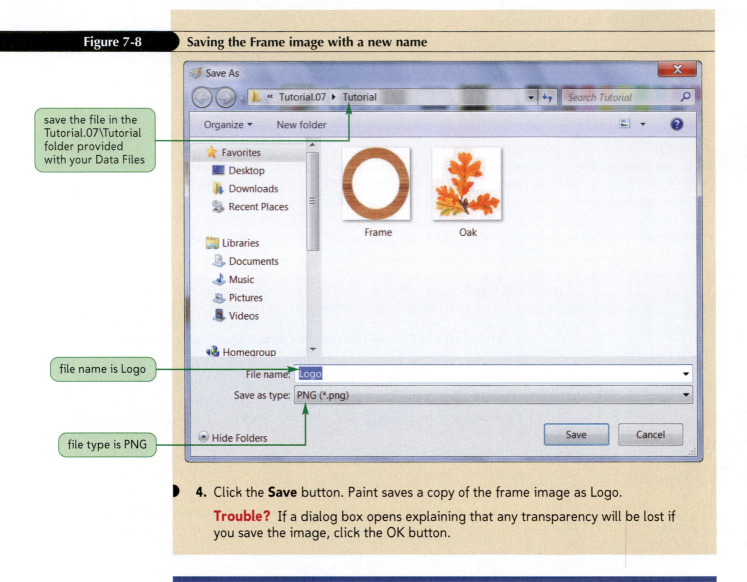

save the file in the Tutorial.07\Tutorial folder provided with your Data Files

file name is Logo

file type is PNG

4. Click the **Save** button. Paint saves a copy of the frame image as Logo.

Trouble? If a dialog box opens explaining that any transparency will be lost if you save the image, click the OK button.

INSIGHT

Saving a Bitmapped Graphic in a Different File Type

In general, you cannot improve the quality of a compressed image by saving it in a different file format. For example, suppose you convert a JPG graphic, which omits some color information to compress the file, to a format such as TIF, which doesn't sacrifice quality to reduce file size. The colors from the original JPG file remain the same, but the file size increases because the TIF file provides an expanded color palette that includes colors not used in the image.

Now you are ready to create the Oak Park logo by combining the picture of the oak leaves with the frame image.

Copying and Pasting to Create a Graphic

One way to insert the oak picture inside the image of the frame is to open the Oak file again, select the entire image, cut or copy it, open the Logo file with the frame image, and then paste the oak picture in the frame. To reduce the number of steps you need to perform, Paint provides a shortcut method, the Paste from command on the Paste button.

You can use this command when you want to copy an entire image from another file and paste it in your current image.

To paste the oak picture in the Logo file:

1. Click the **Paste button arrow**, and then click **Paste from**. The Paste From dialog box opens, which has the same controls as the Open dialog box.

   Trouble? If the Paste From dialog box did not open, you probably clicked the Paste button instead of the Paste button arrow. Click the **Undo** button 🔄 on the Quick Access Toolbar, and then repeat Step 1.

2. In the file list, click **Oak** and then click the **Open** button. The oak image appears in the upper-left corner of the logo picture in a selection box. See Figure 7-9.

Figure 7-9   Pasting the oak picture in the Logo file

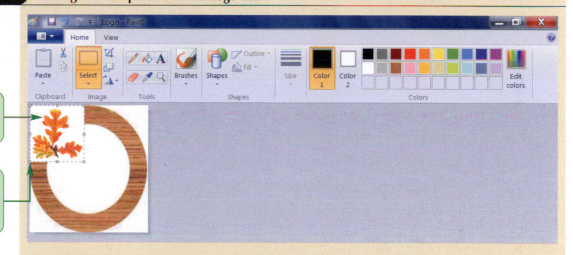

pasted image is selected in the Paint window

dashed lines and handles indicate this is a selection box

Because you need to move the oak picture, do not click anywhere in the Paint window. If you do, you remove the selection box from the oak picture and its pixels replace the ones from the logo picture underneath it.

Trouble? If you click in the Paint window and remove the selection box from the oak picture, click the Undo button 🔄 on the Quick Access Toolbar, and then repeat Steps 1 and 2.

If you make a mistake while working in Paint, click the Undo button on the Quick Access Toolbar. You can reverse your last three actions.

The selection box around the oak image indicates that you can manipulate the image by moving, copying, resizing, or deleting it. You can think of the selected image as floating on top of the frame picture because any changes you make to the oak picture do not affect the Logo file until you click to remove the selection box. You want to show Bernie how to move the oak picture to the center of the frame. You can do so by dragging the selected oak picture.

To move the selected oak image:

1. Point to the selected **oak image**. The pointer changes to ⊕.

2. Drag the **oak image** to the center of the frame, and then release the mouse button. See Figure 7-10. The oak picture is still selected, but it now appears in the middle of the frame.

Figure 7-10   **Moving the oak picture to the center of the frame**

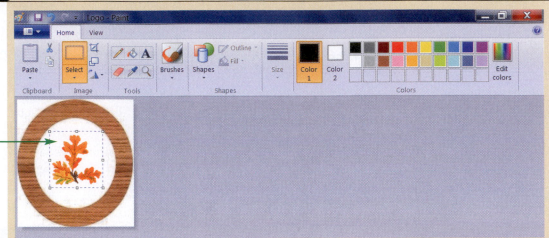

move the oak image to the middle of the frame

3. Click anywhere outside of the selected image to remove the selection box. The oak image is now part of the Logo file.

Now that you have created the first major part of the graphic, you should save the Logo file so you don't inadvertently lose your changes.

To save the Logo graphic:

1. Click the **Save** button 💾 on the Quick Access Toolbar. Paint saves the current image using the same name and location you used the last time you saved the graphic.

Next, you need to add the name of Bernie's company to the graphic to make it a true logo. According to your sketch, the company name should appear in a colored rectangle that extends to the right and left of the circular frame. Right now, there's not enough room in the graphic to accommodate this rectangle. You need to modify the graphic by resizing the canvas and then moving the image to create space for the company name.

Modifying Graphics in Paint

After you create and save an image in Paint, you can modify it by adding graphic elements, such as lines, shapes, and text; changing colors; and cropping, or removing, parts. According to your sketch for the Oak Park Landscaping logo, you need to add a text box below the oak leaves. To provide enough work space for creating the text box, you should first resize the canvas.

Resizing the Canvas and Moving an Image

When you open a graphic, it fills the canvas—the white part of the Paint window—if the graphic is the same size or larger than the canvas. If the graphic is smaller than the canvas, you can resize the canvas to fit snugly around the image. Doing so reduces file size and eliminates a border around your picture. Reducing the width or height of the canvas is one way to **crop**, or remove, a row or column of pixels from an edge of a graphic. You can also resize the canvas if you want to make it larger than the image so you can add more graphic elements to the picture. When you enlarge the canvas, the image remains in the upper-left corner of the Paint window as you drag a selection handle on the canvas to make it longer, wider, or both.

After increasing the size of the canvas, you often need to move the image so it fits more aesthetically within the enlarged space. To move all or part of an image in Paint, you first select the image using the Rectangular selection tool or the Free-form selection tool. With the Rectangular selection tool, you draw a selection box around the area you want to select. With the Free-form selection tool, you draw a line of any shape around the area. To select the entire graphic, you can click the Select button arrow and then click Select all.

TIP

You can also select an entire image by pressing the Ctrl+A keys.

To resize the canvas and then move the logo graphic:

1. Point to the selection handle in the lower-right corner of the canvas so that the pointer changes to ↘, and then begin to drag down and to the right, watching the dimensions in the middle of the status bar. See Figure 7-11.

Figure 7-11   **Resizing the canvas**

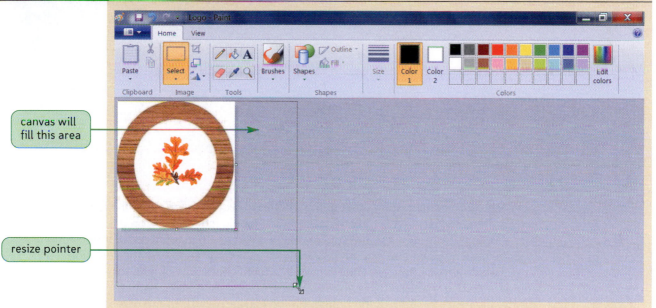

canvas will fill this area

resize pointer

2. When the dimensions are 400 × 500px, release the mouse button.

3. In the Image group, click the **Select button arrow** and then click **Select all** to select the entire graphic.

4. Drag the graphic to the upper-middle part of the canvas. See Figure 7-12.

Figure 7-12 | **Moving the logo graphic**

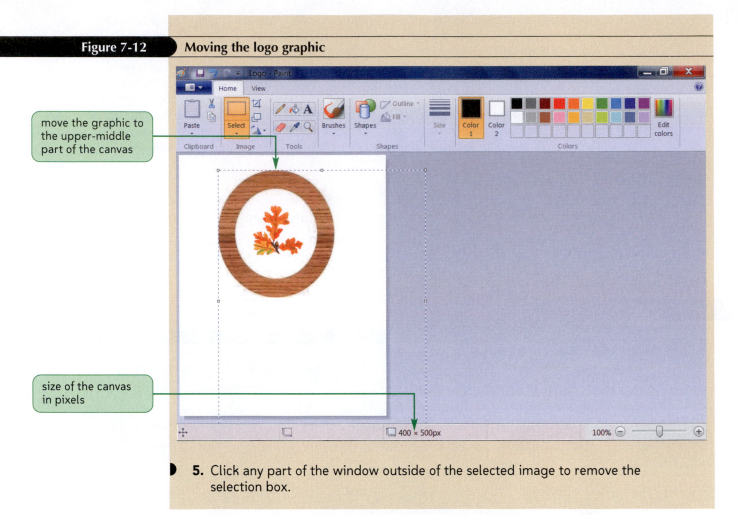

move the graphic to the upper-middle part of the canvas

size of the canvas in pixels

400 × 500px

▶ **5.** Click any part of the window outside of the selected image to remove the selection box.

When you move a graphic, part of the selection box can extend past the edges of the canvas. Because Paint saves only the part of the graphic that appears on the canvas, make sure all parts of a moved graphic appear on the canvas before you remove the selection box. You lose any part that extends past the canvas when you remove the selection.

As you've already noticed, Paint helps you identify and control your location while you are drawing shapes or dragging selections. The pixel coordinates in the status bar specify the exact location of the pointer on the canvas relative to the pixels on your screen. Paint displays the pixel coordinates in an (x,y) format (x represents the horizontal location and y the vertical location). Pixel coordinates of 138 × 25, for example, indicate that the center of the pointer is 138 pixels from the left edge of the screen and 25 pixels from the top. Using these coordinates helps you position a shape or image on the canvas and position graphic elements in relation to one another. In addition, when you draw a shape, you can use the sizing coordinates, which appear immediately to the right of the pixel coordinates, to determine the size of the shape you are dragging. For example, when you draw a text box, you might start at pixel coordinates 15 × 15 and drag with sizing coordinates of 300 × 30—so your text box is long and narrow and appears in the upper-left corner of the graphic.

Resizing the canvas and moving the image provides plenty of room for your next step—adding the company name to the graphic.

Adding Text to a Graphic

To add words to a graphic in Paint, you use the Text tool. You first use the Text tool to create a text box, and then you type your text in this box. The Text Tools Text tab opens on the Ribbon when you select the Text tool so you can select a font, size, and attributes for the text. If your text exceeds the length and width of the text box, you can drag the sizing handles to enlarge the box.

REFERENCE

Adding Text to a Graphic

- Click the Text tool and then drag a text box on the canvas.
- On the Text Tools Text tab, select a font, font size, or attributes (bold, italic, or underline).
- Type the text in the text box, using the sizing handles to resize the text box, if necessary.
- Adjust the font, font size, or attributes, and resize the text box as necessary.
- Click outside the text box.

When you add text to a graphic, by default Paint displays black text on a white rectangle. You can change these colors before you draw a shape or as you are drawing a shape and it's still selected. To do so, you change the Color 1 (foreground) and Color 2 (background) colors, which are shown to the left of the color palette. Paint uses Color 1 for lines, borders of shapes, and text. Paint uses Color 2 for the background of text rectangles and the inside color of enclosed shapes. To set a color, you click the Color 1 or Color 2 button, and then click a color in the palette. If the color palette does not contain a color you want to use, you can select one from your image using the Color picker tool. Click the Color picker tool in the Tools group on the Home tab, and then click a color in the image to change Color 1 to the color you clicked. Do the same with the right mouse button to change Color 2.

REFERENCE

Magnifying a Graphic

- To zoom in, click the Magnifier tool, and then click the graphic one or more times or drag the magnification slider to the right to increase the magnification.
- To zoom out, click the Magnifier tool, and then right-click the graphic one or more times or drag the magnification slider to the left to decrease the magnification.

According to your sketch, *Oak Park Landscaping* should appear in a colored rectangle that crosses the lower part of the round frame in the logo graphic. To match the font and style that Bernie and Hector use for other promotional materials, you'll use Verdana italic as the font and style of the text. You suggest picking a color from the oak leaves as the background color of the text box and using white as the foreground color for the text. When you use the Color picker tool to change a color, it is often helpful to zoom in, or increase the magnification of the image, so you can see the pixels of color more clearly. To do so, you can use the Magnifier tool or you can use the magnification control on the status bar. Increase the magnification by dragging the slider to the right or by clicking the Zoom in button. You can decrease the magnification, or zoom out, by dragging the slider to the left or by clicking the Zoom out button.

To zoom in and pick a color:

1. Click the **Magnifier** tool in the Tools group, and then click the center of the oak leaves image twice to increase the magnification to 300% and center the Paint window on the oak leaves. See Figure 7-13.

Figure 7-13   **Changing the magnification of the image**

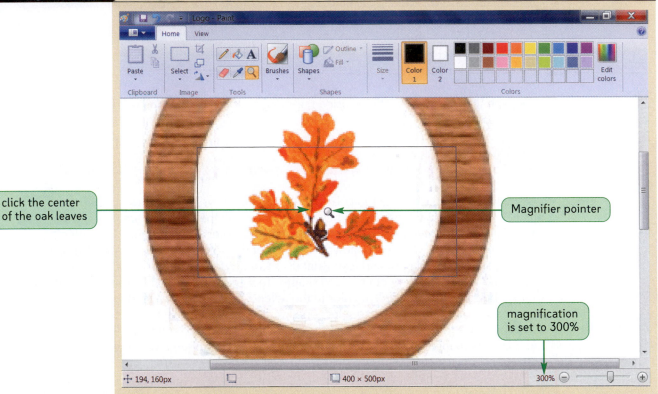

click the center of the oak leaves

Magnifier pointer

magnification is set to 300%

194, 160px   400 × 500px   300%

Trouble? If you magnified a different area of the graphic, use the scroll bars to display the center of the oak leaves as shown in Figure 7-13.

2. Click the **Color picker** tool in the Tools group, and then right-click a **dark orange pixel** in the top leaf. The Color 2 button displays the color you clicked.

Trouble? If you clicked the dark orange pixel with the left mouse button instead of the right, repeat Step 2.

3. Click the **Color 1** button in the Colors group, and then click the **white color square** in the color palette (middle row, first column). The Color 1 button displays white.

4. Click the **Zoom out** button on the status bar twice so the graphic appears at 100% zoom.

Now you are ready to use the Text tool to add the company name to the graphic. To avoid making mistakes in the current logo graphic, you'll create the text box at the bottom of the canvas and then move it. The text box you draw will be dark orange, and the text you type will be white. In addition, the text will appear with the font, size, and attributes shown on the Text Tools Text tab. The font size of the letters is measured in points, where a single point is 1/72 inch. That means a one-inch-tall character is 72 points, and a half-inch-tall character is 36 points. Attributes are characteristics of the font, including bold, italic, underline, and strikethrough. You can change the font, size, and attributes before you type, after you select the text you type, or as you edit the text. When you are satisfied with the text and its appearance, you click outside the text box, and Paint anchors the text into place, making it part of the bitmapped graphic. After the text is anchored in a graphic, you can change the font or its attributes only by deleting the text and starting over with the Text tool.

To add text to the graphic:

1. Click the **Text** tool A in the Tools group.

2. Below the framed oak leaves, drag to create a text box at least 315 pixels wide by 60 pixels tall. Refer to the left-middle part of the status bar for the size coordinates. Then release the mouse button. The Text Tools Text tab appears on the Ribbon. See Figure 7-14.

Figure 7-14   **Creating a text box**

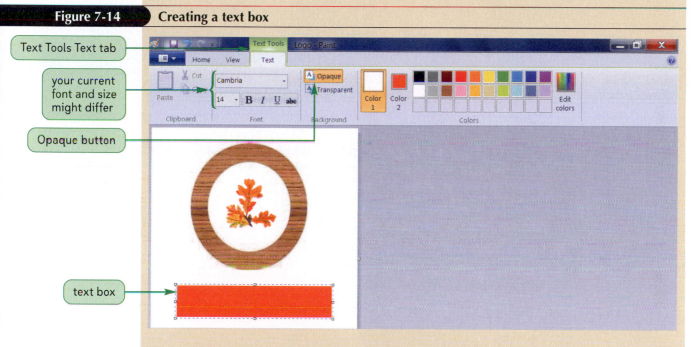

Text Tools Text tab

your current font and size might differ

Opaque button

text box

Trouble? If the text box you created is not at least 315 × 60 pixels, click outside of the selected text box, and then repeat Steps 1 and 2.

3. If necessary, click the **Opaque** button in the Background group to display the orange fill in the text box.

4. Click the **Font family button arrow** Calibri ▾ , scroll the fonts list as necessary, and then click **Verdana**.

5. Click the **Font size button arrow** 11 ▾ button, and then click **16**.

6. Click the **Italic** button I .

7. In the text box, type **Oak Park Landscaping**. See Figure 7-15.

Figure 7-15   **Adding text with the Text tool**

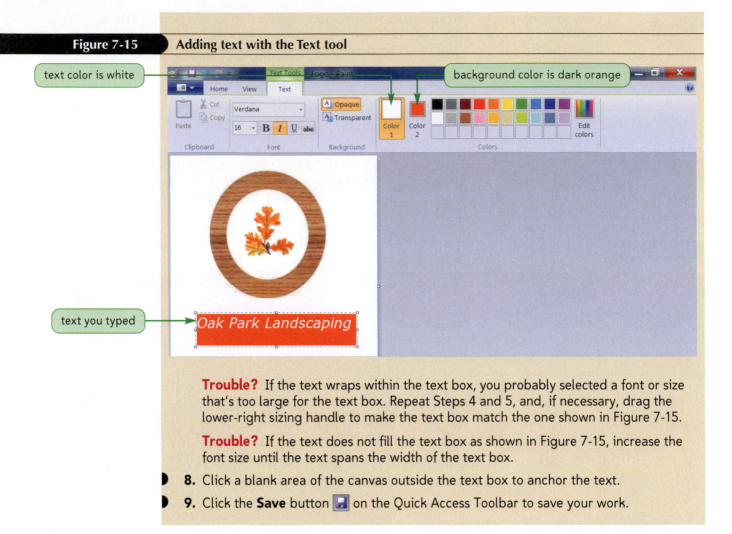

text color is white

background color is dark orange

text you typed

Trouble? If the text wraps within the text box, you probably selected a font or size that's too large for the text box. Repeat Steps 4 and 5, and, if necessary, drag the lower-right sizing handle to make the text box match the one shown in Figure 7-15.

Trouble? If the text does not fill the text box as shown in Figure 7-15, increase the font size until the text spans the width of the text box.

8. Click a blank area of the canvas outside the text box to anchor the text.

9. Click the **Save** button 🖫 on the Quick Access Toolbar to save your work.

Next, you'll show Bernie how to move the text image to another part of the graphic.

Moving Part of a Graphic

To move part of a graphic, you select the area you want to move, and then drag the selection to a new location. You can also move or copy part of a graphic using the Clipboard on the Home tab: select an area, click the Cut or Copy button in the Clipboard group, and then click the Paste button to paste the selection into the graphic, where it floats in the upper-left corner of the canvas until you drag it to the desired location.

Before you move part of a graphic, you might need to change Color 2 so it matches the surrounding area. For example, change Color 2 to white before moving the text box so the area it occupies remains orange after you move it.

When you move or copy part of a graphic using a selection tool, you can select the image with a solid background (the default) or a transparent background. Choose the Transparent selection command on the Select button list to omit the background color from the selection, so any areas using that color become transparent and allow the colors in the underlying picture to appear in its place when you move or copy the selected image. For example, if you use the Transparent selection command when you select and move a shape with a white background, the background becomes transparent when you move it to a colored area of the graphic. When the Transparent selection command is selected, it appears with a check mark on the Select button list. Remove the check mark to include the background color in your selection when you move or paste it somewhere else in the picture.

TIP

To delete an area of a graphic, select the area using a selection tool, and then press the Delete key.

Using a Solid or Transparent Background

INSIGHT

Using the Transparent selection command in Paint can be an effective way to move an image that is not rectangular, such as the oak leaves in the logo graphic. If you select the oak leaves without using the Transparent selection option and move them to an orange area of the graphic, they remain in a white rectangle. If you select them using the Transparent selection command, however, they appear against an orange background when you move them into an orange area. The Transparent selection command works best in a graphic that does not use thousands or millions of colors. A white background in a JPG file, for example, often includes hundreds of shades of white, and only one of those shades is set to be transparent when you use the Transparent selection command.

First, you'll show Bernie how to move the Oak Park Landscaping text to center it within the orange rectangle. You need to select all of the text but as little of the background as possible. To work at this level of detail, you can zoom into the graphic again before selecting the text.

To zoom in and move the text:

1. Click the **Magnifier** tool 🔍 in the Tools group, and then click the **L** in *Landscaping* in the text box. The magnification increases to 200%.

2. Click the **Select button arrow** in the Image group. If the Transparent selection command appears with a check mark, click **Transparent selection** to remove the check mark, and then click the **Select button arrow** again.

3. Click **Rectangular selection**. The pointer changes to ⌖. The Select button displays the Rectangular selection tool, and will do so until you change the type of selection.

4. Drag to select all of the text but only as much background as necessary. Then drag the selected text to the middle of the orange rectangle. See Figure 7-16.

Figure 7-16   **Moving the text within the text box**

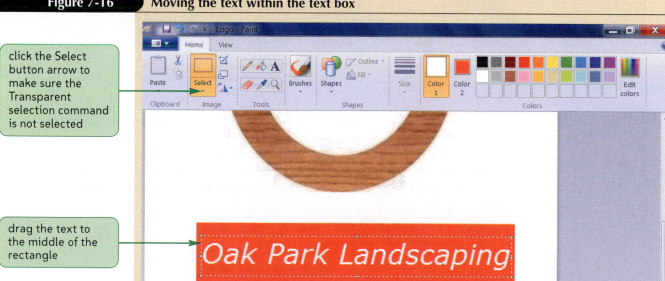

click the Select button arrow to make sure the Transparent selection command is not selected

drag the text to the middle of the rectangle

Trouble? If part of the text remains in its original location, click the Undo button 🔄 on the Quick Access Toolbar, and then repeat Steps 3 and 4.

   5. Click the **Magnifier** tool 🔍 in the Tools group, and then right-click the graphic to return to 100% zoom and remove the selection box from the text.

Because Color 2 (the background color) is still set to orange, moving the text does not introduce new colors into the text box. Before you move the entire text box, however, you need to change Color 2 to white so the area the text box now occupies doesn't remain orange after you move the text box.

To move the text box:

   1. Click the **Color 2** button in the Colors group, and then click the white color box in the palette to change the background color to white.

   2. Click the **Select** button in the Images group to use the Rectangular selection tool.

   3. Drag to select only the Oak Park Landscaping text box. A dashed outline appears around the text box. Don't include any white background in the selection.

   Trouble? If the selection box you created contains some of the white background, click outside of the selection, and then repeat Steps 2 and 3.

   4. Use the ✥ pointer to drag the text box so that it is centered just below the oak leaves. See Figure 7-17.

Figure 7-17 **Moving the text box**

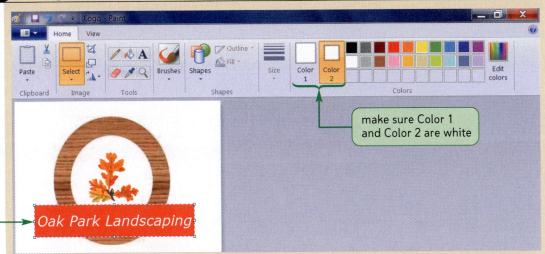

make sure Color 1 and Color 2 are white

move the text box so it doesn't overlap the oak leaves

Oak Park Landscaping

   Trouble? If the text box does not move when you drag it, but the selection box changes size, you probably dragged a sizing handle instead of the entire selection. Click the Undo button 🔄 on the Quick Access Toolbar, and then repeat Step 4.

   Trouble? If part of the orange text box remains in its original location, continue with the steps. You'll remove this part of the graphic when you resize the canvas.

   5. When the text box is in a position similar to the one shown in Figure 7-17, click a blank area of the canvas to anchor the text box into place.

   6. Click the **Save** button 💾 on the Quick Access Toolbar to save your work.

The entire image now matches your original sketch, but you and Bernie discuss adding other graphic elements to enhance the logo. In particular, you suggest adding a row of squares below the text box to balance the image and draw the eye to the company name.

Drawing Shapes

To draw closed shapes, such as squares and circles, you select a shape from the Shapes gallery, and then use it to draw a shape on the canvas. Before or after you draw a shape, you can set the following options:

- Outline: Select a style for the shape's outline. You can use a solid color, crayon, marker, oil, natural pencil, watercolor, or no outline.
- Fill: Select a style for the shape's fill, or inside area. You can use a solid color, crayon, marker, oil, natural pencil, watercolor, or no fill.
- Size: Select a width for the outline, ranging from thin to thick.
- Color 1: Select a color for the shape's outline.
- Color 2: Select a color for the shape's fill.

For example, to draw a rectangle, click the Shapes button, click the Rectangle tool, and then drag diagonally to create the shape. To draw a square, you hold down the Shift key while dragging. Similarly, you draw an ellipse, or oval, by selecting the Ellipse tool and then dragging to create the shape. To draw a circle, hold down the Shift key while dragging. While the shape is selected, you can select an outline and fill style, an outline size, and an outline and fill color. You can also set these options before you draw.

You want to add three filled squares to the left and right of the circular frame, just below the text box. You'll show Bernie how to do so using the Rectangle tool. Before you draw the shapes, you want to select a fill color. Bernie suggests using the same color as the background of the text box. You also want to zoom in on the graphic so you can work accurately.

To draw a square:

1. Click the **Magnifier** tool 🔍 in the toolbox, and then click the word **Oak** twice to magnify the left side of the text box and the area just below it by 300%.

2. Click the **Color picker** tool 🖊 in the Tools group, and then click the background of the text box to change Color 1 to dark orange. Click the **Color picker** tool 🖊 again, and then right-click the background of the text box to change Color 2 to dark orange.

3. Click the **Shapes** button in the Shapes group to display the Shapes gallery, if necessary. See Figure 7-18.

| Figure 7-18 | **Preparing to use the Rectangle tool** |

Rectangle shape

Shapes gallery

Color 2 is dark orange so the outline and fill are the same color

draw the first square here

Oak Park Landscaping

4. Click the **Rectangle** tool ☐ in the Shapes gallery.

5. Click the **Outline** button in the Shapes group, and then click **Solid color**, if necessary.

6. Click the **Fill** button in the Shapes group, and then click **Solid color**, if necessary.

7. Click the **Size** button, and then click the first size, if necessary, which draws a 1-px line.

8. Use the Drawing pointer ✛ to point to the lower-left corner of the text box, and note the pixel coordinates shown on the left side of the status bar.

9. Move the Drawing pointer ✛ about 10 pixels below the text box and at the same horizontal position so the shape you draw is left-aligned with the text box.

10. Hold down the **Shift** key, drag to draw an 11 × 11 pixel square, release the mouse button, and then release the **Shift** key. Figure 7-19 shows the square before releasing the mouse button. Your pixel coordinates may differ.

Figure 7-19 **Drawing a square**

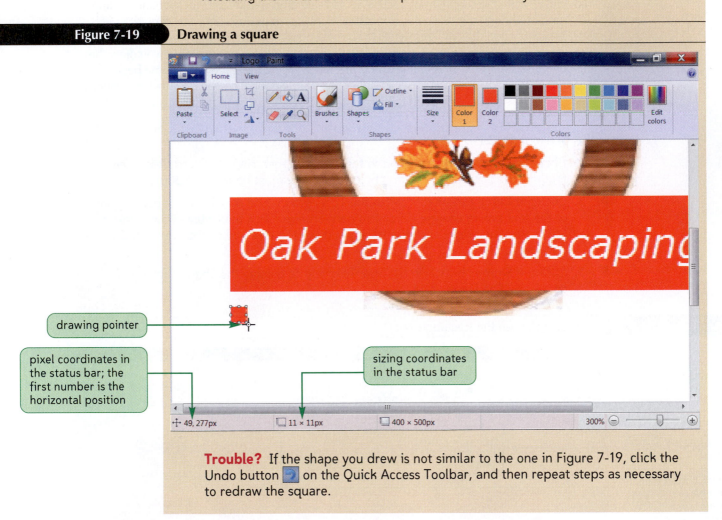

Trouble? If the shape you drew is not similar to the one in Figure 7-19, click the Undo button 🔄 on the Quick Access Toolbar, and then repeat steps as necessary to redraw the square.

The element you added is the right size and shape and is in the right position, but repeating the color from the text box doesn't create enough of a contrast. You can change the square's color to a different one in the oak leaves image to determine if that suits the design of the logo.

Changing Colors

You can add color to a graphic by choosing colors as you draw or applying color to shapes after you finish drawing them. Before you use a drawing tool, you can select a color for the line or shape, as you did when you drew the text box and the square. If you want to add color to an existing image or color a large area of an image, you use the Fill with color tool. When you use the Fill with color tool to click a pixel in a graphic, Paint changes the color of that pixel to Color 1. To change the color to Color 2, right-click a pixel with the Fill with color tool. If adjacent pixels are the same color as the one you clicked, Paint also changes those colors to Color 1. In this way, you can use the Fill with color tool to fill any enclosed area with color. Make sure the area you click is a fully enclosed space. If it has any openings, the new color will extend past the boundaries of the area you are trying to color.

REFERENCE

Filling an Area with Color

- Click the Fill with color tool.
- Click the Color 1 button, if necessary, and then click the desired color in the color palette.
- Click inside the border of the area you want to color.

You suggest to Bernie that a contrasting color, such as the green that appears in the lower-left oak leaf, would make the squares more appealing, and you offer to show him how to quickly change the color of the square you drew.

To change the color of the square:

1. Click the **Color picker** tool in the Tools group, and then click a green pixel in the lower-left oak leaf to change the foreground color to medium olive green.

2. Click the **Fill with color** tool and move the pointer into the graphic. The pointer changes to a paint can , indicating that any pixel you click will change to the foreground color.

3. Click inside the **square** to change its color from dark orange to medium olive green. See Figure 7-20.

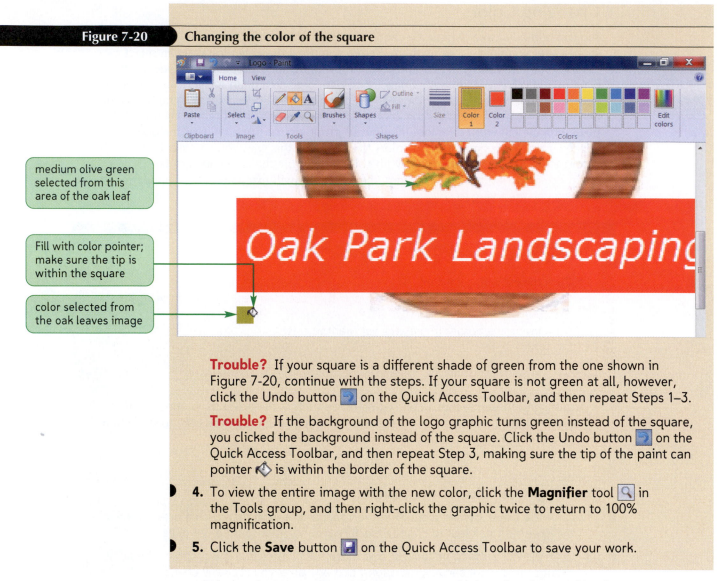

Figure 7-20   Changing the color of the square

medium olive green selected from this area of the oak leaf

Fill with color pointer; make sure the tip is within the square

color selected from the oak leaves image

Trouble? If your square is a different shade of green from the one shown in Figure 7-20, continue with the steps. If your square is not green at all, however, click the Undo button on the Quick Access Toolbar, and then repeat Steps 1–3.

Trouble? If the background of the logo graphic turns green instead of the square, you clicked the background instead of the square. Click the Undo button on the Quick Access Toolbar, and then repeat Step 3, making sure the tip of the paint can pointer is within the border of the square.

4. To view the entire image with the new color, click the **Magnifier** tool in the Tools group, and then right-click the graphic twice to return to 100% magnification.

5. Click the **Save** button on the Quick Access Toolbar to save your work.

Coloring the square green creates contrast, which makes that graphic element more interesting. Now you can complete the logo graphic by copying the square so three squares appear to the left of the circular frame and three appear to the right of the frame.

Copying an Image

Recall that to copy an image, you use a method similar to the one used for moving an image: you select the area you want to copy, copy it to the Clipboard, and then paste it in your graphic. Because the copied image appears in a selection box in the upper-left corner of the graphic, you usually must drag the image to a new location after pasting it. You'll show Bernie how to copy the green square and then paste it to create a row of three squares in the lower-left area of the logo graphic. To create an appealing arrangement, you must make sure that the squares are evenly spaced and that their tops and bottoms are aligned. When the bottoms of the squares are aligned, for example, the lower edge of each square is on the same row of the bitmap grid. To space and align shapes effectively, you can display a grid when positioning the shapes. The grid does not become a part of the graphic—it is only a visual guide that appears in the Paint window. You'll show Bernie how to display the grid when you magnify the graphic to copy and paste the square.

To copy and paste the square:

◗ **1.** Click the **Magnifier** tool 🔍 in the Tools group, if necessary, and then click the **green square** three times to magnify the image 400%.

◗ **2.** Click the **View** tab, and then click the **Gridlines** check box to display a grid in the Paint window.

◗ **3.** Click the **Home** tab on the Ribbon, click the **Select** button in the Image group, and then drag to select only the **green square**. See Figure 7-21.

Figure 7-21   Selecting the square to copy it

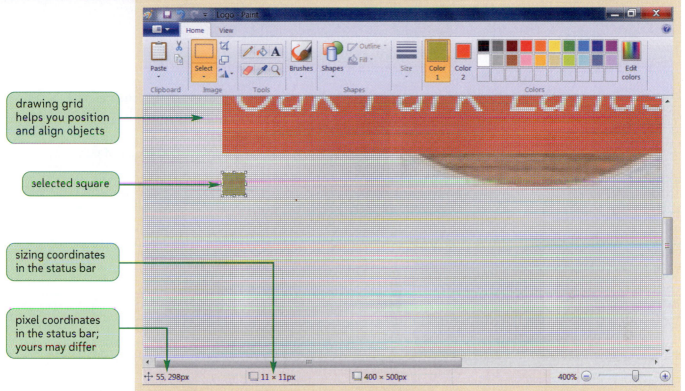

drawing grid helps you position and align objects

selected square

sizing coordinates in the status bar

pixel coordinates in the status bar; yours may differ

55, 298px   11 × 11px   400 × 500px   400%

Trouble? If the selection box includes part of the background or does not include the entire green square, click outside the selection box and repeat Step 3.

◗ **4.** Click the **Copy** button 📋 in the Clipboard group to copy the square to the Clipboard.

◗ **5.** Click the **Paste** button to paste the square in the upper-left corner of the Paint window.

◗ **6.** Drag the selected square next to the first square, leaving about 11 pixels of white space, or 11 dots on the grid, between the two shapes. In other words, the white space between the squares should be the same width as each square. If necessary, drag the selected square up or down to adjust its vertical and align it with the first square. Its lower edge should be on the same row of the grid as the lower edge of the first square.

◗ **7.** Click the **Paste** button again to paste another copy of the square in the upper-left corner of the Paint window.

◗ **8.** Drag the selected square next to the first two squares, again leaving about 11 pixels of white space between the second and third squares and positioning the square vertically to align its bottom with the other two squares. See Figure 7-22.

Figure 7-22   **Pasting and positioning a copy of the square**

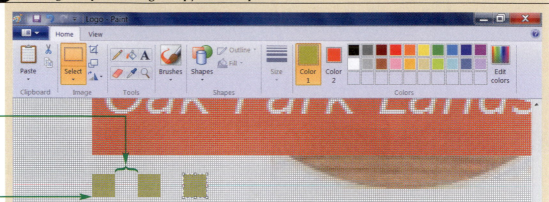

allow about 11 pixels between each square

align the bottoms of the three squares on the same row of the grid

Trouble? If the three squares are not evenly spaced or bottom-aligned, click the Color 2 button, click the white square, use the Select tool to select a square, and then drag it to change its position to match the squares in Figure 7-22.

9. Click outside the selection, and then point to the bottom edge of a green square. Note the vertical coordinate of this pixel (the second number in the pair of numbers on the left side of the status bar).

10. To view the entire image with the three squares, click the **Zoom out** button ⊖ on the status bar three times to return to 100% magnification.

Now you can copy the three squares to the right side of the graphic to balance the image. To copy the squares precisely, you'll magnify the view again.

To copy and paste the three squares:

1. Click the **Magnifier** tool 🔍 in the Tools group, and then click the **middle green square** three times to magnify the image 400%.

2. Click the **Select** button in the Image group, and then drag to select the **three green squares**. This time, it doesn't matter if some of the background is included in the selection box. Be sure, however, that the selection box includes all parts of the three squares.

3. Click the **Copy** button 📋 in the Clipboard group to copy the squares to the Clipboard.

4. Drag the bottom scroll bar to the right to display the right side of the Oak Park Landscaping text box.

5. Click the **Paste** button in the Clipboard group to paste the squares in the upper-left corner of the Paint window.

6. Drag the selected squares below the Oak Park Landscaping text box so that the right edge of the third square aligns with the right edge of the text box, and then click outside of the selection box.

7. Point to the lower-right corner of the third square, and then look in the status bar to find its position. The vertical coordinate should match the one you noted in the previous set of steps. See Figure 7-23.

Figure 7-23 | Displaying the position of the squares

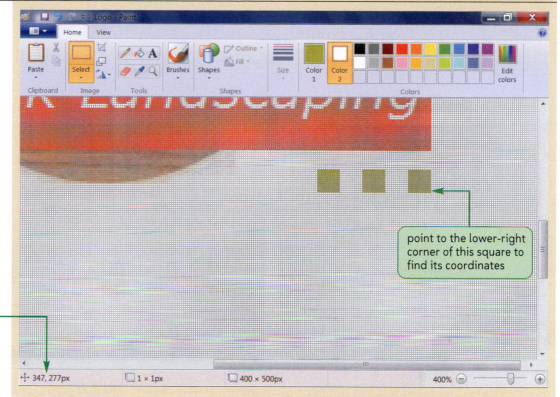

coordinates of far-right square; yours may differ

point to the lower-right corner of this square to find its coordinates

8. If necessary, select the three squares again, click the **Color 2** button in the Colors group, click the **white** square in the palette, and then drag the squares to align with the text box and the three squares on the left side of the graphic.

9. To hide the grid, click the **View** tab, and then click the **Gridlines** check box to remove the grid from the canvas.

10. To view the logo image with all graphic elements, click the **Zoom out** button ⊖ in the Zoom group three times to return to 100% magnification. See Figure 7-24.

Figure 7-24 | Logo with all graphic elements

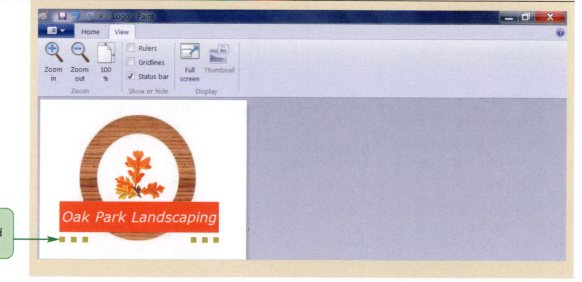

two groups of squares arranged in a row

Your graphic doesn't have to look exactly like Figure 7-24, but it should look similar. Your last task is to position the image on the canvas to minimize the amount of unnecessary white space in the graphic.

Cropping a Graphic

Recall that you can crop an image to remove one or more rows or columns of pixels from the edge of a picture. When you crop a graphic to eliminate unnecessary white space by resizing the canvas, you reduce file size and prevent a border from appearing around your picture when you paste it into another file. Before you crop the white space from the logo graphic, you should move the image into the upper-left corner of the Paint window. Then you can drag the canvas to fit tightly around the image.

To move and crop the logo graphic:

1. Click the **Home** tab, click the **Select button arrow** in the Image group, and then click **Select all**.

2. Drag the image to the upper-left corner of the Paint window, making sure that the entire image appears in the window. See Figure 7-25. Then click outside the canvas to remove the selection.

Figure 7-25 **Dragging the image before cropping**

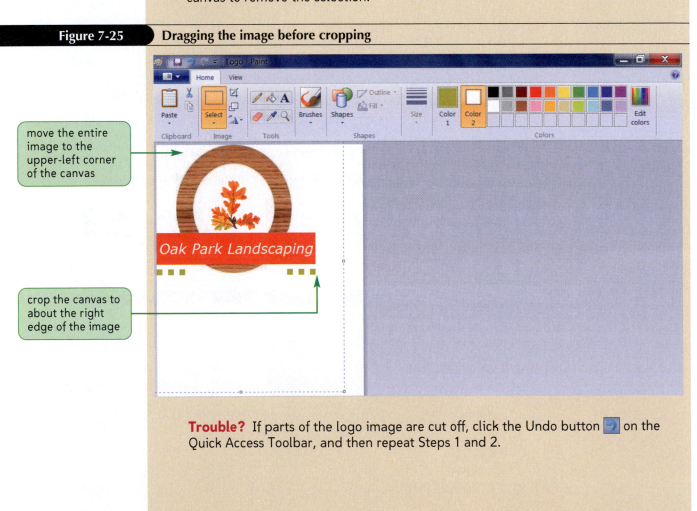

move the entire image to the upper-left corner of the canvas

crop the canvas to about the right edge of the image

Trouble? If parts of the logo image are cut off, click the Undo button ↪ on the Quick Access Toolbar, and then repeat Steps 1 and 2.

3. Point to the sizing handle on the lower-right corner of the canvas, and then drag it to reduce the size of the canvas so that it fits tightly around the graphic without hiding any part of it. See Figure 7-26.

Figure 7-26   **Completed Logo graphic**

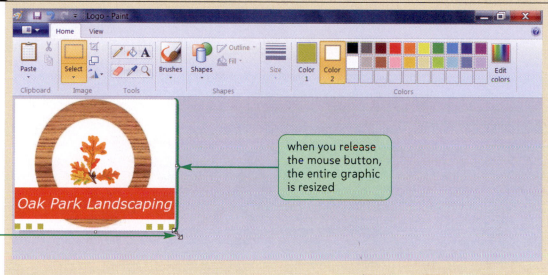

> when you release the mouse button, the entire graphic is resized

> resize pointer

Trouble? If you made the canvas too small so that parts of the logo image are cut off, click the Undo button on the Quick Access Toolbar, and then repeat Step 3.

Cropping is the best way to resize a bitmapped graphic. Although you can resize a graphic in Paint to make the entire image larger or smaller, recall that the results are often disappointing. Because you cannot change the size of an individual pixel, resizing the overall image tends to distort it. For example, when you try to enlarge a bitmapped graphic, Paint duplicates the pixels to approximate the original shape as best it can—often resulting in jagged edges. On the other hand, when you shrink a bitmapped graphic, Paint removes pixels and the graphic loses detail. In either case, you distort the original graphic. Sometimes the resized bitmapped graphic looks fine, such as when it contains many straight lines, but just as often the resized graphic's image quality suffers. For example, Figure 7-27 shows how the current logo image looks when it's enlarged.

Figure 7-27   Enlarging a bitmapped graphic

edges appear jagged

How do you bypass this problem? In Paint, there is no easy solution to resizing graphics because they are all bitmapped. If your work with graphics requires resizing—for example, if you want a graphic that looks good on a small business card and a large poster—using vector graphics is a better choice. Because vector graphics are mathematically based, you can resize them as necessary without sacrificing image quality. You need to buy a graphics program that allows you to work with vector graphics.

You've completed the graphic for Oak Park Landscaping, so you can save the Logo file and close Paint.

To save the file and close Paint:

1. Click the **Save** button 💾 on the Quick Access Toolbar.

2. Close the Paint window.

Now that you've shown Bernie how to use Paint to create and modify bitmapped graphics, you can get ready to work with Hector to develop a multimedia presentation.

REVIEW

Session 7.1 Quick Check

1. Computer graphics come in two fundamental types: vector and _____.
2. Name five graphic file formats you can use in Paint.
3. What command do you use to copy an entire image from another file and paste it in your current image?
4. True or False. Reducing the size of the canvas reduces the file size.
5. When you draw a shape, _____ controls the color of the shape's outline or border, and _____ controls its fill or inside color.
6. To position shapes precisely, you can display _____ in the Paint window.
7. The _____ graphic file format efficiently compresses photographic images.

SESSION 7.2 VISUAL OVERVIEW

The Pictures library toolbar contains tools for working with photos.

Click the Slide show button in the Pictures library to play a simple slide show.

This photo has a problem with **contrast**, which is the difference between the brightest and darkest parts of the picture.

You can organize images in the Pictures library or its folders by Rating, Tag, or Date.

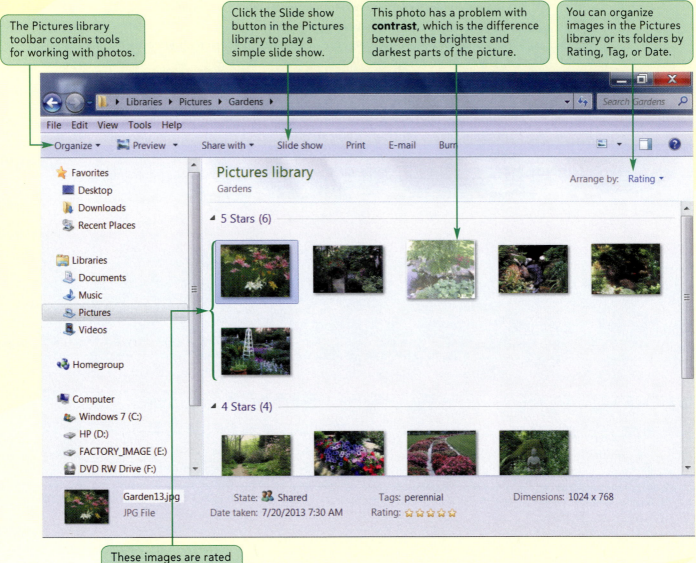

These images are rated with five stars.

WINDOWS 7 PHOTO TOOLS

Windows Media Center is designed to display moving images, such as slide shows and videos.

Click select all to add all photos in this folder to a slide show.

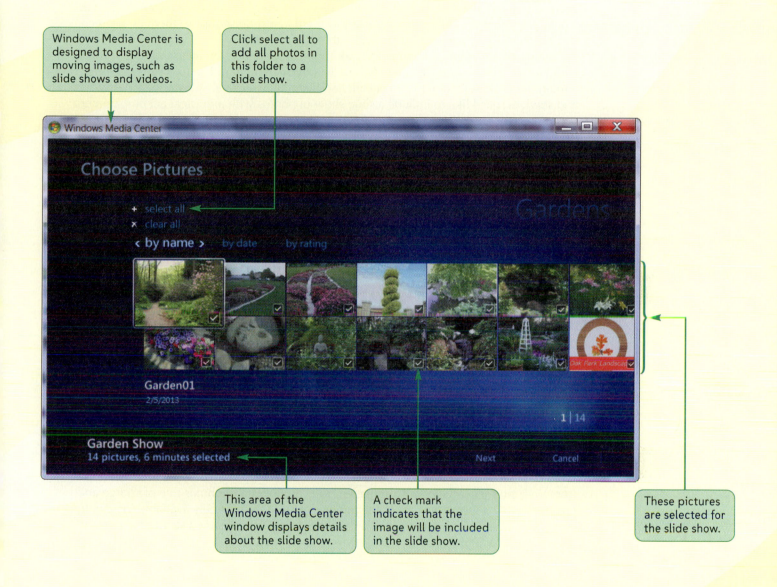

This area of the Windows Media Center window displays details about the slide show.

A check mark indicates that the image will be included in the slide show.

These pictures are selected for the slide show.

Working with Photos

Innovations in digital cameras and computers have transformed the field of photography, letting anyone edit and print photos without using a darkroom or professional photo lab. Instead, you can transfer photos from your digital camera to your Windows 7 computer, where you can fine-tune the images, display them in a slide show, use them as a screen saver or wallpaper, and share them with others.

As a part-time graphic designer for Oak Park Landscaping, you are preparing to work with Hector Torres, one of two partners in the landscaping firm. Hector wants to create a multimedia presentation that Oak Park Landscaping can use to showcase its designs and services. He'd like to include a slide show of photos with a musical accompaniment in the presentation. Hector has already transferred photos of landscaping projects from his digital camera to his computer. You'll show him how to view, organize, and edit the photos so he can assemble them into a slide show to play at landscaping trade shows and expositions.

Acquiring and Importing Photos

Before you can create a slide show on your computer, you need to acquire and then import photos. The most popular way to acquire photos is to use a digital camera to take the photos. Cameras store photos as JPG image files, so you can work with them using any photo editor or painting graphics program. Using a digital camera lets you control the subject matter and maintain the legal rights to the images, two notable advantages. Unless you're a trained photographer, the main disadvantage is that your images are not professional quality, though you often can improve them using digital editing tools. If you are using the photos for the enjoyment of family and friends, you might not need to do more than snap the photos on your digital camera and then transfer them to your Windows 7 computer.

If you need professional photos, such as for a product brochure or company Web site, you have a few options. Hiring a photographer to create and prepare the images can be effective, though expensive. You can also purchase stock photo collections, typically provided on a CD or DVD. These collections usually contain royalty-free images that you can use for any purpose, and cost anywhere from thousands of dollars to under $20 for hundreds or thousands of images. As mentioned earlier, you can also purchase photos from Web sites, usually for a licensing fee. You can download photos free of charge and copyright only if the photos are in the public domain and are freely available for use. If you have conventional photographs printed on paper, you can use a scanner to convert the photos into digital pictures if you own the copyright.

Decision Making: Using Copyright-Protected, Royalty-Free, and Public-Domain Photos

Many school and work projects involve graphics. Where and how to acquire graphics is often a decision you need to make early in the project, one that can have legal consequences. Although you can easily copy photos displayed on Web sites, that doesn't mean that you should. Most photos and other media on the Web are protected by copyright law. A copyright gives photographers (and other types of graphic artists and creators) the exclusive right to control their images. They can decide who can copy, distribute, or derive material from their photographs. Before you can use a copyrighted photo, you must receive permission from the photographer.

Some Web sites and services offer royalty-free photos, meaning that the photographers do not receive payment each time their photos are used. However, the photographers still retain the rights to the photos even if they don't receive royalties for each use. Only photos in the public domain are not protected by copyright law. These include photos for which the copyright has expired, some government images, and those explicitly identified as being in the public domain.

If you want to copy photos from the Web or another digital source, the following guidelines help you respect the photographer's rights:

- Ask the owner of the copyright for permission.
- Find out if the photographer has any stipulations on how the material may be used.
- If explicit guidelines are given, follow them, and credit the source of your material.
- Keep a copy of your request and the permission received.

If you acquire photos from a Web site, CD, or DVD, you only have to copy them to a folder on your computer so you can edit and organize them. However, if you are using a digital camera, including one in your cell phone, you need to perform an additional step of importing the photo files from your camera or cell phone to your computer. One way to do this is to connect the device directly to the computer using a cable that plugs into the computer's USB port. Another way is to import pictures using a memory card reader, a device that plugs into your computer's USB port. Most digital cameras store pictures on a flash memory card. If you have a memory card reader attached to your computer, you can remove the memory card from your camera and then slide it into the card reader to import the photos stored on the card. In either case, Windows 7 should recognize your camera or card (it recognizes most makes and models of digital cameras and cards), and guide you through the steps of importing pictures. You have the chance to add tags to the photo files so you can identify them easily later, to erase the image files on your camera or card so you can use it to store more photos, and to correct your picture's rotation, if necessary. After importing the images, Windows 7 stores them in the Pictures library by default.

Viewing and Organizing Photos

Windows 7 provides a number of tools for working with photos. Although some of these tools have features in common, each one is designed to serve a particular purpose, as explained in the following descriptions:

- Pictures library: The Pictures library and its folders are the best places to store your digital photos because they offer tools that are not available in other folders. For example, you can use the Slide show button to play the photos in the current folder as a full-screen slide show. You can also use the Search box in the Pictures library to quickly find photos stored anywhere on your computer, which is particularly helpful if you have dozens or hundreds of photos, as many people do. Other tools, such as the Windows Media Center, detect the photos stored in the Pictures library so you can quickly create a slide show or touch them up.

- Windows Photo Viewer: Although Windows Photo Viewer is not a separate program you can open from the Start menu, it is a full-featured tool you can open from the Pictures library. When you double-click a photo in a folder window, it opens in Windows Photo Viewer by default. The Pictures library and Windows Photo Viewer share many features. For example, you can view pictures, print pictures, and see a slide show of your pictures from either the Pictures library or Windows Photo Viewer. However, while the Pictures library is designed to help you find and organize photos by displaying all of them in one place, Windows Photo Viewer lets you concentrate on each photo one at a time. You can rotate photos, zoom in, and view photos at full size.
- Windows Media Center: This tool is designed to be the entertainment hub of your computer. You can record and play television shows, play home videos, import photos from your digital camera, and view the photos stored in the Pictures library. Similar to the Pictures library and Windows Photo Viewer, you can create a slide show; though in Windows Media Center, you can play music or audio files at the same time.
- Windows Live Photo Gallery: Part of Windows Live Essentials, Windows Live Photo Gallery lets you import, organize, edit, and share photos and videos. You can download Windows Live Photo Gallery from the Windows Live Web site (*home.live.com*). Because the other three tools included with Windows 7 provide many of the same features, this tutorial does not cover Windows Live Photo Gallery.

You might have additional photo-editing tools installed on your computer. These tools are often provided by digital camera and computer manufacturers.

Your first task in developing a presentation with Hector is to review the photos he has taken of Oak Park Landscaping's gardening and landscaping projects. Start by copying the photos in your Tutorial folder to a subfolder of the Pictures library.

To copy photo files to the Pictures library:

1. Open a folder window that displays the contents of the Tutorial.07\Tutorial folder provided with your Data Files.

2. Copy the 13 garden photos (**Garden01–Garden13**) to a new folder in the Pictures library named **Gardens**.

3. Open and maximize the **Gardens** folder window.

Be sure to create the Gardens folder in the Pictures library so you can use tools special to the Picture library.

Now you can show Hector how to use the Pictures library and Windows Photo Viewer to display, examine, and organize photos.

To examine photos using the Pictures library:

1. In the Gardens folder window, switch to Details view, if necessary, by clicking the **Change your view button arrow** and then clicking **Details**.

2. Make sure the Name, Date modified, Tags, Size, and Rating columns are displayed in the Gardens folder window. If necessary, right-click a column heading and then click to check or uncheck column names so they match the ones shown in Figure 7-28.

Figure 7-28   **Displaying the Gardens folder photos in the Pictures library**

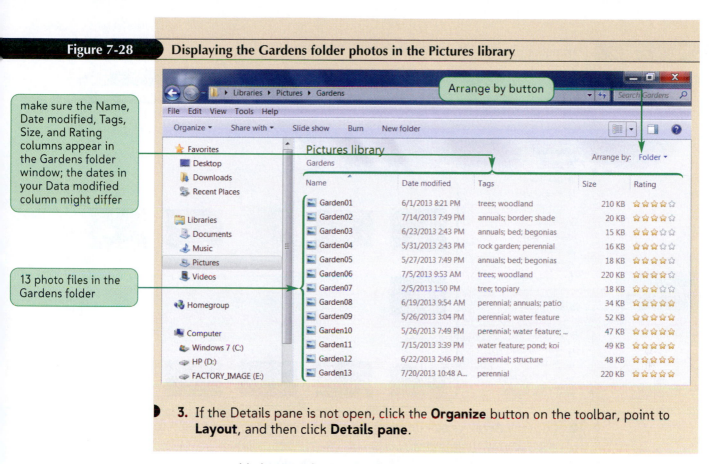

make sure the Name, Date modified, Tags, Size, and Rating columns appear in the Gardens folder window; the dates in your Data modified column might differ

13 photo files in the Gardens folder

Arrange by button

Pictures library

Arrange by: Folder ▼

Name	Date modified	Tags	Size	Rating
Garden01	6/1/2013 8:21 PM	trees; woodland	210 KB	☆☆☆☆☆
Garden02	7/14/2013 7:49 PM	annuals; border; shade	20 KB	☆☆☆☆☆
Garden03	6/23/2013 2:43 PM	annuals; bed; begonias	15 KB	☆☆☆☆☆
Garden04	5/31/2013 2:43 PM	rock garden; perennial	16 KB	☆☆☆☆☆
Garden05	5/27/2013 7:49 PM	annuals; bed; begonias	18 KB	☆☆☆☆☆
Garden06	7/5/2013 9:53 AM	trees; woodland	220 KB	☆☆☆☆☆
Garden07	2/5/2013 1:50 PM	tree; topiary	18 KB	☆☆☆☆☆
Garden08	6/19/2013 9:54 AM	perennial; annuals; patio	34 KB	☆☆☆☆☆
Garden09	5/26/2013 3:04 PM	perennial; water feature	52 KB	☆☆☆☆☆
Garden10	5/26/2013 7:49 PM	perennial; water feature; ...	47 KB	☆☆☆☆☆
Garden11	7/15/2013 3:39 PM	water feature; pond; koi	49 KB	☆☆☆☆☆
Garden12	6/22/2013 2:46 PM	perennial; structure	48 KB	☆☆☆☆☆
Garden13	7/20/2013 10:48 A...	perennial	220 KB	☆☆☆☆☆

3. If the Details pane is not open, click the **Organize** button on the toolbar, point to **Layout**, and then click **Details pane**.

Hector added tags and ratings to these photos when he imported them to the computer. You can use the tags, ratings, and other details to arrange the photos so they are easier to reference. For example, Hector often needs to refer to garden photos by date so he can see which photos show gardens at their peak in May, for example. He might also want to select all the photos of gardens with water features or all those he rated with five stars. You'll show him how to use the Pictures library to arrange the photos.

To arrange the garden photos:

1. Click the **Arrange by** button, which displays *Folder* by default, and then click **Rating**. The photos are arranged into three sections: 5 Stars, 4 Stars, and 3 Stars. See Figure 7-29.

Figure 7-29 ▶ **Arranging photos by Rating**

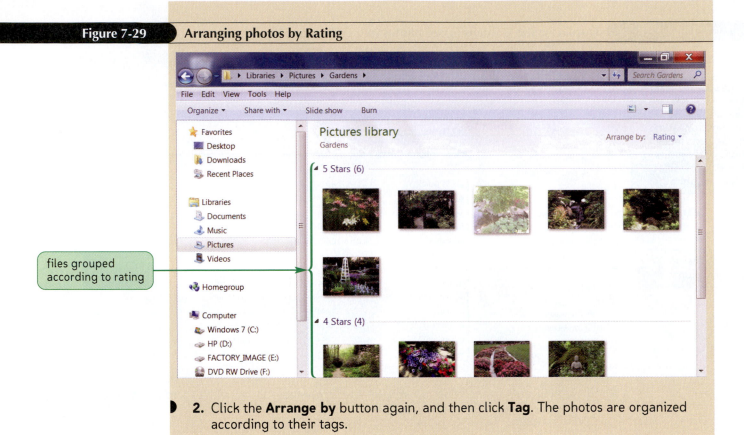

files grouped according to rating

2. Click the **Arrange by** button again, and then click **Tag**. The photos are organized according to their tags.

3. To return to folder view, click the **Arrange by** button, and then click **Folder**.

As you've seen, the Pictures library lets you see all your photos in one place and then arrange them by date, rating, or other criteria. Now you want to show Hector how to use Windows Photo Viewer so he can compare the two tools.

To view photos using Windows Photo Viewer:

1. In the Gardens folder window, click the **Garden01** photo, and then click the **Preview** button on the toolbar. The photo opens in Windows Photo Viewer. See Figure 7-30.

   Trouble? If the Garden01 photo does not open in Windows Photo Viewer, click the Garden01 photo, click the Preview button arrow on the toolbar, and then click Windows Photo Viewer.

Figure 7-30   Windows Photo Viewer

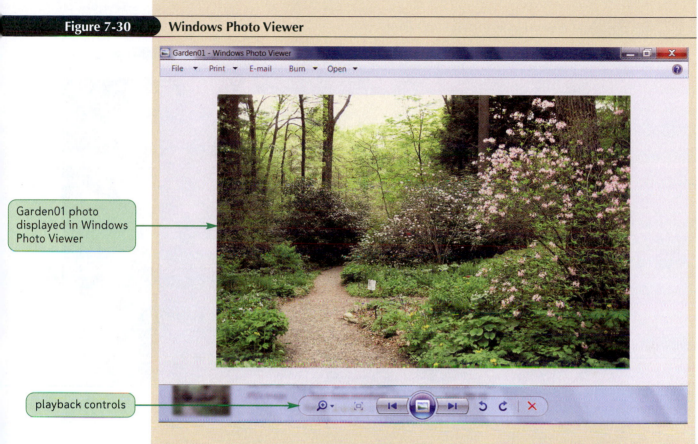

Garden01 photo displayed in Windows Photo Viewer

playback controls

2. To view the photos in the Gardens folder in sequence, click the **Next (Right arrow)** button ▶| on the navigation bar six times, until you display the Garden07 photo, which shows a topiary tree. This photo needs to be rotated.

3. Click the **Rotate counterclockwise** button ↺ on the navigation bar. Now the tree appears upright as it should.

4. Continue clicking the **Next (Right arrow)** button ▶| on the navigation bar until you display the Garden13 photo, which shows a garden of lilies. Hector wants to zoom in on the light pink flowers in the background.

5. Click the **Changes the display size** button ⊕▾ on the navigation bar, and then drag the slider button about halfway up the slider bar.

6. Point to the photo to display a hand pointer 🖐 and then drag the photo to the left to bring the light pink flowers into view. See Figure 7-31. Now Hector can identify those as miniature roses.

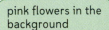

Figure 7-31 Magnified view of Garden13 photo

pink flowers in the background

hand pointer in Windows Photo Viewer; drag the image to scroll

Fit to window button

Changes the display size button

▶ **7.** To display this photo at its original size, click the **Fit to window** button 🔲 on the navigation bar.

Besides examining and rotating photos, you can play a simple slide show in Windows Photo Viewer. Hector wants to play a slide show of Oak Park Landscaping projects when he and Bernie go to gardening and landscaping expositions.

Playing a Simple Slide Show

You can play a simple slide show in the Pictures library by clicking the Slide Show button on the toolbar, or in Windows Photo Viewer by clicking the round Play Slide Show button on the navigation bar. In either case, the slide show includes all the photos in your current folder and its subfolders, and plays the photos one after another at various speeds. You can also create more sophisticated slide shows and save them on a CD or DVD, which you will do later in this session.

REFERENCE

Playing a Slide Show

- In the Pictures library window, click the Slide show button on the toolbar.

or

- In Windows Photo Viewer, click the Play slide show button on the navigation bar.

During a slide show, Windows Photo Viewer displays photos as a full-screen slide show that runs automatically. The slide show plays all the photos in the current folder, starting with the selected photo or the first one if none is selected. While a slide show is running, you can right-click a photo to pause the show, adjust the speed, go forward or backward, and choose whether pictures are shown randomly or sequentially.

While you are playing the simple slide show, you can examine Hector's photos again and see if any need adjustments to fix problems such as washed-out colors.

To play a simple slide show:

1. In Windows Photo Viewer, click the **Play slide show** button 🖼 on the navigation bar. The monitor darkens, and then Windows Photo Viewer fills the screen with the current photo, displays it for a few seconds, and then displays the next photo.

2. To slow the slide show so you can examine the photos, right-click a slide and then click **Slide Show Speed - Slow** on the shortcut menu.

3. After viewing one photo that appears washed out (Garden09, a pond with dark pink flowers) and another that could be cropped (Garden04, a rock garden), right-click a slide, click **Slide Show Speed - Medium** on the shortcut menu to return to the default speed, and then press the **Esc** key to end the slide show.

4. Close Windows Photo Viewer.

Hector says that a simple slide show isn't catchy enough to attract new customers. He also wants to play music while displaying the photos. You'll show him how to create such a slide show later. Right now, you want to edit a couple of photos in the Gardens folder. You found at least two photos that could be improved with a few touch-ups. You'll show Hector how to fix these photos next.

Editing Photos

Windows Media Center is included in most editions of Windows 7, including Home Premium, Professional, Ultimate, and Enterprise. If you connect your computer to a high-definition TV, you can use a Media Center remote to control the television shows you watch, pause, and record. You can also use Media Center to view photos and videos in a TV-like environment. To get the most out of your photos, Media Center provides photo-editing tools for correcting common problems such as red eye from flash photos, dark or washed-out images, and unbalanced composition. You can touch up photos in Windows Media Center in the following ways:

- Red Eye: If you used a flash when snapping a photo of one or more people, their eyes might appear red in the picture, a common problem caused by the flash reflecting off the eyes. Reduce or eliminate this effect by replacing the red with a more natural black.
- Contrast: Photos with inaccurate contrast are too bright or too dark. Correct this problem by letting Media Center adjust the contrast (the difference between the brightest and darkest parts of the picture).
- Crop: Improve the composition of your picture by trimming distracting or unnecessary elements. You crop a picture by dragging to select the part of the picture you want to keep.

The first time you start Windows Media Center, a setup page opens with information about various features, as well as two setup options: Express and Custom. If you have not already set up Media Center, click the Express option unless your instructor specifically instructs you not to do so. You can return to the Custom setup later by running setup again, if necessary.

Now you can show Hector how to improve the quality of a couple of photos. The colors in Garden09 are washed out, which probably means the contrast is unbalanced. You think you can also improve the composition of the rock garden in Garden04 by cropping that photo.

To use Windows Media Center to touch up photos:

1. Click any photo in the Gardens folder window.

2. Click the **Preview button arrow** on the toolbar, and then click **Windows Media Center**. Windows Media Center starts and displays the folders in the Pictures library, including the Gardens folder.

   Trouble? If this is the first time you are starting Windows Media Center, click the Express option on the setup page. Follow any instructions to import media and return to the main Media Center page. If necessary, click Pictures + Videos to open the Pictures library.

3. Click **Gardens** to open that folder in Windows Media Center.

4. Point to the photos until you find Garden09, which is washed out. Right-click **Garden09**, and then click **Picture Details** on the shortcut menu.

5. Click **Touch Up** to display Garden09 in the Media Center window, ready to be touched up. See Figure 7-32.

Figure 7-32   **Fixing a photo problem in Windows Media Center**

your window might open maximized or in a different size

photo with a contrast problem

options for fixing photos

your playback controls appear here when you first open the window

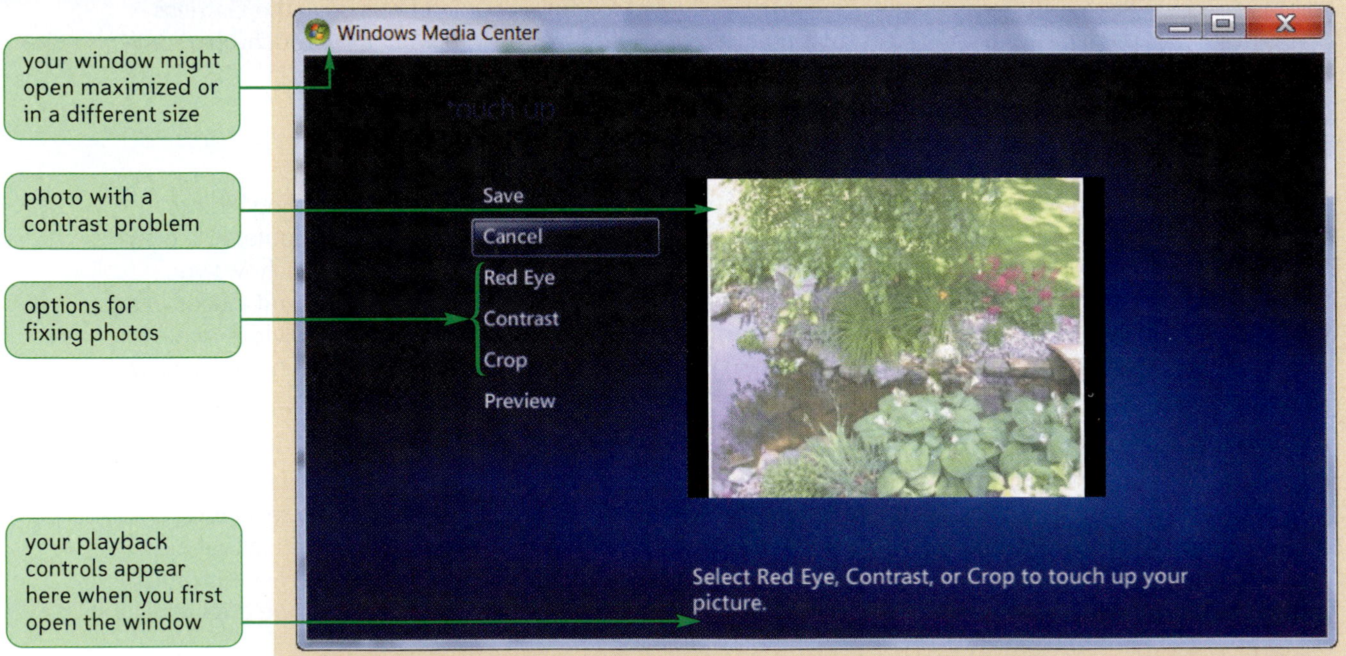

6. To correct the contrast problems in this photo, click **Contrast**. Windows Media Center corrects the contrast problem.

7. Click **Save** to keep the changes, and then click the **Yes** button to confirm.

8. Point to the Media Center window, and then click the **Back** button to return to the Gardens folder.

Touching up the Garden09 file fixed the contrast problems in the photo of a pond. Now you're ready to improve the composition of the rock garden photo. You want to crop out most of the rocks on the right side of the photo so the focus is on the three plants.

To crop a photo:

1. Right-click **Garden04**, which shows a rock garden, click **Picture Details** on the shortcut menu, and then click **Touch Up**.

2. Click **Crop** to crop the photo. A cropping frame appears in the middle of the photo. The area you want to preserve is taller than it is wide, so you need to rotate the frame.

3. Click the **Rotate Frame** button 🔄. The cropping frame now appears taller than it is wide.

4. Click the **Left Arrow** button ◀ as many times as necessary to move the cropping frame to the left edge of the photo. See Figure 7-33.

Figure 7-33	Cropping a photo

rotated cropping frame

click an arrow button to move the frame

depending on how you set up Media Center, you might see additional controls at the bottom of the window

click a magnifier button to increase or decrease the size of the frame

Rotate Frame button

Trouble? If your cropping frame is not in the same position as the one shown in Figure 7-33, repeat Step 4 to reposition the frame.

5. Click the **Zoom out** button 🔍 four times to select the left half of the photo.

6. Click **Save**, and then click the **Yes** button to confirm. A cropped version of the photo appears in the picture details window. See Figure 7-34.

Figure 7-34	Completed rock garden photo

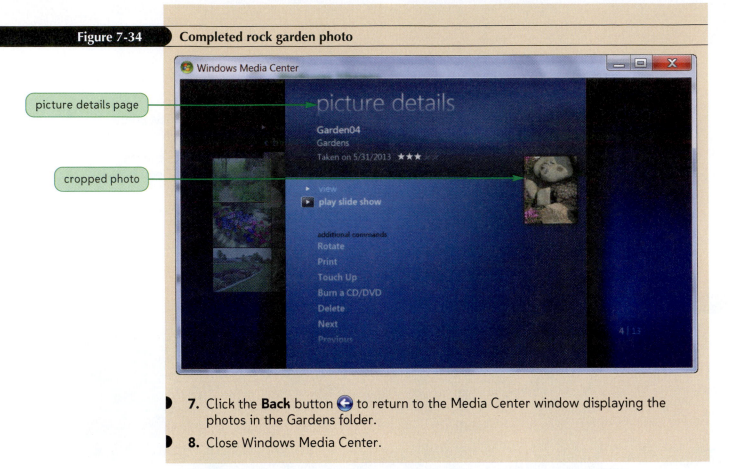

picture details page

cropped photo

> **7.** Click the **Back** button ⬅ to return to the Media Center window displaying the photos in the Gardens folder.

> **8.** Close Windows Media Center.

Now that you've improved some of Hector's photos, you want to show him how to share the photos with potential clients.

Sharing Photos

When you share your photos, you make them available for other people to view on their computers. The most popular ways to share photos are to post them on a photo-sharing Web site, send them to others in e-mail, or print them. A photo-sharing Web site lets you share and store pictures, often free of charge. (Check the Web site's policies before copying your files to an online album.) You can then invite others to visit the Web site and view your photo albums.

Although Windows 7 does not provide tools for posting your photos on a Web site, it does help you e-mail and print your photos.

Distributing Photos via E-Mail

Although it seems natural to share your photos with others using e-mail, photos taken by digital cameras are usually large files, even if they are saved in JPG format. Files you attach to e-mail messages should be as small as possible so you can transfer the files efficiently. Using the E-mail button on the Pictures library toolbar or the Windows Photo Viewer toolbar can solve this problem by compressing the photos before you attach them to an e-mail message. Your e-mail is then transferred more quickly and takes up less space on your recipient's computer. Compressing the photos in this way does not affect the original files.

Before you can send photos by e-mail, you need to make sure that an e-mail program is specified as the default on your computer. To set an e-mail program as the default, click the Start button on the taskbar, click Default Programs, click Set your default programs, click an e-mail program in the Programs list, click Set this program as default, and then click the OK button.

Hector and Bernie often receive e-mail messages from potential clients requesting information about their designs and services. Hector is ready to respond to a message he received earlier today asking for examples of water features the company has designed and installed. He wants to send a few appropriate photos along with his response. You'll show him how to find photos of water features and then send them via e-mail. You'll find the photos by searching their tags in the Pictures library, which displays tags in the Details pane in all views or listed in the folder window in Details view. Although you can use the Search box in the Pictures library the same way you search for any type of file in a folder window, recall that you can use the Arrange by button to quickly find photos in the current folder by date taken, rating, or tag.

To find and e-mail photos:

1. Make sure the Gardens folder you created in the Pictures library is open.

2. Click the **Arrange by** button, and then click **Tag**. Windows organizes the photos according to their tags.

3. Scroll down, if necessary, and then double-click **water feature**. Three photos appear in the file list, arranged by Day. See Figure 7-35.

Figure 7-35   **Arranging pictures by tags**

three photos to be selected for e-mailing

photos with water features

TIP

You can also send a photo via e-mail from Windows Photo Viewer by displaying the photo and then clicking the E-mail button on the toolbar.

4. Select the **three photos**, and then click the **E-mail** button on the toolbar. The Attach Files dialog box opens, estimating the size of the attachment.

5. Click the **Picture size** button, and then click **Smaller: 640 × 480**. This doesn't change the size of the original photo; it only resizes the version you are sending by e-mail.

6. Click the **Attach** button. Windows 7 opens your default e-mail program, such as Windows Live Mail, and attaches the three photos to the new message.

7. Enter your e-mail address to send the message to yourself, type **Water feature photos** as the subject, and then click the **Send** button to send the message and attachments.

8. Click the **Back** button ⬅ to return to the Gardens folder window.

9. Click the **Arrange by** button, and then click **Folder** to display all the garden photos in Details view.

Hector is also planning to meet with a client who wants Oak Park Landscaping to build a fence and freestanding trellis for a climbing rose. He wants to print a copy of the Garden12 photo to provide an example of a fence and trellis that Oak Park Landscaping could build. You'll show Hector how to print that photo from the Pictures library.

Printing Photos

To print your photos, you can use your own printer, order the prints online, or use a store or Web site that offers digital photo-printing services. To print sharp, appealing photos, you need a photo-quality printer and photo paper. Inkjet and dye-sublimation print-ers can produce high-quality photos when you print them on photo paper. Using the Pictures library or Windows Photo Viewer, you can print a single photo, more than one photo on a page, or a contact sheet, which is a page of thumbnails arranged in a grid.

Because the paper and ink required for printing photos is expensive, especially if you print often, many people prefer to use a store or online service to print their photos. In many places, you can take your camera's memory card or a CD containing your photos to a store that provides digital photo-printing services. Some stores have self-serve photo kiosks that let you edit and print photos yourself. Look for retailers in your area that pro-vide photo kiosks or digital photo-printing services.

To use an online photo-printing service, you copy your photo files to a Web site, and then order prints in a variety of sizes and formats. For example, you can print your photos on a calendar, mug, or t-shirt. You can also order prints directly from Windows Photo Viewer. To do so, select the pictures you want to print, click the Print button on the toolbar, and then click Order prints. Windows 7 connects to the Internet and displays a Web page listing photo-printing companies. Select the company you want to use, and then click Send Pictures. Follow the instructions provided by the printing company to complete your order.

Hector wants to print an 8 × 10-inch copy of the Garden12 photo so he can give it to a client. After loading photo paper in the printer and making sure this photo-quality printer is connected to your computer and turned on, you are ready to show Hector how to print this photo.

To print a photo:

1. In the Pictures library window displaying the contents of the Gardens folder, click **Garden12** to select that photo.

2. Click the **Print** button on the toolbar. The Print Pictures dialog box opens. See Figure 7-36.

Figure 7-36   **Print Pictures dialog box**

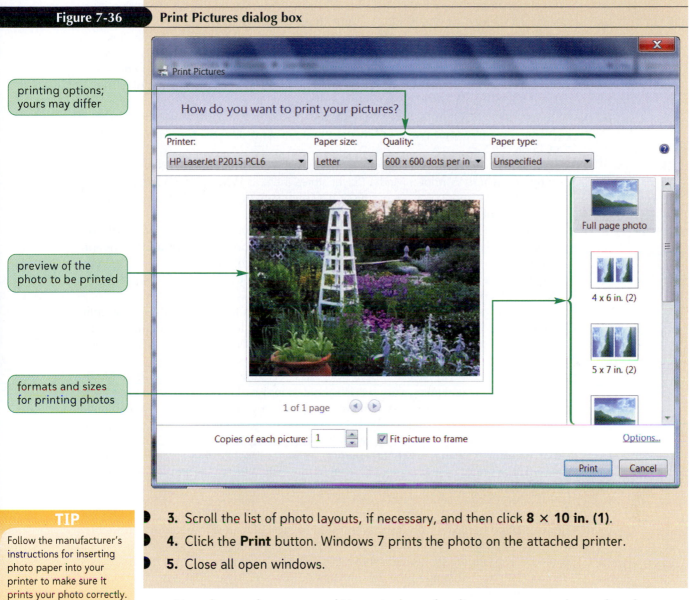

printing options; yours may differ

preview of the photo to be printed

formats and sizes for printing photos

3. Scroll the list of photo layouts, if necessary, and then click **8 × 10 in. (1)**.

4. Click the **Print** button. Windows 7 prints the photo on the attached printer.

5. Close all open windows.

Now that you have prepared Hector's photos for clients, you are ready to select the music for a multimedia slide show that he can play at expositions and trade shows.

Playing and Organizing Music Files

To play and organize digital music files on your Windows 7 computer, use the Windows Media Player. You can find and play music stored on your computer, CDs, or Web sites; download music files you've purchased from online stores; and create your own albums of songs and burn them onto CDs or sync them to a portable music player, such as an MP3 player or your cell phone. You can use Windows Media Player to perform some or all of the following tasks:

- Play an audio or video file: To play a music or video file stored anywhere on your computer, right-click the file and then click Play. You can play music and videos stored in a variety of media file formats, including Windows Media Audio (WMA), Windows Media Video (WMV), Audio Video Interleave (AVI), MPEG-1 Audio Layer 3 (MP3), and Waveform audio format (WAV).

- Play a CD or DVD: To play an audio CD, you only need to insert the CD in your CD drive, and then choose the Play audio CD using Windows Media Center option if an AutoPlay dialog box opens. Do the same to play a video DVD.
- Organize your media collection in the library: Even if you store your media files in many folders on your computer, you can organize your media collection in the Windows Media Player library. Then you can easily find and play a file, or choose content to burn to a CD or sync to a portable device. You can also create **playlists**, lists of media files, such as songs, that you want to play in a specified order.
- Burn your own CDs and DVDs: If you have a drive that can read and write CDs or DVDs, you can copy a playlist of media files to a CD or DVD, a process called *burning* a CD or DVD.
- Rip music from a CD: You can copy, or *rip*, tracks from your audio CDs onto your computer, where Windows Media Player stores them as WMA or MP3 files. As with graphics, make sure you have permission to duplicate tracks on a CD or you might be in violation of copyright law.
- Sync songs to a portable music player: If your portable music player can play WMA or MP3 songs, you can use Windows Media Player to copy, or **synchronize** (*sync* for short) files from your Player library to the portable device. To do so, you connect your portable player to your computer, usually by plugging a cable into a USB port, and then start Media Player.

  If the storage capacity of your portable music player is less than 4 GB or your entire library cannot fit on the device, Windows Media Player lets you sync manually. You select the files or playlists you want to sync each time you connect the device to your computer.
- Shop for music and movies at online stores: Use Windows Media Player to find and subscribe to music, video, radio services, and other media content from online stores. If you download songs or other content, it appears in your library. Before you purchase or download files, make sure you understand the usage rights that the store grants you. The content that stores provide is typically protected by media usage rights, which specify what you can do with the content. For example, these rights might specify that you cannot burn the file to an audio CD, or they might limit the number of times you can burn or sync the file.

Hector wants to find music he can use with his promotional slide show, but he's not sure what type of music would work best. You suggest playing a few sample music files provided in the Windows 7 Music library to get a feel for the style and musical genre that would be appropriate for his slide show. First, you'll show him how to start Windows Media Player and store all of the default Windows 7 sample music files in the Windows Media Player library.

To start Windows Media Player:

▶ 1. Click the **Windows Media Player** button ▶ on the taskbar. The Windows Media Player window opens.

   Trouble? If this is the first time you are running Windows Media Player, a dialog box opens before the main program windows does, giving you the option to choose Recommended settings or Custom settings. Unless your instructor specifies otherwise, click Recommended settings.

▶ 2. If necessary, maximize the window. See Figure 7-37. Your window might contain different music or might not contain any music yet.

Figure 7-37   **Windows Media Player window**

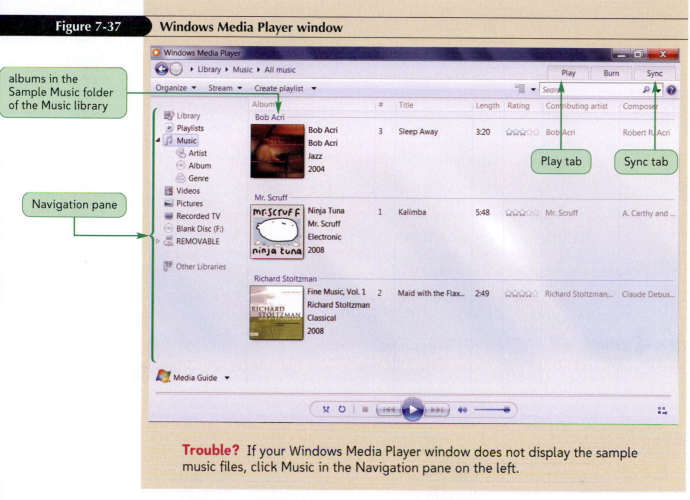

albums in the Sample Music folder of the Music library

Navigation pane

Play tab

Sync tab

Trouble? If your Windows Media Player window does not display the sample music files, click Music in the Navigation pane on the left.

Although Windows Media Player initially displays the songs in the Sample Music library, it monitors the Music library and updates your collection when you add or remove files. (This is a good reason to store your music files in the Music library or its subfolders.) It also adds any music files you play on your computer or the Internet and music that you rip from a CD or download from an online store.

Playing Music

To play music in Windows Media Player, double-click a song, an album, or a playlist. While a song is playing, Windows Media Player provides information and controls at the bottom of the window. A progress bar and timer track the progress of the song, and information such as the song title, album title, musician name, and composer name flashes in the lower-left corner of the window as the song plays. You can use the playback controls, which are similar to the controls on a CD player, to play, stop, rewind, fast-forward, mute, or change the volume.

If you click the Switch to Now Playing button in the lower-right corner of the Media Player window, you can view **visualizations**, which are patterns of colors and abstract shapes that move with the music you are playing. To view visualizations in Now Playing view, right-click the Media Player window, click Visualizations on the shortcut menu, and then select a visualization. To change the appearance of the Media Player window, you can switch to a different display mode: Player library (the default), Now Playing (controls only), skin (a customized design, such as one that matches the Windows XP Media Player), or full screen (display photos or other visuals so they fill the entire screen).

One of the albums in Hector's library is called Bob Acri and is included in the Jazz genre. Hector thinks that sounds promising. He also likes classical music, and notices that a classical album called Fine Music, Vol. 1 is included in the library. You'll show him how to play songs on those albums, which are samples provided by Windows 7 in the Music library.

Before performing the following steps, make sure that your computer has a sound card and speakers, and that the speakers are plugged into a power source, turned on, and connected to your computer. Also make sure that the speaker volume is not muted, but is low enough to hear without disturbing others. If you don't have speakers but do have a sound card, you might be able to plug headphones into a headphone jack to listen to music. If your computer does not have the hardware necessary to play music, you can still perform the following steps, though you won't be able to hear the music.

To play a song:

1. Locate the **Bob Acri** album, and then double-click it. The first song on the album, titled Sleep Away, begins to play, and information appears next to the playback controls. See Figure 7-38.

   Trouble? If the Bob Acri album does not appear in the album list, double-click any other album or song in the Jazz genre.

Figure 7-38   Playing a music file in Windows Media Player

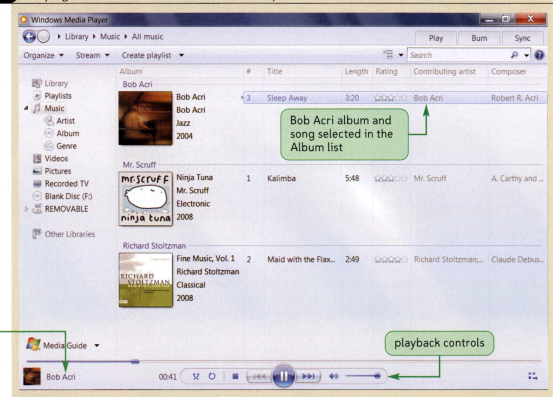

2. Click the **Stop** button ◼ in the playback controls.

3. Double-click the **Fine Music, Vol. 1** album in the album list.

   Trouble? If Fine Music, Vol. 1 does not appear in the album list, double-click any other album or song in the Classical genre.

4. Listen to the music for a few seconds, and then click the **Stop** button ◼.

TIP

To listen to music, you can also click a song or an album and then click the Play button in the playback controls.

Hector thinks both of those albums are good options to accompany his slide show of landscaping projects, but he wants Bernie to listen to the songs as well. Bernie often listens to a portable player as he works, so Hector wants to sync those songs to Bernie's portable player. Then Bernie can choose one of the songs in the playlist for the slide show. You'll show Hector how to add the songs to a new playlist so they are easy to sync.

Creating a Playlist

A playlist contains one or more digital media files and provides a way to organize files that you want to work with as a group. For example, you can create a playlist of lively songs that you play to wake up in the morning or a playlist of your favorite songs that you burn on a CD or transfer to a portable music player. By default, items in a playlist are played in the order they appear in the list. You can change the order of the items by dragging them within the list, or you can shuffle the items in the list, which means they play in a random order.

REFERENCE

Creating a Playlist

- Click the Create playlist button on the Windows Media Player toolbar.
- Enter a name for the playlist.
- Drag albums, songs, and other music from the file list to the List pane.
- Click the Save list button.

You can create two types of playlists in Windows Media Player—regular and auto. A regular playlist does not change unless you add or delete songs or other items in the list. As its name implies, an auto playlist changes automatically according to criteria you specify. For example, you could add any song rated four stars or more to an auto playlist. As Windows Media Player monitors your folders for new songs, it adds any with at least a four-star rating to that auto playlist.

Now that you and Hector have listened to selections from two albums, you'll add these songs to a new regular playlist.

To create a regular playlist:

1. Click the **Play** tab to open the list pane on the right side of the Media Player window.

   Trouble? If songs or a playlist already appear in the list pane, click the Clear list button (or click the Display additional commands button ⟩⟩, if necessary, and then click Clear list).

2. Drag the **Bob Acri** album (or another Jazz album) from the album list to the bottom portion of the list pane. The Sleep Away song (or another song) on that album appears in the new playlist.

   Trouble? If a song you added to the playlist begins to play, click the Stop button ▪ on the playback controls.

3. Drag the **Fine Music, Vol. 1** album (or another Classical album) to the list pane.

4. Click the **Save list** button at the top of the pane.

5. Type **Slide Show Music** and then press the **Enter** key. See Figure 7-39.

Figure 7-39	Saved playlist

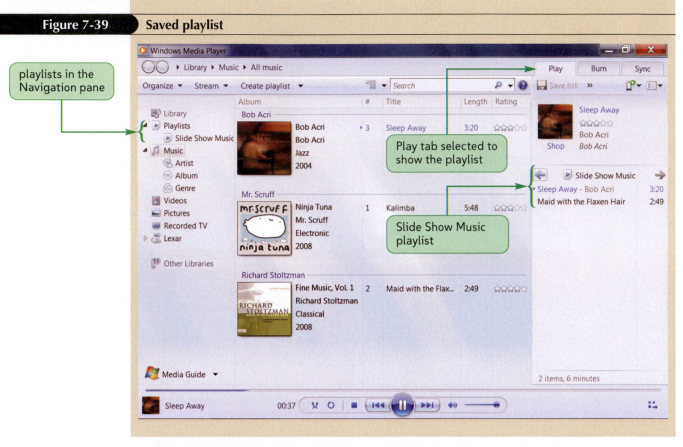

By default, playlists are saved with a .wpl extension in the Playlists folder, which is located in the My Music folder in the Music library.

If you want to change the order of the songs in the playlist, you can drag a song to a new position in the list pane. To play the songs in a playlist in order, right-click the playlist in the Navigation pane and then click Play. To play the songs in random order after you click Play, click the Turn shuffle on button in the playback controls.

Next, you can sync the songs in the Slide Show Music playlist to a portable music device.

Syncing Files to a Portable Device

When you connect a device to your computer for the first time, Windows Media Player selects the sync method that works best for your device, depending on the storage capacity of the device and the size of your library in Windows Media Player. If your portable music device has a storage capacity of more than 4 GB and your entire Media Player library can fit on the device, Windows Media Player offers to sync automatically. If you accept this option, your entire Player library is copied to your device. Every time you connect your device to your computer while Windows Media Player is running, Windows updates the contents of the portable music device to match the contents of the Media Player library. If you add songs to the Media Player library, Windows automatically copies the songs to your device the next time you connect it to your computer. If you delete songs from the Media Player library, Windows deletes those songs from your device the next time you connect it to your computer. You can also choose what to sync automatically by specifying the playlists you want to sync.

To perform the following steps, you can use a USB flash drive or a portable music device. If you are not equipped with the proper hardware, read but do not perform the following steps.

To sync files to a portable device:

1. If you are using a portable music device, turn it on and then connect it to your computer. If you are using a USB flash drive, connect it to your computer.

2. In Windows Media Player, click the **Sync** tab to open the Sync tab in the list pane.

3. Click the **Sync 'Slide Show Music'** link in the list pane. The two songs in the Slide Show Music playlist appear in the Sync list, and Windows 7 displays how much free space is available on the drive.

4. Click **Start sync**. A progress bar appears in the Sync tab.

5. When Windows 7 is finished syncing, close all open windows.

Hector gives Bernie his portable music player and asks him to listen to the new songs. Bernie says that the songs are ideal, and would like to play both during the promotional slide show. Now that you have song selections and touched-up photos, you're ready to create a slide show with music, which you'll do next.

Creating a Multimedia Slide Show with Windows Media Center

You've already seen how to create a simple slide show using the Pictures library or Windows Photo Viewer. This type of slide show covers the entire desktop and displays a group of photos one by one. Using Windows Media Center, you can add a soundtrack to the slide show. In addition, you can select the photos and songs you want to include in the slide show and specify the order in which they play.

If your computer has been recently upgraded to Windows 7, it might need updated drivers to work efficiently with Windows Media Center. Use Windows Update to check for, download, and install the latest drivers for your video and sound hardware before working with Windows Media Center.

Hector wants to include the Logo graphic in the slide show. To do so, you can copy it to the Gardens folder in the Pictures library.

To copy the Logo graphic to the Gardens folder:

1. Open a folder window that displays the contents of the Tutorial.07\Tutorial folder provided with your Data Files.

2. Copy the **Logo** graphic file to the **Gardens** folder in the Pictures library.

3. Close all open windows.

To make it easy to access Windows Media Center, you can add a Media Center gadget to your desktop. This gadget is provided with Windows 7 by default. You'll show Hector how to add the Media Center gadget to his desktop, and then use it to start Windows Media Center and create a slide show with music.

To add the Windows Media Center gadget to the desktop:

1. Right-click the **desktop**, and then click **Gadgets** on the shortcut menu to open the gadgets gallery.

2. If necessary, navigate to the Windows Media Center gadget in the gallery. See Figure 7-40.

Figure 7-40   **Windows Media Center gadget in the gadget gallery**

scroll the pages as necessary to display the Windows Media Center gadget

3. Double-click the **Windows Media Center** gadget. The gadget opens on the desktop and displays a slide show of television programs you can watch with Media Center if your computer is set up to play these programs.

4. Close the gadget gallery.

Now you can use the gadget to start Windows Media Center and then assemble the Oak Park Landscaping slide show with music.

To start Windows Media Center and create a slide show:

1. Click the **Windows Media Center** icon 🔵 in the gadget on the desktop. Windows Media Center opens to the main page.

2. In the Pictures + Videos section, click the **picture library** icon to display the contents of the Pictures library.

   Trouble? If the Pictures + Videos section does not appear on the main page, point to the top or bottom of your screen until an arrow appears, and then click the arrow one or more times to bring the Pictures + Videos section into view.

3. In the row of viewing options near the top of the window, click **slide shows**, if necessary. Move the pointer to the middle of the picture library window, and then click **Create Slide Show**. A text box appears where you can enter the name of the slide show.

4. In the text box, type **Garden Show**, and then click the **Next** button. A list of media sources appears—you can select media files from the Music library or the Pictures library.

5. Click the **Picture Library** option button, and then click the **Next** button to display the files and folders in the Pictures library.

6. Click **Gardens** to display the photos in the Gardens folder. These are the photos you want to use in the slide show. See Figure 7-41.

Figure 7-41	Preparing to create a slide show in Windows Media Center

select all command

Garden01 photo

Logo file copied to the Gardens folder

7. Click **select all** to select all the photos and the Logo graphic, and then click the **Next** button. On this page, you can set the order in which the images appear in the slide show. You want the Logo graphic to appear first.

8. Scroll down in the list of images, and then click the **Move up** button ⌃ next to Logo as many times as necessary to display Logo at the top of the list.

You've selected and organized the image files for the slide show. Now you can add the music for the soundtrack. Because you saved the two songs Hector and Bernie want to play in a playlist, you can add the playlist to the slide show to play the songs in order. If you wanted to change that order, you could do so using Windows Media Player.

To add music to the slide show:

1. In Windows Media Center, point to the right of the image list, and then click **Add More**. The list of media sources appears again. At this point, you can add image files from another folder in the Pictures library or you can add files from the Music library.

2. Click the **Music Library** option button, and then click the **Next** button to display the files and folders in the Music library.

3. In the row of options near the top of the window, click **playlists**, move the pointer to the middle of the window, and then click **Slide Show Music**, which is the playlist that contains the songs for the slide show.

4. Click **select all** to select all the songs in the Slide Show Music playlist, and then click the **Next** button. The Review & Edit Slide Show page displays all the media files you've selected for the slide show. See Figure 7-42.

Figure 7-42	Review & Edit Slide Show page

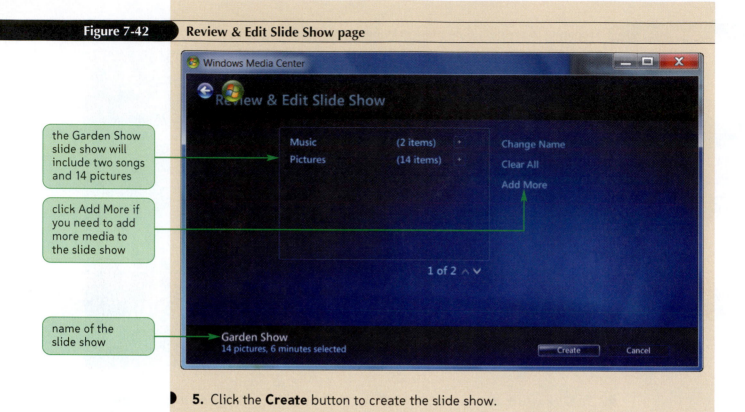

the Garden Show slide show will include two songs and 14 pictures

click Add More if you need to add more media to the slide show

name of the slide show

5. Click the **Create** button to create the slide show.

You can play the Garden Show slide show to review it and see if you need to change anything.

To play the slide show:

1. In the Slide Shows with Music section of the Media Center window, click **Garden Show**.

2. Click **play slide show**. The Garden Show slide show begins to play, displaying first the Logo graphic and then the photos you selected. At the same time, the Sleep Away song (or other jazz song) plays on the soundtrack. See Figure 7-43.

Trouble? If your computer has been recently upgraded to Windows 7 and you have not downloaded and installed the latest drivers for your computer, it might shut down and restart unexpectedly when you are using Windows Media Center. After restarting, Windows 7 displays a message identifying the drivers you need to install. Follow the instructions to install the drivers. See your instructor or support person for additional help.

Figure 7-43   **Playing a slide show in Windows Media Center**

Pause button

song information displayed in the slide show

Stop button

During the slide show, the images are displayed for a certain amount of time and song information occasionally appears in the lower-left corner of the window. Hector wants to slow down the images so customers can view them carefully and he wants to hide the song information.

To customize the slide show:

1. Right-click the slide show, and then click **Settings** on the shortcut menu.

2. Click **Pictures** in the list of settings to change, and then click **Slide Shows**. This page contains options for customizing slide shows. Click the **Stop** button ▣ in the playback controls to stop the show. See Figure 7-44.

Trouble? If your computer has been recently upgraded to Windows 7 and you have not downloaded and installed the latest drivers for your computer, it might shut down and restart unexpectedly when you are using Windows Media Center. After restarting, Windows 7 displays a message identifying the drivers you need to install. Follow the instructions to install the drivers. See your instructor or support person for additional help.

Figure 7-44   Setting options for a slide show

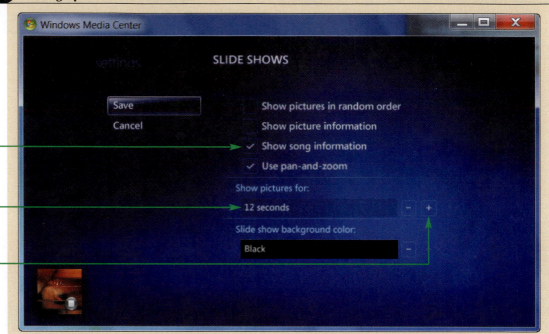

click to remove the check mark and hide song information during the slide show

increase this number to play the slide show more slowly

click the plus sign button to add more time between images

3. In the Show pictures for section, click the **plus sign** button [+] twice to display pictures for 16 seconds each.

4. Click the **Show song information** check box to remove the check mark and turn off the display of the song information for this slide show.

5. Click the **Save** button to save your changes.

6. Click the **Back** button ⬅ as necessary to return to the pictures window displaying the Garden Show slide show. Click **play slide show** to play the slide show again. This time, the images are displayed more slowly and the song information is hidden.

7. Click the **Stop** button 🔲 in the playback controls twice to stop the slide show, and then close Windows Media Center.

Now that the slide show is complete, Hector asks you to review a video he shot of a backyard butterfly garden this summer. He wants to burn the video on a DVD so he can send it to customers. You'll show him how to do so next.

Working with Videos

Windows Media Center is designed to display moving images—slide shows, television programs, and videos. You can play videos created in any of the popular video formats—including 3GP, AAC, AVCHD, MPEG-4, WMV, and WMA. It also supports most AVI, DivX, MOV, and Xvid files. These are file formats most digital video cameras use to save video files and that other videos are stored in, such as those you can download from the Web. All of the copyright and other rules that apply to downloading graphics and photos from the Web apply to videos—you need permission from the video owner to download and use a video unless it's in the public domain.

To play a video in Windows Media Center, copy the video file to the Videos library or one of its folders. Media Center displays all the video files in the Videos library by default, so you will be able to find them easily.

After you click a video file to play it, you can use the playback controls in Windows Media Center or the Media Center remote to control the video. (Many Windows 7 PCs are sold with Media Center remotes.) The steps in this tutorial use the on-screen controls. Point to the Media Center window to display the playback controls. To play the video in slow motion, for example, you can click the Pause button and then click the Fast Forward button once. To speed up the playback, click the Fast Forward button four times.

To prepare to play Hector's video in Windows Media Center, you need to copy this video, which is named Summer, to a folder in the Videos library.

To copy the Summer video to the Videos library:

1. Open a folder window that displays the contents of the Tutorial.07\Tutorial folder provided with your Data Files.

2. Copy the **Summer** video file to a new folder in the Videos library named **Backyards**.

3. Open and maximize the **Backyards** folder window.

Now you can start Windows Media Center again and play the Summer video.

To play the Summer video in Windows Media Center:

1. In the Backyards folder window, click the **Summer** video file, click the **Play button arrow** on the toolbar, and then click **Windows Media Center**. Windows Media Center begins playing the Summer video. See Figure 7-45.

| Figure 7-45 | Playing the Summer video in Windows Media Center |

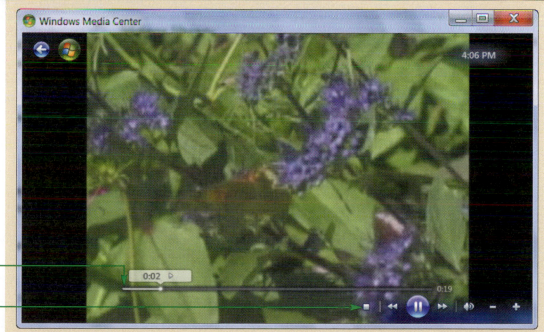

progress bar

playback controls

TIP

You can also right-click a video as it is playing, and then use the shortcut menu to control playback.

2. To pause the video, click the **Pause** button ⏸ in the playback controls to temporarily stop the video.

   Trouble? If the playback controls do not appear in the Media Center window, point to the window until they appear.

3. To play the video in slow motion, click the **Fast Forward** button ⏭ in the playback controls.

4. To resume playing the video at normal speed, click the **Play** button ▶ in the playback controls.

5. Let the video play until it ends. The synopsis window opens. Leave it open for the next set of steps.

Next, you'll show Hector how to burn the Summer video to a DVD so he can send it to customers.

Burning a Video onto a DVD

If you want to share videos with others (and have permission to do so), you can burn a video file onto a CD or DVD. Because video files are often quite large, burning them onto a disc is usually the best way to transfer them to other people. To do so, you need the right kind of drive on your computer and a recordable CD or DVD.

To burn a CD, you must have a rewritable CD drive or a CD burner connected to or installed in your computer. The type of recordable CD you should use depends on the types your CD burner supports and the type of disc you prefer. For instance, you can use either a blank CD-Recordable (CD-R) or CD-Rewritable (CD-RW) disc for burning CDs, though not all CD players can play CD-RW discs.

A DVD can hold much more data than a CD. To burn a DVD, you must have a rewritable DVD drive or a DVD burner connected to or installed in your computer. Most Windows 7 computers come with rewritable DVD drives. Some DVD burners work with a DVD-Recordable (DVD-R or DVD+R) or a DVD-Rewritable (DVD-RW or DVD+RW) disc, while others support only certain ones. Check the information about your DVD drive that came with your computer to learn what your DVD burner can use.

Hector's computer includes a rewritable DVD drive and you have a recordable DVD. You're ready to burn the Summer video onto the DVD.

To perform the following steps, you also need a recordable DVD and a rewritable DVD drive on your computer. If you do not have this equipment, read but do not perform the following steps.

To burn a video on a DVD:

1. In the synopsis window, click **actions**, and then insert a recordable DVD into your DVD drive. Wait a few moments for Windows 7 to recognize the DVD.

2. If an AutoPlay dialog box opens, close the dialog box without selecting an option.

3. In the Windows Media Center window, click **Burn a CD/DVD**.

4. On the Select Disc Format page, click **Video DVD**, and then click the **Next** button.

5. Type **Garden Videos** as the name of your DVD, and then click the **Next** button. The Summer video appears on the Review & Edit List page.

Trouble? If the Summer video does not appear, click Add More, click Video Library, click the Next button, click the Backyards folder, click the Summer video to select it as the video you want to burn, and then click the Next button.

▶ 6. On the Review & Edit List page, click **Burn DVD**. When the Initiating Copy dialog box appears, click the **Yes** button. Windows Media Center burns the selected video onto the DVD, which will take a few minutes. (Do not click the OK button to do anything else while the disc is being burned.) After the disc is burned, the Completing Burn dialog box opens.

▶ 7. Click the **Done** button, remove the DVD from the drive, and close all open windows.

You hand the DVD to Hector so he can give it to an interested customer. He can easily burn other DVDs as necessary when customers request them.

Restoring Your Computer

If you are working in a computer lab or on a computer other than your own, complete the steps in this section to restore the original settings on your computer.

To restore your computer:

▶ 1. Navigate to the **Pictures** library on your computer.

▶ 2. Move the **Gardens** folder to the **Tutorial.07\Tutorial** folder provided with your Data Files. Delete the copies of the **Logo** file and the 13 garden photos in the Tutorial.07\Tutorial folder.

▶ 3. Navigate to the **Music** library on your computer. Open the **Playlists** folder, and then move the **Garden Show** and **Slide Show Music** files to the **Tutorial.07\ Tutorial** folder provided with your Data Files.

▶ 4. Navigate to the **Videos** library on your computer. Delete the **Backyards** folder from the Videos library.

▶ 5. Remove the **Windows Media Center** gadget from the desktop, and close all open windows.

Session 7.2 Quick Check

REVIEW

1. How does Windows Photo Viewer differ from the Pictures library?

2. Why should you generally take advantage of the offer from Windows 7 to compress photos before attaching them to an e-mail message?

3. A(n) _____ is a list of media files, such as songs, that you want to play in a specified order.

4. Name two Windows 7 tools you can use to create a slide show.

5. Using _____, you can create a slide show with a music soundtrack.

6. True or False. Unlike photos, you do not need permission from the video owner to download and use a video you find on the Web.

7. What equipment do you need to burn files onto a DVD?

Practice the skills you learned in the tutorial using the same case scenario.

PRACTICE

Review Assignments

For a list of Data Files in the Review folder, see page WIN 337.

Oak Park Landscaping is conducting a series of seminars on garden design to help promote its business. Hector Torres wants to create a postcard he can mail to current and prospective clients to invite them to attend a seminar. He's found two graphics that he wants to use on the postcard, and he asks you to show him how to combine these into an effective design. Bernie Quinn has taken photos of some of the most popular flowers they feature in gardens, and wants to showcase these in a slide show he can play at the seminar on selecting bedding plants. He asks you to help him prepare the photos and assemble them into a professional slide show. Complete the following steps:

1. Start Paint, open the **Border** picture from the Tutorial.07\Review folder provided with your Data Files, and then save it as **Seminar** in the same folder.

2. Paste the **Plan** picture into the Seminar picture, and center it within the border.

3. Increase the size of the canvas to at least 600 × 400 pixels to create a larger work area.

4. Select a violet blue color from the Border graphic as Color 1, and a light yellow-green color from the Plan graphic as Color 2, the background color.

5. Using the Text tool with an Opaque background, create a text box of about 260 × 40 pixels. Choose Verdana as the font, 14 as the point size, and Italic as the style. Type **Oak Park Landscaping** in the text box. If the text you typed does not span the width of the text box, increase the font size until it does.

6. Move the text to center it in the rectangle. Save your work.

7. Switch the foreground and background colors—make light green Color 1 and violet blue Color 2. (*Hint*: Use the Color picker tool to click a light-green spot and then to right-click a violet-blue spot.)

8. Create a text box of about 300 × 40 pixels. Choose Verdana as the font, the same point size you used in Step 5, and Italic as the style. Type **Garden Design Seminars** in the text box.

9. Move the text to center it in the rectangle. Save your work.

10. Change the background color to white.

11. Arrange the rectangles so that they are right next to each other with no white space between them, the Oak Park Landscaping rectangle on the left and the Garden Design Seminars rectangle on the right. Save your work.

12. Copy the rectangles, which now form a two-color bar, and then resize the canvas to 560 × 250 pixels. If any remnants of the rectangles remain, delete them.

13. Paste the rectangles into the picture, and then move them to the bottom of the canvas, taking care not to extend any part of the rectangles past the borders of the canvas. Save your work.

14. Working in 400% magnified view, draw a 12 × 12 pixel square in the upper-right corner of the picture, using the same shade of light green you used in the rectangles. Fill the square with light green. Change Color 2 to white. Display the grid and move the square so it is 12 pixels to the right of the Border image and 12 pixels from the top of the canvas.

15. Copy and paste the square to create a row of four squares with 12 pixels of white space between each square. Turn off the gridlines. The final picture should look similar to Figure 7-46.

Figure 7-46   **Plan graphic for Oak Park Landscaping**

16. Make any final modifications as necessary, save your work, and then close Paint.

17. Copy the nine flower garden photos from the Tutorial.07\Review folder provided with your Data Files to a new folder in the Pictures library named **Flowers**. (Don't copy the Border, Plan, or Seminar graphics.)

18. Play a simple slide show of the pictures in the Flowers folder.

19. Use Windows Photo Viewer to rotate the Iris photo.

20. Use Windows Media Center to correct the contrast in the Fuchsia photo.

21. Crop the **Rose** photo by rotating the frame to remove about one-third of the photo on the right and one-third on the left.

22. Start Windows Media Player, and then create a playlist named **Flower Slide Show** consisting of Kalimba and Maid with the Flaxen Hair, and then close Windows Media Player.

23. In Windows Media Center, create a slide show named **Seminar Show** that includes all nine photos in the Flowers folder and all the songs in the Flower Slide Show playlist.

24. Play the slide show in Windows Media Center. Press the Alt+Print Screen keys to capture an image of the slide show window, and then paste the image in a new Paint or WordPad file. Save the file as **SlideShowXY** in the Tutorial.07\Review folder provided with your Data Files.

25. Close Windows Media Center. Move the **Seminar Show** and **Flower Slide Show** playlist files from the Playlists folder in the Music library to the Tutorial.07\Review folder provided with your Data Files.

26. Move the **Flowers** folder from the Pictures library to the Tutorial.07\Review folder provided with your Data Files. Delete the nine flower garden photos from the Tutorial.07\Review folder. (Do not delete the Border, Plan, and Seminar files.)

27. Submit the results of the preceding steps to your instructor, either in printed or electronic form, as requested.

Use your skills to manage multimedia files for a stationery shop.

APPLY

Case Problem 1

For a list of Data Files in the Case1 folder, see page WIN 337.

Alpha-Zeta Marianne Zeta owns Alpha-Zeta, a stationery store in Greenwich, Connecticut, that offers paper making, calligraphy, and other hand-printing services. As Marianne's assistant, you help her serve customers, fill orders, and create promotional materials. Marianne asks you to work with two calligraphy images to develop a logo for the store and to create a slide show of female authors. Complete the following steps:

1. Start Paint, open the **Flourish** picture from the Tutorial.07\Case1 folder provided with your Data Files, and then save it as **AZ Logo** in the same folder. (Click the OK button if you are notified that transparency will be lost.)

2. Increase the size of the canvas to at least 400 × 400 pixels.

3. Paste the **Letters AZ** picture from the Tutorial.07\Case1 folder into the AZ Logo picture, and move the Letters AZ picture to a blank spot on the canvas.

4. Working in a magnified view as necessary, select the letters *A* and *Z* again without selecting any white space around them. Move the letters so that they appear about 22 pixels to the right of the middle of the flourish image. Save your work.

5. Near the bottom of the canvas, create a text box of about 120 × 30 pixels and choose 16-point Monotype Corsiva for the text. (If Monotype Corsiva is not available on your computer, select another script font.) Type **Alpha-Zeta** in the text box. Make sure all the text appears on one line. If necessary, change the font size of the text so it spans the width of the text box.

6. Select the text, including as little background as possible, and then move it under the letter *Z*, so that it is right-aligned with the black box containing the letter *Z*.

7. Change Color 1 to a dark red selected from the picture.

8. Near the bottom of the canvas, create another text box of about 160 × 25 pixels and choose 10-point Monotype Corsiva (or the same script font you used in Step 5) for the text. Type **Stationery & Calligraphy**. Make sure the text appears on one line. If necessary, change the font size of the text so it spans the width of the text box.

9. Move the new text under *Alpha-Zeta* so that *Stationery* is left-aligned with *Alpha-Zeta*. Make sure no part of the text extends below the flourish image. Save your work.

10. Resize the canvas so its dimensions are about 240 × 200. The final logo should look similar to Figure 7-47.

Figure 7-47 **Completed AZ Logo graphic**

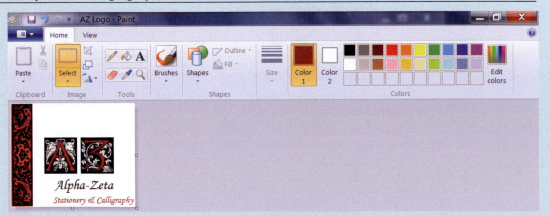

11. Make any final modifications as necessary, save your work, and then close Paint.

12. Copy the seven portraits of female authors (in other words, all the JPG files) from the Tutorial.07\Case1 folder provided with your Data Files to a new folder in the Pictures library named **Authors**.

13. Play a simple slide show of the pictures in the Authors folder.

14. In Windows Photo Viewer, rotate the **Browning** photo so it appears in the correct orientation.

15. Close Windows Photo Viewer.

16. Start Windows Media Center, and then create a slide show named **Author Slide Show**.

17. Display the seven portraits from the Authors folder in the Author Slide Show.

18. Add the Maid with the Flaxen Hair song to the slide show. (*Hint*: In the Choose Music window, first click Songs.) Play the slide show, press the Alt+Print Screen keys to capture an image of the slide show window, and then paste the image in a new Paint or WordPad file. Save the file as **AuthorsXY** in the Tutorial.07\Case1 folder provided with your Data Files.

19. Close Windows Media Center.

20. Move the **Authors** folder from the Pictures library to the Tutorial.07\Case1 folder provided with your Data Files. Delete the seven portraits of female authors from the Tutorial.07\Case1 folder.

21. Open the **Playlists** folder in the Music library and move the **Author Slide Show** file to the Tutorial.07\Case1 folder provided with your Data Files.

22. Submit the results of the preceding steps to your instructor, either in printed or electronic form, as requested.

Use your skills to work with multimedia files for a lighthouse preservation society.

APPLY

Case Problem 2

For a list of Data Files in the Case2 folder, see page WIN 337.

Landmark Lighthouses   Since the United States Coast Guard automated the nation's coastal lights, the federal government has been transferring ownership of lighthouses to state and local governments and to nonprofit organizations. With this in mind, Stanley and Debra Keene started Landmark Lighthouses, a nonprofit company dedicated to preserving historic lighthouses, in Superior, Wisconsin. You volunteer regularly for the organization, and offer to help Stan and Debra create fundraising materials. Stan asks you to show him how to use Paint to create an image for their Web site and to create a slide show they can make available for download. Complete the following steps:

1. Start Paint, open the **Lighthouse** file from the Tutorial.07\Case2 folder provided with your Data Files, and then save it as **Landmark** in the same folder.

2. Increase the size of the canvas to at least 600 × 500 pixels to create a larger work area.

3. Change Color 1 and Color 2 to a shade of pale yellow that appears in the lighthouse lantern. Select the Oval shape tool, and then change the Outline and Fill settings to Solid color.

4. Near the top of the canvas and to the right of the lighthouse, draw a perfect circle about 140 × 140 pixels round with a pale yellow solid outline and a pale yellow solid fill. (*Hint*: Hold down the Shift key as you drag to draw the circle.)

5. Deselect the circle, and then change Color 2 to white.

6. If necessary, move the yellow circle so that its top edge touches the top of the canvas. Save your work.

7. Select the lighthouse, choose the Transparent selection command, and then move the lighthouse to the circle so that the lantern and the first red segment of the lighthouse appear to be surrounded by a halo of yellow light. See Figure 7-48.

Figure 7-48   **Adding a circle of yellow light to the Landmark graphic**

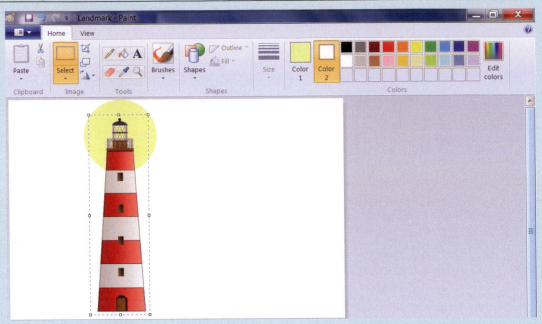

8. Change Color 1 to a shade of light gray selected from the lighthouse, and then change Color 2 to a shade of red selected from the lighthouse.

9. Using a solid 1-px outline with the Marker fill style, draw a rectangle of 300 × 47 pixels in the lower-left corner of the canvas.

10. In the lower-right corner of the canvas, create a text box about 300 pixels wide. Choose an Opaque background and 16-point Book Antiqua for the text. Type **Landmark Lighthouses** in the text box. Make sure the text appears on one line. If necessary, change the font size of the text so it spans the width of the text box.

11. Move the text box to the dark-red rectangle, centering the text in the rectangle. Save your work.

12. Change Color 2 to white. Delete any remaining part of the text box.

13. Select the entire remaining rectangle, deselect the Transparent selection command, and then move the rectangle so it is centered under the lighthouse and no white space appears between the lighthouse and the rectangle.

14. Move the entire image so that the left edge of the rectangle touches the left edge of the canvas. (The top edge of the halo should still touch the top edge of the canvas.)

◆ EXPLORE   15. Use the Rectangular selection tool to point to the lower-right corner of the rectangle and note its pixel coordinates. Click the Paint menu button and then click Properties to open the Image Properties dialog box. Enter the pixel coordinates in the appropriate text boxes, which should be close to 300 for the Width and 450 for the Height. Click the OK button. Your image should look similar to Figure 7-49.

Figure 7-49   Completed Landmark graphic

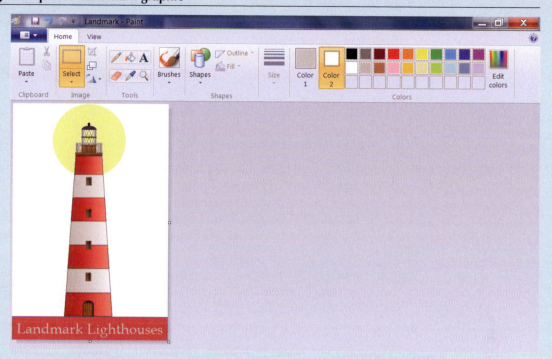

16. Make any final modifications as necessary, save your work, and then close Paint.

17. Copy the eight lighthouse photos and the **Landmark** graphic from the Tutorial.07\ Case2 folder provided with your Data Files to a new folder in the Pictures library named **Lighthouses**.

18. Copy the **Ocean** sound file to a new folder in the Music library named **Ocean Sounds**.

19. In the Pictures library, play a simple slide show of the pictures in the Lighthouses folder.

20. Change the slide show speed to fast.

21. In Windows Photo Viewer, e-mail the LH03 photo to yourself using the smallest picture size. When your e-mail program starts and displays a new message, press the Alt+Print Screen keys to capture an image of the message, and then paste the image in a new Paint or WordPad file. Save the file as **EmailXY** in the Tutorial.07\Case2 folder provided with your Data Files. Close Windows Photo Viewer.

⊕ **E X P L O R E**   22. Open the **Ocean** sound file in Windows Media Player. As the sound plays, click the Turn repeat on button in the playback bar so the sound plays continuously. Close Windows Media Player.

23. Start Windows Media Center, and then create a slide show named **Lighthouse Show**. Include the eight photos and the Landmark graphic from the Lighthouses folder in the Pictures library and the Ocean sound file from the Ocean Sounds folder in the Music library.

24. Play the show, press the Alt+Print Screen keys to capture an image of the slide show window, and then paste the image in a new Paint or WordPad file. Save the file as **LighthouseXY** in the Tutorial.07\Case2 folder provided with your Data Files. Close Windows Media Center.

25. Move the **Lighthouses** folder from the Pictures library to the Tutorial.07\Case2 folder provided with your Data Files. Move the **Ocean Sounds** folder in the Music library to the Tutorial.07\Case2 folder. Delete the eight lighthouse photos, the Landmark graphic file, and the Ocean sound file from the Tutorial.07\Case2 folder.

26. Open the Playlists folder in the Music library and move the **Lighthouse Show** file to the Tutorial.07\Case2 folder provided with your Data Files.

27. Submit the results of the preceding steps to your instructor, either in printed or electronic form, as requested.

Extend what you've learned to work with graphics for a bird supply store.

CHALLENGE

Case Problem 3

For a list of Data Files in the Case3 folder, see page WIN 337.

Backyard Birds   Backyard Birds is a store with two locations in Silver Spring, Maryland, that specializes in wild bird supplies, quality bird seed, field guides, and other distinctive equipment and gifts for birding enthusiasts. Tricia Knowles recently opened her second store in the area and hired you to manage it. When she learned that you have some graphic design training, she asked you to help her design a graphic she can use on her newsletter and business correspondence. She also wants you to develop a slide show highlighting backyard birds. Complete the following steps:

1. Start Paint, open the **Window** picture from the Tutorial.07\Case3 folder provided with your Data Files, and then save it as **Backyard Birds** in the same folder. (Click the OK button if you are notified that transparency will be lost.)

2. Increase the size of the canvas to at least 700 × 500 pixels to create a larger work area.

3. Paste the **Wren** picture into the Backyard Birds picture, and move the bird to a blank spot on the canvas.

⊕ **EXPLORE**

4. With the image of the bird still selected, rotate the image 90 degrees to the right by clicking the Rotate or flip button in the Image group, and then clicking Rotate right 90°. If necessary, drag the selected image so the entire image appears on the canvas.

5. Copy a leaf from the bird image to a blank area of the canvas. When you select the leaf, you will probably include some pixels from the frame or bird.

⊕ **EXPLORE**

6. Make sure Color 2 is white. Select the image of the window frame without selecting any white space around it. Choose the Transparent selection command, and then move the window frame over the bird so that the bird appears mostly in the top two panes. The lower-right frame should contain almost all white space. Save your work.

7. Change Color 1 to a shade of dark olive green that appears in the bird image.

8. In a blank spot on the canvas, create a text box of about 115 × 70 pixels. wide. Select 18-point Goudy Old Style for the text. Type **Backyard Birds** in the text box so that the text appears on two lines. If necessary, change the font size of the text so it spans the width of the text box. Save your work.

9. Move the *Backyard Birds* text into the lower-right pane of the window frame. See Figure 7-50.

Figure 7-50 Positioning the Backyard Birds text

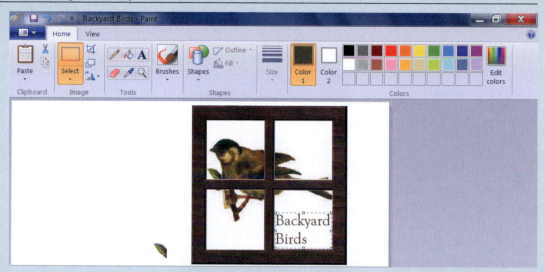

EXPLORE
10. In the copy of the leaf, erase the unnecessary pixels by clicking the Eraser tool, clicking the smallest size in the Size button list, and then clicking the pixels you want to erase from the leaf. Save your work.

11. Move the leaf to the lower-right window pane next to *Birds*.

12. Move the entire image to the upper-left corner of the canvas. No white space should appear above and to the left of the graphic.

EXPLORE
13. Resize the canvas to precisely 340 × 344 by clicking the Paint menu button, clicking Properties, entering **340** in the Width text box and **344** in the Height text box, and then clicking the OK button.

14. Change Color 1 to a shade of light olive green that appears in the bird image.

15. Fill the white part of the canvas outside of the window frame with light olive green. Your image should look similar to Figure 7-51.

Figure 7-51 Completed Backyard Birds graphic

16. Make any final modifications as necessary, save your work, and then close Paint.

17. Copy the **Backyard Birds** graphic and the 10 bird photos from the Tutorial.07\Case3 folder provided with your Data Files to a new folder in the Pictures library named **Birds**. Copy the sound files to a new folder in the Music library named **Bird Sounds**.

18. In the Pictures library, play a simple slide show of the pictures in the **Birds** folder.

19. In Windows Photo Viewer, rotate the **Bird02** photo. Close Windows Photo Viewer.

⊕ **EXPLORE**   20. Navigate to the Bird Sounds folder in your Music library. Right-click a sound file, point to Open with, and then click Windows Media Player. Click the Switch to Library button, if necessary to open the library. Add BirdSong and Waterfowl to a new playlist named **Nature Sounds**. Then close Windows Media Player.

21. Start Windows Media Center, and then create a slide show named **Bird Show**. Add the 11 image files from the Birds folder in the Pictures library.

⊕ **EXPLORE**   22. Add the Nature Sounds playlist from the Bird Sounds folder in your Music library to the slide show. Choose to play all the music in order by title.

23. Play the slide show, press the Alt+Print Screen keys to capture an image of the slide show window, and then paste the image in a new Paint or WordPad file. Save the file as **BirdShowXY** in the Tutorial.07\Case3 folder provided with your Data Files. Close Windows Media Center.

24. Open the **Playlists** folder in the Music library and move the **Bird Show** and **Nature Sounds** files to the Tutorial.07\Case3 folder provided with your Data Files. Move the **Bird Sounds** folder from the Music library to the Tutorial.07\Case3 folder provided with your Data Files.

25. Move the **Birds** folder from the Pictures library to the Tutorial.07\Case3 folder provided with your Data Files. Delete the **Bird01–Bird10** photos, the **Backyard Birds** graphic file, and the **BirdSong** and **WaterFowl** sound files from the Tutorial.07\Case3 folder.

26. Submit the results of the preceding steps to your instructor, either in printed or electronic form, as requested.

Using Figures 7-52 and 7-53 as guides, create a graphic for a farmer's market.

C R E A T E

Case Problem 4

For a list of Data Files in the Case4 folder, see page WIN 337.

Farmer's Market West   Franklin Bieder is the manager of Farmer's Market West in Spokane, Washington. Franklin hired you as his assistant to provide marketing and graphic design services to the organization. He asks you to design a logo he can use in print and online. He'd also like you to create a slide show that promotes the market's products. Complete the following steps:

1. Create a logo for Farmer's Market West using Figure 7-52 as a guide. Save the graphic as **FMWest** in the Tutorial.07\Case4 folder provided with your Data Files.

Figure 7-52 **Creating a logo for Farmer's Market West**

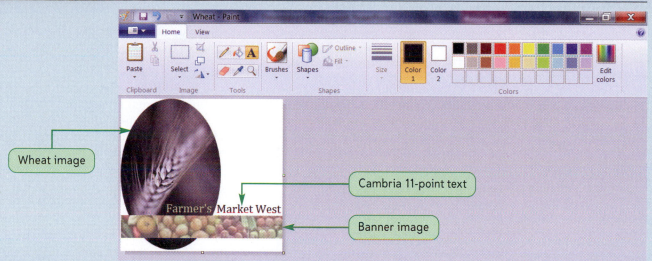

Wheat image

Cambria 11-point text

Banner image

The Wheat and Banner graphics files are in the Tutorial.07\Case4 folder provided with your Data Files. Be sure to save your work after making a significant change to the graphic.

2. Create a slide show named **Market** for Farmer's Market West using Figure 7-53 as a guide. Move the slide show to the Tutorial.07\Case4 folder provided with your Data Files. If you copy any files to a library, move the files to a folder named **Market** in the Tutorial.07\Case4 folder when you're finished.

The eight photos you need are in the Tutorial.07\Case4 folder provided with your Data Files. Select any two song tracks to play during the show.

Figure 7-53 **Creating a title slide**

two songs selected for the Market slide show

eight photos selected for the Market slide show copied from the Tutorial.07\Case4 folder to a folder in the Pictures library

3. Submit the results of the preceding steps to your instructor, either in printed or electronic form, as requested.

SAM: Skills Assessment Manager

ASSESS

For current SAM information, including versions and content details, visit SAM Central (http://samcentral.course.com). If you have a SAM user profile, you may have access to hands-on instruction, practice, and assessment of the skills covered in this tutorial. Since various versions of SAM are supported throughout the life of this text, check with your instructor for the correct instructions and URL/Web site for accessing assignments.

ENDING DATA FILES

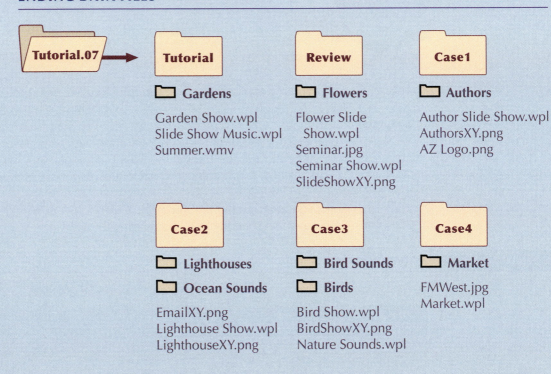

OBJECTIVES

Session 8.1
- Manage mobile computing devices
- Present information to an audience
- Explore network concepts
- Manage network connections

Session 8.2
- Set up and use a homegroup
- Access shared network folders
- Synchronize folders
- Allow remote access to your computer

Connecting to Networks with Mobile Computing

Accessing Network Resources

Case | *KATE Consultants*

Kevin Adelson and Tay Endres are partners in KATE Consultants, a firm in Portland, Oregon, that provides financial and management consulting to businesses throughout western Oregon. You have been working for KATE as an associate for a few months, specializing in helping clients upgrade to Microsoft Windows 7. Kevin and Tay are preparing to configure a wireless network for their client Chamberlain & Klein, a small law firm in Klamath Falls, and ask you to help them. Tay knows how to perform networking tasks in earlier versions of Windows, but not in Windows 7. Because Kevin plans to work on his laptop computer during the five-hour drive to Klamath Falls, he also asks you to change mobility settings on his computer so he can use it during the trip without worrying about losing power or disturbing you and Tay.

In this tutorial, you will explore mobile computing, including maintaining power and accessing other computing resources. You will also examine network concepts and learn how to connect two or more computers in a network, and then use the network to share files, folders, and resources.

STARTING DATA FILES

There are no starting Data Files needed for this tutorial.

SESSION 8.1 VISUAL OVERVIEW

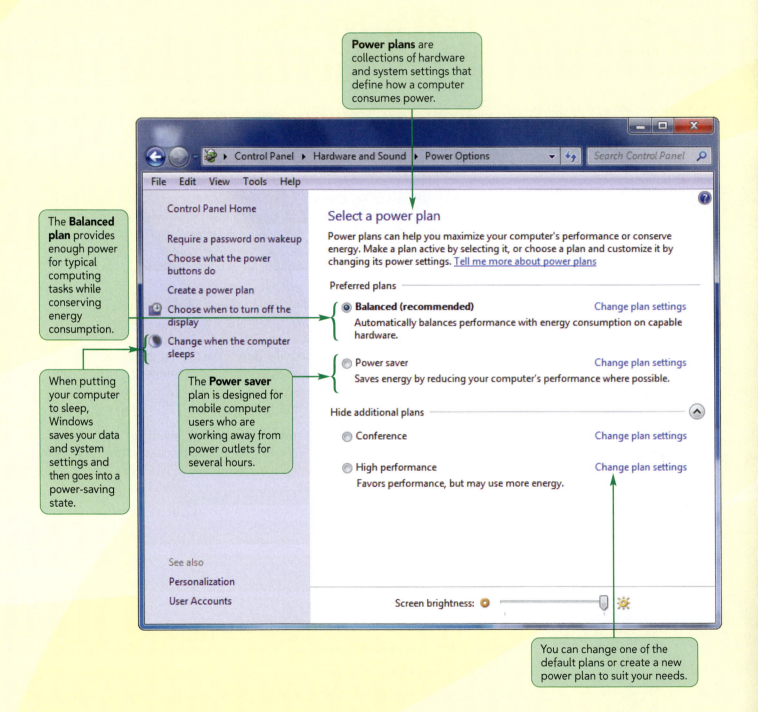

Power plans are collections of hardware and system settings that define how a computer consumes power.

The **Balanced plan** provides enough power for typical computing tasks while conserving energy consumption.

When putting your computer to sleep, Windows saves your data and system settings and then goes into a power-saving state.

The **Power saver** plan is designed for mobile computer users who are working away from power outlets for several hours.

You can change one of the default plans or create a new power plan to suit your needs.

Control Panel ▶ Hardware and Sound ▶ Power Options

Search Control Panel

File   Edit   View   Tools   Help

Control Panel Home

Require a password on wakeup

Choose what the power buttons do

Create a power plan

Choose when to turn off the display

Change when the computer sleeps

See also

Personalization

User Accounts

Select a power plan

Power plans can help you maximize your computer's performance or conserve energy. Make a plan active by selecting it, or choose a plan and customize it by changing its power settings. Tell me more about power plans

Preferred plans

Balanced (recommended)   Change plan settings
Automatically balances performance with energy consumption on capable hardware.

Power saver   Change plan settings
Saves energy by reducing your computer's performance where possible.

Hide additional plans

Conference   Change plan settings

High performance   Change plan settings
Favors performance, but may use more energy.

Screen brightness:

MOBILE COMPUTING

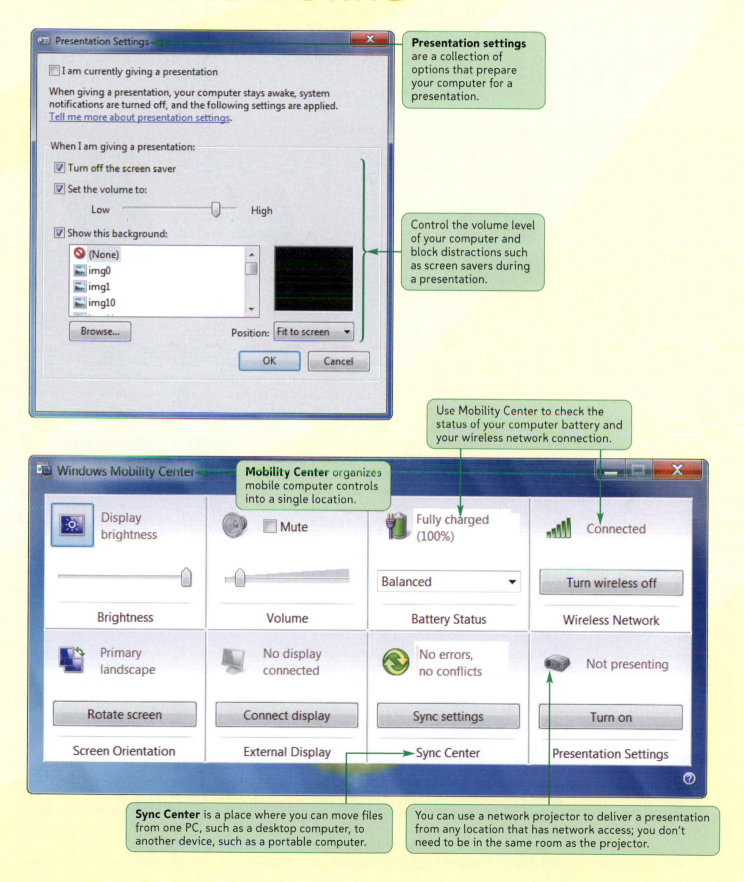

Presentation settings are a collection of options that prepare your computer for a presentation.

Control the volume level of your computer and block distractions such as screen savers during a presentation.

Use Mobility Center to check the status of your computer battery and your wireless network connection.

Mobility Center organizes mobile computer controls into a single location.

Sync Center is a place where you can move files from one PC, such as a desktop computer, to another device, such as a portable computer.

You can use a network projector to deliver a presentation from any location that has network access; you don't need to be in the same room as the projector.

Managing Mobile Computing Devices

A **mobile computing device**, or a **mobile personal computer (PC)**, is a computer you can easily carry, such as a laptop, notebook, or Tablet PC. Currently, more people are buying mobile PCs than desktop PCs, preferring their portability and flexibility. Although a desktop PC must always be plugged into a power source and use cables to connect most of its components and devices, a mobile PC contains all of its necessary parts in a single package, including a display screen, processor, keyboard, and pointing device. See Figure 8-1.

| Figure 8-1 | Comparing desktop and mobile computers |

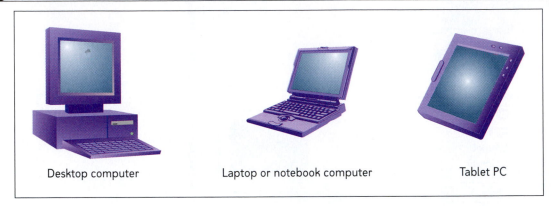

Desktop computer   Laptop or notebook computer   Tablet PC

The terms **laptop computer** and **notebook computer** are interchangeable, although *laptop* is the older term and *notebook* is sometimes associated with a smaller, lighter computer. Both refer to portable computers that are smaller than the average briefcase and light enough to carry comfortably. A laptop or notebook has a flat screen and keyboard that fold together and a battery pack that provides power for a few hours so that you don't have to plug the computer into a wall outlet. A **Tablet PC** is smaller than a laptop or notebook and works like an electronic slate. You use a stylus and a touch screen to make selections and enter information instead of using a keyboard and a pointing device.

Contemporary mobile computers are just as powerful as desktops and let you use your computer almost anywhere, including while traveling and meeting with others. However, the portability of mobile computers introduces two problems that desktop computers typically do not have: managing power and keeping your files synchronized. When you're using a notebook computer while traveling, for example, you need a way to preserve battery power so you don't lose data or have to shut down unexpectedly. If you do some of your work on a mobile computer, such as at a client meeting, and other work at a desktop computer, especially one connected to a network, you need a way to update the files stored on your desktop computer or network with the work you saved on your mobile computer and vice versa.

Windows 7 solves these problems with Mobility Center, power plans, and Sync Center. Windows Mobility Center organizes mobile computer controls into a single location. These controls let you view and adjust the settings on a mobile computer you use most often, including the screen brightness, speaker volume, and battery status. While working in Mobility Center, you can also select a power plan, a collection of hardware and system settings that define how a computer consumes power. For example, you can choose a plan designed to minimize power consumption, maximize system performance, or strike a balance between the two. Mobility Center also provides access to Sync Center, a place where you can move files from one PC, such as a notebook computer, to another device, such as a desktop PC, network computer, portable music player, digital camera, or mobile phone. While moving the files, Sync Center helps you maintain consistency among two or more versions of the same file stored in different locations, so you don't use an out-of-date file on a portable device, for example, when you have a more current version on your desktop PC.

Using Mobility Center

Mobility Center provides a small control panel for managing a mobile computer. Although hardware vendors can add and change features in Mobility Center, by default Windows 7 lets you adjust power settings such as the brightness of the computer screen, the speaker volume, and the current power-saving scheme. If your mobile computer is equipped to access a wireless network, Mobility Center displays your network status (connected or not connected) and lets you quickly open the Network and Sharing Center, which you'll explore later in this tutorial. Mobility Center also lets you manage settings you often need when you are working away from your desk, such as those for synchronizing files, using an external display, and controlling what appears on a projector when you give a presentation. See Figure 8-2.

Figure 8-2   Windows Mobility Center

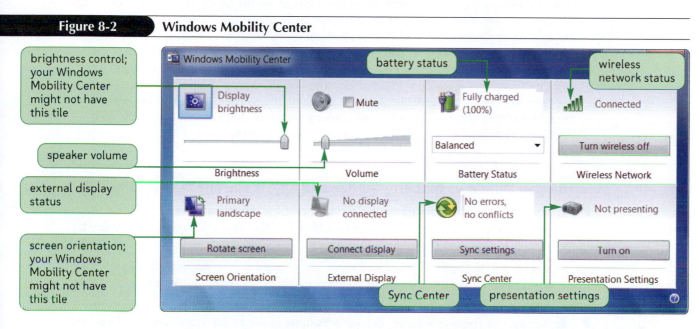

Each control in Mobility Center is called a tile. Some computers do not include the Screen Orientation or Brightness tile. Computer manufacturers sometimes remove these tiles if their hardware provides alternate controls. Figure 8-3 describes the purpose of each tile.

Figure 8-3   Settings in Windows Mobility Center

Tile	Description
Brightness	Dim or increase the brightness of your screen.
Volume	Use the slider to control the volume of the computer's speakers or mute the speakers to turn off the sound completely.
Battery Status	Select a power scheme that suits how you are working with your computer.
Wireless Network	View whether your computer is connected to a wireless network, and access the Network and Sharing Center.
Screen Orientation	Set the screen orientation on your Tablet PC to portrait or landscape.
External Display	Connect your computer to another monitor or projector.
Sync Center	Open Sync Center to identify devices containing files to synchronize and then exchange information.
Presentation Settings	Control what appears on a projector when your computer is connected to one.

Setting Speaker Volume

You can set the speaker volume using the Volume tile in Mobility Center or the speaker icon in your notification area. In both cases, you drag a slider to increase or decrease the volume. As you drag, a ScreenTip displays the current volume setting, which ranges from a low of 0 to a high of 100. When you stop dragging, Windows plays a sound at the current volume so you can hear how loud or soft it is. You can also use the Volume tile or the speaker icon to mute sound, which effectively turns off the speakers. You use the same controls to turn the sound back on.

As you help Kevin prepare for your trip to your client's office in Klamath Falls, Kevin reminds you that he wants to work on his laptop computer during the drive. He is planning to view the presentation he will give to Chamberlain & Klein. Because the presentation includes audio, he wants to turn off the speakers on his laptop during the trip so that the presentation does not distract Tay while he is driving. You'll show Kevin how to test the volume of the speakers and then mute them using Windows Mobility Center. Note the original volume setting so you can restore it later.

In order to perform most of the steps in this session, you need to be working on a mobile PC, such as a laptop computer, or a desktop PC where Windows Mobility Center has been enabled, a process that involves changing registry settings and is beyond the scope of this tutorial. If you are not working on a mobile PC or a desktop PC with Windows Mobility Center, read but do not perform the steps.

To open Windows Mobility Center and adjust the speaker volume:

▶ **1.** Click the **Start** button 🪟 on the taskbar, point to **All Programs**, click **Accessories**, and then click **Windows Mobility Center**. Windows Mobility Center opens as shown in Figure 8-2.

   Trouble? If Windows Mobility Center is not listed on the Accessories menu, click in the Search for programs and files box on the Start menu, type *mblctr*, and then click mblctr in the results list.

▶ **2.** To test the speaker volume, drag the **Volume** slider to **30**. Windows plays a sound at that volume.

   Trouble? If your speakers are already set to 30, drag the Volume slider to 40.

   Trouble? If the sound scheme on your computer is set to No Sounds, no sound will be audible.

▶ **3.** Click the **Mute** check box to insert a check mark. Windows turns the speakers off.

Now that you've shown Kevin how to control the volume of his notebook speakers, you'll demonstrate how to manage battery power with power plans.

Selecting a Power Plan

One advantage of mobile PCs over desktop computers is that you can use mobile PCs without plugging them into a power outlet. Instead, mobile PCs get the power they need from a battery, which is usually installed within the computer case. However, even with recent improvements in battery cell technology, you can use a mobile computer powered by a battery for only a limited time before you need to recharge the battery. You can track the status of the battery charge in Windows Mobility Center and in the notification area of the taskbar. Both places display a battery meter icon that shows how much charge remains in the battery. See Figure 8-4.

Figure 8-4　　**Battery status**

battery status displayed in Windows Mobility Center

battery meter icon in the notification area of the taskbar

Although a battery meter icon always appears on the taskbar of a mobile computer, it can also appear on a desktop computer that is plugged into an uninterruptible power supply (UPS) or other short-term battery device. If your computer has more than one battery, you can click the battery meter icon in the notification area of the taskbar to display the charge remaining on one battery, click it again to see the charge remaining on the second battery, and so on. Point to the battery meter icon to see the combined charge.

You can also point to the battery meter icon to display the amount of time and percentage of battery power remaining. The battery meter icon changes appearance to display the current state of the battery so that you can see how much charge remains even when you are not pointing to the icon. When the battery charge is higher than 25 percent, the battery image in the icon is completely or mostly white. When the battery charge reaches 25 percent, a yellow warning sign appears on the icon. When the charge is 10 percent or lower, a critical sign appears and Windows displays a notification so you can recharge the battery. See Figure 8-5.

Figure 8-5　　**Changes in the battery meter icon**

Your mobile PC is plugged in and the battery is charging	Battery is fully charged	Your mobile PC is running on battery power	Battery charge is low	Battery charge is critical

Besides displaying the percentage of charge remaining in the battery, the battery meter icon and the Battery Status tile in Mobility Center display your current power plan. Recall that a power plan is a collection of hardware and system settings that manages how your computer uses and conserves power. To match how you are using your mobile computer with how it consumes energy, you select a power plan. Windows 7 provides three default plans that let you save energy, maximize system performance, or balance energy conservation with system performance. The three default plans are called Balanced, Power saver, and High performance, and are described in Figure 8-6. Some computer manufacturers set up additional power plans, so your computer might have different plans.

Figure 8-6   **Default power plans**

Power Plan	Description
Balanced	Balances energy consumption and system performance by adjusting your computer's processor speed to match your activity
Power saver	Saves power on your mobile computer by reducing system performance and extending battery life
High performance	Provides the highest level of performance on your mobile computer but consumes the most energy

You can select a power plan by clicking the Battery Status arrow button in Mobility Center, or by clicking the battery icon in the notification area of the taskbar and then clicking a power plan option button. Most mobile computers include the kind of hardware Windows 7 expects to support power management settings. However, if your computer does not have the proper kind of hardware or if Windows cannot identify it, the Battery Status arrow button or battery icon menu displays only the plans your computer supports.

REFERENCE

Selecting a Power Plan

- Click the Start button, point to All Programs, click Accessories, and then click Windows Mobility Center.
- Click the Battery Status arrow button, and then click a power plan.

or

- Click the battery icon in the notification area of the taskbar.
- Click a power plan option button.

Because Kevin will have to run his laptop computer on battery power during the trip to Klamath Falls, you show him how to monitor his power consumption by pointing to the battery meter icon in the notification area of the taskbar. Next, you'll show him how to change his power plan to Power saver, which is designed for mobile computer users who are working away from power outlets for several hours. Note your original settings so you can restore them later.

To perform the following steps, you need to be working on a PC with a battery power source such as a laptop computer. If you are not working on such a PC, read but do not perform the steps.

To change the power plan:

1. In Windows Mobility Center, click the **Battery Status** arrow button, and then click **Power saver**.

   Trouble? If your Battery Status is already set to Power saver, skip Step 1.

   Trouble? If the Power saver setting is not available when you click the Battery Status arrow button, skip Step 1.

2. Minimize the Windows Mobility Center window.

To extend battery life, the Power saver plan slows system performance and lowers the brightness of the display.

INSIGHT

Choosing a Power Plan

When working with mobile computers or desktop computers that are connected to a battery, choose a battery plan that best fits your current activities to conserve battery power and to save energy in general. If you are engaging in activities that don't require a lot of power, such as reading e-mail messages or listening to music, switch to the Power saver plan. If you need a lot of computing power, such as when you are working with complex spreadsheets or creating movies, use the High performance plan. If you are performing a variety of tasks, select the Balanced power plan so that the processor can run at full speed when you are playing a game or watching a video, but slow down to save power when you are checking your e-mail.

Kevin thinks the Power saver plan is perfect for conserving the battery charge while he's traveling. He can then change to the Balanced plan when he arrives in Klamath Falls, but he wants to fine-tune that plan to suit his needs. During his presentation, he wants to use power settings that are not offered in any of the default plans, so you'll show him how to modify a default plan.

Customizing Power Options

If the default power plans provided by Windows 7 or your computer manufacturer do not address your power needs, you can change one of the default plans. All of the plans specify how long the computer can be idle before Windows turns off the display and how long to wait before Windows puts the computer to sleep when you are using battery power or a wall outlet. When putting your computer to sleep, Windows saves your data and system settings in temporary memory and then suspends operations as it goes into a power-saving state. During sleep, the screen is blank and the computer does not perform any activities, which conserves power. In fact, while a mobile computer is asleep, it typically uses 1 to 2 percent of battery power per hour, which is a fraction of what it uses when running on full power. (You can put a computer to sleep yourself by clicking the Shut down arrow button on the Start menu then clicking Sleep, pressing a sleep button if your mobile device has one, or closing the lid on your notebook computer.) To wake a mobile computer from sleep, you usually press the hardware power button. To wake a desktop computer, you usually move the mouse or press a key. In a few seconds, Windows displays the desktop in its presleep state, including open windows and running programs.

Besides changing sleep settings and displaying turn-off times for each default power plan, you can specify advanced settings such as how long to wait before hibernating. **Hibernation** is a power-saving state designed for laptop computers. It saves your work to your hard disk, puts your computer into a power-saving state, and then turns off your computer. Of the three power-saving states in Windows 7, hibernation uses the least amount of power. Because the sleep states require some power, Windows automatically puts a mobile computer into hibernation after a specified period of time. Windows also puts a mobile PC into hibernation when the battery charge is critically low. If you know that you won't use your mobile computer for a while and you can't charge the battery during that time, you should put your computer into hibernation yourself. To do so, click the Shut down arrow button on the Start menu, and then click Hibernate.

Hybrid sleep is an alternative to sleep designed for desktop computers. As its name suggests, hybrid sleep is a combination of sleep and hibernation. Windows saves your open documents and programs to temporary memory and to your hard disk, and then goes into a low-power state without turning off the power. You resume from hybrid sleep the same way and almost as quickly as from sleep. The advantage is that if a power failure occurs while your computer is asleep, Windows can restore your documents because it saved them to your hard disk. If the hybrid sleep option is selected (which it is by default on desktop computers) and you click the Power button on the Start menu, Windows puts your computer into hybrid sleep instead of standard sleep.

In short, power plans include settings that determine how long Windows should wait before putting your computer into a power-saving state: sleep, hibernation, or hybrid sleep. You can also put your computer to sleep or into hibernation yourself by using a button on the Start menu.

PROSKILLS

Decision Making: Choosing a Power-Saving State

Sleep, hybrid sleep, and hibernation are three power-saving states Windows uses to conserve battery power on mobile computers. Selecting the right option for your computer and your usage style can help you work more efficiently. Keep the following guidelines in mind when choosing a power-saving state:

- *Sleep*. If you do not plan to use your computer for several hours, Microsoft recommends putting it to sleep rather than turning it off. Sleep is preferable to turning off your computer because when you're ready to use your computer again, it wakes quickly so you can resume your work where you left it. If you put a computer to sleep yourself, be sure to save your data first so you don't lose it in case of a power failure. Even if you let Windows put your computer to sleep after a specified amount of idle time, standard sleep is the best power-saving state for average computing because it resumes operations faster than hybrid sleep or hibernation.
- *Hibernation*. When you are finished working and know you won't use your mobile computer for up to a day, and that you won't have a chance to recharge the battery during that time, put the computer into hibernation yourself. Otherwise, you can generally let Windows determine when to use hibernation. If you don't plan to use the computer for more than a day, you save wear and tear on your electronic components and conserve energy by turning the computer off. However, most computers redisplay the desktop more quickly after hibernating than being turned off.
- *Hybrid sleep*. If you are concerned that you might lose power while the computer is asleep, such as when your battery charge is low and you cannot recharge it, turn on hybrid sleep so that Windows saves your data on the hard disk before it puts your computer to sleep.

Modifying a Power Plan

When you modify a power plan, you can adjust up to two basic settings and dozens of advanced settings that apply when your computer is running on battery power and when your computer is plugged into a power outlet. For example, in the Balanced plan, Windows is set to turn off the display after five minutes of idle time if the computer is using battery power and after 10 minutes of inactivity if the computer is plugged into an outlet. You can increase or decrease these times in the Edit Plan Settings window, which you open from the Power Options category in the Control Panel. To change advanced settings, such as whether to use hybrid sleep instead of standard sleep, you open the Power Options dialog box from the Edit Plan Settings window.

Modifying a Power Plan

- Click the Start button, and then click Control Panel.
- In Category view, click Hardware and Sound, and then click Power Options. In Large icons or Small icons view, click Power Options.
- Click Change plan settings for the power plan you want to modify.
- Click a button for a power setting, and then click the amount of time to wait before applying the setting.
- Click Change advanced power settings.
- Expand an advanced setting, change the setting, and then click the OK button.
- Click the Save changes button.

Kevin wants to make two changes to the Balanced power plan on his mobile computer. First, he wants Windows to wait for more than 10 minutes of idle time before it turns off the display when his computer is plugged in. During his presentation, members of the audience might raise questions that lead him to step away from his computer for 20–30 minutes of discussion. Also, because he has only one copy of the presentation on his laptop, he wants to take an extra precaution to prevent losing that document if a power outage occurs while his computer is asleep. You'll show Kevin how to change basic and advanced settings for the Balanced power plan.

TIP

You can also open the Power Options window by clicking the battery icon in the notification area and then clicking More power options.

To change basic power plan settings:

1. Click the **Start** button 🔵, click **Control Panel**, click **Hardware and Sound**, and then click **Power Options**. The Power Options window opens. See Figure 8-7.

Figure 8-7   **Power Options window**

preferred power plans on this computer; yours might differ

summary of how the plan balances battery life and system performance

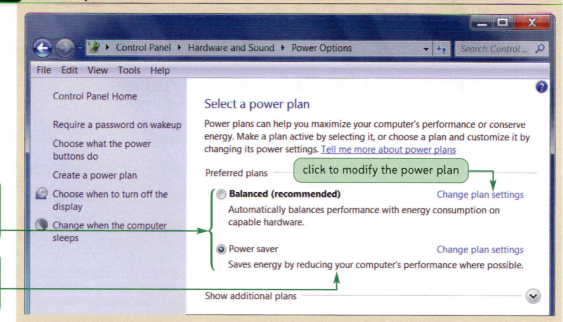

This window lists power plans and summarizes how each plan balances battery life with system performance.

Trouble? If your Control Panel window opens to Large icons or Small icons view, click Power Options instead of clicking Hardware and Sound.

2. Click **Change plan settings** for the Balanced power plan. The Edit Plan Settings window opens for the Balanced plan. See Figure 8-8. Your settings might differ. If you are using a desktop computer, your options also differ.

Figure 8-8   Edit Plan Settings window

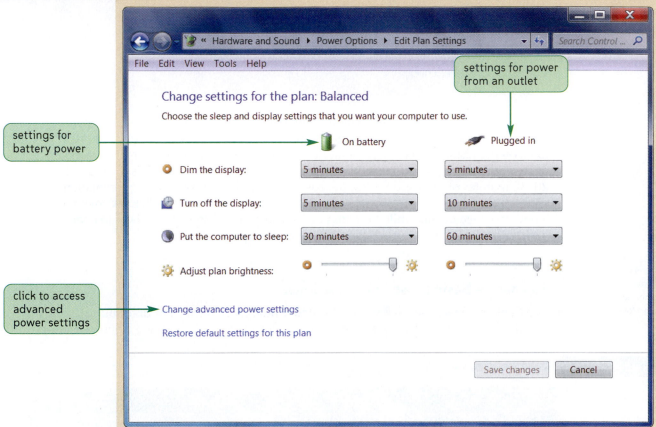

settings for power from an outlet

settings for battery power

click to access advanced power settings

3. For the Turn off the display setting, click the **arrow button** in the Plugged in column, and then click **30 minutes**.

Trouble? If you are working on a desktop computer, click the arrow button for the Turn off the display setting, and then click 30 minutes.

4. Click the **Save changes** button. Windows saves the new setting and returns to the Power Options window.

You can change the other basic power plan settings the same way—click a button for a setting such as Turn off the display or Put the computer to sleep, and then select an amount of idle time Windows should wait before activating that setting. You can turn off the setting by selecting Never. For example, if you do not want Windows to put the computer to sleep when it's plugged in, click the arrow button in the Plugged in column for the Put the computer to sleep setting, and then click Never. However, you might lose data if you prevent a mobile computer from sleeping or hibernating and the battery runs out of power.

Next, you'll show Kevin how to customize the hibernation setting on his laptop computer as an extra precaution to prevent losing updates he makes to his presentation. To do so, you need to change an advanced power plan setting.

To change advanced power plan settings:

▶ **1.** In the Power Options window, click **Change plan settings** for the Balanced power plan to open the Edit Plan Settings window again.

▶ **2.** Click **Change advanced power settings** to open the Power Options dialog box. See Figure 8-9.

Figure 8-9	Power Options dialog box

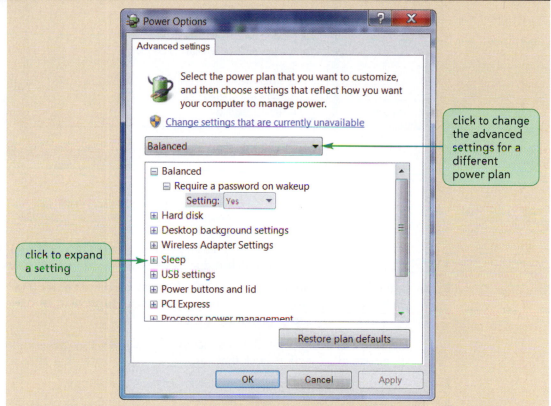

▶ **3.** Click the **expand** button ⊞ for the Sleep setting, and then click the **expand** button ⊞ for the Hibernate after setting. See Figure 8-10.

Figure 8-10   **Preparing to allow hibernation**

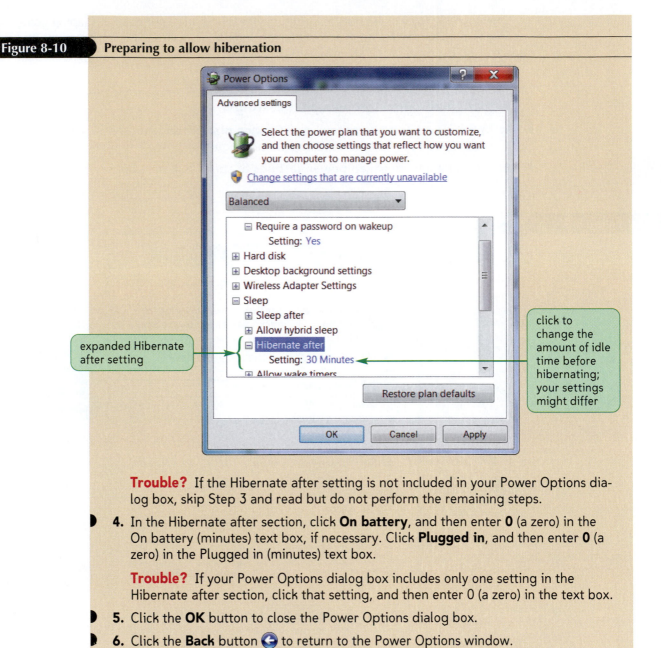

expanded Hibernate after setting

click to change the amount of idle time before hibernating; your settings might differ

Trouble? If the Hibernate after setting is not included in your Power Options dialog box, skip Step 3 and read but do not perform the remaining steps.

4. In the Hibernate after section, click **On battery**, and then enter **0** (a zero) in the On battery (minutes) text box, if necessary. Click **Plugged in**, and then enter **0** (a zero) in the Plugged in (minutes) text box.

Trouble? If your Power Options dialog box includes only one setting in the Hibernate after section, click that setting, and then enter 0 (a zero) in the text box.

5. Click the **OK** button to close the Power Options dialog box.

6. Click the **Back** button ⬅ to return to the Power Options window.

You've changed basic and advanced settings in Kevin's Balanced power plan. Next, you'll show him how to change other power options.

Selecting Other Power Options

Besides using power plans, you can control other power settings, such as what Windows should do when you press the hardware power button or close the lid on your mobile PC. You can apply the following settings to all of your power plans or only to a specific plan.

- Define power button and lid settings. Recall that by default, Windows puts a mobile computer to sleep when you press the hardware power button or close the lid. It also puts the computer to sleep when you press the hardware sleep button (if your computer has one). You can change the power button, sleep button, and lid settings to hibernate, shut down, or do nothing when your computer is running on battery power or is plugged in.

- Require a password on wakeup. If you log on to your computer by providing a password, Windows locks your computer for security when it sleeps and requires that password to unlock the computer when it wakes from sleep. This is especially helpful if you need to protect confidential information on your computer. However, if you're the only one who uses your computer and you use it at home or another private place, you can change this setting if you don't want to enter a password every time your computer wakes.

Kevin is in the habit of using the Shut down arrow button on the Start menu to put his notebook computer to sleep and likes having the computer go to sleep when he closes the lid, which he does when he moves the computer. However, if his computer is running on battery power, he wants to save the battery charge by having the computer hibernate and eventually turn off when he presses the hardware power button on the computer case. In addition, although he wants to maintain password protection during the trip to Klamath Falls, he wants to know how to turn off the password protection on wake-up setting so he doesn't need to provide the password when he works from home. You'll show Kevin how to change the power button and password protection on wake-up settings.

To change power options:

1. In the Power Options window, click **Choose what the power buttons do** in the left pane. The System Settings window opens. See Figure 8-11. If you are using a desktop computer, your options differ.

| Figure 8-11 | System Settings window |

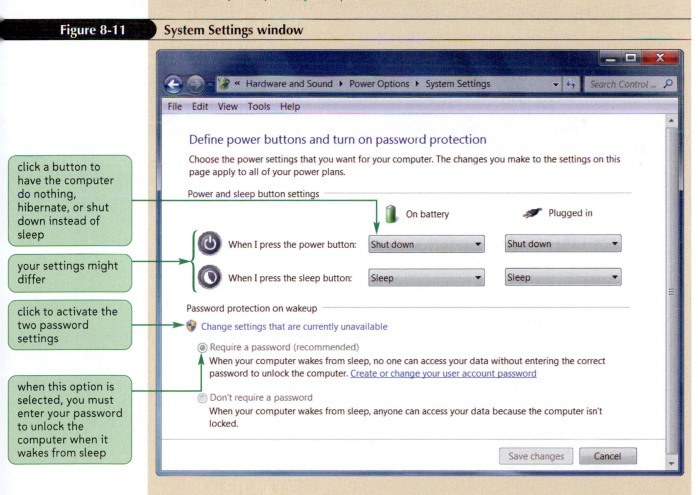

click a button to have the computer do nothing, hibernate, or shut down instead of sleep

your settings might differ

click to activate the two password settings

when this option is selected, you must enter your password to unlock the computer when it wakes from sleep

Trouble? If the name of the command in your Power Options window is Choose what the power button does, click that command.

▶ **2.** For the When I press the power button setting, click the **arrow button** in the On battery column, and then click **Hibernate**.

Trouble? If you are using a desktop computer, your window does not have two columns of buttons. Click the arrow button for the When I press the power button setting, and then click Hibernate.

▶ **3.** Click the **Change settings that are currently unavailable** link, if necessary, to make the Password protection on wakeup settings available.

▶ **4.** Click the **Don't require a password** option button. This means that when your computer wakes from sleep, it is unlocked and anyone can access your data and settings.

▶ **5.** Click the **Require a password (recommended)** option button. This means that when your computer wakes from sleep, it is locked and you or another user must enter your Windows password to unlock it.

▶ **6.** Click the **Save changes** button.

▶ **7.** Close the Power Options window.

The change you made to the power button now applies to all of the power plans on Kevin's computer. To make these changes to only a particular power plan, you open the Advanced settings tab in the Power Options dialog box as you did earlier, and then change the Require a password on wakeup and Power buttons and lid settings.

If you turn off the setting to require a password to wake your computer from sleep, you should also turn off your screen saver password. (A screen saver password locks your computer when the screen saver is on. The screen saver password is the same as the one you use to log on to Windows.) To turn off the screen saver password, open the Control Panel, click Appearance and Personalization, click Change screen saver, and then click the On resume, display logon screen check box to remove the check mark.

Now that you've shown Kevin how to control the power state of his mobile PC, you're ready for the trip to Klamath Falls. When you arrive, you can help him prepare his computer for the presentation to Chamberlain & Klein.

Presenting Information to an Audience

Giving a presentation is a common practice in business and education. When you use a computer to give a presentation to an audience, you can combine images, text, animation, sound and visual effects, and audio to educate, inform, or train others. You can give a presentation to a small or large group of people while you are in the same room, or you can present the information remotely to people with whom you share a network connection. To create a presentation, you can use Microsoft PowerPoint, Windows Live Movie Maker, the slide show feature in the Pictures folder, or any other presentation program. You can then connect your computer to a projector to broadcast the presentation. To start and control the presentation, you use the keyboard and pointing device on your computer and the tools provided in the presentation program to perform tasks such as switching from one image or slide to another and ending the presentation.

Before you give a presentation, you can use Windows Mobility Center to adjust presentation settings, which are a collection of options that prepare your computer for a presentation. For example, you can control the volume level of your computer and block distractions such as notifications and reminders. You can also use Mobility Center to connect your computer to an external display, such as a larger monitor or projector. To connect to a network projector, which is a projecting device connected to your network, you can use the Connect to a Network Projector wizard, an accessory program available on the Start menu.

Preparing a Computer for a Presentation

Using Windows Mobility Center, you can specify the settings that Windows 7 uses when you are giving a presentation. When you turn on presentation settings, your computer stays awake and Windows blocks system notifications, such as notices about available software updates. You can also choose to turn off the screen saver, adjust the speaker volume, and change your desktop background image. Windows saves these settings and applies them when you turn on presentation settings in Windows Mobility Center. To turn on presentation settings, you can click the Turn on button in the Presentation Settings tile of Windows Mobility Center. Windows also turns on presentation settings when you connect your mobile PC to a network projector or additional monitor. To turn off presentation settings, you can click the Turn off button in Mobility Center. Windows also turns off presentation settings when you disconnect your computer from a projector or when you shut down or log off from your PC.

Now that you, Kevin, and Tay have arrived in Klamath Falls, you have some time to prepare for Kevin's presentation, which he'll give in the Chamberlain & Klein conference room. First, you'll customize the presentation settings to turn off the screen saver, turn up the volume, and change the desktop background to black. Then you'll show Kevin how to turn the presentation settings on and off. Note your original settings so you can restore them later.

To customize presentation settings:

1. Restore the Windows Mobility Center window.

2. In the Presentation Settings tile, click the **Change presentation settings** icon ⬕. The Presentation Settings dialog box opens. See Figure 8-12.

Figure 8-12 | Presentation Settings dialog box

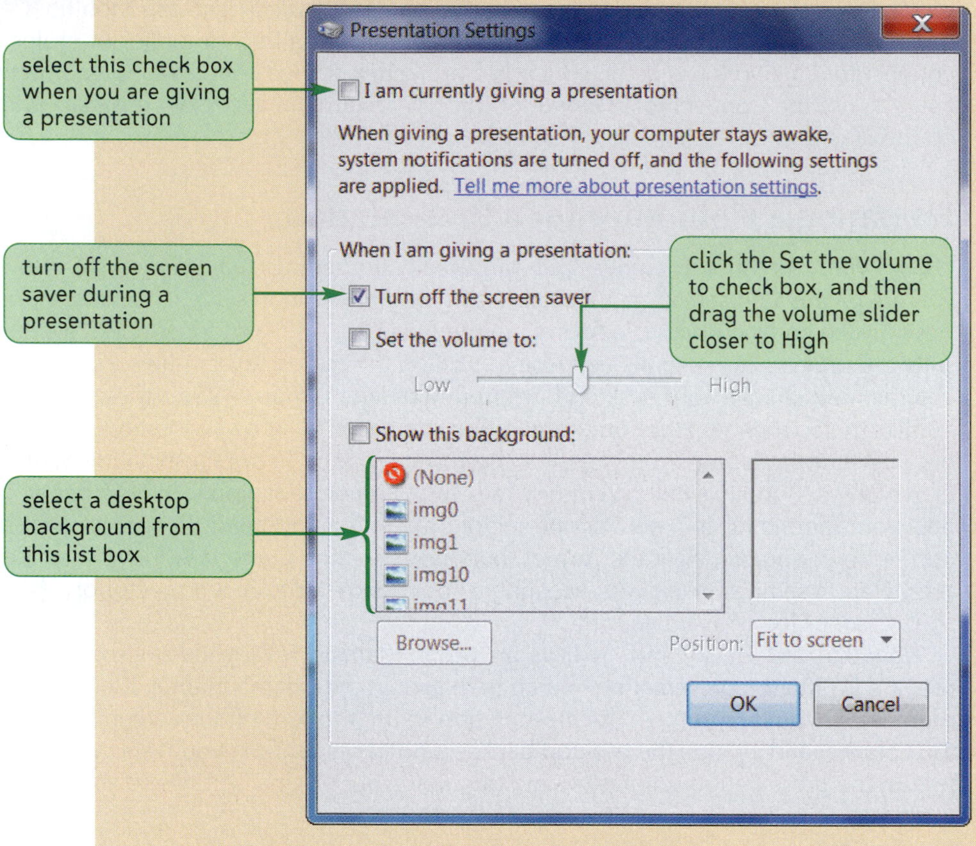

select this check box when you are giving a presentation

turn off the screen saver during a presentation

click the Set the volume to check box, and then drag the volume slider closer to High

select a desktop background from this list box

3. If necessary, click the **Turn off the screen saver** check box to insert a check mark.

4. Click the **Set the volume to** check box, and then drag the slider to **85**.

5. Click the **Show this background** check box, and then click **(None)**.

6. Click the **OK** button.

Now Windows will turn off the screen saver, turn up the speaker volume, and display a black desktop background when Kevin turns on the presentation settings, which you'll show him how to do next.

To turn presentation settings on and off:

1. In the Presentation Settings tile, click the **Turn on** button. The desktop, taskbar, and window borders turn black. See Figure 8-13.

Figure 8-13 | **Turning on presentation settings**

black desktop background

Presentation Settings tile indicates you are presenting

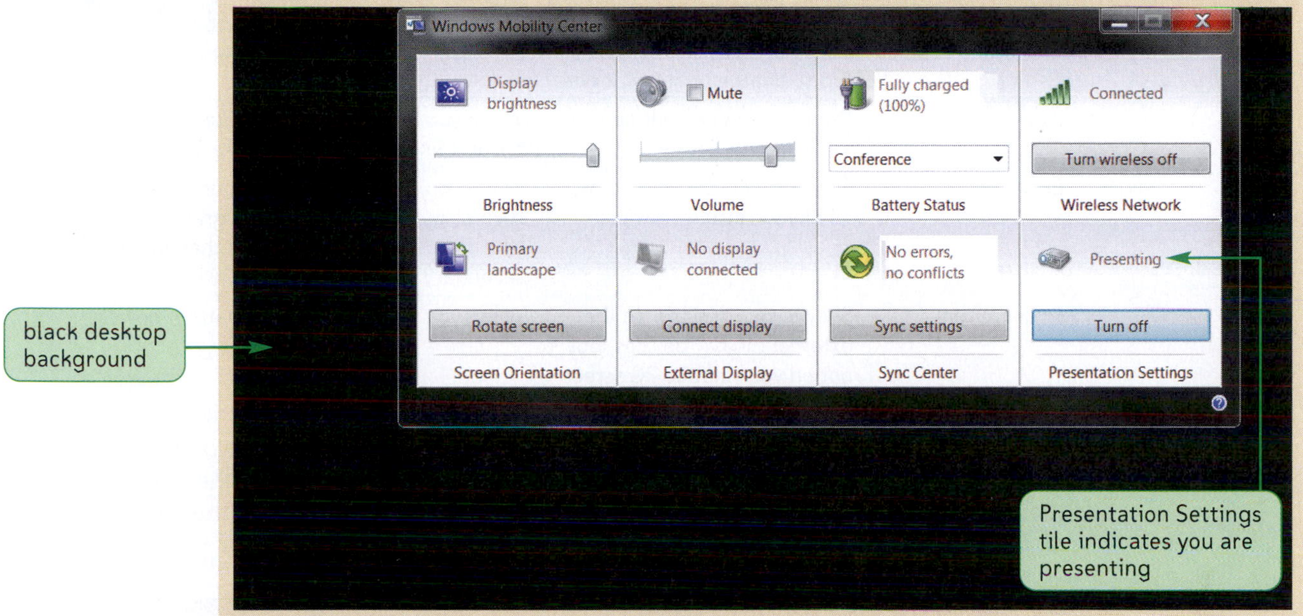

It's not yet time for Kevin's presentation, so you can turn off the settings for now.

2. In the Presentation Settings tile, click the **Turn off** button. The desktop returns to its pre-presentation state.

Next, you'll help Kevin select display settings when he connects his notebook computer to a projector.

Displaying Information on an External Display Device

TIP

You can also click the Connect display button in the External Display tile in Mobility Center to select an external projector or monitor.

When you connect a mobile PC to a projector or any other type of additional display device such as a flat-screen monitor, Windows 7 detects the extra display and recommends the video settings that correspond to that device. See Figure 8-14.

Figure 8-14 | **Selecting a display option**

Duplicate and Projector only settings are appropriate for giving presentations

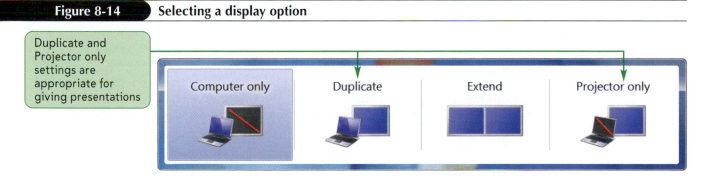

Figure 8-15 describes what each option in this dialog box means.

Figure 8-15   **Display options when you connect an external display**

Display Option	Description	When to Use
Computer only	Does not extend your desktop to another display device	When you are using your computer as usual
Duplicate	Duplicates your desktop on each display device	When you are giving a presentation on a projector or a fixed display, such as a TV-type monitor
Extend	Extends your desktop across all of your display devices	When you want to increase your work space, such as by displaying one program window on your primary monitor and another window on a secondary monitor
Projector only	Shows your desktop on the external display devices, but not on your mobile PC screen	When you want to conserve battery power

When you disconnect the external display device, Windows restores the original display settings to your main computer monitor. The next time that you connect the same monitor, Windows automatically applies the display settings that you used the last time that you connected that monitor.

Before adding a second display device to your computer, make sure that you have a video card that supports multiple monitors or that your computer has more than one video card. A video card that supports multiple monitors has two video ports—check the back of your computer to find these ports.

Turn off your computer before connecting the second display device. When you turn on your computer, Windows should recognize the secondary monitor and open the window with buttons for duplicating, extending, or showing your desktop on the external display only.

Kevin connects his notebook computer to the projector in the conference room. When the window shown in Figure 8-14 opens, you click the Duplicate setting. Kevin's desktop is now displayed on his notebook and is projected on a large white screen in the conference room.

Connecting to a Network Projector

As you'll learn shortly, you can share resources such as Internet access and a printer if you connect your computer to one or more other computers to form a network. (**Network resources** are files, folders, software, and hardware devices that computers on a network can access.) If you are connected to a network that includes a projector as one of its shared resources, you can use that network projector to give a presentation from a desktop or mobile computer. That means you can deliver a presentation from any location that has network access, whether a private office or a conference room where the projector is located.

To do so, you use the Connect to a Network Projector Wizard, which guides you through the steps of connecting to any available projector on your network. You can use the wizard to connect to a network projector in one of two ways: select from a list of available projectors or enter the network address of the projector. See Figure 8-16.

| Figure 8-16 | Starting the Connect to a Network Projector Wizard |

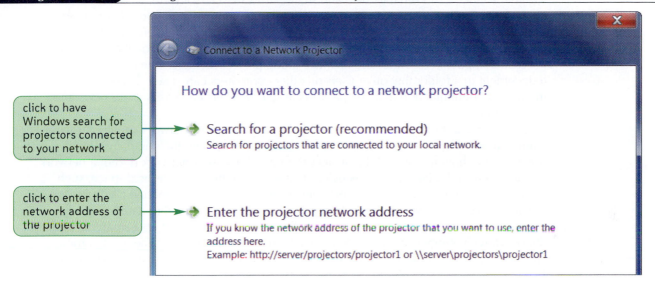

When you choose to search for a projector with the Connect to a Network Projector Wizard, Windows searches for projectors on your network and then displays up to five projectors that you have used recently. (The wizard can only find a network projector if the projector is connected to the same network segment to which your computer is connected.) To use one of these projectors, you select it from the list. If you want to use a different projector, you can enter the projector's network address, which you can enter as a URL such as *http://server/projectors/projector01*, or as a path such as *\\server\projectors\projector01*. You might need to ask your network administrator for the correct network address. When you enter a projector's network address, the wizard can find the projector regardless of where it's located on the network.

REFERENCE

Connecting to a Network Projector

- Click the Start button on the taskbar, point to All Programs, click Accessories, and then click Connect to a Network Projector.
- If you are asked for permission to connect, click Yes. If you are then asked for permission to continue, click the Continue button.
- If a dialog box opens with a message that Windows Firewall is blocking the network projector, click Allow the network projector to communicate with my computer.
- Select Search for a projector (recommended) or Enter the projector network address.
- Click an available projector in the list or enter the network address, enter the projector password, if necessary, and then click the Connect button.

After you finish using the wizard to connect to a network projector, a Network Presentation icon appears in the notification area of the taskbar. You can click the icon to open the Network Presentation dialog box to pause, resume, or end your presentation by disconnecting your computer from the network projector.

Because Kevin can use the projector in Chamberlain & Klein's conference room, he doesn't need to use a network projector. However, after you help Tay configure the law firm's network, Kevin can use the Connect to a Network Projector Wizard to remotely connect to the law firm's projector if necessary.

Exploring Network Concepts

As you know, a network is a collection of computers and other hardware devices linked together so they can exchange data and share hardware and software. Networks offer many advantages. Groups of computers on a network can use the same printer, so you don't have to purchase a printer for each computer. Network computers can also share an Internet connection, so you don't need to purchase and install a broadband modem for each computer. Networks also facilitate group projects because one person can save a document in a folder that other users on other computers can access. A network also improves communication in a company because coworkers can easily share news and information.

Large companies that want to connect their computers on a network usually hire a team of network specialists to determine what type of hardware the company should purchase and how to connect the devices to form a **local area network (LAN)**, a network of computers and other hardware devices that reside in the same physical space, such as an office building. Small office and home users can set up a simplified LAN to enjoy the advantages of networking. Like large companies, you also need to decide what type of network technology and hardware you will use if you want to set up a small network. (**Network technology** is the way computers connect to one another.) The most common types of network technology for a small office or home network are wireless, Ethernet, Home Phone Network Alliance (HPNA), and Powerline. Figure 8-17 compares network technologies.

Figure 8-17	Comparing network technologies

Network Technology	How It Sends Information Between Computers	Pros	Cons
Wireless	Uses radio waves, microwaves, or infrared light	Setting up the network and moving computers are easy because there are no cables.	Wireless technology is more expensive and often slower than Ethernet or HPNA. Wireless connections can be interrupted by interference.
Ethernet	Uses Ethernet cables	Ethernet is a proven and reliable technology, and Ethernet networks are inexpensive and fast.	Ethernet cables must connect each computer to a hub, switch, or router, which can be time consuming and difficult when the computers are in different rooms.
HPNA	Uses existing home telephone wires	You can connect computers without using hubs or switches.	You need a phone jack in each room where you want to have a computer, and all jacks must be on the same phone line.
Powerline	Uses existing home electrical wiring to send information between computers	You don't need hubs or switches to connect more than two computers in a Powerline network.	You need an electrical outlet in each room where you want to have a computer, and Powerline networks can be affected by interference and noise on the line.

Small office and home networks use a variety of special hardware, including the following devices:

- Network adapters. Also called network interface cards (NICs), these adapters connect computers to a network. Network adapters are often installed inside your computer, though you can also plug one into a USB port. See Figure 8-18.

Figure 8-18   **Network interface card**

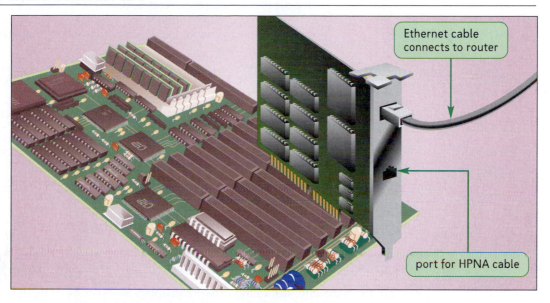

Ethernet cable connects to router

port for HPNA cable

- Network hubs and switches. Used on an Ethernet network, these devices connect two or more computers to the network.
- Routers or access points. Routers connect computers and networks to each other and let you share a single Internet connection among several computers. They are called routers because they direct network traffic. An access point provides wireless access to a wired Ethernet network. An access point plugs into a wired router and sends out a wireless signal, which other wireless computers and devices use to connect to the wired network. Most home networks share access to the Internet by connecting a wireless router to a modem and to a computer with an Internet connection.
- Modems. To connect your computer to the Internet, you need a modem, which sends and receives information over telephone or cable lines.
- Cables. On an Ethernet or HPNA network, cables connect computers to each other and to other devices, such as hubs and routers.

Figure 8-19 describes the hardware required for each type of network technology.

Figure 8-19	Hardware needed for each type of network technology

Network Technology	Hardware Required
Wireless	• Wireless network adapter installed on each computer in the network • Wireless access point or router
Ethernet	• Ethernet network adapter on each computer in the network • Ethernet hub or switch if you want to connect more than two computers • Ethernet router if you want to connect more than two computers and share an Internet connection • Ethernet cables • Crossover cable if you want to connect two computers directly to each other and not use a hub, switch, or router
HPNA	• Home phone line network adapter on each computer in the network • Telephone cables
Powerline	• Powerline network adapter for each computer on your network • Ethernet router to share an Internet connection • One electrical outlet for each computer on your network

Setting Up a Small Office or Home Network

After you determine what type of network you want and acquire the hardware you need, you can set up a small office or home network by performing the following tasks:

- Install the hardware. Install the network adapters in the computers that need them, if necessary.
- Set up an Internet connection. If you want the network computers to access the Internet, set up a connection to the Internet. (See Appendix A for complete instructions.)
- Connect the computers. On an Ethernet network, you can use crossover cables to connect two computers in the same room. If you want to connect more than two computers or link computers in different rooms on an Ethernet network, you need a hub, switch, or router to connect the computers. Use a router to share an Internet connection. Connect the router to the computer that is connected to the modem.

  If you only want to share an Internet connection on a wireless network, you can set up a wireless router and then use Windows 7 to connect to that network. If you want to also share files and printers, run the Set up a wireless router or access point wizard to guide you through the steps of adding computers and other devices to the network.

  On an HPNA network, use cables to connect two or more computers.

- Test the connections. Turn on all the computers and devices, and then open the Network window by clicking the Start button, clicking your user name, and then clicking Network in the left pane. In the Network window, an icon should appear for your computer and all the other computers and devices connected to the network.

  If you only want to share an Internet connection on a wireless network, you need to complete two steps:

- Configure the wireless router to broadcast signals.
- Set up Windows 7 on each computer to receive the signals.

  In the first step, you install a wireless router and configure it to start broadcasting and receiving information to and from your computer. To have the router start broadcasting radio signals, you need to run the setup software provided with your router. The steps to run this software vary depending on your router, but usually you need to provide a network name, or service set identifier (SSID), which is a name you use to identify your wireless network. You'll see this name later when you use Windows 7 to connect to your wireless network. The setup software also lets you turn on security settings to encrypt your data when you transmit it, which helps to prevent unauthorized people from accessing your data or your network. To do so, you need to provide a password so that you can access the network. See Figure 8-20.

| Figure 8-20 | Wireless network sharing an Internet connection |

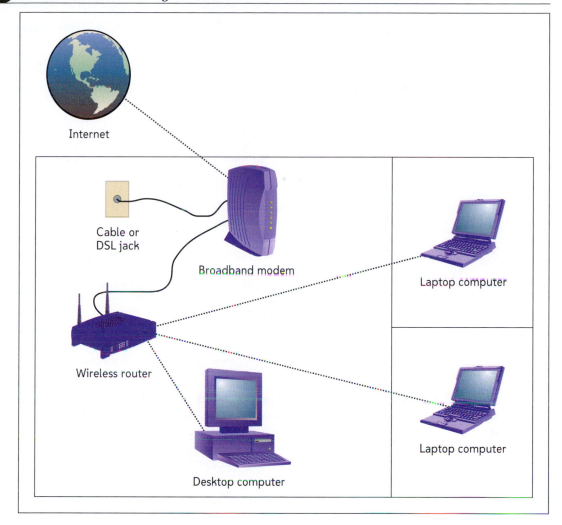

The following section shows you how to set up Windows 7 to receive the wireless signals.

If you want to share files and printers as well as an Internet connection on a wireless network, you can set up a homegroup, which is discussed later in this tutorial.

Managing Network Connections

After you connect two or more computers through cables or wireless connections, you can use Windows 7 to monitor and manage your network connections. If your network is set up to share a network printer or an Internet connection, Windows works behind the scenes to organize requests to use these resources. For example, if two people want to print documents at the same time on the network printer, Windows lines up the printer requests in a queue and prints the documents one after the other. It also lets all the network users share a single Internet connection so they can visit Web sites and exchange e-mail without interrupting each other. For other networking tasks, such as verifying you are connected to a network, finding and connecting to a wireless network, and determining which other computers are connected, you use the Network and Sharing Center window. See Figure 8-21.

Figure 8-21 **Network and Sharing Center window**

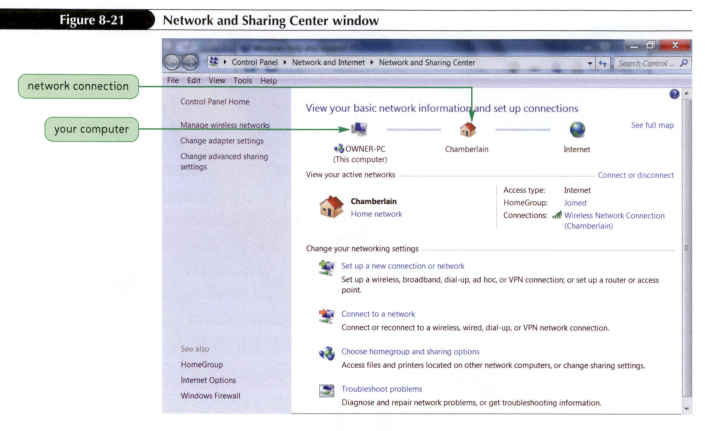

You can now show Tay how to connect his mobile PC to the Chamberlain & Klein wireless network. He has prepared some sample network policy documents and wants to copy them to a folder on the network that the Chamberlain & Klein partners can access. Tay might also need to retrieve a document stored on their network. Before he can perform those tasks, he needs to connect to the wireless network.

Connecting to a Wireless Network

If you have a mobile PC with a wireless network adapter, you can display a list of available wireless networks and then connect to one of those networks, whether it's your own private wireless network or a public one. You'll show Tay how to use Mobility Center to open the Connect to a network window, which you can use to connect to available wireless networks. Windows displays the following information about each available wireless network:

- Network name. This is the SSID you or someone else provided when the network was set up. Because wireless signals extend past the boundaries of your home or office, the wireless adapter in your computer often detects more than one network within its range.
- Security. Unsecured networks don't require a password, whereas security-enabled networks do. Security-enabled networks also encrypt data before transmitting it, meaning that unauthorized people cannot intercept sensitive information such as a credit card number when you send it across the network. When you set up a wireless network, you should create a strong password or passphrase (more than one word). A strong passphrase includes at least 20 characters and is not a common phrase that other people are likely to know. If you don't create a passphrase, the network is protected with a network security key, which is usually a series of hexadecimal numbers.

- Signal strength. Windows displays a series of bars that indicate the strength of the signal. The more bars highlighted, the stronger the connection. Having the strongest signal (five bars highlighted) means that the wireless network is nearby or there is no interference. To improve the signal strength, you can move your computer closer to the wireless router or access point, or move the router or access point away from sources of interference such as brick walls or walls that contain metal support beams.

Unless you are accessing a public network, such as in an airport or hotel, be sure to connect only to the wireless network you are authorized to use, even if you can access an unsecured private network. If you are authorized to connect to more than one wireless network, you should generally use the one with the strongest signal. However, even if an unsecured network has a stronger signal than a security-enabled one, keep in mind that it's safer for your data to connect to the security-enabled network, as long as you are an authorized user of that network.

The Chamberlain & Klein law firm already has a wireless network set up in its offices. Tay asks you to help him perform some basic tasks to manage the Chamberlain & Klein network by connecting his mobile computer to the law firm's wireless network. Frank Chamberlain gives you the passphrase to access the network, which is C&Kuser10 klamath Law01.

The following steps assume you are not connected to a network and are equipped to connect to a wireless network named Chamberlain. Substitute the name of your network and your network password when you perform the following steps. If you are already connected to a network or are not equipped to connect to a wireless network, read but do not perform the following steps.

To connect to a wireless network:

1. In Windows Mobility Center, click the **Change wireless network settings** icon. The Connect to a network window opens. See Figure 8-22.

Figure 8-22   **Connect to a network window**

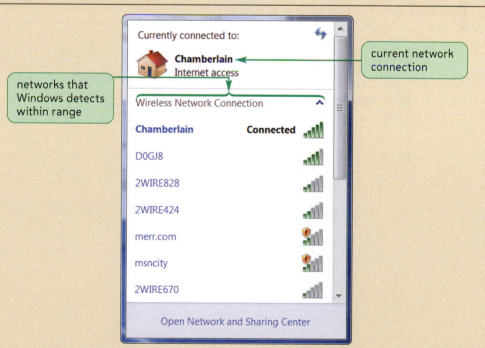

Make sure you are connected to a network to perform the rest of the steps in this tutorial.

2. Click your network name, such as **Chamberlain**, in the list of available networks, and then click the **Connect** button. If a Disconnect button appears, you are already connected to the network. Read but do not perform the remaining steps.

Trouble? If your network is not listed in the Connect to a network window, the signal strength might be low. Move your computer closer to the wireless router or access point, if possible, and then click the Refresh button 🔁.

Trouble? If your network is not listed in the Connect to a network window, but one or more networks are listed as *Unnamed network*, click an Unnamed network, click Connect, and then enter the network's name.

3. If a dialog box opens requesting your security key or passphrase, enter your passphrase, such as **C&Kuser10 klamath Law01**, and then click the **OK** button. Windows connects to the network.

Trouble? If a Set Network Location dialog box opens requesting you to select a network type, click Home network. If the Create a Homegroup window opens, click the Cancel button.

4. To verify that you are connected, click the **Change wireless network settings** icon 📶 in Windows Mobility Center again, and then click the **Open Network and Sharing Center** link. The Network and Sharing Center window now shows your computer connected to the network.

TIP

You can also connect to or disconnect from a network in the Network and Sharing Center window.

Tay's mobile computer is now connected to the Chamberlain & Klein wireless network. Because older cordless phones and other devices can interfere with a wireless connection, you should periodically check the status of the connection. You can do so by opening the Network and Sharing Center or Windows Mobility Center, or by using the network icon in the notification area of the status bar. You'll show Tay how to check the status using the Mobility Center and the network icon. The Mobility Center indicates whether your computer is connected to or disconnected from the network. The ScreenTip for the network icon provides more information, including the name of the network and the type of access you have, such as Chamberlain *Internet access*.

To check the status of a wireless connection:

1. Display the Windows Mobility Center window, if necessary. The Wireless Network tile indicates whether your computer is connected to or disconnected from the network.

2. Point to the **network** icon 📶 in the notification area of the taskbar. A small notification window shows the status of your network connection. See Figure 8-23. Your network status might differ.

Figure 8-23   **Computer connected to the network**

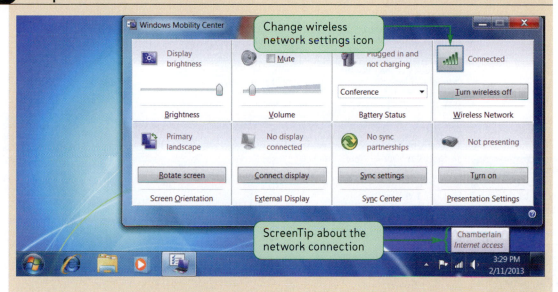

3. Close all open windows.

Now that you've helped Tay connect to the Chamberlain & Klein wireless network, you are ready to perform some typical network tasks, which involve connecting to and sharing files with other computers on the network. You'll do that in the next session.

Session 8.1 Quick Check

REVIEW

1. A computer you can easily carry, such as a laptop, notebook, or Tablet PC, is a(n) _____.

2. Which of the following settings is *not* included in the Windows Mobility Center?
   a. Battery status
   b. Name of wireless network
   c. Speaker volume
   d. Presentation settings

3. A(n)_____ _____ is a collection of hardware and system settings that manages how your computer uses and conserves power.

4. Name two settings you can set before you give a presentation.

5. When Windows saves your open documents and programs and then goes into a low-power state without turning off the power, it is called _____.

6. Common types of network technology for a small office or home network are _____, Ethernet, home phone line (HPNA), and Powerline.

7. When you point to the network icon in the notification area of the taskbar, what two details does the ScreenTip display?

SESSION 8.2 VISUAL OVERVIEW

If you don't want to share the selected folder with other homegroup users, change the permission level to Nobody.

A **homegroup** is a group of computers on a home network that can share files and printers.

Use the options on the Share with button list to select who can access shared folders.

After a homegroup is created on a computer, other users can **join** the homegroup, which means they make their folders and other resources available to other users on the home network.

By default, Windows gives homegroup users **Read access** to the libraries, which means they can open the files in the libraries, but they can't change them.

If you want to share pictures, music, videos, documents, and printers with other people on your home network, use a homegroup.

When you are connected to a network, the network computers are displayed in the Navigation pane.

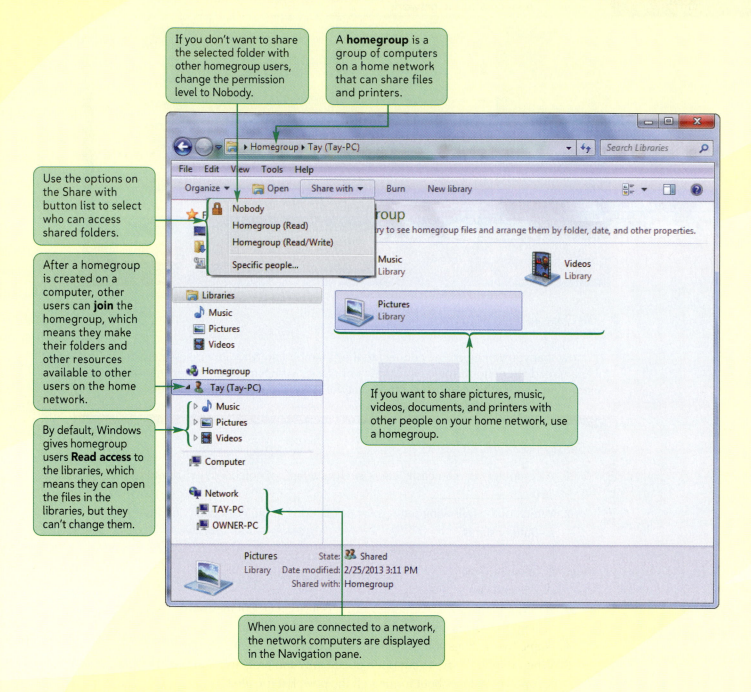

SHARING FILES

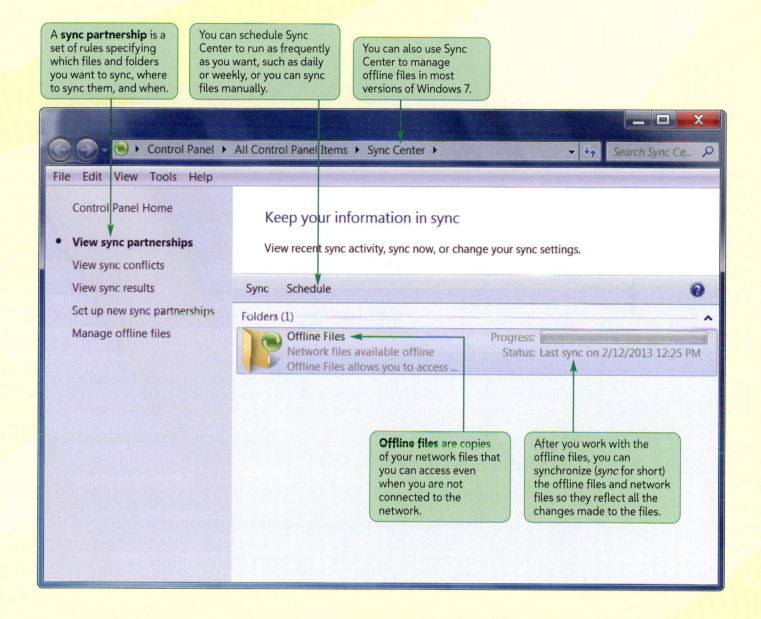

A **sync partnership** is a set of rules specifying which files and folders you want to sync, where to sync them, and when.

You can schedule Sync Center to run as frequently as you want, such as daily or weekly, or you can sync files manually.

You can also use Sync Center to manage offline files in most versions of Windows 7.

Control Panel ▸ All Control Panel Items ▸ Sync Center ▸

File   Edit   View   Tools   Help

Control Panel Home

● **View sync partnerships**
   View sync conflicts
   View sync results
   Set up new sync partnerships
   Manage offline files

Keep your information in sync

View recent sync activity, sync now, or change your sync settings.

Sync   Schedule

Folders (1)

Offline Files
Network files available offline
Offline Files allows you to access ...

Progress:
Status: Last sync on 2/12/2013 12:25 PM

Offline files are copies of your network files that you can access even when you are not connected to the network.

After you work with the offline files, you can synchronize (*sync* for short) the offline files and network files so they reflect all the changes made to the files.

Using a Windows Homegroup

When you set up a Windows 7 computer, Windows creates a homegroup for you (unless one has already been created on your home network). Other user accounts on Windows 7 computers on your home network can then join the homegroup, which is the easiest and safest way to share files and printers on a home network. You select the libraries that you want to share with others. If you want to keep some files private, you can prevent certain files and folders in those libraries from being shared. You can protect the entire homegroup with a password, which each user must enter to connect to other computers.

Only computers running Windows 7 (not earlier versions of Windows) can participate in a homegroup. Computers running Windows 7 Starter or Home Basic can join a homegroup, but cannot create one. In addition, homegroups are only available for home networks. To make sure your network uses the Home network location, open the Network and Sharing Center and check the location. If you change the location from Work or Public to Home, Windows might start creating a homegroup for you.

Creating a Homegroup

Although Windows 7 creates a homegroup when you first set up your computer, you can create one manually if necessary. Now that Tay is connected to the wireless network at Chamberlain & Klein, you suggest he create a homegroup with the desktop computer in the conference room. The first step is to create a homegroup from Tay's laptop computer. Next, he can select the libraries he wants to share with other homegroup users. He might want to keep files in the Documents library private, so he will share all the libraries except the Documents library.

The steps in this section assume you are working on a home network and can create and join a homegroup on the network. If you are not working on a home network or cannot join a homegroup on the network, read but do not perform the steps in this section. In the following steps, you create a homegroup on a laptop computer.

To create a homegroup:

▶ **1.** Click the **Start** button 🏁 on the taskbar, and then click **Control Panel** to open the Control Panel window.

▶ **2.** Click in the Search box, type **homegroup**, and then click **HomeGroup** in the Control Panel window. If a homegroup has not been created on your computer, a window opens where you can create a homegroup. See Figure 8-24.

| Figure 8-24 | Creating a homegroup |

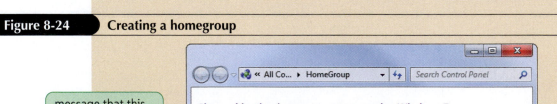

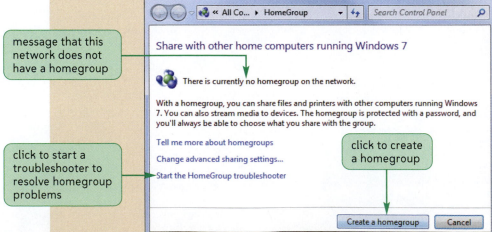

Trouble? If the window indicates that a homegroup has already been created on your computer and Windows asks if you want to join or leave the homegroup instead of creating one, skip Steps 3–7.

3. Click the **Create a homegroup** button. A window opens where you select the libraries you want to share with the other computers in the homegroup.

4. Click the check boxes as necessary to select the printers and all of the libraries except the Documents library as shown in Figure 8-25.

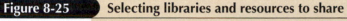

Figure 8-25   Selecting libraries and resources to share

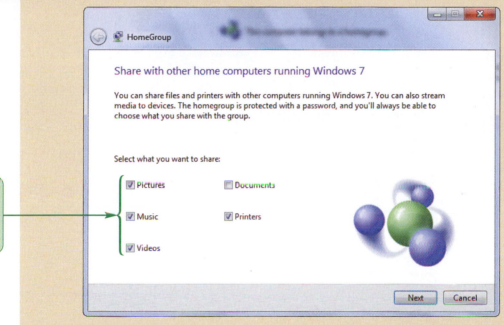

select the libraries and resources you want to share with other users in the homegroup

5. Click the **Next** button. Windows creates the homegroup and generates a password. Other users on the network need this password to join the homegroup, so you should print it.

6. Click the **Print password and instructions** link, and then click the **Print this page** button to print the password, if requested by your instructor.

7. Click the **Finish** button.

You can change the password to one that's easier to remember. In the HomeGroup window, click the Change the password link, and then follow the steps in the wizard to change the password.

Adding Other Computers to a Homegroup

After you create a homegroup, you add the other computers on your home network to it. You can do so by working at the other computers to join the homegroup, or the other users can join the homegroup without your help. Joining involves using the HomeGroup window to select files and resources for sharing and then entering the homegroup password. After other users join the homegroup, you can access the files they've selected for sharing.

Now that you've created a homegroup for Tay on his laptop computer, you can work on the desktop computer in the conference room and join the homegroup. You'll share all the libraries on the desktop computer because none of those files need to be kept private.

To join a homegroup:

1. On a computer in the homegroup (other than the laptop that you used to create the homegroup), open the HomeGroup window. The window includes a message indicating that another user created a homegroup on the network. See Figure 8-26.

Figure 8-26 Joining a homegroup

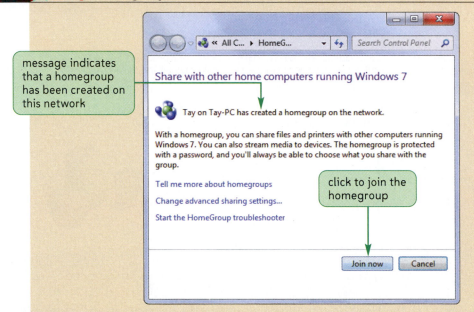

message indicates that a homegroup has been created on this network

Share with other home computers running Windows 7

Tay on Tay-PC has created a homegroup on the network.

With a homegroup, you can share files and printers with other computers running Windows 7. You can also stream media to devices. The homegroup is protected with a password, and you'll always be able to choose what you share with the group.

Tell me more about homegroups

Change advanced sharing settings...

Start the HomeGroup troubleshooter

click to join the homegroup

Join now   Cancel

Be sure to click Join now so you can perform the rest of the steps in this section.

2. Click the **Join now** button. A window opens where you can select the libraries and resources you want to share.

Trouble? If a Join now button is not displayed in the window, a homegroup might not be available. Read but do not perform the remaining steps.

3. Click the check boxes as necessary to select all of the libraries and printers, and then click the **Next** button. A window opens requesting the homegroup password.

4. Type the homegroup password you received in the previous set of steps, and then click the **Next** button.

Trouble? If you do not remember the password, click the *Where can I find the homegroup password?* link, follow the instructions for retrieving it, and then repeat Step 4.

5. When a window appears indicating you successfully joined the homegroup, click the **Finish** button.

Next, you'll show Tay how to use his laptop computer to access the libraries he made available for sharing on the desktop computer in the conference room.

Sharing Files with a Homegroup

After you set up a homegroup with two or more computers, you can share files using Windows Explorer. Click or expand Homegroup in the Navigation pane to display the other users in your homegroup. Click or expand a user icon to display the libraries that the user selected for sharing. Then you navigate the libraries and folders as you usually do to find the file you want to access.

Working on the conference room computer, you'll show Tay how to open the Pictures library on his laptop computer. This computer is named Tay-PC and the user account is named Tay. When you perform the following steps, substitute the name of a computer and user account on your homegroup for *Tay-PC* and *Tay*.

TIP

Keep in mind that if a homegroup computer is turned off, hibernating, or asleep, it won't appear in the Navigation pane.

To access shared files on a homegroup:

1. On a computer in the homegroup (other than the laptop where you created the homegroup), click the **Windows Explorer** icon 🗂 on the taskbar to open a folder window.

2. In the Navigation pane, click **Homegroup**. The Navigation pane displays the users in your homegroup.

3. In the Navigation pane, click the **Tay (Tay-PC)** user (or any user on the computer where you created the homegroup) to display the libraries available for sharing on that computer. See Figure 8-27.

Figure 8-27   **Displaying libraries available for sharing**

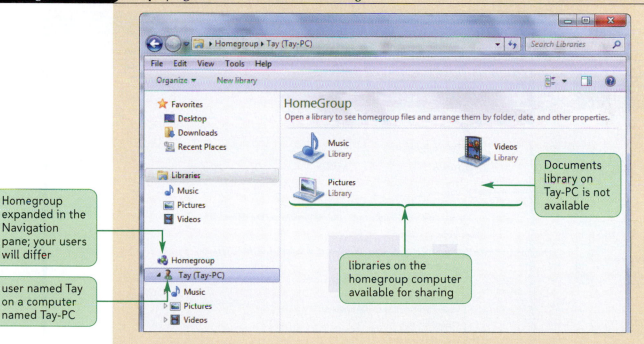

4. Double-click the **Pictures** library to display the files and folders stored in that library.

TIP

To include a shared folder from a homegroup user's computer in your own library, right-drag the folder to your library, and then click Include in library on the shortcut menu.

When you select the libraries you want to share with other people in your homegroup, Windows gives other homegroup users Read access to the libraries. You can change the level of access to **Read/Write access** so that homegroup users can open and change the files. You change the permission level for a library, folder, or file using the Share with button on a folder window toolbar.

You can also exclude libraries, folders, and files from being shared. To stop sharing the Pictures library, for example, you open the HomeGroup window and then remove the check mark from the Pictures check box. To stop sharing a folder named Surprise Project stored in the Pictures library, you use the Share with button on a folder window toolbar to change the permission level to Nobody, which means no one else can access the folder or file.

When you created the homegroup for Tay, you did not make the Documents library on his laptop computer available for sharing. You'll show him how to include the Documents library with the other shared libraries, and then create and exclude a folder named KATE. You need to return to the laptop where you created the homegroup to perform the following steps.

To include a library with other shared libraries in the Homegroup:

▶ 1. Open the HomeGroup window. The window displays a page where you can change the homegroup settings.

▶ 2. Click the **Documents** check box. See Figure 8-28.

Figure 8-28   **Changing homegroup settings**

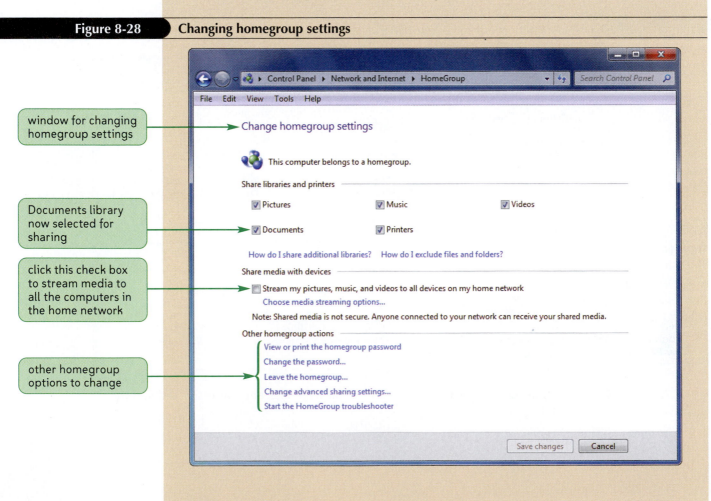

> **3.** Click the **Save changes** button to make the Documents library available for sharing.

Now you'll create a folder named KATE in the Documents library on Tay's laptop computer and then exclude it from sharing. That way, only he can access the files he stores in the KATE folder.

To exclude a folder from sharing:

> **1.** Display the folder window showing the Documents library on a homegroup computer. In the Navigation pane, click the **Documents** library on your computer.

> **2.** Click the **New folder** button on the toolbar to create a new folder in the My Documents folder in your Documents library, type **KATE** as the folder name, and then press the **Enter** key.

> **3.** Click the **KATE** folder, and then click the **Share with** button on the toolbar. See Figure 8-29.

Figure 8-29   Excluding a folder from sharing

click Nobody to prevent the selected folder from being shared

click to select specific people to share the folder with

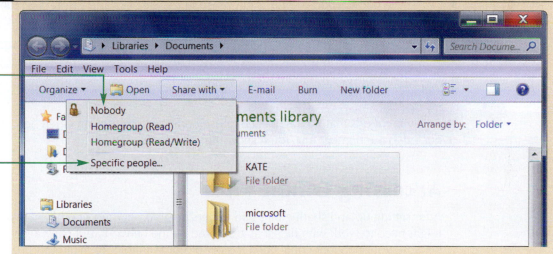

> **4.** Click **Nobody** to exclude the KATE folder from sharing.

When you choose Nobody on the Share with button list, you prevent the file or folder from being shared with anyone in the homegroup. If you want to share the file or folder with some people but not others, click Specific people on the Share with button list, and then select the people who can share access to the file or folder.

Sharing a Printer with a Homegroup

If a printer is connected to a homegroup computer using a USB cable or wireless connection, the printer can be shared with the homegroup. After the printer is shared, you can access it through the Print dialog box in any program, just like any printer directly connected to your computer.

Windows can connect to most types of printers automatically. If it cannot, you can connect the printer manually by installing it in the homegroup. First, on the homegroup computer connected to the printer, make sure that the Printers check box is selected in the HomeGroup window so it can be shared with others. Next, on the homegroup computer from which you want to print, open the HomeGroup window, click Install printer, and then complete the wizard to manually install the printer. If your HomeGroup window does not include an Install printer link and Windows has not installed the printer automatically, press the F1 key to find help for installing the printer.

The following steps assume that a printer is connected to a computer on your homegroup. If that is not the case, read but do not perform the following steps. Both the printer and the homegroup computer connected to it should be turned on. Perform the following steps using the laptop where you created the homegroup.

To connect to a homegroup printer:

▶ **1.** Click the **Start** button 🪟 on the taskbar, and then click **Devices and Printers**. If Windows can automatically connect to the printer, it appears in the Devices and Printers window.

> **Trouble?** If Devices and Printers does not appear on your Start menu, click Control Panel, click Hardware and Sound, and then click Devices and Printers.

▶ **2.** If the homegroup printer is not listed in the Devices and Printers window, click the **Windows found a homegroup printer** message to connect to the printer.

> **Trouble?** If the Devices and Printers window does not display a message or the homegroup printer, the printer needs to be installed on the homegroup. Skip Step 2.

▶ **3.** Close the Devices and Printers window.

Tay mentions that he might need to use homegroup files even when he's not connected to the homegroup. You'll show him how to do so next.

Accessing Offline Files

After setting up and sharing files and folders on a homegroup or other network, you might need to work with files that are stored on the network, but can't access them because your network connection is slow or not available. To avoid this problem, you can create offline files, which are copies of your network files that you store on your computer and use when you are not connected to the network.

To create offline files, you first enable offline files on your computer, and then navigate to the folder or file stored on a network computer other than your own. After you choose the network files you want to make available offline, Windows creates copies of these files for you on your computer. Every time you connect to the network folder, Windows updates, or synchronizes, the offline files so they remain exact duplicates of the network files. When you are not connected to the network, you can open the offline files on your computer knowing that they have the same content as the network files. When you're finished working with the offline files, you can use Sync Center to synchronize the offline files and network files yourself, or you can wait for Windows to do it the next time you access the network files.

You can synchronize files whenever you copy and save network files to your computer. When you first create offline files, Windows 7 transfers the files from the network to a specified folder on your hard disk. After that, when you connect to the network folder that contains the files you've also stored offline, Windows makes sure that both the folder containing the offline files and the network folder contain the most recent versions of the files.

You explain to Tay that offline files are especially popular with mobile computer users. You'll show him how to set up his notebook to use offline files, and then you'll make a Public folder on the Chamberlain & Klein network available to him offline.

Setting Up a Computer to Use Offline Files

Before you specify that a network file or folder should be available offline, make sure that offline files are enabled on your computer, which they are by default. When this feature is turned on, Windows synchronizes the offline files on your computer with the network files as soon as you reconnect to the network. Perform the following steps on the laptop where you created the homegroup.

To make sure offline files are enabled on your computer:

1. Click the **Start** button 🟦, click **Control Panel**, click in the Search box, type **Offline**, and then click **Manage offline files**. The Offline Files dialog box opens. See Figure 8-30.

Figure 8-30   **Offline Files dialog box**

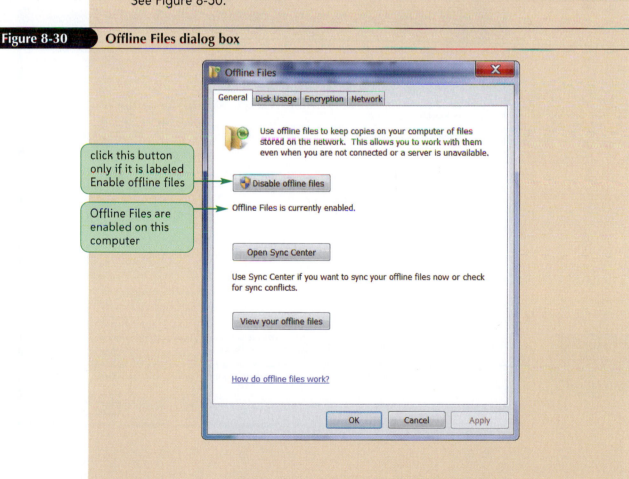

click this button only if it is labeled Enable offline files

Offline Files are enabled on this computer

Trouble? If offline files are disabled on your computer, click the Enable offline files button, and then follow the instructions to restart your computer.

2. Click the **OK** button to close the dialog box.

3. Close the Control Panel window.

Before you share files or folders in one of the Windows 7 Public folders, you should make sure that Public folder sharing is turned on. To do so, you use the Advanced sharing settings window, which you open from the Network and Sharing Center.

To make sure Public folder sharing is turned on:

1. Click the **network** icon ▦ or ▦ in the notification area of the taskbar, and then click **Open Network and Sharing Center**. The Network and Sharing Center window opens.

2. In the left pane, click **Change advanced sharing settings**. The Advanced sharing settings window opens. See Figure 8-31.

Figure 8-31   Advanced sharing settings window

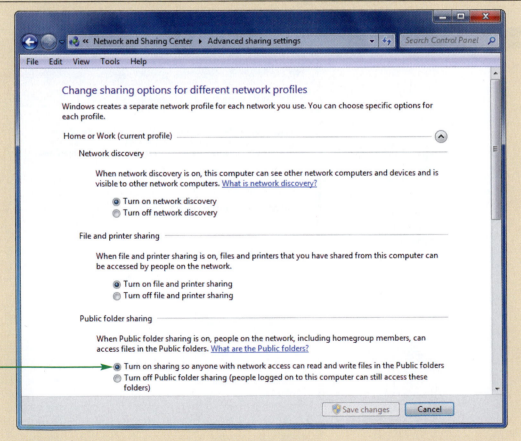

this option should be selected to share files in the Public folder

3. In the Home or Work (current profile) section, click the **Turn on sharing so anyone with network access can read and write files in the Public folders** option button, if necessary, and then click the **Save changes** button.

4. Close all open windows.

Next, you'll access a network folder and make it available to Tay offline.

Making a File or Folder Available Offline

To use a file or folder offline, you specify that it is always available offline. (When you make a folder available offline, all the files in the folder are also available offline.) Afterwards, you will be able to open the file or folder even if the network version is unavailable. You'll show Tay how to use offline files and folders by making the Public Documents folder on the conference room computer available offline.

The following steps assume that a computer named Conference-PC is connected to your network. If your network does not include a computer named Conference-PC, substitute the name of a different network computer that you can access in the following steps. The steps also assume that you have permission to access the Public Documents folder on the network computer. If you do not have permission to access this folder, ask your instructor which folder you can make available offline. Perform the following steps on a homegroup computer (other than the laptop where you created the homegroup).

To make network files available offline:

1. Open the Control Panel in Category view, and then click **Network and Internet**.

2. In the Network and Internet window, click **View network computers and devices** to open the Network window.

3. Double-click the **Conference-PC** computer (or any computer listed on your network) to display the users and resources on the computer.

4. Double-click the **Users** folder, and then double-click the **Public** folder.

5. Right-click the **Public Documents** folder, and then click **Always available offline** on the shortcut menu if this command is not checked.

   Trouble? If the Always available offline command does not appear on the shortcut menu, navigate to and right-click a folder you have permission to access offline. If you do not have permission to access any folders offline, read but do not perform the remaining steps.

6. Close the folder window.

TIP

To view all your offline files, open the Offline Files dialog box, and then click the View your offline files button.

Now you can show Tay how to work with the files in the Public Documents folder offline.

If you made a different folder available offline, substitute that folder for the Public Documents folder in the following steps. If you did not make any folders available offline, read but do not perform the following steps.

To work with offline files:

1. Navigate to the Public folder on the network again, and then open the **Public Documents** folder.

TIP

When you are finished working offline, click the Work online button on the toolbar to sync the changes you made with the files on the network.

▶ **2.** Click the **Work Offline** button on the toolbar. This button appears only if you have already made this folder available offline.

▶ **3.** Close the folder window.

When you lose your network connection, Windows turns on offline files and copies to your computer the files you designate as offline files so you can work on them. When you are reconnected to the network, Windows syncs the two copies. You can find out if you're working offline by opening the network folder that contains the file you are working on, and then looking in the Details pane of the folder window. If the status is offline, you are working with a copy of the file on your computer. If the status is online, you are working with the file on the network.

Synchronizing Folders

Recall that keeping files in sync is one of the problems mobile computer users often have that desktop computer users do not. If you use more than one computer, such as a desktop computer and a mobile PC, it can be difficult to keep track of all your files. To make sure that you have the most recent versions of your files on your mobile PC before you travel, for example, you can synchronize information on your mobile PC, desktop computer, and other devices by using Sync Center. To do so, you create a set of rules that tells Sync Center what files you want to sync, where to sync them, and when. In this way, Sync Center makes it easy to move files from one computer to another device, such as another computer, network server, portable music player, digital camera, or mobile phone. Besides copying files from one device to another, Sync Center can maintain consistency among two or more versions of the same file stored in different locations. If you add, change, or delete a file in one location, Sync Center can add, overwrite, or delete an earlier version of the file in other locations.

You can also use Sync Center to manage offline files in Windows 7 Home Premium, Professional, and Ultimate editions. In this case, Sync Center compares the size and time stamp of an offline file with a network file to see if they are different. For example, suppose you have changed an offline file, but have not made the same changes in the network copy. Sync Center copies the offline file to the network so both versions are identical. If Sync Center finds a new file in an offline folder, for example, it copies the file to the network folder. The same is true for deleted files. If Sync Center finds that a file has been deleted from the network folder, for example, it deletes the same file in the offline folder.

Sometimes, Sync Center discovers a conflict, which means that you have changed both a network file and its offline copy. A sync conflict occurs whenever differences can't be reconciled between a file stored in one location and a version of the same file in another location. A sync conflict stops the sync from being completed. This usually happens when a file has changed in both locations since its last sync, making it difficult to determine which version should be left unchanged (or kept as the master copy) and which should be updated. In this case, Sync Center asks you to select the version you want to keep.

When you are synchronizing a mobile device, such as a portable music player, and your computer, Sync Center gives you the option of setting up a one-way or two-way sync. In a one-way sync, every time you add, change, or delete a file or other information in one location, such as the Music folder on your hard disk, the same information is added, changed, or deleted in the other location, such as your portable music player. Windows does not change the files in the original location, such as the Music folder on your hard disk, because the sync is only one way.

In a two-way sync, Windows copies files in both directions, keeping files in sync in two locations. Every time you add, change, or delete a file in either location, the same change is made in the other sync location.

Using Sync Center

At one time, the synchronizing process was so complex, especially in work environments, that companies relied on a system administrator to set up synchronizations for their employees. Now you can use Sync Center to set up the sync yourself by specifying which files and folders you want to sync, where to sync them, and when. This set of rules—which represents a partnership between two or more sync locations—is called a sync partnership. To perform the following steps, you must be working on a mobile computer. If you are not working on a mobile computer, read but do not perform the following steps. Perform the following steps on the laptop where you created the homegroup.

To open Sync Center and sync offline files:

1. Open the Windows Mobility Center window.

2. Click the **Change synchronization settings** icon 🔄 in the Sync Center tile. The Sync Center window opens. See Figure 8-32.

Figure 8-32   Sync Center window

click to set up a sync partnership, if necessary

files that need to be synced

3. Click **View sync partnerships** in the left pane, if necessary, to display the Offline Files icon, and then click the **Offline Files** icon to select it. See Figure 8-33.

Figure 8-33   Preparing to sync offline files

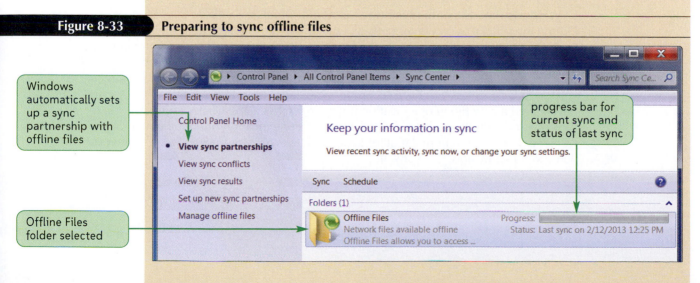

Windows automatically sets up a sync partnership with offline files

progress bar for current sync and status of last sync

Offline Files folder selected

▶ **4.** Click the **Sync** button. Windows synchronizes the files. See Figure 8-34.

Figure 8-34 **Synchronizing files**

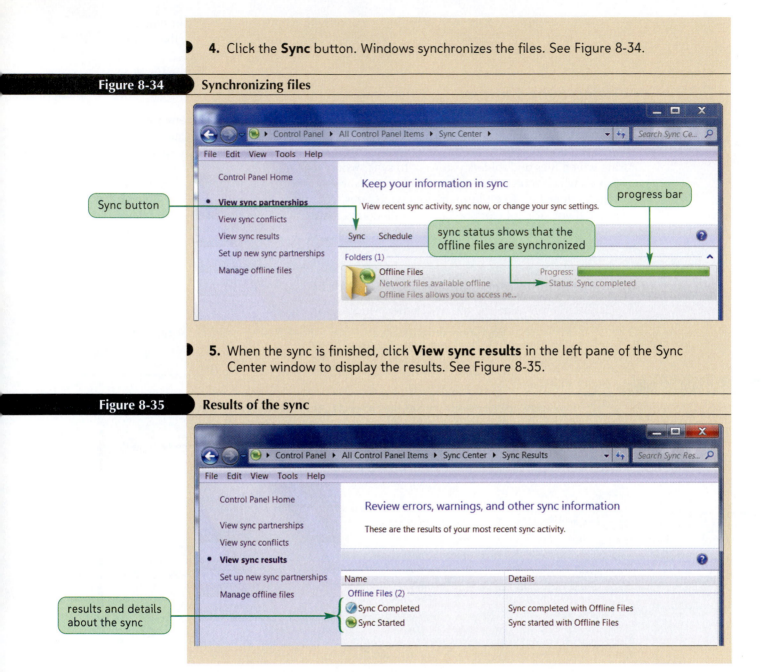

Sync button

progress bar

sync status shows that the offline files are synchronized

▶ **5.** When the sync is finished, click **View sync results** in the left pane of the Sync Center window to display the results. See Figure 8-35.

Figure 8-35 **Results of the sync**

results and details about the sync

Windows reports that the sync was successful, which streamlines your sync tasks. During the sync, if Sync Center finds that the offline file is identical to the network file, Sync Center does nothing because the files are already in sync. If Sync Center finds that an offline file differs from its network version, Sync Center determines which version of each file to keep and copies that version to the other location. It selects the most recent version to keep unless you have set up the sync partnership to sync differently. If you have added a new file in one location but not the other, Sync Center copies the file to the other location. If you have deleted a file from one location but not the other, Sync Center deletes the file from the other location. If Sync Center finds a conflict, however, you should know how to resolve it.

Resolving Synchronization Conflicts

If Windows performs a sync and Sync Center finds that a file has changed in both locations since the last sync, Sync Center flags this as a sync conflict and asks you to choose which version to keep. You must resolve this conflict so that Sync Center can keep the files in sync. When Sync Center detects one or more conflicts, it displays a message similar to the one shown in Figure 8-36.

Figure 8-36	Conflict window

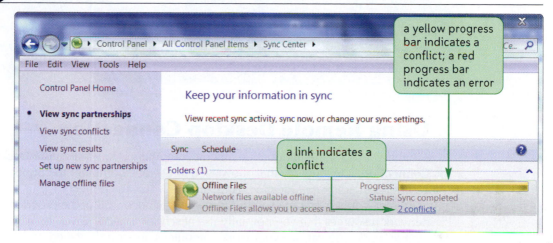

To resolve the conflicts, you click the conflict link, select the offline files, and then click the Resolve button. When you do, the Resolve Conflict dialog box opens for each file in conflict and asks if you want to keep this version and copy it to the other location, or if you want to delete both copies. See Figure 8-37.

Figure 8-37	Resolving sync conflicts

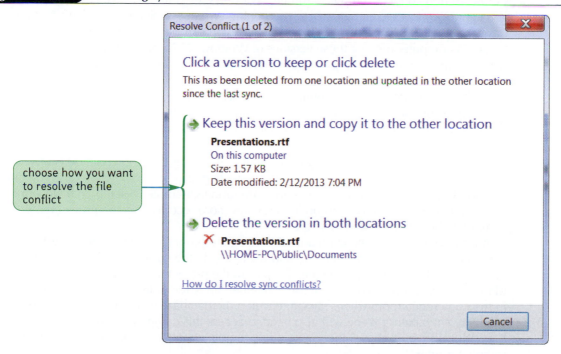

Click the appropriate option, and then click the OK button.

Problem Solving: Distinguishing Between Sync Conflicts and Sync Errors

A sync conflict occurs when differences can't be reconciled between a file stored in one location and a version of the same file in another location. This stops the sync from being completed for this file until you decide how to reconcile the differences. You don't need to resolve all sync conflicts, but it improves the integrity of your files if you do so.

In contrast, a sync error is a problem that usually prevents the sync from being completed, such as a mobile device that is not plugged in or turned on, or a network server that is unavailable. Unlike sync conflicts, sync errors are not caused by problems reconciling two versions of a file. Rather, sync errors usually occur when there is a problem with the device, computer, or folder you are trying to sync with. To complete a sync successfully, you must resolve all sync errors.

Using Remote Desktop Connection

Another way to share information among computers is to use **Remote Desktop Connection**, a technology that allows you to use one computer to connect to a remote computer in a different location. For example, you can connect to your school or work computer from your home computer so you can access all of the programs, files, and network resources that you normally use at school or work. If you leave programs running at work, you can see your work computer's desktop displayed on your home computer, with the same programs running.

Suppose you are planning to use a mobile computer at home and want to connect to your computer at work. To use Remote Desktop Connection, the home computer and work computer must both be running Windows and must be connected to the same network or to the Internet. Remote Desktop must also be turned on, and you must have permission to connect to your work computer. However, you cannot use Remote Desktop Connection to connect computers running Windows XP Home Edition. Furthermore, you cannot connect to a computer if it is running Windows 7 Starter, Windows 7 Home Basic, or Windows 7 Home Premium. However, you can establish an outgoing connection on a computer running those versions of Windows 7. If you are using a computer at work or school, firewall settings at those locations may prevent you from connecting to another computer using Remote Desktop Connection.

Setting up Remote Desktop Connection is a two-part process. First, you allow remote connections on the computer to which you want to connect, such as your work computer. Next, you start Remote Desktop Connection on the computer you want to connect from, such as your home computer. You can allow connections from computers running any version of Remote Desktop Connection, including those in earlier versions of Windows. If you know that the computers connecting to your computer are also running Windows 7, allow connections only if they are running Remote Desktop with Network Level Authentication (NLA). This option provides more security and can protect remote computers from hackers and malware.

After viewing the presentation and discussing the proposal, the Chamberlain & Klein partners decide that they want Kevin and Tay to create the custom database described in their proposal. Tay will be managing this part of the project, and will spend some time in Klamath Falls to work on the database. Chamberlain & Klein are providing a computer in the conference room where Tay can develop the database when he is in Klamath Falls. Tay anticipates that he will also need to access this computer when he is not in Klamath Falls. You'll show him how to allow remote connections on that conference room computer.

First, you need to determine whether the conference room computer is running a version of Remote Desktop with NLA. Perform the following steps on a homegroup computer other than the laptop where you created the homegroup.

To see if your computer is running a version of Remote Desktop with NLA:

1. Click the **Start** button, start typing **Remote Desktop Connection** in the Search programs and files box, and then click **Remote Desktop Connection**. The Remote Desktop Connection dialog box opens. See Figure 8-38.

Figure 8-38 Remote Desktop Connection dialog box

click this icon and then click About

2. Click the **Remote Desktop Connection** icon in the title bar, and then click **About**. A window opens describing Remote Desktop Connection. See Figure 8-39. Look for the phrase *Network Level Authentication supported.*

Figure 8-39 About Remote Desktop Connection window

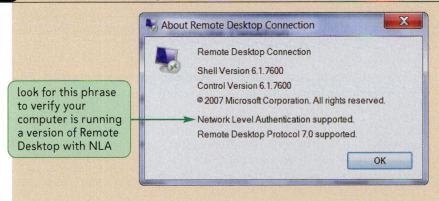

look for this phrase to verify your computer is running a version of Remote Desktop with NLA

3. Click the **OK** button.

4. Click the **Close** button to close the Remote Desktop Connection window.

Now you are ready to set up your computer to allow a remote desktop connection from another computer. Before performing the following steps, log on to your laptop computer as an Administrator. If you are not allowed to use an Administrator account on your computer, read but do not perform the following steps.

To set up Remote Desktop Connection:

1. Click the **Start** button 🪟, click **Control Panel**, click **System and Security**, and then click **System**. The System window opens.

2. In the left pane, click **Remote settings**. The System Properties dialog box opens to the Remote tab. See Figure 8-40.

   Trouble? If you are asked for an administrator password or confirmation, type the password or provide confirmation.

Figure 8-40 Remote tab in the System Properties dialog box

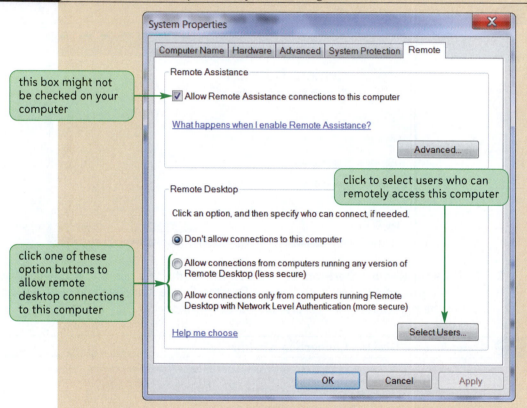

3. Click the **Allow connections only from computers running Remote Desktop with Network Level Authentication (more secure)** option button.

   Trouble? If a dialog box opens regarding your power settings, click the OK button.

   Trouble? If a Remote Desktop dialog box opens with a message about sleep and hibernation, click the OK button.

4. Click the **Select Users** button. The Remote Desktop Users dialog box opens.

5. Make sure the Administrator account, such as the Owner account, already has access on the computer, and then click the **OK** button to close the Remote Desktop Users dialog box.

6. Click the **OK** button to close the System Properties dialog box. Close the System window.

To allow users other than the Administrator to use a remote desktop connection to your computer, click the Add button in the Remote Desktop Users dialog box, enter the name of the user or computer who can access your computer, and then click the OK button. The name you entered appears in the list of users in the Remote Desktop Users dialog box. After you set up Remote Desktop Connection on your remote computer, such as the one at work, you can start Remote Desktop Connection on the computer you want to work from, such as the one at home. Before you do, you need to know the name of the computer to which you want to connect. To find the name of a computer, you open the System window by opening the Control Panel, click System and Security, and then click System. The computer name is listed in the Computer name, domain, and work-group settings section.

The following steps assume that you are set up to connect to a remote computer. To do so, you need to know the name of the computer to which you want to connect. If you are not set up to connect to a remote computer, read but do not perform the following steps. Perform the following steps using the laptop computer where you created the homegroup.

To start Remote Desktop Connection to connect to a remote computer:

1. Open the Remote Desktop Connection dialog box.

2. In the Computer text box, type **Conference**. This is the name of the computer in the Chamberlain & Klein conference room.

Trouble? If the name of the remote computer to which you want to connect is not named Conference, enter its name instead of Conference in the Computer text box.

3. Click the **Connect** button to connect to that computer on your network.

Trouble? If a Remote Desktop Connection dialog box opens asking if you want to connect even though the identity of the remote computer cannot be verified, click the Yes button.

4. Enter your user name and password, and then click the **OK** button to establish the connection.

5. Click the **Close** button, and then click the **OK** button to disconnect.

Now Tay and his associate can access the computer in the Chamberlain & Klein conference room when they are working in the KATE offices in Portland.

Restoring Your Settings

If you are working in a computer lab or on a computer other than your own, complete the steps in this section to restore the original settings on your computer.

To restore your settings:

▶ 1. Open the Windows Mobility Center, and then drag the **Volume** slider to its original setting.

▶ 2. If necessary, click the **Mute** check box to remove the check mark and turn the speakers on.

Trouble? If your speakers were turned off when you originally opened Windows Mobility Center in Session 8.1, skip Step 2.

▶ 3. Click the **Change power settings** icon 🔋 in the Battery Status tile to open the Power Options window, and then click **Balanced**.

▶ 4. Click **Change plan settings** for the Balanced power plan, and then click **Restore default settings for this plan**.

▶ 5. Click the **Yes** button to restore the settings, and then click the **Back** button ⬅ to return to the Power Options window.

▶ 6. In the Windows Mobility Center window, click the **Change presentation settings** icon 💻, and then restore the screen saver, volume, and background controls to their original settings. Click the **OK** button.

▶ 7. Navigate to the Network window, and then navigate to the Public Documents folder on the network. Right-click the **Public Documents** folder, and then click **Always available offline** on the shortcut menu to remove the check mark. Close the folder window.

▶ 8. Open the Network and Sharing Center window. Click **Choose homegroup and sharing options**, click **Leave the homegroup**, and then click **Leave the homegroup** to confirm you want to leave.

▶ 9. Open the Remote Desktop Connection dialog box. In the Computer text box, select the name of the computer to which you have a remote desktop connection, such as **Conference**, and then click the **Disconnect** button, if necessary.

▶ 10. Delete the **KATE** folder from the Documents folder, and then close all open windows.

Session 8.2 Quick Check

REVIEW

1. A(n) _____ is a group of computers on a home network that can share files and printers.

2. What type of window do you open to share libraries with other users in your homegroup?

3. The first major step in setting up Remote Desktop Connection is to allow remote connections on the computer to which you want to connect. What is the second step?

4. How do you make a network folder available offline?

5. To exclude a folder from sharing with others in a homegroup, you click the folder, click the Share with button on the toolbar, and then click _____.

6. Identify an advantage Sync Center offers if you work on more than one computer, such as a mobile computer and a network computer.

7. _____ _____ are copies of your network files that you can access even when you are not connected to the network.

Practice the skills you learned in the tutorial using the same case scenario.

PRACTICE

Review Assignments

There are no Data Files needed for the Review Assignments.

You are now working with Tay Endres to help him prepare for a meeting with a client in Eugene, Oregon—a small video production studio named Eugene Video. Tay asks you to help him prepare his mobile computer for the trip and for a presentation he plans to make to Eugene Video when he arrives. Kevin Adelson also requests your help with connecting his Windows 7 notebook computer to the Eugene Video wireless network and sharing some of its resources. Complete the following steps, noting your original settings so you can restore them later:

1. Open the Windows Mobility Center, change the speaker volume to 25, and then mute the speakers.

2. In the Power Options window, change the plan settings for the Power saver plan so that the display turns off after five minutes of idle time when running on battery power and after 15 minutes when plugged in. (If you are not using a mobile computer, set the Power saver plan to turn off the display after 15 minutes of idle time.) Save your changes. Also set the plan to hibernate after 45 minutes of idle time on any type of power.

3. Display the settings for the Power saver plan, arrange the Power Options dialog box so it is clearly visible, and then press the Alt+Print Screen keys to capture an image of the window. Paste the image in a new Paint file, and save the file as **Saver** in the Tutorial.08\Review folder provided with your Data Files.

4. Change what the hardware power button does so that when you press the power button when running on battery power, your computer hibernates. (If you are not using a mobile computer, do the same for the default type of power.) Press the Alt+Print Screen keys to capture an image of the window. Paste the image in a new Paint file, and save the file as **Power Button** in the Tutorial.08\Review folder provided with your Data Files. Save your changes, and then close the Power Options window.

5. Change presentation settings so that when you give a presentation, you turn off the screen saver, set the volume to 75, and show img11 as the desktop background. Press the Alt+Print Screen keys to capture an image of the window. Paste the image in a new Paint file, and save the file as **Presentation** in the Tutorial.08\Review folder provided with your Data Files.

6. Connect to an available wireless network, entering a security key or passphrase as necessary. (If you are not equipped to connect to a wireless network, connect to a wired network.) Capture an image of the Network and Sharing Center window. Paste the image in a new Paint file, and save the file as **Wireless** in the Tutorial.08\Review folder provided with your Data Files.

7. If necessary, connect to an available homegroup or create a new homegroup. Change the homegroup settings to share all libraries and printers and to share media with devices. Press the Alt+Print Screen keys to capture an image of the window. Paste the image in a new Paint file, and save the file as **Homegroup** in the Tutorial.08\Review folder provided with your Data Files.

8. Make offline files available for sharing in the Public Downloads folder, if possible. Press the Alt+Print Screen keys to capture an image of the window showing the Public Downloads folder. Paste the image in a new Paint file, and save the file as **Offline** in the Tutorial.08\Review folder provided with your Data Files.

9. Copy a file from the Sample Pictures folder on your computer to the Public Downloads folder on a homegroup computer, if possible.

10. Open Sync Center and synchronize the offline files. When the sync is finished, view the sync results and then press the Alt+Print Screen keys to capture an image of the window. Paste the image in a new Paint file, and save the file as **Sync** in the Tutorial.08\Review folder provided with your Data Files. Close all open dialog boxes.

11. Open the System Properties dialog box, and then allow connections only from computers running Remote Desktop with NLA. Press the Alt+Print Screen keys to capture an image of the dialog box with this setting. Paste the image in a new Paint file, and save the file as **Remote Desktop** in the Tutorial.08\Review folder provided with your Data Files. Close all open dialog boxes.

12. Restore your original settings. Change the speaker volume to its original setting, and then turn on the speakers. Change the Power saver plan to its default settings, and then select your original plan. Restore the original action to the hardware power button. Restore the presentation settings to their original form. Turn off sharing for the Public Downloads folder on the network computer. Disconnect from the network, if necessary, and then close all open windows.

13. Submit the results of the preceding steps to your instructor, either in printed or electronic form, as requested.

Use your skills to enhance mobile computing for a visiting nurse service.

APPLY

Case Problem 1

There are no Data Files needed for this Case Problem.

Tempe Visiting Nurse Service   Sarah Shepard is the director of the Tempe Visiting Nurse Service (TVNS) in Tempe, Arizona. During flu season in the fall, TVNS sets up mobile clinics in offices throughout the city to provide flu shots and give presentations on avoiding the flu, pneumonia, and other viruses. Sarah recently hired you to train her and her staff in using Windows 7 to perform mobile computing tasks, including managing power options and connecting to wireless networks when working at offices in Tempe. Complete the following steps, noting your original settings so you can restore them later:

1. Open the Windows Mobility Center and then mute the speakers.

2. Change the plan settings for the Balanced plan so that the display turns off after 10 minutes of idle time when running on battery power and after 1 hour when plugged in.

3. Set the Balanced plan to hibernate after 60 minutes whether running on battery or another type of power. Arrange the Power Options dialog box and the Edit Plan Settings window so you can see the settings in both windows, and then press Print Screen to capture an image of the desktop. Paste the image in a new Paint file, and save the file as **Power Plans** in the Tutorial.08\Case1 folder provided with your Data Files. Save your changes.

4. Set the computer to require a password when waking from sleep. Press the Alt+Print Screen keys to capture an image of the window. Paste the image in a new Paint file, and save the file as **Password** in the Tutorial.08\Case1 folder provided with your Data Files. Save your changes, and then close the Power Options window.

5. Change presentation settings so that when you give a presentation, the volume is set to High, the screen saver is turned off, and the background displays img2. Press the Alt+Print Screen keys to capture an image of the Presentation Settings dialog box. Paste the image in a new Paint file, and save the file as **Preset** in the Tutorial.08\ Case1 folder provided with your Data Files. Save your changes.

6. Display a list of wireless networks within range of your computer. Capture an image of the window. Paste the image in a new Paint file, and save the file as **Connect** in the Tutorial.08\Case1 folder provided with your Data Files.

7. Open the Advanced sharing settings window. Press the Alt+Print Screen keys to capture an image of the window. Paste the image in a new Paint file, and save the file as **Advanced** in the Tutorial.08\Case1 folder provided with your Data Files.

8. Open the Remote Desktop Connection dialog box, and then determine whether your computer supports Network Level Authentication. Press the Alt+Print Screen keys to capture an image of the window that provides this information. Paste the image in a new Paint file, and save the file as **NLA** in the Tutorial.08\Case1 folder provided with your Data Files. Close all Control Panel windows.

9. Restore your original settings by turning on the speakers. Change the Balanced power plan to its default settings, and then select your original plan. Remove password protection on wakeup. Restore the presentation settings to their original form. Close all open windows.

10. Submit the results of the preceding steps to your instructor, either in printed or electronic form, as requested.

Use your skills to set up mobile computing for an event planner.

APPLY

Case Problem 2

There are no Data Files needed for this Case Problem.

Celebration Event Planners   Alissa Hanley started Celebration Event Planners in Omaha, Nebraska, to serve families and businesses that sponsor events such as anniversaries, retirement parties, and product introductions. Alissa often travels around Omaha to meet with potential clients and vendors, so she wants to know more about the Windows 7 mobile computing features. Many of the events she organizes involve slide shows that run on a notebook computer. As Alissa's assistant, you help her with a wide range of tasks, including planning events and managing the company's computers. She asks you to help her use Windows 7 to perform mobile computing tasks, including managing power options and giving presentations. Complete the following steps, noting your original settings so you can restore them later:

1. Change the speaker volume to 30, and then mute the speakers.

2. Change the plan settings for the Power saver plan so that the display turns off after five minutes of idle time when running on battery power and after 30 minutes when plugged in. (If you are not using a mobile computer, set the display to turn off after 30 minutes of idle time.)

EXPLORE
3. For the Power saver plan, turn on hybrid sleep instead of sleep for all types of power. Arrange the Power Options dialog box and the Edit Plan Settings window so you can see the settings in both windows, and then press the Print Screen key to capture an image of the desktop. Paste the image in a new Paint file, and save the file as **Events** in the Tutorial.08\Case2 folder provided with your Data Files.

4. Set the computer to always hibernate when you press the hardware power button. Make sure a password is required to access your computer when it wakes up. Press the Alt+Print Screen keys to capture an image of the window. Paste the image in a new Paint file, and save the file as **Hibernate** in the Tutorial.08\Case2 folder provided with your Data Files. Save your changes, and then close the Power Options window.

5. Change presentation settings so that when you give a presentation, the volume is set to 80, the screen saver is turned off, and a black background is displayed. Press the Alt+Print Screen keys to capture an image of the Presentation Settings dialog box. Paste the image in a new Paint file, and save the file as **Dark** in the Tutorial.08\Case2 folder provided with your Data Files. Save your changes.

EXPLORE
6. Open the Advanced sharing settings window. In the settings for your home or work network, turn on media streaming, if necessary, and then display the media streaming options. Press the Alt+Print Screen keys to capture an image of the window. Paste the image in a new Paint file, and save the file as **Streaming** in the Tutorial.08\Case2 folder provided with your Data Files.

7. Determine whether your printer is shared by other users on your network. Open the window displaying this information, and then press the Alt+Print Screen keys to capture an image of the window. Paste the image in a new Paint file, and save the file as **Printer** in the Tutorial.08\Case2 folder provided with your Data Files.

8. Open a window that displays the four options for connecting to an external display. Press the Alt+Print Screen keys to capture an image of the window. Paste the image in a new Paint file, and save the file as **External** in the Tutorial.08\Case2 folder provided with your Data Files.

9. Restore your original settings. Change the speaker volume to its original setting, and then turn on the speakers. Change the Power saver plan to its default settings, and then select your original plan. Restore the presentation settings to their original form. Close all open windows.

10. Submit the results of the preceding steps to your instructor, either in printed or electronic form, as requested.

Extend what you've learned to set up mobile computing for a researcher.

CHALLENGE

Case Problem 3

There are no Data Files needed for this Case Problem.

Amity Market Research Ron Amity is a marketing analyst who consults with companies that need market research to improve sales or develop new products. His company, Amity Market Research in Hartford, Connecticut, employs researchers who often work on mobile computers at their clients' offices. As a project assistant, part of your job is to make sure the researchers are using their computers effectively. Ron asks you to show him how to use Windows 7 to perform mobile computing tasks, including conserving battery power, connecting to networks, and sharing files. Complete the following steps, noting your original settings so you can restore them later:

⊕ **EXPLORE**

1. Open the Power Options window, click a link to learn more about power plans, and then click a link to learn how to conserve power. Read the Help topic about conserving battery power. Leave the Help window open.

2. In the Windows Mobility Center, change settings to conserve as much power as you can on your computer. Press the Print Screen key to capture an image of the desktop. Paste the image in a new Paint file, and save the file as **Conserve** in the Tutorial.08\Case3 folder provided with your Data Files.

⊕ **EXPLORE**

3. Change the High performance power plan to turn off the display after five minutes of idle time when running on battery power and after 15 minutes when plugged in. (If you are not using a mobile computer, set the display to turn off after 15 minutes of idle time.) Also set the plan to put the computer to sleep after 30 minutes of idle time when using any type of power. If possible, dim the display after 10 minutes of idle time when using any type of power. Press the Alt+Print Screen keys to capture an image of the window. Paste the image in a new Paint file, and save the file as **Amity** in the Tutorial.08\Case3 folder provided with your Data Files.

4. Change presentation settings so that when you give a presentation, the volume is set to 75, the screen saver is turned off, and img16 is shown as the desktop background. Press the Alt+Print Screen keys to capture an image of the window. Paste the image in a new Paint file, and save the file as **Show** in the Tutorial.08\Case3 folder provided with your Data Files.

5. Connect to an available wireless network, entering a security key or passphrase as necessary. (If you are not equipped to connect to a wireless network, connect to a wired network.)

⊕ **EXPLORE**   6. Start a wizard that troubleshoots Internet connections, and then capture an image of the desktop. Paste the image in a new Paint file, and save the file as **Diagnose** in the Tutorial.08\Case3 folder provided with your Data Files.

⊕ **EXPLORE**   7. Turn on an advanced sharing setting for the Public Documents folder so that anyone with network access can read and write files in the Public folder. Press the Alt+Print Screen keys to capture an image of the window that shows Public folder sharing turned on. Paste the image in a new Paint file, and save the file as **Public** in the Tutorial.08\Case3 folder provided with your Data Files. Close the Network and Sharing Center window.

8. Make sure offline files are enabled on your computer. If possible, make the Public Documents folder on a network computer always available offline.

9. Open Sync Center and synchronize the offline files. When the sync is finished, view the sync results, resize the columns to show the date of the sync, and then press the Alt+Print Screen keys to capture an image of the window. Paste the image in a new Paint file, and save the file as **Sync Center** in the Tutorial.08\Case3 folder provided with your Data Files.

10. Change the homegroup settings on your computer to share only documents. Capture an image of the window. Paste the image in a new Paint file, and save the file as **Shared** in the Tutorial.08\Case3 folder provided with your Data Files.

11. Restore your original settings. Restore the High performance power plan to its default settings, and then select your original plan. Restore the presentation settings to their original form. Restore the original sharing setting for the Public Documents folder on the network computer. Close all open windows.

12. Submit the results of the preceding steps to your instructor, either in printed or electronic form, as requested.

Case Problem 4

Use your skills and the Internet to research networks.

RESEARCH

There are no Data Files needed for this Case Problem.

Columbia City Planning   The city planning office for Columbia, Missouri, is considering connecting its computers on a network. The planning office has the following characteristics and requirements:

- There are nine users—seven on mobile computers and two on desktop computers.
- All computers are running Windows 7.
- Most of the city planners use their computers outside of the office.
- All users often distribute large files to other users.

Nelson Ochoa is the lead project manager and asks you, an administrative assistant, to help him research small office networks using the Internet and Windows Help and Support. Complete the following steps:

1. Use the Internet to research appropriate networks for the Columbia City planning office. Choose two types of networks to recommend. Create a document with four column headings: **Network Technology**, **Hardware Requirements**, **Speed**, and **Cost**. Complete the columns according to the following descriptions:

Network Technology	Hardware Requirements	Speed	Cost
List two types of networks.	List devices and other hardware required.	List speed considerations or rates.	List cost considerations.

2. Save the document as **Networks** in the Tutorial.08\Case4 folder provided with your Data Files.

3. Submit the results of the preceding steps to your instructor, either in printed or electronic form, as requested.

SAM: Skills Assessment Manager

ASSESS

For current SAM information, including versions and content details, visit SAM Central (http://samcentral.course.com). If you have a SAM user profile, you may have access to hands-on instruction, practice, and assessment of the skills covered in this tutorial. Since various versions of SAM are supported throughout the life of this text, check with your instructor for the correct instructions and URL/Web site for accessing assignments.

ENDING DATA FILES

Tutorial.08

Review
Homegroup.png
Offline.png
Power Button.png
Presentation.png
Remote Desktop.png
Saver.png
Sync.png
Wireless.png

Case1
Advanced.png
Connect.png
NLA.png
Password.png
Power Plans.png
Preset.png

Case2
Dark.png
Events.png
External.png
Hibernate.png
Printer.png
Streaming.png

Case3
Amity.png
Conserve.png
Diagnose.png
Public.png
Shared.png
Show.png
Sync Center.png

Case4
Networks.doc

OBJECTIVES

Session 9.1
- Back up and restore files
- Create a system restore point
- Install and uninstall software
- Set default programs

Session 9.2
- Maintain hard disks
- Enable and disable hardware devices
- Install and update device drivers
- Adjust monitor settings and set up multiple monitors
- Install and set up printers

Maintaining Hardware and Software

Managing Software, Disks, and Devices

Case | *Northbrook Farmers Market*

The Northbrook Farmers Market is a grocery store in Manchester, New Hampshire, that specializes in fresh food grown and raised on nearby New England farms. Julie McCormick is the general manager of the store. When she needs to complete office work, she conducts much of her business on her Windows 7 PC. As her assistant back office manager, one of your responsibilities is to maintain the hardware and software at the store.

In this tutorial, you will back up and restore files and folders, and create a schedule to perform these functions automatically. You will also prepare to install new programs, and then install software and view your updates. You will manage a hard disk by checking for problems and learn to improve performance. You will also learn how to maintain the devices attached to a computer, including your monitor and printer.

STARTING DATA FILES

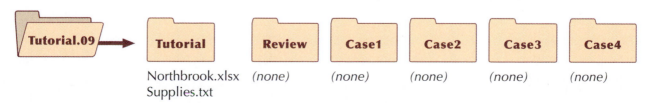

Tutorial.09 → Tutorial
Northbrook.xlsx
Supplies.txt

Review
(none)

Case1
(none)

Case2
(none)

Case3
(none)

Case4
(none)

SESSION 9.1 VISUAL OVERVIEW

A **system image** is an exact copy of a drive.

When you create a **backup file**, you create a copy of one or more files and store it in a compressed folder on an external medium such as an external hard drive.

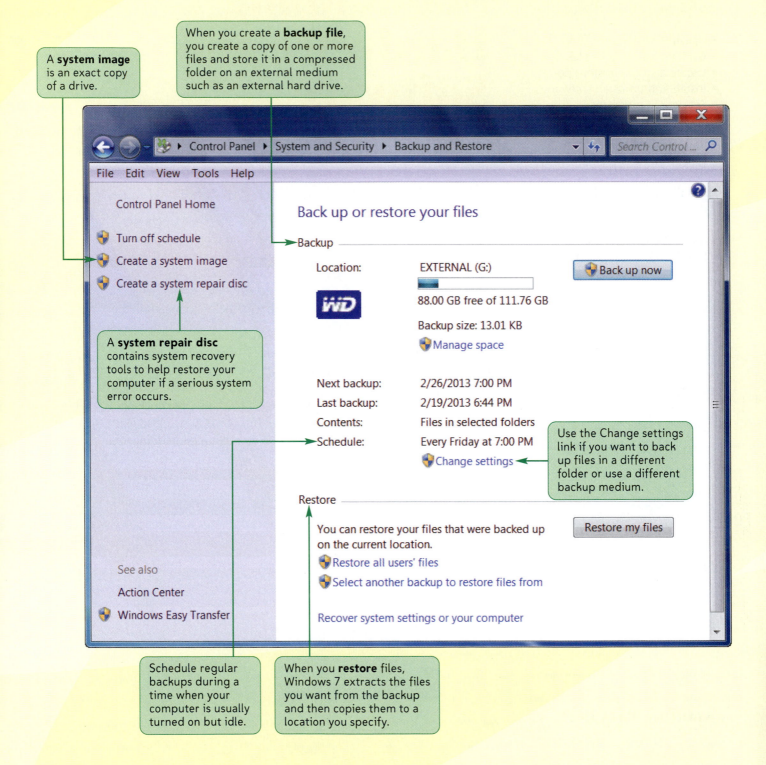

A **system repair disc** contains system recovery tools to help restore your computer if a serious system error occurs.

Use the Change settings link if you want to back up files in a different folder or use a different backup medium.

Schedule regular backups during a time when your computer is usually turned on but idle.

When you **restore** files, Windows 7 extracts the files you want from the backup and then copies them to a location you specify.

MANAGING DATA AND SOFTWARE

Installed updates are updates to Windows 7 that have been installed on your computer.

Uninstalling a program removes it completely from your computer.

If a program is not running correctly, you can change or repair the installation.

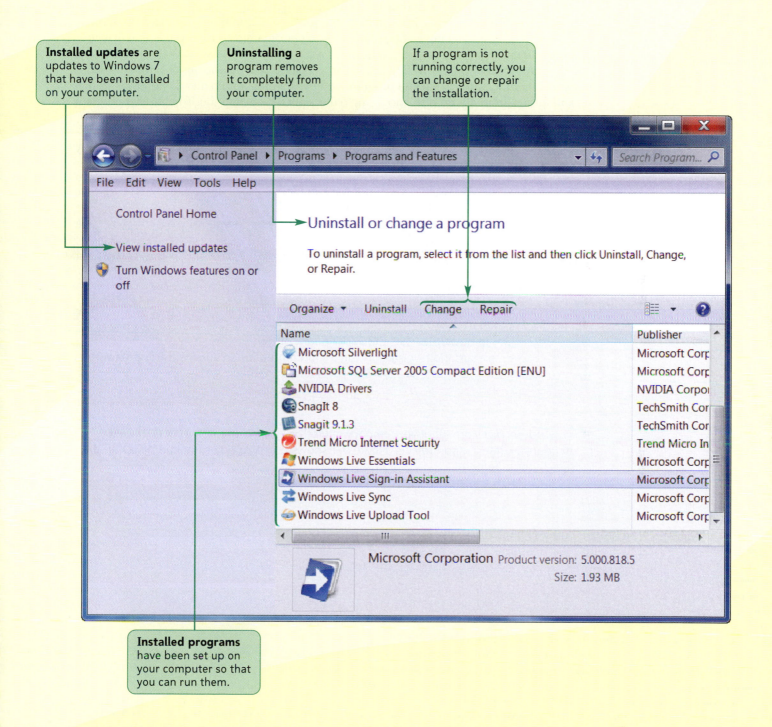

Installed programs have been set up on your computer so that you can run them.

Backing Up and Restoring Files

No one is safe from computer problems that result in data loss. Problems such as a power surge, a power loss, a failed section of a hard disk, or a computer virus can strike at any time. Rather than risk disaster, you should make copies of your important files regularly. You have already learned how to copy data to and from your hard disk and a removable disk. Making a copy of a file or folder on a removable disk is one way to protect data.

To protect data on a hard disk, however, you should use a backup program instead of a copy procedure. A **backup program** copies and then automatically compresses files and folders from a hard disk into a single file, called a backup file. The backup program stores a backup file on a **backup medium** such as an external or internal hard disk, a writeable CD or DVD, or a removable USB flash drive. To back up files in Windows 7, you use Windows Backup, which guides you through the following steps of backing up your files:

- Specify where you want to save your backup file.
- Select the folders and files you want to back up.
- Indicate how often you want to create a backup.

REFERENCE

Backing Up Files

- Click the Start button, click Control Panel, click System and Security, and then click Backup and Restore.
- Click Set up backup or click the Back up now button.
- Follow the steps in the wizard. If you are prompted for an administrator password or confirmation, type the password or provide confirmation.

Suppose you store all of your important files on drive C in three folders named Accounts, Clients, and Projects. Figure 9-1 shows how Windows Backup backs up the files in these folders.

Figure 9-1   **Backing up data**

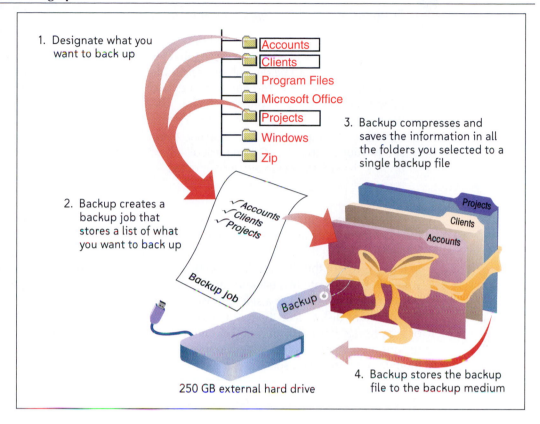

1. Designate what you want to back up

- Accounts
- Clients
- Program Files
- Microsoft Office
- Projects
- Windows
- Zip

2. Backup creates a backup job that stores a list of what you want to back up

✓ Accounts
✓ Clients
✓ Projects

Backup job

250 GB external hard drive

3. Backup compresses and saves the information in all the folders you selected to a single backup file

Projects
Clients
Accounts

Backup

4. Backup stores the backup file to the backup medium

Backing up files is different from copying files because Windows Backup copies files into a single, compressed file, whereas a copy simply duplicates the files. Figure 9-2 points out the differences between copying and backing up, showing why backing up files is a faster, easier, and better data-protection method than copying files.

Figure 9-2   **Comparing copying and backing up files**

Copy	Backup
Copying your files can be time consuming and tedious because you must navigate to and select each file and folder that you want to copy.	Using Windows Backup is faster because you select the files and folders in one step, and Windows Backup navigates to the folders and selects the files during the backup.
Because a copy of a file occupies the same amount of space as the original file, making a copy of all the files on a hard disk is impractical.	Windows Backup can back up your entire computer and store the contents in a compressed file, which is much smaller than the original files combined.
You need to manually track which files and folders have changed since your last backup.	Windows Backup keeps track of which files and folders are new or modified. When you create a backup, you can back up only the files that have changed since your last backup.
You need to set reminders on your own to create backups periodically.	If you set up automatic backups, Windows regularly backs up your files and folders so that you don't have to remember to do it.
If you do lose data because of a computer failure, it is not easy to locate a file you need in your backups.	Windows Backup keeps track of the files you have backed up, and makes it easy to find and recover a file.

INSIGHT

Determining Which Files to Back Up

The most valuable files on your computer are your data files—the documents, pictures, videos, projects, and financial records that you create and edit. You should back up any data files that would be difficult or impossible to replace, and regularly back up files that you change frequently. You don't need to back up programs because you can download them from the vendor's Web site again or use the original product discs to reinstall them, and programs typically take up a lot of space on backup media. However, you should create a system image (a backup of your entire computer system) when you first set up your computer and then periodically after that. Microsoft recommends that you update the system image every six months.

After you back up files, you should store the backups in a safe place where unauthorized people cannot access them. For example, if you create a backup of your personal folder by burning those files on a CD, you should store the CD away from the computer, in a place where the CD is unlikely to be tampered with or damaged. For your most valuable files, create two backups and store one off site, such as through an online backup service or even in a safe deposit box. If you accidentally delete or replace files on your hard disk or lose them due to a virus or worm, software or hardware trouble, or a complete hard disk failure, you can restore your files from the backup. When you restore files, Windows 7 extracts the files you want from the backup and then copies them to a location you specify.

Specifying Where to Save Your Backup File

With Windows 7, you can create backups on a hard drive, USB flash drive, writeable CD or DVD, or a network folder. To select the location that is best for you, consider the hardware installed on your computer and the number and size of files that you want to back up. You can back up files to any of the following locations:

- Internal hard drive: If you have an additional internal hard drive in your computer, you can use it to back up files. However, Windows does not let you back up files to a folder on the same hard drive on which the operating system is installed. If your computer suffers a virus or software failure, you might have to reformat the drive and reinstall Windows to recover from the problem.
- External hard drive: If your computer has a USB port, you can attach an external hard drive to it and then back up files to the external drive. If you plan to back up your entire computer, the external hard drive must have plenty of space for your backups; at least 200 GB is often recommended. You need less storage space if you plan to back up only selected files. For extra security, keep your external hard drive in a fireproof location separate from the computer. Because of its portability, capacity, and ease of use, backing up to an external hard drive is the option experienced computer users prefer.
- USB flash drive: If you are backing up data only (not a system image), you can use a USB flash drive that can store more than 1 GB of data. USB flash drives are inexpensive and convenient, so they are a good choice for documents and other personal files. However, they are less reliable than external hard disks, so they are not suitable for long-term file storage.
- Writeable disc: If your computer has a CD or DVD burner, you can back up your files to writeable CDs or DVDs. (A writeable CD means that you can add, delete, or change its contents.) Windows Backup estimates how much space you need each time you perform a backup. If you are backing up to writeable discs, make sure you have enough discs to store the complete backup.

- Network folder: If your computer is on a network, you can create a backup on a network folder. You need to have permission to save files in the folder and set sharing options so that unauthorized users cannot access the backup.

If your computer is not equipped with an extra internal hard disk, USB port, or disc burner, or if you are not connected to a network, you can purchase this hardware or use an Internet-based file storage service. These services let you store personal, password-protected backups, usually on a server you can access via the Internet.

Selecting the Folders and Files to Back Up

When you use Windows Backup, you can select personal data files to back up, such as documents, financial records, pictures, and projects. Besides backing up these personal files, you can back up your entire computer, including programs and system settings, by creating a system image. In Windows 7, you create a system image of the drive where Windows is installed. The image includes a copy of your programs, system settings, and files and a record of their original locations. You can then use the system image to restore your computer if it stops working. Microsoft recommends that you update the system image every six months. Figure 9-3 compares backing up files and backing up your entire computer by creating a system image.

Figure 9-3   **Backing Up Files or Your Entire Computer**

Backup Option	What It Backs Up	When to Use
Back up files	Personal files such as pictures, music, and documents	On a regular schedule and before you make system changes
System image	All the files, folders, and settings on your computer	When you first set up your computer and every six months afterward

When you back up personal files, Windows Backup lets you back up the most common file types, including documents, pictures, music, and compressed folders. It does not let you back up system files, program files, Web e-mail not stored on your hard disk, files in the Recycle Bin, temporary files, or user profile settings. In addition, you cannot back up files that have been encrypted using the Encrypting File System (EFS), which is a Windows feature that allows you to store information on your hard disk in an encrypted format. (EFS is not fully supported in Windows 7 Home Premium.) Furthermore, you can back up only files stored on hard disks formatted with the NT File System (NTFS), not the earlier versions of the file allocation table (FAT) file system.

When you back up an entire computer, the system image contains copies of your programs, system settings, and files. Although a system image includes your personal files, you should use Windows Backup to back up these files so you can restore files and folders as needed. When you restore your computer from a system image, it is a complete restoration; you can't choose individual items to restore, and all of your current programs, system settings, and files are replaced. The system image is usually a very large backup file that you can use to restore the contents of your computer if your hard disk or entire computer stops working.

Indicating How Often to Back Up

Windows Backup lets you create automatic backups on a daily, weekly, or monthly basis. You can also create backups manually at any time. You should back up your personal files regularly, preferably at least once a week. If you're working on an important project and can't afford to lose even a few hours of work, back up your files once or twice a day. You should also back up your files before making any system changes, such as adding new hardware or making significant changes to Windows, by installing a service pack, for example. If you create many files at a time, such as dozens or hundreds of digital photos you took at a special occasion, back up those files as soon as you can.

You should create a system image when you first set up your computer, when it contains only programs and files provided by the computer manufacturer. Microsoft recommends that you update the system image every six months.

When you back up your personal files and your complete computer, you need media with enough space to store the files. Windows Backup can create a backup file that spans more than one optical disc, so you can back up your complete computer using a few DVDs, for example. Note that you need to be available to insert additional discs as necessary during the backup. If you run out of discs, you can suspend the backup and finish it later. After you create the first backup file, Windows keeps track of the files that have been added or modified since your last backup so you only have to update the existing backup, which saves time and space on your backup media.

Before you create a backup file, you want to copy files to Julie's computer so that Windows includes them in the backup. You'll store the files in a folder named Julie so that you can find them easily later.

To copy files to the Julie folder:

▶ **1.** Navigate to the **My Documents** folder in the **Documents** library on the hard disk of your computer.

▶ **2.** Click the **New folder** button on the toolbar.

▶ **3.** Type **Julie** as the name of the folder.

▶ **4.** Copy the files from the Tutorial.09\Tutorial folder provided with your Data Files to the Julie folder.

▶ **5.** Close the folder window.

Now you're ready to back up Julie's documents.

Backing Up Files

Before you back up your personal files, make sure you know where you want to store the backup file, which files you want to back up, and when you want to schedule automatic backups. The first time you back up files, the Setup backup Wizard guides you through the steps. The first dialog box in the wizard lets you choose where to save your backup. The wizard searches your computer and displays a list of all locations you can use for the backup. Windows 7 cannot create backups in the following types of locations:

- Tape drives
- The hard disk on which Windows 7 is installed
- CD-ROM or a read-only DVD drive (you must use a writeable CD or DVD drive)

Most of the work Julie does on her computer involves documents, such as text documents and spreadsheets, and she has not backed up these documents on her Windows 7 computer yet. You'll show her how to back up the files onto an external hard drive named EXTERNAL on drive G. Substitute the name of your backup location for EXTERNAL (G:) in the following steps.

To perform the steps, your computer needs access to an additional internal hard drive, an external hard drive, a network folder, a USB flash drive, or a writeable CD or DVD drive. You also need to log on to the computer using an Administrator account. If your computer cannot access these locations, or you cannot log on as an Administrator, read but do not perform the following steps. Note the original settings so you can restore them later.

To back up personal files:

1. If necessary, insert a writeable CD or DVD into the appropriate drive or attach an external hard drive or USB drive to your computer by plugging it into a USB port. Close any dialog boxes that open.

2. Click the **Start** button 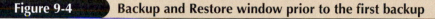 on the taskbar, click **Control Panel**, and then click **Back up your computer** in the System and Security category. The Backup and Restore window opens as shown in Figure 9-4.

Figure 9-4   **Backup and Restore window prior to the first backup**

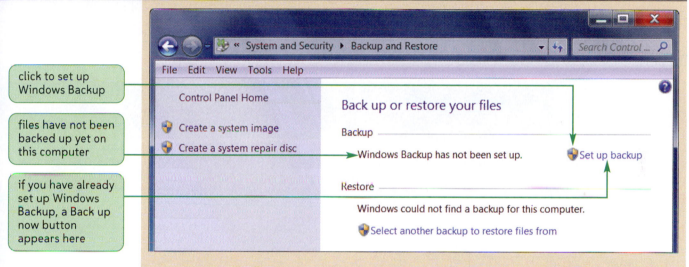

click to set up Windows Backup

files have not been backed up yet on this computer

if you have already set up Windows Backup, a Back up now button appears here

3. Click the **Set up backup** link. The Set up backup Wizard starts and asks where you want to save your backup. See Figure 9-5.

   Trouble? If Windows Backup is already set up on your computer, click the Change settings link in the Backup and Restore window.

Figure 9-5   **Selecting the backup location**

select a backup destination

4. In the Backup Destination column, click **External (G:)** (or another destination). Click the **Next** button. The next dialog box asks what you want to back up.

5. Click the **Let me choose** option button, and then click the **Next** button. In the next wizard dialog box, you select the types of files to back up.

6. In the Data Files section, click the **Back up data for newly created users** check box to remove the check mark, if necessary. Also click the **Libraries** check box for each user to remove the check mark, if necessary.

7. Click the **expand** icon ▷ next to your Windows 7 hard disk icon, such as Windows 7 (C:), click the **expand** icon ▷ next to the Users folder, and then continue clicking the **expand** icon ▷ to navigate to the Documents library, and then the Julie folder. See Figure 9-6.

Figure 9-6 | **Selecting folders to back up**

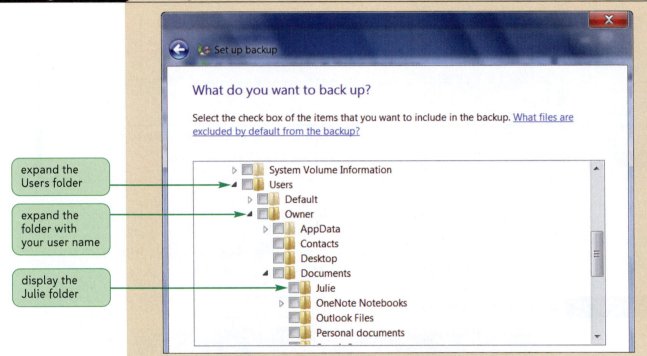

8. Click the **Julie** check box to select it, and then click the **Next** button. The next window summarizes what you will back up, and displays a schedule for the backups. See Figure 9-7.

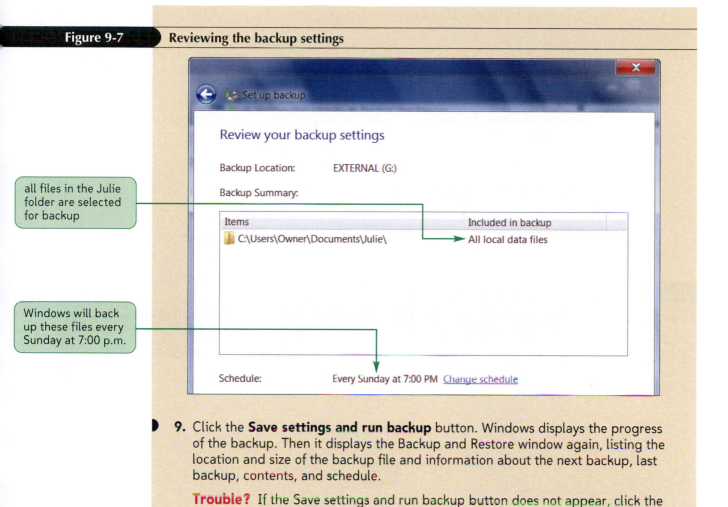

Figure 9-7   Reviewing the backup settings

all files in the Julie folder are selected for backup

Windows will back up these files every Sunday at 7:00 p.m.

9. Click the **Save settings and run backup** button. Windows displays the progress of the backup. Then it displays the Backup and Restore window again, listing the location and size of the backup file and information about the next backup, last backup, contents, and schedule.

Trouble? If the Save settings and run backup button does not appear, click the Save settings and exit button. Then, click the Back up now button in the Backup and Restore window.

After you back up files at least once, you can quickly back up your files using the same settings by opening the Backup and Restore window and then clicking the Back up now button. Click the Change settings link if you want to back up files in a different folder, use a different backup medium, or change the automatic backup schedule.

If you let Windows choose what to back up, you back up all data files saved in libraries, on the desktop, and in default Windows folders. This is considered a full backup of your files. When you make a full backup, Windows creates a backup folder and labels it with the current date. As you add updates, the date in the label stays the same, though your backup is up to date. The next time you make a full backup, Windows creates a new backup folder and labels it with the new current date, and then adds any updates to the new backup folder. You should not delete the current backup folder because Windows uses it to track the files that have changed on your computer.

After Windows 7 makes the first full backup, it backs up only files that have changed since your last backup. That means it doesn't need as much storage space to create the subsequent backups. Eventually, after many files have changed, Windows 7 will indicate it needs to create another full backup, which it stores in a different folder. As you add personal files to the folders on your computer, each full backup might require more storage space than the last full backup, so keep additional storage media handy.

Changing Your Backup Settings

After you create a backup, you can change any backup settings, including the location of the backup file, the types of files to back up, and the schedule for automatic backups. You do so by selecting Change settings in the Backup and Restore window, which starts the Set up backup Wizard.

The current schedule for backups on Julie's computer is every Sunday at 7:00 p.m. Julie decides that she wants to schedule automatic backups on Fridays at 7 p.m. instead of Sundays.

To change backup settings:

1. Make sure your computer can still access your backup media.

2. If necessary, make the Backup and Restore window the active window. It now displays the results of your last backup. See Figure 9-8.

Figure 9-8 Details about your last backup

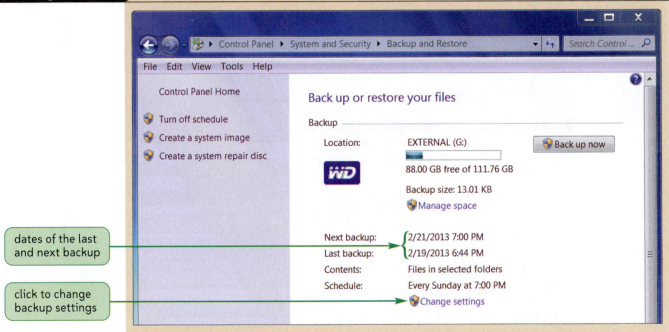

3. Click **Change settings**. A setup window opens briefly, and then the Set up backup Wizard starts, displaying the dialog box where you select a destination for the backup files.

4. Click **EXTERNAL (G:)** or another backup disk, if necessary, and then click the **Next** button. Click the **Let me choose** option button, if necessary, and then click the **Next** button. Navigate to the Julie folder, click to insert a check mark, if necessary, and then click the **Next** button. The next wizard dialog box opens, displaying the current backup schedule.

5. Click the **Change schedule** link. The next wizard dialog box opens, asking how often you want to back up. See Figure 9-9.

Figure 9-9   **Scheduling backups**

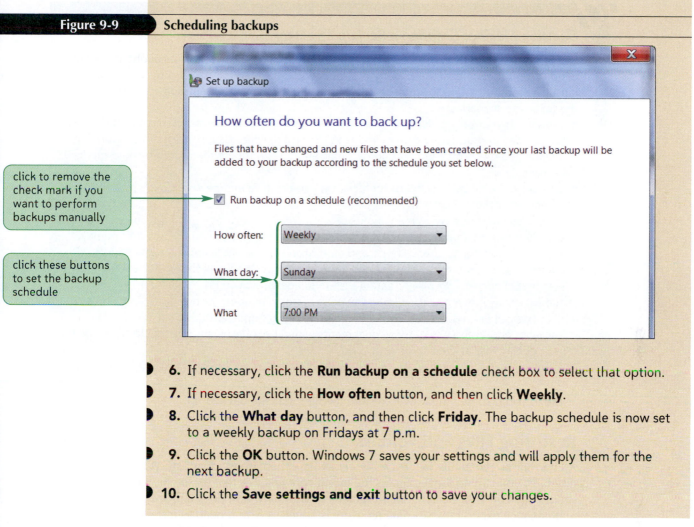

click to remove the check mark if you want to perform backups manually

click these buttons to set the backup schedule

6. If necessary, click the **Run backup on a schedule** check box to select that option.

7. If necessary, click the **How often** button, and then click **Weekly**.

8. Click the **What day** button, and then click **Friday**. The backup schedule is now set to a weekly backup on Fridays at 7 p.m.

9. Click the **OK** button. Windows 7 saves your settings and will apply them for the next backup.

10. Click the **Save settings and exit** button to save your changes.

If you want Windows to back up files on your computer automatically late at night, remember to leave your computer turned on during the scheduled time. Windows can't make backups if your computer is turned off.

You can quickly verify that Windows created a backup folder on your removable disk. Open a folder window, navigate to the removable disk, and then look for a folder with a backup icon [icon] and a name that includes the name of your computer, such as *Owner-PC*. This folder contains all of the backups that you make on your computer until you reach the disk's storage capacity. Right-click the file and then click Open to open the Owner-PC folder (yours might have a different name) to display one or more backup folders, which are named and saved in the following format: *backup location\ computer name\Backup Set year-month-day time*. For example, if your computer name is Owner-PC, your backup location is G, and you backed up on April 12, 2013, at 10:16:00, that backup is named Backup Set 2013-04-12 101600 and is stored in G:\ Owner-PC.

Decision Making: Creating a Backup Strategy

Before you back up files, develop a backup strategy that you can follow throughout the life of your computer. A backup strategy is a routine you develop for creating backups regularly. The most effective strategy balances security, efficiency, and storage space. Consider the following scenarios:

- *Security*: If your only concern is security, you could create a full backup of your files a few times a day and update a system image at the end of every day. However, this approach devotes too much time to creating backups, and does not take the cost of backup media into account.
- *Efficiency*: If your main concern is efficiency, you could save time and money by backing up only your most important files occasionally, such as once or twice a year. The drawback is that you risk losing many hours of work with that strategy. Instead, you should set a backup routine that secures your data without costing you too much time and money.
- *Low computer usage*: If you create and modify only a few documents a week, you could create a full backup once, and then create a backup once a week that includes only the files that changed. Likewise, create a system image when you first start working with a computer, and then update it before making system changes, such as installing software.
- *High computer usage*: If you create and modify many important documents each day, however, and losing any of those documents would be a hardship, you should back up your documents at the end of each day.

Next, you'll show Julie how to restore the files that she backed up.

Restoring Files and Folders

All hard disks eventually fail, even if you maintain them conscientiously. When a hard disk fails, you can no longer access the files it contains. For that reason alone, you should back up your personal files regularly. If your hard disk does fail, and a computer maintenance expert believes data recovery is hopeless, you'll need to install a new hard disk or reformat the one that you have. Practically everyone who has been using computers for very long has a data loss story to tell. Many computer owners who now make regular backups learned the hard way how important it is to protect data. Backing up your files is one of the most effective ways to save time and maintain data integrity when you are working on a computer. Create the first backup file, and then set up an automatic schedule to update it regularly. If you do lose data, your backup file allows you to easily restore the files you lost.

When you restore personal files, Windows 7 extracts the files you want from the backup media and then copies them to a location you specify. You can restore individual files, groups of files, or all files that you have backed up. In addition to selecting the files and folders you want to restore and specifying where you want to restore them, you can also set other restore options. For example, you can specify that you do not want Windows 7 to replace any current files on your computer, or to replace files only if the ones on the hard disk are older. Either option prevents you from overwriting files you might need.

You restore files using the Restore Files Wizard, which you also start from the Backup and Restore window. If you want to restore files from your latest backup or an older one, you click the Restore my files button. You can also restore the files of all users on a computer or restore files created on another computer running an older version of Windows. In any case, you specify the files to restore by adding files and folders from the backup file to a list. You can also search for files to restore. Windows 7 restores all the files you add to the list. You can restore the files to their original location (that is, the location from which you backed them up) or a different location you specify.

When you restore files from a system image, you are restoring the entire computer, so you don't need to choose files or folders to restore. Windows 7 replaces all of your current programs, system settings, and files.

You'll show Julie how to restore the documents she backed up using her latest backup.

To restore files from a backup:

▶ **1.** In the Backup and Restore window, click the **Restore my files** button. The Restore Files Wizard starts and asks what you want to restore.

▶ **2.** Click the **Browse for folders** button. The next window displays the backup folders on your backup medium. See Figure 9-10.

Figure 9-10   Selecting files and folders to restore

backup file stored on an external hard drive

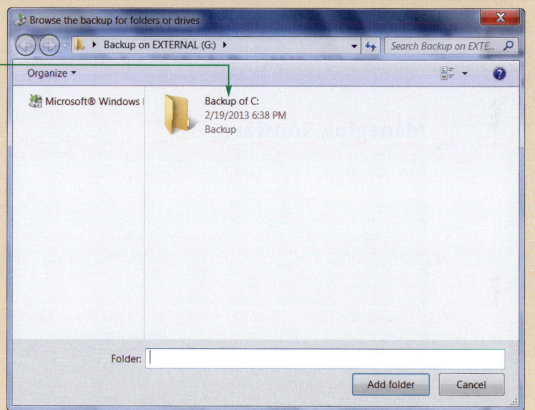

▶ **3.** Double-click the **Backup of C:** folder, and then navigate to and click the **Julie** folder in your Documents library. Click the **Add folder** button. The Julie folder is added to the list of files and folders to restore.

▶ **4.** Click the **Next** button. The next wizard dialog box asks where you want to restore your files.

▶ **5.** Click the **In the original location** option button, if necessary, and then click the **Restore** button. The Copy File dialog box opens and indicates the Julie folder already includes a file with the same name.

▶ **6.** Click **Copy and Replace** twice to replace the Northbrook and Supplies files. Windows restores the files from the backup. Restoring might take a few minutes, depending on the size of the files you backed up.

7. When a dialog box opens indicating the files were successfully restored, click the **Finish** button.

8. Close all open windows.

To recover a complete system, most computer manufacturers provide a set of system recovery options, usually on a CD. This CD is called a system repair disc. This disc contains files your computer needs to start and display recovery options (it does not contain the Windows operating system, other programs, or your data files). If your computer has major problems, such as a virus infection or a corrupt file system, you use the system repair disc to start the computer and display options for recovering the system. Then, you can use the system image to restore your computer. If you don't have a system repair disc, you can create one using the Backup and Restore window. In the left pane of the window, click Create a system repair disc, and then follow the steps. After you insert a CD or DVD into the appropriate drive, Windows copies the necessary files onto the disc, which you should store in a safe place.

Besides restoring files that you have backed up manually or through an automatic backup, you can restore files that Windows 7 creates when you create a restore point, which you'll explore next.

Managing Software

Although your personal files are the most valuable files you have on a computer, they are useful to you only if you have the right programs to open, edit, and otherwise enhance those files. To safeguard your data and your programs, recall that you can create a system image using the Backup and Restore window. To save system files without affecting your personal files, you can use **System Restore**, a Windows tool that helps you restore your computer's system files to an earlier point when your system was working reliably. If your system becomes unstable or starts to act unpredictably after installing software, you can try uninstalling the software to see if that solves your problem. If uninstalling does not solve your problem, you can undo system changes by restoring your computer to an earlier date when the system worked correctly.

When you use System Restore, it tracks changes to your computer's system files and uses a feature called System Protection to create a **restore point**, which is a snapshot of your computer's system files. A restore point contains information about these system files and settings in the **registry**, which is a database of information about your computer's configuration. If your system becomes unstable, use System Restore to return your computer settings to a particular restore point. System Restore creates restore points at regular intervals (typically once a day) and when it detects the beginning of a change to your computer, such as a Windows Update. You can also create a restore point yourself at any time.

Because System Restore reverts to previous system settings without affecting your personal files, it usually cannot help you recover a personal file that has been lost or damaged. To protect your data, you still need to back up your files regularly. However, when System Protection is turned on (which it is by default for all the hard disks on your computer), Windows does save copies of data files that you've modified since it created the last restore point. These files are called **shadow copies**, or previous versions of your files. You can use shadow copies to restore files that you accidentally modified, deleted, or damaged. For your own data files, you can open the shadow copy, save it to a different location, or restore a previous version. (Only Windows 7 Business, Ultimate, and Enterprise editions create shadow copies.)

Selecting a Tool to Restore Your Files

Windows 7 offers a few tools for restoring files. If you accidentally delete a file, the easiest way to recover it is to retrieve it from the Recycle Bin. If you've already emptied the Recycle Bin, the most reliable way to recover the file is to restore it from a backup. If you don't have a backup that contains the file you need, your next step is to restore a shadow copy, which provides a previous version of the file.

System Restore helps you manage system software; however, you can also use other Windows 7 tools to manage your applications. To make sure the programs provided with Windows are running smoothly and include the latest features, you can use Windows Update to install a software update. You can also install other programs, such as office productivity suites, games, and security programs. Typically, you install programs from a CD, DVD, Web site, or network. If you no longer use a program or if you need to free up space on your hard disk, you can uninstall a program. You'll learn how to do both later in this section.

Creating a System Restore Point

Although Windows 7 automatically creates system restore points periodically and before a significant system event such as installing new software, you can create a restore point yourself at any time. When a restore point is created, Windows saves images of its system files, programs, and registry settings. It might also save images of files that help to run programs, such as scripts and batch files. As with backup files, Windows can only create restore points on NTFS disks, not FAT disks. To create restore points, you need at least 300 MB of free space on a hard disk that has at least 1 GB of storage space. System Restore might use from 3–5 percent of the space on each disk. As this space fills up with restore points, System Restore deletes older restore points to make room for new ones. Also note that Windows 7 does not recognize restore points created in earlier versions of Windows because it uses a different method to create them.

Creating a System Restore Point

- Click the Start button, click Control Panel, click System and Security, and then click System
- In the left pane, click System protection to open the System Properties dialog box.
- Click the System Protection tab, if necessary, and then click the Create button.
- Enter a description to help you identify the restore point, and then click the Create button.
- Click the Close button.

Julie's computer is working well right now, so you'll show her how to create a restore point to protect her system. Before you do, you want to make sure that System Protection is turned on for her computer.

To make sure System Protection is turned on:

► **1.** Click the **Start** button 🌐, click **Control Panel**, click **System and Security**, and then click **System**. The System window opens.

► **2.** In the left pane, click **System protection**. The System Properties dialog box opens. See Figure 9-11. The Available Drives list shows for which drives System Protection is turned on. Make sure that System Protection is turned on for the drive where Windows 7 is installed on your computer.

Figure 9-11   **System Properties dialog box**

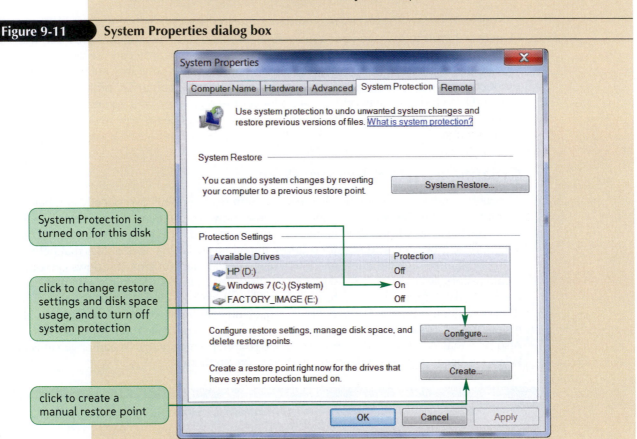

Trouble? If a User Account Control dialog box opens requesting your permission or a password to continue, enter the password or click the Continue button.

You can use this dialog box to create a restore point yourself.

To create a restore point:

► **1.** In the System Properties dialog box, click the **Create** button. The System Protection dialog box opens.

► **2.** Type **Julie** as the description for this restore point. Windows will add the current date and time automatically.

► **3.** Click the **Create** button. Windows creates a restore point, which might take a few minutes, and then displays a message indicating it was created successfully.

► **4.** Click the **Close** button.

At any point after you or Windows 7 creates a restore point, you can select one to undo changes made to your system up to that restore point. Every time you use System Restore, Windows creates a restore point before proceeding, so you can undo the changes if reverting to a restore point doesn't fix your problem. If you need to restore your computer, Windows recommends using the most recent restore point created before a significant change, such as installing a program. You can also choose from a list of restore points. It's a good idea to select restore points in descending order, starting with the most recent. If that doesn't solve your problem, try the next most recent, and so on. Although System Restore doesn't delete any of your personal files, it removes programs installed after the restore point you select, requiring you to reinstall those programs.

You'll show Julie how to restore her computer in case she has system problems and wants to revert to a previous point. You won't actually restore her computer in the following steps because it doesn't need it right now. You'll work as far as you can through the System Restore dialog boxes, and then click the Cancel button instead of the Finish button. You also inform Julie that she should save any open files and close any running programs before using System Restore.

TIP

You can also open the System Restore dialog box by clicking the Start button, pointing to All Programs, clicking Accessories, clicking System Tools, and then clicking System Restore.

To begin restoring a computer:

1. In the System Properties dialog box, click the **System Restore** button. The System Restore Wizard starts.

2. Click the **Next** button. The next System Restore dialog box opens, where you can choose a restore point. See Figure 9-12.

Figure 9-12   Choosing a restore point

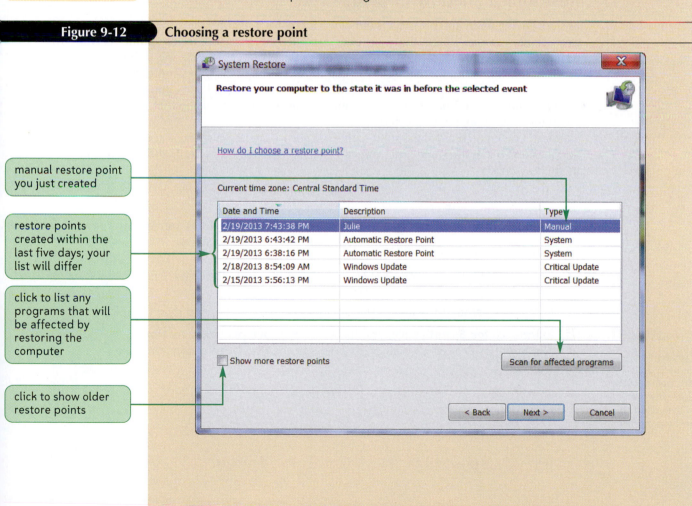

manual restore point you just created

restore points created within the last five days; your list will differ

click to list any programs that will be affected by restoring the computer

click to show older restore points

3. Click the **second restore point** in the list, which is probably the one Windows created when you backed up Julie's documents, and then click the **Next** button. The last System Restore dialog box opens so you can confirm your restore point. At this point, you can also click the Scan for affected programs link to identify the programs added since Windows created that restore point.

4. Click the **Cancel** button to close the dialog box without restoring the computer.

Trouble? If you clicked the Finish button instead of the Cancel button, confirm that you want to restore your computer, and then wait until System Restore finishes and restarts your computer. Open the System Properties dialog box, click the System Restore button, click Undo System Restore, click Next, click Finish, and then click Yes.

5. Close all open windows.

Recall that Windows 7 saves restore points until they fill up the hard disk space reserved by System Restore. (You can change the amount of space allocated for System Restore in the System Protection dialog box.) As you and Windows create new restore points, System Restore deletes old ones. If you turn off System Protection on a disk, Windows deletes all the restore points from that disk. When you turn System Protection back on, Windows starts creating new restore points.

Restoring a Shadow Copy of a File

Besides saving an image of your system when it creates a restore point, Windows 7 also saves shadow copies of files that have been modified since the last restore point. As with restore points, Windows creates shadow copies of files on a hard disk only if System Protection is turned on for that disk. You can restore a single file or an entire folder. Note that Windows saves only one version of a file as a shadow copy. For example, if you modify a file several times in one day, Windows saves only the version that was current when the restore point was created.

When you created a restore point earlier, Windows created a shadow copy of the Supplies text file at the same time. You can change this file now, save it, and then restore its shadow copy.

To change the Supplies file and then restore a previous version:

1. Open the **Julie** folder window.

2. In the Julie folder window, double-click **Supplies**. The Supplies file opens in the default text editor, such as Notepad.

3. Enter your name at the end of the document, save the file, and then close it.

4. Right-click the **Supplies** file, and then click **Restore previous versions**. The Supplies Properties dialog box opens to the Previous Versions tab. See Figure 9-13.

TIP

If the file you want to restore has been mistakenly deleted from a folder, you can right-click that folder and then select Restore previous versions.

Figure 9-13   **Previous Versions tab in the Supplies Properties dialog box**

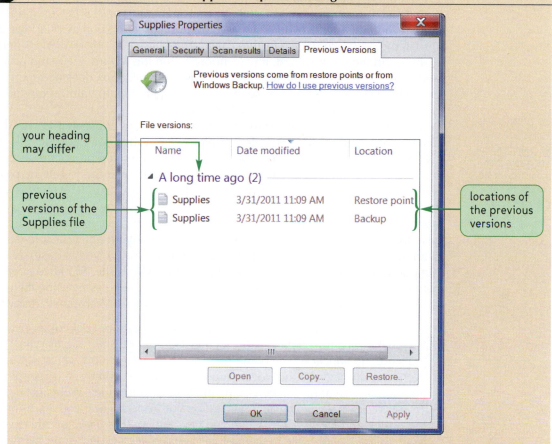

your heading
may differ

previous
versions of the
Supplies file

locations of
the previous
versions

This dialog box lists two previous versions—one created when you set a restore point, and the other in the backup folder. You'll restore the previous version created by the restore point.

5. Click the **Supplies** file created by the restore point, and then click the **Restore** button. The Previous Versions dialog box opens, asking you to confirm that you want to restore this version of the Supplies.txt file. Note that restoring the file replaces the current version and cannot be undone.

6. Click the **Restore** button. After restoring the file, Windows displays a message indicating that the file was successfully restored.

7. Click the **OK** button.

8. In the Julie folder window, open the **Supplies** text file again. Note that your name does not appear at the end of the document. Close the file.

9. Click the **OK** button to close the Supplies Properties dialog box.

10. Close all open windows.

Next, you want to show Julie how to install software on her computer.

Installing Software

You can install software from at least three locations: from a CD or DVD, a Web site, or a network folder. Installing typically involves starting a setup program, copying the files you need from the installation medium to a folder on your computer, and then changing

Windows 7 settings so that the program runs properly. Most programs come with a setup wizard that asks you for some information, such as where you want to store the program, and then takes care of the rest of the tasks.

If the software you want to install is provided on a CD or DVD, you insert the disc into the appropriate drive on your computer. In most cases, as soon as Windows detects the disc in the drive—through a feature called AutoPlay—a dialog box opens and asks if you want to run the setup wizard. If you choose to run the wizard, the Setup program starts and guides you through the installation steps. If a dialog box does not open to ask about the setup wizard, you can browse the disk and open the program's setup file yourself by double-clicking a file named Setup.exe or Install.exe.

You can install a program from a Web site by using your browser to visit the Web site and then clicking a link to download the program. When you click the link, a dialog box usually opens and gives you the choice of running the setup program now or saving it to install the program later. If you choose Run (or Open), you can install the program immediately by following the instructions in a dialog box or wizard. However, if your transmission is interrupted, you might need to start downloading the program again. Because downloading and running a program in the same step can introduce a virus, choosing to save the program file when you download it is safer—your antivirus software can then scan the file for known viruses or you can do so yourself. In either case, be sure you trust the publisher of any program you download from a Web site. You have already learned some ways to determine the legitimacy of a Web site, such as by using the phishing filter. In addition, use the following guidelines to determine if a Web site is trustworthy:

TIP

Avoid downloading and running a program in the same step because doing so increases the risk of triggering a virus.

- The Web site is certified by an Internet trust organization. Look for a privacy certification seal from a trust organization such as TRUSTe, BBB*OnLine*, or WebTrust. These seals usually appear on the home page of the Web site. However, some unscrupulous Web sites display fake trust logos. You can find out if a Web site is registered with an Internet trust organization by visiting the trust organization's Web site.
- The Web site is owned by an organization you know well. If you are using a Web site for a brick-and-mortar store where you have shopped or if you or others you know have visited the Web site in the past with no problems, you can probably trust the files provided by the Web site.

In contrast, be wary of downloading files from Web sites you are invited to visit in an e-mail message sent by someone you don't know, Web sites that offer objectionable content, and those that make offers that seem too generous, indicating a possible sale of illegal or pirated software.

You know that Microsoft provides a handy calculator program that converts weights and measurements, and you think Julie might find it useful. You'll show Julie how to download this program from the Microsoft Web site and then install it.

To perform the following steps, make sure you have permission to download software from a Web site. If your school does not allow you to download files, read but do not perform the following steps.

To download a program from the Microsoft Web site:

▶ **1.** Start Internet Explorer.

▶ **2.** Type **www.microsoft.com/downloads** in the Address bar, and then press the **Enter** key. The Microsoft Download Center Web page opens.

▶ **3.** In the Search All Download Center box, type **Calculator Plus**, and then press the **Enter** key. The search results include a link to the Microsoft Calculator Plus program.

4. Click the **Microsoft Calculator Plus** link. The Microsoft Calculator Plus page opens. See Figure 9-14.

Figure 9-14   **Microsoft Download Center Web page**

name of the program you are downloading

description of the program

click to read system requirements

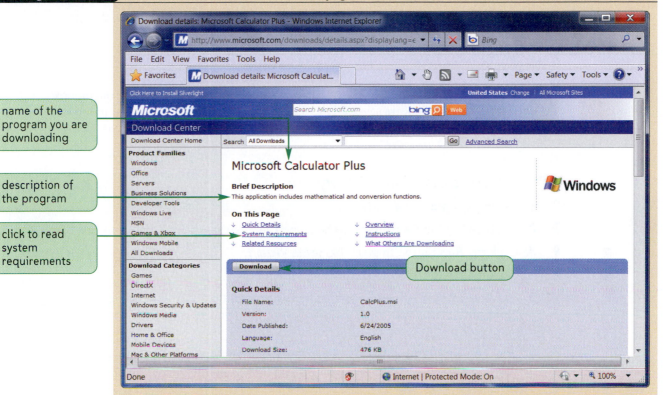

Trouble? If the Microsoft Calculator Plus link or a similar link does not appear in the search results, click the Next button to view another page of search results. If you do not find a link to the Microsoft Calculator Plus page, close Internet Explorer and then read but do not perform the remaining steps.

5. Click the **Download** button. The Microsoft Web site begins to download the file, and then opens the File Download – Security Warning dialog box. See Figure 9-15.

Figure 9-15   **File Download – Security Warning dialog box**

click to save the files on your computer and run the setup program later

click to run the setup program immediately

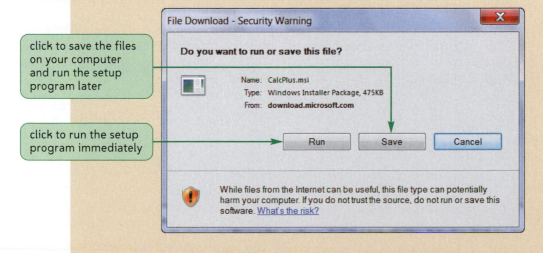

> 6. Click the **Save** button. The Save As dialog box opens.
>
> 7. Navigate to the **Julie** folder in the Documents library, and then click the **Save** button. The Microsoft Web site finishes downloading the file, which might take a few minutes, and then closes the dialog box.
>
>   **Trouble?** If the Download Complete dialog box does not close, click the Close button.
>
> 8. Close Internet Explorer.

Be sure to save the file in the Julie folder so you can find it later.

When you use the Save option in the File Download – Security Warning dialog box to download files, Windows saves all the files it needs to install the program in the folder you specify. To install the program, you double-click the file you downloaded.

To install the downloaded program:

> 1. Navigate to the **Julie** folder.
>
> 2. Double-click the **CalcPlus** file. The Open File – Security Warning dialog box opens.
>
> 3. Click the **Run** button to start the Setup Wizard.
>
> 4. Click the **Next** button to continue in the Setup Wizard.
>
> 5. Read the License Agreement, click the **I Agree** option button, and then click the **Next** button. The wizard displays the path to the folder where the Calculator Plus program will be installed.
>
> 6. Click the **Next** button to start the installation. Windows 7 installs the program, displays a progress bar, and then displays an Installation Complete dialog box.
>
> 7. Click the **Close** button.
>
> 8. Close the Julie folder window.

Now you can show Julie how to start the Microsoft Calculator Plus program. Like any other Windows 7 program, it is available on the Start menu. After starting this program, you can demonstrate it to Julie and see if she wants to keep it on her computer. You'll show her how to use the program to convert kilograms to pounds.

To start Calculator Plus:

> 1. Click the **Start** button ⊞ on the taskbar. The new program is highlighted on the Start menu. The All Programs command is also highlighted, indicating that you can start the new program from the All Programs list if it doesn't appear on the Start menu.

2. Click **Microsoft Calculator Plus** to start the program.

   Trouble? If Microsoft Calculator Plus does not appear on your Start menu, point to All Programs, click the Microsoft Calculator Plus folder, and then click Microsoft Calculator Plus.

3. Click the **Category** button, and then click **Weights**.

4. Click the **Convert from** button, and then click **kilograms**, if necessary. Click the **Convert to** button, and then click **pounds**, if necessary.

5. Click in the text box, and then type **1** to convert 1 kilogram to pounds.

   Trouble? If you make a typing error, click the Backspace button below the text box to delete the error.

6. Click the **Convert** button to display the results.

7. Close the Calculator Plus program.

Julie isn't sure that she'd use the new program, so you'll show her how to uninstall it.

TIP

For some programs, you can point to the program name on the Start menu, and then click an uninstall command to uninstall the program.

Uninstalling a Software Program

You can uninstall a program from your computer if you no longer use it. Doing so frees up space on your hard disk, sometimes a significant amount of space, depending on the program. You can use the Programs and Features window to uninstall programs. Uninstalling removes the program's files and any changes made to Windows system settings, such as in the registry.

You can also use the Programs and Features window to change a program's configuration by adding or removing certain options. Usually this means that you turn optional features of the program on or off. Not all programs let you change their features. To determine whether you can, click the program name in the Programs and Features window, and then look for the Change or Repair button on the toolbar.

You'll show Julie how to uninstall the Microsoft Calculator Plus program using the Programs and Features window.

To uninstall a program:

1. Click the **Start** button, click **Control Panel**, and then click **Uninstall a program** in the Programs category. The Programs and Features window opens and now includes the Microsoft Calculator Plus program in the list of installed programs. See Figure 9-16.

Figure 9-16 **Programs and Features window**

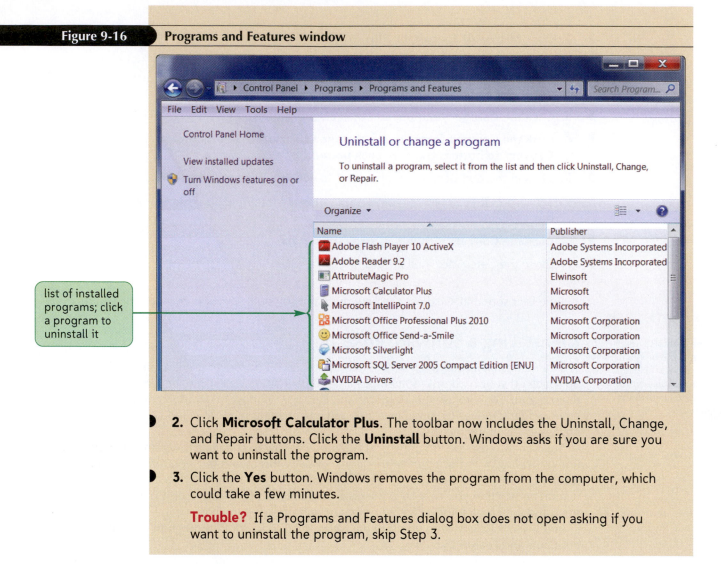

list of installed programs; click a program to uninstall it

2. Click **Microsoft Calculator Plus**. The toolbar now includes the Uninstall, Change, and Repair buttons. Click the **Uninstall** button. Windows asks if you are sure you want to uninstall the program.

3. Click the **Yes** button. Windows removes the program from the computer, which could take a few minutes.

   Trouble? If a Programs and Features dialog box does not open asking if you want to uninstall the program, skip Step 3.

Installing and Uninstalling a Software Update

You should install updates to Windows 7 as they become available. Important updates provide significant benefits, such as improved security and reliability. To do so, you can turn on automatic updating. If an update is available, Windows will download and install it the next time your computer is turned on. You can also set Windows to automatically install recommended updates, which can address noncritical problems and help enhance your computing experience. You can also check for optional updates using the Windows Action Center on your own. Windows Update does not download or install optional updates automatically. You can use the Programs and Features window to verify which updates have been installed on your computer.

To view installed updates:

1. In the left pane of the Programs and Features window, click **View installed updates**. Windows scans your computer for updates, and then displays them sorted by program. See Figure 9-17.

Figure 9-17   **Viewing installed updates**

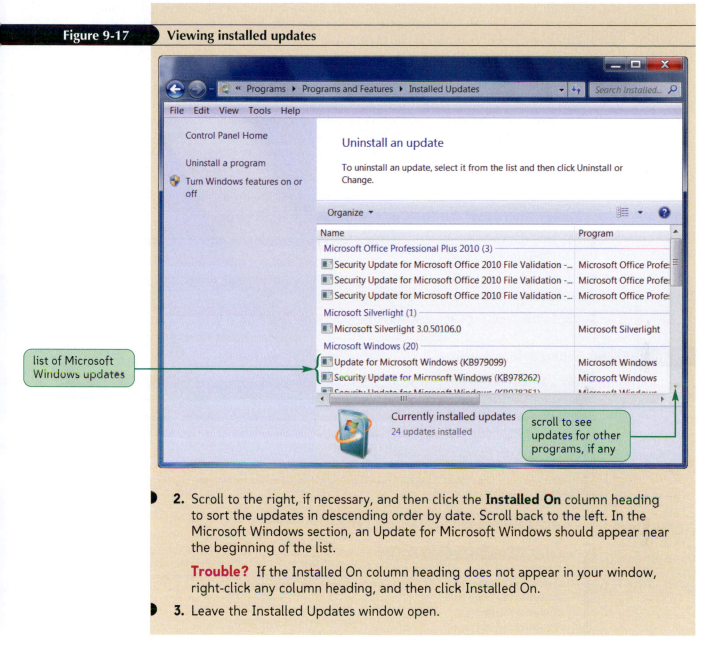

list of Microsoft
Windows updates

Currently installed updates
24 updates installed

scroll to see
updates for other
programs, if any

▶ **2.** Scroll to the right, if necessary, and then click the **Installed On** column heading
to sort the updates in descending order by date. Scroll back to the left. In the
Microsoft Windows section, an Update for Microsoft Windows should appear near
the beginning of the list.

Trouble? If the Installed On column heading does not appear in your window,
right-click any column heading, and then click Installed On.

▶ **3.** Leave the Installed Updates window open.

Julie's copy of Windows 7 seems to be up to date, and she verifies that she has automatic updating turned on, so you are confident she has the latest software updates.

Setting Default Programs

When you double-click a data file such as a graphic or text document, a program starts
and opens the file. Most computers have more than one program that can open certain
types of files. For example, to open a photo file with a .jpg extension, you can use programs including Paint, Windows Photo Viewer, and Windows Media Center. How does
Windows choose the program to start when you double-click the .jpg file? It chooses
the one set as the default program for that file type.

You can set default programs by using the Default Programs tool in the Control Panel
to associate file types with an installed program. For example, if you associate .jpg files
with Windows Photo Viewer and .png files with Paint, you can use two default programs
for working with graphics files. You can also set the default program you want to use for

certain activities, such as browsing the Web. For example, if you have more than one browser installed on your computer, you can select the one you want to use by default. That browser will open when you click a Web page link in a document, for example.

Julie has two e-mail programs on her computer: Microsoft Outlook and Windows Live Mail. She wants to set Microsoft Outlook as the default program for creating and reading e-mail. She also reviews graphics for Northbrook ads in the .png file format. Because she often needs to edit the graphics, she wants Paint to open when she double-clicks a .png file. You'll show her how to perform both tasks using the Default Programs tool.

You need to log on using an Administrator account to perform the steps in this section. If you are not allowed to log on as an Administrator, read but do not perform the following steps.

To set Microsoft Outlook as the default e-mail program:

1. In the Installed Updates window, click **Programs** in the Address bar to display the Programs window.

2. In the Default Programs category, click **Set your default programs**. The Set Default Programs window opens.

3. In the Program list, click **Microsoft Outlook**. See Figure 9-18.

Figure 9-18	Setting default programs

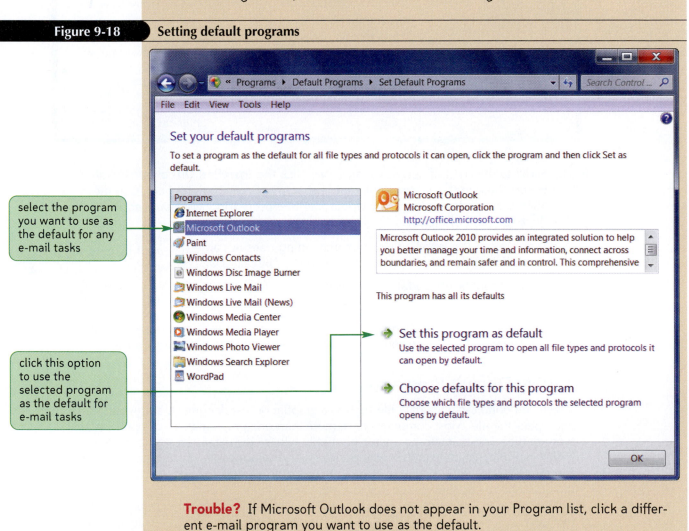

select the program you want to use as the default for any e-mail tasks

click this option to use the selected program as the default for e-mail tasks

Trouble? If Microsoft Outlook does not appear in your Program list, click a different e-mail program you want to use as the default.

4. Click **Set this program as default**, and then click the **OK** button. The Default Programs window opens.

Now when Julie clicks a link or button on a Web page, for example, to create an e-mail message, Microsoft Outlook will start and open a new message window.

Next, you'll show Julie how to associate files in the .png format with Paint so that when she double-clicks a .png file, Paint starts instead of a different graphics program.

To set Paint as the default program for opening .png files:

1. In the Default Programs window, click **Associate a file type or protocol with a program**. The Set Associations window opens, listing hundreds of file types associated with the programs on your computer.

2. Scroll down, click **.png** in the list of file types and protocols, and then click the **Change program** button. The Open with window opens and displays the programs you can use to open .png files. See Figure 9-19.

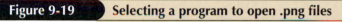

Figure 9-19   Selecting a program to open .png files

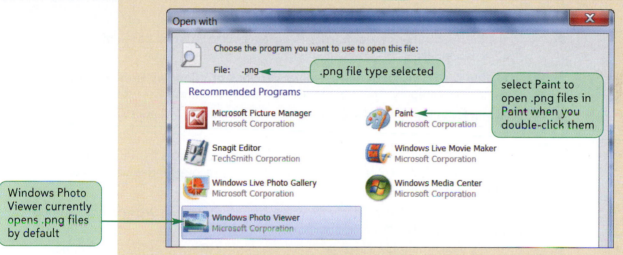

3. Click **Paint** in the Recommended Programs list, and then click the **OK** button.

4. Leave the Set Associations window open.

Now when Julie double-clicks a .png file, Paint will start so she can edit the graphic if necessary.

Setting Up a Program for Compatibility

If you install programs written for earlier versions of Windows, such as Windows Vista or Windows XP, chances are that they will run properly. However, some older programs might run poorly or not run at all. When you run an older program, the Program Compatibility Assistant dialog box might open if it detects known compatibility issues. The dialog box notifies you about the problem and offers to fix it the next time you run the program.

If the Program Compatibility Assistant dialog box does not appear when you run an older program, you can use the Program Compatibility troubleshooter to select and test compatibility settings that might fix the problems in the older program. You can let Windows apply recommended settings or you can troubleshoot the program manually. When you troubleshoot manually, you can choose an operating system recommended for the program or one that previously supported the program correctly. After you apply recommended settings or select an operating system, you can start the older program to see if the new settings solve the problem. If they don't, you can return to the troubleshooter and try other settings.

Microsoft advises that you should not use the Program Compatibility troubleshooter on older antivirus programs, disk utilities, or other system programs because it might remove data or create a security risk.

Julie installed a Windows XP program called Electronic Organizer on her Windows 7 computer, and it has not displayed menus or title bars correctly since she installed it. You'll run the Program Compatibility troubleshooter and select the Electronic Organizer program to run it with compatibility settings, and see if that solves the problem.

The following steps select compatibility settings for a program named Electronic Organizer. Ask your instructor to identify a program on your computer that you can use instead of Electronic Organizer. The program should not be an antivirus program, disk utility, or other system program. Substitute the name of that program for *Electronic Organizer* when you perform the following steps.

To use the Program Compatibility troubleshooter:

1. In the Set Associations window, click **Programs** in the Address bar to display the Programs window.

2. Click **Run programs made for previous versions of Windows** in the Programs and Features category. The Program Compatibility troubleshooter starts.

3. Click the **Next** button. The next dialog box lists programs installed on your computer.

4. Click the **Electronic Organizer** (or other program name), and then click the **Next** button. Windows 7 gives you two options: Try recommended settings or Troubleshoot program.

   Trouble? If your list of programs does not include Electronic Organizer, click the program your instructor recommended.

5. Click **Try recommended settings**. Windows detects which operating system the program is designed for and then applies settings, if possible. See Figure 9-20.

TIP

You can also start the Program Compatibility troubleshooter by right-clicking a program icon and then clicking Troubleshoot compatibility.

Figure 9-20   **Program Compatibility window**

Windows detected that this program was created for Windows XP (Service Pack 2)

click to start the program and test the new settings

6. Click the **Start the program** button. If a User Account Control dialog box opens, click the **Yes** button. Electronic Organizer (or other program) starts.

   Trouble? If the older program does not start or run correctly, close the program window, if necessary, and then read but do not perform the following steps.

   Trouble? If a User Account Control dialog box opens requesting your permission or a password to continue, enter the password or click the Continue button.

7. Close the program, and then click the **Next** button. The next wizard dialog box asks if the program has been fixed.

8. Click **Yes, save these settings for this program**. Windows saves the settings, and then displays a summary.

9. Click the **Close** button to close the Program Compatibility window.

10. Close all open windows.

You're finished showing Julie how to back up and restore files and manage her software. In the next session, you'll examine how to maintain hard disks and monitors and work with device drivers.

Session 9.1 Quick Check

REVIEW

1. Describe why you should use a backup program instead of a copy procedure to protect data on a hard disk.
2. To back up your entire computer, including programs and system settings, you create a(n) _____.
3. True or False. If your computer becomes unstable, you can undo system changes using a full backup.
4. A(n) _____ is a copy of a data file that you've modified since Windows made the last restore point.
5. How can you make sure that when you double-click a .jpg file, the Paint program starts?
6. True or False. You can view a list of the updates Windows Updates has installed on your computer, including the date they were installed.
7. If an older program doesn't run correctly in Windows 7, what can you do?

SESSION 9.2 VISUAL OVERVIEW

Hardware is any physical piece of equipment, called a **device**, that is both connected to your computer and controlled by your computer.

A **local disk** is installed in your computer.

Windows 7 must be installed on a disk using the **NTFS file system**, which is the underlying structure a computer uses to organize data on a hard disk.

As part of a regular maintenance program, you should be familiar with the properties of your hard disk, including how much free space it has.

The **Disk Cleanup tool** frees disk space by deleting unnecessary files such as temporary files.

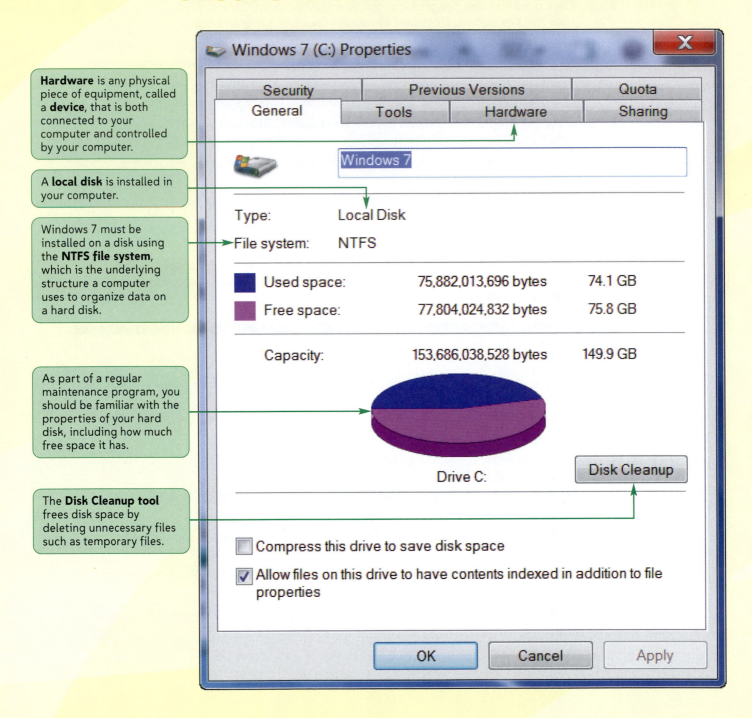

MANAGING HARDWARE

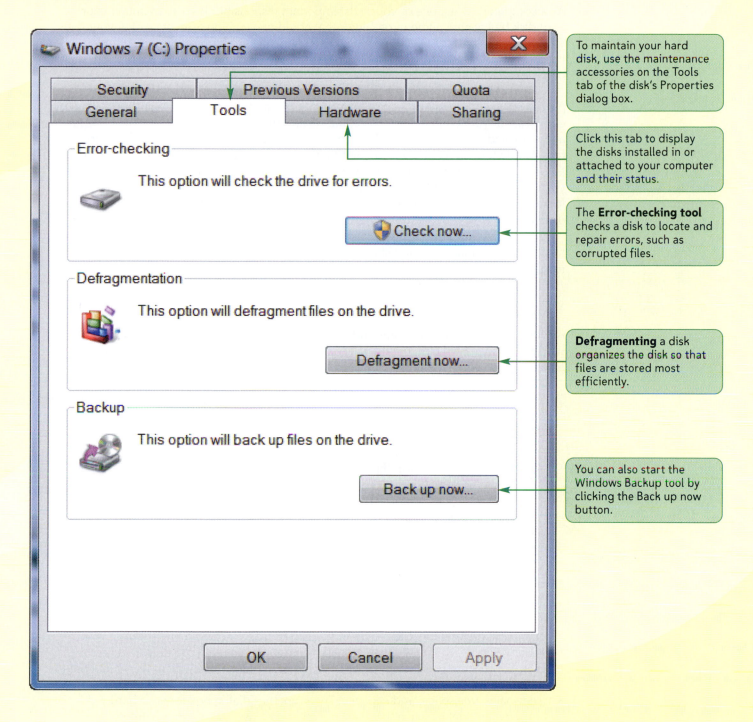

Windows 7 (C:) Properties

| Security | Previous Versions | Quota |
| General | Tools | Hardware | Sharing |

Error-checking

This option will check the drive for errors.

Check now...

Defragmentation

This option will defragment files on the drive.

Defragment now...

Backup

This option will back up files on the drive.

Back up now...

OK   Cancel   Apply

To maintain your hard disk, use the maintenance accessories on the Tools tab of the disk's Properties dialog box.

Click this tab to display the disks installed in or attached to your computer and their status.

The **Error-checking tool** checks a disk to locate and repair errors, such as corrupted files.

Defragmenting a disk organizes the disk so that files are stored most efficiently.

You can also start the Windows Backup tool by clicking the Back up now button.

Maintaining Hard Disks

As a computer owner, one of your most important responsibilities is to maintain your hard disk by keeping it free of problems that could prevent you from accessing your data. The failure of a hard disk can be a headache if you have backups of your data and a disaster if you don't. Windows 7 helps you prevent disk failure from occurring in the first place by providing some valuable disk maintenance accessories.

As part of a regular maintenance program, you should become familiar with the properties of your hard disk, including whether it is partitioned. Next, you should check each disk on your computer to locate and repair errors, such as parts of corrupted files and damaged sections on the disk. Then you should defragment each disk. If you are responsible for maintaining a computer that is used all day, you should probably run these maintenance procedures on a weekly or even daily basis. On the other hand, if you use your computer less frequently—for example, if you use a home computer only for correspondence, games, and maintaining your finances—you might only need to run disk maintenance procedures once every month or so.

Julie has not performed any maintenance tasks on her computer, so you'll guide her through the cleanup tasks and show her how to make sure they are completed on a regular basis.

Viewing Hard Disk Properties

As you know, all of the programs and system files on your computer are stored on your hard disk. You should periodically check the amount of free space on your hard disk to make sure the computer does not run out of room.

REFERENCE

Viewing Hard Disk Properties

- Click the Start button, and then click Computer.
- Right-click a hard disk in the Computer window.
- Click Properties on the shortcut menu.

View the properties of your hard disk to learn the following information:

- File system: Recall that Windows 7 must be installed on a disk using the NTFS file system. NTFS supports file system recovery (in the case of a hard disk failure) and can access disk drives up to 2 terabytes in size. NTFS is the preferred file system if your disk drive is larger than 32 gigabytes. Your computer might also be able to access a disk that uses the FAT32 file system, which uses an older, less efficient method of organizing data on the disk.
- Used space, free space, and capacity: The Properties dialog box for your hard disk shows the amount of space that files and other data use, the amount of free space remaining, and the total capacity of the disk.
- All disk drives: The Hardware tab of a disk's Properties dialog box lists all the disks installed in or attached to your computer. If you are having trouble with a disk, you can view more details about it, such as its status, which indicates whether it is working properly.

You'll start your maintenance session with Julie by viewing the properties of her hard disk. In the following steps, the hard disk is named Windows 7 (C:). Substitute the name of your hard disk if it is different.

To view the properties of a hard disk:

1. Click the **Start** button on the taskbar, and then click **Computer**. The Computer window opens.

2. Right-click **Windows 7 (C:)**, and then click **Properties** on the shortcut menu. See Figure 9-21. The space details on your computer will differ.

Figure 9-21   **Windows 7 (C:) Properties dialog box**

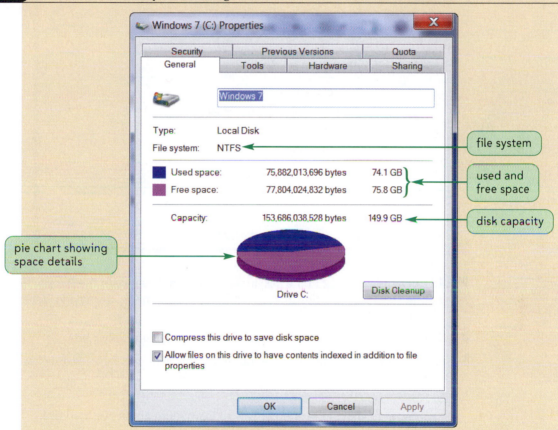

pie chart showing space details

file system

used and free space

disk capacity

Trouble? If the hard disk where Windows 7 is installed has a different name, right-click that disk icon, and then click Properties.

3. Click the **Hardware** tab to display the disks attached to your computer. See Figure 9-22.

Figure 9-22 **Hardware tab of the Windows 7 (C:) Properties dialog box**

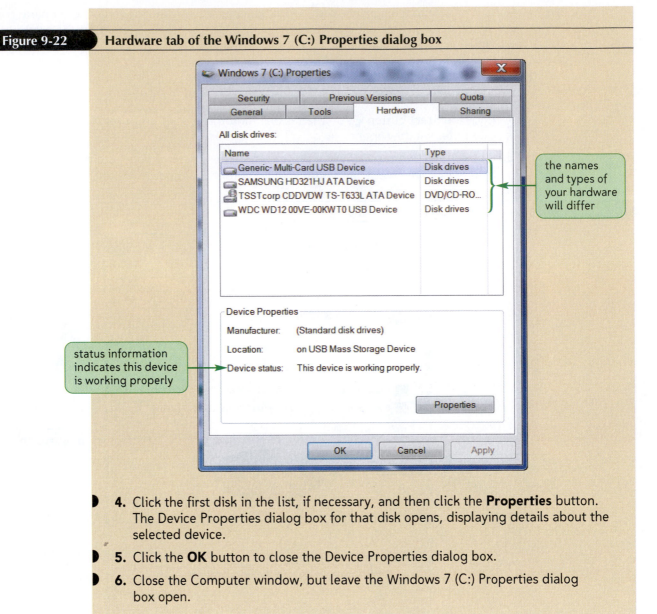

4. Click the first disk in the list, if necessary, and then click the **Properties** button. The Device Properties dialog box for that disk opens, displaying details about the selected device.

5. Click the **OK** button to close the Device Properties dialog box.

6. Close the Computer window, but leave the Windows 7 (C:) Properties dialog box open.

You want to show Julie another way to learn more about her hard disk.

Checking for Partitions

A **partition** (sometimes called a **volume**) is part of a hard disk that works like a separate disk—it can be formatted with a file system and identified with a letter of the alphabet. A hard disk needs to be partitioned and formatted before you can store data on it. Computer manufacturers usually perform this task for you, and set up the hard disk as a single partition that equals the size of the hard disk. Partitioning a hard disk into several smaller partitions is not required, but it can be useful for organizing data on your hard disk. Some users prefer to have separate partitions each for the Windows operating system files, programs, and personal data. You can also create partitions if you want to install more than one operating system on your computer.

You can use the Disk Management window to view the partitions on your system. One partition is the system partition, which contains the hardware-related files that tell a computer where to look to start Windows. Another partition is the boot partition, which contains the Windows operating system files. These files are located in the Windows file folder. Usually, the system partition and boot partition are the same partition, especially if you have only one operating system installed on your computer. If you have more than one operating system on your computer, such as Windows 7 and Windows Vista (called a dual-boot or multiboot computer), you have more than one boot partition. The other partitions are for your programs and data.

You'll show Julie how to view the partitions on her hard disk and identify the system partition in the Disk Management window. Usually, only experienced computer administrators work in this window, but you can open it to view basic information about your hard disk.

You need to log on using an Administrator account to perform the following steps. If you are not allowed to log on as an Administrator, read but do not perform the following steps.

To view the partitions on a hard disk:

1. Click the **Start** button on the taskbar, click **Control Panel**, and then click **System and Security**.

2. Scroll to the Administrative Tools category, and then click **Create and format hard disk partitions**. The Disk Management window opens. See Figure 9-23. The information in your Disk Management window will differ.

Figure 9-23   Disk Management window

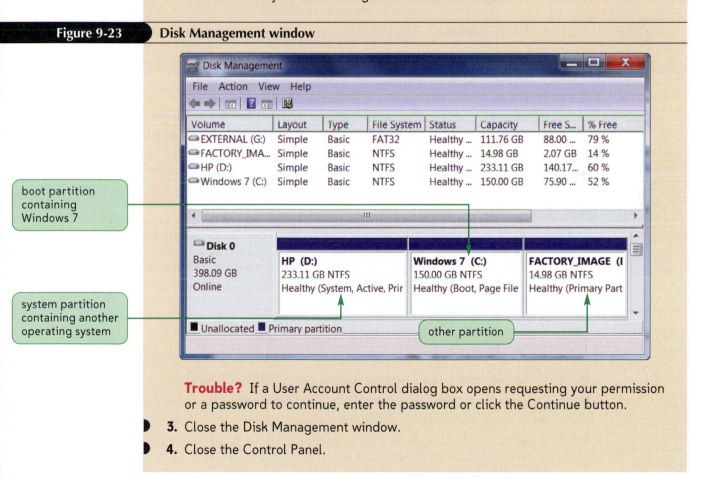

boot partition containing Windows 7

system partition containing another operating system

other partition

Trouble? If a User Account Control dialog box opens requesting your permission or a password to continue, enter the password or click the Continue button.

3. Close the Disk Management window.

4. Close the Control Panel.

Now that you and Julie are acquainted with her hard disk, you can start performing maintenance tasks. The first one is to remove unnecessary files using Disk Cleanup.

Deleting Unnecessary Files with Disk Cleanup

When you work with programs and files in Windows 7, unnecessary files, such as temporary Internet and setup files, accumulate on your hard disk and impair system performance. The Disk Cleanup tool helps you free disk space by permanently deleting these files. When you start Disk Cleanup, it searches your disk for unnecessary files, and then lists the types of files it found in the Disk Cleanup dialog box. Figure 9-24 describes the typical types of files Disk Cleanup can remove when you choose to clean your files to free space on your hard disk. Your Disk Cleanup dialog box might include a different set of files depending on your computer activity.

Figure 9-24 | **Typical types of files to remove when using Disk Cleanup**

Category	Description
Downloaded program files	Program files downloaded automatically from the Internet when you view certain Web pages
Temporary Internet files	Web pages stored on your hard disk for quick viewing, stored in the Temporary Internet Files folder
Offline Web pages	Web pages stored on your computer so you can view them without being connected to the Internet
Hibernation File Cleaner	Information about your computer stored in the Hibernation file; removing this file disables hibernation
Recycle Bin	Files you deleted from your computer, which are stored in the Recycle Bin until you delete them
Setup log files	Files Windows created during setup
Temporary files	Files generated by programs to be used temporarily; usually these are deleted when you close the program; but if the program isn't shut down properly, the temporary files remain on your disk
Thumbnails	Copies of your picture, video, and document thumbnails if you are using Windows Aero

You can also choose to clean files for all users on a computer if you are using an Administrator account. In that case, the Disk Cleanup dialog box includes an additional tab named More Options. Using the More Options tab, you can uninstall programs that you no longer use and delete all but the most recent restore point on the disk.

You'll clean Julie's hard disk by starting the Disk Cleanup tool from the Windows 7 (C:) Properties dialog box.

To use Disk Cleanup:

1. In the Windows 7 (C:) Properties dialog box, click the **General** tab.
2. Click the **Disk Cleanup** button. If you have not used Disk Cleanup on your computer, a dialog box opens asking which files to clean up.
3. If necessary, click the **Drives** arrow button, click the drive where Windows 7 is installed, such as Windows 7 (C:), and then click the **OK** button. Disk Cleanup calculates how much space you can free and then opens the Disk Cleanup for Windows 7 (C:) dialog box. See Figure 9-25. The information in your Disk Cleanup dialog box will differ.

TIP
You can also start Disk Cleanup by clicking the Start button, clicking All Programs, clicking Accessories, clicking System Tools, and then clicking Disk Cleanup.

| Figure 9-25 | Disk Cleanup for Windows 7 (C:) dialog box |

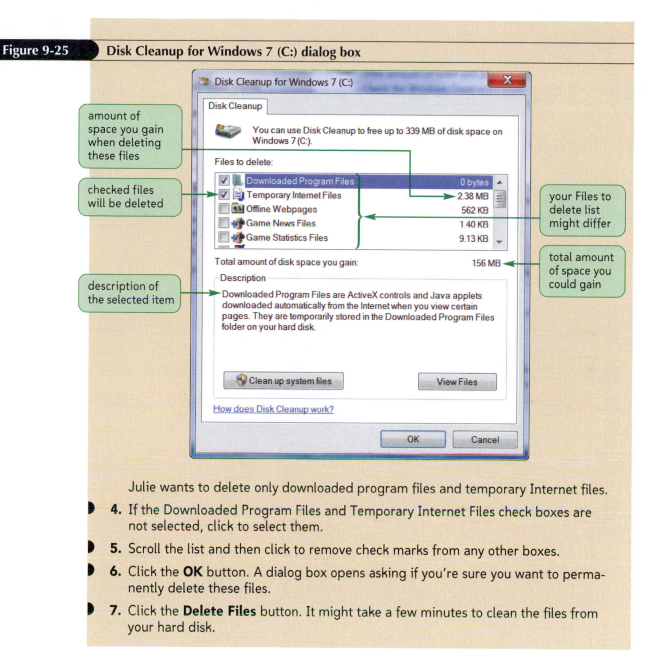

Julie wants to delete only downloaded program files and temporary Internet files.

4. If the Downloaded Program Files and Temporary Internet Files check boxes are not selected, click to select them.

5. Scroll the list and then click to remove check marks from any other boxes.

6. Click the **OK** button. A dialog box opens asking if you're sure you want to permanently delete these files.

7. Click the **Delete Files** button. It might take a few minutes to clean the files from your hard disk.

Next, you'll check Julie's hard disk for errors and other problems.

Checking a Hard Disk for Errors

A computer hard disk is a magnetic storage device that contains several metal platters that are usually sealed in your computer. Sections of the magnetic surface of a disk sometimes get damaged. Regularly scanning your disks for errors can be an effective way to head off potential problems that would make data inaccessible. The Windows 7 Error-checking tool not only locates errors on a disk, but it also attempts to repair them. If it can't repair them, the tool marks the defective portions of the disk so that Windows doesn't try to store data there. In earlier versions of Windows, the Error-checking tool was called Check Disk or ScanDisk.

To understand what problems the Error-checking tool looks for and how it repairs them, you need to understand the structure of a disk. A hard disk is organized as a concentric stack of disks or platters. Each platter has two surfaces, and each has its own read/write head, which reads and writes data magnetically on the surface. The data is stored on concentric circles on the surfaces called **tracks**. An individual block of data is one **sector** of a track, as shown in Figure 9-26.

Figure 9-26	Single platter on a hard disk

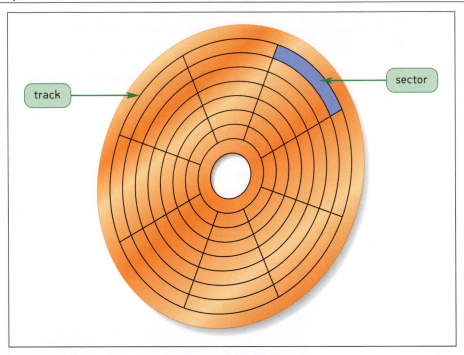

Corresponding tracks on all surfaces on a drive, when taken together, make up a cylinder. The number of sectors and tracks depends on the size of the disk. A 40 GB hard disk, for example, has 16,384 cylinders. Each cylinder has 80 heads, with one head per track. Each track has 63 sectors, with 512 bytes per sector. That makes 42,278,584,320 bytes, which is considered 40 GB.

Although the physical surface of a disk is made up of tracks and sectors, a file is stored in clusters. A **cluster** is one or more sectors of storage space—it represents the minimum amount of space that an operating system reserves when saving the contents of a file to a disk. Most files are larger than 512 bytes (the size of one sector). That means a file is often stored in more than one cluster. A file system error known as a **lost cluster** occurs if Windows loses track of which clusters contain the data that belongs to a single file. The Error-checking tool identifies file system errors and can repair them if necessary.

INSIGHT

Checking for Errors After Power Failures

If your computer suffers a power surge, a power failure, or any problem that locks it up, Windows might lose one or more clusters from a file that was open when the problem occurred, and you might lose the data stored in those clusters. The presence of lost clusters on a disk is not damaging, but lost clusters do take up valuable space, and having too many of them can lead to other types of file system errors. To prevent an accumulation of file system errors, you should check your hard disk for errors immediately after a power failure.

When you use the Windows 7 Error-checking tool to scan your disk for errors, you can specify whether you want it to automatically repair problems with files that the scan detects, such as lost clusters, or only report problems and not fix them. You can also perform a thorough disk check by scanning for and repairing physical errors on the hard disk itself, including **bad sectors**, which are areas of the disk that do not record data reliably. Performing a thorough disk check can take much longer to complete.

You'll show Julie how to check her hard disk for file system errors. Because her computer is still relatively new, it's unlikely the hard disk has any bad sectors. But after she's used her computer awhile, she should check the hard disk for bad sectors as well as file system errors.

To check the hard disk for errors:

1. In the Windows 7 (C:) Properties dialog box, click the **Tools** tab. See Figure 9-27.

Figure 9-27   **Tools tab of the Windows 7 (C:) Properties dialog box**

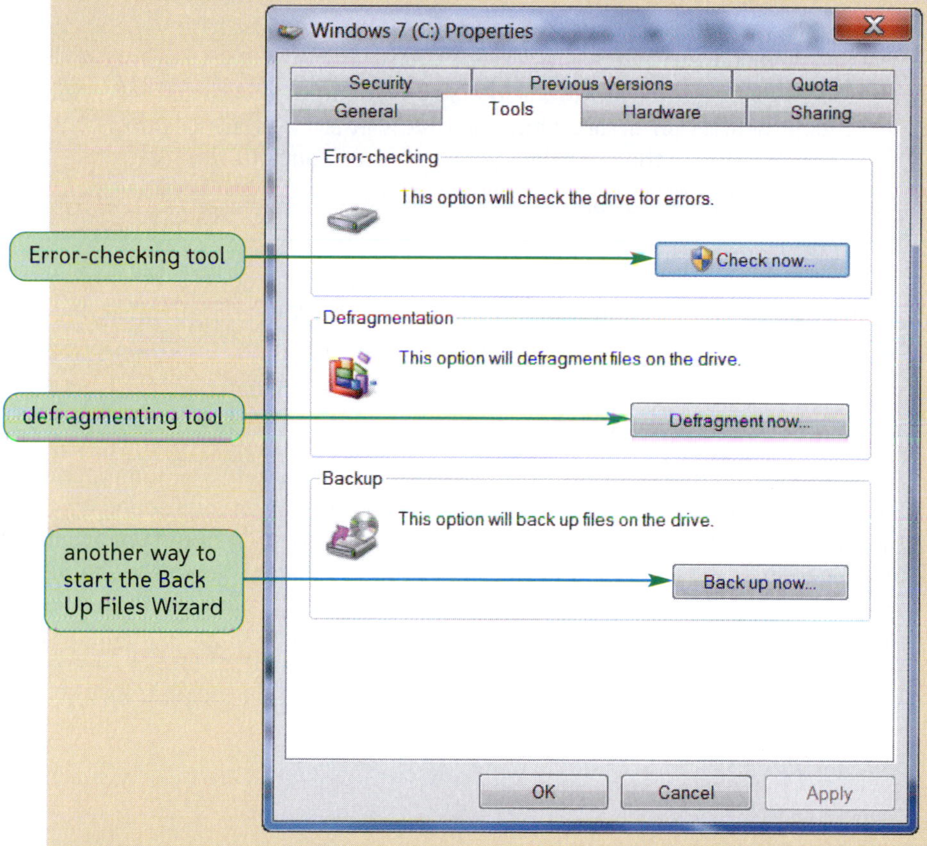

▶ **2.** Click the **Check now** button. The Check Disk Windows 7 (C:) dialog box opens. See Figure 9-28.

Figure 9-28   **Check Disk Windows 7 (C:) dialog box**

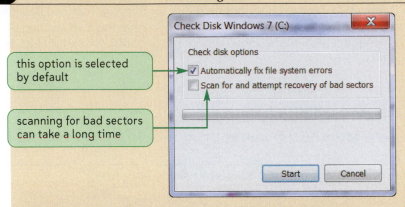

this option is selected by default

scanning for bad sectors can take a long time

▶ **3.** Make sure that only the Automatically fix file system errors box is checked, and then click the **Start** button. A dialog box opens indicating that Windows can't check the disk for errors while the disk is in use and asks if you want to check for hard disk errors the next time you start your computer.

▶ **4.** Click the **Cancel** button.

Julie doesn't need to check her disk now, but when she does, she can click the Schedule disk check button. Windows will then check the disk the next time she starts her computer.

Defragmenting a Disk

After correcting any errors on your hard disk, you can use Disk Defragmenter to improve the disk's performance so that programs start and files open more quickly. When you save a file, Windows 7 stores as much of the file as possible in the first available cluster. If the file doesn't fit into one cluster, Windows locates the next available cluster and puts more of the file in it. Windows attempts to place files in contiguous clusters whenever possible. The file is saved when Windows has placed all the file data into clusters. Figure 9-29 shows two files named Address and Recipes saved on an otherwise unused platter on a hard disk.

Figure 9-29   **Two files saved on a hard disk**

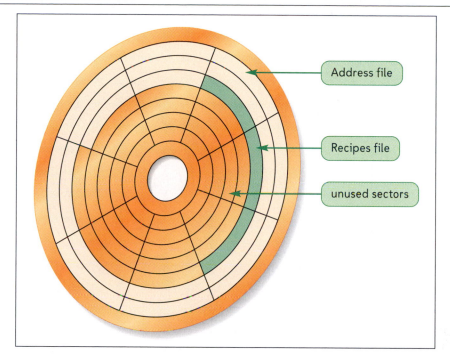

Address file

Recipes file

unused sectors

As you create and save new files, more clusters are used. If you delete a file or two, those clusters are freed. Figure 9-30 shows the disk after you save a new file, Memo, and then delete Recipes.

Figure 9-30   **Adding one file and deleting another file**

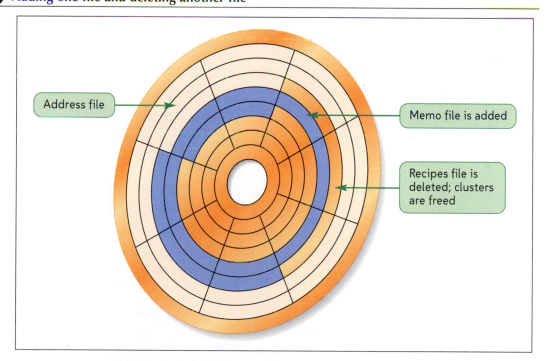

Address file

Memo file is added

Recipes file is deleted; clusters are freed

The next time you save a file, Windows 7 searches for the first available cluster, which is now between two files. Figure 9-31 shows what happens when you save a fourth file, Schedule—it is saved to clusters that are not adjacent.

Figure 9-31 **Adding a new file in fragmented clusters**

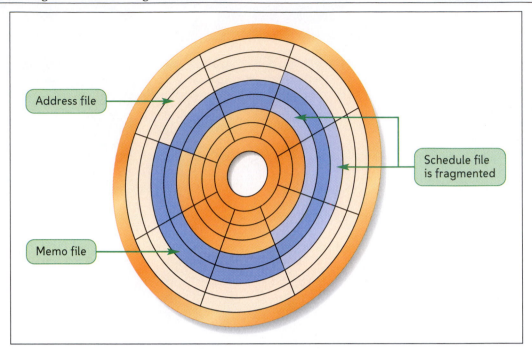

The more files you save and delete, the more scattered the clusters for a file become. A disk that contains files whose clusters are not next to each other is said to be **fragmented**. The more fragmented the disk, the longer Windows 7 takes to retrieve the file, and the more likely you are to have problems with the file. Figure 9-32 shows a fragmented disk. When a program tries to access a file on this disk, file retrieval takes longer than necessary because the program must locate clusters that aren't adjacent.

Figure 9-32 **Fragmented files**

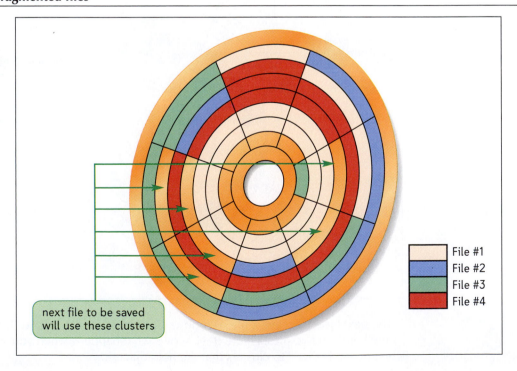

Whenever a disk has been used for a long time, it's a good idea to defragment it. Defragmenting rearranges the clusters on the disk so each file's clusters are adjacent to one another. To do so, you use Disk Defragmenter, which rearranges the data on your hard disk and reunites fragmented files so your computer can run more efficiently. In Windows 7, Disk Defragmenter runs on a schedule so you don't have to remember to run it, although you can still run it manually or change the schedule it uses.

You'll show Julie how to start Disk Defragmenter and examine its schedule. Because defragmenting a hard disk can take a long time and you must close all programs, including antivirus software, before defragmenting, you won't defragment now.

To start Disk Defragmenter:

1. On the Tools tab of the Windows 7 (C:) Properties dialog box, click the **Defragment now** button. The Disk Defragmenter dialog box opens. See Figure 9-33.

   Trouble? If a dialog box opens with a message that Disk Defragmenter was scheduled using a different program, click the Cancel button, and then read but do not perform the remaining steps.

| Figure 9-33 | Disk Defragmenter dialog box |

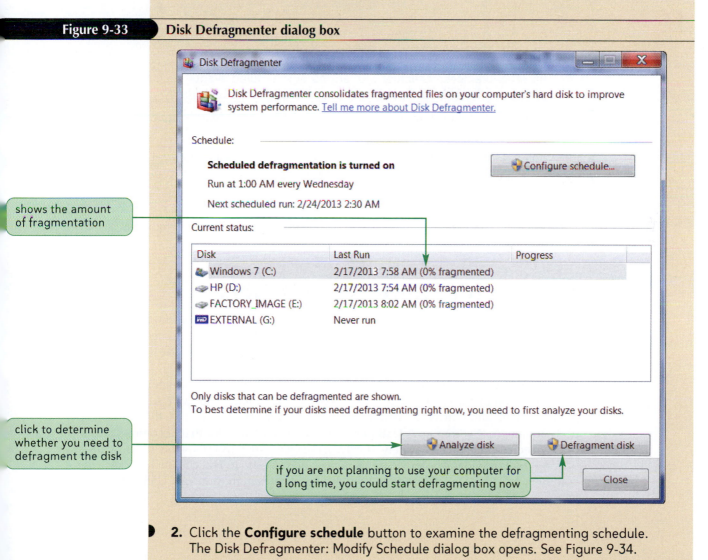

shows the amount of fragmentation

click to determine whether you need to defragment the disk

if you are not planning to use your computer for a long time, you could start defragmenting now

2. Click the **Configure schedule** button to examine the defragmenting schedule. The Disk Defragmenter: Modify Schedule dialog box opens. See Figure 9-34.

Figure 9-34 Disk Defragmenter: Modify Schedule dialog box

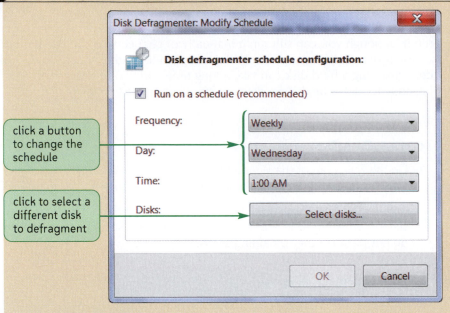

click a button to change the schedule

click to select a different disk to defragment

This schedule doesn't conflict with any other scheduled events, such as an antivirus scan, so Julie doesn't need to change it.

3. Click the **Cancel** button to close the Disk Defragmenter: Modify Schedule dialog box.

4. Click the **Close** button to close the Disk Defragmenter dialog box.

5. Close the Windows 7 (C:) Properties dialog box.

By default, Disk Defragmenter is set to run every week to make sure your disk is defragmented.

Working with Devices and Drivers

Hardware devices include external equipment such as keyboards, printers, and scanners, which remain outside the case of the computer, and internal equipment, such as disk drives, modems, and network adapter cards, which are placed inside the case of the computer.

External devices are connected to your computer through a **port**, which is a physical connection that is visible on the outside of the computer. Windows 7 supports serial, parallel, and Universal Serial Bus (USB) ports for external devices, though USB ports are the most common. A **USB port** is a thin, rectangular slot that accommodates a high-speed connection to a variety of external devices, such as removable disks, scanners, keyboards, video conferencing cameras, and printers. To use USB technology, your computer must have a USB port, and the device you install must have a USB connector, which is a small, rectangular plug. See Figure 9-35.

Figure 9-35   USB and other external ports

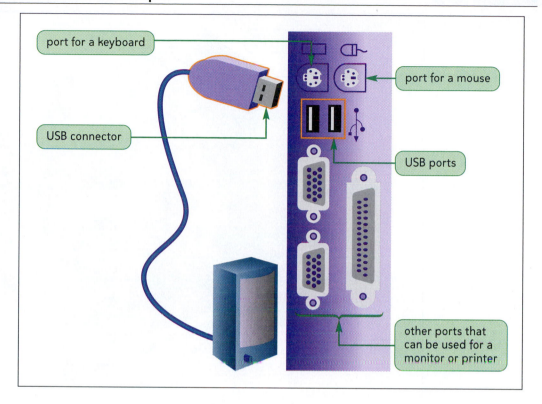

When you plug the USB connector into the USB port, Windows 7 recognizes the device and allows you to use it immediately. You can also "daisy-chain" up to 127 devices together, meaning that you plug one device, such as a scanner, into the USB port, and then plug a second device, such as a speaker, into the scanner, so you are no longer limited by the number of ports on your computer. Instead of daisy-chaining devices, you can also connect multiple devices to a single inexpensive **USB hub**. A hub is a box that contains many USB ports—you plug the hub into your computer, and then plug your USB devices into the hub. USB devices communicate with your computer more efficiently—a USB port transfers data many times faster than other types of ports. You can also connect and disconnect USB devices without shutting down or restarting your computer.

Internal devices are connected to the **motherboard**, a circuit board inside your computer that contains the **microprocessor** (the "brains" of your computer), the computer memory, and other internal hardware devices. Internal devices are connected either directly to the motherboard (such as the microprocessor and your memory chips) or via a socket in the motherboard called an **expansion slot**. You can insert devices such as network adapter cards or sound cards into expansion slots. Devices that you insert into expansion slots are often called **expansion cards** or **adapter cards** because they "expand" or "adapt" your computer and they look like large cards. See Figure 9-36.

Figure 9-36   **Internal devices**

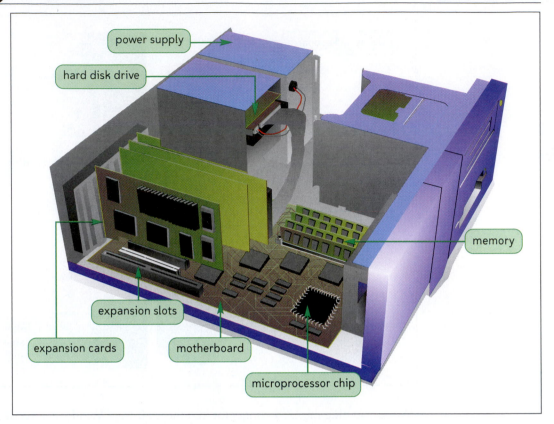

power supply

hard disk drive

memory

expansion slots

expansion cards

motherboard

microprocessor chip

Understanding Device Resources

Windows 7 assigns each device a set of system resources to help it work with the computer. Windows can assign up to four resources to a device: an IRQ, a DMA channel, an I/O address, and a memory range. When two devices share a particular resource, a **device conflict** can occur, rendering one or both of the devices unusable.

A hardware device often needs to use the microprocessor in the computer to send or receive information. When you are trying to complete several computer tasks at once (for example, when you search for a Web page while you are printing a document and playing an audio CD), Windows needs a way to handle these simultaneous requests. It does so by assigning each device an **interrupt request (IRQ) line** number that signals the microprocessor that the device is requesting an action. Windows 7 makes 16 IRQ numbers, numbered from 0 to 15, available to hardware devices. Lower numbers have higher priority and receive attention first. One common hardware headache is to have more devices than available IRQs, resulting in an IRQ conflict. If you use USB devices, however, Windows 7 only uses one set of resources for all USB devices, meaning you don't have to resolve these types of IRQ conflicts.

If the device does not need to use the microprocessor, information can be transferred directly between the device and the system's memory. This channel for transferring data is called the **direct memory access (DMA) channel**. Most computers have four DMA channels, numbered from 0 to 3, available for your devices.

When the computer receives information from one of its devices, it needs a place to store that data in the computer's memory. It does this by reserving a specific section of the computer's memory for each device. The section of the computer's memory devoted to the different devices on a computer is called the **I/O address**. Each device requires a different I/O (input/output) address.

Finally, some devices, such as video cards, require additional computer memory for their own use (not related to communicating with the microprocessor). For example, a video card needs additional memory to manage video and graphics that are not essential to the operating system. This resource is called the **memory address** or **memory range**.

Your computer uses all four types of system resources—IRQs, DMA channels, I/O addresses, and memory addresses—to communicate between hardware and software.

Understanding Device Drivers

Each hardware device requires a **driver**, a software file that enables Windows 7 to communicate with and control the operation of the device. In most cases, drivers come with Windows or can be found by going to Windows Update in the Control Panel window and checking for updates. If Windows doesn't have the driver you need, you can find it on the disc that came with the hardware or device you want to use, or on the manufacturer's Web site. Hardware manufacturers update drivers on a regular basis to improve device performance and speed. If you are having trouble with a device, you can use Windows Update or check the manufacturer's Web site to download and install an updated driver.

A **signed driver** is a device driver that includes a digital signature. Recall that a digital signature is an electronic security mark that can indicate the publisher of the software, as well as whether someone has changed the original contents of the driver package. If a publisher signed a driver by verifying its identity with a certification authority, you can be confident that the driver actually comes from that publisher and hasn't been altered. Windows 7 alerts you if a driver is not signed, was signed by a publisher that has not verified its identity with a certification authority, or has been altered since it was released.

Installing a USB Device

Before installing new hardware, check the instructions included with the device to determine whether a driver should be installed before you connect the device. Typically, Windows detects a new device after you connect it, and then installs the driver automatically. However, some devices require you to install the driver before plugging the device in. Although most devices that have power switches should be turned on before you connect them, others require that you turn them on during the installation process. Differences like this one make it a good idea to read the instructions included with a new device before you connect it.

To install new devices of any type, you typically can plug the device into a port or install a new add-on card in your computer, and Windows 7 detects the hardware, automatically installs the correct driver, and notifies you when installation begins and when it's complete. The first time you plug a USB device into a USB port, Windows installs a driver for that device. After that, you can disconnect and reconnect the device without performing additional steps.

Julie has a new USB flash drive that she wants to use with her computer. You'll show her how to install this new device. Her computer has a USB port on the front of its case, making it convenient for Julie to use her new USB flash drive because she plans to connect and disconnect the device frequently.

To perform the following step, you need a USB device that you have not yet used with your computer. If you do not have such a USB device, read but do not perform the following step.

To install a USB device:

▶ **1.** Plug the device into the USB port. Windows detects the device, installs a device driver automatically, and indicates that the device is ready to use.

  Trouble? If an AutoPlay dialog box opens, close it.

Next, you can show Julie how to use Device Manager to manage her new USB flash drive.

Enabling and Disabling Devices

Device Manager is a Windows tool that lets you manage the external and internal devices your computer uses. Using Device Manager, you can determine which devices are installed on your computer, update driver software for your devices, check to see if hardware is working properly, and modify hardware settings.

REFERENCE

Enabling and Disabling Devices

- Click the Start button, click Control Panel, click System and Security, and then click Device Manager in the System category. If you are prompted for an administrator password or confirmation, type the password or provide confirmation.
- Expand the list of devices as necessary, and then click a device.
- If the device is disabled, click the Enable button on the toolbar to enable it. If the device is enabled, click the Disable button on the toolbar to disable it.

You can use Device Manager to change how your hardware is configured and interacts with your programs. Advanced users can use the diagnostic features in Device Manager to resolve device conflicts and change resource settings. Typically, however, you use Device Manager to update device drivers and troubleshoot problems by checking the status of your devices. Suppose you occasionally have trouble burning files to a disc in your CD-RW drive. You can check the status of that drive in Device Manager and try to repair it by disabling it and then enabling it. When troubleshooting, you might also disable a device instead of uninstalling it to see if that device is causing a larger system problem. If the problem persists, you can enable the device and disable a different device. When you disable a device, you turn it off. When you enable a device, you turn it on.

You'll start Device Manager and show Julie how to disable and then enable her new USB flash drive.

To perform the following steps, you need to log on using an Administrator account. The USB device you installed in the preceding set of steps should also be available and plugged into a USB port. If you cannot log on using an Administrator account or if you do not have a USB device, read but do not perform the following steps.

To disable a USB device:

▶ **1.** If necessary, open the System and Security window, and then click **Device Manager** in the System category. The Device Manager window opens. See Figure 9-37.

Figure 9-37   **Device Manager window**

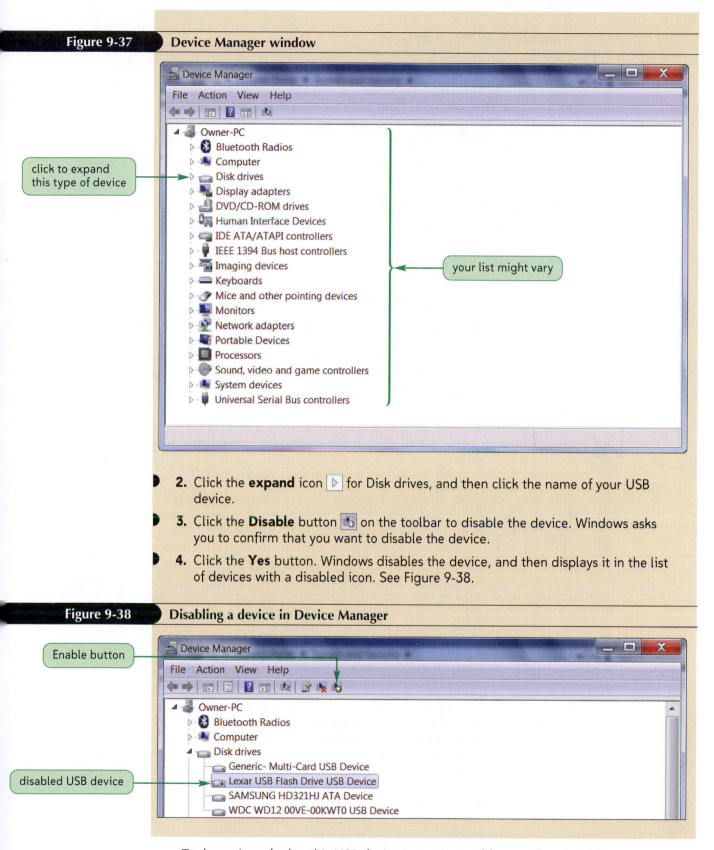

2. Click the **expand** icon ▷ for Disk drives, and then click the name of your USB device.

3. Click the **Disable** button 🜷 on the toolbar to disable the device. Windows asks you to confirm that you want to disable the device.

4. Click the **Yes** button. Windows disables the device, and then displays it in the list of devices with a disabled icon. See Figure 9-38.

Figure 9-38   **Disabling a device in Device Manager**

To determine whether this USB device is causing problems with your system, you could troubleshoot to see if your system now works properly with this device disabled. Julie is not really having any problems with this USB device, so you can enable it again.

To enable a disabled device:

▶ **1.** In the Device Manager window, click the disabled **USB device**, if necessary.

▶ **2.** Click the **Enable** button on the toolbar to enable the device. Windows turns on the device so you can use it.

Trouble? If an AutoPlay dialog box opens, close it.

Another way to troubleshoot a hardware problem is to install or update device drivers.

Installing and Updating Device Drivers

If a hardware device isn't working properly, or if a program that you're installing indicates that it requires newer drivers than you currently have installed, first check Windows Update for updated drivers. Windows Update automatically installs the device drivers you need as it updates your computer. In some cases, such as when technical support personnel ask you to install drivers from a disc or from the device manufacturer's Web site, you can also manually update drivers for your device using Device Manager.

To install or update a device driver, you can use the Properties dialog box for the hardware device. The Driver tab in this dialog box lets you update the driver, roll it back, disable it, or uninstall it. You can also find out if a driver is signed. If you want to update a driver, you can have Windows search your computer and the Internet for the appropriate files. If you have a CD or DVD that contains the updated driver, you can navigate to and install the driver files yourself.

PROSKILLS

Problem Solving: Installing Device Drivers on Your Own

Sometimes, you install a device in Windows 7 and find that it is working well. Then, when you visit the manufacturer's Web site, you notice that they've provided a newer driver that you can download and install. However, if you're not having any problems with the device, you might not need to download and install that updated driver. Newer drivers are not necessarily better. They might not have any improvements to help your hardware run better. Device drivers that are not available when you use Windows Update typically add support for new products or technologies you don't have. For example, a manufacturer might provide new drivers when it releases new high-speed DVD devices. One of the drivers might also support the older DVD driver that you purchased from the manufacturer. Unless you have one of the new DVD drives, you probably won't benefit from the new driver. If the driver hasn't been fully tested with your older DVD driver, it might cause problems with the hardware.

In case Julie needs to update a device driver on her own, you'll show her how to check for and manually install an updated driver.

To perform the following steps, you need to log on using an Administrator account. The USB device you installed in the preceding set of steps should also be available and plugged into a USB port. If you cannot log on using an Administrator account or if you do not have a USB device, read but do not perform the following steps.

To update and install a device driver:

1. In the Device Manager window, double-click the **USB device**. Its Properties dialog box opens. See Figure 9-39.

Figure 9-39	Properties dialog box for a USB device

Driver tab provides driver details and lets you update a driver

device type, manufacturer (if provided), and location

current status of the driver

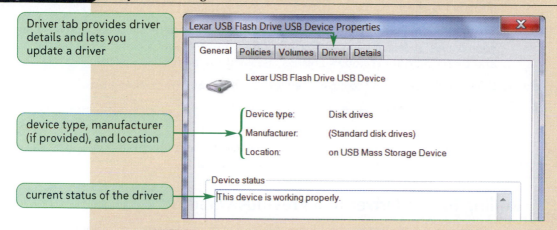

2. Click the **Driver** tab. You can use this tab to find out if a driver is signed, update the driver, roll it back, disable it, or uninstall it. See Figure 9-40.

Figure 9-40	Driver tab in the Properties dialog box for a USB device

click to view information about the driver file

click to update the driver with a newer version

if enabled, click to reinstall the previous version of the driver

click to uninstall the device driver

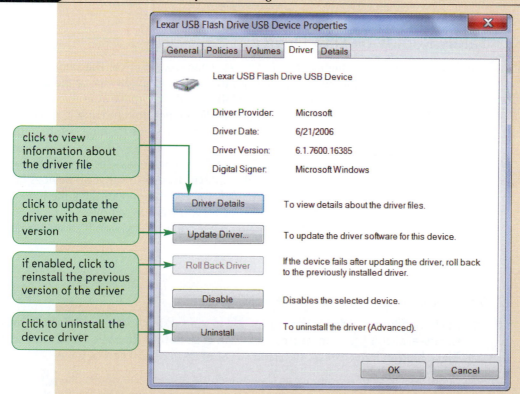

3. Click the **Driver Details** button. The Driver File Details dialog box opens, displaying the name, location, and other details about the driver file.

4. Click the **OK** button to close the Driver File Details dialog box.

5. Click the **Update Driver** button. A dialog box opens asking how you want to search for driver software.

6. Click **Search automatically for updated driver software**. Windows searches your computer and the Internet for the latest version of the driver software. For Julie's USB device, it determined that the best driver software for the device is already installed.

   Trouble? If Windows determines that you need to update the driver software for your device, it asks if you want to install the software now. Click the Yes button, and then wait until Windows finishes installing the driver.

7. Click the **Close** button to close the Update Driver Software dialog box.

8. Close all open windows.

Sometimes, installing an updated driver can cause more problems than it solves. In that case, you can restore the driver to a previous version.

Rolling Back a Driver to a Previous Version

If your computer or device has problems after you upgrade a driver, try restoring, or rolling back, the driver to a previous version. In many cases, that solves the problem. To roll back a driver, you use the Roll Back Driver button on the Driver tab of the device's Properties dialog box. (If this button is not available, that means no previous version of the driver is installed for the selected device.) Windows restores the previous version of the driver.

Safely Removing USB Devices

You can remove and unplug most USB devices whenever you like. The same is true for PC cards, which some mobile computers use to connect to a network or the Internet. When unplugging storage devices, such as USB flash drives, make sure that the computer has finished saving any information to the device before removing it. If the device has an activity light, wait for a few seconds after the light stops flashing before unplugging the device.

You know you can remove a USB device or PC card when you see the Safely Remove Hardware icon in the notification area of the taskbar. This means that all devices have finished all operations in progress and are ready for you to remove. Click the icon to display a list of devices, and then click the device you want to remove.

Julie is finished using the USB flash drive on her computer, so you'll show her how to safely remove it.

To remove a USB device from a computer:

1. Click the **Show hidden icons** button ▲ in the taskbar, click the **Safely Remove Hardware** icon 📇, if necessary, and then click **Safely Remove Hardware and Eject Media**, if necessary, to display a list of devices you can remove.

   Trouble? If your hidden icons do not include an icon that looks like 📇, point to the icons to display their names in a ScreenTip, and then click the Safely Remove Hardware icon.

2. Click **Eject USB Flash Drive**. (The wording of your notification might differ.) The Safe To Remove Hardware notification appears, indicating that you can now safely remove the device from the computer.

3. Unplug the USB device from the USB port.

Now that you've examined how to maintain hard disks and other hardware devices, you'll learn how to maintain another important component in your system: your monitor.

Maintaining Your Monitor

When your monitor is installed, Windows chooses the best display settings for that monitor, including screen resolution, refresh rate, and color. If you start having display problems with your monitor or want to improve its display, you can change the following settings or restore them to their defaults:

- Brightness and contrast: For the best results, you can use a calibration device to adjust brightness, contrast, and color settings. You usually attach the device to the front of your monitor to read light and color levels, and then use a program that came with the device to optimize your monitor's display. You can also adjust brightness and contrast manually (though not as precisely) by using the hardware controls, which are usually placed on the front of the monitor.
- Display resolution: You can adjust the screen resolution to improve the clarity of the text and images on your screen. Recall that at higher resolutions, computer images appear sharper. They also appear smaller, so more items fit on the screen. At lower resolutions, fewer items fit on the screen, but they are larger and easier to see. At very low resolutions, however, images might have jagged edges.

  For an LCD monitor, use its **native resolution**—the resolution a monitor is designed to display best, based on its size. The monitor manufacturer usually ships the computer with the monitor set to the native resolution, which is usually the highest available resolution. Although LCD monitors can technically support lower resolutions than their native resolution, the image might look stretched, or it might be small, centered on the screen, and edged with black.
- Color settings: The number of colors determines how realistic the images look. However, the higher the resolution and color setting, the more resources your monitor needs; the best settings for your computer balance sharpness and color quality with computer resources. Windows colors and themes work best when you have your monitor set to 32-bit color.
- Screen refresh rate: To reduce or eliminate flicker, you can adjust the screen refresh rate. If the refresh rate is too low, the monitor can flicker. Most monitor manufacturers recommend a refresh rate of at least 75 hertz.
- Screen text and icons: To make text and icons easier to see on your screen, you can change their size without changing the screen resolution of your monitor or laptop screen.

Julie already knows how to adjust the brightness, contrast, and screen resolution. You'll show her how to maintain her monitor by adjusting the display refresh rate and selecting color settings.

Adjusting the Display Refresh Rate

A flickering monitor can contribute to eyestrain and headaches. You can reduce or eliminate flickering by increasing the **screen refresh rate**, which determines how frequently the monitor redraws the images on the screen. The refresh rate is measured in hertz. A refresh rate of at least 75 hertz generally produces less flicker.

REFERENCE

Adjusting the Display Refresh Rate

- Right-click the desktop, and then click Screen resolution on the shortcut menu.
- Click the Advanced settings link.
- Click the Monitor tab.
- Click the Screen refresh rate button, and then click a refresh rate.

You might need to change your screen resolution before changing the refresh rate because not every screen resolution is compatible with every refresh rate. The higher the resolution, the higher your refresh rate should be. Recall that to change your screen resolution, you can right-click the desktop, click Screen resolution on the shortcut menu, click the Resolution button, and then drag the slider.

Julie recently increased the screen resolution on her monitor from 1024 × 768 to 1280 × 720 to improve the clarity of her icons. However, the screen flickers slightly since she changed that setting. You'll show her how to increase the screen refresh rate to reduce monitor flicker.

TIP

You can also open the Screen Resolution window by opening the Control Panel, clicking Adjust screen resolution, and then clicking Advanced settings.

To change the screen refresh rate:

1. Right-click the desktop, and then click **Screen resolution** on the shortcut menu. The Screen Resolution window opens.

2. Click the **Advanced settings** link. The Properties dialog box for your monitor opens.

3. Click the **Monitor** tab to display the monitor properties. See Figure 9-41.

Figure 9-41   **Monitor tab in the Properties dialog box for a monitor**

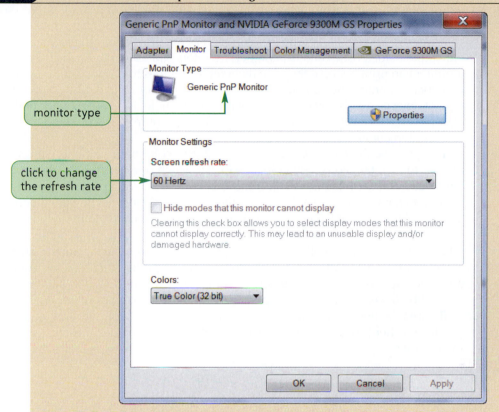

4. Click the **Screen refresh rate** button, and then click **75 Hertz**.

   Trouble? If your list of refresh rates does not include 75, click any other refresh rate the same or higher than your current refresh rate.

5. Click the **Apply** button to apply the new setting. Windows asks if you want to keep these display settings.

6. Click the **Yes** button, and leave the Monitor Properties dialog box open.

   Trouble? If you could not change the screen refresh rate, skip Steps 5 and 6.

Next, you'll show Julie how to manage the color settings on her computer. She is planning to update and print a four-color ad for the Northbrook Farmers Market and wants to make sure the colors she sees on her monitor are the same colors that print in the ad.

Selecting Color Settings

You can use the Monitor Properties dialog box to make sure that the colors displayed on your monitor match the colors produced on a color printer, for example. To do so, you use the Windows 7 color management settings.

Hardware devices that produce color, such as monitors and printers, often have different color characteristics and capabilities. Monitors can't show the same set of colors that a printer can print because they use different techniques to produce color on a screen or on paper. Scanners and cameras also have different color characteristics. Even the same type of device can display color differently. For example, the LCD monitor built into a laptop computer might display different shades of color from the LCD monitor attached to a desktop computer.

To overcome these differences, Windows 7 uses color management settings and color profiles to maintain consistent colors no matter which device produces the color content. Hardware manufacturers can create a color profile, which is a file that describes the color characteristics of a device. Profiles can also define viewing conditions, such as low-light or natural lighting. When you add a new device to your computer, the color profile for that device is included with the other installation files, so you don't need to add or remove a color profile. In addition, the default color management settings almost always produce the best results; therefore, only color professionals, such as compositors and typographers, should change them. However, you can use the Monitor Properties dialog box to verify that your computer is using the default color management settings.

Before Julie updates and prints her four-color ad for the Northbrook Farmers Market, you'll show her how to make sure her computer is using the default settings for color management.

To verify the color management settings:

1. In the Properties dialog box for your monitor, click the **Color Management** tab, and then click the **Color Management** button. The Color Management dialog box opens to the Devices tab, which identifies your hardware display and lists its color profiles, if any.

2. Click the **Advanced** tab to display the color management settings. See Figure 9-42, which shows all of these settings set to the system default. Your settings might differ.

Figure 9-42   **Advanced tab in the Color Management dialog box**

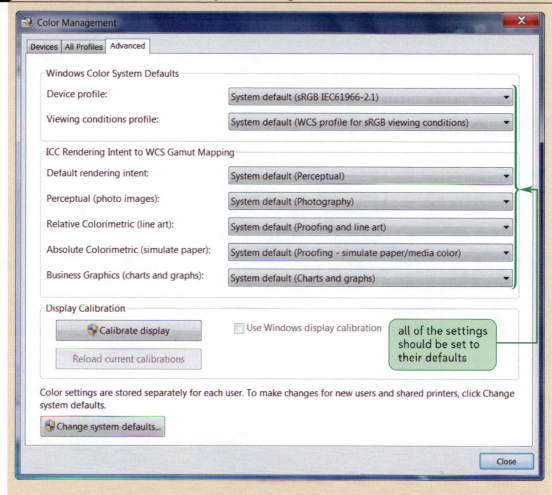

3. Click the **Close** button to close the Color Management dialog box.

4. Click the **OK** button to close the Properties dialog box for your monitor.

Using the Screen Resolution window, you can also change the size of text and other items on your screen.

Changing the Size of Icons and Text

You can increase or decrease the size of text, icons, and other items on your screen without changing the screen resolution. If you're using an LCD monitor or laptop, Microsoft recommends that you set your screen to its native resolution to avoid blurry text. (Recall that the native resolution is the optimal resolution for an LCD monitor or laptop screen.) You can choose the Smaller setting, which is the default for most monitors; Medium, which sets text and other items to 125 percent of normal size; or Larger, which sets text and other items to 150 percent of normal size. The Larger option is available only if your monitor supports a resolution of at least 1200 × 900 pixels.

To change this setting, use the Make text and other items larger or smaller link in the Screen Resolution window. After you change the size of icons and text, you will have to log off and then log on again before the new setting can take effect.

Setting Up Multiple Monitors

If you have an extra monitor, you can double your desktop workspace by connecting the extra monitor to your computer. Windows 7 can stretch the desktop across both monitors so you can display a presentation or report on the primary monitor, for example, and browse the Internet on the secondary monitor. Windows can also split the desktop between the two monitors or display the desktop on only one monitor. Figure 9-43 illustrates these options. In the figure, the laptop computer display is the primary monitor, and the flat-screen display is the secondary monitor.

Figure 9-43   Options for displaying the desktop with multiple monitors

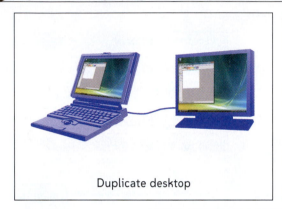

Duplicate desktop

Extended desktop

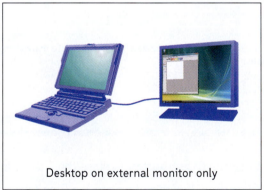

Desktop on external monitor only

To use multiple monitors, your computer should have a video card with at least two ports. When you plug in a second monitor, Windows detects and identifies it, and then applies the video settings that are best suited to the new display. When you disconnect the additional monitor, Windows restores the original display settings, including screen size, resolution, and color depth, and then moves all open files and program windows to your primary monitor. If you connect that monitor again, Windows applies the same display settings you used when you last connected the monitor.

By default, when you connect an external monitor to a laptop, the same image (a duplicate, or mirror image) of your desktop appears on the external monitor. Before you can drag a window from your laptop monitor to the external monitor, you must extend your desktop by using the Screen Resolution window to change your display settings. However, when you connect another monitor to a desktop PC, the display is set to extended by default, so you can drag a window from one monitor to the other without changing any settings.

When you plug two monitors into a desktop PC or one monitor into a laptop, Windows usually detects each new monitor and lets you choose one of the following:

- Computer only or Projector only: Choose one of these settings to make one monitor blank while showing the desktop on the other monitor. You might use this setting with a laptop computer if you want to keep your laptop screen blank after you connect to a large desktop monitor.
- Duplicate: This option displays the same desktop on both monitors. For a laptop, this is the default setting. This is useful if you're giving a presentation with your laptop connected to a projector or large monitor.
- Extend: This spreads your desktop over both monitors and lets you drag items between the two screens. This is the default setting for a desktop PC.

When Julie works on her ad, she needs to follow detailed instructions that her printing company provided. To avoid switching frequently from the program window containing the ad image to the program window containing the instructions, she wants to use two monitors. She can then display the current version of the ad on her primary monitor and the instructions on her secondary monitor. You'll show her how to set up an additional monitor on her laptop computer. To perform the following steps, you need an extra monitor. Your computer also needs to have a video card with at least two ports. (Check the back of your computer for an additional video port.) If you do not have the required hardware, read but do not perform the following steps.

TIP

If you're using multiple monitors, the taskbar appears on only one monitor.

To extend the desktop to an additional monitor:

1. Physically connect the extra monitor to your computer by plugging the monitor into an available video port. Windows 7 detects the extra monitor and displays the options shown in Figure 9-44.

Figure 9-44   Detecting a new display

click the Extend option to extend the desktop across two monitors

your option may be called Disconnect Projector

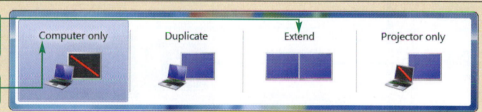

Trouble? If the Screen Resolution window opens instead of the window shown in Figure 9-44, click the Connect to a projector link in the Screen Resolution window. If the options shown in Figure 9-44 do not appear, click the Start button 🔵. Type *connect* in the Search for programs and files box, and then click Connect to an external display.

2. Click the **Extend** option. Windows extends your desktop across the two monitors.

If Windows can't identify the monitor that you connect, it applies the last display settings that you used (if any) for that type of monitor and asks whether you want to keep the settings. Click OK to keep the settings. If you click Cancel or do nothing, the Screen Resolution window opens so that you can choose the display settings yourself. You'll examine how to adjust the resolution of the secondary monitor next.

Setting the Resolution of a Secondary Monitor

When you connect an additional monitor to your computer, you don't have to use the same display settings that you use for the primary monitor. You can use the Screen Resolution window to adjust the resolution, color depth, and other options. You can also use the Screen Resolution window to set up three or more monitors connected to your desktop computer. When you connect one additional monitor, Windows can automatically detect it. If you connect two or more additional monitors, you must use the Screen Resolution window to designate the primary display, arrange your desktop, and apply display settings. The next time that you connect these monitors, Windows identifies the primary display and applies the settings that you specified.

You'll show Julie how to examine the display settings to specify which monitor is the primary monitor and to set the resolution of the secondary monitor. If you did not connect a second monitor, read but do not perform the following steps.

To set display settings for multiple monitors:

▶ **1.** Open the Screen Resolution window, if necessary.

▶ **2.** Click the monitor identified as **1**. The window displays resolution settings available for this monitor.

▶ **3.** Click the monitor identified as **2** to display settings available for that monitor. See Figure 9-45.

Figure 9-45	Changing resolution settings for multiple monitors

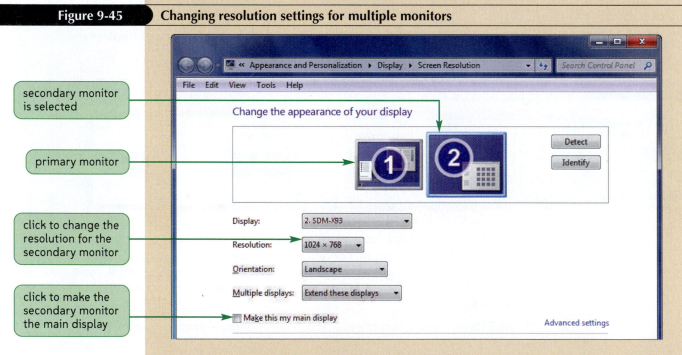

secondary monitor is selected

primary monitor

click to change the resolution for the secondary monitor

click to make the secondary monitor the main display

▶ **4.** Click the **Resolution** button, and then drag the slider as necessary to change the resolution of Monitor 2. The preview window displays the effect of your changes.

▶ **5.** Click the **OK** button to accept your changes and close the dialog box. The Display Settings dialog box opens to confirm that you want to keep these display settings.

▶ **6.** Click the **Keep changes** button.

Julie doesn't need to use the additional monitor right now, so you can disconnect it. The next time she connects the extra monitor to her computer, Windows will apply the same settings so she can start using the monitor immediately.

If you did not connect a second monitor to your computer, read but do not perform the following step.

To disconnect the extra monitor:

▶ **1.** Unplug the monitor from the video port in the back of the computer.

Now you can turn to a final hardware task: installing and setting up a printer.

Installing and Setting Up a Printer

Before you can print anything from your computer, you either need to connect a printer directly to your computer, making it a **local printer**, or create a connection to a network or shared printer. Before using Windows 7 to install a printer, check the manual that came with your printer. For some printers, you plug the printer into your computer, usually using a USB port, turn on the printer, and then Windows 7 detects the new printer and installs its driver. For other printers, you need to install their software first, and then plug in and turn on the printer.

Most contemporary printers are USB printers, meaning you connect them by plugging the printer's cable into a USB port on your computer. Older printers use a parallel cable that connects to your computer's printer port (also called the LPT1 port). If you are installing a second or third printer, you might need to use a parallel cable if you are using the computer's USB ports for other devices.

After you physically connect a local printer, you open the Devices and Printers window and start the Add Printer Wizard, which guides you through the steps of installing the printer and its drivers. You use the same wizard to set up a network printer for which you've turned on printer sharing.

Installing a Local Printer

Using the printer manufacturer's directions, attach or connect the printer to your computer. Windows usually installs the printer without further action from you. If Windows does not recognize the printer, you can open the Devices and Printers window from the Control Panel to install it yourself.

REFERENCE

Installing a Local Printer

- Follow the printer manufacturer's instructions to connect the printer to your computer.
- If Windows does not automatically detect the printer and install its drivers, click the Start button, and then click Devices and Printers.
- Click the Add a printer button on the toolbar.
- In the Add Printer Wizard, click Add a local printer.
- Click the Next button to accept the existing printer port.
- Select the printer manufacturer and the printer name, and then click the Next button.
- Enter a printer name, and then click the Next button.
- Click the Finish button.

Julie already uses a network laser printer that is connected to her network, and she needs to connect a color printer to her computer using a USB cable plugged into the printer port. You'll show Julie how to install her Hewlett-Packard color laser printer, which is called HP Color LaserJet 2800 Series PS.

If you are working on a school or institutional network, you probably cannot install a printer on your computer. In that case, read but do not perform the following steps.

To install a local printer:

 1. Physically connect your printer to your computer. The Devices and Printers window opens. See Figure 9-46.

Figure 9-46 **Devices and Printers window**

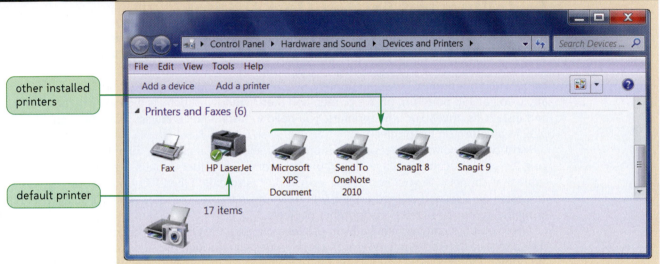

other installed printers

default printer

Trouble? If you plugged the printer into a USB port, Windows might detect the printer and install the drivers automatically. In that case, the printer is ready to use. Read but do not perform the following steps.

Trouble? If the Devices and Printers window does not open, click the Start button , and then click Devices and Printers.

 2. Click the **Add a printer** button on the toolbar. The Add Printer Wizard starts and lets you choose whether to add a local or network printer.

 3. Click **Add a local printer**. The next wizard dialog box opens, where you can choose a printer port.

 4. Make sure the Use an existing port option button is selected, and then click the **Next** button. The next wizard dialog box opens, where you can select the manufacturer and model of your printer. See Figure 9-47.

Figure 9-47   **Installing the printer driver**

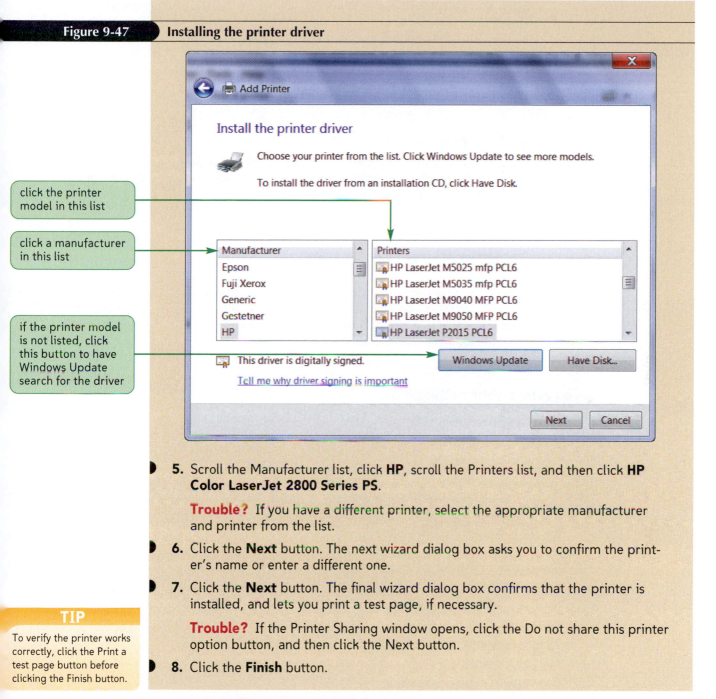

click the printer model in this list

click a manufacturer in this list

if the printer model is not listed, click this button to have Windows Update search for the driver

5. Scroll the Manufacturer list, click **HP**, scroll the Printers list, and then click **HP Color LaserJet 2800 Series PS**.

   Trouble? If you have a different printer, select the appropriate manufacturer and printer from the list.

6. Click the **Next** button. The next wizard dialog box asks you to confirm the printer's name or enter a different one.

7. Click the **Next** button. The final wizard dialog box confirms that the printer is installed, and lets you print a test page, if necessary.

   Trouble? If the Printer Sharing window opens, click the Do not share this printer option button, and then click the Next button.

8. Click the **Finish** button.

TIP

To verify the printer works correctly, click the Print a test page button before clicking the Finish button.

After you successfully install the color laser printer for Julie, she notices that it is now the default printer, meaning that all the documents she prints will be directed to that printer unless she changes that setting using the Print dialog box. She prints far more often on the black-and-white laser printer. You'll show her how to specify that printer as the default.

Changing the Default Printer

If you have more than one printer connected to your computer, you can select the one you want to use by default. When you use Windows or your programs to print, a Print dialog box opens and lets you select settings, including a printer. The Print dialog box selects the default printer automatically, though you can change it if you like. In some programs, when you click a Print button, the content prints on the default printer without opening a Print dialog box. You should therefore select the printer you use most often as your default printer. You can do so in the Devices and Printers window.

Julie wants to make her black-and-white laser printer the default instead of her color printer. You'll show her how to change her default printer using the Devices and Printers window.

To change the default printer:

▶ **1.** In the Devices and Printers window, right-click the **HP LaserJet** printer icon, and then click **Set as default printer** on the shortcut menu. Windows displays a default icon ✅ on the HP LaserJet.

Restoring Your Settings

If you are working in a computer lab or on a computer other than your own, complete the steps in this section to restore the original settings on your computer. If a User Account Control dialog box opens requesting an Administrator password or confirmation after you perform any of the following steps, enter the password or click the Continue button.

To restore your settings:

▶ **1.** Click the **Start** button 🔵 on the taskbar, click **Control Panel**, and then click **Back up your computer**.

▶ **2.** Click **Change settings**.

▶ **3.** Click the drive containing your backup medium, click the **Next** button, and then click the **Let Windows choose (recommended)** option button if this option was originally set on your computer.

▶ **4.** Click the **Next** button, click **Change schedule**, and then restore the original setting, which is weekly on Sundays at 7 p.m. by default. Click the **OK** button, and then click the **Save settings and exit** button. Close the Backup and Restore window.

▶ **5.** Move the **backup** folder (which has a name such as *Owner-PC*) containing your backup file from your removable disk to the Tutorial.09\Tutorial folder provided with your Data Files.

▶ **6.** Move the **Julie** folder in your Documents library to the Tutorial.09\Tutorial folder provided with your Data Files.

▶ **7.** Right-click the desktop, and then click **Screen resolution** on the shortcut menu.

▶ **8.** Click the **Advanced settings** link, and then click the **Monitor** tab. Click the **Screen refresh rate** button, and then click your original refresh rate, such as **60 Hertz**. (Your refresh rates might differ.) Click the **OK** button to close the Properties dialog box for your monitor. Click the **OK** button to close the Screen Resolution window.

▶ **9.** Click the **Start** button 🔵, and then click **Devices and Printers**.

▶ **10.** Right-click the extra printer you installed in this tutorial, and then click **Remove device** on the shortcut menu. Click the **Yes** button to confirm that you want to remove the device.

▶ **11.** Close all open windows.

REVIEW

Session 9.2 Quick Check

1. You can use the _____ tool to free disk space by deleting unnecessary files.
2. True or False. Defragmenting a disk organizes its files so that they are stored most efficiently.
3. You can reduce or eliminate flickering on your monitor by increasing the screen _____ rate.
4. Name two ways to update a device driver.
5. When you are using multiple monitors, which display option is best if you are giving a presentation?
6. The printer directly connected to your computer is called the _____ printer.
7. True or False. Windows 7 most often detects a new device after you connect one, and then installs the driver automatically.

Review Assignments

There are no Data Files needed for the Review Assignments.

You are now working with Stuart Hansen, the front-end manager of the Northbrook Farmers Market. He has recently acquired a new Windows 7 computer and asks you to show him how to maintain its hardware and software. He is particularly concerned about protecting the photos he uses to promote the market and its products. Complete the following steps, noting your original settings so you can restore them later:

1. Attach a USB flash drive or an external hard drive to your computer by plugging it into a USB port.

2. Open the Backup and Restore window, and then change the backup settings to save your backup to the USB flash drive or external hard drive that you prepared in Step 1. Choose to back up only the files in the Pictures library on your computer. With the Review your backup settings window open showing the types of files you are backing up, press the Alt+Print Screen keys to capture an image of the window. Paste the image in a new Paint file, and save the file as **Pictures Backup** in the Tutorial.09\Review folder provided with your Data Files. To save time and disk space, click the Cancel button to close the window without creating a backup.

3. Create a restore point named **Stuart**. With the System Restore window open and displaying the restore points on your computer, press the Alt+Print Screen keys to capture an image of the window. Paste the image in a new Paint file, and save the file as **System Restore** in the Tutorial.09\Review folder provided with your Data Files.

4. Display the installed updates on your computer. Sort the updates by the date they were installed, and then press the Alt+Print Screen keys to capture an image of the window. Paste the image in a new Paint file, and save the file as **Updates** in the Tutorial.09\Review folder provided with your Data Files.

5. Set Paint to open .bmp files by default. With the Set Associations window open, press the Alt+Print Screen keys to capture an image of the window. Paste the image in a new Paint file, and save the file as **BMP** in the Tutorial.09\Review folder provided with your Data Files.

6. Display the amount of free space and used space on your hard disk. With the dialog box open showing this information, press the Alt+Print Screen keys to capture an image of the window. Paste the image in a new Paint file, and save the file as **Disk Space** in the Tutorial.09\Review folder provided with your Data Files.

7. Open the Disk Cleanup dialog box for your hard disk, and then choose to clean up only your temporary files (not temporary Internet files). Press the Alt+Print Screen keys to capture an image of the window. Paste the image in a new Paint file, and save the file as **Disk Cleanup** in the Tutorial.09\Review folder provided with your Data Files.

8. Display the schedule for defragmenting your hard disk. Press the Alt+Print Screen keys to capture an image of the window. Paste the image in a new Paint file, and save the file as **Defragment** in the Tutorial.09\Review folder provided with your Data Files.

9. Install a USB device you have not used with your computer, or plug it into a USB port you have not yet used with the device. After installing it successfully, disable the device. With the Device Manager window open, press the Alt+Print Screen keys to capture an image of the window. Paste the image in a new Paint file, and save the file as **Disabled** in the Tutorial.09\Review folder provided with your Data Files. Enable and then disconnect the USB device.

10. Display the refresh rate of your monitor, and then press the Alt+Print Screen keys to capture an image of the Monitor Properties window. Paste the image in a new Paint file, and save the file as **Refresh** in the Tutorial.09\Review folder provided with your Data Files.

11. Install a local printer named **Office** in the Devices and Printers window. (*Hint*: You can install a local printer even if it is not connected to your computer.) Do not share the printer or set it as the default. With the Devices and Printers window open, press the Alt+Print Screen keys to capture an image of the window. Paste the image in a new Paint file, and save the file as **Office Printer** in the Tutorial.09\Review folder provided with your Data Files.

12. Restore your settings by removing the Office printer from the Devices and Printers window. Close all open windows.

13. Submit the results of the preceding steps to your instructor, either in printed or electronic form, as requested.

Use your skills to maintain the hardware and software for a symphony orchestra.

APPLY

Case Problem 1

There are no Data Files needed for this Case Problem.

Sarasota Symphony Orchestra   Martin Prago is the business director of the Sarasota Symphony Orchestra, and he has recently hired you to help him automate the orchestra's business operations and marketing efforts. Martin has been using a Windows 7 laptop for a few months, and asks you to help him properly maintain its hardware and software. Complete the following steps, noting your original settings so you can restore them later:

1. Attach a USB flash drive or an external hard drive to your computer by plugging it into a USB port.

2. Open the Backup and Restore window, and then change the backup settings to save your backup to the drive that you prepared in Step 1. Choose to back up only files in the Music library on your computer. With the Review your backup settings window open showing the files you are backing up, press the Alt+Print Screen keys to capture an image of the window. Paste the image in a new Paint file, and save the file as **Music Backup** in the Tutorial.09\Case1 folder provided with your Data Files. To save time and disk space, click the Cancel button to close the window without creating a backup.

3. Create a restore point named **Martin**. With the System Restore window open and displaying the restore points on your computer, press the Alt+Print Screen keys to capture an image of the window. Paste the image in a new Paint file, and save the file as **Martin Restore** in the Tutorial.09\Case1 folder provided with your Data Files.

4. In the Programs and Features window, display the programs installed on your computer. Select a program that lets you change or repair its settings, and then press the Alt+Print Screen keys to capture an image of the Programs and Features window. Paste the image in a new Paint file, and save the file as **Programs** in the Tutorial.09\Case1 folder provided with your Data Files.

EXPLORE

5. Start the Program Compatibility troubleshooter and display the list of programs in the Program Compatibility window. Press the Alt+Print Screen keys to capture an image of the window. Paste the image in a new Paint file, and save the file as **Compatible** in the Tutorial.09\Case1 folder provided with your Data Files.

6. Open the Properties dialog box for your local hard disk. Display all the disk drives attached to your computer. With the dialog box open showing this information, press the Alt+Print Screen keys to capture an image of the window. Paste the image in a new Paint file, and save the file as **Disk Drives** in the Tutorial.09\Case1 folder provided with your Data Files.

7. Use Device Manager to check for an updated driver for any device on your computer. After checking, press the Alt+Print Screen keys to capture an image of the dialog box showing the results. Paste the image in a new Paint file, and save the file as **Driver** in the Tutorial.09\Case1 folder provided with your Data Files. If Windows found an updated driver, do not install it.

8. Increase the resolution of your monitor, and then increase the screen refresh rate, if possible. With the Screen Resolution window open, press the Alt+Print Screen keys to capture an image of the window. Paste the image in a new Paint file, and save the file as **Resolution** in the Tutorial.09\Case1 folder provided with your Data Files.

9. Install a local printer named **Sarasota** in the Devices and Printers window. (*Hint*: You can install a local printer even if it is not connected to your computer.) Do not share the printer or set it as the default. With the Devices and Printers window open, press the Alt+Print Screen keys to capture an image of the window. Paste the image in a new Paint file, and save the file as **Sarasota** in the Tutorial.09\Case1 folder provided with your Data Files.

10. Restore your settings by removing the Sarasota printer from the Devices and Printers window and restoring your original screen resolution. Close all open windows.

11. Submit the results of the preceding steps to your instructor, either in printed or electronic form, as requested.

Use your skills to manage the hardware and software for a semiprofessional hockey team.

APPLY

Case Problem 2

There are no Data Files needed for this Case Problem.

Salem Hockey Ducks   Guy Larousse is the owner of the Hockey Ducks, a semi-professional hockey team in Salem, Oregon. You are a part-time assistant for the Hockey Ducks and primarily help Guy perform computer tasks using his Windows 7 computer. Guy recently lost some data during a power failure and asks you to help him back up the files in his libraries. He is also concerned about maintaining the software on his computer. You'll show him how to complete these maintenance tasks. Complete the following steps, noting your original settings so you can restore them later:

1. Attach a USB flash drive or an external hard drive to your computer by plugging it into a USB port.

2. Open the Backup and Restore window, and then change the backup settings to save your backup to the drive that you prepared in Step 1. Choose to back up the libraries on your computer. Change the schedule to back up files every Sunday at 10 p.m. With the Review your backup settings window open showing the files you are backing up, press the Alt+Print Screen keys to capture an image of the window. Paste the image in a new Paint file, and save the file as **Library Backup** in the Tutorial.09\Case2 folder provided with your Data Files. To save time and disk space, click the Cancel button to close the window without creating a backup.

⊕ **EXPLORE**

3. In the left pane of the Backup and Restore window, click Create a system repair disc, insert a CD or DVD in the appropriate drive, click the Create disc button, and then follow the on-screen instructions to create a repair disc. When the system repair disc is complete, press the Alt+Print Screen keys to capture an image of the window. Paste the image in a new Paint file, and save the file as **Repair** in the Tutorial.09\Case2 folder provided with your Data Files.

4. Open a document in the Documents library or any of its folders and modify it by inserting your name at the beginning of the document. Display previous versions of the document. With the Previous Versions tab open in the Properties dialog box for the document, press the Alt+Print Screen keys to capture an image of the window. Paste the image in a new Paint file, and save the file as **Versions** in the Tutorial.09\Case2 folder provided with your Data Files.

5. Begin restoring Guy's computer by choosing the first automatic restore point in the list. With the System Restore window open and displaying the restore points on your computer, press the Alt+Print Screen keys to capture an image of the window. Paste the image in a new Paint file, and save the file as **Automatic** in the Tutorial.09\Case2 folder provided with your Data Files. Click the Cancel button to close the System Restore window.

✛ **EXPLORE**

6. Use Windows Update to check for optional updates to your computer, including device drivers. (*Hint*: Open the Windows Update window, click Check for updates, and then wait while Windows looks for the latest updates for your computer.) Display the optional updates available, and then press the Alt+Print Screen keys to capture an image of the window. Paste the image in a new Paint file, and save the file as **Updates** in the Tutorial.09\Case2 folder provided with your Data Files. Close the Windows Update window without installing any updates.

✛ **EXPLORE**

7. From the Programs and Features window, display the Windows features that are turned on and off on your computer. Press the Alt+Print Screen keys to capture an image of the window. Paste the image in a new Paint file, and save the file as **Features** in the Tutorial.09\Case2 folder provided with your Data Files.

✛ **EXPLORE**

8. Display the partitions on your computer. Maximize the window, and then press the Alt+Print Screen keys to capture an image of the page. Paste the image in a new Paint file, and save the file as **Partitions** in the Tutorial.09\Case2 folder provided with your Data Files.

9. Install a local printer named **Salem** in the Devices and Printers window. Do not share the printer or make it the default. With the Devices and Printers window open, press the Alt+Print Screen keys to capture an image of the window. Paste the image in a new Paint file, and save the file as **Salem** in the Tutorial.09\Case2 folder provided with your Data Files.

10. Restore your settings by removing the Salem printer from the Devices and Printers window. Close all open windows.

11. Submit the results of the preceding steps to your instructor, either in printed or electronic form, as requested.

Extend what you've learned to maintain the hardware for a group of designers.

CHALLENGE

Case Problem 3

There are no Data Files needed for this Case Problem.

Pacific Design Group   Ali Johanssen is the founder of the Pacific Design Group in West Hollywood, California. The Pacific Design Group is a cooperative venture that shares design and office space for interior and industrial designers. Ali has hired you to help her maintain the computer hardware for the Pacific Design Group members. Complete the following steps, noting your original settings so you can restore them later:

1. Install a USB flash drive or external hard disk on your computer.

2. Display the amount of free space and used space on the removable disk. With the dialog box open showing this information, press the Alt+Print Screen keys to capture an image of the window. Paste the image in a new Paint file, and save the file as **Free Space** in the Tutorial.09\Case3 folder provided with your Data Files.

3. Open the Disk Cleanup dialog box for the removable disk, and display the files you can delete. Press the Alt+Print Screen keys to capture an image of the dialog box. Paste the image in a new Paint file, and save the file as **Cleanup** in the Tutorial.09\Case3 folder provided with your Data Files. If you cannot perform a Disk Cleanup on a removable disk, open the Disk Cleanup dialog box for your local hard drive instead.

✛ **EXPLORE**

4. Display the schedule for defragmenting your removable disk, and then click the Analyze disk button. When the analysis is complete, press the Alt+Print Screen keys to capture an image of the window. Paste the image in a new Paint file, and save the file as **Defrag** in the Tutorial.09\Case3 folder provided with your Data Files.

⊕ **EXPLORE**   5. Click the ReadyBoost tab in the Properties dialog box for the removable disk. Settings on this tab let you use a USB flash drive to boost your available memory. Test the device, if possible, and then press the Alt+Print Screen keys to capture an image of the window. Paste the image in a new Paint file, and save the file as **ReadyBoost** in the Tutorial.09\Case3 folder provided with your Data Files.

6. Check the removable drive for errors, and automatically fix file system errors only. When Windows is finished checking the drive, press the Alt+Print Screen keys to capture an image of the window. Paste the image in a new Paint file, and save the file as **Error Check** in the Tutorial.09\Case3 folder provided with your Data Files.

⊕ **EXPLORE**   7. Open the Device Manager window, and then display all the devices by connection. (*Hint*: Click View on the menu bar, and then click Devices by connection if it is not selected.) Press the Alt+Print Screen keys to capture an image of the window. Paste the image in a new Paint file, and save the file as **Devices** in the Tutorial.09\Case3 folder provided with your Data Files. Return the view to Devices by type.

⊕ **EXPLORE**   8. From the System and Security window, click Schedule tasks to explore the settings you can use to start a program according to a schedule (rather than manually from the Start menu, for example). Press the Alt+Print Screen keys to capture an image of the Task Scheduler window. Paste the image in a new Paint file, and save the file as **Task Scheduler** in the Tutorial.09\Case3 folder provided with your Data Files.

9. Install a local printer named **Ali** in the Devices and Printers window. Do not share the printer or make it the default. With the Devices and Printers window open, press the Alt+Print Screen keys to capture an image of the window. Paste the image in a new Paint file, and save the file as **Ali** in the Tutorial.09\Case3 folder provided with your Data Files.

10. Restore your settings by removing the Ali printer from the Devices and Printers window and removing the USB device from your computer. Close all open windows.

11. Submit the results of the preceding steps to your instructor, either in printed or electronic form, as requested.

Use your skills and the Internet to research accessibility features.

RESEARCH

Case Problem 4

There are no Data Files needed for this Case Problem.

Council for the Hearing and Visually Impaired   Rose Mellenhoff is the director of the Council for the Hearing and Visually Impaired in Columbia, Missouri. You volunteer for the council, usually by performing data entry, computer hardware maintenance, and other computer-related tasks. Rose is interested in learning more about making computers accessible to her clients and asks you to research the hardware and software accessibility features of Windows 7. Complete the following steps:

1. Use your favorite search engine to find information about how to make a computer easier to use for the hearing and visually impaired. Try searching for information about the following types of information:
   - Accessible computing
   - Assistive technology
   - Accessibility features

2. Use Windows Help and Support and your favorite search engine to find information about the features Windows 7 provides for the hearing and visually impaired.

3. Select two or three features that interest you, and then write a paragraph about each feature. Be sure to explain how to use the feature and how to change the setting, if any, in Windows 7. Also describe the benefits the feature provides to the hearing or visually impaired.

4. Save the paragraphs in a document named **Accessible** in the Tutorial.09\Case4 folder provided with your Data Files.

5. Submit the results of the preceding steps to your instructor, either in printed or electronic form, as requested.

SAM: Skills Assessment Manager

For current SAM information, including versions and content details, visit SAM Central (http://samcentral.course.com). If you have a SAM user profile, you may have access to hands-on instruction, practice, and assessment of the skills covered in this tutorial. Since various versions of SAM are supported throughout the life of this text, check with your instructor for the correct instructions and URL/Web site for accessing assignments.

ENDING DATA FILES

Tutorial.09 →

Tutorial

📁 **Owner-PC**
(backup folder)

📁 **Julie**

Review

BMP.png
Defragment.png
Disabled.png
Disk Cleanup.png
Disk Space.png
Office Printer.png
Pictures Backup.png
Refresh.png
System Restore.png
Updates.png

Case1

Compatible.png
Disk Drives.png
Driver.png
Martin Restore.png
Music Backup.png
Programs.png
Resolution.png
Sarasota.png

Case2

Automatic.png
Features.png
Library
  Backup.png
Partitions.png
Repair.png
Salem.png
Updates.png
Versions.png

Case3

Ali.png
Cleanup.png
Defrag.png
Devices.png
Error Check.png
Free Space.png
ReadyBoost.png
Task Scheduler.png

Case4

Accessible.doc

TUTORIAL **10**

OBJECTIVES

Session 10.1
- Optimize computer performance
- Monitor system tasks
- Examine system information
- Increase memory capacity with ReadyBoost

Session 10.2
- Troubleshoot typical computer problems
- Respond to software and operating system errors
- Use the Problem Steps Recorder
- Manage remote assistance

Improving Your Computer's Performance

Enhancing Your System and Troubleshooting Computer Problems

Case | SafeRecords

SafeRecords in Indianapolis, Indiana, provides secure storage facilities for local businesses. In addition to storing documents and other records in a climate-controlled warehouse, SafeRecords shreds, recycles, and tracks paper documents and electronic media. You work for SafeRecords as a computer specialist, and your supervisor is Amar Gupta, the company's system administrator. Your job is to help Amar keep the SafeRecords computers running at peak performance. Amar is familiar with system maintenance and troubleshooting tools in earlier versions of Windows, but he is new to Windows 7.

In this tutorial, you will improve your computer's performance by optimizing system settings and increasing memory capacity. You'll monitor system performance and diagnose and repair computer problems. You'll also use the Problem Steps Recorder and request remote assistance.

STARTING DATA FILES

There are no starting Data Files needed for this tutorial.

SESSION 10.1 VISUAL OVERVIEW

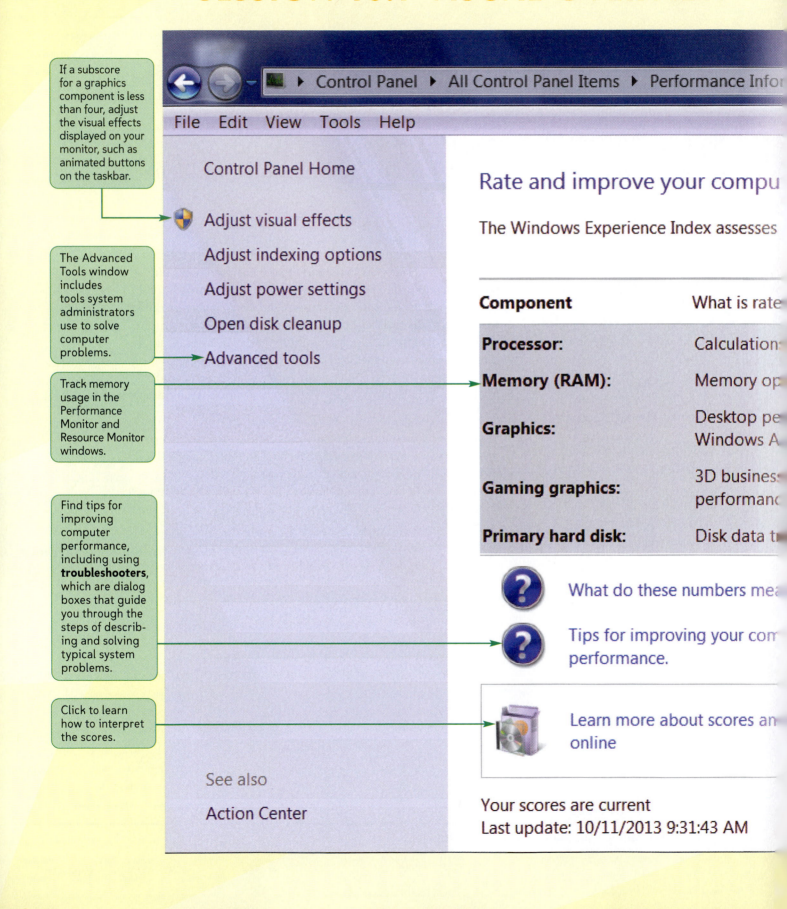

If a subscore for a graphics component is less than four, adjust the visual effects displayed on your monitor, such as animated buttons on the taskbar.

The Advanced Tools window includes tools system administrators use to solve computer problems.

Track memory usage in the Performance Monitor and Resource Monitor windows.

Find tips for improving computer performance, including using **troubleshooters**, which are dialog boxes that guide you through the steps of describing and solving typical system problems.

Click to learn how to interpret the scores.

Control Panel ▸ All Control Panel Items ▸ Performance Infor

File   Edit   View   Tools   Help

Control Panel Home

Adjust visual effects

Adjust indexing options

Adjust power settings

Open disk cleanup

Advanced tools

See also

Action Center

Rate and improve your compu

The Windows Experience Index assesses

Component	What is rate
Processor:	Calculation
Memory (RAM):	Memory op
Graphics:	Desktop pe Windows A
Gaming graphics:	3D busines performanc
Primary hard disk:	Disk data t

What do these numbers mea

Tips for improving your com performance.

Learn more about scores an online

Your scores are current
Last update: 10/11/2013 9:31:43 AM

TRACKING SYSTEM PERFORMANCE

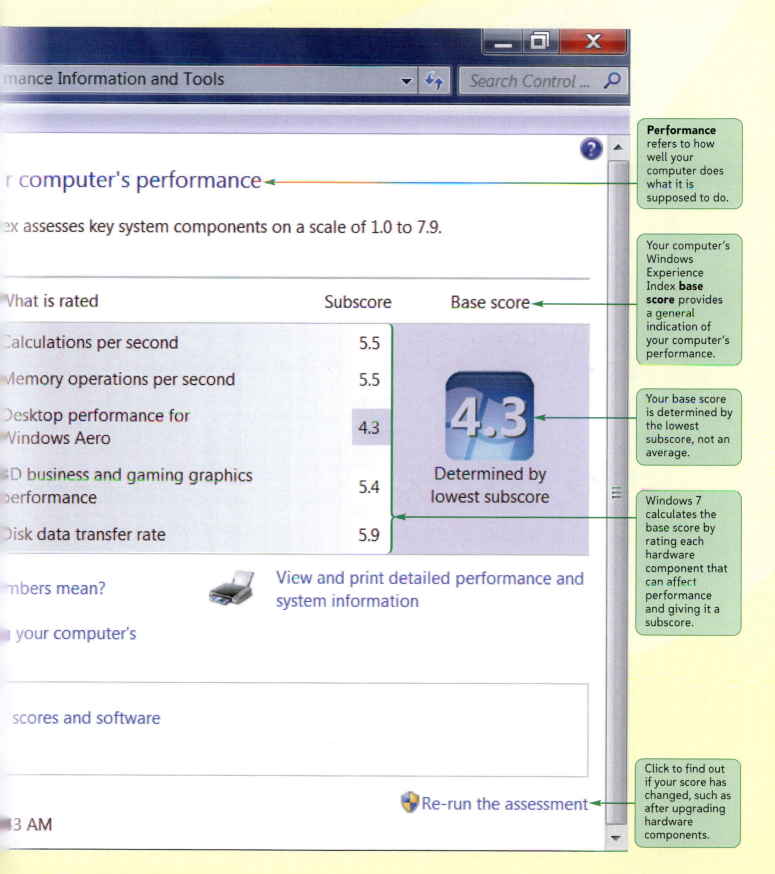

mance Information and Tools

Search Control ...

r computer's performance

ex assesses key system components on a scale of 1.0 to 7.9.

What is rated	Subscore	Base score
Calculations per second	5.5	
Memory operations per second	5.5	
Desktop performance for Windows Aero	4.3	**4.3** Determined by lowest subscore
3D business and gaming graphics performance	5.4	
Disk data transfer rate	5.9	

View and print detailed performance and system information

mbers mean?

your computer's

scores and software

Re-run the assessment

3 AM

Performance refers to how well your computer does what it is supposed to do.

Your computer's Windows Experience Index **base score** provides a general indication of your computer's performance.

Your base score is determined by the lowest subscore, not an average.

Windows 7 calculates the base score by rating each hardware component that can affect performance and giving it a subscore.

Click to find out if your score has changed, such as after upgrading hardware components.

Improving System Performance

After using your computer for a while, and especially after installing software or saving and deleting files, you might notice changes in your system performance. These changes usually mean that your computer is not as quick to respond to your actions or to perform system tasks as it was when Windows 7 was first installed. In that case, you can improve system performance by completing certain maintenance tasks. Start by opening the Performance Information and Tools window from the Control Panel, shown in the Visual Overview for this session.

The Performance Information and Tools window lets you view and complete the information and performance tasks described in Figure 10-1.

| Figure 10-1 | Tasks and information provided in the Performance Information and Tools window |

Task or Information	Description	How to Use
Windows Experience Index base score	View your score to learn the capability of your computer's hardware and software to run Windows 7 and perform computing tasks	Click the Re-run the assessment link to calculate your base score
Adjust visual effects	Modify how Windows displays menus and windows to improve performance	Use the Performance Options dialog box to optimize how Windows displays menus and windows
Adjust indexing options	Set indexing options to help you quickly find files on your computer	Use the Indexing Options dialog box to specify which locations to index
Adjust power settings	Modify how Windows consumes or conserves power, which directly affects performance, especially for mobile computers	Use the Power Options window to change power plans and their settings
Open disk cleanup	Remove temporary or unnecessary files that can take up too much storage space	Use the Disk Cleanup tool to delete unnecessary files
Advanced tools	Examine advanced performance information to avoid related problems	Use the Advanced Tools window to view notifications about performance problems and how to solve them

You have already explored some of these tools in earlier tutorials. This tutorial discusses each item in the Performance Information and Tools window to help improve the performance of your computer.

Rating Your Computer's Performance

Your computer's Windows Experience Index base score reflects the speed and performance of your computer's components, including the processor, random access memory (RAM), graphics card, and hard disk. A higher base score generally means that your computer performs better and faster than a computer with a lower base score, especially when working on more advanced and resource-intensive tasks. Windows 7 calculates the base score by rating each hardware component that can affect performance and giving it a subscore. The base score is the lowest subscore, not an average. If the subscore for your general graphics component is 3.7 but all the other subscores are 5.5 or higher, the base score for your computer is 3.7.

Viewing and Calculating Your Base Score

- Click the Start button, click Control Panel, click System and Security, and then click Check the Windows Experience Index in the System category.
- In the Performance Information and Tools window, view the Windows Experience Index base score and subscores for your computer. If these scores are not displayed, click Rate this computer.
- To find out if your score has changed, click Re-run the assessment.

When you open the Performance Information and Tools window, it displays the base score calculated the last time Windows 7 rated the hardware components on your computer. If it has never rated the components, you can click the Rate this computer link to score the computer. After you install new hardware, you can recalculate the rating by clicking the Re-run the assessment link to update the score.

Software publishers other than Microsoft might identify the minimum base score your computer needs to run their software. You can therefore use the base score to make decisions when purchasing software. For example, if your computer has a base score of 5.1, you can confidently purchase software designed for Windows 7 that requires a computer with a base score of 5 or lower. If you want to use a particular program or feature of Windows 7 that requires a higher score than your base score, note the lowest subscore in the Performance Information and Tools window. You might need to upgrade the component with that subscore to meet the necessary base score.

You can generally interpret your computer's base score according to the descriptions in Figure 10-2.

Figure 10-2   Interpreting base scores

Maximum Base Score	What the Computer Can Do
2	Complete general computing tasks, such as running office productivity programs and searching the Internet, but not use Aero themes or the advanced multimedia features of Windows 7
3	Respond more quickly than computers in the 1–2 range while running the same types of programs; some computers with a base score of 3 or lower can run Aero themes, though performance might decline
4–5	Run Aero themes and new Windows 7 features at a level adequate for most computer users
6–8	Play HDTV content, and run high-end, graphics-intensive programs, such as multiplayer games

In addition, consider how you use your computer when interpreting the subscores. If you use your computer primarily to perform office productivity tasks by working with word processing, spreadsheet, e-mail, and Web browsing software, then your processor and memory components should have high subscores. If you use your computer to play games or run high-end graphics programs, such as a video editor, then your RAM, graphics, and gaming graphics components should have high subscores. If you use your computer as a media center, such as to play multimedia slide shows or record digital TV programs, then your processor, hard disk, and graphics components need high subscores.

SafeRecords mostly uses office productivity programs and custom databases to track the documents and other files it handles. Amar wants to make sure that his base score is high enough to use Aero themes and that his subscores are appropriate for his typical tasks, which involve producing spreadsheets and reports that analyze the SafeRecords storage capacity. You'll show Amar how to view and calculate the Windows Experience Index base score for the first time on his Windows 7 computer.

To view and calculate a computer's base score:

▶ 1. Click the **Start** button 🟦, and then click **Control Panel**. The Control Panel window opens.

▶ 2. Click the **System and Security** category, and then click **Check the Windows Experience Index** in the System category. The Performance Information and Tools window opens.

▶ 3. If possible, click the **Rate this computer** link to assess the hardware and calculate a base score, which might take a few minutes. Windows displays the subscores and base score in the Performance Information and Tools window. See Figure 10-3.

Figure 10-3   Results of calculating the base score

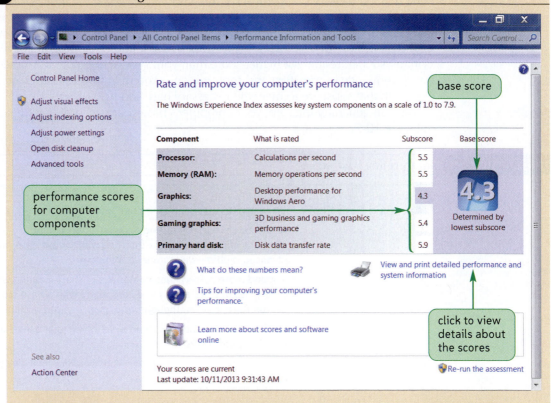

Trouble? If Windows 7 has already calculated a base score, the Rate this computer link does not appear. Instead, you can click Re-run the assessment to have Windows recalculate the base score.

TIP

To further interpret the scores, click Learn more about scores and software online.

The subscores for Amar's computer are high for the processor, memory, and hard disk, which is appropriate for the type of tasks he performs. His graphics score of 4.3 is the lowest subscore, and is therefore his base score. This is an appropriate score for his current computing needs. However, because he has decided to add another monitor to improve his productivity, he will need to increase this score by upgrading his graphics components. You suggest that Amar view the details about those components so he knows what to upgrade.

To view system details:

1. In the Performance Information and Tools window, click **View and print detailed performance and system information**. The More details about my computer window opens, displaying detailed information about Amar's system. See Figure 10-4.

Figure 10-4   **Displaying system details**

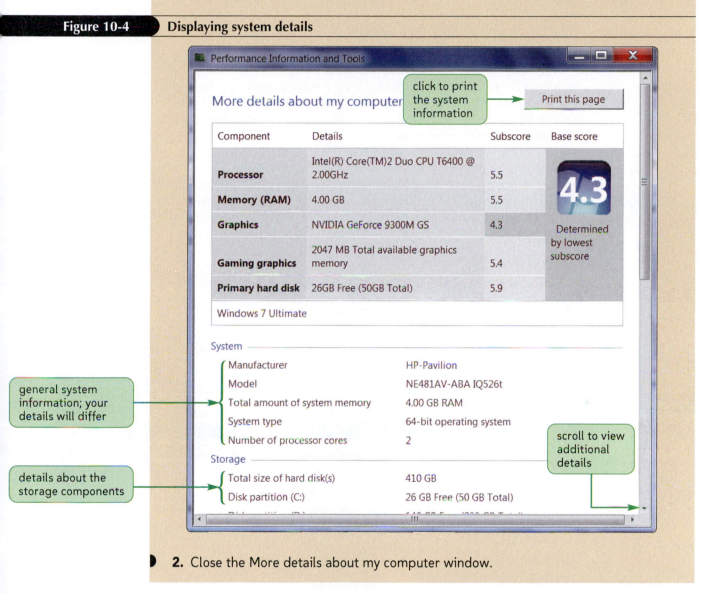

2. Close the More details about my computer window.

Amar has noticed that his computer is performing more slowly than it was when he first started using it. It is particularly slow to restart and wake up from sleep. You'll help him identify ways to improve his computer performance.

Using the Performance Troubleshooter

You can use the security tools in the Action Center to keep your computer and its data secure. The Action Center also includes tools for maintaining your computer, including a collection of troubleshooters. Although troubleshooters are not designed to address every computer problem, they are a good place to start to keep your computer in excellent running condition.

Using a Troubleshooter

- Click the Action Center icon in the notification area of the taskbar.
- Click Open Action Center, and then click Troubleshooting.
- In the list of troubleshooters, select a troubleshooter, or click a category and then select a troubleshooter.
- Follow the instructions in the troubleshooter dialog boxes.

When you run a troubleshooter, it might ask you some questions or reset common settings as it works to fix the problem. If the troubleshooter fixes the problem, you can close the troubleshooter dialog box. If it can't fix the problem, you can display options and then go online to find an answer. In either case, you can display a complete list of changes the troubleshooter made.

The first dialog box in each troubleshooter includes an Advanced link. Click this link to display a selected Apply repairs automatically check box. Clear this check box to select a solution from a list of fixes instead of applying them automatically.

To optimize Windows performance, you can use the Performance troubleshooter to automatically find and fix problems that might be slowing down your computer's performance, such as too many programs running at the same time.

To use the Performance troubleshooter:

1. In the left pane of the Performance Information and Tools window, click **Action Center** in the See also section.

2. In the Action Center window, click **Troubleshooting**. The Troubleshooting window opens. See Figure 10-5.

| Figure 10-5 | Troubleshooting window |

categories of common computer problems

select this check box to access the latest troubleshooters from a Windows Web site

3. Click **Check for performance issues** in the System and Security category to start the Performance troubleshooter. The first dialog box in the troubleshooter opens. See Figure 10-6.

Figure 10-6   Performance troubleshooter

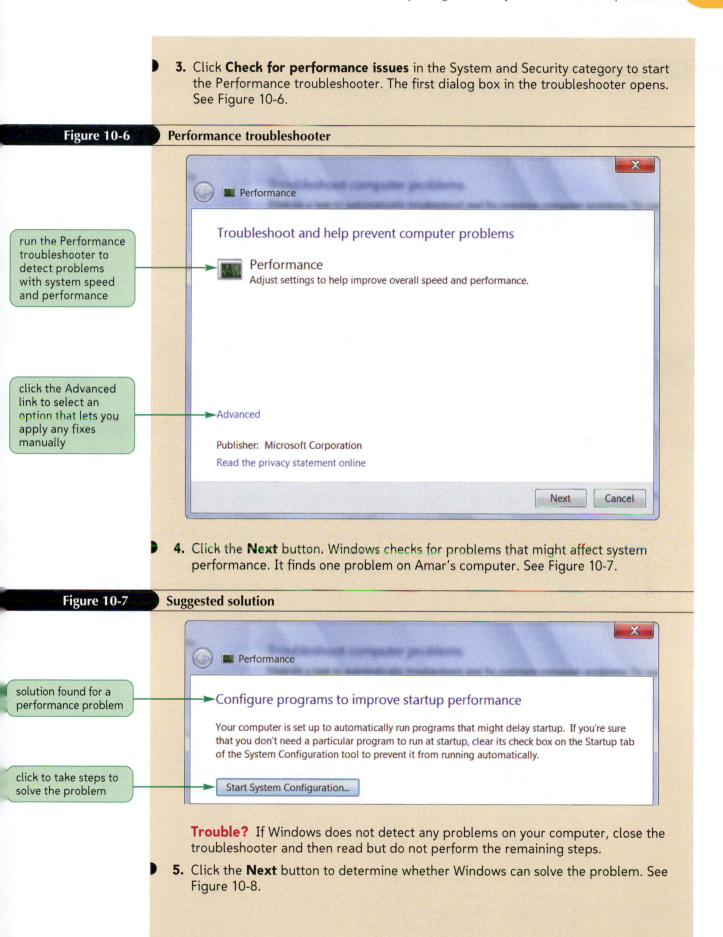

run the Performance troubleshooter to detect problems with system speed and performance

click the Advanced link to select an option that lets you apply any fixes manually

4. Click the **Next** button. Windows checks for problems that might affect system performance. It finds one problem on Amar's computer. See Figure 10-7.

Figure 10-7   Suggested solution

solution found for a performance problem

click to take steps to solve the problem

Trouble? If Windows does not detect any problems on your computer, close the troubleshooter and then read but do not perform the remaining steps.

5. Click the **Next** button to determine whether Windows can solve the problem. See Figure 10-8.

Figure 10-8   Results of the troubleshooter

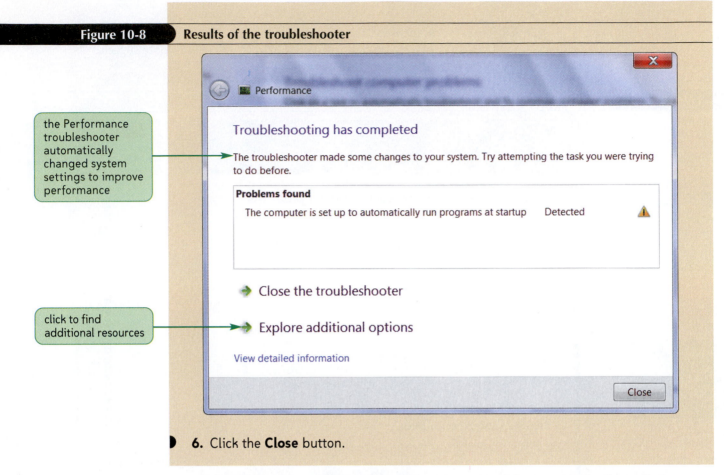

the Performance troubleshooter automatically changed system settings to improve performance

click to find additional resources

> 6. Click the **Close** button.

Windows found a problem with Amar's computer and then automatically applied a solution. If Windows does not detect a problem, you can explore other options. These include using Windows Help and Support, searching for answers or posting a question in a Windows online community, or finding related troubleshooters. If the problem persists, you can use other tools to get assistance or you can use System Recovery to revert your computer to a previous working state.

Recall that the base score for Amar's computer is 4.3, reflecting the lowest subscore for his graphics component. Until Amar can upgrade his graphics hardware, he can improve his computer's performance by adjusting its visual effects.

Optimizing Visual Effects and Other Options

Windows 7 uses visual effects to enhance your computing experience, especially if you are using an Aero theme. For example, it shows thumbnails instead of icons to help you identify files in a folder window. It also fades menu items after you click them to reinforce your selection. However, these visual effects consume system resources related to the general graphics and gaming graphics components. If a subscore for one of these components is less than 4, your computer might be working especially hard to display visual effects. In that case, you can improve performance by displaying some effects and not others, using the Visual Effects tab in the Performance Options dialog box. This tab lists settings for visual effects such as animating windows when minimizing and maximizing. It also provides the following four option buttons:

- Let Windows choose what's best for my computer: Windows selects the visual effects to balance appearance and performance for your computer hardware.
- Adjust for best appearance: Use all the visual effects listed.
- Adjust for best performance: Use none of the visual effects listed.
- Custom: Select only the visual effects you want to use.

You'll show Amar how to turn off window animation to improve performance.

To adjust visual effect settings:

▶ 1. Click **Control Panel** in the Address bar, click **System and Security**, and then click **Check the Windows Experience Index** in the System category to open the Performance Information and Tools window again.

▶ 2. In the left pane, click **Adjust visual effects**. The Performance Options dialog box opens to the Visual Effects tab. See Figure 10-9.

| Figure 10-9 | Performance Options dialog box |

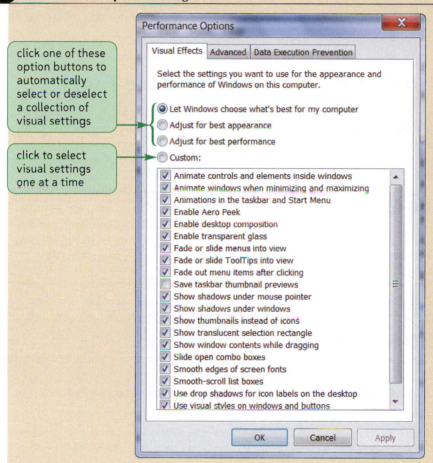

click one of these option buttons to automatically select or deselect a collection of visual settings

click to select visual settings one at a time

Trouble? If a User Account Control dialog box opens requesting your permission or a password to continue, enter the password or click the Continue button.

▶ 3. Click the **Animate controls and elements inside windows** box to remove the check mark. This automatically selects the Custom option button.

▶ 4. Click the **Animate windows when minimizing and maximizing** box to remove the check mark.

▶ 5. Click the **OK** button to change the visual effects Windows uses.

The Performance Information and Tools window also includes other tools you can use to improve performance. Recall that you can set indexing options to help you find files on your computer. In the left pane of the Performance Information and Tools window, click Adjust indexing options to open the Indexing Options dialog box, where you can specify which folders to include in your indexed locations. You can search more efficiently and improve performance by excluding folders from your indexed locations and including only those that you commonly use. To remove a folder from the indexed locations, click the folder name in the Indexing Options dialog box, click the Modify button, clear the check box for the folder in the Change selected locations list, and then click OK.

Changing your power settings also affects performance. In the left pane of the Performance Information and Tools window, click Adjust power settings to select a default power plan or create a new one. The High performance plan chooses settings that optimize performance and minimize battery life.

You can use the Disk Cleanup tool to delete temporary and other unnecessary files. In the left pane of the Performance Information and Tools window, click Open disk cleanup. Windows 7 calculates how much space you can free by permanently deleting files such as temporary Internet files and downloaded program files. You can also select other types of files, such as those in the Recycle Bin. After you select the files to remove, click the OK button to delete the files.

Using Advanced Performance Tools

System administrators and information technology (IT) professionals often use advanced system tools, such as Event Viewer and System Information, to solve problems. These performance tools are listed in the Advanced Tools window, which notifies you about performance issues and suggests how to address them. For example, if Windows detects that a driver is reducing performance, the Advanced Tools window displays a notification you can click to learn which driver is causing the problem and to view help on how to update the driver. Performance issues are listed at the top of the Advanced Tools window in order of importance. In other words, issues at the beginning of the list affect the system more than issues at the end of the list. The Advanced Tools window also provides access to the advanced performance tools described in Figure 10-10.

Figure 10-10   Advanced performance tools

Advanced Tool	Description
Event Viewer	Event Viewer tracks details of system events that might affect your computer's performance.
Performance Monitor	This monitor displays graphs of system performance.
Resource Monitor	This monitor collects data about resource usage.
Task Manager	Task Manager provides details about programs, processes, and how your computer is using system resources, such as RAM.
System Information	This tool displays details about the hardware and software components on your computer.
Performance Options	This dialog box is the same one used to adjust visual effects. You can also use it to manage memory and Data Execution Prevention (DEP), a Windows 7 tool that protects against damage from viruses and other security threats.
Disk Defragmenter	Use the Disk Defragmenter window to schedule disk defragmentation or to immediately start defragmenting.
System Diagnostics	This tool generates a report about the status of hardware resources, system response times, and other system information, and provides suggestions for maximizing performance.

You'll explore these advanced performance tools with Amar shortly. Right now, you want to open the Advanced Tools window to see if it detects any performance issues.

To view performance issues:

1. In the Performance Information and Tools window, click **Advanced tools** in the left pane. The Advanced Tools window opens. See Figure 10-11. Windows identifies one issue that might affect the performance of Amar's computer.

Figure 10-11   **Advanced Tools window**

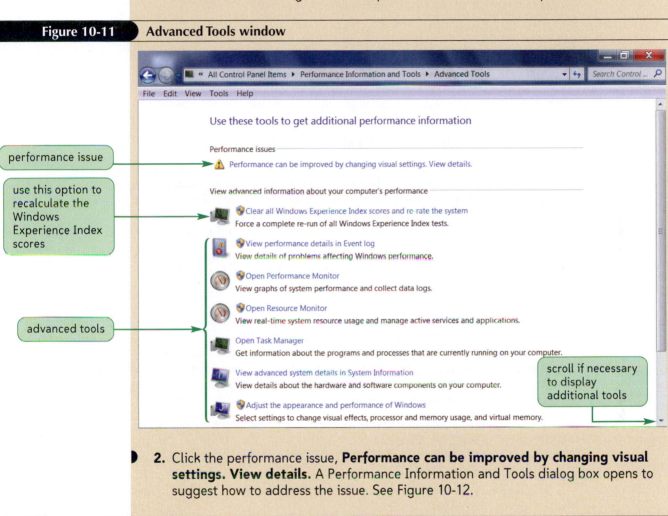

2. Click the performance issue, **Performance can be improved by changing visual settings. View details.** A Performance Information and Tools dialog box opens to suggest how to address the issue. See Figure 10-12.

Figure 10-12   **Suggested resolutions for performance issue**

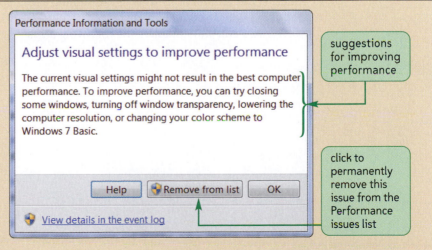

Trouble? If a different performance issue is listed first in your Advanced Tools window, click that issue. If no issues are listed in your Advanced Tools window, read but do not perform the remaining steps.

Trouble? If the Performance Information and Tools dialog box opens as a minimized window, click its button on the taskbar to open the window on the desktop.

3. Click the **Help** button to open a Windows Help and Support window that describes how to improve display quality.

4. Read the suggestions, and then close the Windows Help and Support window.

5. Click the **OK** button to close the Performance Information and Tools dialog box.

Next, you will explore some of the advanced performance tools that Amar has not used before.

Viewing Details About System Events

When you are troubleshooting problems with Windows and other programs, it is often helpful to view details about system events, such as a program closing unexpectedly. Windows records these system events in an **event log**, a special text file that contains details about the event. You can read event logs by using Event Viewer, an advanced performance tool that tracks system events, including the following types:

- Program events. Windows classifies the severity of each program event as critical, error, warning, or information. A critical event indicates that a failure has occurred from which the application or component cannot automatically recover. An error indicates a significant problem, such as loss of data. A warning is an event that might indicate a potential problem. An information event indicates that a program, driver, or service performed successfully.
- Security events. These events are called audits and are either successful or failed. For example, when you log on to Windows, Event Viewer records that as a successful audit.
- System events. Similar to program events, Windows classifies each system event as critical, error, warning, or information.

To view details about an event, double-click it in the Event Viewer window to open the Event Properties window, which describes the event and provides details helpful to a PC professional. You can copy the event properties to the Windows Clipboard, and then paste it in a text file or e-mail message to send to a computer technician, for example.

You'll show Amar how to open the Event Viewer window and find information about critical events.

To perform the following steps, you must be logged on using an Administrator account. If you are not logged on as an Administrator, you can only change settings that apply to your user account, and you might not be able to access some event logs. However, you can still complete the following steps.

To use Event Viewer:

1. In the Advanced Tools window, click **View performance details in Event log**. A message appears briefly indicating that Windows is setting up the program, and then the Event Viewer window opens. See Figure 10-13. The layout of your Event Viewer window might differ.

Figure 10-13	Event Viewer window

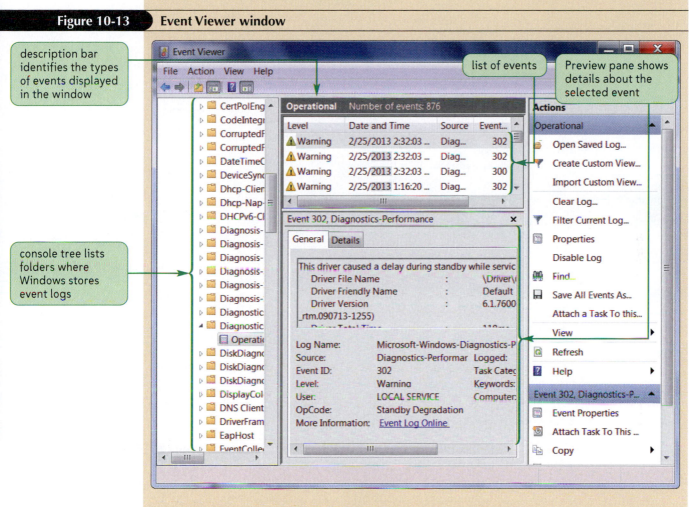

description bar identifies the types of events displayed in the window

list of events

Preview pane shows details about the selected event

console tree lists folders where Windows stores event logs

Trouble? If a User Account Control dialog box opens requesting your permission or a password to continue, enter the password or click the Continue button.

2. Scroll the list of events, and then double-click a **Critical** event. The Event Properties window opens. See Figure 10-14. Note that this particular event has an Event ID of 100. If necessary, you could provide the Event ID to a PC technician trying to troubleshoot your computer.

Figure 10-14   Event Properties window

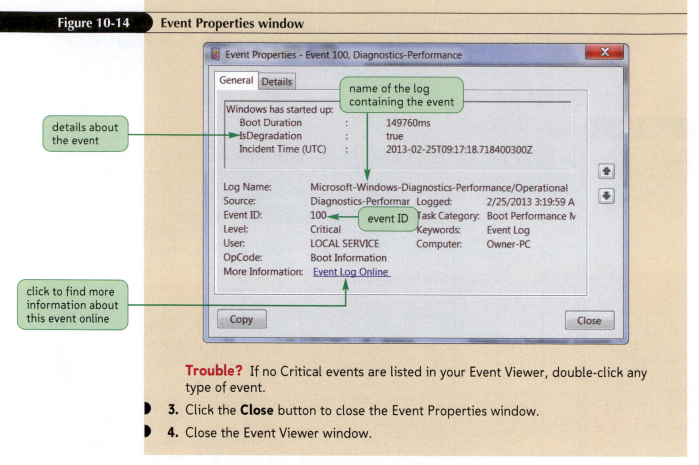

Trouble? If no Critical events are listed in your Event Viewer, double-click any type of event.

3. Click the **Close** button to close the Event Properties window.

4. Close the Event Viewer window.

Next, you want to show Amar how to use Performance Monitor to view graphs of system performance.

Monitoring System Performance

A common complaint from computer users is that their computer seems to be running more slowly than usual. If you are experiencing this same symptom, too many programs might be running at the same time, causing a loss of performance. Or the computer might be low on memory or require an upgrade to a faster processor. To determine the cause, you need to measure the performance of the system in numerical terms.

REFERENCE

Monitoring System Performance

- Click the Start button, click Control Panel, click the System and Security category, and then click Check the Windows Experience Index in the System category.
- Click Advanced tools in the left pane.
- Click Open Performance Monitor.
- In the left pane, expand the Monitoring Tools folder, if necessary.
- Click Performance Monitor to graph system performance.

One way of accomplishing this task is to use the Windows Performance Monitor, which analyzes system performance. You can monitor the performance of programs and hardware, customize the data you want to collect in logs, and generate reports.

When you open the Performance Monitor window, it displays an overview describing the Performance Monitor tool. A system summary provides statistics and other information about memory, your network interface, your physical disk (or hard disk), and processor performance. You can also use Performance Monitor to produce a graph that reflects system performance. See Figure 10-15.

| Figure 10-15 | Performance Monitor tracking performance indicators |

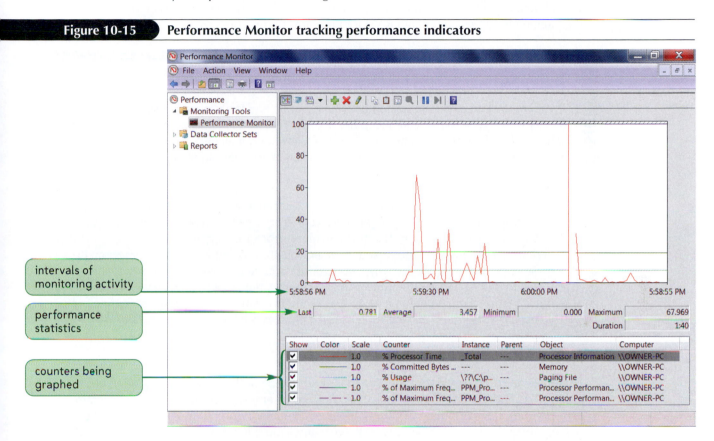

intervals of monitoring activity

performance statistics

counters being graphed

By default, Performance Monitor tracks the percentage of time your processor is working, which is one measure of how busy your system is. You can also track other performance indicators, such as how fast your computer retrieves data from the hard disk. Tracking performance information can locate the source of trouble in a slow system, and can help you determine what needs to be done to speed up the system.

To track performance indicators other than processor time, you add an item, called a **counter**, to measure a particular part of the system performance and track the values of the counter in the graph. The counter is updated at intervals you specify—usually every few seconds. To add a counter to the graph, you click the Add button on the Performance Monitor toolbar to open the Add Counters window. This window lists performance counters that are included with Windows 7.

You'll show Amar how to use Performance Monitor to track processor time. In this case, the graph in the Performance Monitor window measures the percentage of time that the processor is not idle. A value near 100% suggests that the processor is almost never idle. If so, that indicates the processor might be so busy that it can't perform tasks efficiently. If a SafeRecords employee reports a computer is working slowly, you and Amar can track the processor time to see if the employee is running too many programs or processes at the same time.

Another common problem that affects performance is low memory. Your computer has two types of memory: RAM and virtual memory. All programs use RAM; so if you have many programs running or are using a program that requires a lot of RAM, Windows might not have enough RAM to run a program. In that case, Windows temporarily moves information that it would normally store in RAM to a file on your hard disk called a

paging file. The paging file is a hidden file on the hard disk that Windows uses to hold parts of programs and data files that do not fit in RAM. Windows moves data from the paging file to RAM as needed and moves data from RAM to the paging file to make room for new data. Because Windows swaps data in and out of the paging file, it is also known as a swap file. The amount of information temporarily stored in a paging file is called **virtual memory**. Using virtual memory—in other words, moving information to and from the paging file—frees up enough RAM for programs to run correctly.

INSIGHT

Preventing and Solving Low Memory Problems

If you try to open a menu or dialog box in a program and the program responds slowly or seems to stop working, your computer is probably low on memory. You can prevent or solve low memory problems by observing the following guidelines:

- Run fewer programs at the same time, especially those that run at startup and those that show signs of requiring lots of memory.
- Increase the size of the paging file. Windows increases virtual memory the first time your computer becomes low on memory, but you can increase it up to the amount of RAM installed. However, this might cause your programs to run more slowly overall.
- Determine if a program uses too much memory. Track the paging file usage in Performance Monitor or Task Manager when you are running a particular program. If these tools show frequent activity, check for updates to the program and install them.
- Install more RAM. Open the System window to view the amount of RAM your computer has installed, and then look on the computer manufacturer's Web site to find out if you can install more. Because this solution involves purchasing and installing RAM, try the other solutions first.

Besides tracking processor time on Amar's computer, you'll also track the paging file usage to diagnose memory problems. If a SafeRecords employee indicates that a program is responding slowly or that Windows reports a low memory problem, you can track the paging file usage and increase its size, if necessary. (You'll learn how to increase the size of the paging file shortly.)

To perform the following steps, you must be logged on using an Administrator account. If you are not logged on as an Administrator, read but do not perform the following steps.

To track processor time:

1. In the Advanced Tools window, click **Open Performance Monitor**. The Performance Monitor window opens.

2. In the left pane of the Performance Monitor window, expand the **Monitoring Tools** folder, if necessary, and then click **Performance Monitor**. The Performance Monitor graph appears in the right pane, tracking the percentage of time that the processor is in use each second. See Figure 10-16. The graph on your computer will show different activity.

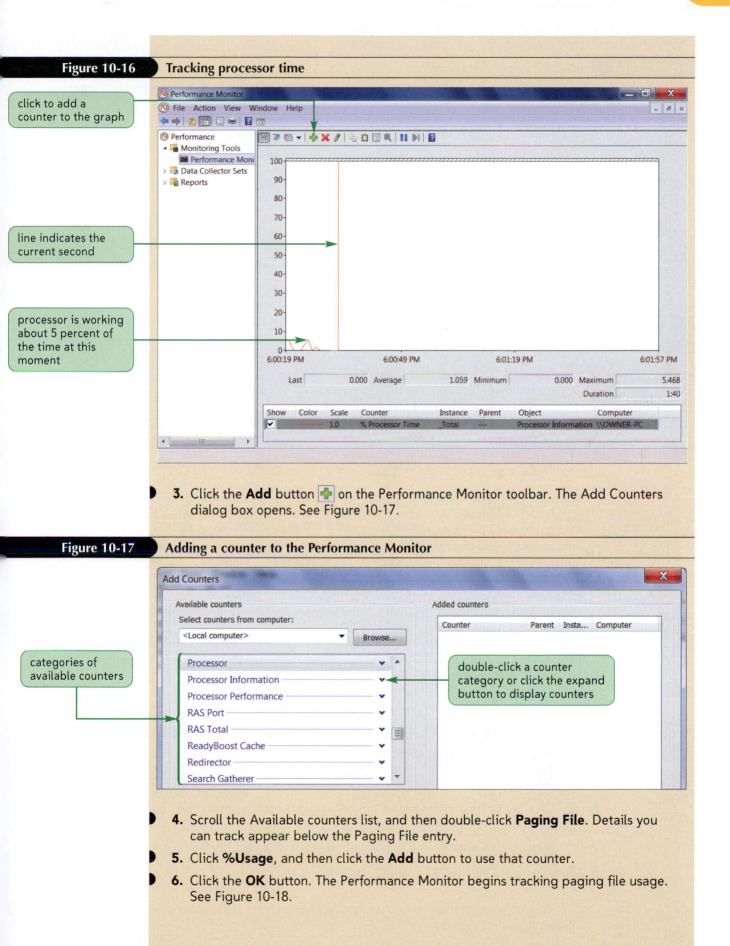

Figure 10-16 Tracking processor time

click to add a counter to the graph

line indicates the current second

processor is working about 5 percent of the time at this moment

3. Click the **Add** button ![plus] on the Performance Monitor toolbar. The Add Counters dialog box opens. See Figure 10-17.

Figure 10-17 Adding a counter to the Performance Monitor

categories of available counters

double-click a counter category or click the expand button to display counters

4. Scroll the Available counters list, and then double-click **Paging File**. Details you can track appear below the Paging File entry.

5. Click **%Usage**, and then click the **Add** button to use that counter.

6. Click the **OK** button. The Performance Monitor begins tracking paging file usage. See Figure 10-18.

Figure 10-18   **Tracking paging file usage**

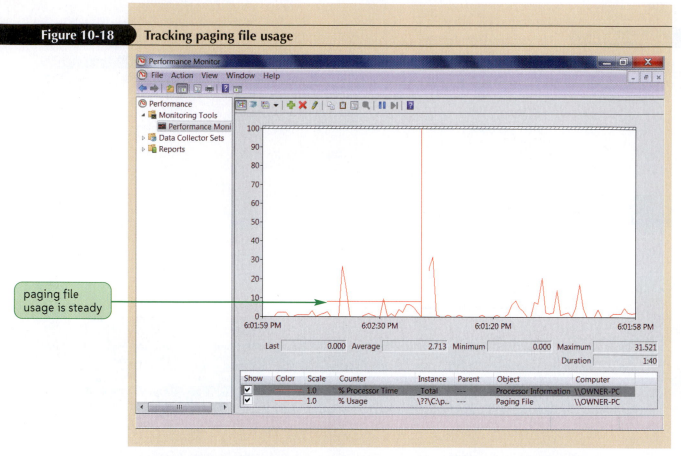

The graph shows that the paging file usage is steady. This number usually increases significantly when you start a program that uses many system resources, such as a Microsoft Office program. If the paging file usage does not decrease by that same amount when you close the program that means the program is leaving temporary files or processes open in memory, which can cause problems. Windows usually recovers that memory after a few minutes of idle time. If it does not, a temporary solution is to restart your computer to clear everything from RAM and make the maximum amount of memory available to your computer. The long-term solution is to install updates to the program that is not handling memory efficiently.

Performance Monitor on Amar's computer is tracking two system indicators, but both lines in the graph are red. You'll show Amar how to change the % Usage counter to a contrasting color so he can distinguish one counter from the other.

To change the color of the % Usage counter:

1. Below the graph, right-click the **% Usage** counter, and then click **Properties** on the shortcut menu. The Performance Monitor Properties dialog box opens to the Data tab.

2. Click the **Color button arrow**, and then click **blue** (the third color from the top of the list).

3. Click the **OK** button. The % Usage indicator line is now displayed in blue.

4. Close the Performance Monitor window.

Next, you'll show Amar how to use another advanced tool to track system performance: Resource Monitor.

Using Resource Monitor

Another tool you can use to measure system performance is Resource Monitor. On the Overview tab of the Resource Monitor window, you can view four graphs to track the usage of the CPU, disk, network, and memory as your computer is using these resources. The Overview tab also includes four bars, one for each system resource. You can click a bar or an expand button to display details about each resource. For example, click the Memory bar to display a summary of memory usage.

The CPU graph shows how much of the central processing unit (CPU) is being used at any given moment. The CPU is the main circuit chip in a computer, and performs most of the calculations necessary to run the computer. A high percentage of CPU usage means that the currently running programs or processes require a lot of CPU resources, which can slow the performance of your computer. If the CPU usage appears frozen at or near 100%, then some programs might not be responding. You can use Task Manager to stop running the program, which you'll do shortly. Click the CPU bar to view the processes, or images, that are using CPU resources. (A **process** is a task performed by a program and usually contains information about starting the program.)

The Disk graph and bar indicate how active your hard disk is, measured by the number of times a program reads (retrieves) data from the hard disk or writes (stores) data on the hard disk. Click the Disk bar to see which files are reading or writing data to your hard disk.

The Network graph and bar indicate the amount of network activity your computer is experiencing, measured in kilobytes per second (Kbps). Click the Network bar to see the network address of the programs exchanging information with your computer.

The Memory graph and bar display the percentage of RAM currently being used and the number of hard faults occurring per second. A hard fault, or page fault, occurs when a program retrieves data from RAM and stores it on the hard disk. If a program is responding slowly to your commands, look here for a high number of hard faults, which indicates that the program is continually reading data from disk rather than RAM.

SafeRecords employees occasionally report to you or Amar that their computers are suddenly running more slowly than normal. You'll show Amar how to open the Resource Monitor window and view the resources Windows is currently using to diagnose the problem with an employee's computer.

To perform the following steps, you must be logged on using an Administrator account. If you are not logged on as an Administrator, read but do not perform the following steps.

TIP

To determine the type of CPU installed on your computer, open Control Panel, click System and Security, click System, and then look for the CPU speed and type in the System section under Processor.

To examine an overview of resource usage:

1. In the Advanced Tools window, click **Open Resource Monitor**. The Resource Monitor window opens to the Overview tab. See Figure 10-19.

Figure 10-19   **Overview tab in the Resource Monitor window**

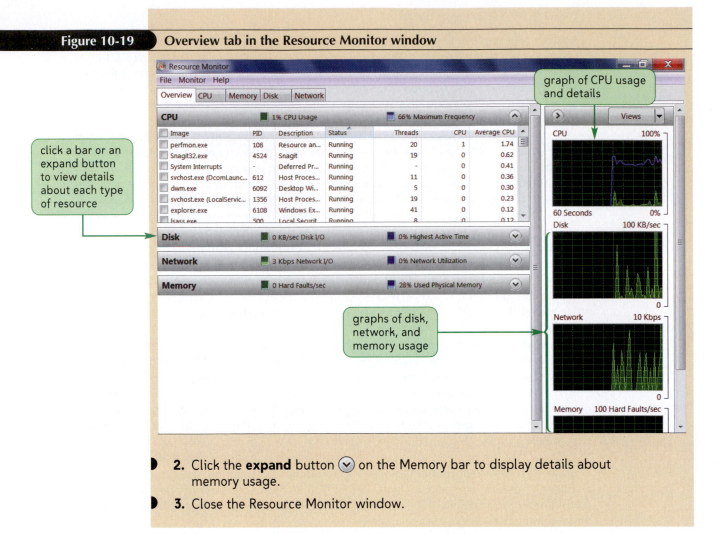

click a bar or an expand button to view details about each type of resource

graph of CPU usage and details

graphs of disk, network, and memory usage

> **2.** Click the **expand** button ⊙ on the Memory bar to display details about memory usage.

> **3.** Close the Resource Monitor window.

The resources on Amar's computer do not indicate any performance problems. However, you and Amar can track these resources to diagnose problems for the SafeRecords employees.

Using Task Manager to Examine System Information

Besides using the Performance Monitor to track system information, you can also use Task Manager to view information about the programs and processes running on your computer. Task Manager does not provide as much information as the Performance and Resource Monitors, but any user can open Task Manager, whereas only Administrators can use the Performance and Resource Monitors.

You can use Task Manager to monitor your computer's performance or to close a program that is not responding. If you are connected to a network, you can also use Task Manager to view the network status and see how your network is functioning. If more than one user is connected to your computer, you can see who is connected and what they are working on, and you can send them a message.

The Windows Task Manager dialog box contains the tabs described in Figure 10-20.

Figure 10-20   **Tabs in the Windows Task Manager dialog box**

Task Manager Tab	Description
Applications	Lists the programs running on your computer, including those that are not responding
Processes	Lists the processes running on your computer
Services	Lists current services, which are the background programs or processes that support other programs
Performance	Provides details about how your computer is using system resources, such as RAM and the CPU
Networking	Provides details about network connections
Users	Identifies the current users of the computer and their status

You typically use the first four tabs to troubleshoot system problems and improve performance. The Applications tab displays each currently active program and its status, which is either Running or Not Responding. If a program has a Not Responding status, you can close the program by clicking it and then clicking the End Task button. However, closing a program this way discards any unsaved changes you made with that program.

Although viruses and other malware rarely appear as programs listed on the Applications tab, they sometimes appear on the Processes tab. To learn more about a process, right-click it on the Processes tab, and then click Properties on the shortcut menu. Click the Details tab in the Properties dialog box to view a description of the file, the program it's associated with, and its copyright information. Typically, the Details tab for malware files does not provide any information. You can also search Windows 7 Help or the Internet for more information about the files listed on the Processes tab. If you are sure a process is associated with malware, click the file, and then click the End Process button. If you don't know the purpose of a process, don't end it. If you end a process associated with an open program, such as a word-processing program, the program closes without saving your data. If you end a process associated with a system service, some part of the system might not function properly.

Recall that a **service** is a program or process running in the background that supports other programs; currently running services appear on the Services tab in the Windows Task Manager dialog box. If a process is associated with a service, you can right-click a service on the Services tab, and then click Go to Process on the shortcut menu. (This command is available only for services associated with an active process.) The Processes tab opens and selects the process associated with that service.

Similar to the Performance Monitor window, the Performance tab displays graphs to illustrate how your computer is using system resources, including CPU and RAM. The status bar in the Windows Task Manager dialog box also displays the percentage of CPU and physical memory (RAM) currently being used. Recall that if the CPU Usage percentage appears frozen at or near 100%, a program might not be responding. In that case, you should open the Applications tab and end that program as previously described.

PROSKILLS

Decision Making: Selecting a Tool to Solve Performance Problems

The term *performance* refers to how efficiently your computer is working and how quickly Windows responds to your requests and commands. If your computer is performing poorly, you waste time waiting for it to complete tasks such as opening files and folders. A computer's performance normally decreases over time as you install programs and save files. However, if a computer is performing so slowly that it significantly affects your productivity, you need to know how to identify and solve the problem. You might need to add memory, remove a troublesome device driver, or replace the entire system. How do you know what to do to fix the problem? You use a performance monitor tool that Windows provides. The two most common tools are Performance Monitor and Task Manager. Each one is designed to provide certain types of information.

Performance Monitor is the main tool you use to diagnose problems with system performance. System administrators typically use Performance Monitor with a new system to set baselines. They select key counters for memory, the network interface, the paging file, the physical disk, and the processor. They graph them a few times during a typical day, and then save the graph and data. You can also set baselines to create a record of your computer when it is performing well. If you notice your computer is working more slowly than normal, select the same counters and graph them again. Then compare the baseline information to the new information to diagnose the problem. For example, the Pages/Sec counter shows how often the system accesses the paging file. In a high-performing system, this value is zero or close to zero. Consistently high values probably mean that your system does not have enough RAM, so adding RAM could solve the performance problem. Performance Monitor's drawback is that it includes hundreds of counters. Although you can search online for information about each one, you need to understand what each counter measures to accurately interpret the data, which takes time and technical knowledge.

Task Manager provides a simplified version of Performance Monitor. Although it does not save information so you can compare it later, the Performance tab in Task Manager provides immediate and clear information related to system performance. For example, the Commit values show how many demands programs and files are making on available resources. If the first Commit value is close to the second one, close programs and large files to improve performance. As with the Performance Monitor counters, you can search online for more information about the values on the Performance tab.

You'll explore the first four tabs in the Windows Task Manager dialog box with Amar to show him the kinds of information they provide.

TIP

You can also open Task Manager by right-clicking the taskbar and then clicking Start Task Manager.

To explore Task Manager:

1. In the Advanced Tools window, click **Open Task Manager** to open the Windows Task Manager dialog box.

2. Click the **Applications** tab, if necessary, to display a list of programs running on your computer. See Figure 10-21. Your list of applications might differ.

Figure 10-21   **Applications tab in the Windows Task Manager dialog box**

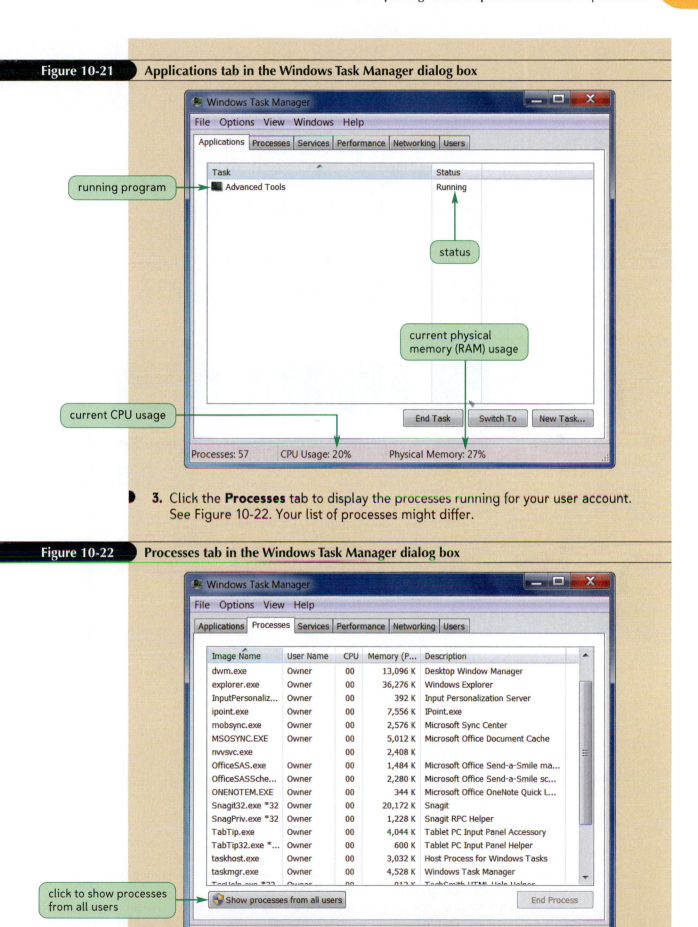

3. Click the **Processes** tab to display the processes running for your user account. See Figure 10-22. Your list of processes might differ.

Figure 10-22   **Processes tab in the Windows Task Manager dialog box**

4. Right-click **explorer.exe** and then click **Properties** on the shortcut menu. The explorer Properties dialog box opens.

5. Click the **Details** tab to view details about the explorer.exe process file. This file is associated with the Windows Explorer program.

6. Click the **OK** button to close the explorer Properties dialog box.

7. Click the **Services** tab in the Windows Task Manager dialog box to display the services associated with the programs and processes running on your computer.

8. Click the **Performance** tab to display graphs of CPU and RAM usage. See Figure 10-23.

Figure 10-23   **Performance tab in the Windows Task Manager dialog box**

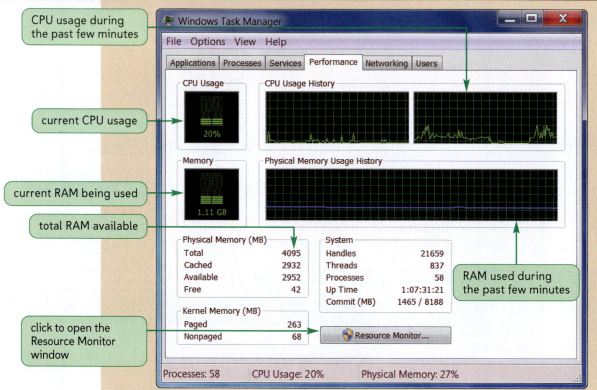

CPU usage during the past few minutes

current CPU usage

current RAM being used

total RAM available

click to open the Resource Monitor window

RAM used during the past few minutes

9. Close the Windows Task Manager dialog box.

Although Task Manager provides information about software running on your computer and displays some resource information also included in the Performance Monitor, you can use another window to examine a summary of hardware on your computer.

Examining System Information

The System Information window collects detailed information about your computer system, some of which is also provided in other windows, including Device Manager and the System window. Advanced users often find it more convenient to use the System Information window to learn details such as the computer name, operating system version, processor type, and total amount of RAM.

Although Amar is comfortable using Device Manager to view hardware information, including device conflicts, drivers, and component names, you'll show him how to use the System Information window to view this same hardware information as well as other system details that computer administrators often need to know.

To examine system information:

▶ **1.** In the Advanced Tools window, click **View advanced system details in System Information** to open the System Information window. By default, this window opens to show a system summary. See Figure 10-24.

Figure 10-24	System Information window

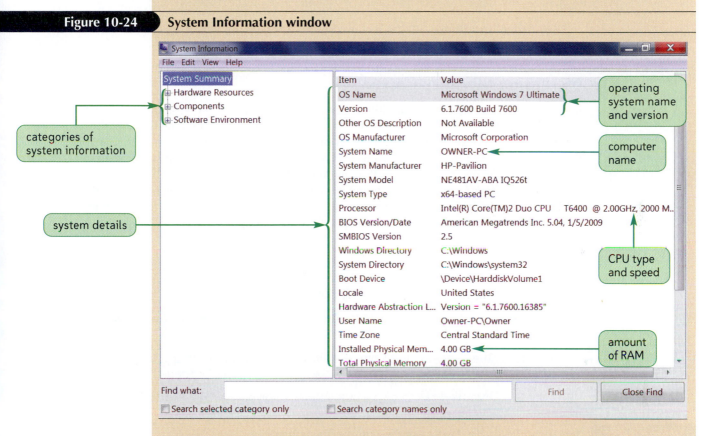

Trouble? If your System Information window does not open showing a system summary, click System Summary in the left pane.

▶ **2.** Click the **expand** icon ⊞ next to Hardware Resources, and then click **IRQs** to display a list of hardware resources, including the IRQ number, device, and status. (Recall that Windows assigns each hardware device an IRQ number and ranks the devices, giving lower numbers higher priority so they receive attention first.)

▶ **3.** Click the **expand** icon ⊞ next to Components to display in the left pane a list of the types of devices installed on your computer.

▶ **4.** Click **CD-ROM** in the Components list to display details about this device, including its drive letter and location of its driver file.

Trouble? If CD-ROM does not appear in your Components list, click any other device type.

▶ **5.** Click the **expand** icon ⊞ next to Software Environment to display a list of software details.

▶ **6.** Click **Running Tasks** in the Software Environment list to display a list of running processes, similar to the one displayed in the Windows Task Manager dialog box.

7. Click **Startup Programs** in the left pane to display details about programs that start when Windows does. Recall that the Advanced Tools window in Figure 10-7 listed a problem with a startup program as a performance issue. If that continues to cause problems, you can examine the programs in the System Information window and then change or repair a program using the Programs tools in the Control Panel.

8. Close the System Information window.

Now that you've shown Amar a few ways to track the paging file usage, you can explore how to increase the size of this file when necessary.

Increasing Memory Capacity

If you receive warnings that your virtual memory is low, you can increase the minimum size of your paging file. Windows sets the initial minimum size of the paging file at the amount of RAM installed on your computer plus 300 MB. It sets the maximum size at three times the amount of RAM installed on your computer. If you see warnings at these recommended levels, then increase the minimum and maximum sizes.

Although Amar's computer has enough virtual memory to perform efficiently, you'll show him how to increase the minimum and maximum size of the paging file for future reference. To do so, you use the Performance Options dialog box, which is the same dialog box you used to select visual effects.

To increase the size of the paging file:

1. In the Advanced Tools window, click **Adjust the appearance and performance of Windows** to open the Performance Options dialog box.

Trouble? If a User Account Control dialog box opens requesting your permission or a password to continue, enter the password or click the Continue button.

2. Click the **Advanced** tab to display paging file information. See Figure 10-25.

Figure 10-25   Advanced tab in the Performance Options dialog box

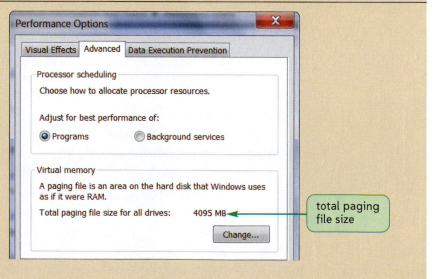

3. Click the **Change** button to open the Virtual Memory dialog box. See Figure 10-26.

Figure 10-26 **Virtual Memory dialog box**

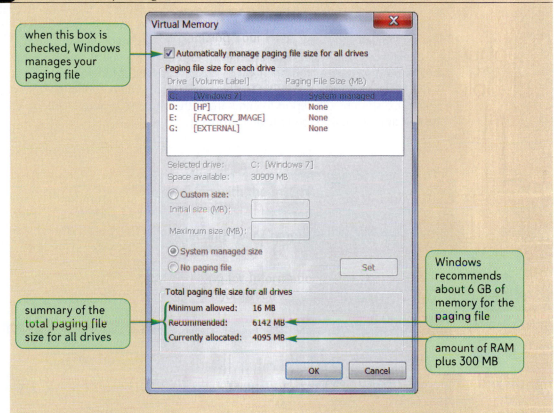

when this box is checked, Windows manages your paging file

summary of the total paging file size for all drives

Windows recommends about 6 GB of memory for the paging file

amount of RAM plus 300 MB

If Amar wanted to manage the paging file size himself, he could click the Automatically manage paging file size for all drives box to remove the check mark, click the drive he wants to manage, click the Custom size option button, enter the initial (minimum) and maximum size for the paging file, and then click the Set button.

4. Click the **Cancel** button to close the Virtual Memory dialog box without making any changes.

5. Click the **OK** button to close the Performance Options dialog box.

The Virtual Memory dialog box shows that Amar has about 4 GB of RAM on his computer, but Windows recommends about 6 GB for the paging file on all drives. If Amar notices a decline in performance on his computer, the first solution he should try is adding 2 GB of RAM.

Two tools remain in the Advanced Tools window: Disk Defragmenter and a system health report. You and Amar already know how to defragment a disk—you open the Disk Defragmenter dialog box and then click the Defragment disk button or set a schedule to have Windows defragment a disk automatically. You'll show Amar how to generate a system health report next.

Generating a System Health Report

To have Windows collect data about your system and diagnose any problems, you can generate a system health report titled System Diagnostics Report. This report includes nine sections. The first section identifies the computer, the date of the report, and the length of time Windows needed to collect the data for the report. The second section, Diagnostic Results, is especially helpful to system administrators. This section lists problems found on the computer, if any, and assigns them a severity, such as Critical or Warning. The Diagnostic Results section also shows the results of basic system checks, such as a survey of the attributes of the operating system, and a resource overview, such as CPU and network usage. Other sections, including the Software Configuration and Hardware Configuration sections, provide details about these checks. The last section, Report Statistics, lists details about the computer, files, and events.

Because Amar's system is performing well right now, you'll generate and save a system health report to use as a baseline, which is a snapshot of the computer's performance when it's running at a normal level. When the system has problems, Amar can generate another system health report to compare to the baseline report. Using baseline reports, he can anticipate and then prevent problems.

To generate a system health report:

1. In the Advanced Tools window, click **Generate a system health report**. The Resource and Performance Monitor window opens and displays a progress bar as Windows collects data about your system for 60 seconds. When it's finished collecting data, Windows generates and displays the System Diagnostics Report. See Figure 10-27.

Figure 10-27	System Diagnostics Report

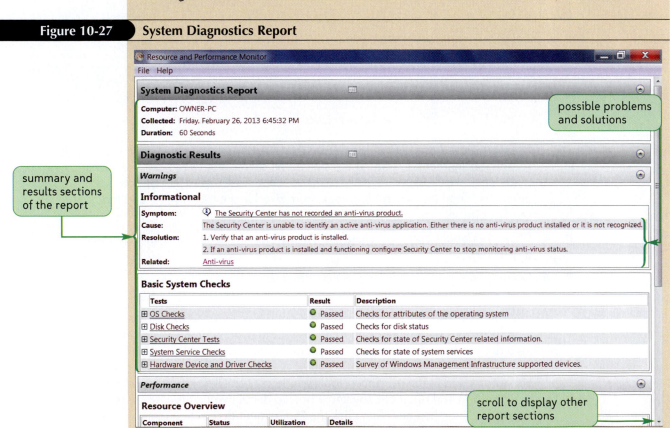

Trouble? If a User Account Control dialog box opens requesting your permission or a password to continue, enter the password or click the Continue button.

2. Click **File** on the menu bar, and then click **Save As** to open the Save As dialog box.

3. Navigate to the Tutorial.10\Tutorial folder provided with your Data Files, type **Diagnostics** as the name of the report, and then click the **Save** button.

4. Close the report window.

5. Close the Advanced Tools window.

You now want to show Amar another useful way to increase memory capacity using a USB flash drive and a feature called ReadyBoost.

Using ReadyBoost to Increase Memory Capacity

Windows ReadyBoost can use storage space on some removable media devices, including USB flash drives, to speed up your computer. When you insert a device with this capability, the AutoPlay dialog box offers you the option to speed up your system using Windows ReadyBoost. If you select this option, you can then choose how much memory to use for this purpose, up to a maximum of 256 GB of additional memory.

In some situations, however, you may not be able to use all of the memory on your storage device to speed up your computer. If your computer has a hard disk that uses solid-state drive (SSD) technology, it might be too fast to benefit from ReadyBoost. In this case, the AutoPlay dialog box does not provide a Windows ReadyBoost option. Some USB storage devices contain both slow and fast flash memory, and Windows can only use fast flash memory to speed up your computer. If your device contains both slow and fast memory, keep in mind that you can only use the fast memory portion for this purpose. USB flash drives eventually wear out after a certain number of uses, so using ReadyBoost can eventually wear out the USB drive. This generally takes a few years, however.

Keep in mind that ReadyBoost is not a replacement for an adequate amount of system memory. The surest way to improve computer performance is to invest in additional RAM. In addition, ReadyBoost is not a replacement for the paging file. ReadyBoost works with the paging file to maximize the amount of memory your computer can use. For certain types of tasks, ReadyBoost provides extra memory that the computer can access much more quickly than it can access data on the hard drive. For other types of tasks, Windows uses the paging file more efficiently.

The recommended amount of memory to use for ReadyBoost acceleration is one to three times the amount of RAM installed in your computer. For instance, if your computer has 2 GB of RAM and you plug in an 8 GB USB flash drive, setting aside from 2 GB to 6 GB of that drive offers the best performance boost.

You can turn ReadyBoost on or off for a flash drive or other removable storage device, as long as the removable media device contains at least 256 MB of space to work with Windows ReadyBoost.

To perform the following steps, you need a USB flash drive that has at least 50 percent of its storage space free. If you do not have such a device, read but do not perform the following steps.

To use ReadyBoost:

1. Plug a USB flash drive into an available USB port on your computer. The AutoPlay dialog box opens. See Figure 10-28.

TIP

You can also open the Computer window, right-click a USB flash drive, click Properties, and then click the ReadyBoost tab.

Figure 10-28 AutoPlay dialog box

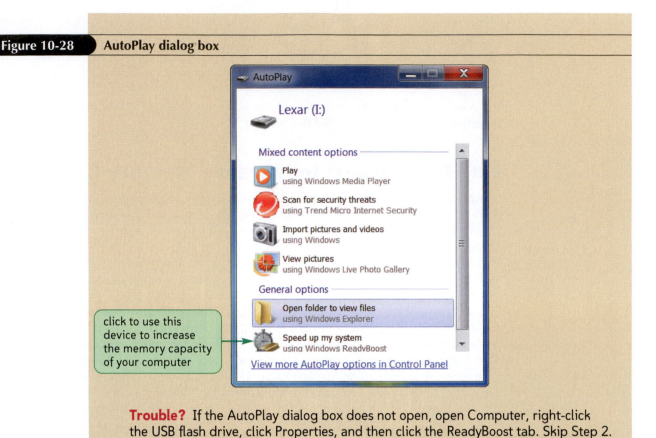

click to use this device to increase the memory capacity of your computer

Trouble? If the AutoPlay dialog box does not open, open Computer, right-click the USB flash drive, click Properties, and then click the ReadyBoost tab. Skip Step 2.

2. Click **Speed up my system** to open the Properties dialog box for the USB flash drive. If necessary, click the **ReadyBoost** tab. See Figure 10-29.

Figure 10-29 USB flash drive's Properties dialog box open to the ReadyBoost tab

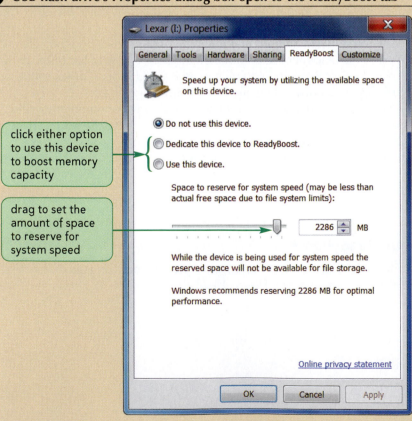

click either option to use this device to boost memory capacity

drag to set the amount of space to reserve for system speed

Trouble? If the Speed up my system option does not appear on the AutoPlay dialog box, the USB flash drive might not have the required performance characteristics for boosting memory. Find a different USB flash drive and repeat Step 1.

▶ **3.** Click the **Use this device** option button to turn on ReadyBoost.

▶ **4.** Drag the slider to the far right, if possible, to select the maximum amount of available space on your USB flash drive to reserve for boosting your system speed.

▶ **5.** Click the **OK** button.

▶ **6.** Close all open windows.

Each time Amar attaches that USB flash drive to his computer, he will have more than 2 GB of extra memory that Windows can use to improve system performance. The settings you select in the AutoPlay dialog box apply to that USB flash drive until you open the Properties dialog box for the drive, click the ReadyBoost tab, and then select the Do not use this device option button.

REVIEW

Session 10.1 Quick Check

1. What is system performance?

2. A(n) _____ is a series of dialog boxes that guides you through the steps of describing and solving typical system problems.

3. True or False. The Windows Experience Index base score is the lowest subscore, not an average.

4. Name two tools you can use to find the list of processes running on your computer.

5. What can you do if you receive warnings that your virtual memory is low?

6. A Windows tool called _____ can use storage space on some removable media devices, including some USB flash drives, to speed up your computer.

7. If you open Task Manager and find that the CPU Usage percentage appears frozen at or near 100%, what can you do to solve the problem?

SESSION 10.2 VISUAL OVERVIEW

The **Microsoft Solution Centers** provide support information for Microsoft product users.

Search for answers in the Solution Centers by entering one or more keywords.

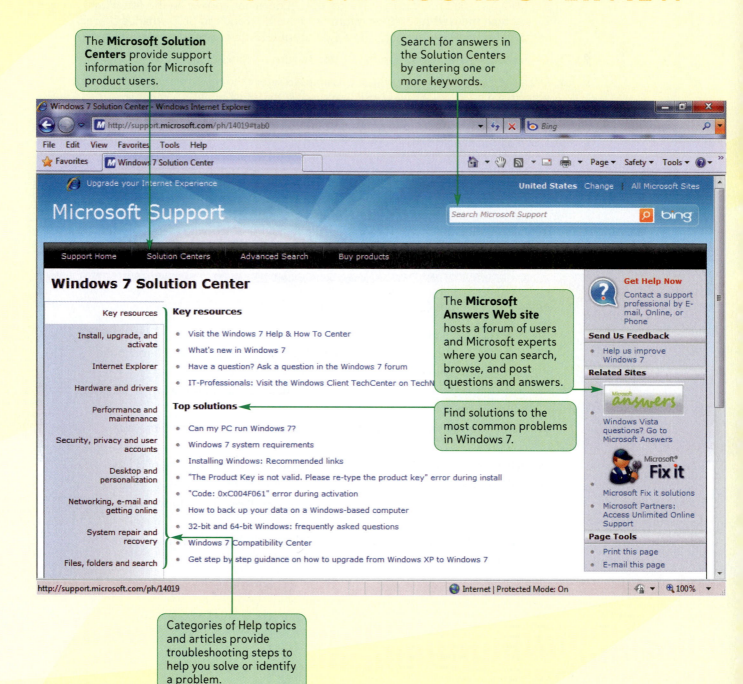

The **Microsoft Answers Web site** hosts a forum of users and Microsoft experts where you can search, browse, and post questions and answers.

Find solutions to the most common problems in Windows 7.

Categories of Help topics and articles provide troubleshooting steps to help you solve or identify a problem.

SOLVING SYSTEM PROBLEMS

Windows archives messages it displayed about system problems; select an archived message to see if a solution is now available.

The Maintenance section of the Action Center window lists tools to help you keep your computer running smoothly.

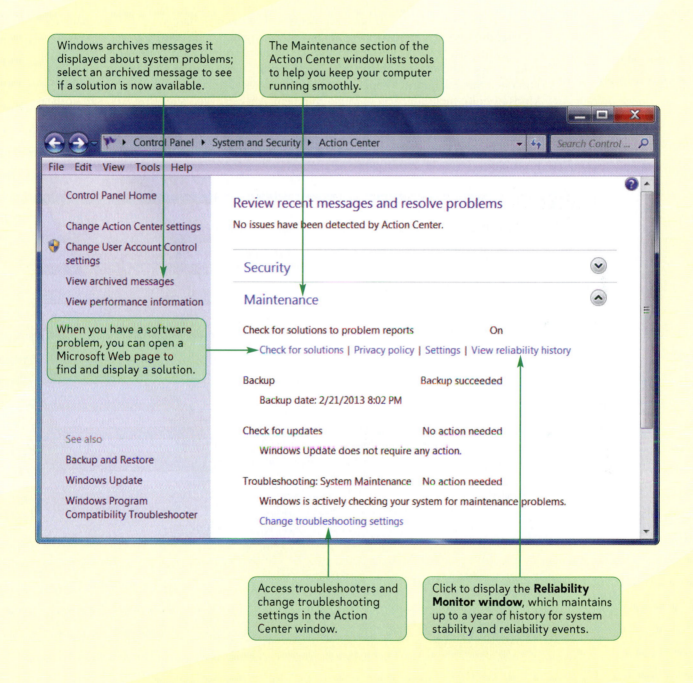

When you have a software problem, you can open a Microsoft Web page to find and display a solution.

Access troubleshooters and change troubleshooting settings in the Action Center window.

Click to display the **Reliability Monitor window**, which maintains up to a year of history for system stability and reliability events.

Finding Troubleshooting Information

When you have problems with Windows, its programs, your computer, or other hardware, you can find troubleshooting information in at least two resources: the Troubleshooting window in the Control Panel and the Microsoft Solution Centers on the Web. You have already used a troubleshooter to identify and solve performance problems. You can use similar troubleshooters if you have problems with programs, hardware devices, networking and the Internet, appearance and display, and system and security tools.

You can also use Windows Help and Support to find Help topics designed to help you troubleshoot and solve problems. On the Windows Help and Support home page, you can click the Ask button to open a page listing ways to get customer support or other kinds of help, including access to the Microsoft Answers Web site. This Web site hosts a forum of users and Microsoft experts where you can search, browse, and post questions and answers. It also provides access to the Microsoft Solution Centers, which include Help topics and articles that provide troubleshooting steps to help you solve or identify a problem.

PROSKILLS

Problem Solving: Troubleshooting System Problems

When you suspect a problem on your computer, take a systematic approach to solving it. Complete the following problem-solving steps so you can troubleshoot problems thoroughly and consistently.

- *Define the problem.* Describe the trouble that you observe, being as specific as possible. For example, if you are having trouble printing, note when the trouble occurs, such as when you try to print from a particular program or with a certain print setting.
- *Identify possible causes.* Look for obvious causes first, such as a loose cable connecting a printer to your computer. Next, determine when the system was last performing normally and what has changed since then. Did you download and install a new driver from Windows Update? Did you install new hardware? These are possible causes of the problem.
- *Test the causes.* For each cause, determine what you can do to see if it is the source of the problem. For example, if you suspect a loose cable is causing printing problems, reconnect the cable. If you installed a new printer driver, try reverting to a previous version. Systematically testing each cause solves most computer problems.
- *Find additional help.* If the problem persists, refer to other resources for solutions. For example, does the Devices and Printers window or the Device Manager window display a message about the printer? Does Windows Help and Support provide information about the problem or a similar one? Can you find possible solutions on the printer manufacturer's Web site?
- *Apply solutions.* As you did when testing causes, try each solution you find, starting with the solutions that affect your system the least. For example, try installing a new printer driver before using System Restore to restore your system. Before you make any major changes to your computer, set a system restore point and back up your data so you don't lose important work.

Amar wants to train SafeRecords employees to use Windows Help and Support to troubleshoot typical computer problems, such as those involving network connections and hardware. You'll show him how to find troubleshooters that employees can use to solve these problems.

To troubleshoot Internet problems:

1. Click the **Action Center** icon 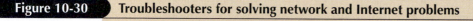 in the notification area of the taskbar, and then click **Open Action Center** to open the Action Center window.

2. Scroll down, if necessary, click **Troubleshooting** to open the Troubleshooting window, and then click **Network and Internet** to open the Troubleshoot problems – Network and Internet window. See Figure 10-30.

Figure 10-30   Troubleshooters for solving network and Internet problems

network and Internet troubleshooters

troubleshooter for the network printer

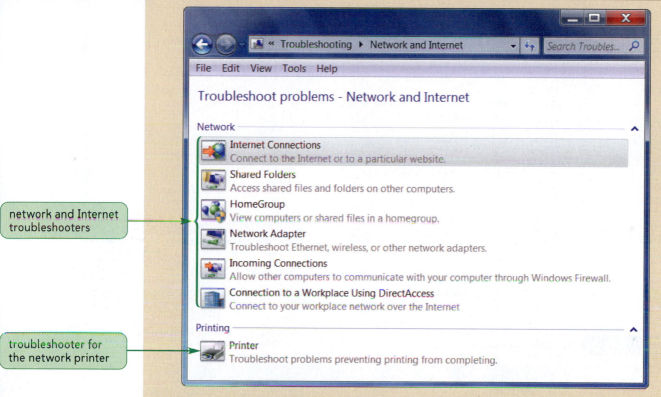

3. Click **Internet Connections** to open the Internet Connections dialog box.

   Amar wants to review changes and repairs before Windows applies them, so you need to display an advanced option.

4. Click the **Advanced** link to display advanced options. See Figure 10-31.

Figure 10-31 Troubleshooter for Internet connection problem

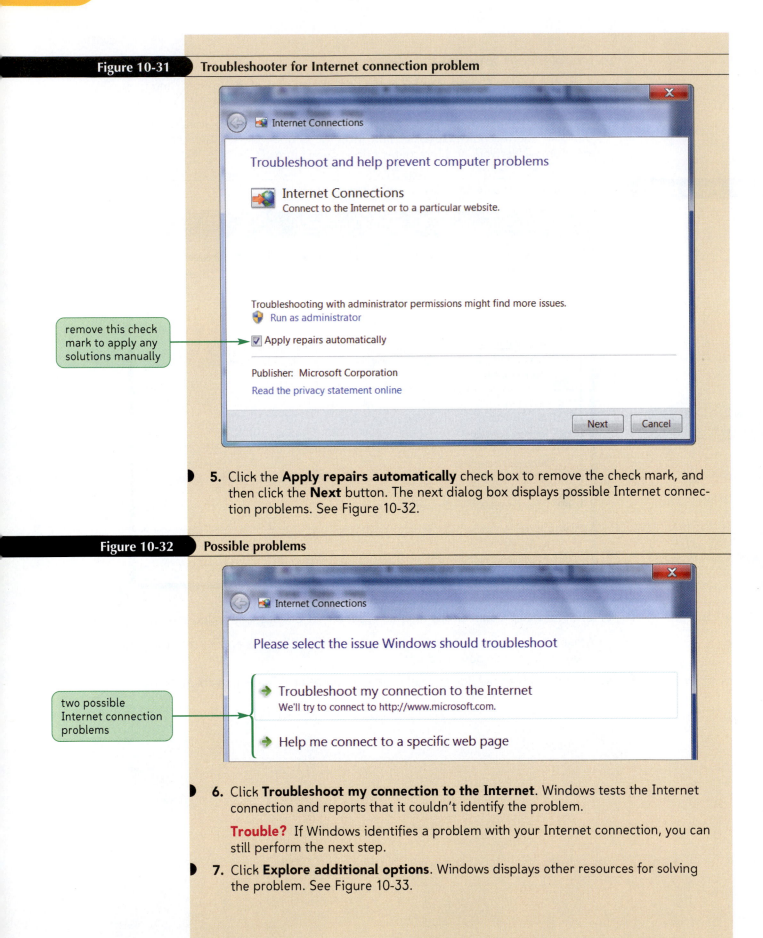

remove this check mark to apply any solutions manually

Internet Connections

Troubleshoot and help prevent computer problems

Internet Connections
Connect to the Internet or to a particular website.

Troubleshooting with administrator permissions might find more issues.
Run as administrator

☑ Apply repairs automatically

Publisher: Microsoft Corporation
Read the privacy statement online

Next   Cancel

5. Click the **Apply repairs automatically** check box to remove the check mark, and then click the **Next** button. The next dialog box displays possible Internet connection problems. See Figure 10-32.

Figure 10-32 Possible problems

Internet Connections

Please select the issue Windows should troubleshoot

two possible Internet connection problems

→ Troubleshoot my connection to the Internet
We'll try to connect to http://www.microsoft.com.

→ Help me connect to a specific web page

6. Click **Troubleshoot my connection to the Internet**. Windows tests the Internet connection and reports that it couldn't identify the problem.

Trouble? If Windows identifies a problem with your Internet connection, you can still perform the next step.

7. Click **Explore additional options**. Windows displays other resources for solving the problem. See Figure 10-33.

Figure 10-33   **Additional resources**

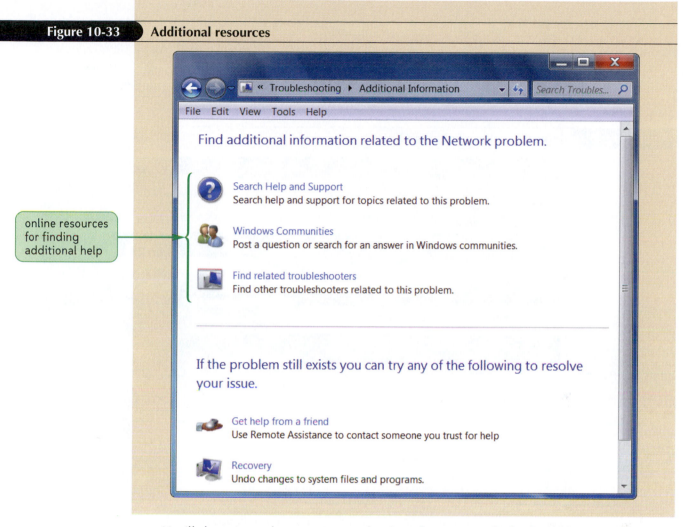

online resources for finding additional help

You'll show Amar the next step to take if employees can't find solutions to their problems using a troubleshooter.

Searching the Microsoft Solution Centers

Because the Microsoft Solution Centers contain support information about all Microsoft software products, they are a valuable resource when you are troubleshooting computer problems. However, it can sometimes be difficult to pinpoint the answer to your question. Just as you search for information on the Internet, you search for answers in a Solution Center by entering one or more keywords. The Solution Center then displays the support articles associated with those keywords.

A SafeRecords employee recently asked Amar why Windows no longer displays the Internet Explorer icon on the desktop. You'll show Amar how to use the Microsoft Solution Centers and the Microsoft Answers online forum to find answers to this question.

To find information in the Microsoft Solution Centers:

1. In the Additional Information window, click **Search Help and Support**. A Windows Help and Support window opens with the troubleshooting search text displayed in the search box.

2. Click the **Ask** button on the Windows Help and Support toolbar. The More support options window opens.

3. Click **Microsoft Customer Support**. Internet Explorer starts and opens the Microsoft Support Web page.

4. Click the **Solution Centers** button on the navigation bar, and then click **Windows Internet Explorer 8** in the Internet and MSN category. The Internet Explorer Solution Center opens. See Figure 10-34.

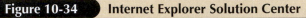

Figure 10-34 | Internet Explorer Solution Center

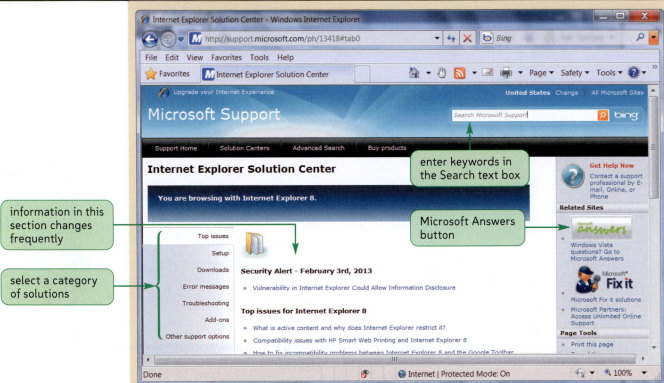

5. Scroll down to find a question or problem related to the Internet Explorer icon not appearing on the desktop.

The Internet Explorer Solution Center does not list a solution to this problem. You can try the Microsoft Answers Web site to see if it provides an answer.

To find information in Microsoft Answers:

1. In the Related Sites section, click the **Microsoft Answers** button. The Welcome to Windows Answers Web page opens. See Figure 10-35.

TIP

You can also open Windows Help and Support, and then click Microsoft Answers.

Figure 10-35 **Microsoft Answers Web site**

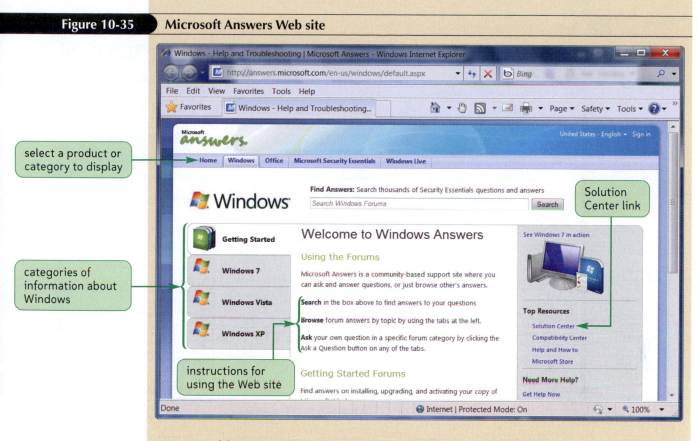

Trouble? If the Web page that opens has a different name or layout, you can still complete the following steps. Information on the Web changes frequently.

2. In the Search Windows Forums text box, type **Internet Explorer icon**, and then press the **Enter** key. A list of search results appears on a new Web page.

3. Click **Internet Explorer icon missing from the desktop?** to display a solution to the problem. See Figure 10-36.

Figure 10-36   **Answer from a community member**

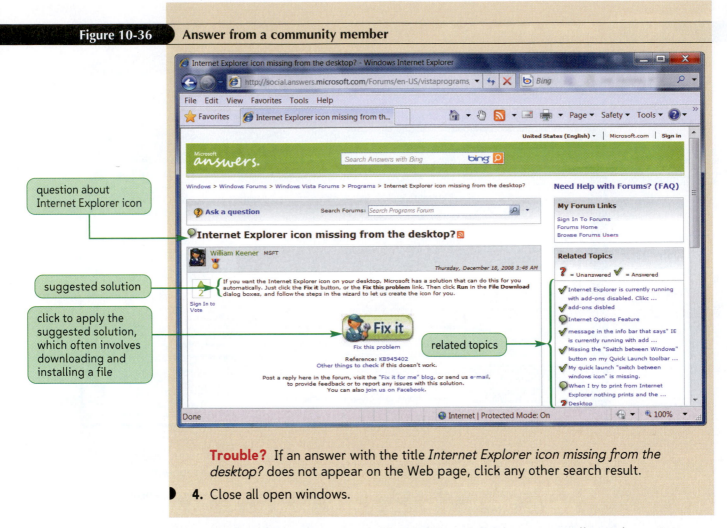

question about Internet Explorer icon

suggested solution

click to apply the suggested solution, which often involves downloading and installing a file

related topics

Trouble? If an answer with the title *Internet Explorer icon missing from the desktop?* does not appear on the Web page, click any other search result.

4. Close all open windows.

When SafeRecords employees have trouble with hardware, it usually involves printers. You'll show Amar how to troubleshoot printing errors so he can help his employees solve those problems.

Troubleshooting Printing Errors

You have already learned how to use the Devices and Printers window to install a printer and select the default printer to use with Windows programs. Besides using a trouble-shooter to detect and repair problems for you, you can also use the Devices and Printers window to troubleshoot some typical printing errors, such as problems with print quality. You need to address certain printing problems, such as running out of paper or clearing a print jam, directly at the printer. For example, when the printer runs out of paper, you need to restock the paper tray with printer paper. To clear a jam, you need to follow the printer manufacturer's recommendations, which might involve pressing a button to clear the jam or opening the printer to remove paper.

However, these printing errors can also cause problems with the **print queue**, which is the list of documents waiting to be printed. While you clear a printer jam, for example, you might need to pause and then restart the print jobs in the print queue. The print queue also displays information about documents that are waiting to print, such as the printing status, document owner, and number of pages to print. You can use the print queue to view, pause, resume, restart, and cancel print jobs.

Amar has not been able to print with a laser printer installed on his system. You'll try printing to the laser printer, and then show Amar how to troubleshoot the problem using the Devices and Printers window and the print queue. To simulate a printing problem and perform the following steps, turn off the printer to which your computer is connected, if possible. The following steps use *Laser Printer* as the name of the printer causing problems. Substitute the name of the printer you turned off for *Laser Printer*. If you cannot turn off a printer connected to your computer, read but do not perform the following steps.

To troubleshoot printing errors:

1. Turn off your printer, start Notepad, and then type your name in the Notepad document.

2. Click **File** on the menu bar, click **Print** to open the Print dialog box, click **Laser Printer** in the Select Printer list, and then click the **Print** button.

3. In the Notepad window, press the **Enter** key and type today's date.

4. Repeat Step 2 to print the document, and then minimize the Notepad window.

5. Click the **Start** button 🪟, and then click **Devices and Printers** to open the Devices and Printers window.

6. If necessary, click the **Change your view arrow button** 📄▾, and then click **Details** to display the window in Details view. Scroll down to display the Printers and Faxes category, if necessary, and then click **Laser Printer**. See Figure 10-37.

Figure 10-37   **Devices and Printers window in Details view**

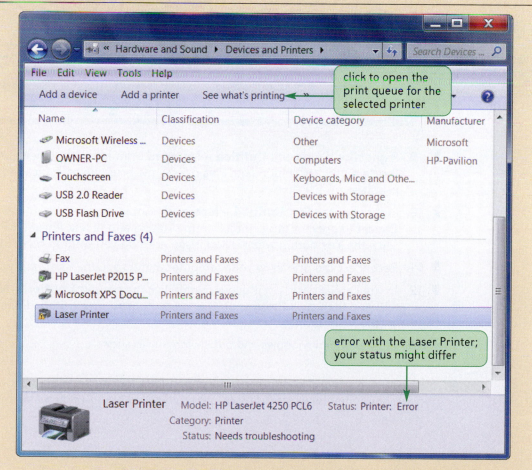

7. Double-click **Laser Printer** to open the Laser Printer window.

8. Double-click **See what's printing** to open the print queue. See Figure 10-38.

Figure 10-38   Laser Printer print queue

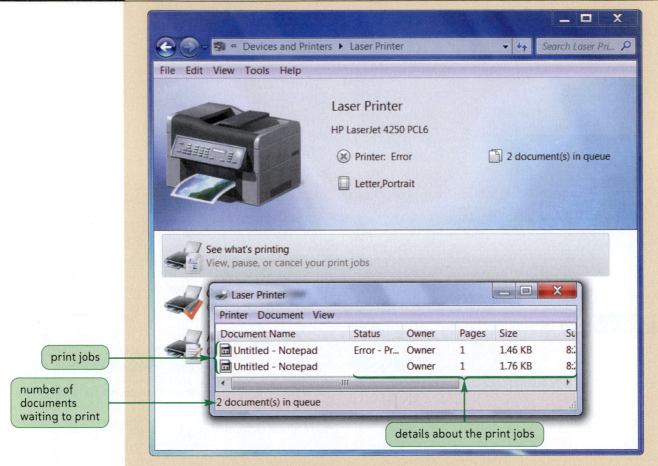

9. Right-click the second **Untitled – Notepad** print job in the queue, and then click **Pause** on the shortcut menu. This pauses the print job so you can solve the printer problem.

10. Right-click the first **Untitled – Notepad** print job in the queue, and then click **Cancel** to prevent this print job from printing and delete it from the print queue. Click the **Yes** button when asked if you are sure you want to cancel the document.

11. Reconnect the printer to your computer and turn it on, if necessary.

12. In the Laser Printer print queue, right-click the paused **Untitled – Notepad** print job, and then click **Resume** on the shortcut menu. The Notepad document prints on the Laser Printer.

13. Close all open windows without saving any changes.

Software errors also cause occasional problems for SafeRecords employees. You'll now show Amar how to report software problems to Microsoft and find and apply solutions.

Recovering from Software Errors

To keep your computer running at peak performance, you need to know how to recover from two types of software errors: those produced by programs and those produced by Windows 7 itself. You have already learned to use Task Manager to respond to a program that stops working or responding to your actions. Recall that you can open the Applications tab in Task Manager to identify unresponsive programs and then click the End Task button to close the program. Another way to recover from software errors is to use the Programs and Features window to change the installed features of a program or to try to repair the installation. (To do so, you open Control Panel, click Programs, click Programs and Features, click the troublesome program, and then click the Repair button.) A third way to respond to software problems is to report the problem to Microsoft and have Windows check for a solution. Windows then notifies you if you should take steps to prevent or solve the problem, or if Microsoft needs more information to find or create a solution.

REFERENCE

Checking for Solutions to Software Problems

- Open the Action Center window. (Click the Action Center icon in the notification area of the taskbar, and then click Open Action Center.)
- Expand the Maintenance section, if necessary, and then click Check for solutions.
- Follow any steps Windows provides.

In addition to reporting problems and checking for solutions, you can use the Action Center window to check for new solutions to past problems, to view your problem history, to change maintenance settings, and to produce a reliability report.

Reporting and Solving Software Errors

You can report software problems and check for solutions in three ways: set Windows to report problems and check for solutions automatically, check for solutions only when a problem occurs, or report problems and check for solutions at any time. When you report a software problem, Windows assembles and sends a description of the problem to Microsoft to try to match the description to a known solution. If Windows finds a solution, it indicates what steps you can take to solve the problem or to find more information. If a solution is not available yet, Microsoft stores the problem report and uses it to find or create a new solution. If you have Windows set to check for solutions automatically, it notifies you about steps you can take immediately after a problem occurs. If Windows is not set to check for solutions automatically, you can manually check for a solution.

Although Amar has sent reports to Microsoft about software problems, he hasn't used the Action Center window yet to repair a software installation. You'll show him how to do so next. First, however, you want to make sure that Windows is set to report software problems and check for solutions automatically on Amar's computer.

To set Windows to check for software solutions automatically:

▶ 1. Click the **Action Center** icon 🏳 in the notification area of the taskbar, and then click **Open Action Center**. The Action Center window opens. Expand the Maintenance section, if necessary. See Figure 10-39.

Figure 10-39 **Maintenance options in the Action Center window**

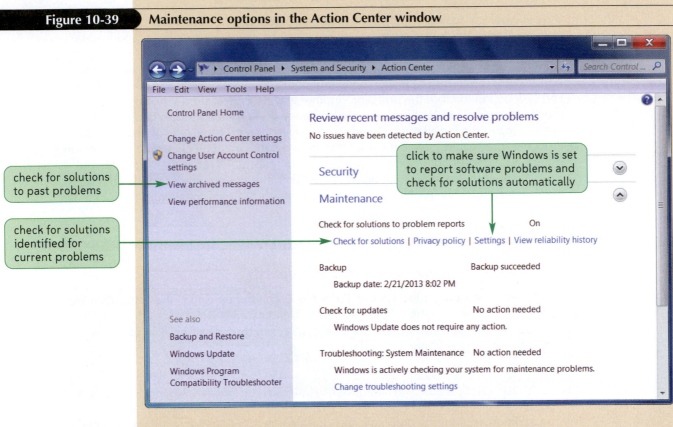

2. Click **Settings** to open the Problem Reporting Settings window.

3. Click the **Automatically check for solutions (recommended)** option button, if necessary, to select it.

> **Trouble?** If you cannot change settings in the Problem Reporting Settings window, skip Step 3.

4. Click the **OK** button.

Now you are sure that Windows will notify Amar about any steps he can take to prevent or solve software problems. You can view any problems that Windows has identified with Amar's software, and then check for new solutions.

To view problems Windows has identified:

1. Click **Maintenance** to expand the Maintenance section in the Action Center window.

2. Click **View archived messages** in the left pane. The Archived Messages window opens. See Figure 10-40.

Figure 10-40   **Problems Windows has identified**

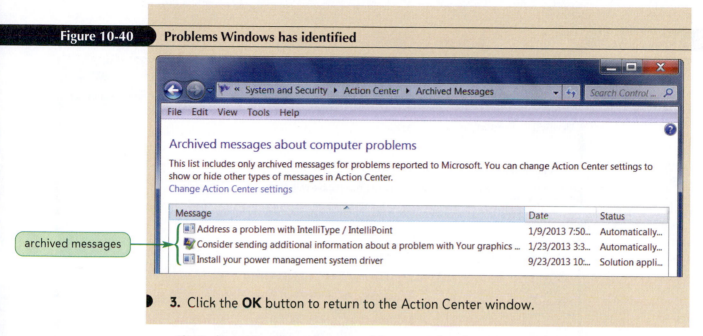

archived messages

3. Click the **OK** button to return to the Action Center window.

If Windows identifies software problems, as it has for Amar's computer, you can use the Action Center window to check for solutions. You'll show Amar how to check for new solutions and then use them to install updated drivers.

To check for new solutions and install them:

1. Click **Maintenance** to expand the Maintenance section in the Action Center window, if necessary.

2. Click **Check for solutions**. Windows contacts Microsoft online and searches for solutions. This might take a few minutes if Windows has identified many problems on your computer. Windows then lists the solutions in the Action Center window.

Trouble? If Windows 7 displays *No new solutions found* instead of listing new solutions, click the Close button.

3. Double-click a solution to display details about it. See Figure 10-41, which shows a solution to a driver problem.

Figure 10-41 | **Solution details**

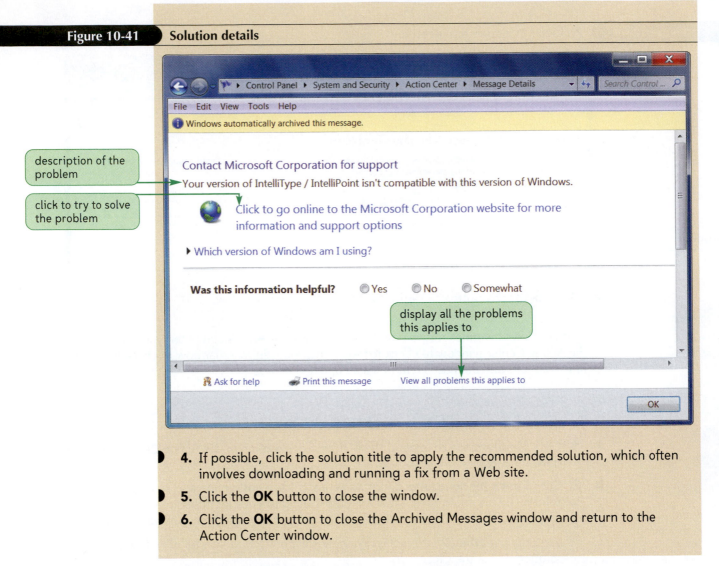

description of the problem

click to try to solve the problem

display all the problems this applies to

4. If possible, click the solution title to apply the recommended solution, which often involves downloading and running a fix from a Web site.

5. Click the **OK** button to close the window.

6. Click the **OK** button to close the Archived Messages window and return to the Action Center window.

The solution to Amar's problem is to download software to update the driver for his mouse. Because you often need to restart a computer after applying this type of solution, you advise Amar to wait to apply this fix until he doesn't need his computer for awhile.

Viewing Reliability History

The Reliability Monitor window includes a chart tracking the stability of your computer. It maintains up to a year of history for system stability and reliability events. For example, this tool tracks program failures, such as a program shutting down unexpectedly, and problems with the hard disk and memory. It then displays these events on a chart, assigning each event a number from 1 (least stable) to 10 (most stable). You'll show Amar how to use this tool to identify events that affected the stability and reliability of his computer.

To view the System Stability chart:

1. Expand the Maintenance section of the Action Center window, if necessary, and then click **View reliability history**. The Reliability Monitor window opens and displays a chart.

2. Click the **Weeks** link to view the chart by weeks. See Figure 10-42. The chart and other system information on your computer will differ.

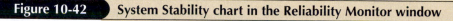

Figure 10-42 | **System Stability chart in the Reliability Monitor window**

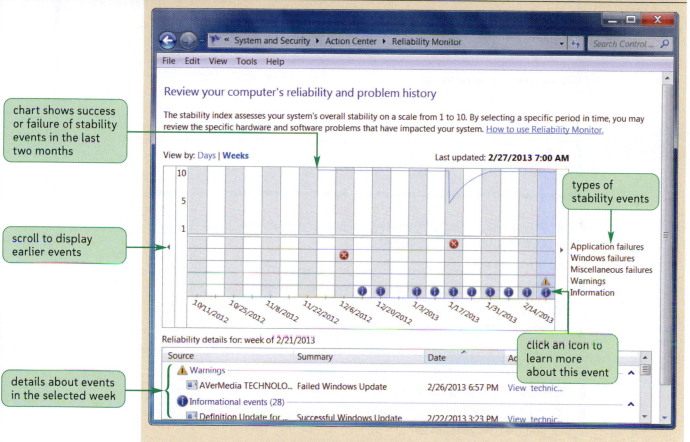

chart shows success or failure of stability events in the last two months

scroll to display earlier events

types of stability events

click an icon to learn more about this event

details about events in the selected week

3. Click an **Information** icon on the chart. Details about that event appear in the Reliability details list. See Figure 10-43.

Figure 10-43   **Viewing information about a system stability event**

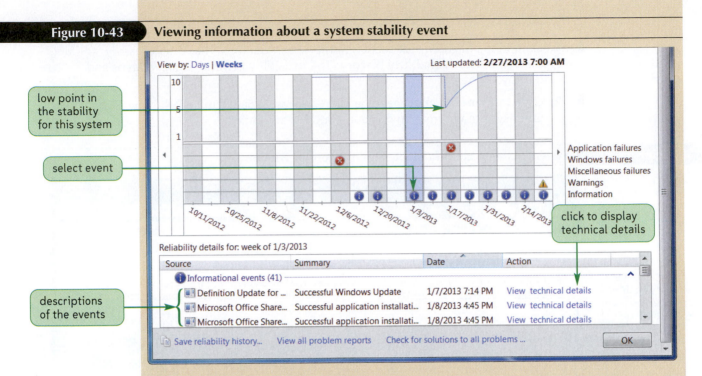

4. If possible, click the first **View technical details** link in the Action column to view details about the problem or event.

5. Click the **OK** button to return to the Reliability Monitor window.

6. If possible, click a **Critical** icon ⊗ in the chart.

7. In the Action column, click **Check for a solution**. The Problem Reporting dialog box opens and checks for solutions online.

   Trouble? If the Action column does not include a Check for a solution link, click any link in the Action column.

8. Close the dialog box to return to the Reliability Monitor window.

9. Click the **OK** button to close the Reliability Monitor window and return to the Action Center window.

The chart showed that the stability of Amar's computer is often 10, though it dipped as low as 5. Overall, this means his system has been fairly stable and reliable over the past year.

Recovering the Operating System

If Windows 7 doesn't start correctly or runs erratically, you can try the troubleshooting steps shown in Figure 10-44 to solve the problem. These solutions are listed in order of complexity, with the simplest solution listed first.

Figure 10-44   **Recovering the operating system**

Tool	Description	How to Access
System Restore	You can use System Restore to restore your computer's system files to an earlier point in time.	1. Click the Start button, point to All Programs, click Accessories, click System Tools, and then click System Restore. 2. Click the Next button twice to accept the most recent restore point. 3. Click the Finish button.
Last Known Good Configuration	This advanced startup option starts Windows using the registry settings and drives that were in use the last time the computer started successfully.	1. Restart your computer. 2. Press and hold the F8 key before the Windows logo appears. 3. On the Advanced Boot Options screen, select Last Known Good Configuration, and then press the Enter key.
Safe mode	If the Last Known Good Configuration option doesn't work, use safe mode to try to identify and fix the problem. If your computer starts only in safe mode, try disabling recently installed hardware or programs.	1. Restart your computer. 2. Press and hold the F8 key before the Windows logo appears. 3. On the Advanced Boot Options screen, select Safe Mode, and then press the Enter key.
Startup Repair	In extreme cases, you can use Startup Repair to fix missing or damaged system files that might prevent Windows from starting.	1. Insert the Windows installation disc. 2. Restart your computer. 3. Select your language settings, and then click the Next button. 4. Click Repair your computer. 5. Select the operating system to repair, and then click the Next button. 6. On the System Recovery Options menu, click Startup Repair.
Reinstall Windows	If your system has been severely damaged, you might need to reinstall Windows. A custom (clean) installation of Windows permanently deletes all of the files on your computer and reinstalls Windows, so only use this option if all other recovery options have been unsuccessful. After the installation, you must reinstall your programs and restore your files from backup copies.	1. Insert the Windows installation disc. 2. Restart your computer. 3. On the Install Windows page, follow any instructions, and then click Install now. 4. Follow the instructions that appear on your screen.

Last Known Good Configuration, Safe mode, and Startup Repair are advanced startup options that let you select settings before Windows 7 starts. **Last Known Good Configuration** uses the most recent system settings that worked correctly. Every time you turn your computer off and Windows shuts down successfully, it saves important system settings in the registry. If those new settings are faulty, you can bypass the settings when you restart the computer by selecting the Last Known Good Configuration option on the advanced startup menu. When you do, Windows loads the settings it saved the second-to-last time you shut down the computer (the time before you shut down the computer after selecting the faulty new system settings.) You can then disable a device or uninstall a program that is causing problems. Be sure you select the Last Known Good Configuration option before you log on to Windows—you must press the F8 key right after the computer starts and before Windows does. If you log on to Windows or start and wait for the desktop to appear, the Last Known Good Configuration will include the faulty new settings.

Safe mode is a troubleshooting option for Windows that starts your computer with only basic services and functionality. If a problem you experienced earlier does not reappear when you start Windows in safe mode, you can eliminate the default settings and basic device drivers as possible causes. While in safe mode, you can use Device Manager to disable a problematic device or restore a driver to its previous version. You can also restore your computer to an earlier point using System Restore.

Startup Repair is a Windows recovery tool that can fix problems such as missing or damaged system files, which might prevent Windows from starting. This tool is provided on the Windows installation disc and, depending on your computer, might also be stored on your hard disk.

INSIGHT

Selecting a Restore Point or the Last Known Good Configuration

If your operating system is running erratically, the two least disruptive solutions to try are reverting to a restore point or using the Last Known Good Configuration. These two options are often confused. Choose System Restore when you notice your system behaving strangely and Windows is still running. Then you can select a restore point to return the system to an earlier point in time when things worked correctly. Unlike Last Known Good Configuration, you can undo the changes made with System Restore, so troubleshoot operating system problems by selecting a restore point first. Choose Last Known Good Configuration if you can't start Windows, but it started correctly the last time you turned on the computer.

Using the Problem Steps Recorder

If you are having trouble performing a task in Windows, you can use the Problem Steps Recorder to record the steps you take on a computer. The Problem Steps Recorder captures the screen each time you click, saves the screen image, and then includes a text description of where you clicked. After you capture these steps, you can save them to a zipped file and then send it to a support professional or someone else helping you with a computer problem.

When you record steps on your computer, anything you type is not recorded. If what you type is an important part of recreating the problem you're trying to solve, use the Comment feature to highlight where the problem is occurring. You can also use the Comment feature to provide other types of explanations or descriptions.

Amar is having trouble installing a driver for a hardware device. He has been using Windows Update to download and install the driver, but each time he tries, Windows reports the update failed. You'll show him how to use the Problem Steps Recorder to record the steps he takes to update the driver. He can then send the report to other system experts at SafeRecords to see if they can help him troubleshoot the problem.

To use the Problem Steps Recorder:

▶ 1. In the Action Center window, click in the **Search Control Panel** box, type **problem steps**, and then click **Record steps to reproduce a problem** in the search results. The Problem Steps Recorder window opens. See Figure 10-45.

Figure 10-45   **Problem Steps Recorder window**

click to start recording your steps

2. Click the **Start Record** button. The Problem Steps Recorder starts recording your steps.

   Trouble? If a Problem Steps Recorder warning dialog box opens indicating you might need to run the Problem Steps Recorder as an administrator, click the OK button.

3. Click the **Start** button 🌐 on the taskbar, point to **All Programs**, and then click **Windows Update**.

4. Click the link for optional updates, and then click the **check box** for an optional update. See Figure 10-46.

Figure 10-46	Recording the steps to install an optional Windows update

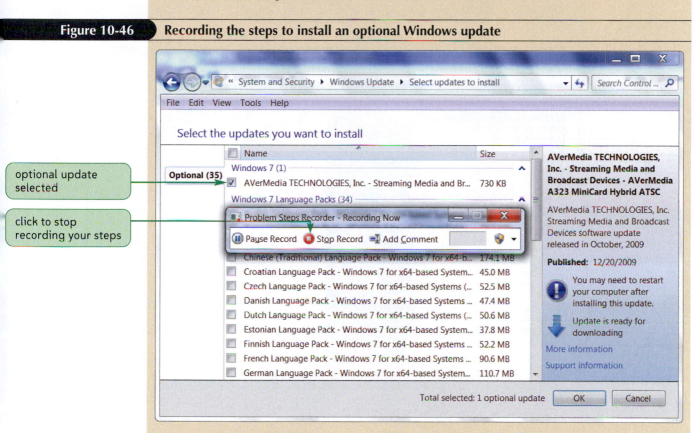

optional update selected

click to stop recording your steps

5. Click the **OK** button, and then click **Install updates**. Wait while Windows prepares and then installs the update or fails to do so.

6. In the Problem Steps Recorder window, click the **Stop Record** button. The Save As dialog box opens.

7. Save the recorded steps as a Zip file named **Update** in the Tutorial.10\Tutorial folder provided with your Data Files.

8. Close the Problem Steps Recorder and then the Windows Update window.

Before you send the zipped report to someone else at SafeRecords, you want to review the steps the Problem Steps Recorder captured.

To review the Problem Steps Recorder report:

1. Navigate to the Tutorial.10\Tutorial folder.

> **2.** Double-click the **Update** Zip folder, and then double-click the problem file. (The filename starts with *Problem*.) The steps open in your browser. Scroll down to review the steps. See Figure 10-47.

Figure 10-47   **Captured steps displayed in an HTML document**

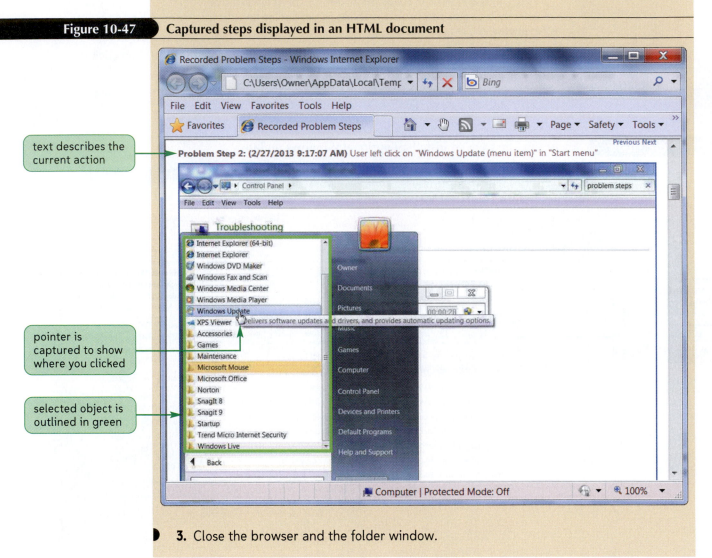

text describes the current action

pointer is captured to show where you clicked

selected object is outlined in green

> **3.** Close the browser and the folder window.

You will e-mail this problem to another SafeRecords employee later.

Requesting and Managing Remote Assistance

If you are experiencing a computer problem and can't find a solution yourself, you can use Windows Remote Assistance to have someone show you how to fix a problem. Windows Remote Assistance is a convenient way for someone you trust, such as a friend or technical support person, to connect to your computer and step you through a solution—even if that person isn't nearby. To help ensure that only people you invite can connect to your computer using Windows Remote Assistance, all sessions are encrypted and password protected.

To request remote assistance, send an instant message or e-mail to invite someone to connect to your computer. After connecting, that person can view your computer screen and chat with you about what you both see on your computer screen. With your permission, your helper can even use a mouse and keyboard to control your computer and show you how to fix a problem. You can also help someone else the same way.

Before you can use Windows Remote Assistance to connect two computers, you must enable the feature. You'll show Amar how to enable Remote Assistance connections so that he can request help from you and vice versa.

To enable Remote Assistance connections:

1. In the Address bar of the Control Panel window, click the **arrow button** ▶ after Control Panel, and then click **System and Security**.

2. In the System and Security window, click **System**. The System window opens.

3. Click **Remote settings** in the left pane. The System Properties dialog box opens to the Remote tab.

   Trouble? If a User Account Control dialog box opens requesting your permission or a password to continue, enter the password or click the Continue button.

4. If necessary, click the **Allow Remote Assistance connections to this computer** box to insert a check mark.

TIP

Windows automatically allows the Remote Assistance program through Windows Firewall so you can receive assistance.

When you allow Remote Assistance connections to your computer, you can send and receive Remote Assistance invitations using e-mail or a file. You can also use instant messaging to correspond with your Remote Assistance partner. To disable Remote Assistance invitations, you remove the check mark from the Allow Remote Assistance connections to this computer box on the Remote tab of the System Properties dialog box.

You can also use the Remote tab in the System Properties dialog box to access advanced Remote Assistance settings. For security reasons, you might want to limit the amount of time that a Remote Assistance invitation is available so that an unauthorized person cannot control your computer without your knowledge.

To select advanced Remote Assistance settings:

1. On the Remote tab of the System Properties dialog box, click the **Advanced** button. The Remote Assistance Settings dialog box opens. See Figure 10-48.

Figure 10-48   **Remote Assistance Settings dialog box**

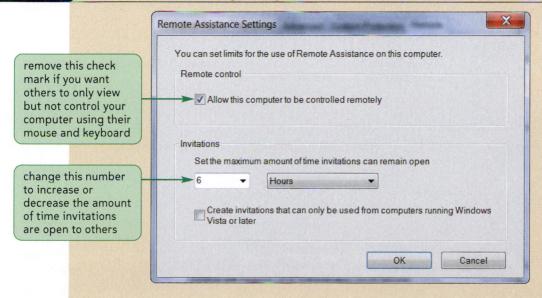

remove this check mark if you want others to only view but not control your computer using their mouse and keyboard

change this number to increase or decrease the amount of time invitations are open to others

2. Click **6** in the Set the maximum amount of time invitations can remain open box, and then type **4** to reduce the amount of time a Remote Assistance invitation is available.

3. Click the **OK** button to close the Remote Assistance Settings dialog box.

4. Click the **OK** button to close the System Properties dialog box.

Although Amar doesn't need to establish a Remote Assistance session now, you'll show him how to request assistance using the Windows Remote Assistance Wizard.

Requesting Remote Assistance

When you need help from someone else, you can request Remote Assistance using the Windows Remote Assistance Wizard. The easiest way to start this wizard is from the Windows Help and Support window.

You'll show Amar how to use the Windows Remote Assistance Wizard to send you an e-mail message inviting you to help him troubleshoot a problem on his computer. When you perform the following steps, substitute the e-mail address of a friend or classmate for the e-mail address used in the steps.

TIP

You can also start Remote Assistance by clicking the Start button, pointing to All Programs, clicking Maintenance, and then clicking Windows Remote Assistance.

To request Remote Assistance:

1. Click the **Start** button , and then click **Help and Support**. The Windows Help and Support window opens.

2. Click the **Ask** button on the toolbar.

3. In the Ask a person for help section of the window, click **Windows Remote Assistance**. The Windows Remote Assistance Wizard starts. See Figure 10-49.

Figure 10-49   **Starting the Windows Remote Assistance Wizard**

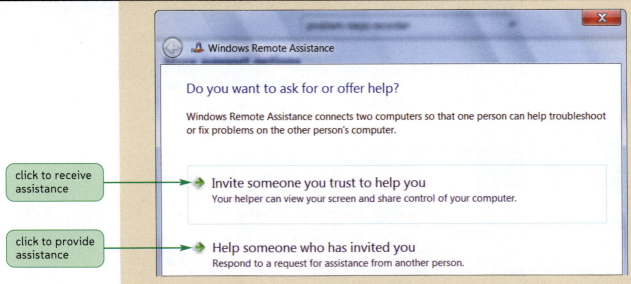

click to receive assistance

click to provide assistance

4. Click **Invite someone you trust to help you**. The next wizard dialog box opens, asking how you want to invite someone to help you.

5. Click **Use e-mail to send an invitation**. Remote Assistance opens an invitation e-mail in your default e-mail program. See Figure 10-50.

Figure 10-50 | **E-mail with Remote Assistance invitation**

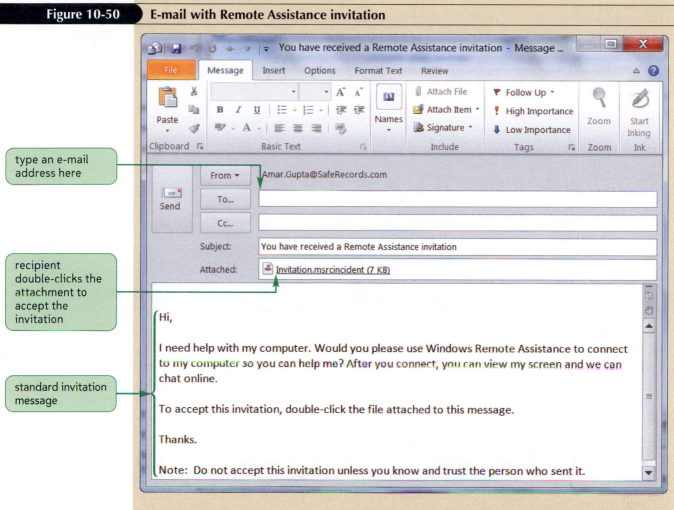

type an e-mail address here

recipient double-clicks the attachment to accept the invitation

standard invitation message

Trouble? If you do not have a default e-mail program set up on your computer, Windows asks you to select an e-mail program to use. Select the program and wait for the invitation e-mail to open, and then continue with Step 6.

6. Enter the e-mail address of a friend or classmate, such as **Helper@SafeRecords.com**, in the To box, and then click the **Send** button. A window opens displaying a connection password. Wait for your helper to receive and open the invitation. Tell your helper the password, which he or she enters to connect to your computer. A Remote Assistance dialog box opens on your computer, asking if you want to allow your helper to connect to your computer.

7. Click the **Yes** button to allow the connection. Your helper can now see your desktop. Windows might also change the theme to Windows Basic. See Figure 10-51.

Figure 10-51   Remote Assistance in action

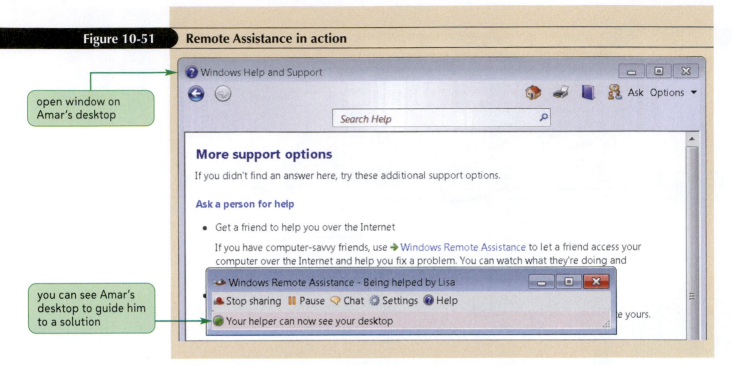

open window on Amar's desktop

you can see Amar's desktop to guide him to a solution

You can now perform the steps that you are having trouble with. Your helper can see your computer screen and chat with you (using the online Chat tool). With your permission, your helper can control your computer to show you how to fix the problem.

To end the Remote Assistance session:

1. If your helper clicked the Request control button in the Remote Assistance window on their computer, click the **Stop sharing** button. Your helper no longer has access to your computer.

2. Close the Remote Assistance window to end the Remote Assistance session.

3. Close all other open windows.

Now that you're finished helping Amar improve his computer's performance and troubleshoot system problems, you should restore your system settings.

Restoring Your Settings

If you are working in a computer lab or on a computer other than your own, complete the steps in this section to restore the original settings on your computer. If a User Account Control dialog box opens requesting an Administrator password or confirmation after you perform any of the following steps, enter the password or click the Continue button.

To restore your settings:

1. Click the **Start** button, click **Control Panel**, click **System and Security**, and then click **Check the Windows Experience Index**.

2. Click **Adjust visual effects** in the left pane.

3. Click the **Let Windows choose what's best for my computer** option button, and then click the **OK** button to close the Performance Options dialog box.

4. Open the Computer window, right-click the **USB flash drive**, and then click **Properties** on the shortcut menu.

5. Click the **ReadyBoost** tab, and then click **Do not use this device**. Click the **OK** button to close the Properties dialog box.

6. In the Control Panel window, navigate to the System window. Click **Remote settings** in the left pane.

7. On the Remote tab of the Remote Assistance Settings dialog box, restore your original settings in the Remote Assistance and Remote Desktop sections.

8. Click the **Advanced** button, and then restore your original setting, which is **6** by default, for the maximum amount of time Remote Assistance invitations can stay open. Click the **OK** button to close the Remote Assistance Settings dialog box.

9. Click the **OK** button to close the System Properties dialog box.

10. Close all open windows.

Session 10.2 Quick Check

REVIEW

1. The Microsoft _____ are repositories of support information for Microsoft product users, and include Help topics and articles that provide troubleshooting steps to help you solve or identify a problem.

2. True or False. A print queue is a list of printers waiting to provide printing services.

3. What types of problems does the Reliability Monitor window track?

4. True or False. The Problem Steps Recorder captures the screen each time you click, saves the screen image, and then includes a text description of where you clicked.

5. Besides using Task Manager to end a task or the Programs and Features window to repair a software installation, what else can you do to troubleshoot a software problem?

6. Which is a more complex or extreme solution to a Windows 7 startup problem: Last Known Good Configuration or Startup Repair?

7. If you are experiencing a computer problem and can't find a solution yourself, why might you use Windows Remote Assistance?

Practice the skills you learned in the tutorial using the same case scenario.

PRACTICE

Review Assignments

There are no Data Files needed for the Review Assignments.

Now that you've helped Amar Gupta improve system performance and troubleshoot hardware and software problems on his computer, he asks you to show another SafeRecords manager, Lani Eggers, how to optimize her computer. Complete the following steps, noting your original settings so you can restore them later:

1. Open the Control Panel, open the Performance Information and Tools window, and then rerun the assessment tool to calculate your computer's Windows Experience Index base score. Press the Alt+Print Screen keys to capture an image of the window. Paste the image in a new Paint file, and save the file as **Base Score** in the Tutorial.10\ Review folder provided with your Data Files.

2. To improve performance, adjust the visual effects on your computer. Do not animate controls and elements inside windows. In addition, do not animate windows when minimizing and maximizing. With the Performance Options dialog box open to the appropriate tab, press the Alt+Print Screen keys to capture an image of the window. Paste the image in a new Paint file, and save the file as **Visual** in the Tutorial.10\ Review folder provided with your Data Files.

3. Open the Advanced Tools window to display any issues that Windows identifies as detracting from the performance of your computer. Press the Alt+Print Screen keys to capture an image of the window. Paste the image in a new Paint file, and save the file as **Advanced** in the Tutorial.10\Review folder provided with your Data Files.

4. Open the Event Viewer window and display details about a critical event. If your Event Viewer window does not list any critical events, display details about an error. Press the Alt+Print Screen keys to capture an image of the window. Paste the image in a new Paint file, and save the file as **Critical** in the Tutorial.10\Review folder provided with your Data Files.

5. Open the Task Manager dialog box and display the processes running for your user account. Open the Properties dialog box for a process and display the Details tab. Arrange the dialog boxes to completely display both of them, and then press the Print Screen key to capture an image of the desktop. Paste the image in a new Paint file, and save the file as **Process** in the Tutorial.10\Review folder provided with your Data Files. Close the Properties dialog box for the process.

6. Display graphs of CPU and RAM usage in the Task Manager dialog box. Press the Alt+Print Screen keys to capture an image of the dialog box. Paste the image in a new Paint file, and save the file as **Graphs** in the Tutorial.10\Review folder provided with your Data Files.

7. Use the System Information window to display a system summary that shows details about the display on your computer. Press the Alt+Print Screen keys to capture an image of the window. Paste the image in a new Paint file, and save the file as **Summary** in the Tutorial.10\Review folder provided with your Data Files.

8. Display the size of the paging file on your computer. Press the Alt+Print Screen keys to capture an image of the dialog box. Paste the image in a new Paint file, and save the file as **Paging** in the Tutorial.10\Review folder provided with your Data Files.

9. Generate a system health report for your computer. Save the report as **System** in the Tutorial.10\Review folder provided with your Data Files.

10. Increase the memory capacity of your system by turning on ReadyBoost. Select the maximum amount of available space on your USB flash drive to reserve for boosting your system speed. Press the Alt+Print Screen keys to capture an image of the dialog box. Paste the image in a new Paint file, and save the file as **ReadyBoost** in the Tutorial.10\Review folder provided with your Data Files.

11. Search the Microsoft Windows 7 Solution Center for articles about ReadyBoost. Display the search results, and then press the Alt+Print Screen keys to capture an image of the window. Paste the image in a new Paint file, and save the file as **Solutions** in the Tutorial.10\Review folder provided with your Data Files.

12. Use the Action Center window to view the archived problem messages on your computer. Press the Alt+Print Screen keys to capture an image of the window. Paste the image in a new Paint file, and save the file as **Problems** in the Tutorial.10\Review folder provided with your Data Files.

13. Display your computer's reliability and problem history. View this information by Weeks. Select the current week, and then press the Alt+Print Screen keys to capture an image of the window. Paste the image in a new Paint file, and save the file as **Reliability** in the Tutorial.10\Review folder provided with your Data Files.

14. Use the Problem Steps Recorder to record the steps for opening an accessory on your computer, such as the Calculator. Save the steps in a Zip file named **Accessory** in the Tutorial.10\Review folder.

15. Set the maximum amount of time Remote Assistance invitations can stay open to **5** hours. Press the Alt+Print Screen keys to capture an image of the dialog box. Paste the image in a new Paint file, and save the file as **Remote** in the Tutorial.10\Review folder provided with your Data Files.

16. Restore your computer by completing the following tasks:

    a. Adjust the visual effects on your computer by letting Windows choose what's best for your computer.

    b. Turn off ReadyBoost.

    c. Return the maximum amount of time Remote Assistance invitations can stay open to its original setting, which is 6 hours by default.

17. Close all open windows.

18. Submit the results of the preceding steps to your instructor, either in printed or electronic form, as requested.

Use your skills to optimize computers for a marketing research company.

APPLY

Case Problem 1

There are no Data Files needed for this Case Problem.

Bodette Partners   Kathleen Bodette owns a marketing research company named Bodette Partners in Salinas, California. Kathleen hired you as a computer specialist and is particularly interested in getting your help to improve the performance of her company's computers. She also wants to know how to find troubleshooting information for problems with Windows Media Player. Complete the following steps, noting your original settings so you can restore them later:

1. Display details about your computer, including its Windows Experience Index base score, processor, and memory. Press the Alt+Print Screen keys to capture an image of the window. Paste the image in a new Paint file, and save the file as **Details** in the Tutorial.10\Case1 folder provided with your Data Files.

2. To improve performance, adjust the visual effects on your computer to deselect settings that involve fading or sliding menus into view and fading or sliding ToolTips into view. With the Performance Options dialog box open to the appropriate tab, press the Alt+Print Screen keys to capture an image of the window. Paste the image in a new Paint file, and save the file as **Fade** in the Tutorial.10\Case1 folder provided with your Data Files.

3. Open the Event Viewer window and display details about a warning. Press the Alt+Print Screen keys to capture an image of the window. Paste the image in a new Paint file, and save the file as **Warning** in the Tutorial.10\Case1 folder provided with your Data Files.

4. Display a resource overview, including graphs of CPU, Disk, Network, and Memory usage. Press the Alt+Print Screen keys to capture an image of the window. Paste the image in a new Paint file, and save the file as **Overview** in the Tutorial.10\Case1 folder provided with your Data Files.

5. Open the Task Manager dialog box and display the programs running on your computer. Press the Alt+Print Screen keys to capture an image of the window. Paste the image in a new Paint file, and save the file as **TaskMan** in the Tutorial.10\Case1 folder provided with your Data Files.

6. In the System Information window, display a list of hardware resource conflicts. Press the Alt+Print Screen keys to capture an image of the window. Paste the image in a new Paint file, and save the file as **Conflicts** in the Tutorial.10\Case1 folder provided with your Data Files.

7. Increase the memory capacity of your system by turning on ReadyBoost. Select the minimum amount of available space on your USB flash drive to reserve for boosting your system speed. Press the Alt+Print Screen keys to capture an image of the dialog box. Paste the image in a new Paint file, and save the file as **Minimum** in the Tutorial.10\Case1 folder provided with your Data Files.

8. Use a Windows troubleshooter to find troubleshooting information about common problems with settings in the Windows Media Player program. In the wizard, do not have Windows apply repairs automatically. Press the Alt+Print Screen keys to capture an image of the wizard listing a suggested fix for Windows Media Player settings. Paste the image in a new Paint file, and save the file as **Media Player** in the Tutorial.10\Case1 folder provided with your Data Files.

9. Search the Microsoft Solution Centers for Help topics and articles about Windows Media Player. Display the Windows Media Player Solution Center, and then press the Alt+Print Screen keys to capture an image of the window. Paste the image in a new Paint file, and save the file as **WMP** in the Tutorial.10\Case1 folder provided with your Data Files.

10. Search the Microsoft Answers Web site to find information about playing MP3 files with Windows Media Player. With the first page of answers displayed, press the Alt+Print Screen keys to capture an image of the window. Paste the image in a new Paint file, and save the file as **MP3 Answers** in the Tutorial.10\Case1 folder provided with your Data Files.

11. Start the Windows Remote Assistance Wizard and prepare to send an invitation to your instructor. Press the Alt+Print Screen keys to capture an image of the open e-mail invitation. Paste the image in a new Paint file, and save the file as **Invitation** in the Tutorial.10\Case1 folder provided with your Data Files.

12. Restore your computer by adjusting the visual effects so that Windows chooses what's best for your computer. Turn off ReadyBoost.

13. Close all open windows.

14. Submit the results of the preceding steps to your instructor, either in printed or electronic form, as requested.

Use your skills to improve the performance of a real estate group's computers.

APPLY

Case Problem 2

There are no Data Files needed for this Case Problem.

CG Real Estate Group   Luis Cortes and Alex Gavin are partners in CG Real Estate Group in Santa Fe, New Mexico. Luis and Alex upgraded their computers to Windows 7 a few months ago, and have noticed that the computers are not running as efficiently as they were when Windows 7 was first installed. As the general manager of CG Real Estate Group, you share responsibility for optimizing the computers. Luis asks you to help him improve the performance of his computer and to troubleshoot problems he's having playing audio files. Complete the following steps, noting your original settings so you can restore them later:

1. Find the hardware component with the lowest Windows Experience Index subscore on your computer, and then display details about it. Press the Alt+Print Screen keys to capture an image of the window. Paste the image in a new Paint file, and save the file as **Lowest** in the Tutorial.10\Case2 folder provided with your Data Files.

⊕ **EXPLORE**

2. Find more information about the Windows Experience Index online. Press the Alt+Print Screen keys to capture an image of the Web page displaying this information. Paste the image in a new Paint file, and save the file as **Index** in the Tutorial.10\Case2 folder provided with your Data Files.

⊕ **EXPLORE**

3. Open Task Manager to display a list of running programs. Sort the list of processes by memory, with the process requiring the most amount of memory at the top of the list. Press the Alt+Print Screen keys to capture an image of the dialog box. Paste the image in a new Paint file, and save the file as **Memory** in the Tutorial.10\Case2 folder provided with your Data Files.

4. Open the Event Viewer window and display details about an error. Press the Alt+Print Screen keys to capture an image of the window. Paste the image in a new Paint file, and save the file as **Error** in the Tutorial.10\Case2 folder provided with your Data Files.

5. Open the Performance Monitor window and graph the percentage of time your processor is working. Add a counter to graph the percentage of paging file usage. Change the color of the % Usage counter to blue. After the Performance Monitor graphs the two counters for a few seconds, press the Alt+Print Screen keys to capture an image of the window. Paste the image in a new Paint file, and save the file as **Counters** in the Tutorial.10\Case2 folder provided with your Data Files.

6. In the System Information window, display details about the sound devices on your computer. Press the Alt+Print Screen keys to capture an image of the window. Paste the image in a new Paint file, and save the file as **Sound Device** in the Tutorial.10\Case2 folder provided with your Data Files.

7. Open the Action Center window and display the archived problem messages. Display the solution to a message, and then press the Alt+Print Screen keys to capture an image of the window. Paste the image in a new Paint file, and save the file as **Message Details** in the Tutorial.10\Case2 folder provided with your Data Files.

8. Use a Windows troubleshooter to troubleshoot problems with playing audio files. In the wizard, do not have Windows apply repairs automatically. Press the Alt+Print Screen keys to capture an image of the window listing the results. Paste the image in a new Paint file, and save the file as **Sound** in the Tutorial.10\Case2 folder provided with your Data Files.

9. Search the Microsoft Solution Centers for articles about sound cards. Display the search results, and then press the Alt+Print Screen keys to capture an image of the window. Paste the image in a new Paint file, and save the file as **Sound Cards** in the Tutorial.10\Case2 folder provided with your Data Files.

10. Use the Problem Steps Recorder to record the steps of opening the Control Panel, clicking Hardware and Sound, and then clicking Sound to open the Sound dialog box. Save the recorded steps as a file named **Sound Problem** in the Tutorial.10\Case2 folder provided with your Data Files.

11. Close all open windows.

12. Submit the results of the preceding steps to your instructor, either in printed or electronic form, as requested.

Extend what you've learned to optimize computers for a business form processor.

CHALLENGE

Case Problem 3

There are no Data Files needed for this Case Problem.

Volunteer Business Forms Kelly Sato manages Volunteer Business Forms in Chattanooga, Tennessee, and works primarily on her Windows 7 computer. Recently, she has noticed that new software is running erratically and that Windows is starting slowly after she shuts it down. As her office assistant, you offer to help her solve these problems. Complete the following steps, noting your original settings so you can restore them later:

EXPLORE 1. Display details about your computer, including its Windows Experience Index base score, subscores, processor, memory, and storage details. Open a Windows Help and Support window explaining what these scores mean. Display details about your computer's subscores. Press the Alt+Print Screen keys to capture an image of the Windows Help and Support window. Paste the image in a new Paint file, and save the file as **Subscores** in the Tutorial.10\Case3 folder provided with your Data Files.

EXPLORE 2. In the System Information window, display a list of running tasks. Note the names of tasks listed in the right pane.

EXPLORE 3. Open Task Manager to display the currently running processes. Sort the processes alphabetically by Image Name. Click a filename you displayed in the previous step. Arrange the windows on the desktop so you can see the System Information and Task Manager windows clearly. Press the Print Screen key to capture an image of the desktop. Paste the image in a new Paint file, and save the file as **Tasks** in the Tutorial.10\Case3 folder provided with your Data Files.

4. Display system information about print jobs on your computer. Use the Devices and Printers window to display the same information about print jobs. Arrange the windows on the desktop so you can see the System Information window and the dialog box showing the print queue. Press the Print Screen key to capture an image of the desktop. Paste the image in a new Paint file, and save the file as **Printing** in the Tutorial.10\Case3 folder provided with your Data Files.

5. Open the Reliability Monitor and select a day when the reliability index is less than 10. Press the Alt+Print Screen keys to capture an image of the window. Paste the image in a new Paint file, and save the file as **History** in the Tutorial.10\Case3 folder provided with your Data Files.

EXPLORE 6. Open the Performance Monitor window and graph the percentage of time your processor is working. Add a Memory counter to graph the percentage of committed bytes in use. Change the color of the Memory counter to green. After the Performance Monitor graphs the two counters for a few seconds, press the Alt+Print Screen keys to capture an image of the window. Paste the image in a new Paint file, and save the file as **Memory Counter** in the Tutorial.10\Case3 folder provided with your Data Files.

7. In the System Information window, display details about the startup programs on your computer. Press the Alt+Print Screen keys to capture an image of the window. Paste the image in a new Paint file, and save the file as **Startup** in the Tutorial.10\Case3 folder provided with your Data Files.

8. Search the Microsoft Solution Centers for articles about Last Known Good Configuration in Windows 7. Display one article or Help topic that discusses this startup option, and then press the Alt+Print Screen keys to capture an image of the window. Paste the image in a new Paint file, and save the file as **Last** in the Tutorial.10\Case3 folder provided with your Data Files.

9. Search the Microsoft Solution Centers for articles about Safe mode. Display one article or Help topic that discusses using Safe mode (not Office safe mode), and then press the Alt+Print Screen keys to capture an image of the window. Paste the image

in a new Paint file, and save the file as **Safe Mode** in the Tutorial.10\Case3 folder provided with your Data Files.

10. Close all open windows.

11. Submit the results of the preceding steps to your instructor, either in printed or electronic form, as requested.

Use your skills and the Internet to research Internet connection problems.

RESEARCH

Case Problem 4

There are no Data Files needed for this Case Problem.

Topp Land Surveyors   Benson Topp owns Topp Land Surveyors in Columbia, South Carolina. He recently set up a small network in his office so he and his staff can share computer resources. Everyone at Topp Land Surveyors has Windows 7 installed on their computers. Benson uses a broadband digital subscriber line (DSL) to connect to the Internet, but the connection is frequently interrupted. Benson's Internet service provider suspects he is having Winsock2 problems. As Benson's business manager, you offer to research how to solve his Internet connection problems. Complete the following steps:

1. Use Windows Help and Support to find information about and suggested solutions for Benson's Internet connection problems.

2. Search the Microsoft Web resources for similar troubleshooting information, including articles about Winsock2 problems.

3. Use your favorite search engine to find a description of Winsock2.

4. Based on your research, write one to two pages recommending how Benson can solve his problem. List the possible causes along with suggested steps to solve his problem. Save the document as **Internet** in the Tutorial.10\Case4 folder provided with your Data Files.

5. Submit the results of the preceding steps to your instructor, either in printed or electronic form, as requested.

ASSESS

SAM: Skills Assessment Manager

For current SAM information, including versions and content details, visit SAM Central (http://samcentral.course.com). If you have a SAM user profile, you may have access to hands-on instruction, practice, and assessment of the skills covered in this tutorial. Since various versions of SAM are supported throughout the life of this text, check with your instructor for the correct instructions and URL/Web site for accessing assignments.

ENDING DATA FILES

Tutorial

Diagnostics.html
Update.zip

Review

Accessory.zip
Advanced.png
Base Score.png
Critical.png
Graphs.png
Paging.png
Problems.png
Process.png
ReadyBoost.png
Reliability.png
Remote.png
Solutions.png
Summary.png
System.html
Visual.png

Case1

Conflicts.png
Details.png
Fade.png
Invitation.png
Media Player.png
Minimum.png
MP3 Answers.png
Overview.png
TaskMan.png
Warning.png
WMP.png

Case2

Counters.png
Error.png
Index.png
Lowest.png
Memory.png
Message Details.png
Sound Cards.png
Sound Device.png
Sound Problem.zip
Sound.png

Case3

History.png
Last.png
Memory Counter.png
Printing.png
Safe Mode.png
Startup.png
Subscores.png
Tasks.png

Case4

Internet.doc

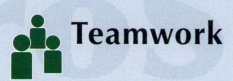 **Teamwork**

Preparing a Team Presentation

Most of your professional work will likely involve participating in a variety of groups and teams. According to *The American Heritage Dictionary*, a team is a "group organized to work together." When you are part of a team, you collaborate with other team members to reach a common goal or outcome. You take advantage of the complementary skills, talents, and abilities that each team member contributes to produce results that are greater than those a single person could achieve. Because so many businesses and other organizations use teams to perform many day-to-day and special tasks, learning to be a contributing member of a successful team is a professional skill everyone needs to develop. Employers look for strong teamwork skills when hiring new employees and promoting current employees to leadership positions.

In this ProSkills exercise, you work with a team to create a presentation that trains other people to use Windows 7. To be effective, your team needs to be more than a collection of people performing similar tasks. Because a team's efforts center on reaching a goal, your team should start by discussing your goal and brainstorming about how to reach it. Because team members ideally complement each other, your team should also strengthen the bonds between each member. To keep your team running smoothly, keep the following guidelines in mind as you work together to complete tasks:

- Remember that everyone brings something of value to the team.
- Respect and support each other as you work toward the common goal.
- When criticisms or questions arise, try to see them from the other person's perspective before taking offense or jumping to conclusions.
- When a team member needs assistance, seek ways to encourage or support him or her so the team's work is not affected.
- Decide early how the team will keep in touch and communicate with each other.
- Deal with negative or unproductive attitudes immediately so they don't damage the team's energy and attitude.
- Get outside assistance if team members can't move beyond the obstacle facing them.
- Provide periodic positive encouragement or rewards for contributions.

PROSKILLS

Training Others to Use Windows 7

Explaining a concept to someone else or teaching a person how to perform a task is often the most effective way to retain information yourself. To make sure you thoroughly understand Windows 7, you can train other people to use it productively. Because you can do so much with Windows 7, a training effort is more practical if you collaborate with other people and form a team. Working as a team, assign tasks for completing the following project:

1. Select the features your team will cover. Each team member should be responsible for at least two Windows 7 features: one general feature (such as the taskbar) and one feature covered in Tutorials 7–10 of this book.

ProSkills

2. Select a format for the presentation. For example, you could create a slide show, a series of informative graphics, an illustrated document, or a movie. (See Appendix B for steps on using Windows Live Movie Maker to create a movie.)

3. Select the software you will use to create the presentation. For example, you can create a slide show using Windows Media Center, Windows Live Movie Maker, or Microsoft PowerPoint.

4. Based on your selections, prepare a presentation designed to train people how to use Windows 7. Assume your audience has worked with computers before, but not with Windows 7. The purpose of the presentation is to introduce people to Windows 7 features that can increase their efficiency and productivity.

5. Include the following types of information in the presentation:
   - Title and introduction, including the names of everyone on the team
   - Graphics, such as photos and screen shots, of each Windows tool your team describes
   - Description of the programs, tools, and other features of Windows 7 you are covering, including their features and benefits
   - Step-by-step explanations of how to perform a typical task using the tool
   - Conclusion or summary

6. Prepare the presentation as a file your instructor can view.

7. Submit the presentation to your instructor, either in printed or electronic form, as requested.

OBJECTIVES

- Prepare to connect to the Internet
- Set up a broadband connection
- Set up a wireless connection
- Set up a dial-up connection
- Troubleshoot your Internet connection

Connecting Computers to the Internet

Setting Up an Internet Connection

Windows 7 makes it easy to connect to the Internet, whether your computer uses a DSL modem, cable modem, or dial-up connection. This appendix is designed for you if you are working with your own computer and want to connect to the Internet. It discusses the most popular types of technologies for connecting to the Internet, and explains what you must do to prepare. It also discusses the pros and cons of the various connection methods. This appendix provides step-by-step instructions for setting up a broadband Internet connection in Windows 7, a wireless Internet connection, and a dial-up Internet connection. Finally, the appendix lists suggestions for troubleshooting these types of connections if you have problems accessing the Internet.

STARTING DATA FILES

There are no starting Data Files needed for this tutorial.

APPENDIX A VISUAL OVERVIEW

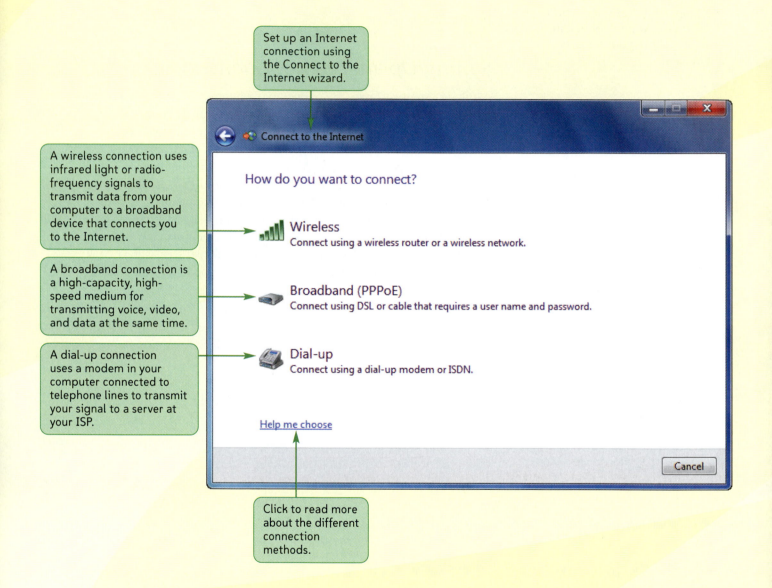

Set up an Internet connection using the Connect to the Internet wizard.

A wireless connection uses infrared light or radio-frequency signals to transmit data from your computer to a broadband device that connects you to the Internet.

A broadband connection is a high-capacity, high-speed medium for transmitting voice, video, and data at the same time.

A dial-up connection uses a modem in your computer connected to telephone lines to transmit your signal to a server at your ISP.

Connect to the Internet

How do you want to connect?

Wireless
Connect using a wireless router or a wireless network.

Broadband (PPPoE)
Connect using DSL or cable that requires a user name and password.

Dial-up
Connect using a dial-up modem or ISDN.

Help me choose

Cancel

Click to read more about the different connection methods.

CONNECTING TO THE INTERNET

Message indicates that this computer is not connected to a wireless network.

A **wireless network** is a way to share Internet access, files, and printers among a group of computers.

Click the Refresh icon to refresh the list of wireless networks your computer can detect.

The number of green bands reflects the strength of the wireless signal.

The security icon indicates an **unsecured network**, which does not require a user name and password to use.

A **network adapter** is a hardware device that translates electronic signals between your computer and your network connection.

If you are away from your wireless home network, your computer can find wireless networks within range by detecting **hotspots**, public spaces equipped with wireless Internet access, such as a hotel or airport.

Not connected

Connections are available

Wireless Network Connection

Chamberlain

2WIRE828

D0GJ8

2WIRE424

matsumoto

2WIRE486

merr.com

madcitybroadband

Open Network and Sharing Center

Windows Network Diagnostics

There might be a problem with one or more network adapters on this computer

➜ Plug a cable into the network adapter "Local Area Connection"
Click here when you are done so that Windows can check if the problem is resolved.

➜ Click for information on how to find wireless networks in range of this computer

Cancel

Preparing to Connect to the Internet

Windows 7 makes communicating with computers easier than ever because it provides tools that allow you to connect your computer to other computers and to the Internet. If you are using a computer on a university or institutional network or any other type of local area network (LAN), you are probably already connected to the Internet, and you can skip this appendix. This appendix is useful for people who are not connected to the Internet but who have their own computer and devices designed for accessing the Internet, including a modem and phone line or cable connections. Figure A-1 describes what you need to set up an Internet connection.

| Figure A-1 | What you need to set up an Internet connection |

Device or Service	Type	Description
Internet service provider (ISP)	National or local	An ISP provides access to the Internet. You sign up for an account with an ISP as you do for telephone service or utilities. Some ISPs serve a broad area, while others are more limited.
Hardware	Broadband modem	A broadband modem is a high-capacity, high-speed device that is usually included as part of the start-up hardware from your ISP when you sign up for a broadband account.
	Dial-up modem	A dial-up modem is a device that usually comes installed in your computer and lets you connect to an ISP via telephone lines.
	Cables	Cables connect your modem to your computer or phone jack.

To access the Internet, you need to connect your computer to an Internet service provider (ISP), which is a company that provides Internet access. ISPs maintain servers that are directly connected to the Internet 24 hours a day. You use hardware attached to your computer—either broadband or dial-up devices—to contact your ISP's server and use its Internet connection. You pay a fee for this service, most often a flat monthly rate.

After you set up a computer with the appropriate hardware and establish an account with an ISP, you can use Windows 7 to manage the connection to the Internet. This appendix explains how to use the tools in Windows 7 to set up a broadband or dial-up connection to the Internet.

Using a Broadband Connection

As the popularity of the Internet has increased, the technologies for connecting to the Internet have improved, providing faster and more reliable connections. If you want to use the Internet to listen to Web radio stations, download music and videos to your computer, send digital photographs to family and friends, play online games, or browse animated Web sites, you need an Internet connection that lets you transfer data quickly. The most popular technology that provides a fast Internet connection is called a broadband connection, which is a high-capacity, high-speed medium for transmitting voice, video, and data at the same time. The two most common and practical broadband connections for home and small office users are digital subscriber line (DSL) and digital cable connections. DSL and digital cable connections are fast because they have a lot of **bandwidth**, which is the amount of data that can be transmitted per second through a connection. The bandwidth for digital cable allows speeds from 64 kilobits per second (Kbps) to 20 megabits per second (Mbps), and DSL allows between 128 Kbps and 7.5 Mbps.

A DSL connection uses telephone lines to connect your computer to your ISP. See Figure A-2. Your ISP usually installs a DSL splitter at your home or office and provides a DSL modem for your computer. The modem is plugged in to your computer on one end and a telephone jack on the other. When you connect to the Internet, the DSL splitter separates the computer data signals from your voice telephone signals, so a DSL connection does not interrupt your phone service. The DSL splitter at your ISP connects to the public phone lines on one end and to a DSL access multiplexer (DSLAM) on the other end. The splitter uses these connections to exchange computer data with your ISP, which provides Internet access to you.

Figure A-2	DSL connection

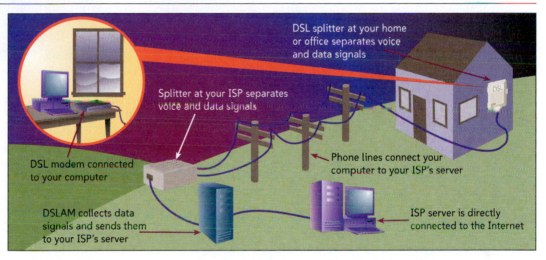

One advantage of a DSL connection is that it is always on, maintaining a constant high-speed, high-bandwidth connection to the Internet. The speed and bandwidth vary, however, depending on the distance between your DSL modem and the DSLAM. The greater the distance, the lower the bandwidth and speed of your connection. The maximum feasible distance is about three miles.

A digital cable connection is also a fast and popular way to connect to the Internet, and like a DSL connection, it is always on. This broadband technology uses a cable modem attached to cable television lines to connect your computer to your ISP. See Figure A-3. One consideration for digital cable is that users within a certain geographic location, such as an apartment or neighborhood, share bandwidth. When only a few people in that location are online, the digital cable connection can be very fast. However, when many people in that location are online, the connection often slows. Because the performance of digital cable can vary, people who are seeking broadband connections and live within range of a DSLAM often opt for DSL over digital cable.

Figure A-3   **Digital cable connection**

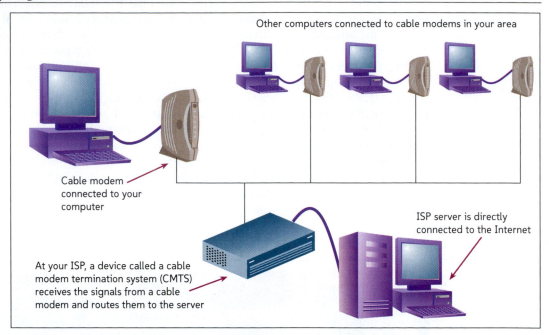

Other computers connected to cable modems in your area

Cable modem connected to your computer

At your ISP, a device called a cable modem termination system (CMTS) receives the signals from a cable modem and routes them to the server

ISP server is directly connected to the Internet

As mentioned earlier, before you can use a broadband service to connect to the Internet, you need to find an ISP that works with DSL or digital cable. The ISP often provides the special equipment you need, such as a cable modem, and establishes an account you use to connect to its server. The ISP also provides account information, including a user name and password, to identify you to the ISP's server. You need this information to set up an Internet connection in Windows 7.

Using a Wireless Connection

Many personal computers, especially laptops and other mobile computers, use a wireless connection to access the Internet. A wireless connection uses infrared light or radio-frequency signals, rather than cables, to transmit data from your computer to a broadband device that connects you to the Internet. To establish a wireless Internet connection in your home, you typically need the following equipment:

• Broadband Internet connection: Establish at least one physical connection to the Internet through a broadband connection, such as a DSL or cable modem.
• Wireless router: A **wireless router** is a computer device that converts the signals from your Internet connection into a wireless broadcast.
• Computer with wireless capabilities: Your computer needs a wireless network adapter or a built-in wireless network card to communicate with the router. This wireless device detects and interprets the wireless broadcast signals transmitted by your wireless router. Most recent computers, especially portable computers, provide built-in wireless capabilities. If your computer does not have built-in wireless capabilities, you can use a wireless network adapter, which typically plugs in to a USB port on a desktop computer or a card slot on a laptop.

After you acquire the equipment you need for a wireless connection, you need to set up a wireless network, which is a way to share Internet access, files, and printers among a group of computers. If you are setting up a wireless network at the same time that you establish a broadband connection to the Internet, your ISP might configure the network for you. Even if your ISP does not provide this service, you can establish a wireless network by connecting your wireless router to your DSL or cable modem, as shown in Figure A-4.

Figure A-4   **Setting up a wireless Internet connection**

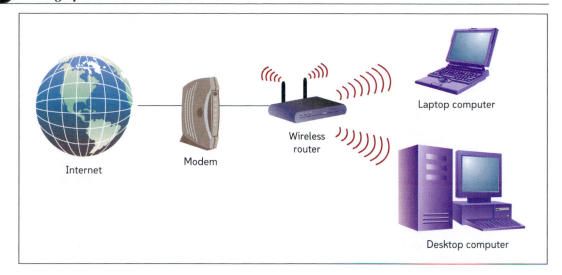

After you set up a wireless network at home, the wireless card or adapter on your computer detects the network so you can use it to connect to the Internet.

If you are away from your wireless home network, you can connect to the Internet without cables through a hotspot. To do so, you need a computer, typically a laptop, with wireless capabilities. As mentioned earlier, most new laptops come equipped with wireless technology. Older laptops require a wireless access card. When you are in range of a hotspot, you can turn on your computer and check to see if you're receiving a network signal. You might need to sign in with information such as user name, password, and method of payment. After you do so, you are connected to the Internet.

Using a Dial-Up Connection

If affordable broadband service is not available in your area, you can connect to the Internet using a **dial-up connection**, which uses a modem in your computer connected to standard telephone lines to transmit your signal to a server at your ISP. See Figure A-5.

Figure A-5   **Phone line connection to the Internet**

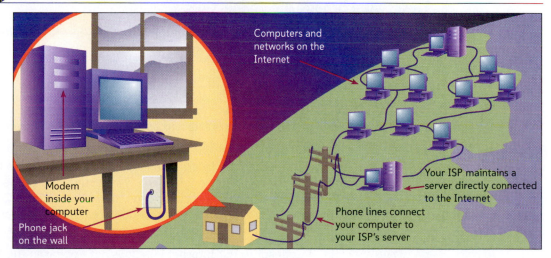

To establish a dial-up connection, you attach the modem in your computer to a phone jack and set the modem to dial the ISP's server, which is directly connected to the Internet. Although regular phone lines are often the only practical choice for some home and small business users, using a dial-up connection has a few drawbacks. Unlike a broadband connection, which is always on, you maintain a dial-up connection only as long as you need to access the Internet because it uses the same telephone lines that you use to make phone calls—if you want to talk on the phone while you are online, you need a second phone line. Phone connections are also less reliable than broadband connections. If there are any problems with the phone connection, you can lose data. Furthermore, the bandwidth of a dial-up connection is much lower than broadband connections. Although it is adequate for reading textual information and transferring small files, a dial-up connection can be inefficient when you want to work with multimedia files online. In some areas, **Integrated Services Digital Network (ISDN)** lines, which are telephone wires that provide a completely digital path from one computer to another, offer the only high-speed connection to the Internet. ISDN lines offer much more bandwidth and speed than regular phone lines, though you must still establish dial-up connections to use them to access the Internet. ISDN lines are rapidly being replaced by DSL.

Setting Up a Broadband Connection

After you set up an account with an ISP and configure the hardware you need to make a broadband connection to the Internet, you're ready to use Windows 7 to access the Internet. If your ISP sends a service person to your home or office to set up a broadband Internet connection, you do not need to set it up yourself. Your broadband connection will be configured by the service person and will be ready to use.

If you need to set up a broadband connection yourself, you can do so by using the Connect to the Internet wizard. This wizard guides you through the steps of connecting to the Internet using a broadband, wireless, or dial-up connection. You choose the broadband method if your computer is connected directly to a broadband modem (a DSL or cable modem) and you have a Point-to-Point Protocol over Ethernet (PPPoE) Internet account. With this type of account, you must provide a user name and password to connect. (Your ISP indicates what type of account it is providing when you sign up for an account.)

To set up a broadband connection:

1. Click the **Start** button 🔵 on the taskbar, and then click **Control Panel**. The Control Panel opens in Category view.

   Trouble? If the Control Panel opens in Large icons or Small icons view, click the View by button, and click Category.

2. In the Network and Internet category, click **Connect to the Internet**. The Connect to the Internet wizard starts and asks how you want to connect to the Internet. See Figure A-6.

   Trouble? If the Connect to the Internet link does not appear in the Network and Internet category, your computer might already be connected to the Internet. If you still want to set up a broadband connection, disconnect from the Internet first by clicking the network icon 🖥 in the notification area of the taskbar, clicking the name of the network, and then clicking the Disconnect button. Repeat Step 2.

   Trouble? If the Connect to the Internet link does not appear in the Network and Internet category and you are not connected to the Internet, click Network and Internet in the Control Panel, click Network and Sharing Center, click Set up a new connection or network, click Connect to the Internet, and then click the Next button.

Figure A-6   **Connect to the Internet wizard**

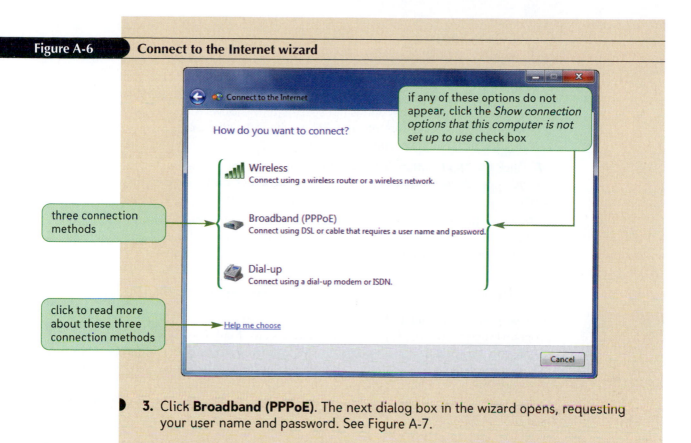

three connection methods

if any of these options do not appear, click the *Show connection options that this computer is not set up to use* check box

click to read more about these three connection methods

3. Click **Broadband (PPPoE)**. The next dialog box in the wizard opens, requesting your user name and password. See Figure A-7.

Figure A-7   **Providing your user name and password**

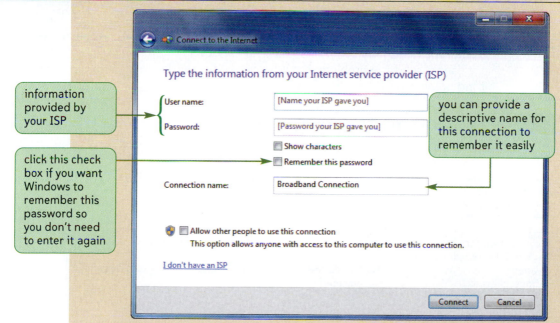

information provided by your ISP

click this check box if you want Windows to remember this password so you don't need to enter it again

you can provide a descriptive name for this connection to remember it easily

Trouble? If Broadband (PPPoE) does not appear as an option, it is probably because your computer does not have the hardware necessary for this type of connection. Click Show connection options that this computer is not set up to use, and then repeat Step 3.

4. In the User name text box, type the user name your ISP gave you. This is often your first and last name combined without any spaces.

5. In the Password text box, type the password your ISP gave you.

6. Click the **Connect** button. Windows 7 sets up a broadband connection to the Internet, and then displays a dialog box indicating the connection was successful.

   Trouble? If the connection is not successful, Windows might identify the reason it cannot connect to the Internet. Follow the instructions or suggestions in the dialog box to solve the problem.

7. Click the **Next** button. Windows tests your Internet connection and lets you know you are connected to the Internet. Click the **Close** button.

To verify the connection, start a program that uses the Internet, such as Internet Explorer. A network icon also appears in the notification area of the taskbar to indicate your computer is connected to the Internet.

Troubleshooting a Broadband Connection

After you set up a broadband Internet connection, you can access the Internet with programs such as Internet Explorer and Windows Live Mail. Even if you shut down and restart your computer, you can access the Internet simply by starting Internet Explorer, for example—you don't need to contact your ISP to make a connection to its server first.

If your broadband connection is interrupted, make sure all the cables and wires are connected properly. If that doesn't solve the problem, you can perform the following steps to repair the connection.

To troubleshoot a broadband connection:

1. Right-click the **network** icon in the notification area of the taskbar, and then click **Troubleshoot problems**. Windows communicates with your network device and repairs the connection if possible. If Windows requires you to take action or if it cannot solve the problem, the Windows Network Diagnostics window opens, listing possible problems. See Figure A-8. Your problems might differ.

Figure A-8 **Diagnosing broadband connection problems**

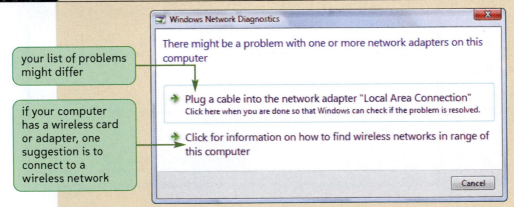

your list of problems might differ

if your computer has a wireless card or adapter, one suggestion is to connect to a wireless network

2. Read the possible problems to find the one that seems the most likely for your computer. Take the suggested action, and then click the option, if necessary.

3. If you still cannot connect to the Internet after attempting to repair the connection, perform the following troubleshooting tasks:

   - Check the status indicator lights on your DSL or cable modem to make sure that it is connected to your ISP.
   - Put the DSL or cable modem on standby (most modems have a Standby button or one with a similar name), and then make the modem active again. Wait a few minutes, and then test your Internet connection.
   - Note the actions you have already performed, and then contact your ISP.

Setting Up a Wireless Connection

You set up a wireless Internet connection using the Connect to the Internet wizard. When you do, you choose the wireless method if you are using a wireless router or network or if you're connecting to a hotspot (even if you also have a broadband connection).

To set up a wireless connection:

1. Open the **Control Panel** in Category view, and then click **Connect to the Internet** in the Network and Internet category. The Connect to the Internet wizard starts and asks how you want to connect to the Internet.

   Trouble? If the Connect to the Internet link does not appear in the Network and Internet category, your computer might already be connected to the Internet. If you still want to set up a wireless connection, disconnect from the Internet first by clicking the network icon 🖥 in the notification area of the taskbar, clicking the name of the network, and then clicking the Disconnect button. Repeat Step 1.

   Trouble? If the Connect to the Internet link does not appear in the Network and Internet category and you are not connected to the Internet, click Network and Internet in the Control Panel, click Network and Sharing Center, click Set up a new connection or network, click Connect to the Internet, and then click the Next button.

2. Click **Wireless**. The next dialog box in the wizard opens, listing the wireless networks nearby. See Figure A-9. Your list of wireless networks will differ.

   Trouble? If Wireless does not appear as an option, it is probably because your computer does not have the hardware necessary for this type of connection. Click Show connection options that this computer is not set up to use, and then repeat Step 2.

Figure A-9 ▶ **Selecting a wireless network**

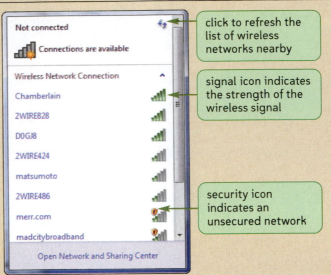

3. Click the wireless network to which you want to connect, and then click the **Connect** button.

4. If you are connecting to a secured network, type the network security key or pass-phrase you need to connect to this network. (Usually, the person who sets up the network gives you this security information.) Then click the **Connect** button.

If you are connecting to an unsecured network, a dialog box opens indicating this network is unsecured. Click **Connect Anyway** to connect to the unsecured network.

Trouble? If you do not want to connect to the unsecured network, click Connect to a different network to return to the dialog box shown in Figure A-9, and then repeat Steps 3 and 4.

Windows attempts to connect to the network, and then displays a dialog box indicating the connection was successful.

To troubleshoot a wireless connection, follow the steps in the "Troubleshooting a Broadband Connection" section.

Setting Up a Dial-Up Connection

You set up a dial-up Internet connection using the Connect to the Internet wizard. When you do, you choose the dial-up method if you are using a dial-up modem (not a DSL or cable modem) or an ISDN line to connect your computer to the Internet.

To set up a dial-up connection:

▶ **1.** Open the **Control Panel** in Category view, and then click **Connect to the Internet** in the Network and Internet category. The Connect to the Internet wizard starts and asks how you want to connect to the Internet.

Trouble? If the Connect to the Internet link does not appear in the Network and Internet category, your computer might already be connected to the Internet. If you still want to set up a dial-up connection, disconnect from the Internet first by clicking the network icon 🖳 in the notification area of the taskbar, clicking the name of the network or the connection, and then clicking the Disconnect button. Repeat Step 1.

Trouble? If the Connect to the Internet link does not appear in the Network and Internet category and you are not connected to the Internet, click Network and Internet in the Control Panel, click Network and Sharing Center, click Set up a new connection or network, click Connect to the Internet, and then click the Next button.

▶ **2.** Click **Dial-up**. The next dialog box in the wizard opens, requesting information about your ISP account. See Figure A-10.

Figure A-10   **Setting up a dial-up connection**

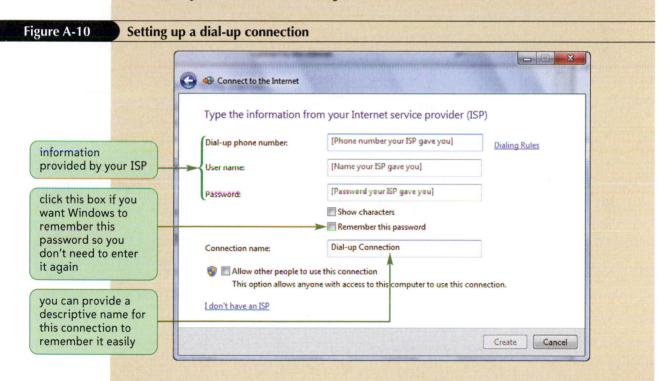

information provided by your ISP

click this box if you want Windows to remember this password so you don't need to enter it again

you can provide a descriptive name for this connection to remember it easily

> **Trouble?** If Dial-up does not appear as an option, it is probably because your computer does not have a dial-up modem. Click Show connection options that this computer is not set up to use, and then repeat Step 2.

3. In the Dial-up phone number text box, type the phone number your ISP gave you. This is the number your modem dials to contact your ISP.

4. In the User name text box, type the user name or account name your ISP gave you.

5. In the Password text box, type the password your ISP gave you.

6. Click the **Connect** button. Windows 7 sets up a dial-up connection to the Internet, and then displays a dialog box indicating the connection was successful.

   > **Trouble?** If a Create button appears instead of a Connect button, click the Create button.

7. Click the **Next** button. Windows tests your Internet connection and lets you know you are connected to the Internet. Click the **Close** button.

Your dial-up account remains connected until you disconnect from your account. In some cases, your ISP might disconnect you automatically if your computer is idle for several minutes.

To disconnect a dial-up connection:

1. Right-click the **network** icon in the notification area of the taskbar, and then click **Disconnect**.

Troubleshooting a Dial-Up Connection

If your dial-up connection is interrupted, refer first to the "Troubleshooting a Broadband Connection" section for steps to solve the problem. If you are still having trouble making and maintaining a dial-up connection to the Internet, try performing the following steps:

- Make sure that you are dialing the correct number, including any required access numbers (such as 9), and that the number is not busy.
- Make sure that the phone jack is working by plugging in a working phone and checking for a dial tone. Similarly, make sure that the phone cable is working properly by plugging a working phone into the telephone jack of your modem and verifying you receive a dial tone.
- Make sure that the phone cable is plugged in to the line jack on your modem, not the telephone jack.
- If you have call waiting, try disabling it, and then try the connection again.
- If someone picked up the phone while you were online, you might have been automatically disconnected. Try connecting again.
- Make sure that your modem is working properly. For more information, check the documentation that came with your modem or go to the manufacturer's Web site.
- Contact your telephone company to verify the quality of your line.

ENDING DATA FILES

There are no ending Data Files needed for this tutorial.

OBJECTIVES

- Change sound and other hardware settings
- Explore Windows Touch and Tablet PC settings
- Set parental controls
- Use Ease of Access options
- Use Windows Live Movie Maker and other Windows Live Essentials

Exploring Additional Windows 7 Tools

Using Control Panel Tools and Windows Live Essentials

Windows 7 provides a wealth of tools and programs for maintaining and enjoying your computer, and for making it more productive. You have already used many Control Panel tools, including those in the System and Security, Network and Internet, Hardware and Sound, User Accounts and Family Safety, and Appearance and Personalization categories. In this appendix, you will learn about a System and Security tool called BitLocker Drive Encryption, and then you will work with tools in the Hardware and Sound category to set AutoPlay options, customize sound schemes, and explore Windows Pen and Touch features. You will also examine ways to protect your computer with user accounts and parental control settings. To optimize your Windows experience, you will use Ease of Access tools, including a narrator and a magnifier.

In addition to the tools provided in the Control Panel, you can download and install Windows Live Essentials, a free suite of programs including Photo Gallery and Movie Maker, which you will explore in this appendix.

STARTING DATA FILES

There are no starting Data Files needed for this appendix.

APPENDIX B VISUAL OVERVIEW

Use the Control Panel to change settings that control nearly everything about how Windows looks and works.

If you have a **multitouch monitor**, which lets you control your computer with your fingertips, adjust its settings using a Hardware and Sound tool.

One useful System and Security tool is **BitLocker Drive Encryption**, which protects the data on hard drives and removable drives.

Use the Sound tool to select a **sound scheme**, which is a collection of sounds Windows plays when system events occur.

AutoPlay is a Hardware and Sound feature that lets you choose which program to use to play media.

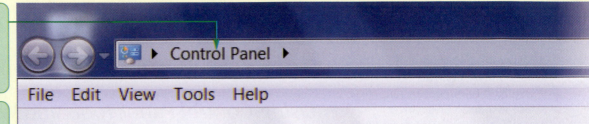

Control Panel

File   Edit   View   Tools   Help

Adjust your computer's settings

System and Security
Review your computer's status
Back up your computer
Find and fix problems

Network and Internet
View network status and tasks
Choose homegroup and sharing options

Hardware and Sound
View devices and printers
Add a device

Programs
Uninstall a program

CONTROL PANEL TOOLS

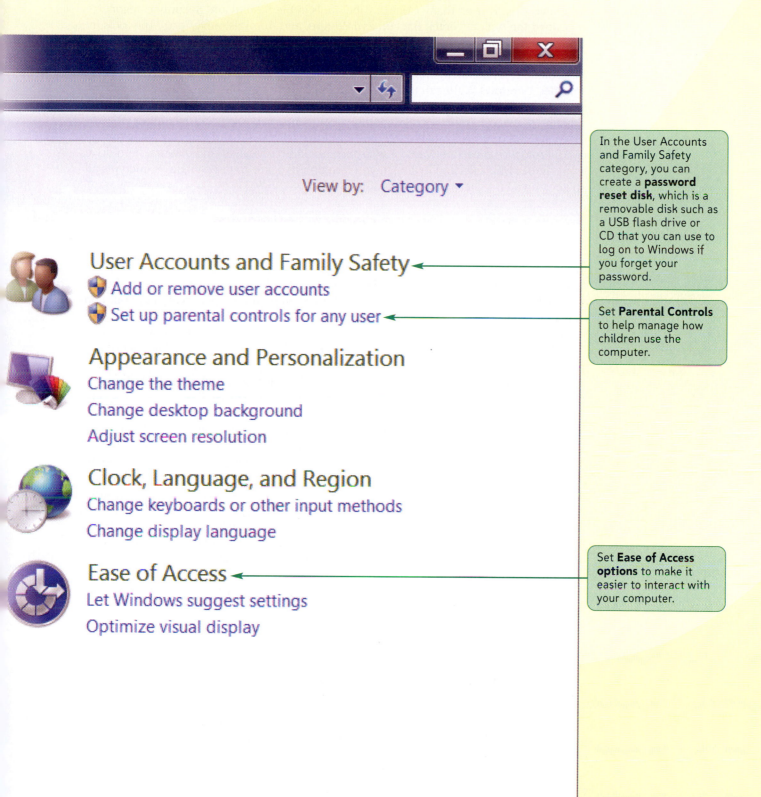

View by: Category ▾

User Accounts and Family Safety
🛡 Add or remove user accounts
🛡 Set up parental controls for any user

Appearance and Personalization
Change the theme
Change desktop background
Adjust screen resolution

Clock, Language, and Region
Change keyboards or other input methods
Change display language

Ease of Access
Let Windows suggest settings
Optimize visual display

In the User Accounts and Family Safety category, you can create a **password reset disk**, which is a removable disk such as a USB flash drive or CD that you can use to log on to Windows if you forget your password.

Set **Parental Controls** to help manage how children use the computer.

Set **Ease of Access options** to make it easier to interact with your computer.

Using BitLocker Drive Encryption

You have already used many Control Panel tools in the System and Security category, including the Action Center, Backup and Restore, and Administrative Tools. The tools in this category help you maintain your computer and keep it secure. Another useful System and Security tool is BitLocker Drive Encryption (BitLocker for short), which helps protect your data from loss, theft, and hackers. BitLocker encrypts the entire drive where you installed Windows 7. (Recall that encrypting means to scramble the contents of files to protect them from unauthorized access.) After you turn on BitLocker, Windows encrypts any files you save on that drive, including documents, passwords, and temporary files. Note that BitLocker is available only for Windows 7 Ultimate and Enterprise editions.

To protect data on removable media such as USB flash drives and external hard drives, you can use BitLocker To Go. When you turn on BitLocker To Go, Windows encrypts all the personal and system files on the removable drive.

Turning BitLocker On and Off

To encrypt the drive where Windows is installed, your computer must have two partitions: a system, or boot, partition (which contains the files needed to start your computer) and an operating system partition (which contains Windows). BitLocker encrypts the operating system partition and then leaves the system partition unencrypted so your computer can start. When you turn on BitLocker for the first time, Windows creates these partitions for you, if necessary, using 200 MB of available disk space for the system partition.

When you turn on BitLocker for the drive containing Windows, BitLocker checks your computer during startup for any conditions that might present a security risk, such as changes to a startup file. If it detects a potential security risk, BitLocker locks the Windows drive until you enter a recovery key to unlock the drive. (You can still log on to your user account with your regular password if you have one.)

If you encrypt a drive that does not contain Windows, such as an internal hard drive or a USB flash drive containing data files, you can unlock the encrypted drive with a password or smart card (a plastic card containing a computer chip encoded with identifying information). You can also set the drive to unlock automatically when you log on to the computer.

To detect changes to the startup process on the operating system drive, BitLocker uses the Trusted Platform Module (TPM) hardware. The TPM is a microchip your computer needs to take advantage of advanced security features, such as BitLocker. If you want to use BitLocker to protect your Windows drive, check the information that came with your computer to make sure the TPM is installed.

You can turn off BitLocker at any time, either temporarily by suspending it or permanently by decrypting the drive.

In the following steps, you turn on BitLocker To Go for a USB flash drive.

> **TIP**
>
> Make sure that you create the recovery key when you turn on BitLocker for the first time; otherwise, you could permanently lose access to your files.

To turn on BitLocker To Go for a USB flash drive:

1. If necessary, insert a USB flash drive into a USB port on your computer.

2. Click the **Start** button 🔵 on the taskbar, click **Control Panel**, click **System and Security**, and then click **BitLocker Drive Encryption** to open the BitLocker Drive Encryption window. See Figure B-1.

| Figure B-1 | **BitLocker Drive Encryption window** |

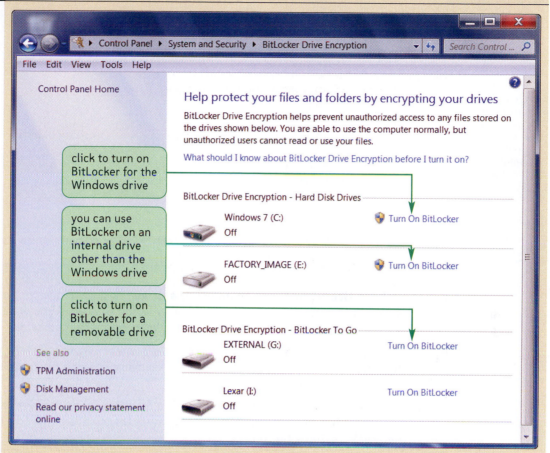

3. Next to your USB flash drive in the BitLocker Drive Encryption – BitLocker To Go section, click **Turn On BitLocker**. Windows initializes BitLocker and then starts the BitLocker Setup Wizard. In the first dialog box of the wizard, you select how you want to unlock the drive. See Figure B-2.

   Trouble? If a User Account Control dialog box opens requesting your permission or a password to continue, enter the password or click the Continue button.

Figure B-2	Selecting how to unlock a drive

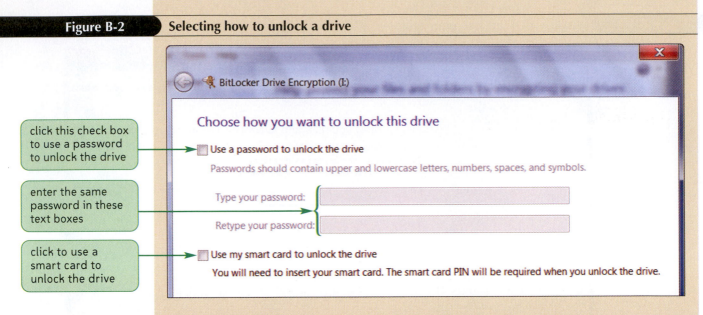

click this check box to use a password to unlock the drive

enter the same password in these text boxes

click to use a smart card to unlock the drive

4. Click the **Use a password to unlock the drive** check box, click in the Type your password text box if necessary, and then type the password you want to use. Click in the Retype your password text box, and then retype the password.

5. Click the **Next** button to display a dialog box where you specify how you want to store your recovery key. You can save the recovery key to a file on your hard disk, or you can print the recovery key.

6. Click **Save the recovery key to a file**. The Save BitLocker Recovery Key as dialog box opens. Navigate to the folder where you want to save the recovery key, and then click the **Save** button.

7. Click the **Next** button to display a dialog box asking you to confirm you are ready to encrypt this drive.

8. Click the **Start Encrypting** button. BitLocker encrypts the drive you selected, which takes a few minutes.

9. When the encryption is complete, click the **Close** button.

To keep the recovery key secure, be sure to save it on a password-protected drive or store the printed key in a safe place. When BitLocker requests the recovery key, enter the BitLocker Recovery Key (not the Recovery key identification). If you store the recovery key on removable media, such as a USB flash drive, you can insert the USB flash drive when BitLocker requests the recovery key. Be sure to store the USB flash drive in a secure place.

You can turn off BitLocker on a system drive in two ways: by suspending BitLocker or by decrypting the drive. Decrypting the drive means removing BitLocker protection entirely, which can take a long time on a system drive. If you suspend BitLocker instead, the drive is still encrypted, but Windows can read the information on the drive. You might suspend BitLocker so you can update a startup file, which you cannot access when BitLocker is turned on.

To turn off BitLocker on a drive that does not contain Windows, you must decrypt the drive. If the drive contains many gigabytes of data, decrypting can be time consuming.

In the following steps, you turn off BitLocker for the same USB flash drive you used in the previous set of steps.

To turn off BitLocker on a USB flash drive:

1. With the USB flash drive attached to your computer, open the BitLocker Drive Encryption window, if necessary, which shows the drives on your computer. See Figure B-3.

| Figure B-3 | Turning off BitLocker for a removable drive |

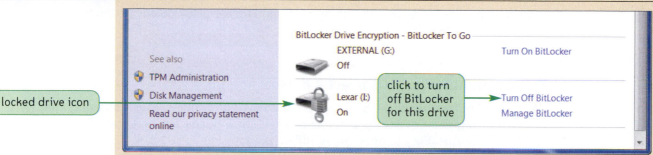

2. Next to your USB flash drive in the BitLocker Drive Encryption – BitLocker To Go section, click **Turn Off BitLocker**. The BitLocker Drive Encryption dialog box opens.

   Trouble? If a User Account Control dialog box opens requesting your permission or a password to continue, enter the password or click the Continue button.

3. Click the **Decrypt Drive** button. BitLocker decrypts the drive, which can take several minutes.

4. When decryption is complete, click the **Close** button.

Keep in mind that after you decrypt a drive, the files on it are no longer protected.

Changing Hardware and Sound Settings

The Hardware and Sound category in the Control Panel contains four tools you have not explored in previous tutorials: AutoPlay, Sound, Pen and Touch, and Tablet PC settings. AutoPlay is a Windows feature that lets you choose which program to use to play media content, such as music stored on a CD or photos stored on a DVD. For example, if you have more than one media player installed on your computer, AutoPlay asks which one you want to use when you play a music CD for the first time. You can change AutoPlay settings for each type of media file on your computer.

The Sound tool in the Hardware and Sound category lets you set the volume of the computer sound (which you learned to do in a previous tutorial). You can also change other sound settings, including the sounds Windows plays to signal program events, such as new e-mail arriving in your Inbox, a program pausing because of an error, or the Recycle Bin emptying.

The Pen and Touch tools let you select options for working with a computer screen that responds to touches from a pen or your fingertips. The Tablet PC tools let you select additional settings for working with a tablet PC, including training the computer to recognize your handwriting.

Selecting AutoPlay Defaults

When you turn AutoPlay on in the Control Panel, you can choose what should happen when you insert different types of digital media into your computer. When AutoPlay is turned off, Windows displays the AutoPlay dialog box when you insert digital media and asks you to choose what you want to do. The AutoPlay dialog box also appears if the Ask me every time setting is selected for the media you insert or if no default has been selected yet. You can prevent the dialog box from opening by selecting a default for the type of media you plan to use.

In the following steps, you turn on AutoPlay, and then select a default action to play audio CDs using Windows Media Player.

To turn on AutoPlay and select a default action:

1. In the Address bar of the BitLocker Drive Encryption window, click **Control Panel** to return to the Control Panel Home window. Click **Hardware and Sound**, and then click **AutoPlay** to open the AutoPlay window. See Figure B-4.

| Figure B-4 | AutoPlay window |

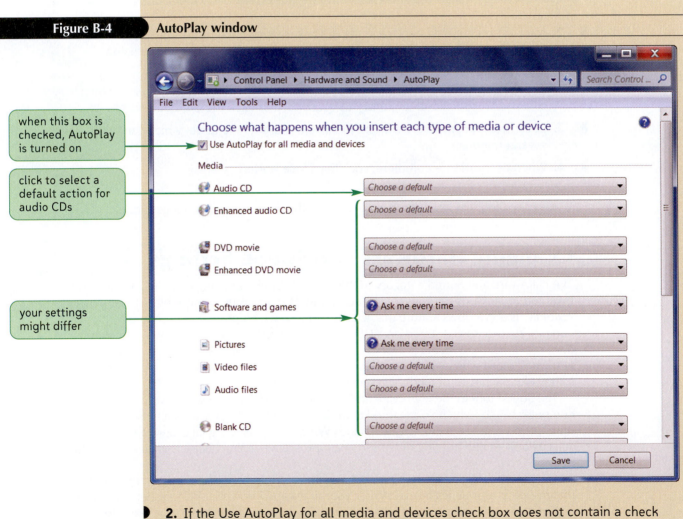

2. If the Use AutoPlay for all media and devices check box does not contain a check mark, click the **Use AutoPlay for all media and devices** check box to turn AutoPlay on.

3. Click the **Audio CD** button to display a list of default actions Windows can take with this type of device. See Figure B-5.

Figure B-5	Selecting a default action

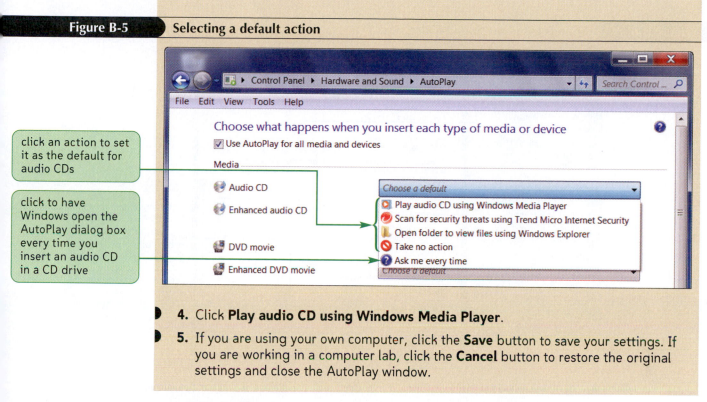

click an action to set it as the default for audio CDs

click to have Windows open the AutoPlay dialog box every time you insert an audio CD in a CD drive

4. Click **Play audio CD using Windows Media Player**.

5. If you are using your own computer, click the **Save** button to save your settings. If you are working in a computer lab, click the **Cancel** button to restore the original settings and close the AutoPlay window.

Other hardware settings you can change include sound options, which you'll adjust next.

Changing the Sound Scheme

By default, Windows 7 plays certain sounds to signal program events, such as when you log on or connect a device to your computer. Windows stores these sounds in a sound scheme. You can create a sound scheme by selecting different sounds and saving them as a new scheme. If you are using a desktop theme other than the default Windows 7 Aero or Basic theme, it might also have its own sound scheme that you can select in the Sound dialog box.

One way to test whether your sound devices are working is to open the Sound dialog box and play a program sound. You'll do that in the next set of steps. Then you'll change a sound for a program event and save the sounds as a new scheme.

Before performing the following steps, note the original settings in case you need to restore them.

To change a sound scheme:

1. In the Hardware and Sound window, click **Sound** to open the Sound dialog box.

2. Click the **Sounds** tab to display the sound schemes.

3. Click **Asterisk** in the list of program events. See Figure B-6.

Figure B-6 ▶ **Sounds tab in the Sound dialog box**

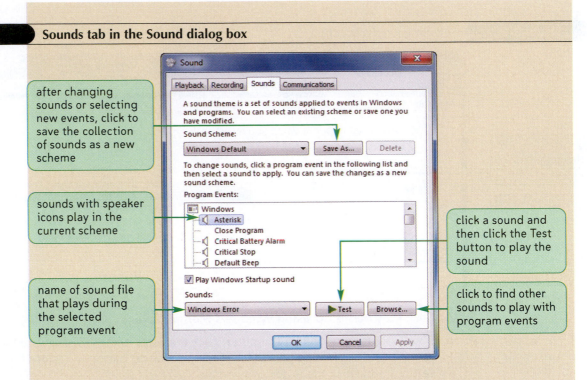

after changing sounds or selecting new events, click to save the collection of sounds as a new scheme

sounds with speaker icons play in the current scheme

name of sound file that plays during the selected program event

click a sound and then click the Test button to play the sound

click to find other sounds to play with program events

▶ **4.** Click the **Test** button. The sound stored in the Windows Error file plays.

> **Trouble?** If a sound does not play on your computer speakers, click the Volume or Speakers icon in the notification area, and then click the Mute button, if necessary, to turn on the speakers. Repeat Steps 3 and 4. If a sound still does not play and you are using external speakers, make sure the speakers are properly connected to your computer and are plugged into a power source, if necessary.

▶ **5.** Scroll the Program Events list, and then click **Open Program** to assign a sound that plays when you start a program.

▶ **6.** Click the **Sounds arrow button**, and then click **tada**.

▶ **7.** Click the **Test** button to play the tada sound.

▶ **8.** Click the **Save As** button to open the Save Scheme As dialog box.

▶ **9.** Type **Program Open** as the name of the new sound scheme, and then click the **OK** button. Program Open is now the current sound scheme on your computer.

▶ **10.** Click the **OK** button to close the Sound dialog box.

Next, you can examine the Pen and Touch options designed for interacting with multitouch monitors and those that let you use a special type of pen as a pointing device.

Using a Multitouch Monitor

Using Windows 7 and a multitouch monitor, you can control your computer with your fingertips. Previous versions of Windows let you use a single finger to select an object at one touch point. In Windows 7, you can take advantage of multitouch monitors, which let you use more than one finger and touch point to perform computer tasks. For example, you can zoom into a map or photo by placing two fingers on a multitouch screen and then spreading them apart. The feature in Windows 7 that lets you use multitouch monitors is called Windows Touch. Many people who use Windows Touch say it is a more natural way to interact with your computer.

If you have the Home Premium, Professional, or Ultimate edition of Windows 7 and a computer with a multitouch monitor, you can change Pen and Touch settings to take advantage of Windows Touch. After you turn on Windows Touch, the icons on the Start menu and taskbar are slightly larger so you can touch each one easily. Windows programs also include Windows Touch features. For example, you can fingerpaint in Paint and use Windows Touch techniques to zoom into Web pages in Internet Explorer.

Instead of pointing and clicking with a mouse, you use gestures that mimic clicks and drags. A gesture is a motion you make with one or two fingers on the screen. Figure B-7 summarizes Windows Touch gestures.

Figure B-7   **Windows Touch gestures**

Mouse Action	Gesture	How to Perform	Sample Use
Click	Tap	Touch the screen	Select a file in a folder window
Double-click	Double-tap	Touch the screen twice in quick succession	Open a file or folder
Right-click	Press and tap	Press and hold with one finger, and then tap with another	Display a shortcut menu
	Press and hold	Press, wait for a blue ring to appear, and then release	Display a shortcut menu
Drag	Drag	Drag with one finger horizontally	Select a paragraph of text
Scroll	Pan	Drag with one or two fingers vertically	Display a hidden section of a window that includes scroll bars
Ctrl+scroll mouse wheel	Zoom out	Touch two points on an object, and then pinch your fingers together	Display a larger area of a map or picture
	Zoom in	Touch two points on an object, and then stretch your fingers apart	Show a smaller area of a map or picture in more detail
Drag rotation handle	Rotate	Touch two points on an object, and then move the object in the direction that you want to rotate it	Turn a shape
Click Back or Forward button	Flick	Quickly drag a finger up, down, right, or left	Display the last Web page you visited

Some programs also use a two-finger tap to perform a specific action. For example, in Internet Explorer, you can tap the screen with two fingers to zoom into a spot, usually one with many links. Magnifying the window helps you tap the link you want. To zoom out, you tap the screen with two fingers again.

Some features new to Windows 7 are particularly easy to use with Windows Touch. For example, recall that you can use Aero Snap to maximize a window by dragging it to the top of the screen. Using Windows Touch, you can touch a window's title bar with your fingertip, and then drag the window up. See Figure B-8.

Figure B-8   Using Windows Touch with Aero Snap

use a fingertip to drag a window to the top of the screen to quickly maximize the window

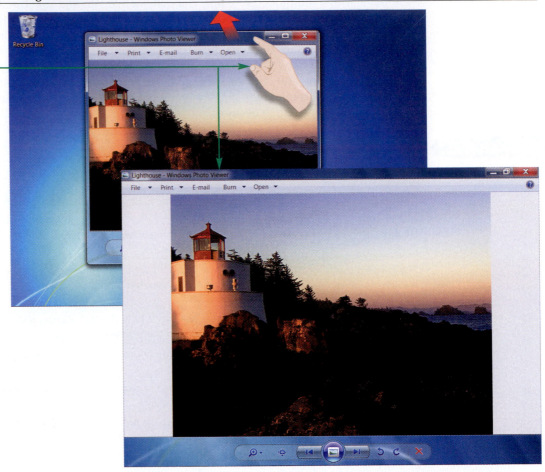

Using Aero Shake is also more natural with Windows Touch—you touch and hold the title bar of a window, and then shake your hand to close all other open windows. To use Aero Peek to preview the contents of minimized windows, you can slide your fingertip along a row of thumbnails on the taskbar. Programs such as Windows Media Center were actually designed for a multitouch monitor. The text and buttons in Media Center windows are large and widely spaced so you can easily tap them with a fingertip. Flick a list of photos or videos to quickly scroll them across the window.

If you have a Tablet PC or a computer monitor that supports Windows Touch, you can use the Pen and Touch tool in the Control Panel to turn on Windows Touch. You can also adjust gesture settings and customize flicks for actions you use often. For example, if you frequently cut text to temporarily store it on the Clipboard, you can assign the Cut action to a flick, such as when you flick your finger toward the upper-left corner of the screen.

To turn on Windows Touch and adjust settings:

1. In the Hardware and Sound window, click **Pen and Touch** to open the Pen and Touch dialog box.

   Trouble? If Pen and Touch does not appear in the Hardware and Sound window, your computer does not support a touch monitor. Read but do not perform the remaining steps.

2. Click the **Touch** tab to display settings for Windows Touch. See Figure B-9.

Figure B-9   Pen and Touch dialog box

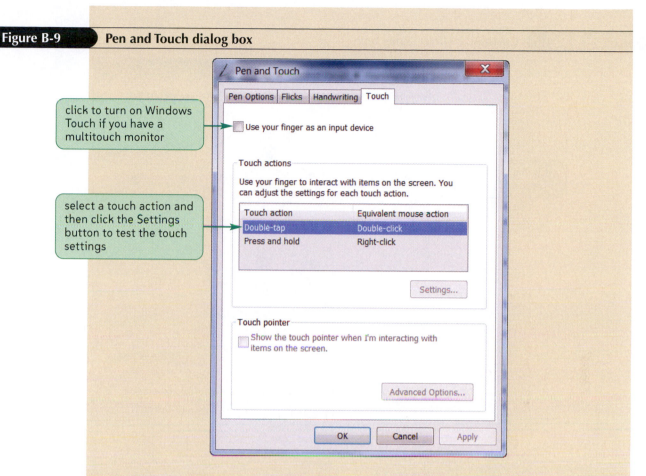

click to turn on Windows Touch if you have a multitouch monitor

select a touch action and then click the Settings button to test the touch settings

3. If a check mark does not appear in the Use your finger as an input device check box, click the **Use your finger as an input device** check box. Windows Touch is now turned on for your computer. You can use the mouse or your fingertip to complete the remaining steps. If you are using your fingertip, tap instead of click to perform the steps.

4. Click **Double-tap** in the Touch action list, and then click the **Settings** button to open the Double-Tap Settings dialog box. Double-tap the graphic to test the settings, and then click the **OK** button.

5. Click **Press and hold** in the Touch action list, and then click the **Settings** button to open the Press and Hold Settings dialog box. Press and hold the graphic to test the settings, and then click the **OK** button.

6. In the Pen and Touch dialog box, click the **Flicks** tab to display the flick options, and then click the **Use flicks to perform common actions quickly and easily** check box, if necessary, to insert a check mark.

7. Click the **Navigational flicks and editing flicks** option button, and then click the **Customize** button to open the Customize Flicks dialog box. See Figure B-10.

Figure B-10   **Customize Flicks dialog box**

click to change what this type of flick does

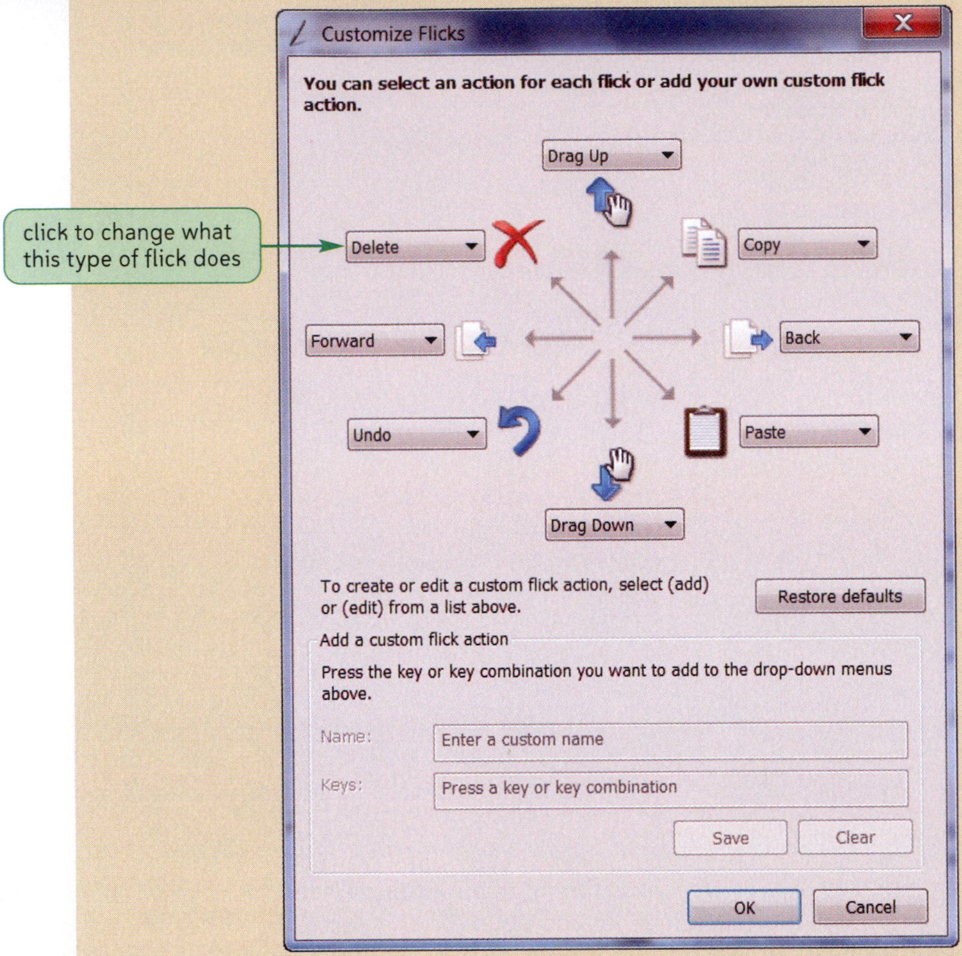

8. Click the **Delete** button, and then click **Cut** to assign the Cut action to this flick.

9. If you are not working on your own computer, click the **Restore defaults** button to restore the default flick settings.

10. Click the **OK** button to close the Customize Flicks dialog box, and then click the **OK** button to close the Pen and Touch dialog box.

After you turn on flicks, you can view your flick settings by clicking (or tapping) the Flicks icon in the notification area of the taskbar.

Adjust Tablet PC Settings

A Tablet PC is a handheld computer that includes a special screen you can use like a slate and write on with a stylus. If you have a Tablet PC, you can use Windows 7 tools designed for this type of computer. For example, you can use the Tablet PC Input Panel to enter text without using a standard keyboard, which can increase your productivity on a Tablet PC. Instead of pressing keys on a physical keyboard, you enter text by tapping keys with your stylus or with your fingertips. A Tablet PC uses the same touch settings for gestures and flicks that you set for multitouch monitors. If you want to turn on or customize flicks on your Tablet PC, for example, you open the Pen and Touch dialog box as you did in the previous set of steps.

To make the most of a Tablet PC, you can calibrate the screen and the pen so that the Tablet PC correctly recognizes the position of your pen.

To open and use the Input Panel:

1. In the Hardware and Sound window, click **Tablet PC Settings** to open the Tablet PC Settings dialog box. See Figure B-11.

Figure B-11   **Tablet PC Settings dialog box**

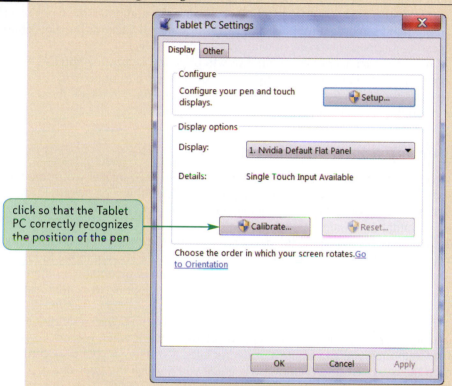

click so that the Tablet PC correctly recognizes the position of the pen

2. On the Display tab, click the **Calibrate** button to test the pen and screen.

   Trouble? If a User Account Control dialog box opens requesting your permission or a password to continue, enter the password or click the Yes button.

3. Follow the instructions on the screen to tap the crosshair each time it appears on the screen.

4. Press the **Esc** key to end the test.

5. Click the **OK** button to close the Tablet PC Settings dialog box.

Calibrating the pen often helps to improve handwriting recognition. You can also configure the Tablet PC for use with your dominant hand, which makes it easier to write on the screen without blocking menus with your hand. For example, if you are left-handed, you should make sure the Tablet PC is set to left-handedness. To do so, open the Tablet PC Settings dialog box, click the Other tab, and then click the Left-handed option button. Click the Right-handed option button if you are right-handed.

Changing User Accounts and Family Safety Settings

You've already used the User Accounts window to add a new user to a computer and to select settings such as the user picture, account name, account type, and password. You can also use the User Accounts window to perform advanced tasks to enhance privacy and security. To prevent you or another user from permanently losing or forgetting a password, you can create a password reset disk.

To preserve the privacy of user accounts, you can set Parental Controls. If children use your computer, set up an account for each child. Then use the Parental Controls feature to set limits on the hours that the children can use the computer, the types of games they can play, and the programs they can run. Using Parental Controls prevents children from accessing inappropriate content with your computer.

Credential Manager offers another way to protect your privacy. You use this tool to store passwords that you frequently use to access Web sites or networks. If you save these passwords using Credential Manager, you don't have to retype them each time you return to the Web site or network.

Creating a Password Reset Disk

Two common problems users often experience with account passwords are entering a password that Windows doesn't recognize and forgetting a password. If you enter a password to log on to Windows, but Windows does not recognize it, check the obvious potential causes first. Make sure the Caps Lock key is not on; Windows passwords are case sensitive, so typing the password with the Caps Lock key on could change the correct capitalization of your password. Also make sure you are trying to log on to your own account—you might have clicked the user name or picture for a different account. Finally, if your computer is on a network, check with your network administrator, who can change your password if necessary.

If you forget your account password, you can use a password reset disk to create a new one. The best time to create a password reset disk is when you create your password, although you can create a reset disk later. If you forget your password, you can insert the reset disk and Windows will guide you through the steps of using it to log on to your account.

To create a password reset disk, you need a USB flash drive or an external hard drive you can use to store the password information. The following steps use Removable Disk (G:) as the name of the drive. Substitute the name of the drive containing your reset disk when you perform the steps. You must be logged on using an Administrator account to create a password reset disk. If you cannot do so, read but do not perform the following steps.

To create a password reset disk:

1. Insert a USB flash drive or external hard drive in the appropriate drive, if necessary.

2. In the left pane of the Hardware and Sound window, click **User Accounts and Family Safety** to open the User Accounts and Family Safety window.

3. Click **User Accounts** to open the User Accounts window, which you have worked with in a previous tutorial. In the left pane, click **Create a password reset disk** to start the Forgotten Password Wizard.

4. Click the **Next** button. The next wizard dialog box opens, where you can select the drive for storing the password reset disk.

5. Make sure **Removable Disk (G:)** is selected in the text box, and then click the **Next** button. The Current User Account Password dialog box opens.

6. In the Current user account password box, type your password, and then click the **Next** button. The Creating Password Reset Disk dialog box opens, displaying the progress of creating the disk.

7. When Windows is finished creating the password reset disk, click the **Next** button. The final dialog box in the wizard opens.

8. Click the **Finish** button.

Be sure to store the password reset disk in a safe place where unauthorized users cannot access it and it cannot be damaged.

If you forget your password after creating a password reset disk, log on to Windows and enter any password. When Windows displays a message that the password is incorrect, click the OK button, insert your password reset disk, click Reset password, and then follow the steps in the Password Reset Wizard to create a new password.

Setting Parental Controls

You can use Parental Controls to set limits on the hours that children can use the computer, the types of games they can play, and the programs they can run. Time limits prevent children from logging on during specified hours, such as very late at night. If children are allowed to use the computer on weekend nights but not weeknights, for example, you can set different hours for every day of the week. You can also use Parental Controls to prevent children from playing certain games, such as those not suited for their age, or from running programs, such as utilities that could damage data on your computer.

Before you set Parental Controls, make sure that each child using the computer has a Standard user account—you can apply Parental Controls only to Standard accounts. Then you can select the settings shown in Figure B-12 to limit a child's access to the computer:

Figure B-12   **Parental controls**

Setting	Use to
Time limits	Set time limits to prevent children from logging on during specified hours. If they are already logged on during a restricted time, Windows logs them off. You can set different logon hours for every day of the week.
Games	Control access to games, choose an age rating level, choose the types of content you want to block, and allow or block unrated or specific games.
Allow and block specific programs	Prevent children from running programs that you don't want them to run.

Before performing the following steps, you need to be logged on using a password-protected Administrator account. You apply the settings to a Standard user account. If one is not available on your computer, create a new Standard account. If you cannot log on as an Administrator or change the settings for a Standard account, read but do not perform the following steps.

The following steps use a Standard account named New User. If the Standard account you are using has a different name, substitute that name as you perform the steps. You'll set Parental Controls on the New User account so that this user can use the computer only until 8 p.m. on weeknights and 9 p.m. on weekends.

To turn on Parental Controls for a Standard user account:

1. In the User Accounts window, click **Parental Controls** in the See also section of the left pane. The Parental Controls window opens. See Figure B-13.

Figure B-13   **Parental Controls window**

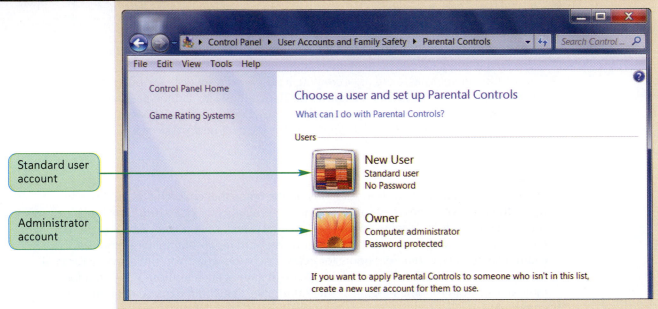

Trouble? If a User Account Control dialog box opens requesting your permission or a password to continue, enter the password or click the Yes button.

2. Click **New User** to open the User Controls window.

   Trouble? If a Windows Live Safety Filter dialog box opens so you can sign in to set up Family Safety, click the Close button ❌ to close the dialog box.

3. Click the **On, enforce current settings** option button. See Figure B-14.

Figure B-14   **User Controls window**

4. Click **Time limits** in the Windows Settings section. The Time Restrictions window opens.

   Trouble? If a Windows Parental Controls dialog box opens indicating that Windows detects a FAT drive, click the OK button.

5. For Sunday, drag from the first **12** to the second **6** and from the second **9** to the last **12**. Do the same for Saturday.

6. For Monday, drag from the first **12** to the second **7** and from the second **8** to the last **12**. Do the same for the remaining weekdays.

7. Click the **OK** button to close the Time Restrictions window.

8. Click the **OK** button to close the User Controls window.

9. In the Parental Controls window, click **User Accounts and Family Safety** in the Address bar to display the User Accounts and Family Safety window again.

Another Control Panel tool you can use to preserve your privacy is the Credential Manager.

Managing Credentials

Besides storing the password for your user account on a reset disk, you can also store credentials, such as user names and passwords, that you use to log on to Web sites or networks. Windows saves your credentials in special folders on your computer called vaults. When you log on to Web sites or other computers on a network, Windows and programs, such as a Web browser, can securely provide the credentials in the vaults so you can log on automatically.

In the following steps, you store the user name and password for logging on to a fictitious financial Web site named Bank.com. Substitute the name of the Web site or network location for which you want to store a password.

To manage network passwords:

1. In the User Accounts and Family Safety window, click **Credential Manager** to open the Credential Manager window. See Figure B-15.

Figure B-15   **Credential Manager window**

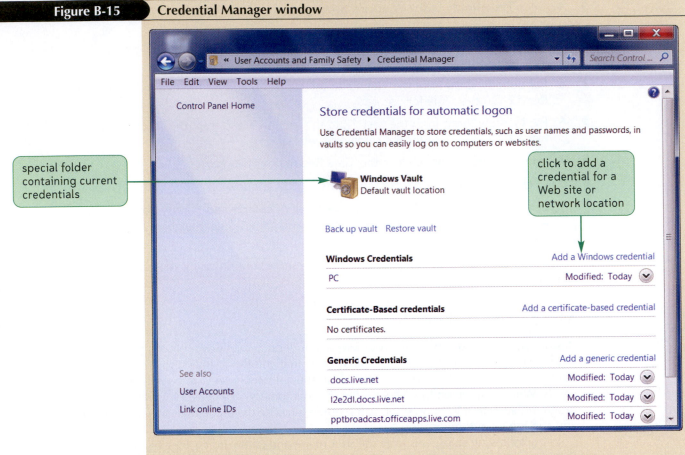

special folder containing current credentials

click to add a credential for a Web site or network location

2. In the Windows Credentials section, click **Add a Windows credential**.

3. In the Add a Windows Credential window, type **www.bank.com** in the Internet or network address text box.

4. In the User name text box, type **New User**.

5. In the Password text box, type **password**.

6. Click the **OK** button. The new vault appears in the Credential Manager window.

The next time you use your browser to visit *www.bank.com*, Windows will provide your user name and password so you can log on automatically, if the site allows you to do so.

Another way to make the hardware and other settings work for you is to use Ease of Access settings to enhance the accessibility of your computer.

Setting Ease of Access Options

Ease of Access options are Windows 7 settings that you can change to make it easier to interact with your computer. Although designed primarily for users with special vision, hearing, and mobility needs, any user might find it helpful to adjust Ease of Access settings when working with software such as graphics programs that require more control over mouse and keyboard settings or when working in a poorly lit or noisy room.

To use Ease of Access options, you open the Ease of Access Center from the Control Panel. In this window, you can adjust settings that make it easier to see your computer, and use the mouse, keyboard, or other input devices. Figure B-16 summarizes some of the accessibility settings you can change using the Ease of Access Center. When you turn on an Ease of Access option, it applies as soon as you log on to Windows.

| Figure B-16 | Ease of Access options |

Option	Description
Use the computer without a display	
Turn on Narrator	Have Narrator read on-screen text aloud and describe some computer events, such as error messages.
Turn on Audio Description	Have Audio Description describe the action displayed in videos.
Make the computer easier to see	
Choose a High Contrast theme	Set a high-contrast color scheme to make some text and images on your screen more distinct.
Turn on Magnifier	Point to an area of the screen to have Magnifier enlarge it.
Use the computer without a mouse or keyboard	
Use On-Screen Keyboard	Display a visual keyboard with all the standard keys, which you can click to enter text.
Use Speech Recognition	Control the computer with your voice.
Make the mouse easier to use	
Turn on Mouse Keys	Control the movement of the mouse pointer by using the numeric keypad.
Activate a window	Make it easier to select and activate a window by pointing to it with the mouse rather than clicking it.
Make the keyboard easier to use	
Turn on Sticky Keys	Select keyboard combinations such as Ctrl+Alt+Del by pressing only one key at a time.
Turn on Toggle Keys	Play an alert each time you press the Caps Lock, Num Lock, or Scroll Lock keys.
Turn on Filter Keys	Set Windows to ignore keystrokes that occur in rapid succession, or keystrokes that are held down for several seconds unintentionally.
Use text and visual alternatives for sounds	
Turn on visual notifications for sounds	Replace system sounds with visual cues, such as a flash on the screen, so that system alerts are noticeable even when they're not heard.
Turn on text captions for spoken dialog	Have Windows display text captions in place of sounds to indicate that activity is happening on your computer (for example, when a document starts or finishes printing).
Make it easier to focus on tasks	
Remove background images	Turn off all unimportant, overlapped content and background images to help make the screen easier to see.
Choose how long Windows notification dialog boxes stay open	Choose how long notifications are displayed on the screen before they close.

You can open the Ease of Access Center to explore its options.

To open the Ease of Access Center:

1. In the left pane of the Credential Manager window, click **Control Panel Home** to return to the Control Panel Home page, and then click **Ease of Access** to open the Ease of Access window.

2. Click **Ease of Access Center**. The Ease of Access Center window opens. A narrator might explain what you can do with this window as Windows moves a selection box in the Ease of Access Center window so you can easily make a selection. See Figure B-17.

Figure B-17 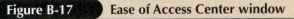 Ease of Access Center window

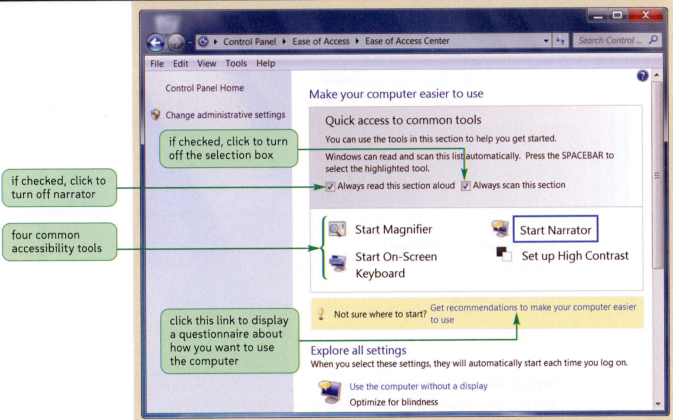

3. To turn off the narrator for now, click the **Always read this section aloud** check box to remove the check mark, if necessary. Click the **Always scan this section** check box to turn off the selection box.

4. Maximize the Ease of Access Center window.

The Ease of Access Center window includes three sections. In the Quick access to common tools box, you can quickly turn on tools that make your computer easier to use: Magnifier, Narrator, On-Screen Keyboard, and High Contrast. When you turn on a tool, it stays on until you log off.

The second section includes a Get recommendations to make your computer easier to use link. Click the link to display a questionnaire about how you want to use your computer. When you submit the questionnaire, Windows provides a list of settings that can make your computer easier to use. You can then select the settings you want.

The third section, Explore all settings, contains the seven categories of accessibility tools listed in Figure B-16. When you select these tools and set their options, they start each time you log on.

You can start a couple of Ease of Access tools to determine whether they improve your computing experience.

To use Ease of Access tools:

1. In the Ease of Access Center window, click **Start Magnifier**. The Magnifier dialog box opens. If necessary, click the **Plus** button ⊕ to increase the magnification to 200%.

2. Click the **Minimize** button ▬ to minimize the dialog box. The screen is now magnified to make it easier to see. See Figure B-18.

Figure B-18   Using Magnifier to make the screen easier to see

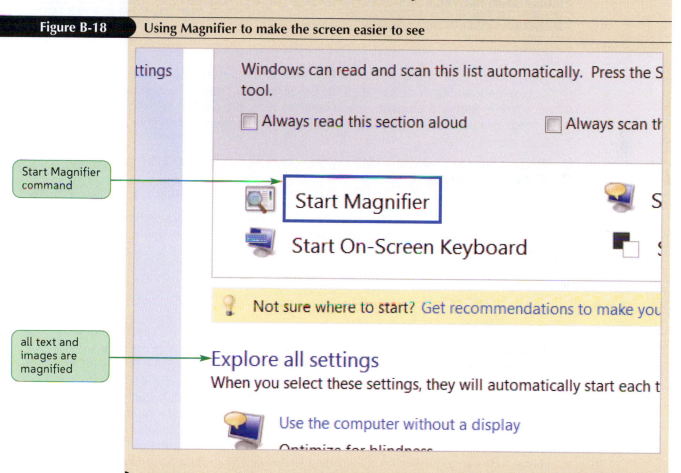

Start Magnifier command

all text and images are magnified

3. Move the pointer around the desktop.

4. Move the pointer to the bottom of the screen to display the taskbar, and then click the taskbar to turn off Magnifier.

   Trouble? If clicking the taskbar does not turn off Magnifier, click the Magnifier program button 🔍 on the taskbar to open the Magnifier dialog box, and then click the Close button ✖ to close the dialog box and turn off the Magnifier. You can also hold down the Windows logo key and then press the Esc key to turn off Magnifier.

5. Click **Start On-Screen Keyboard** to open the On-Screen Keyboard window. See Figure B-19.

Figure B-19   **Using the On-Screen Keyboard to enter data**

click a key instead of typing on the physical keyboard

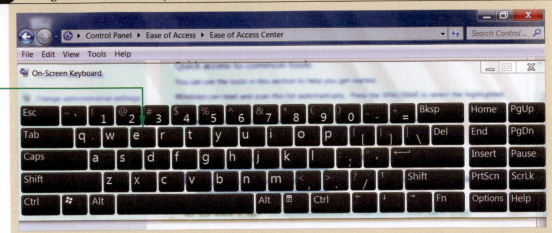

6. If necessary, drag the On-Screen Keyboard to the bottom of the screen. Open Notepad, and then click keys on the On-Screen Keyboard to enter your name in a new Notepad document. As you begin to type, the On-Screen Keyboard might display a key containing your name. If so, click the key to insert your name in the Notepad window.

7. Close Notepad without saving any changes, and then close the On-Screen Keyboard window.

You can also use the Ease of Access Center window to change accessibility settings, such as those that optimize the visual display, adjust settings for the mouse or other pointing device, and set up alternatives to sound. You'll explore one of these windows to change accessibility settings next.

Making the Computer Easier to See

If you want to optimize the visual display on your computer, you can open a window where you can select settings to turn on High Contrast, read aloud screen text or video descriptions, or turn on the Magnifier tool when you log on to Windows. By default, High Contrast uses large white letters on a black background and increases the size of the title bar and window control buttons, making objects and text stand out. If you have limited vision or if you're in a dark office, using a High Contrast color scheme can make it easier to see what's on your screen. You can also select a different High Contrast color scheme to use instead of the default white-on-black scheme. After selecting a High Contrast color scheme, you can turn it on by pressing the Left Alt+Left Shift+Print Screen keys.

If you are having problems seeing text on a screen or viewing a video, you can turn on the Narrator or Audio Description, which narrates the action in a video. (This feature is available only for videos that provide audio descriptions.) You can also select settings to turn on the Magnifier tool when you log on to Windows, set the thickness of the blinking insertion point, and remove background images when they appear in windows.

You'll turn on the High Contrast color scheme, and then explore other settings that make your computer easier to see.

To make your computer easier to see:

1. In the Ease of Access Center window, click **Make the computer easier to see** in the Explore all settings list. A window opens providing options for optimizing the visual display.

2. To test the current High Contrast color scheme, turn it on by pressing the **Left Alt+Left Shift+Print Screen** keys. A dialog box opens asking if you want to turn on High Contrast.

3. Click the **Yes** button. The desktop color scheme changes to the default High Contrast scheme. See Figure B-20.

Figure B-20	Default High Contrast color scheme

change this setting if you do not want to use a keyboard shortcut to turn High Contrast on or off

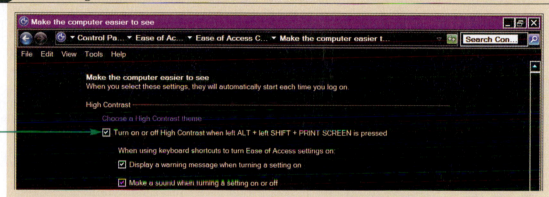

4. Press the **Left Alt+Left Shift+Print Screen** keys to turn off High Contrast.

5. Scroll the window, if necessary, to display the options in the Make things on the screen easier to see section.

6. Click the **Set the thickness of the blinking cursor** button (which displays a 1 by default), and then click **3**. The sample insertion point in the Preview box is thicker.

7. Click the **Set the thickness of the blinking cursor** button, and then click **1** to restore this setting.

8. Close all open windows.

Now that you have learned how to use many useful tools in the Control Panel, you can explore a few optional programs that let you create and share information with other people.

Using Windows Live Essentials

Windows Live Essentials is a suite of free software that you can use for a variety of personal and professional tasks. You already used one Windows Live Essentials program—Windows Live Mail—in a previous tutorial to send and receive e-mail. Recall that you downloaded the program from the Windows Live Web site and then installed it on your computer. All the Windows Live Essentials programs work the same way. Figure B-21 identifies and describes each program.

| Figure B-21 | Windows Live Essentials programs |

Program	Use to
Family Safety	Manage and monitor children's online activities
Mail	Send, receive, and organize e-mail messages and manage multiple e-mail accounts
Messenger	Chat online with friends and family on your computer or your mobile phone
Movie Maker	Organize your photos into slide shows and turn your video clips into movies complete with titles and credits
Photo Gallery	View, organize, fix, and share your photos
Toolbar	Quickly access Search and other online tools you use often
Writer	Compose a blog, add photos and video, and then post it on the Web

To see if any Windows Live Essentials programs are installed on your computer, click the Start button, type *Windows Live* in the search box, and then look in the search results to see if they contain a Windows Live Essentials program. You might have Windows Live Mail installed on your computer, for example. If you want to install another Windows Live Essentials program, you can download it for free from the Windows Live Web site.

This appendix explains how to use Windows Live Photo Gallery and Windows Live Movie Maker. If they are not already installed on your computer, you can download both programs at the same time.

To download and install Windows Live Essentials:

1. Start your Web browser, such as Internet Explorer, type **http://download.live.com** in the Address bar, and then press the **Enter** key to open the Windows Live Essentials home page.

2. Click the **Download** button to display the File Download – Security Warning dialog box, and then click the **Run** button. The Windows Live Essentials program files begin to download from the Web site. If a User Account Control dialog box opens asking if you want to allow the program to make changes to the computer, click the **Yes** button. After a few moments, the Welcome to Windows Live window opens and prepares the installer.

3. When a window opens listing programs you can install, make sure the Movie Maker and Photo Gallery check boxes are selected. If you do not want to download any other Windows Live Essentials programs, click all the other check boxes to deselect them.

4. Click the **Install** button. If a window opens asking you to close an open program such as Internet Explorer, click the **Close these programs for me** option button, if necessary, and then click the **Continue** button. Wait a few minutes while Windows Live Movie Maker and Photo Gallery are installed on your computer.

5. When installation is complete, a Windows Live window opens asking you to select settings. Click the **Continue** button to accept the default settings.

6. When a window opens welcoming you to Windows Live, click the **Close** button.

7. Close your Web browser.

Now you can start by exploring Windows Live Photo Gallery.

Using Windows Live Photo Gallery

You use Windows Live Photo Gallery to edit and share photos. After you take digital photos and import them onto your computer, you can fix common problems, such as unbalanced contrast and color, incorrect orientation, and red eye. You can also use Windows Live Photo Gallery to produce creative effects by combining two or more photos to create a single panoramic picture, for example. When you're satisfied with your photos, you can publish them to a photo album on a photo Web site.

Now that you've downloaded and installed Windows Live Photo Gallery on your computer, you can start the program and view the photos and videos in the Pictures and Videos libraries, which Photo Gallery displays by default.

To start and explore Windows Live Photo Gallery:

1. Click the **Start** button 🔵 on the taskbar, point to **All Programs**, click **Windows Live**, and then click **Windows Live Photo Gallery**.

   Trouble? If a dialog box opens asking about opening file types, click the No button.

   Trouble? If a Sign in to Windows Live dialog box opens, click the Cancel button.

2. In the Navigation pane on the left, click the **Public Pictures** folder to display the pictures in that folder in the Windows Live Photo Gallery window. See Figure B-22.

| Figure B-22 | Windows Live Photo Gallery |

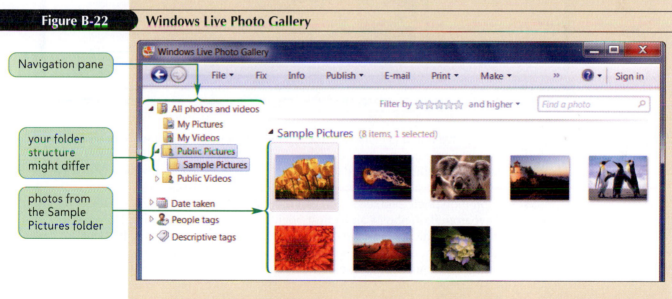

Navigation pane

your folder structure might differ

photos from the Sample Pictures folder

3. Point to the picture of the koala bear to display an enlarged preview displaying information about the picture.

4. Click the **View details** button 📋 on the status bar to display information about each picture, such as the file size, date taken, dimensions, and rating.

5. Click the **Info** button on the toolbar to open the Info pane on the right side of the window. See Figure B-23.

Figure B-23   Info pane in the Windows Live Photo Gallery window

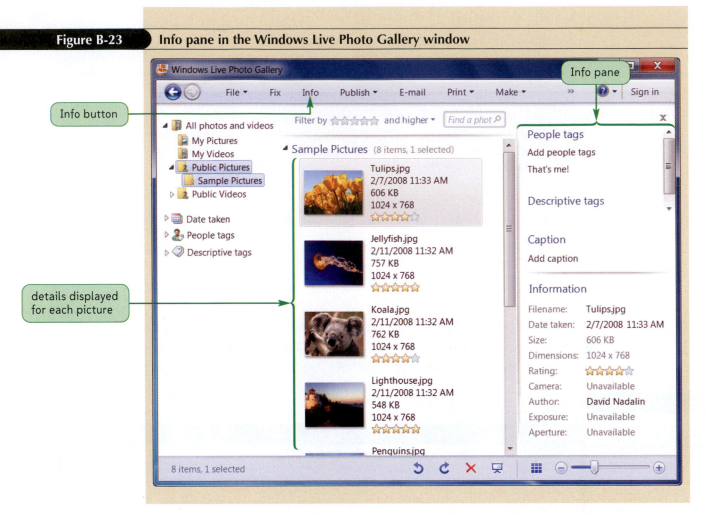

The Windows Live Photo Gallery window is similar to a folder window because it includes a Navigation pane, toolbar, Search box, and file list. The Info pane and the Editing pane provide tools specialized for working with photos. For example, you use the tools in the Info pane to add tags to photos and enter ratings and other information.

To solve common photo problems, you can use the tools in the Editing pane to remove red eye from flash photos and adjust brightness, contrast, and color. The easiest way to fix these problems is to use the Auto adjust tool. This tool automatically selects the best settings for light exposure and color. Try using Auto adjust before selecting any other repair method. If Auto adjust doesn't fix the problem with the photo, you can change one of the other settings yourself:

- Adjust exposure: Photos with inaccurate exposure are too bright or too dark. Correct this problem by changing the brightness (the amount of light displayed in the picture) or the contrast (the difference between the brightest and darkest parts of the picture).
- Adjust color: Change up to three color settings. To set the overall tone of the picture, change the color temperature to make the image appear warmer (with more red tones) or cooler (with more blue tones). If one color dominates your picture and makes the other colors look inaccurate—an effect called color cast—adjust the tint by adding or removing a color. If the colors in your photo look too vivid or dull, change the saturation, which determines the amount of color in an image.

You can also use other tools in the Editing pane to remove red eye and crop a picture.

To use the Windows Live Photo Gallery editing tools:

1. In Windows Live Photo Gallery, click the **Desert.jpg** photo, and then click the **Fix** button on the toolbar. The Editing pane opens. See Figure B-24.

| Figure B-24 | Editing pane in the Windows Live Photo Gallery window |

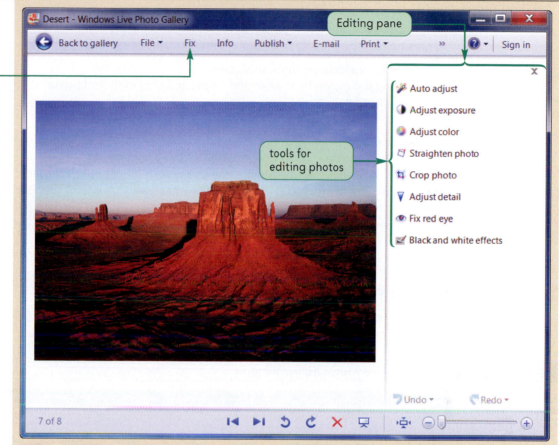

2. Click **Adjust exposure** to display the Adjust exposure options for Brightness, Contrast, Shadows, Highlights, and Histogram.

3. Drag the **Brightness** slider to the right. The Desert photo now looks washed out.

4. Click the **Scroll down** button ⌄ in the Editing pane, if necessary, and then click **Adjust color** to display the Adjust color options for Color temperature, Tint, and Saturation.

5. Drag the **Color temperature slider** to the left to make the colors in the Desert photo cooler, which emphasizes blue hues.

6. Click the **Undo button arrow** at the bottom of the Editing pane, then click **Undo all** to restore the Desert photo to its original exposure and colors.

7. Close all open windows.

To crop a picture in Windows Live Photo Gallery, you click Crop photo in the Editing pane, drag the cropping handles to select the area you want to crop, and then click Apply. To fix photos with red eye, click Fix red eye in the Editing pane, and then drag a rectangle around the eye you want to adjust.

Using Windows Live Movie Maker

If you have a digital video (DV) camera, you can use Windows Live Movie Maker to import audio and video to your computer from your DV camera, and then assemble the imported content into a movie. You can also import existing audio, video, and still pictures into Movie Maker to use in movies and slide shows. Each piece of media you use in Movie Maker is called a clip. You can also include **transitions** between each photo or video clip to control how your movie or slide show plays from one video clip or picture to the next. For example, a video clip can start by fading in from a black screen or one picture can slide across the screen to reveal another picture.

Creating a movie typically involves completing three major steps:

1. Importing video, pictures, and music
2. Editing the movie to arrange and fine-tune video clips and pictures, add transitions, and coordinate music
3. Publishing the edited movie or slide show

If you need help making a movie, add some photos and videos, choose a song, and then click AutoMovie—Windows Live Movie Maker automatically creates a movie for you.

Keep in mind that creating movies can consume a lot of hard disk space. A 10-minute movie consisting of video clips and transitions can easily take up 2 or more gigabytes, so make sure you have enough hard disk space before you start creating a movie. Also, the video card on your computer must support Microsoft DirectX 9c or later and Pixel Shader 2.0 or later with video drivers for Windows 7.

To start Windows Live Movie Maker and play a video:

▶ 1. Click the **Start** button 🔵 on the taskbar, point to **All Programs**, click **Windows Live**, and then click **Windows Live Movie Maker**. See Figure B-25.

Figure B-25   Windows Live Movie Maker window

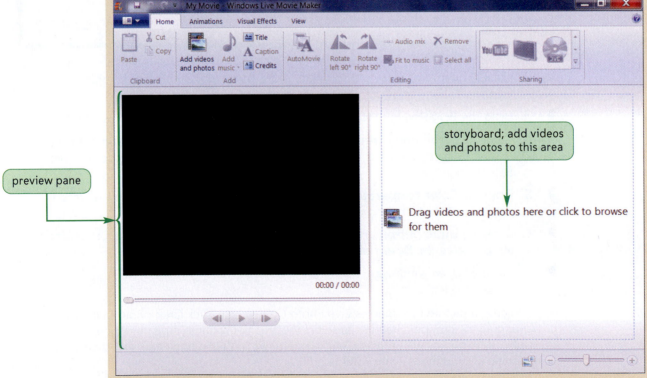

preview pane

storyboard; add videos and photos to this area

2. On the **Home** tab in the Add group, click the **Add videos and photos** button. The Add Videos and Photos dialog box opens.

3. In the Navigation pane, click the **Videos** library. Double-click the **Sample Videos** folder to display its contents.

4. Double-click the **Wildlife** video to add it to the Movie Maker storyboard. See Figure B-26.

| Figure B-26 | Adding a video clip to the storyboard |

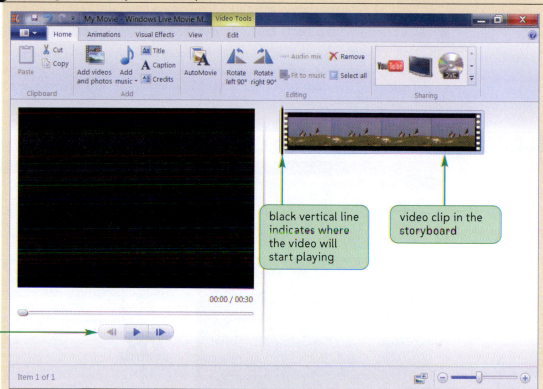

playback controls

black vertical line indicates where the video will start playing

video clip in the storyboard

5. Click the **Add videos and photos** button in the Add group again, navigate to the **Pictures** library, open the **Sample Pictures** folder, and then double-click the **Penguins** picture to add it to the storyboard.

6. To play the video, click the beginning of the video clip in the storyboard, and then click the **Play** button ▶ in the playback controls on the left side of the window.

7. After playing a few seconds of the video, click the **Pause** button ❚❚ in the playback controls. Before you make changes to the video, save it with a different name.

8. Click the **Movie Maker menu** button ▤▾ , click **Save project as**, navigate to the **Videos** library, if necessary, type **My Movie XY** (where XY are your initials), and then click the **Save** button.

When you save a project, you save all the clips in the storyboard and any other information you added to the storyboard, including transitions and timings.

As you've seen, the Movie Maker window includes a preview pane on the left, where you play the movie, and a storyboard on the right. In the storyboard, you set the order of your clips, edit them, and add visual effects. The storyboard is your workspace for linking media clips in logical order. You can fine-tune the arrangement by dragging media from one spot on the storyboard to another. You can also split video clips in two and trim a video.

The sample video you selected is about 30 seconds long. To make it shorter, you can trim the video clip, which means you hide any parts of the video that you don't want to show in your final movie. You can trim the My Movie XY video so it shows the horses running and birds flying during the first 7 seconds of the video.

To trim the video clip:

1. If necessary, click the beginning of the video clip again. The vertical black bar in the storyboard should appear at the beginning of the video clip.

2. Click the **Video Tools Edit** tab, and then click the **Set start point** button in the Editing group.

3. In the preview pane, prepare to set the end point by dragging the **playback slider** to the right to about the 00:07 second mark, just before the seals appear. See Figure B-27.

| Figure B-27 | Preparing to set the end point |

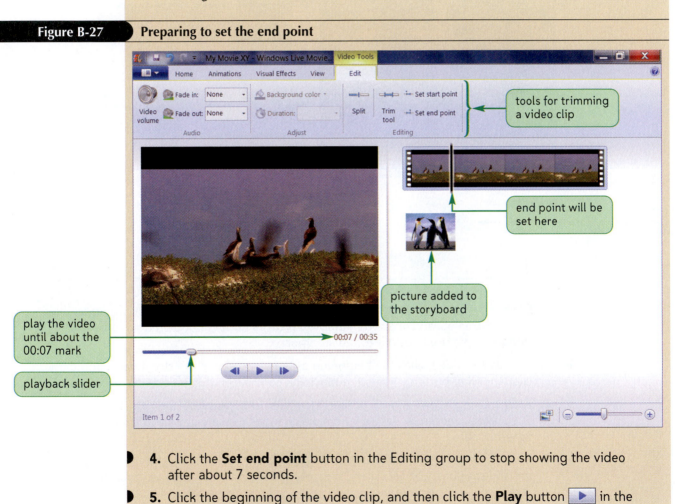

4. Click the **Set end point** button in the Editing group to stop showing the video after about 7 seconds.

5. Click the beginning of the video clip, and then click the **Play** button ▶ in the playback controls to view the edited video clip.

To let viewers know basic information about your movie, such as when, where, and what happened, you can add a title to the movie.

To add a title to the movie:

1. Click the beginning of the video clip, click the **Home** tab, and then click the **Title** button in the Add group. A black title slide appears to the left of the video clip in the storyboard.

2. Type **My First Movie** to add text to the title slide in the preview pane.

3. To change the background color of the title slide, click the **Background Color button** in the Adjust group to display the Background Color gallery. See Figure B-28.

Figure B-28   **Changing the background color of a title clip**

Dark blue theme color

black background will change to the color you select

text that appears in the title clip

title clip text box

My First Movie

4. Click the **Dark blue** theme color in the first row to apply that color to the background of the title slide.

5. To change the amount of time the title slide plays, click the **Text duration** text box in the Adjust group, and then change the time to **3.00**. Now the title slide will play for 3 seconds.

6. In the storyboard, drag the **My First Movie** text box so it is centered below the title slide. The vertical black bar moves with the text box to indicate that the text would start playing immediately if you clicked the Play button now. You'll move the black bar to the beginning of the title slide in the next step.

7. Click the **Save** button 💾 on the Quick Access Toolbar, click the beginning of the title slide in the storyboard, and then click the **Play** button ▶ in the playback controls to view the movie.

Now that you have three clips in the storyboard, you can add transitions between them. You can also add an effect to change the appearance of a clip. For example, you can apply a Blur effect to make a photo look blurred. A transition plays as one clip ends and the next clip starts, while a visual effect is applied for the entire duration of a clip. You can add multiple visual effects to the same clip and customize the order of effects. For still photos, you can add pan and zoom effects to create the illusion of motion. If you no longer want to use a transition or special effect, you can remove it.

To add a transition between the title slide and the video:

▶ **1.** Click the **title slide**, if necessary to select it, hold down the **Shift** key, and then click the **Penguins photo** to select all three clips. With all clips selected, the transition you select will play between each clip.

▶ **2.** Click the **Animations** tab to display the transition options. See Figure B-29.

| **Figure B-29** | **Selecting a transition** |

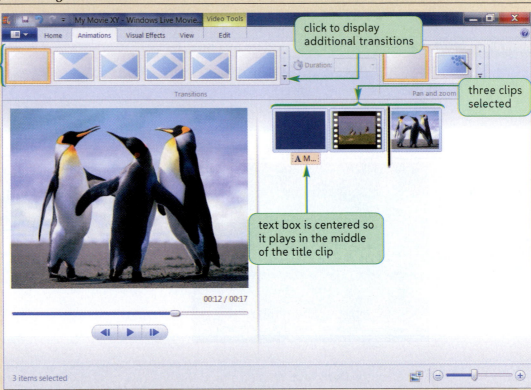

Callouts:
- transitions to apply to the selected clips
- click to display additional transitions
- three clips selected
- text box is centered so it plays in the middle of the title clip

00:12 / 00:17

3 items selected

▶ **3.** Point to the **Bow tie – horizontal** box in the Transitions group to preview this transition.

▶ **4.** Click the **Bow tie – horizontal** box to apply the transition to the selected clips.

▶ **5.** To lengthen the duration of the transition, click the **Duration** list arrow in the Transitions group, and then click **1.50**.

▶ **6.** Click the **Save** button on the Quick Access Toolbar to save your work, click the beginning of the title slide, and then click the **Play** button in the playback controls to view the movie.

Next, you can apply a visual effect to the photo of the penguins at the end of the movie.

To add a visual effect to a photo:

▶ **1.** Click the **Penguins photo** in the storyboard to select the photo clip.

▶ **2.** Click the **Visual Effects** tab to display the visual effects options. See Figure B-30.

Figure B-30   **Applying a visual effect**

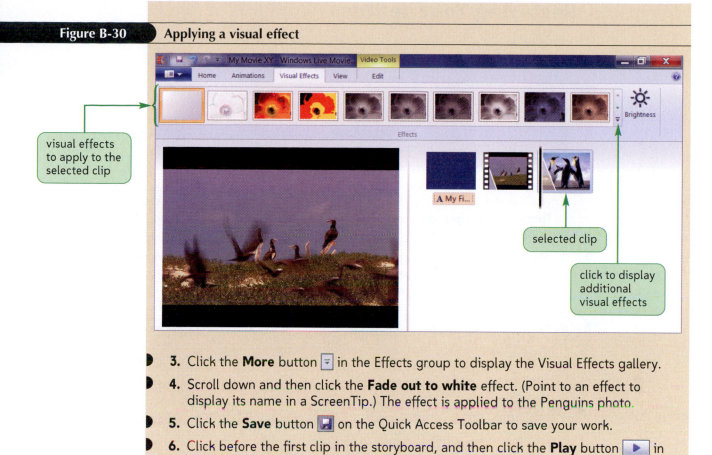

visual effects to apply to the selected clip

selected clip

click to display additional visual effects

3. Click the **More** button in the Effects group to display the Visual Effects gallery.

4. Scroll down and then click the **Fade out to white** effect. (Point to an effect to display its name in a ScreenTip.) The effect is applied to the Penguins photo.

5. Click the **Save** button on the Quick Access Toolbar to save your work.

6. Click before the first clip in the storyboard, and then click the **Play** button in the playback controls to view the movie.

Once your movie looks and sounds the way you want, you can publish the project file as a movie on the Web or save it as a WMV movie file. Windows Live Movie Maker offers different types of compression for WMV files. You select the type when you save the file depending on how you plan to store or distribute the movie. For example, select the For e-mail or instant messaging option if you plan to send the movie using e-mail. If you want to save your work as a movie file, you can complete the following steps.

To save the movie file:

1. Click the **Movie Maker menu** button , point to **Save movie**, and then click **For e-mail or instant messaging**. The Save Movie dialog box opens, displaying the contents of the My Videos folder.

2. Type **Published Movie XY**, where XY are your initials, and then click the **Save** button. After the movie is published, you can play the movie, open the folder where it's stored, or close the dialog box.

3. Click the **Close** button to close the dialog box.

4. Close all other open windows.

You're finished exploring some of the tools available in Windows 7 and Windows Live Essentials.

Restoring Your Settings

If you are working in a computer lab or on a computer other than your own, complete the steps in this section to restore the original settings on your computer.

To restore your settings:

▶ **1.** Open the Hardware and Sound window in the Control Panel, click **Sound**, click the **Sounds** tab, click the **Sound Scheme** button, click **Windows Default**, and then click the **OK** button.

▶ **2.** In the Hardware and Sound window, click **Pen and Touch**, if possible, click the **Touch** tab in the Pen and Touch dialog box, and then click the **Use your finger as an input device** check box to remove the check mark and turn off Windows Touch.

▶ **3.** Navigate to the User Accounts and Family Safety window, click **Add or remove user accounts**, click **New User** (or the name of the new user you created in this appendix), click **Delete the account**, click the **Delete Files** button, and then click the **Delete Account** button to confirm you want to delete the account.

▶ **4.** Return to the User Accounts window, and then click **Manage your credentials** in the left pane. In the Windows Credentials section of the Credential Manager window, click the **expand** button ⊙ for *www.bank.com*, if necessary, click **Remove from vault**, and then click the **Yes** button to confirm you want to remove the credential.

▶ **5.** Navigate to the Videos library, and then delete the **My Movie XY** project file. Delete the **Published Movie XY** from the My Videos folder or move it to a removable disk.

▶ **6.** Close all open windows.

ENDING DATA FILES

There are no ending Data Files for this appendix.

GLOSSARY/INDEX

Note: Boldface entries include definitions.

A

Accelerator A tool in Internet Explorer that makes it easier to find information provided on the Web without navigating to other Web sites. WIN 175, WIN 194–196

access point, WIN 433

access to computer, controlling, WIN 274–275

Action Center A Control Panel tool that helps you manage security from a single window. WIN 228, WIN 230–240
    antivirus software, WIN 238–240
    features, WIN 230–231
    opening, WIN 231
    troubleshooting performance, WIN 547–550
    Windows Firewall, WIN 232–235
    Windows Update, WIN 235–237

active program The program you are currently working with. WIN 14

ActiveX control A small, self-contained program you can run in other programs, especially Internet Explorer. WIN 257

adapter cards. *See* expansion card

add-on A program offered by any software vendor that provides enhancements such as a toolbar or improved search feature to another program. WIN 261–262

Address bar The bar at the top of a folder window that shows the location of the current window. WIN 30, WIN 33, WIN 57, WIN 312
    navigating using, WIN 63–64

Address toolbar, WIN 154

advanced performance tools, WIN 552–571
    Disk Defragmenter, WIN 552, WIN 569
    Event Viewer, WIN 552, WIN 554–556
    Performance Monitor, WIN 542, WIN 552, WIN 556–560
    Performance Options, WIN 552, WIN 568–569
    Resource Monitor, WIN 542, WIN 552, WIN 561–562
    System Diagnostics, WIN 552, WIN 569–571
    System Information window, WIN 552, WIN 566–568
    Task Manager, WIN 552, WIN 562–566

Advanced Tools window, WIN 542, WIN 553

adware A type of spyware that changes your browser settings to display advertisements. WIN 240

Aero The user interface in Windows 7. WIN 5

Aero Flip 3D (Flip 3D) A feature available in the Aero experience that displays all your open windows in a three-dimensional stack so you can *see* the windows from the side. WIN 15, WIN 17

Aero Peek A feature available in the Aero experience that lets you preview the desktop and open windows. WIN 141
    managing desktop, WIN 144–146
    tools, WIN 142

Aero Shake A feature available in the Aero experience that lets you quickly minimizes all open windows on the desktop by shaking the title bar of the window you want to focus on. WIN 141, WIN B12
    managing desktop, WIN 146
    tools, WIN 142

Aero Snap A feature in Windows 7 that lets you arrange and resize windows by dragging them to the edge of the desktop. WIN 141, WIN B11–B12
    arranging windows side by side, WIN 143–144
    tools, WIN 142

alert message A notice about security and maintenance settings that need your attention. WIN 229

antispyware program A program that can detect and remove spyware. WIN 229, WIN 230

antivirus software, WIN 230, WIN 238–240

Appearance and Personalization category, Control Panel, WIN 126

application Software that a computer uses to complete tasks; also called a program. WIN 4

Applications tab, Windows Task Manager dialog box, WIN 563, WIN 564–565

appointment, scheduling with Windows Live Calendar, WIN 217–219

arrow button, WIN 50

aspect ratio The ratio of the width to the height. WIN 137

attachment, e-mail messages, WIN 213–214

Audio Description, WIN B24

audio file
    playing, WIN 385
    Windows Live Movie Maker, WIN B30–B35

AutoPlay A Windows feature that lets you choose which program to use to play media. WIN B2, WIN B7, WIN B8–B9

B

Back A button that takes you back to your previous location in your sequence of opened locations; appears next to the address bar in a folder window. WIN 50, WIN 57

background
    solid, WIN 357
    transparent, WIN 357

background color The color used for the inside of enclosed shapes and the background of text in Paint. WIN 339

backup file A copy of one or more files stored in a compressed folder on an external medium such as an external hard drive. WIN 55, WIN 468, WIN 470–482, WIN 483
    changing backup settings, WIN 478–480
    copying compared, WIN 471
    frequency of backing up, WIN 473–474
    locations for, WIN 472–473
    restoring files and folders, WIN 480–482
    selecting files and folders to back up, WIN 472, WIN 473
    strategy, WIN 480

backup medium A separate medium, such as an external or internal hard disk, a writeable CD or DVD, or a removable USB flash drive on which backup files are saved. WIN 470

backup program A program that copies and then automatically compresses files and folders from a hard disk into a single file, called a backup file. WIN 470

bad sector An area of a hard disk that does not record data reliably. WIN 507

Balanced plan A power plan that provides enough power for typical computing tasks while conserving energy consumption. WIN 412

bandwidth The amount of data that can be transmitted, measured in kilobits or megabits per second, through a connection. WIN A5

base score A measure of the speed and performance of a computer's components, including the processor, random access memory (RAM), graphics card, and hard disk. WIN 543, WIN 544–546

BitLocker Drive Encryption A System and Security tool that protects the data on hard drives and removable drives. WIN B2, WIN B4–B7
   turning on and off, WIN B4–B7

bitmapped graphic A graphic made up of small dots called pixels that form an image. Also called a bitmap graphic. WIN 338, WIN 340
   saving in different file type, WIN 348
   vector graphics compared, WIN 341

Blocked Senders list, WIN 249

BMP. *See* Windows Bitmap Format (BMP)

Boolean filter A word such as AND, OR, or NOT that lets you combine search criteria. WIN 287, WIN 304–305
   combining with file properties, WIN 307

broadband connection A high-capacity, high-speed medium for connecting to the Internet. WIN 178, WIN A2
   preparing to connect, WIN A4–A6
   setting up, WIN A8–A10
   troubleshooting, WIN A10–A11

browser A program that locates, retrieves, and displays Web pages. WIN 174, WIN 178

Brushes button, Paint, WIN 344

burning CDs and DVDs, WIN 386, WIN 398–399

C

cable, WIN 433

calendar. *See also* Calendar
   printing, WIN 219

Calendar In Windows Live Mail, the electronic version of a daily planner. WIN 198, WIN 216–219
   scheduling appointments, WIN 217–219
   starting, WIN 216–217

Calendar gadget, WIN 114

canvas
   Paint window, WIN 343
   resizing, WIN 350–351

CD
   burning, WIN 386, WIN 398–399
   playing, WIN 386

certificate A digital document that verifies the security of a Web site you visit. WIN 257

Change your view A button that changes the size of the icons in a folder window. WIN 31

check box, WIN 30

click To press a mouse button and immediately release it. WIN 7
   gesture, WIN B11

Clipboard A temporary storage area for files and information that you have copied or moved from one place and plan to use somewhere else. WIN 70
   copying files, WIN 72

Clipboard group button, Paint, WIN 343, WIN 344

Clock dialog box, WIN 115–116

Clock gadget, WIN 114–116

Clock, Language, and Region category, Control Panel, WIN 126

Close button, WIN 20

closing
   Paint, WIN 368
   programs from taskbar, WIN 17–18

cloud computing Providing and using computer tools, such as software, via the Internet (or the cloud). WIN 177

cluster One or more sectors of storage space on a hard disk. WIN 506

collaboration. *See* Windows Live Groups

color
   changing in Paint, WIN 361–362
   desktop, setting, WIN 131–134
   filling areas, WIN 361
   monitor settings, WIN 524–525
   picking in Paint, WIN 354

Color 1 button, Paint, WIN 344

Color 2 button, Paint, WIN 344

Color palette button, Paint, WIN 344

Color picker button, Paint, WIN 344

Colors group, WIN 339

Colors group buttons, Paint, WIN 343, WIN 344

column heading A title for a column in a folder window that can be clicked to sort a list of files and folders. WIN 31

command
   adding to right side of Start menu, WIN 160–161
   selecting, WIN 8

compatibility, setting up programs for, WIN 495–497

compressed file, WIN 92–95

compressed folder A folder that reduces the size of the files it contains so they take up less disk space. WIN 74

compression A space-saving technique used to store data in a format that takes less space. WIN 346

computer icon An icon in the Navigation pane of a folder window that shows the drives on your computer. WIN 50

Computer window A tool that you use to view, organize, and access the programs, files, and drives on your computer. WIN 11
   navigating with, WIN 32–34

Connect to a Network Projector Wizard, WIN 431

contact A collection of information about a person or organization, such as name and e-mail address. WIN 199
   adding to Windows Live Contacts, WIN 214–216

Contents list, Windows Help and Support, selecting topics, WIN 41

contrast The difference between the brightest and darkest parts of an image. WIN 370
   photos, WIN 379

control A graphical or textual object used for manipulating a window and for using a program. WIN 18–19
   dialog boxes, WIN 28
   Ribbon, WIN 24

Control Panel A window that contains specialized tools you use to change the way Windows 7 looks and behaves. WIN 11, WIN 124–136
   Action Center. *See* Action Center
   activating screen savers, WIN 134–136
   categories, WIN 126
   changing desktop background, WIN 129–131
   changing desktop colors and fonts, WIN 131–134
   Hardware and Sound category. *See* Hardware and Sound category, Control Panel
   opening, WIN 125
   saving themes, WIN 136
   selecting themes, WIN 127–129

cookie A small file that records information about you when you visit a Web site. WIN 262
   privacy settings, WIN 262–265

copy To place a file in a new location that you specify without removing it from its current location. WIN 69
    backing up compared, WIN 471
    backup. *See* backup file
    files, WIN 69, WIN 71–72
    folders, WIN 69, WIN 71
    images in Paint, WIN 362–366

copy and paste method, creating graphics, WIN 348–350

Copy button, Paint, WIN 344

copyright The originator's exclusive legal right to reproduce, publish, or sell intellectual property. WIN 197

copyright-protected photo, WIN 373

counter A performance indicator that measures a particular part of the system performance. WIN 557

CPU graph, WIN 561

CPU Meter gadget, WIN 114

cracker A hacker with criminal intent. WIN 230

credentials, managing, WIN B19–B20

crop To remove a row or column of pixels from an edge of a graphic to make it smaller or to remove unwanted parts. WIN 350
    graphics, WIN 366–368
    photos, WIN 379, WIN 381–382

Crop button, Paint, WIN 344

CRT (cathode ray tube) monitor, WIN 137

Currency gadget, WIN 114

Customize Flicks dialog box, WIN B13–B14

Customize Start Menu dialog box, WIN 157

customizing
    file list, WIN 89–91
    folder window, WIN 86–92
    gadgets, WIN 115–117
    Navigation pane, WIN 91–92
    slide shows, WIN 395–396
    Start menu, WIN 157–163

Cut button, Paint, WIN 344

D

date
    changing in computer, WIN 147
    filtering search results by date modified, WIN 295–297

Date/Time control An element on the far right side of the taskbar that shows the current date and time and lets you set the clock. WIN 3

default settings A set of standard settings that controls how the screen is set up and how a document looks when you first start typing. WIN 6
    default program, WIN 493–494

defragment To reorganize the clusters on a disk so that files are stored most efficiently. WIN 499, WIN 508–512, WIN 552, WIN 569

Delete Browsing History dialog box, WIN 265

deleting
    e-mail messages, WIN 212–213
    files and folders, WIN 77–78
    parts of graphics, WIN 356
    quarantined files, WIN 243
    shortcut icons, WIN 124
    unnecessary files using Disk Cleanup, WIN 504–505

desktop Your workspace on the screen for projects and the tools that you need to manipulate your projects. WIN 3, WIN 6–10
    background, WIN 129–131
    colors and fonts, WIN 131–134
    extending to additional monitor, WIN 527
    icons. *See* icon
    keeping clean, WIN 119
    managing with Aero tools, WIN 142–146
    number of open windows, WIN 18
    personalizing using Control Panel. *See* Control Panel
    screen resolution, WIN 137–138

desktop background The color or design that appears on the desktop. WIN 107

desktop icon An icon that appears on the desktop and lets you access Windows tools, drives, programs, and documents. WIN 106

Desktop Icons Settings dialog box, WIN 110–111

Desktop toolbar, WIN 154

Details pane The pane at the bottom of a folder window that displays the characteristics of the folder or selected object. WIN 31

device. *See* hardware

device conflict An event that occurs when two devices share an IRQ, DMA channel, I/O address, or memory range, that renders one or both devices unusable. WIN 514

device driver. *See* driver

dialog box A special kind of window in which you enter or choose settings for how you want to perform a task. WIN 24–25, WIN 27–29. *See also* specific dialog boxes
    controls, WIN 28

dial-up connection A way to access the Internet by using a modem connected to a standard telephone line. WIN 178, WIN A2, WIN A7–A8
    setting up, WIN A12–A14
    troubleshooting, WIN A14

digital cable A broadband technology that creates a high-speed connection to the Internet using a cable modem attached to cable television lines. WIN 178

digital signature An electronic security mark that can be added to files. WIN 257, WIN 258

digital subscriber line (DSL) A broadband technology that creates a high-speed connection to the Internet through standard telephone lines. WIN 178, WIN A5–A6

direct memory access (DMA) channel The channel for transferring data directly between a device and system memory without using the microprocessor. WIN 514

disabling a hardware device, WIN 516–518

disk A computer device for storing data. WIN 52

Disk Cleanup tool A Windows 7 tool that frees disk space by deleting unnecessary files, such as temporary files. WIN 498, WIN 504–505

Disk Defragmenter, WIN 511–512, WIN 552

Disk graph, WIN 561

displaying. *See also* viewing
    Desktop toolbar, WIN 154–155
    Favorites list, WIN 188–189
    filename extensions, WIN 89–91
    file path, WIN 60
    pop-up windows, WIN 260
    redisplaying windows, WIN 21
    standard desktop icons, WIN 109, WIN 110–111
    Web pages designed for earlier versions of Internet Explorer, WIN 183

DMA. *See* direct memory access (DMA) channel

document, creating shortcut to, WIN 119–121

domain name An identifier on the Internet that includes one or more IP addresses. WIN 180

double-click To click the left mouse button twice in quick succession. WIN 9
    gesture, WIN B11

downloading Windows Live Essentials, WIN B26

drag To click an object and then press and hold down the mouse button while moving the mouse. WIN 21
    creating shortcuts, WIN 117
    gesture, WIN B11
    to move and copy files, WIN 72

drawing shapes, WIN 359–360

drive A computer device that can retrieve and sometimes record data on a disk. WIN 52
    creating shortcut to, WIN 117–119
    encryption, WIN B2, WIN B4–B7
    opening in right pane, WIN 57
    unlocking, WIN B5–B6
    USB flash drive, WIN 472, WIN B4–B7

driver A software file that enables Windows 7 to communicate with and control the operation of the device. WIN 515
    installing, WIN 518–520
    rolling back to previous version, WIN 520

DSL. *See* digital subscriber line (DSL)

DVD
    burning, WIN 386, WIN 398–399
    playing, WIN 386

E

Ease of Access category, Control Panel, WIN 126, WIN B3, WIN B20–B25

Ease of Access options Settings to make it easier to interact with a computer. WIN B3, WIN B20–B25

Edit colors button, Paint, WIN 339, WIN 344

editing photos, WIN 379–382

Edit Plan Settings window, WIN 422

electronic mail (or e-mail) Electronic messages transferred between users on a network, such as the Internet. WIN 198–216
    addressing, WIN 201
    distributing photos, WIN 382–384
    etiquette, WIN 202
    operation, WIN 200–201
    sending and receiving, WIN 200–201, WIN 206–213
    viruses. *See* virus
    Windows Live Mail. *See* Windows Live Mail

e-mail account The information, such as user name and password, that an e-mail program uses to connect to your e-mail service. WIN 198
    supported by Windows Live Mail, WIN 205

e-mail address The notation that directs a message to its destination. WIN 199

e-mail message A simple text document that you can compose and send using an e-mail program, such as Windows Live Mail. WIN 199
    encrypting, WIN 247

e-mail program A program, such as Windows Live Mail, that allows users to compose, send, and receive e-mail messages. WIN 199

e-mail relay A practice spammers use to take advantage of vulnerabilities in your computer to send spam to other computers without your permission. WIN 247

e-mail server A network computer that transfers e-mail messages. WIN 200

enabling a hardware device, WIN 516–518

encryption, WIN 247
    drives, WIN B2, WIN B4–B7

Eraser button, Paint, WIN 344

error. *See also* troubleshooting system problems
    checking hard disk for, WIN 505–508
    software. *See* software error

Error-checking tool A Windows 7 tool that checks a disk to locate and repair errors, such as corrupted files. WIN 499

Ethernet technology, WIN 432, WIN 433

etiquette, e-mail, WIN 202

event log A special text file that contains details about a system event. WIN 554

Event Properties window, WIN 556

Event Viewer, WIN 552, WIN 554–556

exit To close a program. WIN 13. *See also* closing

expansion card A device that you insert into an expansion slot. Also called an adapter card. WIN 513

expansion slot A socket in the motherboard to which internal devices can be connected. WIN 513

extension A dot followed by three or more characters in a filename that identifies the file's type. WIN 74
    showing, WIN 89–91

external display device, presentations, WIN 429–430

external hard drive, saving backup files, WIN 472

extract To create an uncompressed copy of a compressed file in a folder you specify. WIN 93, WIN 94–95

F

Family Safety program, WIN B26

Favorites bar A toolbar in Internet Explorer that contains buttons for Web Slices and links to Web pages you view often. WIN 174
    adding links and Web slices, WIN 191–193

Favorites Center A pane in Internet Explorer that displays links to your favorites, feeds, and recently visited Web pages. WIN 174

Favorites list, WIN 188–190
    adding items, WIN 189
    displaying, WIN 188–189
    organizing, WIN 190

feed Online content that is updated often. WIN 114

Feed Headlines gadget, WIN 114

file A collection of related information; typical types of files include text documents, spreadsheets, digital pictures, and songs. WIN 4
    adding tags and other details to files, WIN 300–303
    attaching to e-mail messages, WIN 213–214
    backup copy, WIN 55. *See also* backup file
    combining Boolean filters with file properties, WIN 307
    compressed, WIN 92–95
    copying, WIN 69, WIN 71–72, WIN 471
    deleting, WIN 77–78
    deleting using Disk Cleanup, WIN 504–505
    filtering search results by size, WIN 291–293
    finding using Search box, WIN 65–66
    grouping, WIN 85–86
    hidden, WIN 89
    loss, preventing, WIN 83
    making available offline, WIN 451–452
    moving, WIN 69–71
    new, creating, WIN 78–79
    offline, accessing, WIN 448–452
    opening, WIN 81–82
    restoring, WIN 480–482
    restoring shadow copies, WIN 486–487
    saving, WIN 79–81
    searching for, by type, WIN 290
    selecting, WIN 71
    sharing with homegroup, WIN 445–447
    sorting and filtering, WIN 82, WIN 83–85
    where to store, WIN 73

File Download—Security Warning dialog box, WIN 489

file format graphics files, WIN 347

file hierarchy, WIN 53

file icon An icon that indicates a file's type. WIN 51

file list, customizing, WIN 89–91

filename The name given to a file when it is saved; identifies the file's contents. WIN 51, WIN 76–77

file path A notation that indicates a file's location. WIN 51

File Sharing dialog box, WIN 276–277

file system An operating system's hierarchy of folders and files, which ensures system stability and enables Windows to find files quickly. WIN 53, WIN 498

Fill button, Paint, WIN 344

Fill with color button, Paint, WIN 344

filter To display in a folder window only files and folders with a certain characteristic you specify. WIN 82, WIN 83–85
    searching vs. WIN 291
    search results, WIN 292–293

Find toolbar An Internet Explorer toolbar that helps you find specific information on a Web page. WIN 308

first-party cookie A cookie generated from a Web site you visit; contains information the Web site reuses when you return. WIN 262

folder A container that helps to organize the contents of your computer. WIN 9
    assigning permissions, WIN 276–277
    backing up, WIN 473
    copying, WIN 69, WIN 71
    creating, WIN 67–68
    creating shortcut to, WIN 119–121
    deleting, WIN 77–78
    making available offline, WIN 451–452
    moving, WIN 69
    network, saving backup files, WIN 473
    opening. See opening folders
    restoring, WIN 480–482
    selecting, WIN 71
    sharing, WIN 275–277
    synchronizing folders, WIN 452–456
    viewing contents, WIN 57

Folder Options dialog box, WIN 89–91

folder window A window that displays the contents of your computer. WIN 32, WIN 56
    changing layout, WIN 87–89
    customizing, WIN 86–92
    searching in, WIN 289–298

font, desktop, setting, WIN 131–134

foreground color The color used for lines, borders of shapes, and text in Paint. WIN 339

Forward A button that takes you to the next location in your sequence of opened locations; appears next to the address bar in a folder window. WIN 50, WIN 57

fragmented A term describing a disk that contains files whose clusters are not next to each other. WIN 510

G

gadget A miniprogram that you can customize and display on the desktop. WIN 107, WIN 114–115
    customizing, WIN 115–117

GB. See gigabyte (GB)

gestures, multitouch monitors, WIN B10–B14

Get help A button that opens the Windows Help and Support window from any folder window. WIN 31

GIF. See Graphics Interchange Format (GIF)

gigabyte (GB) 1000 megabytes (or 1 billion bytes) of data. WIN 52

graphic A file that displays an image on a computer monitor. Also called a graphic image. WIN 340–342
    adding text, WIN 353–356
    adding to computer, WIN 341
    bitmapped. See bitmapped graphic
    copying and pasting to create, WIN 348–350
    copying in Paint, WIN 362–366
    creating in Paint. See Paint
    cropping, WIN 366–368
    deleting parts, WIN 356
    drawing shapes, WIN 359–360
    file formats, WIN 347, WIN 348
    magnifying, WIN 353
    moving, WIN 366–367
    moving parts, WIN 356–358
    opening in Paint, WIN 345–346
    saving files, WIN 346–348
    vector, WIN 340–341. See vector graphic

graphical user interface (GUI) A type of user interface that displays icons representing items stored on your computer, such as programs and files. WIN 4

Graphics Interchange Format (GIF), WIN 347

graphics program Software that includes drawing and graphics-editing tools. WIN 338

gridlines Horizontal and vertical lines that are used to space and align shapes in Paint. WIN 338

group (computers). See homegroup

group (files) A sequential list of files in a folder window that share a particular detail, such as file type or size. WIN 74, WIN 85–86
    searching vs. WIN 291

group (people). See Windows Live Groups

group (Ribbon) A collection of controls for related actions on a Ribbon's tab. WIN 23

GUI. See graphical user interface (GUI)

H

hacker A person that intends to access a computer system without permission. WIN 230

hard disk A storage device permanently housed inside the computer case. WIN 52, WIN 500–512
    checking for errors, WIN 505–508
    defragmenting, WIN 508–512, WIN 552, WIN 569
    deleting unnecessary files, WIN 504–505
    organizing files and folders, WIN 54
    partitions, WIN 502–503
    viewing properties, WIN 500–502

hardware Any physical piece of equipment that is both connected to your computer and controlled by your computer. Also called a device. WIN 498
    device conflict, WIN 514
    disabling devices, WIN 516–518
    enabling devices, WIN 516–518
    removing USB devices, WIN 520–521
    TPM, WIN B4

Hardware and Sound category, Control Panel, WIN 126, WIN B7–B14
    changing sound scheme, WIN B9–B10
    Pen and Touch options, WIN B7, WIN B10–B14
    selecting AutoPlay defaults, WIN B2, WIN B7, WIN B8–B9
    Tablet PC settings, WIN B14–B15

Help and Support A window that provides articles, video demonstrations, and steps for performing tasks in Windows 7. WIN 11–12, WIN 39–42
    searching Help pages, WIN 41–42
    selecting topics from Contents list, WIN 41
    starting Help, WIN 39
    viewing Windows Basics topics, WIN 40

hibernation A power-saving state in which current data and system settings are saved to the hard disk, the computer is put into a power-saving state, and then the computer is turned off. WIN 419, WIN 420, WIN 423–424

hidden file A file not listed in a folder window, though it is actually stored in that folder. WIN 89

High Contrast, WIN B24

hijack To seize control of a browser. WIN 259

History list, WIN 184–185

hit A link in the list of Internet search results. WIN 308

homegroup A group of computers on a home network that can share files and printers. WIN 440, WIN 442–448
  adding other computers, WIN 443–444
  creating, WIN 442–443
  joining, WIN 444
  sharing files, WIN 445–447
  sharing printers, WIN 447–448

home network, setting up, WIN 434–435

home page The Web page a browser is set to open by default. WIN 178

hotspot A public space equipped with wireless Internet access. WIN A3

HPNA technology, WIN 432, WIN 433

HTTP. *See* Hypertext Transfer Protocol (HTTP)

hybrid sleep A power-saving state in which current data and system settings are saved to temporary memory and to the hard disk and the computer is put into a low-power state without turning off the power. WIN 420

hyperlink (or link) Text or a graphic in a Web document that targets another part of the document or a different document altogether. WIN 175
  adding to Favorites bar, WIN 191–193
  navigating using, WIN 182–183

Hypertext Transfer Protocol (HTTP) The most common way to transfer information around the Web. WIN 180

I

icon A small picture that represents an object available on your computer. WIN 2
  adding to desktop, WIN 109–111
  changing appearance, WIN 111–113
  changing size, WIN 525
  changing view, WIN 34–36

standard, displaying, WIN 109, WIN 110–111
  types, WIN 108

Image group buttons, Paint, WIN 343, WIN 344

IMAP. *See* Internet Message Access Protocol (IMAP)

importing a photo, WIN 372–373

Inbox In Windows Live Mail, the folder that stores the e-mail messages you receive. WIN 198

indexed location One or more folders that Windows indexes so it can search them quickly. WIN 293

Information bar A bar in Internet Explorer that displays information about security, downloads, and blocked pop-up windows. WIN 252

InPrivate Browsing A feature that prevents Internet Explorer from storing data about your browsing session. WIN 252, WIN 265–268
  turning on, WIN 266
  using, WIN 267–268

installed program A program that has been set up on your computer so that you can run it. WIN 469

installed update An update to Windows 7 that has been installed on a computer. WIN 469

installing
  device drivers, WIN 518–520
  local printers, WIN 529–531
  software, WIN 487–491
  software updates, WIN 492–493
  Windows Live Essentials, WIN B26

Integrated Services Digital Network (ISDN) line Telephone wires that provide a completely digital path from one computer to another. WIN A8

internal hard drive, saving backup files, WIN 472

Internet A worldwide collection of computers connected to one another to enable communication. WIN 4
  searching. *See* searching the Internet

Internet connection, WIN A1–A14
  broadband connections, WIN A4–A6, WIN A8–A11
  dial-up connections, WIN A7–A8, WIN A12–A14
  preparation, WIN A4–A8
  wireless connections, WIN A6–A7, WIN A11–A12

Internet Explorer. *See* Microsoft Internet Explorer; Microsoft Internet Explorer security

Internet Message Access Protocol (IMAP), WIN 205

Internet Options dialog box, WIN 263–264

Internet Security dialog box, WIN 259

Internet service provider (ISP) A company that sells Internet access. WIN 178, WIN A4

interrupt request (IRQ) line A number assigned to a device by Windows that signals the microprocessor that the device is requesting an action. WIN 514

I/O address The section of the computer's memory devoted to a particular device on a computer. WIN 514

IP address A unique number that identifies every computer on the Internet; consists of four sets of numbers from 0 to 255 separated by periods, or dots, as in 216.35.148.4. WIN 180

IRQ. *See* interrupt request (IRQ) line

ISDN. *See* Integrated Services Digital Network (ISDN) line

ISP. *See* Internet service provider (ISP)

J

join To become part of a homegroup, and to make folders and other resources available to other users in the homegroup. WIN 440, WIN 444

Joint Photographic Experts Group (JPG or JPEG), WIN 347

Jump List A list of recently or frequently opened files. WIN 140–150

junk mail. *See* spam

K

keyboard shortcut A key or combination of keys that perform a command. WIN 15

keyword A word in an Internet search expression. WIN 309

L

LAN. *See* local area network

laptop computer A portable computer that is smaller than the average briefcase and light enough to carry comfortably. A laptop computer has a flat screen and keyboard that fold together and a battery pack that provides several hours of power. WIN 414

Last Known Good Configuration An advanced startup option that uses the most recent system settings that worked correctly. WIN 591, WIN 592

layout, folder window, changing, WIN 87–89

LCD (liquid crystal display) monitor, WIN 137

library A central place to view and organize files and folders stored anywhere that your computer can access, such as those on your hard disk, removable drives, and network. WIN 33, WIN 58–59

lid setting, defining, WIN 424

link. *See* hyperlink

Links toolbar, WIN 154

list box A box that displays a list of available choices from which you can select one item. WIN 26

local area network (LAN) A network of computers and other hardware devices that reside in the same physical space, such as an office building. WIN 432

local disk A disk that is installed in a computer. WIN 498

local printer A printer connected directly to a computer. WIN 529–531
    installing, WIN 529–531

locking computer, WIN 274–275

log off To end a session with Windows 7 but leave the computer turned on. WIN 12, WIN 43

lost cluster A file system error that occurs if Windows loses track of which clusters contain the data that belongs to a single file. WIN 505

lost file, preventing, WIN 83

M

Magnifier button, Paint, WIN 344

Magnifier dialog box, WIN B23

Magnifier tool, WIN 353

magnifying a graphic, WIN 353

Mail program, WIN B26

malware
    blocking with Protected Mode and security zones, WIN 257–259
    protecting against, WIN 235–240
    types, WIN 235

Maximize button, WIN 20, WIN 21

MB. *See* megabyte (MB)

megabyte (MB) 1 million bytes of data. WIN 52

memory
    increasing capacity using Performance Options dialog box, WIN 568–569
    increasing capacity using ReadyBoost, WIN 571–573
    low, WIN 557–558

memory address or memory range Additional memory required by a device for its own use. WIN 515

Memory graph, WIN 561

menu A group or list of commands. WIN 7

menu bar A bar that lists commands for working in a folder window. WIN 74

menu command Text on a menu that you click to complete a task. WIN 7

message flag In Windows Live Mail, an icon that indicates the status of an e-mail message. WIN 198

Messenger program, WIN B26

microprocessor The "brains" of a computer; a silicon chip that contains a central processing unit. WIN 513

Microsoft Answers Web site A Web site that hosts a forum of users and Microsoft experts where you can search, browse, and post questions and answers. WIN 574

Microsoft Internet Explorer, WIN 178–179
    displaying Web pages designed for earlier versions, WIN 183
    navigating with Internet Explorer tools, WIN 184
    searching the Internet. *See* searching the Internet
    starting, WIN 178–179
    Suggested Sites feature, WIN 193

Microsoft Internet Explorer security, WIN 254–269
    add-on programs, WIN 261–262
    blocking pop-up windows, WIN 259–261
    InPrivate Browsing, WIN 265–268
    privacy settings, WIN 262–265
    Protected Mode, WIN 257–259
    security zones, WIN 258
    SmartScreen Filter, WIN 254–257

Microsoft SmartScreen Filter dialog box, WIN 255–256

Microsoft Solution Centers An online repository of support information for Microsoft product users. WIN 574, WIN 579–582

Microsoft Windows 7 A recent version of the Windows operating system. WIN 4
    starting, WIN 4–5
    turning off, WIN 43–44

Microsoft Windows Explorer
    navigating with, WIN 36–38
    starting, WIN 37

Microsoft Windows Flip, WIN 16

Minimize button, WIN 20–21

mobile computing device A computer that be easily transported, such as a laptop, notebook, or Tablet PC. WIN 414

Mobile PC category, Control Panel, WIN 126

mobile personal computer (PC). *See* mobile computing device

Mobility Center A control panel for managing a mobile computer. WIN 413, WIN 415–419
    power plan selection, WIN 416–419
    speaker volume setting, WIN 416

modem, WIN 433

monitor, WIN 521–529
    color settings, WIN 524–525
    icon and text size, WIN 525
    multiple, WIN 526–529
    multitouch, WIN B10–B14
    screen refresh rate, WIN 522–523
    secondary, setting resolution, WIN 528–529

monitor, changing settings, WIN 137–139

monitoring system performance, WIN 556–560

motherboard A circuit board inside a computer that contains the microprocessor, the computer memory, and other internal hardware devices. WIN 513

mouse The most common type of pointing device. WIN 6

move To remove a file from its current location and place it in a new location. WIN 69–71

Movie Maker program, WIN B26

moving
    graphics, WIN 366–367
    parts of graphics, WIN 356–358
    taskbar, WIN 151–152
    taskbar buttons, WIN 150–151

multimedia slide show, creating with Windows Media Center, WIN 391–399

multitask To work on more than one task at a time and to switch quickly between projects. WIN 14–18

multitouch monitor A monitor that lets you control your computer with your fingertips. WIN B2, WIN B10–B14

music file, WIN 385–391
   playing, WIN 387–389

N

Narrator, WIN B24

narrowing a search, WIN 314–318

native resolution The resolution a monitor is designed to display best, based on its size. WIN 521

navigate To move from one location to another on a computer, such as from one file or folder to another. WIN 32
   Address bar, WIN 63–64
   Computer window, WIN 32–34
   to data files, WIN 60–63
   History list, WIN 184–185
   hyperlinks, WIN 182–183
   Internet Explorer tools, WIN 184
   Windows Explorer, WIN 36–38

Navigation pane The left pane of a folder window that shows icons and links to resources and locations on your computer. WIN 30, WIN 38
   customizing, WIN 91–92

network Two or more computers connected to exchange information and resources. WIN 176
   home, setting up, WIN 434–435
   small office, setting up, WIN 434–435
   wireless, connecting to, WIN 436–439

network adapter A hardware device that translates electronic signals between your computer and your network connection. WIN 433, WIN A3

Network and Internet category, Control Panel, WIN 126

Network and Sharing Center window, WIN 436

network connection, managing, WIN 435–439

Network Firewall, WIN 230

network folder, saving backup files, WIN 473

Network graph, WIN 561

network hub, WIN 433

Networking tab, Windows Task Manager dialog box, WIN 563

network projector, connecting to, WIN 430–432

network resources The files, folders, software, and hardware devices that computers on a network can access. WIN 430–432

network switch, WIN 433

network technology The way computers connect to one another. The most common types of network technology for a small office or home network are wireless, Ethernet, Home Phone Network Alliance (HPNA), and Powerline. WIN 432–434

New folder button, WIN 50

New toolbar, WIN 154

notebook computer. *See* laptop computer

notification area The area on the right side of the taskbar that displays icons corresponding to services running in the background, such as an Internet connection. WIN 3
   monitoring, WIN 148

NTFS file system The file system Windows 7 uses to organize data on a hard disk. WIN 498

O

object, changing size, WIN 138–139

offline file A copy of a network file that you can access even when you are not connected to the network. WIN 441
   accessing, WIN 448–452

Offline Files dialog box, WIN 449

On-Screen Keyboard window, WIN B23–B24

opening
   Action Center, WIN 231
   Control Panel, WIN 125
   drives in right pane, WIN 57
   files, WIN 81–82
   folders. *See* opening folders
   graphics in Paint, WIN 345–346
   Start menu, WIN 7
   Web pages, WIN 179–188

opening folders, WIN 38
   right pane, WIN 57
   using hierarchy of folders, WIN 59–60

operating system Software that manages and coordinates activities on the computer and helps the computer perform essential tasks such as displaying information on the computer screen and saving data on disks. WIN 4
   recovering, WIN 590–592

optimize To add keywords and phrases to a Web page that users are likely to use to find the information on the Web page. WIN 313

organizing files and folders, WIN 52–55, WIN 82–86
   grouping files, WIN 85–86

   need, WIN 53
   planning organization, WIN 55
   sorting and filtering files, WIN 83–85
   strategies, WIN 54–55

organizing photos, WIN 375–376

Outline button, Paint, WIN 344

P

paging file A hidden file on the hard disk that Windows uses to hold parts of programs and data files that do not fit in RAM. WIN 558

Paint. *See also* graphic
   adding text to graphics, WIN 353–356
   changing colors, WIN 361–362
   closing, WIN 368
   copying and pasting to create graphics, WIN 348–350
   copying images, WIN 362–366
   cropping graphics, WIN 366–368
   drawing shape, WIN 359–360
   moving images, WIN 351, WIN 352
   opening graphics, WIN 345–346
   picking colors, WIN 354
   resizing canvas, WIN 350–351
   saving files, WIN 346–348
   starting, WIN 342

Paint window, WIN 342–343

pane A separate area of a menu or window. WIN 2, WIN 10

Parental Controls Settings to help manage how children use a computer. WIN B3, WIN B17–B19

partition A part of a hard disk that works like a separate disk. Also called a volume. WIN 502–503

password A confidential series of characters that you must enter before you can work with Windows 7. WIN 4
   creating, WIN 273
   creating password-protected user accounts, WIN 270
   managing credentials, WIN B19–B20
   reset disk, WIN 274
   strong, WIN 271
   unlocking computer from sleep, WIN 425
   waking computer, WIN 44

password reset disk A removable disk, such as a USB flash drive or CD, that you can use to log on to Windows if you forget your password. WIN B3, WIN B16–B17

Paste button, Paint, WIN 344

Pen and Touch dialog box, WIN B12–B13

Pen and Touch options, WIN B7, WIN B10–B14

Pencil button, Paint, WIN 344

performance How well a computer does what it is supposed to do. WIN 541–549
   advanced performance tools. *See* advanced performance tools
   deleting temporary and unnecessary files, WIN 552
   indexing options, WIN 551–552
   optimizing visual effects, WIN 550–551
   power settings, WIN 552
   rating, WIN 544–547
   selecting tools to solve performance problems, WIN 564
   troubleshooters, WIN 547–550

Performance Information and Tools dialog box, WIN 553–554

Performance Monitor, WIN 542, WIN 552, WIN 556–560

Performance Monitor window, WIN 542

Performance Options, WIN 552, WIN 568–569

Performance Options dialog box, WIN 551

Performance tab, Windows Task Manager dialog box, WIN 563, WIN 566

Performance troubleshooter, WIN 547–550

permission, assigning to folders, WIN 276–277

phishing An attempt to deceive you into revealing personal or financial information when you respond to an e-mail message or visit a Web site. WIN 250–251
   protecting against, WIN 254

photo, WIN 372–382
   acquiring, WIN 372–373
   copyright-protected, WIN 373
   editing, WIN 379–382
   importing, WIN 372–373
   organizing, WIN 375–376
   playing slide shows, WIN 378–379
   printing, WIN 384–385
   public-domain, WIN 373
   royalty-free, WIN 373
   sharing photos, WIN 382–385
   viewing, WIN 373–375, WIN 376–378
   Windows Live Photo Gallery, WIN B27–B29

Photo Gallery program, WIN B26

Picture Puzzle gadget, WIN 114

Pictures library, WIN 373, WIN 374–375

pin To attach a program to the taskbar or Start menu or to attach a file to a program menu. WIN 140
   pinning programs to Start menu, WIN 157–160
   pinning programs to taskbar, WIN 148–151

pixel Short for picture element; one of the tiny dots that make up a computer image. Screen resolution is measured horizontally and vertically in pixels. WIN 137, WIN 340

pixel coordinates A display in the Paint status bar that specifies the exact location of the pointer on the canvas relative to the pixels on the screen. Pixel coordinates are given in an (x,y) format with x representing the horizontal locations and y representing the vertical location. WIN 338

playing
   music, WIN 387–389
   slide shows, WIN 378–379, WIN 394–395

playlist A list of media files, such as songs. WIN 386
   creating, WIN 389–390

PNG. *See* Portable Network Graphic (PNG)

point To use a pointing device to move the mouse pointer over objects on the desktop. WIN 6

pointer A small object, such as an arrow, that moves on the screen when you move your mouse. WIN 2

pointing device A piece of hardware connected to a computer that helps you interact with objects on the desktop. WIN 6

POP3. *See* Post Office Protocol 3 (POP3)

pop-up ad A window that appears while you are viewing a Web page and advertises a product or service. WIN 240
   blocking, WIN 259–261

Pop-up Blocker An Internet Explorer tool that limits or blocks pop-up windows. WIN 252

Pop-up Blocker Settings dialog box, WIN 260–261

port A physical connection that is visible on the outside of the computer to which external devices are connected. WIN 512

Portable Network Graphic (PNG), WIN 347

Post Office Protocol 3 (POP3), WIN 205

power button setting, defining, WIN 424

power failure, checking for errors after, WIN 506

Powerline technology, WIN 432, WIN 433

Power Options dialog box, WIN 423–424

Power Options window, WIN 421

power plan A collection of hardware and system settings that define how a computer consumes power. WIN 412
   customizing, WIN 419–426

Power saver plan A power plan that slows system performance and lowers the brightness of the display to extend battery life for mobile computer users who are working away from power outlets for several hours. WIN 412

presentation settings A collection of options that prepare a computer for a presentation. WIN 413, WIN 426–432
   connecting to network projectors, WIN 430–432
   customizing, WIN 427–429
   displaying information on external display devices, WIN 429–430
   turning on and off, WIN 428–429

Presentation Settings dialog box, WIN 428

Preview pane The pane in a folder window that displays the contents of a selected file. WIN 75

printer
   default, changing, WIN 531–532
   local. *See* local printer
   sharing with homegroup, WIN 447–448

printing
   calendars, WIN 219
   photos, WIN 384–385
   troubleshooting, WIN 582–584

print queue The list of documents waiting to be printed. WIN 582, WIN 584

privacy setting, WIN 262–265

Problem Steps Recorder, WIN 592–594

process A task performed by a program that usually contains information about starting the program. WIN 561

Processes tab, Windows Task Manager dialog box, WIN 563, WIN 565–566

processor time, tracking, WIN 557, WIN 558–560

program Software that a computer uses to complete tasks; also called an application. WIN 4. *See also* operating system
   adding to allowed programs list, WIN 234–235
   closing from taskbar, WIN 17–18

creating shortcut to, WIN 121–122
errors. *See* software error
exiting, WIN 13
installing, WIN 487–491
multiple, running, WIN 14–18
pinning. *See* pin
searching for, from Start menu, WIN 310–312
starting, WIN 12–13
switching between, WIN 15–17
uninstalling, WIN 491–492
updating. *See* software update

program button A button that appears on the taskbar for each open program. WIN 13

Program Compatibility Assistant dialog box, WIN 495–497

program event, viewing details, WIN 554

program menu button, WIN 18

Programs and Features window, WIN 492

Programs category, Control Panel, WIN 126

projector, network, connecting to, WIN 430–432

Properties dialog box, WIN 299–300

property A characteristic of an object, such as a file. WIN 124, WIN 299–303
    adding other details to files, WIN 302–303
    adding tags to files, WIN 300–301

Protected Mode A feature in Internet Explorer that guards against Web sites trying to save files or install malware on your computer. WIN 252
    Microsoft Internet Explorer, WIN 257–259

protocol A standardized procedure used by computers to exchange information. WIN 180

public-domain photo, WIN 373

quarantine To move a file to another location on your computer and prevent it from running until you remove or restore the file. WIN 242–243

Quick Access Toolbar A row of buttons on a program's title bar that give you one-click access to frequently used commands. WIN 18, WIN 19, WIN 25–26

R

Read access A permission level that allows other users to open a file, folder, or library without making any changes. WIN 440

reading e-mail messages, WIN 209–211

Read/Write access A permission level that allows other homegroup users to open and make changes to a file, folder, or a library. WIN 46

ReadyBoost, WIN 571–573

receiving e-mail messages, WIN 209–211

Recent Pages A button that displays a list of recent locations; appears next to the address bar in a folder window. WIN 50, WIN 57

recovering the operating system, WIN 590–592

Recycle Bin An area on your hard disk that holds deleted files until you remove them permanently. WIN 2, WIN 483
    deleting files and folders, WIN 77
    viewing contents, WIN 9

red eye, WIN 379

redisplaying windows, WIN 21

registry A database of information about a computer's configuration. WIN 482

Reinstall Windows tool, WIN 591

Reliability Monitor window A Windows 7 feature that maintains up to a year of history for system stability and reliability events. WIN 575, WIN 588–590

Remote Assistance, requesting, WIN 596–598

Remote Assistance Settings dialog box, WIN 595–596

Remote Desktop Connection A technology that allows you to use one computer to connect to a remote computer in a different location. WIN 456–459

removable media, organizing files and folders, WIN 54

removing. *See also* deleting
    USB devices, WIN 520–521

replying to e-mail messages, WIN 211–212

Resize button, Paint, WIN 344

resizing
    canvas, WIN 350–351
    graphics, WIN 344
    taskbar, WIN 151, WIN 152
    windows, WIN 22–23

Resource Monitor, WIN 542, WIN 552, WIN 561–562

Resource Monitor window, WIN 542

restore To use Windows 7 to extract files you want from a backup file and then copy them to a location you specify. WIN 468

Restore Down button, WIN 20, WIN 21

restore point A snapshot of a computer's system files and registry settings. WIN 482, WIN 483–486
    reverting to, WIN 592

restoring
    computer settings, WIN 95, WIN 399, WIN 459–460, WIN 532, WIN 598–599, WIN B36
    shadow copies of files, WIN 486–487
    windows, WIN 21

Ribbon The area at the top of a program window that provides access to a main set of commands, which are organized by task into tabs and groups. WIN 18, WIN 19, WIN 23–26
    controls, WIN 24
    Paint window, WIN 343

right-click To click an object with the right mouse button. WIN 10
    creating shortcuts, WIN 117
    gesture, WIN B11

right-drag, creating shortcuts, WIN 117, WIN 120

right pane The pane on the right side of a folder window that shows the contents of the object that is selected in the Navigation pane. WIN 30
    opening drives and folders, WIN 57

ripping music from CDs, WIN 386

root directory The location at the top of the file system hierarchy where Windows stores folders and important files that it needs when you turn on the computer. WIN 53

Rotate button, Paint, WIN 344

router, WIN 433

royalty-free photo, WIN 373

S

Safe mode A troubleshooting option for Windows that starts your computer with only basic services and functionality. WIN 591–592

SafeRecords, WIN 545–546

Safe Senders list, WIN 249

Safety Options dialog box, WIN 250

saving
    files, WIN 79–81
    graphics files, WIN 346–348

searches, WIN 297–298
themes, WIN 136
Web pages, WIN 196–197

scanner A device that converts an existing paper image into an electronic file that you can open and work with on your computer. WIN 342

scanning using Windows Defender, WIN 241–243

scheduling appointments, Windows Live Calendar, WIN 217–219

screen refresh rate The frequency, measured in hertz, at which a monitor redraws the images on the screen. WIN 52–523

screen resolution The clarity of the text and images on the screen. WIN 137–138

screen saver A program that causes a monitor to go blank or to display an animated design after a specified amount of idle time. WIN 4
activating, WIN 134–136
security, WIN 134

Screen Saver Settings dialog box, WIN 135–136

ScreenTip On-screen text that appears when you point to certain objects; tells you the purpose or function of the object to which you are pointing. WIN 6

script Programming code that performs a series of commands and can be embedded in a Web page. WIN 257

scroll bar, WIN 26–27

scrolling, gesture, WIN B11

Search box A text box next to the Address bar in a folder window that lets you find a file in the current folder or any of its subfolders. WIN 51, WIN 57, WIN 312
adding advanced criteria, WIN 303–307
finding files, WIN 65–66

search criteria Conditions that the file or folder must meet to have Windows find it. WIN 286, WIN 288–289
advanced, WIN 303–307
combining when searching file contents, WIN 304–307

search engine A program that conducts searches to retrieve Web pages. WIN 174

search expression The word or phrase that best describes the information you want to find. WIN 308

search filter A condition that narrows a search to files that share a specified detail. WIN 286

searching
combining Boolean filters and file properties, WIN 307
combining search criteria when searching file contents, WIN 304–307
filtering search results by date modified, WIN 295–297
filtering search results by size, WIN 291–293
folder windows, WIN 289–298
Help pages, WIN 41–42
Internet. See searching the Internet
for programs from Start menu, WIN 310–312
results, WIN 293–295
saving searches, WIN 297–298
search strategies, WIN 288–289
sorting, filtering, or grouping vs. WIN 291

searching the Internet, WIN 312–321
Internet Explorer search tools, WIN 312
narrowing searches, WIN 314–318
search expressions, WIN 313–314
search providers, WIN 318–321

Search programs and files box A text box at the bottom of the Start menu that helps you quickly find anything stored on your computer, including programs, documents, pictures, music, videos, and e-mail messages. WIN 11

search provider A Web site that specializes in searching the Internet. WIN 309, WIN 312
choosing, WIN 318–321

search results The files that meet the conditions of your search conditions. WIN 286

sector An individual block of data; a segment of a track. WIN 506

security, WIN 227–278
Action Center. See Action Center
Internet Explorer. See Microsoft Internet Explorer security
locking computer, WIN 274–275
phishing messages, WIN 250–251
securing and sharing folders, WIN 275–277
settings, WIN 230
spam. See spam
spyware. See spyware
user accounts, WIN 269–274

security event, viewing details, WIN 554

security icon An icon that indicates you need permission to access and change a setting. WIN 229

Security Status bar The part of the Address bar that indicates the whether the current Web page has a security problem. WIN 253

security zone A collection of security settings Internet Explorer uses for a site. WIN 253, WIN 258

select To point to and then click an object in order to work with it. WIN 8
files and folders, WIN 71

Select button, Paint, WIN 344

selected object An object that has been selected. WIN 30

sending e-mail messages, WIN 207–209

Send to menu, creating shortcut to document, WIN 121

Sent items In Windows Live Mail, the folder that stores message you have sent to others. WIN 198

service A program or process running in the background that supports other programs. WIN 563

Services tab, Windows Task Manager dialog box, WIN 563

shadow copy A copy created by Windows of a data file that has been modified since the most recent restore point. WIN 482
restoring, WIN 486–487

shape, drawing, WIN 359–360

Shapes button, Paint, WIN 344

Shapes group buttons, Paint, WIN 343, WIN 344

sharing
files with homegroups, WIN 445–447
photos, WIN 382–385
printers with homegroups, WIN 447–448
Remote Desktop Connection, WIN 456–459

shortcut icon An icon that provides a quick way to open a file, folder, device, or program without having to find its permanent location. WIN 106, WIN 109
creating, WIN 117–122
deleting, WIN 124
organizing on desktop, WIN 122–124

shortcut menu A list of commands associated with an object that you right-click. WIN 10

shut down To end a session with Windows 7 and turn off the computer. WIN 43, WIN 44

signed driver A device driver that includes a digital signature. WIN 515

Simple Mail Transfer Protocol (SMTP), WIN 205

size, filtering search results by size, WIN 291

Size button, Paint, WIN 344

sizing button, WIN 18, WIN 19

sizing coordinates A display in the Paint status bar that specifies the exact size in pixels of the shape being drawn. Sizing coordinates are given in an (x,y) format with x representing the horizontal size and y representing the vertical size. WIN 338

sleep A low-power state in which Windows saves your work and then turns down the power to your monitor and computer. WIN 12, WIN 42, WIN 420
    hybrid, WIN 420
    unlocking computer from, WIN 425

slide show
    customizing, WIN 395–396
    multimedia, creating with Windows Media Center, WIN 391–399
    playing, WIN 378–379, WIN 394–395

Slide Show gadget, WIN 114

small office network, setting up, WIN 434–435

SmartScreen Filter, WIN 254–257

software. *See* operating system; program

software error, WIN 585–592
    operating system recovery, WIN 590–592
    reporting and solving, WIN 585–588
    viewing reliability history, WIN 588–590

software update
    installing, WIN 492–493
    uninstalling, WIN 493

solid background, WIN 357

sort To list files and folders in a particular order, such as alphabetically by name or type or chronologically by their modification date. WIN 82, WIN 83–85
    searching vs. WIN 291

Sound dialog box, WIN B9–B10

sound scheme A collection of sounds Windows plays when system events occur. WIN B2
    changing, WIN B9–B10

spam Junk e-mail. WIN 247–251
    blocking, WIN 249–250
    phishing messages, WIN 250–251
    Windows Live Mail security settings, WIN 247–249

spoofed Web site A fraudulent site posing as a legitimate one. WIN 254

spyware Software that secretly gathers information about you and your computer actions and passes it to advertisers and others. WIN 228, WIN 240–247
    scanning with Windows Defender, WIN 241–243
    Windows Defender options, WIN 244–247

Start button A button on the far left side of the taskbar that provides access to programs, documents, and information on the Internet. WIN 2

starting
    Microsoft Internet Explorer, WIN 178–179
    Paint, WIN 342
    programs, WIN 12–13
    Windows 7, WIN 4–5
    Windows Defender, WIN 241
    Windows Explorer, WIN 37
    Windows Help, WIN 39
    Windows Live Calendar, WIN 216–217
    Windows Live Mail, WIN 206–207
    Windows Media Player, WIN 386–387

Start menu A menu that provides access to programs, documents, and much more. WIN 7, WIN 10–13, WIN 155–163
    adding commands to right pane, WIN 160–161
    controlling appearance, WIN 155–157
    opening, WIN 7
    pinning programs to, WIN 157–160
    searching for programs, WIN 310–312
    selecting commands, WIN 8
    selecting settings, WIN 161–163
    starting programs, WIN 12–13

Startup Repair A Windows recovery tool that can fix problems such as missing or damaged system files, which might prevent Windows from starting. WIN 591, WIN 592

status bar, WIN 18, WIN 19

store-and-forward technology The practice of an e-mail server storing e-mail messages until the recipients request them, and then forwarding the messages to the appropriate computers. WIN 200

strong password A password that is difficult to guess but easy for you to remember. WIN 271

subfolder A folder contained within another folder. WIN 53

submenu A list of commands that extend from and relate to a main menu command. WIN 7

switching between programs, WIN 15–17

Sync Center A Windows 7 feature that synchronizes files on one PC, such as a desktop computer, with those on another device, such as a desktop PC, network computer, portable music player, digital camera, or mobile phone. WIN 413
    resolving synchronization conflicts, WIN 455–456
    synchronizing folders, WIN 452, WIN 453–454

synchronize (sync for short) To copy files from one computer to another device, such as another computer, network server, portable music player, digital camera, or mobile phone. WIN 386
    distinguishing between sync conflicts and sync errors, WIN 456
    to portable device, WIN 390–391
    resolving synchronization conflicts, WIN 455–456
    synchronizing folders, WIN 452–456

sync partnership A set of rules specifying which files and folders you want to sync, where to sync them, and when. WIN 441

System and Security category, Control Panel, WIN 126

system detail, viewing, WIN 547

System Diagnostics, WIN 552, WIN 569–571

system event, viewing details, WIN 554

system image An exact copy of a drive, including copies of all programs, system settings, and files and a record of their original locations. WIN 468

System Information window, WIN 552, WIN 566–568

System Properties dialog box, WIN 484

system repair disc A disc that contains system recovery tools to help restore a computer if a serious system error occurs. WIN 468

System Restore A Windows tool that restores a computer's system files to an earlier point when the system was working reliably. WIN 482–487, WIN 591
    creating restore points, WIN 482–487, WIN 482–487

T

tab A collection of commands that perform a variety of related tasks on a program's Ribbon. WIN 18, WIN 19, WIN 23, WIN 486-487
  restoring shadow copies of files
  Web pages, closing and reopening, WIN 187–188

tabbed browsing A feature that lets you open more than one Web page in a single browser window. WIN 175

Tablet PC A portable computer that is smaller than a laptop or notebook and that works like an electronic slate; that is, a stylus and a touch screen are used to make selections and enter information instead of a keyboard and a pointing device. WIN 414
  adjusting settings, WIN B14–B15

Tablet PC Input Panel toolbar, WIN 154

Tablet PC Settings dialog box, WIN B15

tag A word or phrase you add to photos and other types of files to describe them. WIN 286
  adding to files, WIN 300–301
  selecting for files, WIN 301

Tagged Image File Format (TIF or TIFF), WIN 347

taskbar A strip that contains the Start button and other buttons that give you quick access to common tools and running programs; appears by default at the bottom of the desktop. WIN 2, WIN 147–153
  closing programs, WIN 17–18
  default selections, WIN 147
  moving, WIN 151–152
  pinning programs to, WIN 148–151
  resizing, WIN 151, WIN 152
  setting appearance properties, WIN 152–153

Taskbar and Start Menu Properties dialog box, WIN 153

taskbar button A button on the taskbar that you can click to open a program, make a program active, or minimize a program. WIN 2
  moving, WIN 150–151

taskbar toolbar A toolbar that appears on the taskbar to provide quick access to programs and icons on the desktop. WIN 141, WIN 153–155
  adding toolbars to taskbar, WIN 154–155

Task Manager, WIN 552, WIN 562–566

task switcher window, WIN 16

text
  adding to graphics, WIN 353–356
  changing size, WIN 138–139, WIN 525

Text button, Paint, WIN 344

Text tool, WIN 355–356

theme A set of desktop backgrounds, window colors, sounds, and screen savers that allow you to personalize the Aero desktop experience. WIN 2
  saving, WIN 136
  selecting, WIN 127–129

third-party cookie A cookie generated from Web site advertisers, who might use them to track your Web use for marketing purposes. WIN 262

thumbnail image A small graphic that previews a file's contents for certain file types. WIN 50

TIF or TIFF. *See* Tagged Image File Format

time, changing in computer, WIN 147

title bar, WIN 18, WIN 19

toolbar A bar that contains buttons that let you perform common tasks; changes to provide buttons appropriate for your current task. WIN 30

Toolbar program, WIN B26

Tools group buttons, Paint, WIN 343, WIN 344

touching up a photo, WIN 379–382

TPM. *See* Trusted Platform Module (TPM) hardware

track One of the series of concentric circles on one of the surfaces of a hard disk platter. WIN 506

transition The effect shown between successive video clips or pictures during a movie or slide. WIN B30

transparent background, WIN 357

Transparent selection command, WIN 356, WIN 357

Trojan horse Malware that hides inside another program, often one downloaded from the Web. WIN 238

troubleshooter A set of dialog boxes that guides you through the steps of describing and solving a system problem. WIN 542

troubleshooting performance, WIN 547–550

troubleshooting system problems, WIN 574–598
  finding troubleshooting information, WIN 576–584

  printing errors, WIN 582–584
  Problem Steps recorder, WIN 592–594
  recovering from software errors, WIN 585–592
  steps, WIN 576
  Windows Remote Assistance, WIN 594–598

Trusted Platform Module (TPM) hardware, WIN B4

U

uniform resource locator (URL) The address that indicates the location of a Web page. WIN 174, WIN 180
  opening Web pages, WIN 180–182

uninstall To completely remove a program from a computer. WIN 469, WIN 491–492
  software updates, WIN 493

Universal Serial Bus port. *See* USB (Universal Serial Bus) port

unlocking a drive, WIN B5–B6

unsecured network A network that does not require a user name and password. WIN A3

update A change to software that can prevent or repair problems, enhance the security of a computer, or improve a computer's performance. WIN 235
  uninstalling, WIN 493
  Windows Update, WIN 235–237

URL. *See* uniform resource locator (URL)

USB flash drive
  encryption, WIN B4–B7
  saving backup files, WIN 472

USB hub A box that contains many USB ports. WIN 513

USB (Universal Serial Bus) port A thin, rectangular slot that accommodates a high-speed connection to a variety of external devices, such as removable disks, scanners, keyboards, video conferencing cameras, and printers. WIN 512

user account A collection of information that indicates the files and folders you can access, the types of changes you can make to the computer, and your preferred appearance settings. WIN 269–274
  levels of control, WIN 270
  password-protected, creating, WIN 270

User Account Control, WIN 230

User Accounts and Family Safety category, Control Panel, WIN 126

user name (or user ID) In Windows Live Mail, the name entered when your e-mail account is set up. WIN 201; in Windows, a unique name that identifies you to Windows 7. WIN 4

Users tab, Windows Task Manager dialog box, WIN 563

V

vector graphic A graphic consisting of shapes, curves, lines, and text created by mathematical formulas. WIN 340–341
    bitmapped graphics compared, WIN 341

video file, WIN 396–398
    burning on DVDs, WIN 398–399
    Windows Live Movie Maker, WIN B30–B35

viewing. *See also* displaying
    changing view, WIN 34–36
    folder contents, WIN 57
    hard disk properties, WIN 500–502
    installed updates, WIN 492–493
    making computer easier to see, WIN B24–B25
    partitions on hard disks, WIN 502–503
    photos, WIN 373–375, WIN 376–378
    Recycle Bin contents, WIN 9
    reliability history, WIN 588–590
    system details, WIN 547
    Windows Basics topics, WIN 40

virtual memory The amount of information temporarily stored in a paging file. WIN 558

Virtual memory dialog box, WIN 569

virus A program attached to a file that runs when you open the file and copies itself to infect a computer. WIN 228
    antivirus software, WIN 238–240
    avoiding, WIN 240
    blocking spam and other junk mail, WIN 249–250
    defending against phishing messages, WIN 250–251
    Windows Live Mail security settings, WIN 247–248

visual effect, optimizing, WIN 550–551

visualization A pattern of colors and abstract shapes that moves with the music being played in Windows Media Player. WIN 387

volume. *See* partition

W

wallpaper The desktop background. WIN 129
    changing, WIN 129–131

Weather gadget, WIN 114

Web (or World Wide Web) A service on the Internet that lets you access linked documents. WIN 176

Web page A hypertext document on the Web. WIN 174
    adding to Favorites list, WIN 189
    designed for earlier versions of Internet Explorer, displaying, WIN 183
    evaluating Web pages in search results, WIN 317
    managing multiple Web pages, WIN 185–188
    opening, WIN 179–188
    printing, WIN 196
    saving, WIN 196–197

Web server An Internet computer that stores Web pages. WIN 177

Web site A collection of Web pages that have a common theme or focus. WIN 177
    checking with SmartScreen Filter, WIN 254–257
    deciding whether to trust, WIN 269

Web Slice A part (or a slice) of a Web page. WIN 175
    adding to Favorites bar, WIN 191–193

wildcard A symbol that stands for one or more unspecified characters in the search criterion. WIN 289

window A rectangular work area on the screen that contains a program, text, graphics, or data. WIN 4
    buttons, WIN 20
    controls, WIN 18–19
    maximizing, WIN 21
    minimizing, WIN 20–21
    redisplaying, WIN 21
    resizing, WIN 22–23
    restoring, WIN 21

Windows Bitmap Format (BMP), WIN 347

Windows Defender
    scanning computer, WIN 241–243
    setting options, WIN 244–247
    starting, WIN 241

Windows Experience Index base score, WIN 543, WIN 544–546

Windows Firewall, WIN 230, WIN 232–235

Windows Help and Support, WIN 576

Windows key, WIN 15

Windows Live Calendar. *See* Calendar

Windows Live Contacts, adding information, WIN 214–216

Windows Live Essentials, WIN B25–B35
    downloading and installing, WIN B26
    Windows Live Movie Maker, WIN B30–B35
    Windows Live Photo Gallery, WIN B27–B29

Windows Live Groups, WIN 321–328
    creating groups, WIN 323–324
    inviting others to join group, WIN 325–238

Windows Live ID, setting up account, WIN 322–323

Windows Live Mail
    attachments, WIN 213–214
    creating messages, WIN 207–209
    deleting messages, WIN 212–213
    reading messages, WIN 209–211
    receiving messages, WIN 209–211
    replying to messages, WIN 211–212
    security settings, WIN 247–248
    sending messages, WIN 207–209
    setting up, WIN 203–206
    starting, WIN 206–207
    window elements, WIN 207

Windows Live Movie Maker, WIN B30–B35

Windows Live Photo Gallery, WIN 374, WIN B27–B29

Windows Media Center, WIN 114, WIN 374
    creating multimedia slide show, WIN 391–399
    playing videos, WIN 397–398
    touching up photos, WIN 380

Windows Media Player, starting, WIN 386–387

Windows Photo Viewer, WIN 374, WIN 376–378

Windows Remote Assistance, WIN 594–598

Windows Task Manager dialog box, WIN 562–563, WIN 564–566

Windows Touch, WIN B11–B14

Windows Update, WIN 230, WIN 235–237

window title, WIN 18

wireless connection A broadband technology that uses infrared light or radio-frequency signals to communicate with devices that are physically connected to a network or the Internet. WIN 178, WIN A2
    preparing to connect, WIN A6–A7
    setting up, WIN A11–A12

wireless network A way to share Internet access, files, and printers among a group of computers. WIN A3
    connecting to, WIN 436–439

wireless network technology, WIN 432, WIN 433

wireless router A computer device that converts the signals from your Internet connection into a wireless broadcast. WIN A6

workspace, WIN 18, WIN 19

World Wide Web. *See* Web (World Wide Web)

worm Harmful computer code that spreads without your interaction. WIN 238

writeable disc, saving backup files, WIN 472

Writer program, WIN B26

Z

zoom, changing, WIN 339

zoom control, WIN 18, WIN 19

Zoom in/Zoom out button, WIN 353

TASK REFERENCE

TASK	PAGE #	RECOMMENDED METHOD
Action Center, open	WIN 231	Click ⚑, click Open Action Center
Action, reverse last in WordPad	WIN 26	Click ↶ on the Quick Access Toolbar
Aero Flip 3D, use	WIN 17	Press and hold the Windows key, press the Tab key
Aero Peek, use	WIN 144	Point to ▮ or click ▮
Aero Shake, use	WIN 146	Click and hold the title bar and shake it by quickly dragging the window to right and left to minimize all the other open windows
Aero Snap, use	WIN 143	Drag a window to the side of the screen
Appointment, schedule in Windows Live Calendar	WIN 218	*See* Reference box: Scheduling an Appointment in Windows Live Calendar
AutoPlay, turn on	WIN B8	Click 🪟, click Control Panel, click Hardware and Sound, click AutoPlay, select Use AutoPlay for all media and devices
Backup and Restore window, open	WIN 475	Click 🪟, click Control Panel, click System and Security, click Backup and Restore
Backup files, restore	WIN 481	Open the Backup and Restore window, click Restore my files, follow the instructions in the Restore Files Wizard
Backup settings, change	WIN 478	Open the Backup and Restore window, click Change settings, follow the instructions in the Set Up Backup Wizard
Base score, view and calculate	WIN 546	*See* Reference box: Viewing and Calculating Your Base Score
BitLocker To Go, turn off for a USB flash drive	WIN B7	Insert the encrypted USB flash drive into a USB port, click 🪟, click Control Panel, click System and Security, click BitLocker Drive Encryption, click Turn Off BitLocker, click Decrypt Drive, click Close
BitLocker To Go, turn on for a USB flash drive	WIN B4	Insert a USB flash drive into a USB port, click 🪟, click Control Panel, click System and Security, click BitLocker Drive Encryption, click Turn On BitLocker, follow the instructions in the wizard
Bold text, enter in WordPad	WIN 26	In the Font group on the Home tab, click **B**
Colors setting, change	WIN 132	Right-click the desktop, click Personalize, click Window Color, click color, click Save changes
Compressed folder, create	WIN 93	In a folder window, select the files and folders to be compressed, right-click the selection, point to Send to on the shortcut menu, click Compressed (zipped) folder, type a folder name, press Enter
Compressed folder, extract all files and folders from	WIN 94	Right-click the compressed folder, click Extract All on the shortcut menu
Computer window, open	WIN 33	Click 🪟, click Computer
Connect a mobile PC to a network projector	WIN 431	*See* Reference box: Connecting to a Network Projector
Connect a mobile PC to a wireless network	WIN 437–438	Click 📶, click network name, click Connect
Connect a mobile PC to an external display device	WIN 430	*See* Reference box: Connecting to an External Display Device

TASK	PAGE #	RECOMMENDED METHOD
Connection, set up broadband	WIN A8	Click 🪟, click Control Panel, click Connect to the Internet, click Broadband (PPPoE), type the user name and password, click Connect, click Next, click Close
Connection, set up dial-up	WIN A13	Click 🪟, click Control Panel, click Connect to the Internet, click Dial-up, type the telephone number and the user name and password, click Connect, click Next, click Close
Connection, set up wireless	WIN A11	Click 🪟, click Control Panel, click Connect to the Internet, click Wireless, select network, click Connect, type network passphrase, click Connect, click Next, click Close
Contact, add in Windows Live Mail	WIN 215	*See* Reference box: Adding a Contact in Windows Live Mail
Control Panel, open	WIN 125	Click 🪟, click Control Panel
Credential Manager, open	WIN B19	Click 🪟, click Control Panel, click User Accounts and Family Safety, click Credential Manager
Default program, set to open a file type	WIN 495	Click 🪟, click Control Panel, click Programs, click Associate a file type or protocol with a program, click a file type, click Change program, click the program to use as the default, click OK
Default, set program as	WIN 494	Click 🪟, click Control Panel, click Programs, click Default Programs, click Set your default programs, click a program, click Set this program as default, click OK
Desktop background, change	WIN 129	Right-click the desktop, click Personalize, click Desktop Background, click image, click Save changes
Desktop colors, change	WIN 132	Right-click the desktop, click Personalize, click Window Color, click color, click Save changes
Desktop icon, change image for	WIN 113	Right-click the desktop, click Personalize, click Change desktop icons, click icon, click Change Icon, click image, click OK
Desktop icons, change location of	WIN 112	Right-click the desktop, point to View, click Auto arrange icons to deselect that option, right-click the desktop, point to View, click Align icons to grid to deselect that option, drag desktop icons to a new location
Desktop icons, change size of	WIN 112	Right-click the desktop, point to View, click a size
Desktop icons, display standard	WIN 109	*See* Reference box: Displaying Standard Desktop Icons
Desktop icons, hide	WIN 112	Right-click the desktop, point to View, click Show desktop icons to deselect that option
Desktop icons, sort	WIN 123	Right-click the desktop, point to Sort by, click sort option
Desktop shortcut, create to drive	WIN 118	Drag the drive icon from a folder window to the desktop
Desktop shortcut, create to file, folder, or program	WIN 120–122	Right-drag the file, folder, or program icon to desktop, click Create shortcuts here
Desktop shortcut, delete	WIN 124	Click the shortcut, press Delete key
Desktop theme, change	WIN 128	*See* Reference box: Selecting a Theme
Desktop theme, save new	WIN 136	Right-click the desktop, click Personalize, click Save theme, enter name, click Save
Details pane, open or close	WIN 88	In a folder window, click Organize, point to Layout, click Details pane

TASK	PAGE #	RECOMMENDED METHOD
Device driver, update and install	WIN 519	Open the Device Manager, double-click the device, click the Driver tab, click Update Driver, click Search automatically for updated driver software, click Yes
Device Manager, open	WIN 516	Click 🪟, click Control Panel, click System and Security, click Device Manager
Device, enable and disable	WIN 516	*See* Reference box: Enabling and Disabling Devices
Disk Cleanup, start	WIN 504	Right-click the disk in a folder window, click Properties, click the General tab, click Disk Cleanup
Disk Defragmenter, start	WIN 511	Right-click the disk in a folder window, click Properties, click the Tools tab, click Defragment now
Display refresh rate, adjust	WIN 522	*See* Reference box: Adjusting the Display Refresh Rate
Documents library, open	WIN 58	In a folder window, click Documents in the Navigation pane
Ease of Access Center, open	WIN B22	Click 🪟, click Control Panel, click Ease of Access, click Ease of Access Center
E-mail message, attach file to	WIN 213	Click the Attach button, double-click file
E-mail message, create	WIN 208	*See* Reference box: Creating and Sending an E-Mail Message
E-mail message, delete	WIN 213	Click a message, click the Delete button
E-mail message, reply to	WIN 212	Click a message, click Reply
Error-checking tool, start	WIN 507	Right-click the disk in a folder window, click Properties, click the Tools tab, click Check now, click Start
Event Viewer, open	WIN 555	Open the Performance Information and Tools window, click Advanced tools, click View performance details in Event log
External display device, connect to	WIN 430	*See* Reference box: Connecting to an External Display Device
Favorites list, add file or folder to	WIN 91	Drag a file or folder to the Favorites list in the Navigation pane
Favorites list, add Web page to	WIN 189	*See* Reference box: Adding a Web Page to the Favorites List
Favorites list, open	WIN 188	Click the Favorites button, click Favorites tab
Favorites list, organize	WIN 190	*See* Reference box: Organizing the Favorites List
File, add tags to	WIN 300	*See* Reference box: Adding Tags to Files
Files, back up	WIN 470	*See* Reference box: Backing Up Files
File, copy	WIN 71	*See* Reference box: Copying a File or Folder in a Folder Window
File, create	WIN 78	Start a program and enter data
File, delete	WIN 77	*See* Reference box: Deleting a File or Folder
File, move	WIN 69	*See* Reference box: Moving a File or Folder in a Folder Window
File, open from folder window	WIN 81	Navigate to the file, double-click the file
File, rename	WIN 77	Right-click the file, click Rename on the shortcut menu, type the new filename, press Enter
Files, restore from backup	WIN 481	Open the Backup and Restore window, click Restore my files, follow the instructions in the Restore Files Wizard
File, restore shadow copy	WIN 486	Right-click a file, click Restore previous versions, click a shadow copy of the file, click Restore, click Restore again to confirm, click OK

TASK	PAGE #	RECOMMENDED METHOD
File, save	WIN 80	Click the program menu button, click Save As, navigate to a location, type the filename, click Save
File, search for within a folder window	WIN 65	Click in the Search box, type the word or phrase to be found in the file or filename
File sharing, turn on	WIN 450	Open Network and Sharing Center, click Change advanced sharing settings, click the Turn on file and printer sharing (in the Home or Work section), click Save changes
Filename extension, show	WIN 89	Click Organize in a folder window, click Folder and search options, click View, click Hide extensions for known file types to deselect the check box
Files, select multiple	WIN 71	Hold down the Ctrl key and click the files
Flip 3D, use	WIN 17	Press and hold the Windows key, press the Tab key
Folder list, expand	WIN 38	Click ▷
Folder window, return to a previously visited location	WIN 64	Click ▾, click a location in the list
Folder window, return to previous location	WIN 64	Click ⬅
Folder, copy	WIN 71	*See* Reference box: Copying a File or Folder in a Folder Window
Folder, create	WIN 67	*See* Reference box: Creating a Folder in a Folder Window
Folder, delete	WIN 77	*See* Reference box: Deleting a File or Folder
Folder, filter files in	WIN 84	In a folder window, click a column heading arrow button, click a filter option
Folder, group files in	WIN 86	Right-click a blank area of a folder window, point to Group by, click a grouping option
Folder, move	WIN 69	*See* Reference box: Moving a File or Folder in a Folder Window
Folder, sort files in	WIN 84	In a folder window, click a column heading
Folders list, close in a dialog box	WIN 80	Click the Hide Folders button
Folders list, open in a dialog box	WIN 80	Click the Browse Folders button
Font size, select in WordPad	WIN 26	In the Font group on the Home tab, click 11 ▾, type text
Gadget, customize	WIN 115	Click 🔧
Graphic file, use as desktop background	WIN 129–130	Right-click desktop, click Personalize, click Desktop Background, click Browse, double-click graphic file, click OK
Hard disk, check for errors	WIN 507	Right-click the disk in a folder window, click Properties, click the Tools tab, click Check now, click Start
Hard disk, clean up	WIN 504	Right-click the disk in a folder window, click Properties, click the General tab, click Disk Cleanup
Hard disk, defragment	WIN 511	Right-click the disk in a folder window, click Properties, click the Tools tab, click Defragment now
Hard disk, view partitions	WIN 503	Click 🪟, click Control Panel, click System and Security, click Create and format hard disk partitions
Hard disk, view properties	WIN 500	*See* Reference box: Viewing Hard Disk Properties

TASK	PAGE #	RECOMMENDED METHOD
Help, find topic	WIN 41	Click 🪟, click Help and Support, click in the Search Help box, type a word or phrase, press Enter
Help, start	WIN 39	Click 🪟, click Help and Support
High contrast color scheme, turn off	WIN B25	Press the Left Alt+Left Shift+Print Screen keys
High contrast color scheme, use on the desktop	WIN B25	Open the Ease of Access Center window, click Make the computer easier to see, press the Left Alt+Left Shift+Print Screen keys, click Yes
Homegroup window, open	WIN 442	Click 🪟, click Control Panel, type homegroup in Search box, click HomeGroup
Homegroup, create	WIN 442–443	Open the Homegroup window, click Create a homegroup, select printers and libraries to share, click Next, click Print password and instructions, click Print this page, click Finish
Homegroup, exclude folder from sharing with	WIN 447	Click the folder to exclude from sharing in a folder window, click Share with, click Nobody
Homegroup, join	WIN 444	Open the Homegroup window, click Join now, select printers and libraries, click Next, click Finish
Homegroup, share files with	WIN 446	Open the Homegroup window, select libraries, click Save changes
Internet Explorer, block all pop-up windows	WIN 260	Start Internet Explorer, click Tools, point to Pop-up Blocker, click Pop-up Blocker Settings, click Blocking level setting, click High: Block all pop-ups
Internet Explorer, delete browsing history in	WIN 264	Start Internet Explorer, click Tools, click Internet Options, click General, click Delete in Browsing history section, click History check box, click Delete
Internet Explorer, manage add-ons in	WIN 261	Start Internet Explorer, click Tools, click Manage Add-ons
Internet Explorer, select privacy settings in	WIN 263	*See* Reference box: Selecting Privacy Settings
Internet Explorer, set SmartScreen Filter	WIN 255	Start Internet Explorer, click Safety, point to SmartScreen Filter, click Turn On SmartScreen Filter
Internet Explorer, start	WIN 178	Click 🌐 on the taskbar
Internet search provider, select	WIN 319	*See* Reference box: Selecting a Search Provider
Link, open in a new tab	WIN 186	Right-click link, click Open in New Tab
Local printer, install	WIN 529	*See* Reference box: Installing a Local Printer
Magnifier, start	WIN B23	Open the Ease of Access Center window, click Start Magnifier, click Minimize
Menu bar, display or hide	WIN 88	In a folder window, click Organize, point to Layout, click Menu bar
Microsoft Answers, search for answer in	WIN 580–581	Click 🪟, click Help and Support, click Ask, click Microsoft Answers, enter a question or topic in the Find Answers text box, click Search, click answer
Microsoft Solutions Center, open	WIN 579–580	Click 🪟, click Help and Support, click Ask, click Microsoft Customer Support, click Solution Centers
Mobility Center, open for a mobile PC	WIN 416	Click 🪟, point to All Programs, click Accessories, click Windows Mobility Center
Multiple monitors, set resolution for	WIN 528	Right-click desktop, click Screen resolution, click the monitor for which to set the resolution, click Resolution, drag the slider, click OK, click Keep changes

TASK	PAGE #	RECOMMENDED METHOD
Multiple monitors, set up	WIN 527	Physically connect the extra monitor to a computer, click an option for using multiple monitors
Multitouch monitor, turn on Windows Touch for	WIN B12–B13	Click ⊞, click Control Panel, click Hardware and Sound, click Pen and Touch, click the Touch tab, select Use your finger as an input device
Music library, open	WIN 33	In a folder window, click Music in the Navigation pane
My Documents folder, open	WIN 38	In a folder window, click ▷ next to Libraries, click ▷ next to Documents, click My Documents
Network files, make available offline	WIN 451	Click ⊞, click Control Panel, click Network and Internet, click View network computers and devices, navigate to and right-click a network folder, select Always available offline
Network passwords, manage	WIN B19–B20	Click ⊞, click Control Panel, click User Accounts and Family Safety, click Credential Manager, click Add a Windows credential, type a URL, user name, and password, click OK
Network projector, connect a mobile PC to	WIN 431	*See* Reference box: Connecting to a Network Projector
New tab, open	WIN 186	Click 🗋
Offline files, enable	WIN 449–450	Click ⊞, click Control Panel, click in the Search box, type Offline, click Manage offline files, click Enable offline Files, click OK
Offline files, sync	WIN 453–454	Open the Sync Center, click Offline Files, click Sync
Offline files, work with	WIN 451–452	Navigate to and click the network folder containing the files, click Work Offline
On-screen keyboard, start	WIN B23	Open the Ease of Access Center window, click Start On-Screen Keyboard
Page Setup dialog box, open in WordPad	WIN 28	In the Print group on the Print preview tab, click Page setup
Paging file, change size	WIN 568	Open the Performance Information and Tools window, click Advanced tools, click Adjust the appearance and performance of Windows, click the Advanced tab, click Change
Paint, add text to a graphic in	WIN 353	*See* Reference box: Adding Text to a Graphic
Paint, copy and paste a portion of the graphic in	WIN 363	Select the portion of the graphic, click 📋, click Paste
Paint, draw a square in	WIN 359–360	Click the Shapes button, if necessary, click ⬜, hold down the Shift key and drag, release the mouse button
Paint, fill an area with color in	WIN 361	*See* Reference box: Filling an Area with Color
Paint, insert an image into the current graphic in	WIN 349	Click the Paste button arrow, click Paste from, navigate to the image file, click the file, click Open
Paint, magnify a graphic in	WIN 353	*See* Reference box: Magnifying a Graphic
Paint, open a graphic file in	WIN 345	Click ▣ ▾, click Open, navigate to the file, click the file, click Open
Paint, resize the canvas in	WIN 367	Drag a sizing handle on the canvas
Paint, select a portion of a graphic in	WIN 357	Click the Select button, drag to select
Paint, start	WIN 342	Click ⊞, point to All Programs, click Accessories, click Paint
Paragraph dialog box, open in WordPad	WIN 24	In the Paragraph group on the Home tab, click ▤

TASK	PAGE #	RECOMMENDED METHOD
Parental controls, turn on	WIN B18	Click 🪟, click Control Panel, click User Accounts and Family Safety, click Parental Controls, click a user, click On, enforce current settings, set options, click OK
Partitions, view for hard disk	WIN 503	Click 🪟, click Control Panel, click System and Security, click Create and format hard disk partitions
Password, create for user account	WIN 273	Click 🪟, click user icon, click Create a password
Password reset disk, create	WIN B16	Click 🪟, click Control Panel, click User Accounts and Family Safety, click User Accounts, click Create a password reset disk, follow the instructions in the Forgotten Password Wizard
Performance details, view and print	WIN 547	Open the Performance Information and Tools window, click View and print detailed performance and system information
Performance Information and Tools window, open	WIN 546	Click 🪟, click Control Panel, click System and Security, click Check the Windows Experience Index
Performance issues, view	WIN 553	Open the Performance Information and Tools window, click Advanced tools
Performance Monitor, open	WIN 556	*See* Reference box: Monitoring System Performance
Permission, assign to folder	WIN 276	Click a folder, click Share with, click Specific people, click the arrow to the right of the first text box, click a user name, click Add, click Permission Level, click a permission level, click Share
Photo, e-mail	WIN 383	In the Pictures library, click a photo, click E-mail, click Picture size, click size, click Attach
Photo, print	WIN 384–385	In the Pictures library, click a photo, click Print
Photo, rotate	WIN 377	Open photo in Windows Photo Viewer, click 🔄 or 🔁
Photo, touch up	WIN 380	In Windows Media Center, right-click a photo, click Pictures Details, click Touch Up, click touch up option, click Save, click Yes
Pictures library, arrange pictures in	WIN 375	In the Pictures library, click the Arrange by button, click picture detail
Power options, change	WIN 425	Click 🪟, click Control Panel, click Hardware and Sound, click Power Options, click Choose what the power buttons do, change settings, click Save changes
Power plan, modify	WIN 421	*See* Reference box: Modifying a Power Plan
Power plan, select	WIN 418	*See* Reference box: Selecting a Power Plan
Pop-up windows, block all	WIN 260	Start Internet Explorer, click Tools, point to Pop-up Blocker, click Pop-up Blocker Settings, click Blocking level setting, click High: Block all pop-ups
Presentation settings, customize for a mobile PC	WIN 427	Open Windows Mobility Center, click 🖥, change settings, click OK
Preview pane, open	WIN 88	In a folder window, click 🗔
Print Preview, close in WordPad	WIN 29	In the Close group on the Print preview tab, click Close print preview
Print Preview, open in WordPad	WIN 28	Click 🗎▾, point to Print, click Print preview
Printer sharing, turn on for network	WIN 450	Open Network and Sharing Center, click Change advanced sharing settings, click the Turn on file and printer sharing (in the Home or Work section), click Save changes button

TASK	PAGE #	RECOMMENDED METHOD
Printer, install local	WIN 529	*See* Reference box: Installing a Local Printer
Printer, set default	WIN 532	Click , click Devices and Printers, right-click a printer, click Set as default printer
Privacy settings, select	WIN 263	*See* Reference box: Selecting Privacy Settings
Problem Steps Recorder, start	WIN 592	Click , click Control Panel, click in the Search Control Panel box, type problem steps, click Record steps to reproduce a problem
Program, check for compatibility	WIN 496	Click , click Control Panel, click Programs, click Run programs made for previous versions of Windows, follow the instructions in the Program Compatibility troubleshooter
Program, close	WIN 13	Click
Program, close inactive	WIN 17	Right-click the program button on the taskbar, click Close window
Program, pin to taskbar	WIN 149	*See* Reference box: Pinning Programs to the Taskbar
Program, start	WIN 12	*See* Reference box: Starting a Program
Program, switch to another open	WIN 15	Click the program button on the taskbar
Program, uninstall	WIN 491	Click , click Control Panel, click Uninstall a program in the Programs category, click the program, click Uninstall, click Yes
Property, add to file	WIN 299	Right-click the file, click Properties, click Details, type property, click OK
Public folder sharing, turn on	WIN 450	Click , click Open Network and Sharing Center, click Change advanced sharing settings, click Turn on sharing so anyone with network access can read and write files in the Public folders (in the Home or Work section), click Save changes
ReadyBoost, use	WIN 571–572	Click , click Computer, right-click a USB flash drive, click Open Autoplay, click Speed up my system, click Use this device, click OK
Recycle Bin, open	WIN 9	Double-click the Recycle Bin icon
Remote Assistance, enable	WIN 595	Click , click Control Panel, click System and Security, click System, click Remote settings, click the Allow Remote Assistance connections to this computer
Remote Assistance, request	WIN 596	Click , click Help and Support, click Ask, click Windows Remote Assistance, follow the instructions in the Windows Remote Assistance Wizard
Remote Desktop Connection, set up	WIN 458	Click , click Control Panel, click System and Security, click System, click Remote settings, click Allow connections only from computers running Remote Desktop with Network Level Authentication (more secure), click OK
Remote Desktop Connection, start and connect to remote computer	WIN 459	Click , start typing Remote Desktop Connection in the Search programs and files box, click Remote Desktop Connection, enter the name of the remote computer, click Connect, enter your user name and password, click OK
Resource Monitor, open	WIN 561	Open the Performance Information and Tools window, click Advanced tools, click Open Resource Monitor
Restore point, create	WIN 483	*See* Reference box: Creating a System Restore Point

TASK	PAGE #	RECOMMENDED METHOD
Screen resolution, change	WIN 137	Right-click the desktop, click Screen resolution, click the Resolution button, drag Resolution slider, click OK
Screen saver, activate	WIN 135	Right-click the desktop, click Personalize, click Screen Saver, click the Screen saver button, click a screen saver, click OK
ScreenTip, view	WIN 6	Position the pointer over an item
Search provider, select	WIN 319	*See* Reference box: Selecting a Search Provider
Search results, filter	WIN 292	*See* Reference box: Filtering Search Results
Search, locate file by type	WIN 290	Click the Search box in a folder window, type a filename extension
Search, locate program	WIN 310	*See* Reference box: Searching for Programs on the Start Menu
Search, save	WIN 298	Click Save search, click Save
Shadow copy, restore file from	WIN 486–487	Right-click a file, click Restore previous versions, click a shadow copy of the file, click Restore, click Restore again to confirm, click OK
Shared files, access on homegroup	WIN 445	Click [icon], click Homegroup, click homegroup computer name, open folder containing the files
Slide show, add music to	WIN 393	In Windows Media Center, select a slide show, click Add More, click a folder containing music, click the music or playlist, click select all (if necessary), click Next, click Create
Slide show, play with music	WIN 394	In Windows Media Center, click a slide show, click play slide show
Slide show, simple, play	WIN 378	*See* Reference box: Playing a Slide Show
Software problems, check for solutions	WIN 585	*See* Reference box: Checking for Solutions to Software Problems
Software update, view installed	WIN 492	Click [icon], click Control Panel, click Programs, click Programs and Features, click View Installed updates
Song, play in Windows Media Player	WIN 388	Click [icon], double-click a song
Sound scheme, create new	WIN B9–B10	Click [icon], click Control Panel, click Hardware and Sound, click Sound, click the Sounds tab, click a Program Event, click the Sounds arrow button, click a sound, click Save As, type a sound scheme name, click OK
Speaker volume, set in Windows Mobility Center	WIN 416	Open Windows Mobility Center, drag the Volume slider
Speakers, mute in Windows Mobility Center	WIN 416	Open Windows Mobility Center, click Mute in Volume tile
Start menu icons, change size	WIN 156	Right-click [icon], click Properties, click Customize, click Use large icons, click OK
Start menu, add command to	WIN 161	Right-click [icon], click Properties, click Customize, select command, click OK
Start menu, open	WIN 7	Click [icon]
Start menu, pin a program to	WIN 158	Click [icon], right-click program name in Start menu, click Pin to Start Menu
Steps, record in Problem Steps Recorder	WIN 592	Click [icon], click Control Panel, click in the Search Control Panel box, type problem steps, click Record steps to reproduce a problem, click Start Record
Sync Center, open	WIN 453	Click [icon], click Control Panel, type sync in Search box, click Sync Center
Synchronize files	WIN 453–454	Open the Sync Center, click Offline Files, click Sync
System details, view and print	WIN 547	Open the Performance Information and Tools window, click View and print detailed performance and system information

TASK	PAGE #	RECOMMENDED METHOD
System Health Report, create	WIN 570	Open the Performance Information and Tools window, click Advanced tools, click Generate a system health report
System information, view	WIN 567	Open the Performance Information and Tools window, click Advanced tools, click View advanced system details in System Information
System performance, monitor	WIN 556	*See* Reference box: Monitoring System Performance
System protection, turn on	WIN 484	Click ⊙, click Control Panel, click System and Security, click System, click System protection, select the drive where Windows is installed
System restore point, create	WIN 483	*See* Reference box: Creating a System Restore Point
System Stability chart, view	WIN 589	Click ▣, click Open Action Center, click View reliability history in the Maintenance section
System, restore	WIN 485	Click ⊙, click Control Panel, click System and Security, click System, click System protection, click System Restore, follow the instructions in the System Restore Wizard
Tablet PC, calibrate screen and pen for	WIN B15	Click ⊙, click Control Panel, click Hardware and Sound, click Tablet PC Settings, click Calibrate, follow the on-screen instructions
Tag, add to file	WIN 300	*See* Reference box: Adding Tags to Files
Task Manager, open	WIN 564	Open the Performance Information and Tools window, click Advanced tools, click Open Task Manager
Taskbar, add Desktop toolbar to	WIN 154	Right-click taskbar, point to Toolbars, click Desktop
Taskbar, hide	WIN 152–153	Right-click taskbar, click Properties, click Auto-hide the taskbar, click OK
Taskbar, move	WIN 151	*See* Reference box: Moving and Resizing the Taskbar
Taskbar, pin program to	WIN 149	*See* Reference box: Pinning Programs to the Taskbar
Taskbar, resize	WIN 151	*See* Reference box: Moving and Resizing the Taskbar
Theme, select	WIN 128	*See* Reference box: Selecting a Theme
Troubleshooter, use	WIN 548	*See* Reference box: Using a Troubleshooter
Update, view for installed software	WIN 492	Click ⊙, click Control Panel, click Programs, click Programs and Features, click View Installed updates
USB device, install	WIN 516	Plug the device into a USB port
USB device, safely remove	WIN 520	Click ▥ in the notification area of the taskbar, click Safely remove USB Device, click the device, click the OK button, unplug the USB device from the USB port
User account, create new	WIN 270	*See* Reference box: Creating a Password-Protected User Account
User picture, change	WIN 156	Click ⊙, click user picture, click Change your picture, click picture, click Change Picture
Video, play in Windows Live Movie Maker	WIN B30–B31	Add a video to the storyboard, click the beginning of the video clip, click ▶
Video, play in Windows Media Center	WIN 397	Click video file in a folder window, click Play button arrow, click Windows Media Center
Video, trim in Windows Live Movie Maker	WIN B32	In the Windows Live Movie Maker storyboard, click where you want the video to start, click the Video Tools Edit tab, click Set start point, click where you want the video to end, click Set end point
View, change in a folder window	WIN 35	*See* Reference box: Changing the Icon View

TASK	PAGE #	RECOMMENDED METHOD
Visual effect settings, adjust	WIN 551	Open the Performance Information and Tools window, click Adjust visual effects, change option settings, click OK
Web page, add to Favorites list	WIN 189	*See* Reference box: Adding a Web Page to the Favorites List
Web page, open using URL	WIN 181	Start Internet Explorer, click Address box, type URL, press Enter
Web page, print	WIN 196	Click 🖶
Web page, return to next	WIN 184	Click ➡
Web page, return to previous	WIN 184	Click ⬅
Web page, return to recent	WIN 184	Click ▼, click a Web page
Web page, return to using History list	WIN 184	Click Favorites, click History, click a date, click a Web page
Window colors, change	WIN 132	Right-click the desktop, click Personalize, click Window Color, click color, click Save changes
Window, maximize	WIN 21	Click ☐
Window, minimize	WIN 20	Click ▬
Window, move	WIN 22	Drag the title bar
Window, resize	WIN 22	Drag an edge or corner of the window
Window, restore	WIN 21	Click ❐
Window, scroll	WIN 27	Click the scroll up or scroll down button, or drag the scroll box
Windows 7, log off	WIN 44	Click 🪟, click the Shut down button arrow, click Log Off
Windows 7, start	WIN 4	Turn on the computer
Windows 7, turn off	WIN 44	Click 🪟, click Shut down
Windows Defender, perform a quick scan with	WIN 241	*See* Reference box: Performing a Quick Scan with Windows Defender
Windows Defender, schedule scan	WIN 244	Start Windows Defender, click Tools, click Options, click Automatic Scanning, click Approximate time
Windows Defender, start	WIN 241	Click 🪟, type Windows Defender, click Windows Defender
Windows Explorer, open	WIN 37	Click 🗂 on the taskbar
Windows Firewall, add program to allowed list	WIN 234	Click 🪟, click Control Panel, click System and Security, click Windows Firewall, click Allow a program or feature through Windows Firewall, click to select a check box, click OK
Windows Live Calendar, schedule appointment	WIN 218	*See* Reference box: Scheduling an Appointment in Windows Live Calendar
Windows Live Group, invite people to join	WIN 325	On the home page of a Windows Live Group, click Invite people, click To box, enter an e-mail address, click Include your own message box, enter a message, click Send
Windows Live Essentials, download and install program from	WIN B26	Using a Web browser, go to *http://download.live.com*, click Download, click Run, select the program, click Install, click Close these programs for me (if necessary), click Continue, click Continue, click Close
Windows Live Mail, add contact to	WIN 215	*See* Reference box: Adding a Contact in Windows Live Mail

TASK	PAGE #	RECOMMENDED METHOD
Windows Live Mail, add sender to Blocked Senders or Safe Senders list	WIN 249	*See* Reference box: Adding a Sender to the Blocked Senders or Safe Senders List
Windows Live Mail, create e-mail message	WIN 208	*See* Reference box: Creating and Sending an E-Mail Message
Windows Live Mail, send e-mail message	WIN 208	*See* Reference box: Creating and Sending an E-Mail Message
Windows Live Mail, set junk e-mail options	WIN 249	Start Windows Live Mail, click 🔲 ▾, click Safety options
Windows Live Mail, start	WIN 206	Click 🟢, point to All Programs, click Windows Live (if necessary), click Windows Live Mail
Windows Live Movie Maker, add a title to a video in	WIN B33	In the Windows Live Movie Maker storyboard, click where the title slide should appear, click the Home tab, click Title in the Add group, enter title text.
Windows Live Movie Maker, add a transition to the storyboard in	WIN B34	In the Windows Live Movie Maker storyboard, click where the transition should appear, click the Animations tab, click transition
Windows Live Movie Maker, add a video or photo to the storyboard in	WIN B31	In Windows Live Movie Maker, click Add videos and photos, navigate to the video or photo, double-click video or photo
Windows Live Movie Maker, add an effect to a photo in	WIN B34	Add a photo to the storyboard, click the photo, click the Visual Effects tab, click an effect
Windows Live Movie Maker, download and install	WIN B26	Using a Web browser, go to *http://download.live.com*, click Download, click Run, select Windows Live Movie Maker, click Install, click Close these programs for me (if necessary), click Continue, click Continue, click Close
Windows Live Movie Maker, play a video in	WIN B30–B31	Add a video to the storyboard, click the beginning of the video clip, click ▶
Windows Live Movie Maker, publish a movie in	WIN B35	Click 🔲 ▾, point to Save movie, click a compression option, navigate to where you want to publish the movie, enter a filename (if necessary), click Save, click Close
Windows Live Movie Maker, save project in	WIN B35	Click 🔲 ▾, click Save project as, navigate to the where the project should be saved, enter filename (if necessary), click Save
Windows Live Movie Maker, start	WIN B30	Click 🟢, point to All Programs, click Windows Live, click Windows Live Movie Maker
Windows Live Photo Gallery, download and install	WIN B26	Using a Web browser, go to *http://download.live.com*, click Download, click Run, select Windows Live Photo Gallery, click Install, click Close these programs for me (if necessary), click Continue, click Continue, click Close
Windows Live Photo Gallery, edit a photo in	WIN B29	Start Windows Live Photo Gallery, click a photo to edit, click Fix, use options in the Editing pane
Windows Live Photo Gallery, start	WIN B27	Click 🟢, point to All Programs, click Windows Live, click Windows Live Photo Gallery
Windows Media Center, burn video to a DVD in	WIN 398	After playing a video in Windows Media Center, click actions, insert DVD into drive, click Burn a CD/DVD, click Video DVD, click Next, enter DVD name, click Next, click Burn DVD, click Yes, click Done

TASK	PAGE #	RECOMMENDED METHOD
Windows Media Player, create a playlist in	WIN 389	*See* Reference box: Creating a Playlist
Windows Media Player, play a song in	WIN 388	Double-click a song
Windows Media Player, start	WIN 386	Click 🔘
Windows Media Player, sync playlist files to portable music device in	WIN 391	Turn on a portable music device and connect it to the computer, click Sync tab, click Sync *Playlist*, click Start sync
Windows Mobility Center, open	WIN 416	Click 🪟, point to All Programs, click Accessories, click Windows Mobility Center
Windows Photo Viewer, view photo in	WIN 376	Click a photo, click Preview
Windows Touch, turn on	WIN B12	Click 🪟, click Control Panel, click Hardware and Sound, click Pen and Touch, click the Touch tab, select Use your finger as an input device
Windows Update, set up	WIN 236	Click 🪟, click Control Panel, click System and Security, click Windows Update, click Change settings
Windows, arrange on desktop	WIN 151	Right-click taskbar, click Cascade Windows, Show Windows Stacked, or Show Windows Side by Side
Wireless connection, check status of	WIN 438	Point to 📶
Wireless network, connect a mobile PC to	WIN 437	Click 📶, click network name, click Connect